DERIVATIVE MARKETS

DERIVATIVE MARKETS

THEORY, STRATEGY, AND APPLICATIONS

Peter Ritchken

Case Western Reserve University

📖 HarperCollins*CollegePublishers*

To Lois, Jake, and Brian

Acquisitions Editors: Kirsten Sandberg and Joan Cannon
Project Editorial Manager: Melonie Salvati
Text Design: Interactive Composition Corporation
Cover Design: Kay Petronio and John Callahan
Art Studio: Interactive Composition Corporation
Electronic Production Manager: Su Levine
Manufacturing Manager: Willie Lane
Electronic Page Makeup: Interactive Composition Corporation
Printer and Binder: R. R. Donnelley & Sons Company
Cover Printer: New England Book Components, Inc.

Derivative Markets: Theory, Strategy, and Applications

Library of Congress Cataloging-in-Publication Data

Ritchken, Peter.
    Derivative markets / Peter Ritchken.
      p.   cm.
    Includes index.
    ISBN 0-673-46017-7
    1. Derivative securities—Marketing.   I. Title.
HG6024.A3R58   1996
332.64′5—dc20
                                95-14277
                                  CIP

96 97 98 9 8 7 6 5 4 3 2

BRIEF
CONTENTS

CONTENTS

PREFACE

To The Student

If you picked up today's copy of the *Wall Street Journal* or the *Financial Times,* you can recount the latest scoop on derivative securities. The financial press often reports fascinating, if not startling, stories about how institutional investors, corporate treasury managers, individual traders, portfolio managers, and other finance practitioners have used, abused, and confused derivative securities and their respective markets in hedging or managing risks—often at great cost. Seemingly at supersonic speed, derivatives continue not only to transform financial markets but also to provide firms with new and more effective risk management tools that were simply nonexistent a few years ago. Major innovations lie ahead, and it is in your power to create and use them.

Actually, derivative contracts have existed for centuries. Why have the derivative markets been so active over the last two decades? In the 1970s, trading was expedited by the development of the theory of option pricing as well as organized stock option exchanges; in the 1980s, continuing deregulation and enhanced market volatilities stimulated activity. More recent catalysts include improved technology: computerized markets are instantaneously linking traders regardless of their geographical location or institutional affiliation, and powerful computer programs are facilitating the design and implementation of new financial instruments and trading strategies. In today's markets, you can design exotic financial contracts precisely to manage almost any specific risk.

Scientific breakthroughs in financial modeling, along with revolutionary changes in the structure of world financial markets and institutions, have created a job-market demand for people who know both the theory and applications of derivative instruments. To be truly marketable, you must be able not merely to identify risk exposures but also to communicate reasons for reducing risk to more manageable levels. You should also be able to identify alternative financial solutions for managing risk. While the solution is frequently obvious, some solutions require you to create new and complex derivative instruments. You should also be able to establish pricing models and trading strategies to attain specified risk management objectives. Finally, you should remember that even though solid pricing models can enable a firm to protect itself, models alone are hardly sufficient. A firm must rely upon sound investment strategies and risk management programs that are immediately responsive to the volatile markets.

To the Instructor

Designed for advanced undergraduates in finance as well as for graduate students and finance professionals, this book assumes that readers have taken introductory courses in finance and in probability and statistics. Students with a quantitative flair—especially those in the newly designed master of science programs in finance — are extremely interested in the content of this book. Most students look forward to a course in derivative markets because of the reported complexities and the high leverage afforded in these markets. This book may supplement advanced investments courses or courses often titled "Futures and Options," "Derivative Securities," "Financial Engineering," "Risk Management Strategies," "Speculative Markets," or "Financial Mathematics." While most introductory finance courses introduce derivatives and the Black-Scholes paradigm to the theory and practice of corporate finance, almost all finance majors seek more than a superficial understanding. To keep up with the scientific breakthroughs in financial modeling, and on top of the continual stream of financial innovations, students and professionals alike need a solid resource on basics of derivatives.

This book provides such a foundation. It serves as a comprehensive introduction to using derivative markets for managing risk in commodity and financial markets. The text provides insights into why practitioners use such contracts, especially as risk-transferring devices. It also features many risk management applications in a variety of settings to illustrate how to use these various contracts effectively. This book differs from most books on options and futures in that it not only provides considerable breadth of coverage but also takes a unifying approach to valuing derivative securities. It carefully illustrates all concepts and strategies with realistic examples. Its highly modular organization enables instructors to select those chapter sequences that best support course objectives and student needs. For even greater flexibility in customizing course content to fit both student ability and instructor interests, some chapters offer appendices of additional details and more rigorous material.

The text features six parts:

Part One, Forward and Futures Markets

Part Two, Option Markets

Part Three, Pricing Derivatives

Part Four, The Wide Variety of Derivative Contracts

Part Five, Interest Rate Derivatives

Part Six, Advanced Topics in Interest Rate Derivatives

Parts One and Two cover the basics of futures and options. Part Three explains how to price options contracts and how to manage risks associated with portfolios containing options. This module is most important not only because of the valuation approaches presented but also because of the risk measures developed. Part Four introduces readers to a wide variety of derivative contracts. It considers options on traded and nontraded assets, such as options on futures, forwards, and even options on options. It also analyzes stock index and foreign exchange contracts in great detail; investigates the use of exchange-traded contracts; describes the role of customized products issued in the over-the-counter market; and looks at contracts with optionlike features, which readers may find in securities issued by firms. Part Five focuses on derivative contracts based on bond prices or interest rates, an enormous market indeed in both the organized and over-the-counter exchanges. This module begins by analyzing the yield curve and identifying the more important interest rate risk management measures. It then examines the more important exchange-traded and over-the-counter contracts. Part Six presents some of the more recent topics in pricing and hedging interest rate risk. It also describes some of the latest techniques for pricing and managing risk and follows up with several applications.

Pedagogical Features

Chapter Openers and Objectives   Most chapters begin with a quick paragraph or two bridging from the previous chapter, and upcoming content is listed so that students know where they have been and where they are heading.

Treatment of Key Equations, Symbols, and Terms   Key equations—equations containing all variables, which are used later in examples to demonstrate how a model works—are numbered so that instructors can reference them during lectures and students can find them quickly when doing homework.

Pedagogical Methodology   The book lays out each key idea according to a consistent five-step format—property, proof, strategy, exhibit, and example. Much like any mathematics text, the book builds upon properties, followed by proofs, sometimes with possible trading strategies, tabular or graphical exhibits, and applied examples. These elements are easy to find, easy to distinguish from general examples without losing track of the key equations, and easy to identify as a group or unit.

Exhibits   Many types of exhibits, lattices, and profit diagrams are presented. Some are tabular and numerical; some are graphs and excerpts from the financial presses. Many exhibits selected from the *Wall Street Journal* include a paragraph explaining how to read this daily.

Conclusion and References   Each chapter ends with a summary for quick review as well as some references and resources for future research.

Problem Sets   Each chapter features a set of challenging exercises and problems, ideal for homework assignment or in-class use. Solutions appear in the Instructor's Manual that accompanies the text.

ComputerSoftware   An easy to use software package is available to instructors who adopt this text.

Development Process and Acknowledgments

Like my first textbook on derivatives, *Options: Theory, Strategy, and Applications,* this expanded version underwent critical review. Users of *Options* recommended that I make my presentation more accessible to advanced undergraduate and MBA-level students by providing more practical examples, explaining underlying corporate intuition, and overviewing derivatives engineering processes. I also wanted to cover futures and other derivatives at a consistent level that readers cannot get when they use different books, and I wanted to add practical applications and realistic examples. The manuscript itself evolved from my lecture notes, developed in teaching an options and futures course in the MBA program at the Weatherhead School of Management at Case Western Reserve University. I covered Parts 1 through 4 and required students to complete two case studies, the first on cross hedges using futures and the second on applications of the Black-Scholes model. In another course on risk management in financial markets, I covered all the material in Parts 5 and 6, with a special emphasis on interest rate risk management. Students in both courses provided much feedback on the level of presentation and the clarity of explanations and applications.

HarperCollins College Publishers secured two rounds of expert advice. The first review panel included both research-oriented users of my *Options* text and teaching-oriented professionals from a range of programs. The second panel consisted of detail-oriented instructors who suggested further editing and minor internal reorganization.

I would like to thank all those who contributed to this development process. First are the many MBA students of my 1990–1993 classes, who really helped me with this project. I would especially like to thank Tina Gregory, Toro Ando, Trond Knudsen, Jeff Penkowski, Charles Vink, Pat Groeller, Saad Zein, and Kirk Teutschbein. I would also like to acknowledge my Ph.D. students Yul Ryu, Betty Simkins, Ivilina Popova, and Ching Pin Liou, who have helped with homework problems and examples. Software development was done with the excellent assistance of Mike Young, Vishi Cusa, and Ivilina Popova. I would also like to acknowledge the assistance of the Chicago Board of Trade. They have always responded to my questions, and their educational programs and brochures are consistently superb. There are many colleagues I would like to acknowledge. Several read chapters and provided helpful advice:

Paul J. Bolster, Northeastern University

G. D'Anne Hancock, University of Missouri

Ayman Hindy, Stanford University

Robert L. Losey, American University

William Margrabe, William Margrabe Group, Inc.

David C. Shimko, JP Morgan Securities, Inc.

Paul D. Weise, University of Missouri

I would especially like to thank my very good friend "Sankar" Sankarasubramanian at Merrill Lynch. We have worked together on research problems for the last six years, and I have learned much from him. He has been a major influence on the way I think about interest rate derivatives, and Parts 5 and 6 are strongly influenced by him.

Thanks to Kirsten Sandberg and Joan Cannon, my acquisitions editors at HarperCollins, for their continous help, enthusiasm, and encouragement throughout all phases of this project. I would also like to thank the Department of Operations Research and the Department of Banking and Finance at Weatherhead School of Management. In particular I would like to thank the chairman of Banking and Finance, David Bowers, for his support in this project, and the Dean of the Weatherhead School of Management, Scott Cowen, who provided a special grant that enabled further software development to take place. Thanks to Tedda Nathan, who has been very helpful in assisting me with some typing and editing earlier drafts. Finally, I would like to thank my family for their support in this project. Actually, this project got done in spite of all their wonderful distractions!

Peter Ritchken

DERIVATIVE MARKETS

PART ONE

Forward and Futures Markets

The first three chapters introduce forward and futures markets. Chapter 1 provides a brief history of these markets and carefully describes the differences between forward and futures contracts. Several institutional features in futures contracts reduce credit risk and enhance liquidity. These features include daily settlement, margin requirements, the role of the clearinghouse, price limit moves, and circuit breakers. Specific examples illustrate how the markets are set up and how trading takes place. Chapter 1 also examines the types of futures contracts that exist worldwide and highlights the ingredients that make particular contracts successful.

Chapter 2 takes a closer look at how prices of forwards and futures are determined. Forward and futures contracts are designed differently, and futures prices are not necessarily equal to forward prices. However, there are some circumstances where the prices are identical. The first part of this chapter investigates these conditions. The second part investigates the cost-of-carry model, which provides an explicit model of futures prices. It explores other properties of futures prices, examines the relationship between futures prices and expected future spot prices, and investigates the determinants of the volatility of futures prices.

Chapter 3 investigates how futures contracts can be used to reduce the risk associated with a given market commitment. A perfect hedge is a strategy that completely eliminates risk. When a perfect hedge is not possible, risk can be reduced but not eliminated. Chapter 3 investigates how risk can be reduced to minimal levels.

CHAPTER 1

Forward and Futures Markets

This chapter provides an introduction to forward and futures markets. The first section outlines the history of these markets. We then begin discussion of forward contracts, which are private agreements between a financial institution and one of its corporate clients or between two financial institutions. These contracts are customized to fit precise needs. Unfortunately, because they are not standardized contracts, they are not usually liquid, and traders often have to maintain their positions until the contracted settlement date. That is, once a position is established, it may be difficult to get out of the position prematurely. In addition, since the contracts are private agreements, both parties are concerned about their partner's ability to make good on the bargain. That is, credit risk is a major concern. Futures contracts attempt to overcome liquidity and credit risk problems by establishing standardized contracts that trade in organized exchanges. Daily settlement, margin requirements, the role of the clearinghouse, price limit moves, and circuit breakers are described and examples of specific contracts are provided. This chapter also examines the types of futures contracts that exist and highlights the ingredients that make particular contracts successful.

The primary objectives of this chapter are the following:

- To introduce the history of forward and futures markets;
- To describe forward contracts; and
- To explain futures contracts and their advantages in reducing risk and enhancing liquidity.

The History of Futures and Forward Markets in the United States

Futures markets arose from the need to reduce price risk in commodity markets. The risk of fluctuating commodity prices became evident during the mid-1800s in the grain market in Chicago. Each fall farmers brought their grains to the city and attempted to sell them to grain merchants. The glut of grain over a short time sharply dampened prices, and farmers who arrived late often had to accept extremely low prices for their products. In the spring, shortages of grain pushed prices to high levels. These wide price swings created huge uncertainties for both suppliers and processors of grain. The fact that there was no centralized marketplace caused the marketing process between buyers and sellers to be inefficient.

Futures markets emerged as a means for buyers and sellers to reduce price risk. In the late 1840s a group of businessmen in Chicago formed the Chicago Board of Trade (CBOT). The goals of the CBOT were twofold. First, it was to maintain a central market so buyers and sellers could do business in an environment where all traders were treated equally and fairly. Second, it was to collect and disseminate commodity and economic information and to establish quality control standards for all deliverable grades of grains.

The establishment of the CBOT created a central point for collecting information about grain. Grain merchants were able to organize deliveries and to enter into contracts with farmers to purchase particular grades of grain, at particular delivery periods, for predetermined prices. These contracts, known as **"to arrive" contracts,** were desired by farmers because they reduced pricing and financing problems. The contract meant that the farmer would not have to ship grain to Chicago at harvest time and hope for the best prices but instead could fix the price, time, and location for delivery. Grain merchants also benefited since these contracts removed price risks.

Unfortunately, during times of heavy surpluses, grain merchants had incentives to break their contracts and to purchase their grains at cheaper market prices. Conversely, in times of unanticipated shortages, farmers had incentives to break their contracts if the market price exceeded their contracted delivery price. To ensure that contractual obligations were met, buyers and sellers were required to deposit good-faith money with third parties. This money became known as **margin money.**

These "to arrive" contracts became more and more standardized. **Speculators,** who used to purchase and then sell grain from their inventories in an attempt to profit, began buying and selling these contracts. Most speculators never owned or intended to own the underlying commodity. Their motive was simply to profit by following trading strategies that reflected their beliefs about the direction of movement in commodity prices. These speculators provided liquidity to the market. As a group, they were prepared to act as buyers of contracts from farmers and as sellers of contracts to manufacturers. That is, they would absorb the risks from traders who were looking to transfer them. Indeed, it was soon recognized that the primary economic function of "to arrive" contracts was to transfer unwanted price risk from farmers and their customers, collectively referred to as **hedgers,** to these speculators, who were willing and able to bear it. Without the active involvement of speculators it would have been difficult to initiate contracts. In general, sellers want the highest possible prices while buyers want the lowest possible prices. Speculators, however, are less concerned about actual price levels. Rather, they base their decisions on the expected change in price levels and hence are more likely to buy or sell from hedgers at all price levels.

By the 1870s the basic structure of trading these contracts had been established. Contract specifications were carefully designed, and the quality and quantity of commodities backing each contract type were established, as was the careful use of margin. In addition, the CBOT adopted rules and regulations to ensure that the marketplace remained free and competitive. The rules governed both the conduct of traders buying and selling contracts on the trading floor and the actual delivery process to be followed.

As the CBOT grew, so did other futures exchanges. The New York and New Orleans Cotton Exchanges served a vital role in the cotton industry. The Butter and Egg Board, forerunner of the Chicago Mercantile Exchange (CME), developed contracts on perishable commodities, where prices responded to seasonal variations.

The development of contracts continued to grow at a steady rate until the early 1970s. By that time futures markets had proved their value as risk-shifting mechanisms. Futures contracts covered such commodities as grains (corn, oats, and wheat); livestock (pork bellies, live hogs, and cattle); timber products (lumber and plywood); cotton; oil and meal (soybean, soymeal, and soy oil); and foodstuffs (cocoa, coffee, orange juice, rice, and sugar). Other contracts involved metals (gold, silver, copper, and platinum) and petroleum products (heating oil, gasoline, crude oil, and propane). For most of these goods, contracts existed for a variety of delivery months. The delivery months were established to maximize the level of trading activity. For agricultural products the contract months were linked to harvest patterns.

In the late 1970s businesses faced risks from high inflation rates, deregulated financial markets, and increasingly volatile interest rates. Futures markets responded to the problems by introducing financial futures contracts. Contracts on short-term Treasury bills, medium-term Treasury notes, and long-term Treasury bonds were introduced. In addition, a very active market developed in Eurodollar deposits. In other countries, financial futures contracts emerged on domestic interest-sensitive securities. For example, in Japan an active market in government bonds exists. Not all contracts that were introduced were successful. For example, a contract based on Government National Mortgage Association (GNMA) bonds began trading in 1975. While it was initially successful, over time the liquidity of the contract dried up as traders found competing products more useful to hedge interest rate risk. Today, interest rate futures contracts account for a significant fraction of all futures contracts traded.

Futures contracts also exist on a variety of foreign currencies. For example, contracts exist on the British pound and the Japanese yen. In the 1980s more types of contracts were introduced. In particular, index futures contracts began trading with cash settlements. These contracts have payouts linked to very specific indices. The majority of these indices are based on stock portfolios, but some contracts have payouts that depend on interest rate indices or foreign stock market indices.

While the futures markets were rapidly expanding, more informal markets were also evolving whereby individual parties could negotiate customized contracts involving future delivery of commodities at predetermined prices. These contracts were typically negotiated between corporate clients and financial institutions. An over-the-counter (OTC) market emerged, consisting of a network of brokers and dealers who negotiated transactions primarily over the telephone. In this market, standardized products tend to slowly emerge, with market makers providing continuous bid and offer quotations. Prior to the 1980s, the primary OTC forward market was the interbank foreign exchange market, involving currency contracts. This market has no regular trading hours, and currency contracts can be bought or sold somewhere 24 hours a day. In the 1980s the OTC market grew rapidly, and a host of new instruments evolved, largely in the interest rate arena. In today's marketplace forward and futures contracts may exist on the same underlying commodities.

The Basics of Forward Contracts

An investor who holds a long (short) position in a forward contract agrees to buy (sell) a specific quantity of a specific asset at a specific date for a specific price. The date at which the actual transaction takes place is called the **delivery date,** and the agreed-upon price is called the **forward price.**

The contract can be viewed as a side bet on the future delivery price. The payoff of this bet is equal to the difference between the forward price and the actual spot price that exists at the delivery date. The contract is simply a sales agreement established in an over-the-counter market in which delivery and payments are deferred.

An investor who considers the forward price to be very low might pay a premium to obtain such a contract. Conversely, if the forward price is considered too high, the contract has inherent value to the seller. Clearly, there is some intermediate price at which the contract will carry zero value. This price corresponds to the forward price. Thus, when a contract is initiated, the forward price is set such that there are no initial cash flows between the parties of the transaction. Let $FO_T(0)$ represent the forward price that exists at time zero, with settlement at time T.

EXAMPLE 1.1   Consider a cereal manufacturer who requires rye in six months and is concerned that prices of rye will rise in the interim. To remove the price uncertainty the manufacturer decides to enter into a forward contract with a particular grain elevator operator. The two parties enter into a contract that specifies the price per bushel that the cereal producer will pay to the grain elevator upon receipt of the agreed-upon quantity at the scheduled delivery date. The quality of the rye that is to be delivered is also specified. The contract may permit some flexibility in the delivery schedule, perhaps allowing the grain elevator operator to dictate the exact day of a specified week for physical delivery to actually take place. Since the contract is a specific contract between two parties, the exact terms are negotiated to reflect their particular needs.

Forward contracts are negotiated contracts that are entered into by two parties. As a result, the exact terms can be customized to individual needs. In particular, the two parties must spell out the quantity and quality of the delivered item, as well as the date and location of delivery. The consequences of failing to meet the obligations should also be laid out. Since each party may default, the creditworthiness of the counterparty is an important issue. The fact that the contract is customized to fit the needs of the two parties has its advantages. Unfortunately, it also has its downside. In particular, since the contract is unique, it may be difficult to establish its fair market value. As a result, if one party wants to terminate the contract prior to the delivery date, establishing the appropriate compensation to the counterparty may be difficult. Also, depending on the terms of the contract, permission may be required to trade the forward contract to another party.

EXAMPLE 1.2   Reconsider Example 1.1. Assume that after four months, the cereal manufacturer realizes that it no longer needs to purchase rye in two months. Unfortunately, the manufacturer has this commitment to purchase in the future. Rather than accept delivery and then resell the rye, the manufacturer is keen to renegotiate the contract with the grain elevator operator. Since rye prices have fallen dramatically over the last four months, the grain elevator operator has little incentive to renegotiate, unless it receives appropriate compensation. Establishing the appropriate level of compensation could be difficult.

The Basics of Futures Contracts

Futures contracts overcome some of the credit risk and market liquidity problems associated with forward contracts. An investor who takes a long (short) position in a futures contract agrees to buy (sell) a specific quantity of a specific asset in a specific time period at a predetermined price called the **futures price.** Like forward prices, the futures price is set such that no payments are made when the contract is initiated.

Like a forward contract, the futures contract can be viewed as a side bet on the future delivery price. However, unlike the case with a forward contract, the payoff, equal to the difference between the final delivery price and the agreed-upon price, is not received in one lump sum at the settlement date but is received in daily amounts. The size of each payment is determined by the daily change in the futures price. If the futures price increases, then the holder of the long position receives a payment from the short for an amount equal to the difference. Conversely, if the futures price declines, the long incurs a loss equal to the drop in futures price. This process of daily resettlements is called **marking to market.** The effect of marking to market is to rewrite the futures contract each day at the closing daily futures price.

Let $F_T(t)$ be the futures price of a contract purchased at time t with delivery date T. The **spot price** (current price) is $S(t)$. Exhibit 1.1 illustrates the daily cash flows from futures contracts for the long position.

At the maturity date T the futures price for immediate delivery must equal the spot price. That is, $F_T(T) = S(T)$. If the futures price were higher than the spot price, an astute investor would buy the spot, sell the futures, and deliver immediately to capture riskless arbitrage profits. Similarly, if the futures price were below the spot price, the astute investor would buy the futures, take immediate delivery, and then sell the spot to earn riskless profits.

Exhibit 1.1 shows that the net cash flow generated by the long position over the period $[0, T]$ equals the sum of the differences in daily settlement prices. Specifically, the net cash flow, $CF(0, T)$, is given by

$$
\begin{aligned}
CF(0, T) &= [F_T(T) - F_T(T - 1)] + [F_T(T - 1) - F_T(T - 2)] \\
&\quad + \cdots + [F_T(1) - F_T(0)] \\
&= F_T(T) - F_T(0) \\
&= S(T) - F_T(0)
\end{aligned}
$$

Note that the net cash flow from the long position to the short position is exactly equal to the cash flow that takes place in a forward contract. However, with futures contracts daily payments or receipts are being made, whereas with forward contracts there are only single, lump-sum payments.

EXHIBIT 1.1 Daily Cash Flows of a Futures Contract

Date	Futures Price	Spot Price	Cash Flow from Futures
0	$F_T(0)$	$S(0)$	—
1	$F_T(1)$	$S(1)$	$F_T(1) - F_T(0)$
2	$F_T(2)$	$S(2)$	$F_T(2) - F_T(1)$
	. . .	. . .	. . .
$T - 1$	$F_T(T - 1)$	$S(T - 1)$	$F_T(T - 1) - F_T(T - 2)$
T	$F_T(T)$	$S(T)$	$F_T(T) - F_T(T - 1)$

EXHIBIT 1.2 Accrued Profit on a Long Position in a Futures Contract

Date	Futures Price	Cash Flow	Accrued Profit (to Date T)
0	$F_T(0)$	—	—
1	$F_T(1)$	$F_T(1) - F_T(0)$	$[F_T(1) - F_T(0)]R^{T-1}$
2	$F_T(2)$	$F_T(2) - F_T(1)$	$[F_T(2) - F_T(1)]R^{T-2}$
3	$F_T(3)$	$F_T(3) - F_T(2)$	$[F_T(3) - F_T(2)]R^{T-3}$
...	...	...	...
$T - 1$	$F_T(T - 1)$	$F_T(T - 1) - F_T(T - 2)$	$[F_T(T - 1) - F_T(T - 2)]R$
T	$F_T(T)$	$F_T(T) - F_T(T - 1)$	$[F_T(T) - F_T(T - 1)]$

Exhibit 1.2 shows the accrued profit to the long position under the assumption that all receipts of cash due to favorable moves in the futures price are invested in interest-bearing securities and losses are financed by borrowing. The interest rates for borrowing and lending are the same and are assumed to be constant. A $1 investment at the riskless rate is assumed to grow to $R over a one-day period. The total accrued profit at date T is given by $\pi(0, T)$, where

$$\pi(0, T) = \sum_{i=0}^{T-1} [F_T(i + 1) - F_T(i)]R^{T-(i+1)} \tag{1.1}$$

Unlike the case with a forward contract, the total profit on a futures position will depend on the sequence of price moves over the period. For example, if futures prices gradually increased and then decreased, the long position would be better off than if futures prices initially decreased and then returned to the same level.

With futures, the difference between the final spot price $S(T)$ and the initial futures price $F_T(0)$ is received or paid in daily installments throughout the life of the contract, whereas with forward contracts no cash flow occurs until settlement. As a result of the daily settling feature, the default risk of a futures-style contract is much smaller than that of a forward contract. Specifically, since a forward contract requires only one cash flow at the delivery date, the chance is high that the amount is large relative to any daily futures cash flow, and there is a greater possibility that the party cannot make the single payment.

EXAMPLE 1.3   A trader enters a long position in 10 gold futures contracts at day 0. The futures price was $370.50 (quoted on the basis of 1 troy ounce). Since each contract controls 100 troy ounces, the actual dollar price is obtained by multiplying the quoted price by 100. At the end of the day the futures price was $371. The futures prices for each of the 5 days remaining to the settlement date are shown below. The accrued profit for holding onto the 10 futures contracts (if the daily interest rate factor, R, is 1.00030) is $7505.85.

Day	Futures Price	Cash Flow (Dollars per Ounce per Contract)	Accrued Profit (to Date *T*)
0	371	0.50	$ 500.75
1	375	4.00	4004.80
2	375	0	0
3	374.5	−0.50	−500.30
4	376.5	2.00	2000.60
5	378	1.50	1500.00
		Total 5-day profit	$7505.85

The change in the futures price on day 0 was 50 cents per ounce, or $50 per contract. Since 10 contracts were purchased, the total profit on day 0 is $500. Investing these funds for 5 days leads to $500.75. The total accrued value over the period is $7505.85. Note that cash flows into and out of the account every day. If the contracts purchased were forward contracts, then one cash flow at day 5 would occur. The size would be ($378 − $370.5) × 100 × 10 = $7500.

Organized Futures Markets

The terms of any futures contracts that trade in the United States are determined by the exchange, subject to the approval of the Commodity Futures Trading Commission. The specifications for each contract are the size, the delivery months, the trading hours, the minimum price fluctuations, the daily price limits, the delivery grades, and the process used for delivery.

As an example of a typical futures contract, consider the corn futures contract that trades on the CBOT. Exhibit 1.3 lists the main features of the contract.

The size of the contract refers to the number of units underlying the contract. The corn futures contract requires delivery of 5000 bushels. If this contract size is too big, a smaller contract is available. In particular, the Mid-America Commodity Exchange, affiliated with the CBOT, has a corn futures contract based on 1000 bushels.

The exchange establishes the grades that are acceptable for delivery. For the corn futures contract there are a number of deliverable grades. The price quotes are all based on no. 2 yellow corn. No. 1 yellow corn is deliverable at a 1/2 cent per bushel premium while no. 3 yellow corn is deliverable at a 1 1/2 cent per bushel discount on the settlement price.

The exchange is responsible for establishing the way in which prices are quoted and the minimum risk size. For the corn futures contract, prices are in cents and quarter cents per bushel, with the tick size equal to 1/4 cent. This translates to (1/4)$5000/100 = $12.50 per contract.

The exchange is also responsible for establishing the delivery months and how far into the future expiration dates should be set. Corn futures trade with delivery months in March, May, July, September, and December. For each expiration

EXHIBIT 1.3   Features of the CBOT Corn Futures Contract

Feature	Terms
Trading unit	5000 bushels
Tick size	1/4 cent per bushel ($12.50 per contract)
Daily price limit	10 cents per bushel ($500 per contract) above or below the previous day's settlement price; no limit in the delivery month
Contract months	March, May, July, September, December
Trading hours	9:30 A.M. to 1:15 P.M. (Chicago time), except on the last trading day of an expiring contract
Last trading day	Seven business days before the last trading day of the delivery month
Delivery dates	Any business day in the delivery month
Deliverable grades	No. 2 yellow corn at par and substitutions at differentials established by the exchange
Locations	Exchange-approved grain elevators

month, the exchange must establish deadlines for trading and for delivery. The last trading day for the corn futures contract is seven business days before the last business day of the delivery month. The last delivery day for this contract is the last business day of the delivery month. Hence, for corn futures, delivery can take place on any business day in the delivery month. The exact process of delivery is specified. Corn delivery takes the form of a warehouse receipt issued by an exchange-approved elevator in Chicago or in Burns Harbor, Indiana. Alternative destinations are in St. Louis, Missouri; Toledo, Ohio; East St. Louis, Illinois; and Alton, Illinois, at a discount of 4 cents per bushel.

Trading takes place during specific times. Corn futures trade from 9:30 A.M. to 1:15 P.M. (Chicago time) except on the last trading day of an expiring contract, when trading closes at noon. During the day, prices fluctuate continuously in response to market information. The exchange imposes a limit on the daily price change. For the CBOT corn futures contract, this limit is 10 cents per bushel above or below the previous day's settlement price. If a contract hits its upper limit, the market is said to be "limit up." The exchange has the authority to change the size of the limits at any time.

Futures prices are reported in the business sections of most big newspapers. Exhibit 1.4 shows the prices as reported in the *Wall Street Journal*. Each row contains information on a particular delivery month. The rows are ranked such that the earliest contract to mature is on the first line and the longest-lived is on the last line. The first three columns give the opening and the high and low prices for each contract. The settlement price is reported next. The settlement price indicates the value of the futures contract at the close of trading. If the futures contract has been actively trading at the end of the session, then the settlement price is probably the last price. However, if the contract has not been trading, then the settlement price may be different from the last traded price. Settlement prices are established by a committee that meets immediately after the market closes. The next column,

FUTURES PRICES

Monday, May 1, 1995.

Open Interest Reflects Previous Trading Day.

GRAINS AND OILSEEDS

CORN (CBT) 5,000 bu.; cents per bu.

	Open	High	Low	Settle	Change	Lifetime High	Lifetime Low	Open Interest
May	250	251¾	249¾	251½	+ 2½	285	228	19,790
July	256½	258¼	256¼	258	+ 2¾	285½	232½	136,360
Sept	260½	263	260½	262¾	+ 3¾	270½	238	30,237
Dec	264	267	264	266½	+ 4	267	235½	124,844
Mr96	270¼	272¾	270	272½	+ 3¾	272¾	249½	12,377
May	274	276¼	274	276¼	+ 3¾	277	259½	946
July	276¼	278¾	276¼	278½	+ 3½	279	254	6,864
Dec	253½	255¼	253½	255	+ 1¾	258½	239	3,914

Est vol 75,000; vol Fri 49,548; open int 335,332, +1,697.

OATS (CBT) 5,000 bu.; cents per bu.

	Open	High	Low	Settle	Change	Lifetime High	Lifetime Low	Open Interest
May	136¾	139¼	136¾	139	+ 2¼	151	122¼	778
July	143	145	143	144¾	+ 2½	145½	127½	10,900
Sept	146½	147	146½	146¾	+ 1½	149	132	1,309
Dec	150	151	149½	150¾	+ 1¾	153	136	2,014
Mr96	154	154	154	154½	+ 1½	157¼	142	312

Est vol 2,500; vol Fri 2,104; open int 15,319, −321.

SOYBEANS (CBT) 5,000 bu.; cents per bu.

	Open	High	Low	Settle	Change	Lifetime High	Lifetime Low	Open Interest
May	567½	576¾	567½	576¼	+ 9¼	705½	553¼	8,972
July	584½	589¾	580	589	+ 9	706½	559¼	61,008
Aug	585¾	594¾	585½	594¼	+ 9	612	562½	10,054
Sept	590	598½	590	598½	+ 9¼	615	564¾	5,575
Nov	597½	606¼	597	605½	+ 9	645	573¼	37,537
Ja96	606	614½	605	613¾	+ 8¼	626½	582½	2,888
Mar	612½	622½	612½	621¾	+ 7¾	632½	590½	847
May	618	626	618	626	+ 8	637	602	255
July	623½	631½	623½	630¾	+ 9¼	641½	599½	1,524
Nov	598½	602	598½	601	+ 3¾	615½	585	2,141

Est vol 55,000; vol Fri 46,044; open int 130,804, −110.

SOYBEAN MEAL (CBT) 100 tons; $ per ton.

	Open	High	Low	Settle	Change	Lifetime High	Lifetime Low	Open Interest
May	162.20	163.80	162.10	163.30	+ 1.40	207.00	155.30	7,410
July	167.50	169.00	167.30	168.40	+ 1.10	206.00	159.80	41,734
Aug	169.80	171.10	169.70	170.30	+ .90	182.60	162.10	10,737
Sept	172.00	173.10	171.80	172.30	+ .90	182.70	164.00	8,539
Oct	173.50	175.00	173.40	174.20	+ 1.00	183.20	166.00	10,615
Dec	176.80	178.00	176.60	177.60	+ 1.20	186.40	169.30	14,140
Ja96	178.30	179.50	178.20	178.80	+ 1.20	187.30	171.00	1,301

Est vol 25,000; vol Fr 35,270; open int 94,515, −142.

SOYBEAN OIL (CBT) 60,000 lbs.; cents per lb.

	Open	High	Low	Settle	Change	Lifetime High	Lifetime Low	Open Interest
May	25.92	26.74	25.90	26.71	+ .85	28.05	22.85	6,133
July	25.85	26.62	25.81	26.60	+ .81	27.85	22.76	35,581
Aug	25.78	26.45	25.75	26.42	+ .71	27.20	22.73	9,604
Sept	25.70	26.35	25.70	26.32	+ .75	26.80	22.75	8,571
Oct	25.55	26.25	25.55	26.22	+ .79	26.60	22.75	6,427
Dec	25.33	26.00	25.33	26.00	+ .76	26.30	22.80	14,471
Ja96	25.33	25.90	25.33	25.95	+ .75	26.10	23.25	751
Mar	25.50	25.60	25.50	25.92	+ .75	25.80	23.85	700

Est vol 30,000; vol Fri 31,497; open int 82,273, −2,226.

	Open	High	Low	Settle	Change	Lifetime High	Lifetime Low	Open Interest
Dec	79.90	80.55	79.25	80.50	+ .80	80.55	66.25	26,953
Mr96	81.10	81.60	80.50	81.60	+ .80	81.60	68.80	7,918
May	81.85	82.20	81.60	82.13	+ .78	82.20	72.70	2,790
Jly	81.90	82.25	81.90	82.25	+ .75	82.25	76.00	1,040
Oct	78.50	79.00	78.50	78.63	+ .08	79.00	77.00	232

Est vol 8,000; vol Fri 6,440; open int 68,897, −341.

ORANGE JUICE (CTN) – 15,000 lbs.; cents per lb.

	Open	High	Low	Settle	Change	Lifetime High	Lifetime Low	Open Interest
May	98.70	100.30	98.50	100.15	+ 1.15	126.50	96.65	1,504
July	103.65	105.30	103.30	105.20	+ 1.25	129.00	100.50	14,375
Sept	107.50	109.25	107.35	109.00	+ 1.50	132.00	102.50	6,385
Nov	107.00	107.50	106.50	107.15	+ .70	129.00	105.00	2,207
Ja96	na	109.15	108.50	109.15	+ 1.15	129.20	106.50	2,588
Mar	na	110.00	110.00	110.00	− .50	130.20	109.00	838
May		....	....	112.00	− 1.25	126.00	113.50	392

Est vol 3,000; vol Fri 2,272; open int 28,287, −621.

METALS AND PETROLEUM

COPPER-HIGH (Cmx.Div.NYM) – 25,000 lbs.; cents per lb.

	Open	High	Low	Settle	Change	Lifetime High	Lifetime Low	Open Interest
May	127.80	128.95	127.40	127.55	− 1.60	139.40	76.85	6,684
June	127.80	127.85	126.45	126.30	− 1.80	136.20	106.30	1,207
July	127.30	126.50	125.10	125.20	− 1.90	134.50	78.00	29,535
Aug		....	....	124.30	− 1.75	131.70	111.40	535
Sept	124.00	124.75	123.40	123.40	− 1.60	130.50	79.10	4,755
Oct		....	....	122.50	− 1.45	127.50	113.00	415
Nov		....	....	121.50	− 1.35	126.30	113.95	351
Dec	121.05	121.70	120.50	120.60	− 1.20	127.00	88.00	3,962
Ja96		....	....	119.60	− 1.10	125.10	88.50	268
Mar	117.75	118.70	117.75	117.60	− .90	123.70	99.20	1,432
May		....	....	115.60	− .90	121.00	107.00	339
July		....	....	113.60	− .90	119.00	105.50	272
Sept		....	....	112.45	− .90	117.00	105.25	195
Dec		....	....	112.45	− .90	116.80	112.00	144

Est vol 9,500; vol Fri 13,279; open int 50,100, −232.

GOLD (Cmx.Div.NYM) – 100 troy oz.; $ per troy oz.

	Open	High	Low	Settle	Change	Lifetime High	Lifetime Low	Open Interest
May		....	....	388.30	+ 1.30	398.20	387.00	34
June	389.90	389.90	388.10	389.80	+ 1.30	430.00	351.00	81,945
Aug	391.70	393.00	391.50	393.20	+ 1.40	414.50	380.50	23,270
Oct	395.80	395.80	394.60	396.60	+ 1.50	419.20	387.20	7,245
Dec	398.70	400.50	398.70	400.20	+ 1.60	439.50	358.00	15,500
Fb96		....	....	403.70	+ 1.60	424.50	393.60	10,508
Apr	402.70	402.70	402.70	407.30	+ 1.60	430.20	398.70	7,128
June	411.00	411.00	410.50	411.00	+ 1.60	447.00	370.90	6,345
Aug		....	....	414.50	+ 1.60	423.00	423.00	634
Oct		....	....	418.30	+ 1.70	432.20	418.00	114
Dec	421.40	422.00	421.40	422.10	+ 1.70	447.50	379.60	4,504
Ju97		....	....	433.80	+ 1.70	456.00	429.20	3,352
Dec		....	....	445.40	+ 1.70	477.00	402.00	3,772
Ju98		....	....	457.20	+ 1.70	489.50	454.70	3,046
Dec		....	....	469.00	+ 1.70	505.00	468.00	3,569
Ju99		....	....	481.10	+ 1.70	520.00	485.30	4,144
Dec		....	....	493.30	+ 1.70	506.00	490.00	1,932

Est vol 24,000; vol Fri 34,389; open int 177,062, −2,339.

	Open	High	Low	Settle	Change	Lifetime High	Lifetime Low	Open Interest
July	18.69	18.82	18.62	18.61	+ .06	18.82	15.71	35,444
Aug	18.35	18.42	18.25	18.26	+ .13	18.42	15.83	19,709
Sept	18.05	18.10	18.01	17.99	+ .16	18.10	15.89	12,599
Oct	17.92	17.93	17.85	17.86	+ .12	17.93	16.10	9,876
Nov	17.80	17.80	17.71	17.70	+ .12	17.80	16.13	3,152
Dec	17.60	17.60	17.57	17.57	+ .12	17.60	15.95	9,965
Ja96		....	....	17.44	+ .09	17.40	16.24	2,808
Feb	17.43	17.43	17.40	17.34	+ .07	17.43	16.18	3,299
Mar		....	....	17.24	+ .05	17.09	16.37	392
Apr	17.10	17.10	17.10	17.10	+ .07	17.30	16.45	1,391
May	17.07	17.07	17.07	17.00	+ .07	17.07	16.86	190

Est vol 44,325; vol Fri 60,145; open int 161,956, −1,530.

GAS OIL (IPE) 100 metric tons; $ per ton

	Open	High	Low	Settle	Change	Lifetime High	Lifetime Low	Open Interest
May	160.50	160.50	158.75	159.00	+ 1.00	167.00	143.25	22,732
June	159.25	159.50	158.25	158.25	+ 1.00	168.75	143.75	28,169
July	158.00	159.25	157.75	157.75	+ 1.00	163.00	145.50	17,361
Aug	160.00	160.00	159.00	159.00	+ 1.25	162.00	147.75	5,855
Sept	161.00	161.00	160.25	160.25	+ 1.25	164.00	149.75	5,232
Oct	163.50	163.50	163.00	162.75	+ 1.50	163.75	151.75	3,465
Nov	165.25	165.25	164.25	164.25	+ 1.00	163.25	154.00	1,901
Dec	167.00	167.00	166.00	166.00	+ 1.25	171.00	155.50	14,014
Ja96		....	....	166.25	+ 1.50	165.50	156.25	1,646
Feb		....	....	166.25	+ 1.50	161.50	157.00	130
Mar		....	....	165.00	+ 1.75	163.50	158.50	641
June		....	....	159.25	+ .75	158.50	158.00	110

Est vol 11,627; vol Fri 19,046; open int 101,256, +3,515.

EXHIBIT 1.4 Price information from the *Wall Street Journal,* May 1, 1995.

Source: Reprinted by permission of the Wall Street Journal © 1995 Dow Jones & Company, Inc. All Rights Reserved Worldwide.

"Change," represents the change in settlement price from the preceding day. The next two columns give the lifetime high and low prices for the contract. The final column, "Open Interest," shows the total number of contracts outstanding for each maturity month. Open interest is discussed more fully later in this chapter.

Opening a Futures Position

Customers wanting to trade futures must first open an account with a broker who is a futures commission merchant. Once this is accomplished, the customer can place a variety of orders. A **market order**, for example, instructs the broker to trade at the best price currently available. A **limit order** is a buy (sell) order that is to be filled at a specific price or lower (higher). A **fill-or-kill order** is a price limit order that must be filled immediately or canceled. A **stop order** becomes a market order only if a specific price is penetrated. A **market-if-touched order** becomes a market order if the futures contract trades at or below the order price. A **day order** is entered for one day only; it is canceled if not filled by the end of the day.

EXAMPLE 1.4   A limit order to buy one December futures with price 3 1/4 is placed with the broker. The order is a day order. If the futures price never drops to $3.25 before the end of the day, the order is canceled.

After receiving an order from a customer, the broker directs it to the appropriate exchange. A broker who represents the firm on the floor of the exchange will attempt to execute the order according to the rules of the exchange.

At the CBOT, trading of futures is conducted in designated areas called **trading pits.** The trading pit consists of one or more consecutive rings of steps dropping toward the center. Trades for each delivery date are informally grouped together. Oftentimes, the contract with the earliest delivery date is the most actively traded and is traded on the topmost step of the pit, close to the phone desks of the futures commission merchants. Alternatively, the pit can be divided like a pie, with different delivery dates trading in different slices.

The broker with the order may trade with another floor broker or with a professional trader. **Floor brokers** execute transactions for customers. In contrast, **professional traders** trade for their own accounts. Professional traders can be classified as position traders, day traders, or scalpers. **Position traders** have definite views of the market and tend to hold onto specific positions over a period of time. For example, a bullish position trader may maintain a large long position in a futures contract, while a bearish position trader may maintain a short position. In contrast, **day traders** usually liquidate their positions at the end of each day. **Scalpers** have very short time horizons and generate income by very active trades, possibly holding onto positions for only a few minutes. Their activity of buying at the bid price and selling at asking prices helps to enhance liquidity. Collectively, professional traders are called **speculators** because they are prepared to take on varying amounts of risk.

Open-Outcry Auctions

The price of a futures contract for a commodity represents the expectations of a large number of buyers and sellers. Their combined knowledge, based on all currently available information, helps establish the futures price. As new events occur, investors' expectations change and the futures price is reset. The actual price determination is established in the trading pits. The trading in the pit is referred to as an **open-outcry auction.** Trading may be quite hectic and noisy because traders face each other and make offers by open outcry to buy or sell an announced number of contracts at an announced price. The bid and offer prices are made openly for the benefit of all potential traders. Traders must be silent if they are not prepared to bid or offer at prices comparable to or better than the best current price. Generally, when the price is vocalized, only the last fraction of the whole price is stated. Grain futures, for example, are traded in ticks of 1/4 cent per bushel, so only the number of ticks is stated.

EXAMPLE 1.5   Our broker has received a market order to buy a July corn futures contract. The broker makes eye contact with another trader who is shouting, "Three at one-half." This trader is offering to sell up to three contracts at $3.50 each. Another trader in the pit might have vocalized a bid, "Four for one-quarter," indicating the desire to buy up to four contracts at $3.25. In any event, our broker accepts the offered price. The customer now has a long position in one futures contract, at a futures price of 3 1/2.

The noise in the trading pit can be very loud, especially in active markets. As a result, a complex set of hand signals has evolved to clarify verbal bids and offers. These hand signals indicate price and quantity information as well as whether the trader is buying or selling.

The open-outcry system is not perfect. In certain pits as many as 400 traders are actively transacting. Simultaneous transactions can occur in different parts of the pit at different prices. Such occurrences, however, are infrequent, and the price discrepancies will be small because all traders on the floor are aggressively searching for the best prices.

Once a deal has been struck, both sides record the number of contracts, the contract type, the price, and the names of the firm and the trader on the other side of the trade. To help speed this process up, traders may wear color-coded clothing or letter-coded badges to identify their firms and their names. The time block at which the trade occurred must also be recorded. The first 30 minutes of trading constitutes block A, the next 30 minutes block B, and so on.

Each trade is therefore recorded twice, once by each side. The transaction is also reported back to the customer. At the conclusion of trading, all traders submit their cards, called **decks,** to their clearinghouses, where all cards are matched up. If any errors are identified, attempts are made to clarify them before trading begins the next day.

EXAMPLE 1.6   **Other Trading Auctions**

The Specialist System
The open-outcry system of auctioning is quite different from the process adopted in the stock market. Typically, all trading in a particular stock is conducted through an individual **specialist.** The specialist maintains a "book" listing all outstanding

limit orders entered by brokers on behalf of their clients. When limit orders can be executed at market prices, the specialist sees to the trade. The specialist also has to maintain a "fair and orderly" market by dealing personally in the stock. At any time, the effective price at which the stock can be bought is the lower of the specialist's offered or ask price and the lowest limit order sell price. Similarly, the effective price at which the stock can be sold is the higher of the specialist's bid price and the highest limit buy order. By standing ready to trade at quoted bid and ask prices, specialists are exposed to exploitation by traders who may have superior information. To reduce this risk, they could in principle widen their bid-ask spreads. However, the exchange officials would not approve if the spread was excessive. Indeed, acceptable spreads are at levels such as 1/4 or 1/2 point. Specialists are compensated for bearing risk by the bid-ask spread and by generating commissions on transactions. They also benefit from proprietary information—they know the limit orders that have been posted in the book.

Electronic Trading

Another form of futures auction is **electronic trading.** In this system bids and offers are made electronically by traders who may be physically located all over the world. Buyers and sellers are matched together based on precise criteria of price and time. Bids and offers remain as standing orders until they are filled, changed, or removed by the trader who entered them or until trading closes. Any unfilled buy or sell orders are filled immediately at the best possible prices. Matching of orders is done on price first, then time of entry.

One international electronic system for futures contracts is Globex, which was developed by Reuters Limited for use by the CBOT and the CME. It allows for electronic trading of futures and options after the close of the exchange's trading floors. Globex is accessible around the world and extends trading hours virtually around the clock.

Electronic trading has several advantages. First, it opens the market to physically distant traders. Second, it improves the speed and fairness of order execution. Third, it creates efficiencies in clearing and matching trades. Fourth, statistical information can be more readily captured and more efficiently distributed. Of course, there may be resistance toward this system from exchange members who have a vested interest in the current market system.

The Clearinghouse

Once a price is negotiated between two brokers on the floor of the exchange, the two parties cease to deal with each other. Instead, they deal with the clearinghouse. The clearinghouse guarantees that all obligations are met, by breaking up every trade and becoming the seller for every buyer and buyer for every seller. Thus, all traders

EXHIBIT 1.5   Breaking Up a Trade

look to the clearinghouse to maintain their side of the bargain rather than to other traders. Since the number of contracts purchased by the clearinghouse equals the number sold, its net position is always zero.

EXAMPLE 1.7   The buyer of the July futures contract need not know the seller. Indeed, after the transaction is made, at a price of $3.25 per bushel, the clearinghouse steps in and breaks up the trade as shown in Exhibit 1.5.

Overall, the clearinghouse has no position in corn. It is obligated to receive and sell corn at the price of $3.25 per bushel.

Because of the clearinghouse, the two parties do not need to trust each other. Rather, they only have to trust the clearinghouse. Since clearinghouses are large, well-capitalized financial institutions, this default risk is small. Nevertheless, the position of the clearinghouse is not completely free of risk. In particular, if either the buyer of seller cannot meet its cash flow obligation and defaults, then the clearinghouse still has to make good on the other side of the transaction. Clearinghouses can guarantee all trades made on the floor of exchanges because they require their members to deposit margin monies based upon its customer positions. These margins act as financial safeguards to ensure that each firm is able to perform on its customers' positions. The size of these margins, called **clearing margins**, is usually based on the overall position of each member that trades on the floor. Before providing more information on the margin system, we address some of the additional benefits this clearing procedure provides.

Closing a Futures Position

So far we have discussed only how an order to buy or sell is initiated. After a position is entered into, the trader can choose either to continue holding the position or to close out the position. If the trader chooses to do nothing, then at the end of each day the position is marked to market and the contract is rewritten at the new futures price. During the course of the day, however, the trader may "unwind" the position by doing a **reversing trade,** as described below.

Trader A buys a futures contract on January 1. The contract requires delivery of the underlying commodity in May. To establish the price for future delivery, there has to be a seller of the May contract. Customer B is the seller of the contract, and the futures price is $100. Once the price is determined, A and B cease to trade with each other. As far as A is concerned, the contract is with the clearinghouse. Now suppose that over the next three weeks prices rise by $5 and the futures price becomes $105. Since the contract is marked to market daily, A has already received a $5 profit (ignoring interest) and now has a commitment to purchase the commodity at $105. This $5 profit has come at the expense of losses experienced by customer B. Customer B now has an obligation to sell at $105. Regardless of whether B defaults on the obligation, A will receive payments from the clearinghouse.

Assume that at this time A wants to unwind the position. To do this A instructs the broker to sell one May contract. Another trader, C, is looking to purchase the contract at the current futures price, $105. As soon as this transaction price is established, A and C cease to deal with each other. Customer A has just entered into a short position with the clearinghouse. A has an obligation to buy at $105 and another, offsetting obligation to sell at $105. The clearinghouse has an obligation to buy from customer B and sell to customer C at the current futures price of $105.

The total number of futures contracts on a given commodity that have not yet been offset by opposite futures transactions is referred to as **open interest.** Open interest differs from **total volume.** Volume refers to the total number of purchases *or* sales made during a specified period of time. Often the volume of transactions is reported over the trading day.

Having a clearinghouse simplifies the tracking of obligations between individual parties. Prior to the existence of a clearinghouse, brokers had to maintain complex accounting records called **rings** to keep track of who would ultimately deliver to whom. In the above example the ring is quite simple, with trader B ultimately dealing with trader C, but with more offsetting transactions the ring would get more complex.

EXAMPLE 1.8   **Offsetting Trades**

1.   On March 1 an investor placed a market order for a July corn futures contract. The price was 3 1/2. A month later the trader placed a stop order instructing the broker to sell the futures contract if prices fell below 3. Later that day this threshold was penetrated, and the order was executed.

2.   On March 1 another trader placed a market order to sell a July corn futures contract at 3 1/2. In May, with the futures price at 3, the trader decided to close out

the position by going long on one July futures contract. Ignoring the marking-to-market profits and losses, as well as any transaction costs, the net profit on this strategy is 50 cents or 2 ticks, worth $25 per contract.

The Delivery Process

If a futures contract is not unwound by an offsetting trade, then delivery will be made against the contract. Over 95 percent of contracts are offset. Most clearinghouses do not make or take delivery. Rather, they provide the mechanism that enables sellers to make delivery to buyers.

EXAMPLE 1.9   The holder of a short position in a corn futures contract wants to make delivery in the delivery month. The clearing firm representing the seller first notifies the clearinghouse that its customer wants to make delivery. The date at which this is done is called the **position day.**

The next day, before the market opens, the clearinghouse matches the seller to a buyer. The rule used for assigning a buyer varies from random selection to selecting the buyer who has been long the longest period of time. The clearing firm representing the seller then sends an invoice to the clearinghouse, and a copy is forwarded to the clearing firm representing the buyer. This is the **notice day.**

The next day the seller receives a check from the buyer's clearing firm and in return receives a warehouse receipt. This is the **delivery day.**

Margin Deposits

As discussed earlier, clearinghouses are able to guarantee all transactions by requiring that all member firms deposit sufficient margin monies to ensure that their customer accounts will perform. The **initial clearing margin** is usually based on the net long or net short position. For example, a clearing member firm with a short position of 100 corn futures and a long position of 50 corn futures is required to deposit margin based on a net short position of 50 contracts. In some exchanges such margin determination by **netting** is not allowed, and margin deposits are required for both the long and short positions.

Typically, margin levels are about 5 percent of the value of the underlying commodity and are sufficient to cover the daily maximum price fluctuations. The clearing margin can be posted in cash, Treasury securities, or letters of credit issued by approved banks. Each evening, the clearinghouse recomputes the margin requirements for each of its members. If margins increase, the member has to provide additional funds before the market opens. If margins decrease, the excess funds can be withdrawn. In periods of great price volatility, the clearinghouse can require its member firms to deposit more initial margin. Indeed, if the volatility rapidly expands, the initial margin could increase to as high as 30 percent of the spot price. Margin requirements vary according to the product and can vary substantially according to the exchange. For example, margin requirements in Japanese exchanges have generally been much higher than in the United States.

Each brokerage firm is responsible for the performance of its clients' positions. To protect itself from customer defaults, the brokerage firm requires a customer who wants to trade in futures contracts to post an **initial margin.** The amount of margin required varies according to the type of contract traded, and the quantity may also vary according to which broker is used. Usually, the margin requirement from individual customers is higher than the margin required from the firm to the clearinghouse.

The daily cash flows that occur due to marking to market are added or subtracted from this account. If losses occur and the level of funds in the account drops below a certain level called the **maintenance margin**, the trader is required to replenish the account, bringing the margin deposit back to its initial level. The amount required to bring the deposit back up is referred to as **variation margin.** If the variation margin is not paid, the broker will close out the futures position. The maintenance margin is usually about 75 percent of the initial margin. Gains above the initial margin level can be withdrawn from the account. The minimum levels for initial and maintenance margins are set by the exchanges. Individual firms may set higher levels for their clients. The exchanges frequently adjust these levels. In particular, if the underlying commodity displays increased volatility, then margin requirements may be increased.

It is the broker's responsibility to make sure these margin requirements are met. The clearinghouse does not deal with individual customers. Rather, it deals with its clearing members. Brokers who are not members of the clearinghouse must therefore arrange to have their trades cleared through other brokers who are members of the clearinghouse.

EXAMPLE 1.10 The initial deposit in the margin account for a buyer of a gold futures contract is $2000. The futures price was $397 per troy ounce, with each contract controlling 100 troy ounces. The underlying spot price was $385. Exhibit 1.6 shows the cash flows in and out of the account, under the assumption that the maintenance margin is $1500. Interest on funds in the margin account is ignored.

The purchase of 100 troy ounces at date 0 would have cost $38,500. The initial margin of $2000 thus represents just over 5 percent of the value of the spot. If the volatility of gold rapidly expanded, then the exchange might very well increase the initial margin to a higher fraction of the spot price.

EXHIBIT 1.6 Margin, Margin Calls, and Variation Margin

Date	Futures Price	Cash Flow	Margin Account	Comments
0	397.00	—	2000	
1	398.00	100	2100	
2	400.00	200	2300	
3	399.50	− 50	2250	
4	398.70	− 80	2170	
5	396.50	−220	1950	
6	396.20	− 30	1920	
7	395.00	−120	1800	
8	393.00	−200	1600	
9	391.50	−150	1450	Margin call issued.
10	392.50	100	1550	$550 of variation margin required (regardless of what happens on day 10).
11	392.60	10	2110	Variation margin received.
12	393.50	90	2200	
13	393.50	—	2200	Investor requests a withdrawal of $200.
			2000	
14	394	50	2050	

Other Features Reducing Default Risk in Futures Contracts

The marking-to-market feature, the role of the clearinghouse, and margin requirements all aim at reducing the credit risk of futures markets. Other institutional
features that also attempt to reduce default risk are daily price limits and circuit
breakers. Price limits control the maximum price move a futures contract can make
in any one day. The sizes of price limits are established by the exchange, which
reserves the right to change them, and indeed, in volatile periods the exchange
usually does expand them. **Circuit breakers** are rules invoked by the exchange to
stop trading if prices are exceedingly volatile. The idea behind circuit breakers is
to temporarily halt trading in cases where panic has set in and "mob psychology"
has driven prices out of line with their fundamental values. The introduction of
circuit breakers and the usefulness of price limits are controversial because they
decouple futures prices from their underlying commodity prices. While these rules
can reduce the magnitudes of loss by traders in any given day, their real value is not
yet well understood.

Current Futures Markets

Exhibit 1.7 lists the major futures exchanges in the United States. The two largest
futures exchanges are the CBOT and the CME. There are four categories of futures
contracts. Physicals are commodities such as grains, livestock, and metals. Futures

EXHIBIT 1.7   U.S. Futures Exchanges

Exchange	Year Founded	Physicals	Interest Rates	Currencies	Index
Chicago Board of Trade (CBOT)	1848	✓	✓		✓
Kansas City Board of Trade (KCBT)	1856	✓			✓
New York Cotton Exchange (NYCE)	1870	✓		✓	✓
New York Mercantile Exchange (NYMEX)	1872	✓			
Chicago Commodity Exchange (formerly the Mid-America Commodity Exchange)	1880	✓	✓	✓	
Minneapolis Grain Exchange	1881	✓			
Coffee, Sugar and Cocoa Exchange	1882	✓			
Chicago Mercantile Exchange (CME)	1919	✓	✓	✓	✓
Commodity Exchange (in New York) (COMEX)	1933	✓			
Citrus Associates, Division of NYCE	1966	✓			
Petroleum Associates, Division of NYCE	1971	✓			
Chicago Rice and Cotton Exchange	1976	✓			
New York Futures Exchange (NYFE)	1979				✓
Financial Instrument Exchange (FINEX), Division of NYCE	1985		✓	✓	✓
Philadelphia Board of Trade	1985			✓	✓

Sources: The *Wall Street Journal* and R. Kolb, *Understanding Futures Markets,* 3d ed., Miami: Kolb, 1991, table 1.6, p. 19.

on interest-sensitive assets and on indices now account for well over 50 percent of the volume of all futures contracts traded. The volume of aggregate business in these areas continues to increase and new products continue to be introduced.

In addition to the U.S. exchanges, approximately 60 other commodity exchanges around the world trade a variety of futures contracts. In England the largest exchanges are the London International Financial Futures Exchange (LIFFE), the London Metals Exchange (LME), the International Petroleum Exchange (IPE), the London Futures and Options Exchange (FOX), and the Baltic International Freight Futures Exchange. The more active futures markets in Europe are the Marché à Terme des Instruments Financiers (MATIF) in France and the Stockholm Options Market (OM) in Sweden. Other exchanges in Europe include the Deutsche Terminboerse (DTB) in Frankfurt, the Financiele Termijnmarkt in Amsterdam, and others in Denmark, Ireland, Switzerland, and Finland. In Japan, financial futures were banned until 1985. Since then the Japanese market has rapidly expanded. The largest futures markets are the Tokyo International Financial Futures Exchange (TIFFE), the Tokyo Stock Exchange (TSE), the Tokyo Commodity Exchange (TCE), and the Osaka Securities Exchange (OSE). In Australia, the Sydney Futures Exchange (SFE) is the largest. Other exchanges in nearby time zones include the New Zealand Futures Exchange (NZFE), the Hong Kong Futures Exchange (HKFE), and the Singapore International Monetary Exchange (SIMEX). In South America, the largest exchange is the São Paulo Commodities Exchange or Bolsa de Marcadorias (BM&F). In Canada, the largest exchanges are

EXHIBIT 1.8   Most Heavily Traded Futures Contracts

1992 Rank	Contract	Exchange	1991 Rank	Average Daily Volume
1	T-bond	CBOT	1	275,600
2	Eurodollar	CME	2	238,300
3	French government bond	MATIF	5	122,300
4	Crude oil	NYMEX	3	83,100
5	Euroyen	TIFFE	6	58,900
6	Interest rate futures	BM&F	—	55,400
7	German government bonds	LIFFE	12	49,600
8	S & P 500	CME	8	48,900
9	3-month Euromarks	LIFFE	—	47,900
10	Nikkei 225 futures	OSE	7	46,900
11	Japan government bond	TSE	4	46,700
12	Deustche mark	CME	13	45,600
13	3-month sterling CD	LIFFE	14	44,400
14	10-year Treasury notes	CBOT	—	44,100
15	Corn	CBOT	9	40,700
16	Soybeans	CBOT	10	35,400

Sources: Futures and Options World: 1991 Annual Worldwide Directory and Review, vol. 9, Surrey, England: Metal Bulletin Journals Ltd., 1991, and publications of the Chicago Board of Trade.

EXHIBIT 1.9   Principal Futures Exchanges

1992 Rank	Exchange	Country	Average Daily Volume	Share of World Volume	1991 Rank
1	CBOT	USA	590,700	21.5	1
2	CME	USA	528,500	19.2	2
3	LIFFE	UK	255,500	9.3	4
4	MATIF	France	218,000	7.9	5
5	NYMEX	USA	185,800	6.8	3
6	BM&F	Brazil	102,000	3.7	13
7	LME	UK	97,400	3.5	8
8	SFE	Australia	69,100	2.5	12
9	TIFFE	Japan	61,100	2.2	9
10	TSE	Japan	57,000	2.1	7
11	TCE	Japan	54,600	2.0	10
12	COMEX	USA	49,900	1.8	11
13	TGE	Japan	48,800	1.8	14
14	SIMEX	Singapore	47,900	1.7	17
15	OSE	Japan	46,900	1.7	6
16	DTB	Germany	42,900	1.6	21
17	IPE	UK	42,000	1.5	16
18	CSCE	USA	36,500	1.3	15
19	OM	Sweden	31,300	1.2	20
20	OGE	Japan	20,900	0.8	19

Sources: Futures and Options World: 1991 Annual Worldwide Directory and Review, vol. 9, Surrey, England: Metal Bulletin Journals Ltd., 1991, and publications of the Chicago Board of Trade.

the Montreal Exchange (ME), the Toronto Futures Exchange (TFE), the Toronto Stock Exchange (TSE), the Vancouver Stock Exchange (VSE), and the Winnipeg Commodity Exchange (WCE). The 15 most heavily traded futures contracts in 1992 are shown in Exhibit 1.8. Several of the top contracts are traded outside the United States.

Exhibit 1.8 clearly shows the dominant position of interest rate futures contracts. Crude oil, corn, soybeans, and (until recently) gold have been the only physicals in the top 15 contracts. Exhibit 1.9 shows the top 20 futures exchanges in the world, ranked by average daily volume.

From Exhibit 1.9 it can be seen that the CBOT and the CME control over 40 percent of the futures market. Actually, their market share is down from 48 percent in 1991. The non-U.S. market is growing much more rapidly than the U.S. market. Indeed, over the last five years the growth rate of the European futures markets has been spectacular. Volume in London's LIFFE, Europe's biggest exchange, now accounts for nearly 10 percent of the world's total, and Paris's MATIF is next largest. Frankfurt's DTB opened in 1990, and its volume continues to expand rapidly.

Design Features of Futures Contracts

In designing a contract, the delivery parameters, such as location, quality, and timing, must be specified in detail. The deliverable item should have certain properties. Specifically, it should be homogeneous, easily identified, and in competitive supply so that no single investor or group of investors can control the supply.

Under the terms of a futures contract, the seller is required to deliver the underlying asset or commodity at the maturity of the contract. At first glance it seems desirable to pin down the contract very precisely so as to eliminate any uncertainty regarding delivery terms and quality characteristics. However, if the contract is too precise, it increases the likelihood of **price squeezes** on the underlying asset. That is, as the delivery date nears, demands for transactions in the underlying spot market may increase dramatically, and this may cause temporary price distortions. To reduce this pressure, many futures contracts have some flexibility with regard to delivery terms and acceptable varieties of the underlying asset that can be delivered.

Different types of contracts have evolved which incorporate these types of flexibilities. For example, the seller of the CBOT corn futures contract is required to deliver 5000 bushels of corn in the delivery month. However, the seller has significant flexibility that allows some variation as to when, where, how much, and what will be delivered. These flexibilities are referred to as the timing option, the location option, the quantity option, and the quality option, respectively.

The **timing option** allows the seller to deliver the contracted asset on any allowable business day in the delivery month. If the asset can be rented profitably during this month, then the seller will delay delivering to capture these profits. For futures on physicals, the timing option is expected to be exercised early since holding of items like metals and agricultural produce is expensive. However, for financial futures, where the underlying instrument may be a coupon-bearing instrument, deferring delivery may be advantageous.

Some contracts have a **quantity option** that allows the seller to deliver an amount that deviates slightly from the requirement. This prevents deliveries being refused for small departures. If less (more) is delivered than the contracted amount, the cash paid by the futures buyer is reduced (increased) by the difference times the prevailing spot price. Since these adjustments are made at current spot prices, there is no advantage to over- or underdeliver. Hence quantity options are relatively unimportant considerations for establishing futures prices.

The **quality option** allows the seller to deliver one of a variety of specified assets. Increasing the number of deliverables against the contract reduces the likelihood of squeezes developing on any specific underlying commodity. The CBOT corn futures contract allows for three deliverable varieties. The benchmark variety is no. 2 yellow corn, which is deliverable at par. No. 1 yellow corn carries a 1/2-cent premium, while no. 3 yellow corn carries a discount of 1 1/2 cents per bushel. Clearly, at delivery time the seller will select that grade which minimizes cost of delivery (the **cheapest-to-deliver variety**).

Wheat futures contracts permit the delivery of 11 different types of wheat, while soybean futures permit 4 varieties of soybean. The CBOT's Treasury bond futures contract has at least 20 different Treasury bonds that can be delivered. Since the cheapest-to-deliver asset changes from time to time, this flexibility provided to the short position is clearly quite valuable.

Futures contracts on commodities specify that delivery may occur at a few specified locations. This provides futures sellers with opportunities to reduce storage and shipment costs associated with the delivery. This is important for agricultural commodities where storage in plentiful seasons can be scarce and costs high. This **location option** reduces the chance that the sellers will be squeezed by expensive local storage areas.

Trading restrictions imposed by the exchange produce additional delivery options, such as the **wildcard option.** It arises if the futures market closes before the spot market. For example, consider the case where a futures market closes at 2 P.M. but the short position has until 5 P.M. to determine whether to deliver or not. Say that on a particular day, after the futures markets closes, a significant event occurs that dramatically changes the prospects for the underlying commodity. While prices in the spot market will respond, the effective futures price remains unchanged at its closing price. The short position may choose to deliver against the contract now and receive the 2 P.M. futures price rather than wait for the next day, when the futures price will adjust to reflect the new information. This ability to choose to deliver based on information that comes out after the close of the futures market has value to the short position.

Since delivery options provided to the seller are valuable, they are reflected in the setting of the futures price. In particular, as the number of delivery options in a futures contract increases, the long position requires increased compensation in the form of a lower futures price.

Innovations, Successes, and Failures

Not every futures contract that has been introduced has been successful. Far from being static, futures exchanges are constantly innovating contracts. In the 1960s, just over 50 new types of exchange-traded contracts were introduced. In the 1970s, over 100 new contracts were introduced, and in the 1980s, the number of innovations was still greater. Not all new futures contracts have been successful. Indeed, it appears that a minority of contracts stand the test of time and emerge as successful innovations. Of all new contracts introduced in the 1960s and 1970s, perhaps one-fourth have had modest or better success. To be successful a contract has to satisfy a clientele of hedgers who find these contracts to be highly efficient for laying off risk that they do not want to bear. Specifically, a new contract has to provide a clear advantage over competing alternatives. This means that the effectiveness of hedging is better with the new contract and the cost of hedging is reduced. Also, these markets should attract speculators who are willing to assume the risk that hedgers want to unload. If the contract is too narrowly defined, then it might be of interest to only a very small, selective group of hedgers, and speculators may not enter the market. Typically, speculators like contracts to have some breadth, or flexibility, in the deliverables. In the industry, they refer to these flexibilities as "dirt." If a contract has a small amount of "dirt," then the group of hedgers is more likely to be diverse and to have different opinions, and the chances are higher that speculators will enter the market. Of course, if the contract contains too much "dirt," then hedgers may conclude that the product does not meet their specific needs, and they may shy away from the product.

Generally speaking, contracts are most likely to succeed when they are based on underlying commodities whose prices can be readily and continuously observed but not manipulated. For example, contracts are less likely to succeed if they have payouts linked to the levels of an index that is updated only periodically (e.g., a futures contract based on a consumer price index is unlikely to be successful if the consumer price index is updated only at certain points in time). For such contracts, information that affects the updates in the index is not known to the same degree by all participants. Less informed traders will shy away from trading since they will feel that they are being exploited by traders who have access to the proprietary information that is required to update the index.

Several types of contracts were initially successful but eventually lost out to newer competing products that had clear advantages. Introducing new futures contracts is expensive for the exchange. Not only does it have research and development costs, but it also has to make sure the appropriate trading and information systems are in place and that the public is well informed about the potential uses of the product. Also, the costs of obtaining regulatory approval for trading can be very high. Of course, the benefits are great for an exchange that introduces an innovative product that is successful. Indeed, once an active market is established, it is very difficult for a second exchange to gain market share by offering competing products.

Over-the-Counter Forward Contract Markets

The alternative to an exchange-traded futures contract is to purchase a tailor-made forward contract from a commercial or investment bank or a brokerage firm. The advantage of doing this is that a precise instrument can be designed to manage the risk of the specific situation. Of course, this customization comes at a cost. Moreover, if circumstances change and the buyer wants to unwind its position, the cost will typically be much higher than the cost of doing this using exchange-traded instruments.

In the last decade, interest in products offered in over-the-counter derivative markets has mushroomed. Products that once were considered highly specialized and were custom-designed for specific applications have now become more standardized. Initially, investment banks and brokerage firms offered these products to their corporate clients at significant markups. However, as these products became more common, dealers began making markets in them by continuously offering to buy and sell them. In this market, dealers communicate their quotes to each other through electronic quotation systems.

The increase in trading in some of these products forced prices to become more competitive. As the markups on these products were lowered, the liquidity benefits of using exchange-traded products diminished, making these products more attractive to firms that had previously been reluctant to use them. In addition, it became possible to terminate these contracts prior to their settlement dates with simple offsetting transactions. As a result, for these products, the differences between forward and futures contracts began to narrow. Of course, since these contracts, unlike futures contracts, are between specific parties, credit risk remains.

Exhibit 1.10 summarizes the basic differences between forward and futures contracts. However, as just discussed, the importance of the differences depends on the particular situation, and in some circumstances, the differences between forward and futures contracts are less acute.

Of course, there are many reasons firms may look to forward markets. First, a firm may not find a suitable futures contract through which it can hedge. There may be no futures contract on the underlying commodity or even on similar types of commodities. Alternatively, the hedger may want to offset a particular risk over a time period that exceeds the longest futures settlement date. Establishing long-dated forward contracts may be more sensible than attempting a risk management strategy that involves rolling over consecutive futures contracts. Finally, the firm may not have the in-house expertise in futures and might prefer to pay a premium in the over-the-counter market for a tailor-made contract that precisely meets its needs. In any case, off-exchange-traded products cannot be ignored. Indeed, over the five-year period ending in 1993, the volume of exchange-traded products grew by just over 38 percent while over-the-counter markets increased by 800 percent. In many cases the decision on which market to use is a difficult one. We certainly will have more to say about this point in future chapters.

EXHIBIT 1.10   Forward Contracts Versus Futures Contracts

	Forward Contract	Futures Contracts
Contract size	Negotiable.	Standardized.
Delivery date	Negotiable.	Standardized.
Trading locations	Over-the-counter dealer-type markets.	Futures exchanges.
Price determination	Negotiated in private by buyer and seller. Resale prices have to be negotiated.	Prices determined by open outcry in an auction-type market at an exchange.
Cash flows	Exchange of cash flows takes place infrequently. Oftentimes, the only cash flow occurs at the delivery date.	Exchange of cash flows occurs daily as the contract is marked to market.
Security deposit	Depends on the credit relationship between buyer and seller. No intermediary or clearinghouse that guarantees performance.	Buyers and sellers post performance margin with the exchange. Daily settlements take place. Clearinghouse guarantees fulfilling futures contract obligation.
Frequency of delivery	Most contracts are held to term. Few contracts are closed out prior to maturity. In some cases it may be difficult to unwind a position.	Most contracts are closed out by offsetting trades prior to the delivery date.
Regulation	Forward markets are self-regulated.	Futures markets are regulated by specific agencies (Commodity Futures Trading Commission, National Futures Association) and by the exchanges.

Conclusion

This chapter has provided an overview of forward and futures markets. A forward contract is a private agreement between a financial institution and one of its corporate clients or between two financial institutions. These contracts are customized to fit precise needs. Unfortunately, because they are not standardized contracts, they are not usually liquid. That is, once entered into, such a contract may not be easily unwound. In addition, since the contract is a private agreement, its credit risk is a major concern. Futures contracts attempt to overcome liquidity and credit risk problems by establishing standardized contracts that trade in organized exchanges and by designing features that reduce credit risk and enhance liquidity (daily settlement, margin requirements, the role of the clearinghouse, price limit moves, and circuit breakers).

We identified the most important futures contracts and the most important futures exchanges. In the early 1990s the most successful futures contracts have been based on interest rate products. Indeed, of the top 10 futures contracts worldwide, 7 are interest rate contracts.

References

The following introductory texts on futures markets all contain good discussions on futures markets. Most exchanges publish material for marketing their products. Interested readers should write to the exchanges for their promotional materials which usually include details on all their contracts, together with applications of risk management for hedgers. The booklets produced by the CBOT, in particular, are very informative and are strongly recommended.

Chance, D. *An Introduction to Options and Futures*. New York: Dryden Press, 1989.

Chicago Board of Trade. *Commodity Trading Manual*. Chicago: CBOT, 1989.

Duffie, D. *Futures Markets*. Englewood Cliffs, N.J.: Prentice-Hall, 1989.

Hull, J. *Introduction to Futures and Options Markets*. Englewood Cliffs, N.J.: Prentice-Hall, 1991.

Kolb, R. *Understanding Futures Markets,* 3d ed. Miami: Kolb, 1991.

Siegel, D., and D. Siegel. *Futures Markets*. New York: Dryden Press, 1990.

Stoll, H. and R. Whaley. *Futures and Options*. Cincinnati, Ohio: South-Western, 1993.

Exercises

1. Suppose that a trader enters into a long position in a gold futures contract for 100 ounces. The contract expires in 100 days. The initial margin is $2000 per contract.
   a. Explain why a trader might enter into a long position.
   b. Ignoring interest on funds in the margin account, compute the value of the account after 14 days, assuming that the futures price increases by $1 per day for 10 days and then remains unchanged.
   c. After 14 days the trader decides to liquidate her position. Explain the process of offsetting the contract, and compute the dollar profit from this investment.
2. A firm enters into a short futures contract to sell 5000 bushels of wheat for 200 cents per bushel. The initial margin is $2500 and the maintenance margin is $2000.
   a. What price change would lead to a margin call?

b. Under what circumstances could $1000 be withdrawn from the margin account?

c. What basic function do the margin rules serve?

3. A trader calls his broker and issues a day order to purchase a silver futures contract. The order is a limit order with price 510 cents.

a. Explain what the broker should do.

b. If the trade is initiated, what sequence of events occurs? In particular, explain what could happen to the open interest. Also explain the role of the clearinghouse.

4. Suppose that a gold dealer has 100,000 ounces of gold and is concerned about price declines over the next three months. The dealer observes that the gold could be delivered against COMEX gold futures contracts.

a. Should the dealer buy or sell futures? How many contracts may be appropriate, and what settlement date would you recommend?

5. A new futures contract on apples is being considered. Three grades of apples are established to satisfy delivery requirements, namely, grades A, B, and C. The recorded futures price is based on grade A. Let F represent the futures price. Adjustments are made to F if grade B or C is delivered. For grade B, the effective futures price is $0.98F$. For grade C, the effective futures price is $0.97F$. Assume that the futures price at the settlement date is $F = \$10$.

a. What should the spot price of A be at the settlement date?

b. If, at the delivery date, the spot prices of grades A, B, and C were $10, $9.70, and $9.70, respectively, then what grade should the short position deliver? Explain why the set of prices seems inconsistent.

6. A corn farmer in Iowa expects to harvest 20,000 bushels of corn in early November and has set a price objective at $1.72 per bushel or better. In April, the futures price for corn is $1.94. Explain the strategy the farmer could follow to lay off price risk. Comment on what could go wrong.

7. The party with a short position in a futures contract has quality, timing, and delivery options. Do these options increase or decrease the futures price? Explain.

8. Comment on what would happen if contracts were marked to market once a week rather than once a day. In particular, comment on the risk borne by the clearinghouse and on adjustments that may have to be made to margin accounts.

CHAPTER 2

Forward and Futures Prices

At the settlement date a futures contract can be converted directly to the underlying asset. At this time, the futures price should equal the spot price. Before settlement, futures and spot prices need not be the same. The difference between the prices— the **basis** of the futures contract—converges to zero as the contract approaches maturity. To understand how futures prices are established, we need to understand the behavior of the basis.

The basis of a forward contract is defined in a similar way. Because of the marking-to-market feature of futures, there is no apparent reason for futures prices to equal forward prices. However, in some circumstances the prices are identical. The first part of this chapter investigates these conditions. The second part takes a closer look at the determinants of the basis in a perfect market. In particular, we investigate the cost-of-carry model, which quantifies the basis and provides an explicit model of futures prices. We explore other properties of futures prices, examine the relationship between futures prices and expected future spot prices, and investigate the determinants of the volatility of futures prices.

The primary objectives of this chapter are the following:

- To explain the basis of forward and futures contracts;
- To explain the relationship between forward and futures prices;
- To examine how futures prices are established;
- To identify arbitrage strategies if futures prices are not within prescribed ranges; and
- To discuss what determines price volatility.

The Basis

The **basis** is defined as the difference between the spot and futures prices. Let $b_T(t)$ represent the size of the basis at date t for a futures contract that settles at date T. Then

$$b_T(t) = S(t) - F_T(t)$$

EXAMPLE 2.1   1.   On October 12 an elevator operator buys corn from a farmer for $2.06 per bushel. The November futures contract is $2.09. The basis is −3 cents. The local grain elevator is said to be "3 cents under" the November contract.

2.   The NYMEX trades a futures contract on crude oil. Actually, the underlying grade of crude oil is West Texas Intermediate (WTI). Exhibit 2.1 shows the prices of WTI and the prices of a futures contract over the lifetime of the contract. The weekly prices are shown for the May 1992 futures contract, from its inception in November 1990. The graph in Exhibit 2.1 clearly shows the volatility of the spot price over this period, in which prices have ranged from about $18 to $32 per barrel. The evolution of the basis over this period is shown in Exhibit 2.2. Note that initially the basis is quite large. Over time, however, it decays, becoming negative,

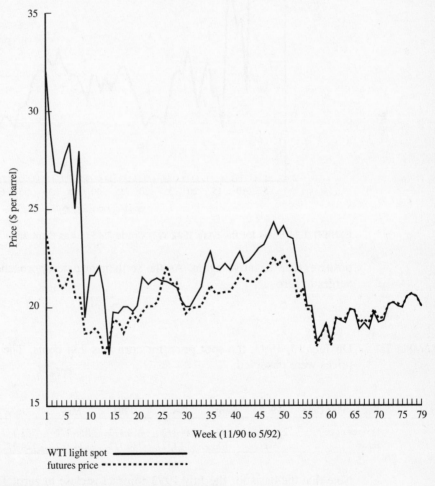

EXHIBIT 2.1 Futures and Spot Prices for WTI

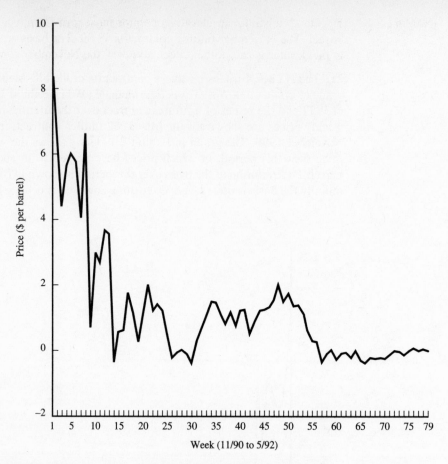

EXHIBIT 2.2 Basis for the May 1992 WTI Crude Oil Futures Contract

positive, then negative again. As the settlement date approaches, the basis converges to zero.

EXAMPLE 2.2 On July 13, 1993, the spot price for corn was 234 cents. The following futures prices were observed:

Settlement Date	July 1993	Sept.	Dec.	March 1994	May	July	Sept.	Dec.
Futures price	234 1/2	242	248 1/2	254 1/2	258 1/2	258 1/2	250	245 1/2
Basis	−1/2	−8	−14 1/2	−20 1/2	−24 1/2	−24 1/2	−16	−11 1/2

Note that the basis for the July 1993 contract is close to zero. The basis for more distant contracts increases in the negative direction and then decreases.

Examples 2.1 and 2.2 show that the basis can be positive or negative and can change direction over time. Further, at any point in time, the basis could be positive for some delivery months and negative for other delivery months. Understanding how futures prices are formed is equivalent to understanding how the basis is established. Before investigating the determinants of the basis, it is worthwhile to establish the relationship between futures and forward prices. Indeed, our first task will be to show that under certain conditions, these two prices are identical. If the appropriate conditions hold, the basis of a futures contract will equal the basis of a forward contract. This fact is useful because it allows us to ignore the marking-to-market feature in futures contracts and to quantify the basis by viewing the contract as a forward contract.

The Valuation of Forward and Futures Contracts

We assume that markets are perfect, with no taxes, transaction costs, or margin requirements. The annualized risk-free rate, r, is known and constant over time, and borrowers and lenders earn the same rate. If \$1 is invested at the riskless rate for 1 day, it grows to \$$R$ where $R = e^{r\Delta t}$ and $\Delta t = 1/365$. Let $M(t, T)$ represent the value of a money fund at the end of day T given that \$1 was invested at the riskless rate $T - t$ days earlier, at date t. In particular, $M(t, T) = R^{T-t}$. Finally, let $B(t, T)$ represent the discount rate for \$1 due at day T, viewed from day t. That is, $B(t, T) = e^{-r(T-t)\Delta t} = 1/R^{T-t}$.

We assume that there are no delivery options in the futures contract. That is, there is one deliverable grade and delivery will take place at a specific settlement date. The underlying security may be a commodity, such as corn or copper, or a financial asset, such as stock or an index. If the underlying instrument provides cash flows, the exact size and timing of these cash flows are assumed to be known.

The assumption that interest rates are known and constant over time may be reasonable for short-term contracts on agricultural commodities and metals, but it is not satisfactory for interest-rate-sensitive futures contracts. We defer discussion of futures contracts that are sensitive to interest rates to Chapter 24.

Let $S(t)$ represent the spot price at time t. The price of a forward contract at time t that calls for delivery of one unit of the commodity at time T is $FO_T(t)$. The price of a futures contract at time t that calls for delivery at time T is $F_T(t)$. The level of the basis at date 0 is $b_T(0)$, where

$$b_T(0) = S(0) - F_T(0) \tag{2.1}$$

Valuing Forward Contracts

Consider a trader who at time 0 enters into a long position in a forward contract with settlement date T, at a forward price of $FO_T(0)$. Recall that this price is established so that the value of the contract is zero. Let $V_0[FO_T(0)]$ be the value at time 0 of this contract. Then

$$V_0[FO_T(0)] = 0 \tag{2.2}$$

EXHIBIT 2.3   Valuing Forward Contracts

Position	Value at Date 0	Value at Date t	Value at Date T
Buy forward at date 0	0	$V_t[FO_T(0)]$	$S(T) - FO_T(0)$
Sell forward at date t	—	0	$-[S(T) - FO_T(t)]$
Value of strategy	0	$V_t[FO_T(0)]$	$FO_T(T) - FO_T(0)$

Over time the value of this contract will change. Let $V_t[FO_T(0)]$ be its value at time t, where $0 \leq t \leq T$. At the settlement date T, the value of the contract will be the difference between the forward and settlement prices. That is,

$$V_T[FO_T(0)] = S(T) - FO_T(0) \tag{2.3}$$

To see this, note that the buyer is obliged to take delivery at price $FO_T(0)$. Since the spot price is $S(T)$, the value of this contract must be the difference.

We now consider the value of the contract at some intermediate time point t, where $0 \leq t \leq T$. Assume that at time t, the investor offsets the long commitment by selling a new forward contract with price $FO_T(t)$. Clearly, the price of this new contract is set so that its value is zero. Hence, by entering into this position, the value of the trader's overall position remains unchanged at $V_t[FO_T(0)]$. At time T, however, the value of the overall position is given by

$$V_T[FO_T(0)] - V_T[FO_T(t)] = [S(T) - FO_T(0)] - [S(T) - FO_T(t)]$$
$$= FO_T(t) - FO_T(0)$$

Exhibit 2.3 summarizes the strategy.

Now, this value is known with certainty at time t. Hence, over the period $[t, T]$, the investor's portfolio is free of risk. Any position that is free of risk should earn the riskless rate of return. As a result, to avoid riskless arbitrage, this portfolio should earn the riskless rate. Hence, the value of this portfolio at time t should be the present value of $FO_T(t) - FO_T(0)$. That is,

$$V_t[FO_T(0)] = [FO_T(t) - FO_T(0)] B(t, T)$$

This leads to Property 2.1.

PROPERTY 2.1

At time t, where $0 \leq t \leq T$, the value of a forward contract entered into at time 0 is just the present value of the change in forward price.

$$V_t[FO_T(0)] = [FO_T(t) - FO_T(0)] B(t, T) \tag{2.4}$$

EXAMPLE 2.3   A forward contract calling for delivery in six months was entered into at a forward price of \$100. Two months later the forward price is \$110. By selling this forward contract, the investor is obliged to buy at \$100 and sell at \$110. Thus, the investor is guaranteed \$10. The current value of the net position is just the present value of \$10. Given $T = 6$, $t = 2$, and assuming the discount rate for four months is given by $B(t, T) = 0.9$, then from equation (2.4) we have

$$V_t[FO_T(0)] = [FO_6(2) - FO_6(0)] B(t, T)$$

$$= [\$110 - \$100]0.9$$

$$= \$9$$

Valuing Futures Contracts

Let $F_T(0)$ be the current futures price for settlement at day T. Like the price of a forward contract, the futures price is established so that its initial value is zero. Hence

$$V_0[F_T(0)] = 0$$

The value accrued at time t of this futures contract position is the sum of the daily gains and losses on the futures position carried forward over the t days. From equation (1.1) the accrued value would be $\pi(0, t)$; hence

$$\pi(0, t) = \sum_{i=0}^{t-1} [F_T(i + 1) - F_T(i)] R^{t-(i+1)} \tag{2.5}$$

PROPERTY 2.2

Futures contracts give the buyer the change in the futures price computed over every day up to the time the position is closed. The exact profit (loss) associated with holding a futures contract over t days will depend on the path of daily closings up to date t.

EXAMPLE 2.4   An investor buys a futures contract at \$150. If at the end of the day the futures price is \$156, the investor makes a \$6 profit. If at the end of the second day the futures price is \$150, the investor loses \$6. The accrued value of holding a futures contract for these two days is $\$6R - \$6$. In contrast, if the futures price dropped \$6 on the first day and then returned to its previous level on the second day, the value of the futures position would be $-\$6R + \$6$. The two numbers would be equal only if the interest rate is zero. Notice that if the interest rate is zero, the value of a futures position held for t days is just the change in the futures price over that period.

The Relationship Between Forward and Futures Prices

Since forward and futures contracts are different, there is no reason for forward prices and futures prices to be equal. Property 2.3 summarizes their relationship.

PROPERTY 2.3

If interest rates are certain, then futures prices and forward prices are equal.

To understand Property 2.3, first consider forward and futures prices with one day to go to delivery. Consider a portfolio consisting of a long position in a forward and a short position in a futures contract. The initial investment is zero. At the end of the day, the value of the forward contract is $S(T) - FO_T(T - 1)$, and the value of the short position in the futures is $F_T(T - 1) - S(T)$. The net portfolio value, $F_T(T - 1) - FO_T(T - 1)$, is certain. Since the initial cost of this portfolio was zero, to avoid riskless arbitrage the terminal value must be zero. Hence, $F_T(T - 1) = FO_T(T - 1)$. That is, with one day to go, futures prices equal forward prices.

Now consider the case with two days to go. Consider the strategy of buying a forward contract and selling $B(T - 1, T)$ futures contracts. Since interest rates are constant, the value $B(T - 1, T)$ is known at date $T - 2$ and is $1/R$. Again the initial investment is zero. At the end of the day, the value of each forward contract is given by the present value of the change in price. That is,

$$[FO_T(T - 1) - FO_T(T - 2)] B(T - 1, T)$$

and the value of each futures contract is

$$F_T(T - 2) - F_T(T - 1)$$

Hence, at the end of the day, the value of the portfolio is

$$[FO_T(T - 1) - FO_T(T - 2)] B(T - 1, T)$$
$$+ [F_T(T - 2) - F_T(T - 1)] B(T - 1, T)$$
$$= [FO_T(T - 1) - FO_T(T - 2) + F_T(T - 2) - F_T(T - 1)] B(T - 1, T)$$
$$= [F_T(T - 2) - FO_T(T - 2)] B(T - 1, T)$$

Viewed from date $T - 2$ this value is known. Again, to avoid riskless arbitrage, this value must be zero. Hence, with two days to go, futures and forward prices must be equal.

If interest rates are deterministic, this argument can be repeated successively to demonstrate that futures and forward prices are equal at all points in time. The result can be obtained only because we can establish the number of futures contracts to sell for every forward bought. (At time $T - 2$, for example, the strategy requires selling $B(T - 1, T)$ futures contracts.) If interest rates are uncertain, the value $B(T - 1, T)$ cannot be known at date $T - 2$ and the appropriate hedge cannot be established.

EXAMPLE 2.5   **Replicating a Forward Contract with Daily Positions in Futures**

Assume that interest rates are constant and over any day an investment of $1 grows to R, where $R = 1.0005$. Now consider futures and forward contracts that have three days to go to settlement. The forward and futures prices are both set at $1000. After one day the prices change to $1200; after two days prices are at $1500 and the settlement price is $1600. The three-day profit on the forward position is $600. The profit on the futures is $200R^2 + 300R + 100 = 603.50.

Now consider the replicating strategy just discussed. With three days to go, buy $1/R^2$ futures contracts and hold them for one day. With two days to go, buy $1/R$ futures contracts and hold them for one day. Finally, with one day to go, buy 1 futures contract. The accrued profit from this strategy is

$$\frac{\$200}{R^2} R^2 + \frac{\$300}{R} R + \$100 = \$600$$

Hence, this rollover position in futures produces the same cash flows as a forward contract. To reemphasize, this replication can work only if interest rates are certain. If they are not certain, then it would not be possible to establish how many futures contracts to purchase. Finally, this example confirms that futures prices must equal forward prices. If the forward price with three days to go was $1100, then an astute investor would sell the contract and initiate the futures rollover strategy, which replicates the forward. Regardless of what prices occur over the remaining time horizon, the investor is guaranteed a $100 profit.

PROPERTY 2.4

1. If futures prices are positively correlated with interest rates, then futures prices will exceed forward prices.
2. If futures prices are negatively correlated with interest rates, then futures prices will be lower than forward prices.
3. If futures prices are uncorrelated with interest rates, then futures prices will equal forward prices.

When interest rates are uncertain, there is no reason for forward prices to equal futures prices. Consider the case when interest rates are not certain and it is known that futures prices and interest rates tend to move in the same direction. Then the long position knows that cash flows generated from an increase in futures prices can more likely be invested at high interest rates, while losses derived from a falling futures price can more likely be financed at a lower interest rate. In this case the long position in a futures contract is at an advantage relative to an otherwise identical forward contract. Of course, the short position is at a disadvantage, and for a fair transaction to be made we would anticipate that the short position would require a higher price than the forward price. Indeed, to entice traders into selling a futures contract, the futures price must be set higher than the forward price. Similarly, when futures prices and interest rates move in opposite directions, profits from rising futures prices will be invested in a falling-interest-rate environment while losses will be financed by borrowing at higher rates. In this case the futures holder is at a disadvantage relative to a forward holder. To entice investors into holding futures, then, the futures price must be set lower than the forward price.

In summary, due to interest rate uncertainty, the setting of futures prices may differ from that of forward prices. Indeed, for a futures contract the total cash flow, together with accrued interest, depends not only on the behavior of the future spot price but also on the joint behavior of the underlying price and interest rates.

EXAMPLE 2.6   Consider a futures contract on a particular bond. If interest rates move down, then up, the price of the bond will increase, then decrease. The long position will make money the first day and invest it at a low interest rate. In contrast, the short position will lose money the first day but will be able to finance this loss at a lower rate. On the second day, the short wins and invests the proceeds at a high rate while the long loses and has to finance the loss at a higher rate.

Relative to a forward contract, the advantage rests with the short position. Of course, the long position realizes this and requires the futures price to be set a bit lower so as to compensate for this disadvantage. Clearly, the magnitude of this compensation depends on the sensitivity of bond prices to the daily interest rate. We shall have much more to say about this relationship in future chapters.

In general, differences between futures and forward prices for short-term contracts with settlement dates less than nine months tend to be very small. That is, the daily marking-to-market process appears to have little effect on the setting of futures and forward prices. Moreover, if the underlying asset's returns are not highly correlated with interest rate changes, then the marking-to-market effects are small even for longer-term futures. Only for longer-term futures contracts on interest-sensitive assets will the marking-to-market costs be significant. Because of this, many studies analyze futures contracts as if they were forwards. In the rest of this chapter we establish pricing relationships for forward contracts, then use Property 2.4 to make statements about futures prices.

Pricing of Forward Contracts on Storable Commodities

To establish the fair price of a forward contract, we need to understand how the basis is determined. Toward this goal, consider an investor who purchases a commodity and caries it over the period $[0, T]$. The cost of carrying the commodity consists of three components. First, if a commodity is held in inventory, funds are tied up that otherwise could generate interest. Let $AI(0, T)$ represent the accrued interest expense over this period: Then

$$AI(0, T) = S(0)[R^T - 1] \qquad (2.6)$$

In addition to the interest expense, there may be storage costs. For agricultural commodities these costs include warehouse rental and insurance charges. Let $\pi(0, T)$ represent the accrued cost of these payments over the period. For example, if rental and insurance premiums for the whole period were $I(0)$ and due at date 0, then

$$\pi(0, T) = I(0)R^T \qquad (2.7)$$

Finally, the commodity being stored may provide some cash flows over the period $[0, T]$. For example, the commodity could be a Treasury bond that pays coupons or a stock that pays dividends. Whenever a payout occurs, the funds are placed in an interest-bearing account. Let $G(0, T)$ be the value of this account at date T. As an example, if a dividend of size d_1 occurs at date t_1, then

$$G(0, T) = d_1 R^{(T-t_1)} \qquad (2.8)$$

The net accrued charges for carrying the commodity are given by $C(0, T)$ where

$$C(0, T) = AI(0, T) + \pi(0, T) - G(0, T) \qquad (2.9)$$

For financial securities, the storage cost, $\pi(0, T)$, may be negligible, but the value of the accrued coupon or dividend account, $G(0, T)$ could be large. Hence the net cost of carry, $C(0, T)$, could be negative.

EXAMPLE 2.7 Consider a trader who borrows \$206,000 to purchase 100,000 bushels of corn. The corn is stored for use in three months. Storage and insurance charges of \$200 are paid at the beginning of each month. These charges are also financed by borrowing. Interest expenses are 10 percent per year, continuously compounded ($r = 0.10$). The finance charge for the purchase is

$$AI(0, T) = S(0)\,[R^T - 1] = (\$206{,}000)\,(e^{r(3/12)} - 1) = \$5214.91$$

The accrued storage cost is

$$\pi(0, T) = \$200\,e^{r(3/12)} + \$200\,e^{r(2/12)} + \$200\,e^{r(1/12)} = \$610.09$$

Since the commodity provides no cash flow over the period, $G(0, T) = 0$, and the net cost of carry is given by equation (2.9). In particular, $C(0, T) = \$5825$.

EXHIBIT 2.4 Cost-of-Carry Strategy

Position	Cash Flow at Date 0	Cash Flow at Date T
Borrow $\$S(0)$.	$S(0)$	Pay back $S(0)$ plus
Buy the commodity.	$-S(0)$	carry cost, $C(0, T)$.
Sell forward.	—	Sell commodity for forward price, $FO_T(0)$.
Net cash flow	0	$FO_T(0) - S(0) - C(0, T)$

The relationship of forward prices to spot prices prior to settlement is determined by the cost of carry. To see this, consider a trader who purchases the underlying commodity by obtaining financing at the riskless rate. At the same time the investor sells a forward contract to lock into a selling price for delivery at time T. Exhibit 2.4 shows the profits from this strategy.

Hence, to avoid riskless arbitrage, the terminal value should be nonpositive. That is,

$$FO_T(0) - S(0) - C(0, T) \leq 0$$

or

$$FO_T(0) \leq S(0) + C(0, T)$$

PROPERTY 2.5

Arbitrage opportunities arise if the forward (futures) price is too high relative to the spot price. In particular, the forward (futures) price should always be bounded above by the spot price plus the net carry charge to the delivery date. That is,

$$FO_T(0) \leq S(0) + C(0, T) \tag{2.10}$$

EXAMPLE 2.8   In the previous example, the cost of a bushel of corn was \$2.06 and the trader's three-month carry charge was \$5,825/100,000 = 5.825 cents per bushel. If the forward price is above \$2.11825 (\$2.06 + \$0.05825) then the trader can lock into a riskless profit. In particular, assume the forward price was \$2.13. By carrying the inventory and selling forward the trader locks into a profit of \$0.01175 (\$2.13 − \$2.11825) per bushel. The total riskless profit would be \$1175.

If the forward price equals the spot price plus carry charge, then the forward price is said to be at **full carry.** In practice the forward price may not be at full carry. This is investigated below.

Reverse Cash-and-Carry Arbitrage

Consider a commodity, such as a financial asset, that can be sold short at the current market price. For this case, consider the strategy of selling the commodity short, investing the proceeds at the riskless rate, and buying the forward contract. At expiration the asset sold short is returned by accepting delivery on the forward contract. In addition the short seller is responsible for any dividends that the commodity pays out over the interim. Assume funds for these cash flows are borrowed. The accrued debt at date T for these payouts is $G(0, T)$. At the settlement date, the investor pays $FO_T(0)$ dollars to receive the commodity back and return it. In addition, the investor pays the debt of $G(0, T)$ dollars. Exhibit 2.5 shows the cash flows from this strategy. Since there is no initial net investment, and since the cash flow at date T is certain, to avoid riskless arbitrage, the terminal value should be nonpositive. That is,

$$S(0) + AI(0, T) - FO_T(0) - G(0, T) \le 0$$

or

$$FO_T(0) \ge S(0) + AI(0, T) - G(0, T)$$

Using equation (2.9) we have

$$FO_T(0) \ge S(0) + C(0, T) - \pi(0, T)$$

PROPERTY 2.6

For a commodity that can be sold short, arbitrage opportunities arise if the forward (futures) price is too low relative to the spot price. In particular, the forward (futures) price should always be bounded below by the spot price plus the net carry charge less the accrued storage charge to the delivery date. That is,

$$FO_T(0) \ge S(0) + C(0, T) - \pi(0, T) \tag{2.11}$$

For most commodities that can be sold short, the storage costs are negligible and equation (2.11) reduces to

$$FO_T(0) \ge S(0) + C(0, T) \tag{2.12}$$

EXHIBIT 2.5   Reverse Cash and Carry

Position	Cash Flow at Date 0	Cash Flow at Date T
Sell commodity short.	$S(0)$	Receive $S(0)$ plus
Invest proceeds at riskless rate.	$-S(0)$	interest, $AI(0, T)$.
Buy forward.	—	Take delivery of asset and return it: $-[FO_T(0) + G(0, T)]$.
Net cash flow	0	$S(0) + AI(0, T) - FO_T(0) - G(0, T)$

Equations (2.10) and (2.12) imply that forward and futures prices for storable commodities that can be sold short should equal the spot price plus the carry charge. This result leads to Property 2.7.

PROPERTY 2.7

For a commodity that has negligible storage costs and can be sold short, forward and futures prices should be set at full carry.

Actually, the ability to sell the commodity short is not essential to prevent forward prices from falling below the spot price plus carry charge. To see this, consider a trader who owns the commodity and plans on holding it for some time. If the forward price dropped below the spot plus carry charge, the trader would sell the commodity, invest the proceeds at the riskless rate, and buy the forward contract. At the settlement date, the trader would take delivery of the asset. In effect, the trader would find this strategy cheaper than storing inventory. If the commodity were in ample supply, other traders who held excess inventory would initiate the same strategy. Their activity would continue until forward prices rose to a level that reflected full carry. This argument suggests that to avoid riskless arbitrage, forward prices on commodities that are abundantly available and storable should reflect full carry charges.

PROPERTY 2.8

If a commodity is in ample supply, then forward and futures prices should reflect full carry charges. That is,

$$FO_T(0) = S(0) + C(0, T) \qquad (2.13)$$

If the underlying commodity provides no cash flows and incurs no storage charges, then the carry charge reflects just the opportunity cost of funds, so

$$FO_T(0) = S(0) + AI(0, T)$$

Substituting equation (2.6) into the above expression yields

$$FO_T(0) = S(0)R^T$$

If the time to delivery T is measured in years rather than days, then the forward price can be expressed as

$$FO_T(0) = S(0) \, e^{rT} \qquad (2.14)$$

If storage charges are incurred continuously and are proportional to the price of the commodity, then the effective cost of carry is increased from the rate r to $r + u$.

Thus

$$FO_T(0) = S(0) + C(0, T) = S(0) \, e^{(r+u)T} \qquad (2.15)$$

where u is the storage cost per year as a proportion of the spot price. For storable commodities, such as financial securities that do not provide cash flows, and for investment commodities, such as gold, the net cost of carry is usually positive, and forward prices typically lie above spot prices.

Finally, if the underlying commodity pays a continuous dividend yield at rate d, the net cost of carry in equation (2.15) is reduced from $r + u$ to $r + u - d$. So

$$FO_T(0) = S(0) \, e^{(r+u-d)T} \qquad (2.16)$$

where u is the net storage cost per year expressed as a proportion of the spot price.

EXAMPLE 2.9 Consider a futures contract on gold. For this product the bulk of the carrying charge is interest expense, with a very small amount required for insurance and storage. The further away the delivery date, the greater the interest expense, so typically forward prices exceed spot prices by an amount that increases with maturity. Below are hypothetical prices of gold forward contracts for delivery in their specified months. The current spot price is $305.

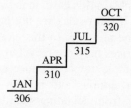

From this information we can infer that the market is saying that the net cost of carrying gold from April to July is $5. If an investor could carry the commodity for under $5 over that period, then riskless arbitrage opportunities could arise if the investor buys the April contract and simultaneously sells the July. This strategy, referred to as a **spread,** locks into a $5 profit less the total cost of borrowing $310 from April to July.

EXAMPLE 2.10 Assume the spot price of a storable commodity is $100, a dividend of $5 is due in six months ($t_1 = 0.5$ year), and interest rates are flat at 5 percent. There are no storage costs and the commodity is in ample supply. Then the forward price of a contract that settles in one year ($T = 1$ year) is

$$FO_T(0) = S(0) \, e^{rT} - d_1 \, e^{r(T-t_1)}$$

$$= \$100 \, e^{0.05} - \$5 \, e^{0.05(0.5)} = \$100$$

EXAMPLE 2.11   Consider a commodity that is currently priced at $100. The commodity is in ample supply. Interest rates are 5 percent. The commodity provides a continuous yield of 8 percent. Storage costs are 1 percent of the commodity price and are charged continuously. Then the forward price of a contract that settles in one year is given by equation (2.16), where $r = 0.05$, $d = 0.08$, and $u = 0.01$. Hence,

$$FO_T(0) = S(0)\ e^{(r+u-d)T} = \$98.01$$

Note that since the cash inflow exceeds the cost of interest and storage, the forward price will be set below the spot price and the basis will be positive.

When cash inflow exceeds the cost of interest plus storage, the basis may be positive. With a lumpy sequence of cash inflows (in the form of dividends or coupon payments), futures prices can be above the spot price sometimes and below the spot price at other times.

Convenience Yields

So far we have assumed that the commodity can be sold short or that it is in abundant supply. In this case, to avoid arbitrage, the forward price reflects the full carry charge. If short sales are not possible, then the reverse cash-and-carry arbitrage cannot be initiated. In this case the futures price has no lower no-arbitrage bound, and prices may not be set at full carry. Of course, if the underlying commodity is in ample supply, producers with large inventories may temporarily relinquish their inventories and purchase forward contracts, and their activity will prevent prices from deviating significantly from the full carry price. However, if the commodity is not abundant, then traders may be reluctant to temporarily relinquish their inventories, and futures prices may not reflect full carry.

Commodities that should reflect full carry include all those that are held for investment purposes, such as stocks, bonds, and gold. The supply of these securities may fluctuate slightly over time, but these fluctuations are small compared to outstanding inventories. The majority of commodities, including all agricultural commodities (such as corn and wheat) and metals (such as copper and zinc), are held for consumption purposes. The supply and demand for these commodities fluctuate over time, and inventories expand and shrink in response. For some commodities, such as agricultural commodities, production is seasonal but consumption is fairly steady. For other goods, such as heating oil, consumption is seasonal while production is continuous. In times of scarcity, holders of such commodities may be reluctant to relinquish their inventories on a temporary basis. By having inventory readily available, suppliers can maintain production processes despite local shortages, or they can generate profits from local price variations that arise during shortages. The owner of inventory has valuable claims that provide the right to liquidate inventory, contingent on price and demand fluctuations. By temporarily relinquishing the inventory, the owner loses these claims. The benefit from owning the physical commodity provides the owner with a yield called the **convenience yield.** Clearly, the size of the convenience yield depends on factors such as the current aggregate levels of inventory, current supply and demand characteristics, and projected future supplies and demands. In addition, the convenience yield depends on risk-reward preferences, with greater inventories being required as risk aversion in the economy increases. Let $k(0, T)$ represent the size of the convenience yield, measured in dollars, accrued up to time T. The futures price on a commodity can then be written as

$$F_T(0) = S(0) + C(0, T) - k(0, T) \qquad (2.17)$$

Futures prices deviate from their full carry values when the convenience yield is significant. Although the actual size of the convenience yield is not observable, we can assume that its benefits to the inventory owner are continuous. Hence, we define κ as the continuous convenience yield per unit time, where κ is a constant proportion of the spot price. Since the convenience yield can be viewed as a nonobservable continuous dividend yield, for the case when storage costs are a constant proportion of the spot price, equation (2.16) yields

$$F_T(0) = S(0)\, e^{(r+u-\kappa)T} \qquad (2.18)$$

If the futures price is observable, we can solve equation (2.18) to obtain the implied convenience yield. Specifically, we obtain

$$\kappa = [\ln(S(0)/F_T(0)) + (r + u)T]/T \qquad (2.19)$$

EXAMPLE 2.12   The futures prices of a storable commodity are shown below. The carry charge for the commodity is 1 percent of the spot price per year ($u = 0.01$) and interest rates are 9 percent. The current time is April, one month prior to the May settlement date. The spot price is \$1.96.

Settlement date	May	July	Sept.	Dec.	March
Futures price	1.95	1.92	1.87	1.89	1.89

The annualized convenience yields, computed using equation (2.19), are shown below.

Settlement date	May	July	Sept.	Dec.	March
Upper bound (using equation (2.10)	1.976	2.0096	2.043	2.095	2.148
Convenience yield	16.13	18.24	21.28	15.45	13.96

Note that by buying a July contract and selling a September contract, the trader is committing to purchase at \$1.92 and sell two months later at \$1.87. Using the cost-of-carry model, we have

$$F_T(t) = F_s(t)\, e^{(r+u-\kappa)(T-s)} \qquad (2.20)$$

where s is the near-term futures delivery date (July), T is the far-term delivery date date (September), and κ is the annualized convenience yield over the time period $[s, T]$. The implied convenience yield over this period can be computed using equation (2.20). For example, the annualized implied convenience yield over the July–September period is 25.83 percent. The implied convenience yields over the successive time periods are shown below.

Time period	April–May	May–July	July–Sept.	Sept.–Dec.	Dec.–March
Implied convenience yield	16.13	19.29	25.83	5.74	10.00

Given the implied convenience yields, it appears that the benefits of holding inventories are greatest over the July–September period and are least over the September–December period.

The Term Structure of Futures Prices and Basis Risk

Futures prices for investment commodities that have low coupons or dividends increase as the settlement date increases. Futures prices for consumption commodities could increase or decrease as the settlement date increases. A downward-sloping term structure of futures prices is especially likely if demand for the commodity is very high and current supplies are limited. In this case, the convenience yield derived by having the commodity in inventory is extremely high.

EXAMPLE 2.13   The diagram illustrates the futures prices of a particular commodity. In effect, the market is paying owners of the commodity to store the commodity for future use.

EXAMPLE 2.14   The term structure of futures prices need not be strictly increasing or decreasing. Other patterns often occur when the futures price for the last delivery month of one marketing year, with its own supply and demand mechanisms, are quite different from the futures price for the first delivery month in the next marketing year. The diagram below shows the futures function on a hypothetical commodity.

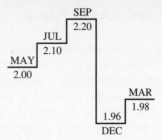

If the futures function increases then decreases, the basis of some contracts may be negative while that of other contracts could be positive. Clearly, significant information can be extracted from this function. In particular, it appears that from May to September the commodity is in abundant supply, and the increasing function is due to interest and storage charges. However, from September to December the sharp dropoff occurs and storing the commodity for future use is penalized.

The magnitude of the basis is determined by the convenience yield and the carry charge to the settlement date. If these charges remain stable over time, then the basis should converge smoothly to zero. However, if the convenience yield or carry charge changes unexpectedly, then the basis will deviate from its smooth path toward zero. The fact that the basis can deviate from its projected path introduces basis risk. We shall return to basis risk in Chapter 3.

Futures Prices for Nonstorable Commodities

The cost-of-carry model requires that the underlying commodity be storable. We now consider the behavior of prices on nonstorable commodities. For example, consider the futures price of electricity. The futures price cannot be directly linked to the spot price through the cost-of-carry model because electricity cannot be stored. In this section we investigate how the futures price is determined. To make matters specific, assume that the market's consensus is that the future spot price at the delivery date will be $100. More precisely, based on all information available, the expected future spot price is $100. If the futures price were significantly lower than $100 (say $90), then some speculators would consider buying the contract with the expectation of making a $10 profit. As the discrepancy between the two prices increases, more speculators participate. Indeed, their very activity prevents prices deviating "too far" from the expected price.

If there is terrific uncertainty about the futures price, the speculator may not purchase the futures contract even if its price is below the expected spot price. For example, if the futures price were $99, speculators might not pursue the $1 expected profit. Indeed, to entice speculators to bear the risk of a futures position, they must be compensated with an appropriate risk premium. As a result, there may not be a simple relationship between futures prices and expected future spot prices.

Speculators, Hedgers, and Futures Prices

Speculators are traders who are prepared to bear risk, in return for which they expect to achieve an appropriate compensation. As a result, speculators will buy (sell) futures contracts only if they expect prices to increase (decrease). Hedgers, on the other hand, are prepared to pay a premium to lay off unwanted risk onto speculators. If hedgers, in aggregate, are short, then speculators are net long, and in this case the futures price will be set below the future expected spot price. This situation is referred to as **normal backwardation.** In contrast, if hedgers are net long, speculators will be net short, and futures prices will be set above the expected future spot price. This situation is known as **contango.**

Of course, the net position of hedgers may change over time. When the contract begins trading, the hedgers may be net short. For example, when a corn futures contract is introduced, farmers may attempt to lock in prices for their crop by selling short. In such a case, the futures price lies below the expected future spot price. Over time, the hedgers gradually offset their positions, and food processors, for example, begin to lock in prices by buying long. As the hedging imbalance moves from net short to net long, the futures price moves from being below the expected spot price to being above the expected spot price.

A price process is said to be a **martingale** if the expectation of its future value equals its current value. If futures prices were martingales, then

$$E_0\{F_T(t)\} = F_T(0) \quad \text{for all} \quad 0 \leq t \leq T$$

In particular, with $t = T$,

$$E_0\{F_T(T)\} = E_0\{S(T)\} = F_T(0)$$

Hence, if futures prices are martingales then the futures price is an unbiased estimator of the expected future spot price. On the other hand, if the market is a normal backwardation or contango market, then prices will not be martingales.

From the above discussion we have no real reason to suspect that futures prices should be martingales. Nonetheless, a substantial number of statistical studies have been performed to test the martingale hypothesis. Many of the early tests were unable to reject this hypothesis. (One reason is that the tests lacked statistical power and hence required overwhelming evidence to reject the hypothesis.) These early results spawned many additional studies, some of which have shown that futures prices may not provide good estimates of future spot prices. But for practical purposes, the futures price is still considered a reasonable estimate for the future expected spot price.

The Volatility of Futures Prices

The current futures price reflects current information about the spot price at delivery time. As information is revealed, futures prices will change. The volatility of price changes clearly is related to the quality and quantity of information revealed over time. If information is revealed more quickly as the delivery date approaches, then one might expect futures prices to show increasing volatility as the maturity approaches. Empirical studies have shown that this type of behavior holds for metal futures, such as gold and copper. For other commodities, the volatility of prices may be seasonal. This is particularly true if important information is revealed over short periods of time. For example, rainfall at crucial points clarifies the supply of agricultural products, and the severity of a winter month clarifies the demand for heating oil. Such seasonality in prices should be less pronounced for financial contracts. However, even there seasonal variability has been uncovered. For example, the volatility of some financial products seems to be larger on Mondays than on other days of the week. Volatility also seems to be related to volume; as uncertainty unfolds, the volume of trade accelerates in response to the volatility.

Conclusion

This chapter has developed the basic principles for pricing futures and forward contracts. Throughout this chapter we have assumed that interest rates are constant. As a result, futures prices and forward prices are identical. The cost-of-carry model and the reverse cash-and-carry model show how futures prices must be linked to their underlying spot prices. In the development of these pricing relationships, we assumed that markets were perfect. Of course, this is not the case. Transaction costs, unequal borrowing and lending rates, margin requirements and restrictions on short selling, and limitations to storage are four imperfections that can affect the pricing relationships. Nonetheless, the cost-of-carry model captures the most important components of the basis. For commodities that cannot be stored, the "expected futures price" framework provides a procedure for thinking about futures prices. Finally, price volatility is greatest when information dissemination on the underlying commodity is most rapid.

References

Cox, J., J. Ingersoll, and S. Ross. "The Relation Between Forward and Futures Prices." *Journal of Financial Economics* 9 (December 1981): 321–46.

Fama, E., and K. French. "Commodity Futures Prices: Some Evidence on Forecast Power, Premiums, and the Theory of Storage." *Journal of Business* 60 (1987): 55–73.

Jarrow, R., and G. Oldfield. "Forward Contracts and Futures Contracts." *Journal of Financial Economics* 9 (December 1981): 373–82.

Kane, E. "Market Incompleteness and Divergences between Forward and Futures Interest Rates." *Journal of Finance* 35 (May 1980): 221–34.

Kolb, R. *Understanding Futures Markets*. Miami: Kolb, 1990.

Park, H., and A. Chen. "Differences Between Futures and Forward Prices: A Further Investigation of Marking to Market Effects." *Journal of Futures Markets* 5 (February 1985): 77–88.

Rendleman, R., and C. Carabini. "The Efficiency of T-Bill Futures Markets." *Journal of Finance* 44 (September 1979): 895–914.

Richard, S., and M. Sundaresan. "A Continuous Time Equilibrium Model of Forward Prices and Futures Prices in a Multigood Economy." *Journal of Financial Economics* (December 1981): 347–71.

Samuelson, P. "Proof That Properly Anticipated Prices Fluctuate Randomly." *Industrial Management Review* 6 (1965): 41–49.

Turnovsky, S. "The Determination of Spot and Futures Prices with Storage Commodities." *Econometrica* 51 (1983): 1363–87.

Working, H. "The Theory of Price of Storage." *American Economic Review* 39 (1949): 1242–62.

Exercises

1. In January, firm ABC enters into a long position in a forward contract with firm DEF as a counterparty. The contract requires delivery in nine months. The forward price is set at $100 per unit, and 1000 units are involved in the transaction. Three months later DEF is offering six-month contracts at a forward price of $80. At this time ABC realizes that it does not need the underlying commodity in the future and is keen to negotiate a price with DEF to terminate the contract. If interest rates are 10 percent per year, continuously compounded, what is the fair compensation ABC should pay DEF?

2. A farmer currently holds 5000 bushels of corn. The local mill is offering a price of $2.18 per bushel. Currently, a three-month futures contract is trading at $2.24. The farmer is considering selling to the local mill or holding the corn in inventory and selling a futures contract. The farmer can store and insure the corn at a total cost of 1 cent per bushel per month. Payment for this cost is due up front, at date 0. Interest rates are 10 percent, continuously compounded. Which alternative should the farmer pursue? Are there any additional factors that need to be considered?

3. Develop a pricing relationship that links the nearby futures price of gold to a more distant futures price. Should this relationship stay stable over time? If the futures contract were a commodity such as wheat, which is produced seasonally but consumed steadily, would the relationship be stable over time? Explain.

4. A forward contract is entered into on a nondividend-paying stock. The stock price is $100, and the settlement date is one year. The interest rate is 10 percent.
   a. Compute the forward price.
   b. After seven months, the stock price is $60. What is the value of the forward contract?

5. The spot price of gold is $400. Interest rates are 10 percent.
   a. Use the cost-of-carry model to establish the futures price of a one-year contract which controls 100 ounces.

b. If transaction costs are introduced into the analysis, then the cost-of-carry model and the reverse cash-and-carry model arguments need to be modified. In this case, bounds on the futures price can be obtained. Reconsider under the assumption that the transaction cost for buying or selling 1 ounce of gold is $1 and the round-trip futures trading cost is $25 per contract. In particular, develop the appropriate bounds on the futures price. (Note that a round-trip cost is the total commission cost associated with buying and then selling or selling and then buying the contract. Assume this cost is paid up front. In your calculations assume that at the delivery date the gold was sold and the futures position offset. As a result another $1 transaction cost per ounce of gold is incurred.)

c. Reconsider Exercise 5b but now add in another market imperfection. Specifically, assume the borrowing rate is 10 percent, but the lending rate is only 8 percent. Establish the new bounds on the futures price.

6. Assume that gold trades at $400. A one-year futures contract has a price of $420. What is the implied cost-of-carry rate?

7. A stock pays a $1 dividend in three months and a second $1 in six months. The stock price is $40. The risk-free rate is 10 percent.
   a. Compute the fair forward price of a contract that requires delivery in seven months.
   b. Four months later, the stock price is $30. What is the new forward price, and what is the value of the original forward contract?

8. The current price of silver is $8 per ounce. Storage costs are 10 cents per ounce per year. Payments are expected in two installments, half the total cost now, with the remaining balance due in six months. Interest rates are constant at 8 percent. Compute the fair futures price of a contract that controls 1 ounce.

9. a. If the futures price of a commodity is greater than the spot price during the delivery period, is there an arbitrage opportunity? If so, construct an appropriate strategy.
   b. If the futures price of a commodity is lower than the spot price during the delivery period, is there an arbitrage opportunity? If so, construct an appropriate strategy.

CHAPTER 3

Hedging with Futures Contracts

In this chapter we investigate how futures contracts can be used to reduce the risk associated with a given market commitment. A **perfect hedge** is a strategy that completely eliminates the risk associated with a future market commitment. To establish a perfect hedge, the trader matches the holding period to the futures expiration date, and the physical characteristics of the commodity to be hedged must exactly match the commodity underlying the futures contract. If either of these features is missing, then a perfect hedge is not possible. In such circumstances, risk can be reduced; in this chapter we investigate how risk can be minimized.

In the first section we revisit basis risk and show how short and long hedges replace price risk with basis risk. We then investigate cross hedges with maturity and asset mismatches. Next we consider simple hedging strategies that minimize the variance of cash flows when the hedge is lifted. A detailed example illustrates how the hedge should be estimated and validated and identifies the economic results that can be anticipated. The final section of this chapter investigates reasons for firms to hedge. Hedging activities should be conducted only after clear economic reasons for reducing risk have been articulated.

The primary objectives of this chapter are the following:

- To explain how futures contracts can be used to reduce risk;
- To illustrate hedging with detailed examples; and
- To explain why firms use hedging strategies.

Basis Risk Revisited

The basis, b, of a futures contract is defined as the difference between the spot and futures prices. At date t, we have

$$b_T(t) = S(t) - F_T(t) \qquad (3.1)$$

Under the cost-of-carry model, the futures price can be expressed as

$$F_T(t) = S(t) + C(t, T) - k(t, T) \qquad (3.2)$$

where $C(t, T)$ is the net cost of carry, which includes the accrued interest expense and storage and insurance costs less the accrued coupon or dividend yield. The term $k(t, T)$ is the convenience yield over the period $[t, T]$. Substituting equation (3.2) into equation (3.1), we obtain

$$b_T(t) = k(t, T) - C(t, T) \tag{3.3}$$

Equation (3.3) states that the basis at date t consists of the positive accrued benefits associated with having the inventory on hand, $k(t, T)$, less the accrued cost of carry. As time advances, the basis changes. Let $\Delta b_T(t)$ represent the change in the basis over a small time increment, and let $\Delta k(t, T)$ and $\Delta C(t, T)$ represent the corresponding changes in the convenience yield and cost of carry. Then

$$\Delta b_T(t) = \Delta k(t, T) - \Delta C(t, T) \tag{3.4}$$

For financial assets and investment commodities such as gold, or for consumption commodities that are in ample supply over the period $[t, T]$, the convenience yield is negligible, and the change in the basis is determined by the change in the cost-of carry term. This term may change in a predictable way. For example, if interest rates remain constant, the cost-of-carry term, $C(t, T)$, smoothly converges to zero.

EXAMPLE 3.1   Assume that nationwide inventories of corn are currently large and that the convenience yield is negligible. In this case the futures price is determined by the direct cost of carry. The current spot and futures prices are $S(0) = \$2.06$, $F_T(0) = \$2.15$, and $T = 3$ months. The net carry of the futures contract is 9 cents over the three-month period, and the basis is

$$b_T(0) = S(0) - F_T(0) = -\$0.09$$

This carry charge reflects the interest and storage changes. Assuming this charge remains stable over time, then the carry charge should equal 3 cents per month. If this assumption holds, then the basis in one month should be -6 cents, in two months it should be -3 cents, and in the last month it should converge to 0.

The basis for a consumption commodity that is currently in short supply (or is anticipated to be in short supply before the delivery date) will reflect a convenience yield. The change in the basis may be less predictable than the corresponding change for a commodity with no convenience yield because of the potential for large unanticipated changes in the convenience yield. In particular, unanticipated imbalances between supply and demand can lead to large shifts in the convenience yield, causing the basis to deviate from its predicted level.

When the basis moves toward zero it is said to be **narrowing.** Conversely, when the basis moves away from zero it is said to be **widening.** In practice the basis very rarely converges smoothly to zero. Exhibit 2.2, which showed the behavior of the basis for West Texas Intermediate oil, indicated a more typical situation, where the path of the basis is quite volatile over the lifetime of the contract before converging to zero. Of course, while the spot and futures prices may display significant volatilities, the pricing relationship between the two usually makes the time series of the basis be more stable. Indeed, the volatility of the basis will usually be an order of magnitude smaller than the volatility of the spot or futures price. As we shall see, this low basis variability is very important for establishing hedging strategies.

Short Hedges

Short hedges are usually initiated by traders who own an asset and who are concerned about prices declining before the sales date. To illustrate a short hedge, consider the problem faced by a grain elevator operator when $S(0) = \$2.06$, $F_T(0) = \$2.15$, the delivery date is three months away, and the basis is predicted to be fairly stable (increasing at a rate of 3 cents per month.)

If the grain elevator planned on selling its corn in three months, it could eliminate all price uncertainty by selling futures contracts to lock in a specific price. The sale of futures contracts against an inventory of the underlying commodity would then be a **perfect hedge.** However, in this example, we shall assume that the sale date is in two months, a full month earlier than the settlement date. To lock into a sale price for corn, the grain elevator sells a futures contract. After two months the grain elevator offsets the transaction in the futures market and sells the corn as planned. The anticipated cash flow at date $t = 2$ is $A(t)$, where

$$A(t) = S(t) - [F_T(t) - F_T(0)]$$
$$= F_T(0) + [S(t) - F_T(t)]$$
$$= F_T(0) + b_T(t)$$

Without the hedge, the anticipated cash flow at date t, $\bar{A}(t)$ say, is given by

$$\bar{A}(t) = S(t)$$

By hedging, the grain elevator has replaced the uncertainty of the commodity price with the uncertainty of the basis. Since basis risk is smaller than commodity price risk, the grain elevator has reduced risk with this hedging strategy. Indeed, if the cost-of-carry relationship stays unchanged, then after two months the basis should be -3 cents, and regardless of what the spot price of corn is, the grain elevator anticipates a cash flow of $\$2.15 - \$0.03 = \$2.12$ per bushel of corn.

EXAMPLE 3.2   Consider the net profit that a grain elevator makes by purchasing corn, storing it for two months, and hedging this inventory by selling three-month futures contracts. Let $C^g(0, t)$ be the net accumulated cost incurred by the grain elevator for financing and carrying the corn inventory over the two-month period. The profit at date $t = 2$ months is given by $\pi(t)$, where

$$\pi(t) = -[S(0) + C^g(0, t)] + S(t) - [F_T(t) - F_T(0)]$$
$$= [S(t) - F_T(t)] - [S(0) - F_T(0)] - C^g(0, t)$$
$$= b_T(t) - b_T(0) - C^g(0, t)$$
$$= \Delta b_T(t) - C^g(0, t)$$

Therefore, the net profit is just the change in the basis less the cost of carry for the grain elevator operator. In this example the change in the basis is expected to be 6 cents per bushel. Hence, if the grain elevator's net cost of financing is less than 6 cents per bushel for the two-month period, then positive returns can be expected.

Of course, the basis may not change in a continuously predictable way determined by the net carry charge. Indeed, due to uncertainty in interest rates or convenience yields, the basis may unexpectedly expand or shrink.

EXAMPLE 3.3   1.   Say that interest rates rise unexpectedly. Then the futures price of corn will increase while the spot price does not. In this case the basis may become more negative. This widening causes the short position to lose more than anticipated.

2.   Suppose that due to unanticipated strong demand for corn, the convenience yield increases, driving the futures price down relative to the spot price. Specifically, the spot price increases by more than the futures price. In this case the basis has become less negative. This narrowing basis causes the short position to profit more than anticipated.

Long Hedges

Long hedges are usually initiated by traders who intend to purchase an asset in the future and are concerned that prices may rise in the interim. To make matters specific, consider a cereal producer who anticipates purchasing corn in $t = 2$ months. Assume the conditions in Example 3.2 apply. The cereal producer purchases a futures contract so as to lock into a price at date t. At date t, the firm sells the futures contract and purchases the spot commodity. The anticipated cash flow with this hedge is

$$A(t) = [F_T(t) - F_T(0)] - S(t)$$
$$= [F_T(t) - S(t)] - F_T(0)$$
$$= -b_T(t) - F_T(0)$$

Without the hedge, the anticipated cash flow at date t is $\bar{A}(t)$, where

$$\bar{A}(t) = -S(t)$$

In comparing cash flows, note that without the hedge the firm is exposed to price risk, whereas with the hedge the risk is reduced to basis risk. If the firm's holding period had coincided with the settlement date, the basis risk would have been eliminated and the hedge would have been perfect.

These examples indicate that the trader who wants to reduce risk should choose a futures contract that has a settlement date close to the trading date. In practice, however, holding onto a futures position in the delivery month may be risky. In

EXHIBIT 3.1 Long Hedge in Silver Futures

Unhedged Position		Hedged Position	
Cost of purchasing silver in November	$80,000	**Futures**	
		Buy 10 futures in June at $5.90.	$59,000
		Sell 10 futures in November at $8.45.	$84,500
		Profit on futures	$25,000
		Cost of purchasing silver in November	$80,000
		Net cost of purchasing silver	$54,500

particular, any long position held in the delivery month runs the risk of having to take delivery of the commodity, at a location that is inconvenient. Long positions can avoid the delivery risk by canceling their positions before the settlement month begins. Even short hedgers should be careful of holding positions in the delivery month, since the price of the contract can sometimes be erratic. If possible, hedgers choose a futures contract that has a slightly longer maturity than the holding period. For example, if the holding period is November, a December futures contract may be appropriate. Of course, liquidity generally decreases as the settlement date lengthens, and this should also be considered in selecting a contract.

EXAMPLE 3.4   A dental supply firm has estimated its demand for silver to be 10,000 troy ounces during December and January. The firm is concerned that prices will rise in the interim and would like to lock in today's price of $5.60 without purchasing the silver today. On June 15, the CBOT's December futures contract trades at $5.90. Since each contract controls 1000 troy ounces, the firm locks into a price of $5.90 by buying 10 contracts. In late November, the spot price has increased to $8 and the futures contract is priced at $8.45. At that time the firm sells the futures contract and purchases the silver at spot prices. Exhibit 3.1 compares this hedging strategy with an unhedged position. The anticipated net price paid equals the contracted futures price of $5.90 plus the basis in November. The basis was −30 cents, and it widened to −45 cents. The resulting cost is $5.90 − $0.45 = $5.45, lower than one might have predicted because the widening basis created profits for the long position.

Rolling the Hedge

In many cases the holding period exceeds the delivery dates of all the active futures contracts. In this case the hedger must set up a rollover strategy. This involves closing out one futures contract just prior to its delivery month, then taking the same position in a futures contract with a longer delivery date.

EXAMPLE 3.5   Implementing a Rollover

In January a firm wishes to establish a short hedge over two years. Futures contracts are traded with settlement dates every month, going out to one year. However, the liquidity of contracts beyond six months is questionable. The firm decides to sell six-month futures and to roll the position over just prior to each delivery month. The sequence of transactions is shown below.

Date	Strategy	
January		Sell June futures.
May	Close out June position.	Sell October futures.
September	Close out October position.	Sell February futures.
January	Close out February position.	

The initial spot price was $23, and the six-month futures contract was $24. The actual futures prices that occurred are shown below.

Date	Initial Price	Close-Out Price (5 Months Later)	Profit from Sale of Futures
January	$24	$22	$2
May	$21	$23	−$2
September	$23	$20	$3

The final spot price in January was $19. The commodity dropped $4 over the period. This loss was partially compensated by a net $3 profit on the futures position. Each time the hedge is rolled over, the trading strategy absorbs basis risk. As a result, the precision of the hedge deteriorates with the number of rollovers.

Example 3.6 illustrates some of the difficulties in managing long-term risks by using successive rollover strategies in shorter-term instruments. Rollover strategies can be very useful in reducing risk, but they do not eliminate it, and if the risks are large enough the firm can still experience cash flow problems.

EXAMPLE 3.6   Maturity Mismatches and Risks with Rollovers

In 1993, Metallgesellschaft AG, a large German engineering and metals conglomerate, revealed that its U.S. trading unit, MG Corp., had incurred losses in energy derivatives of almost $1 billion.[1] The problem began 18 months prior to the

---

[1] For a detailed discussion of this problem see the *Wall Street Journal,* Monday, January 10, 1994.

announcement, when MG began aggressively marketing gasoline, heating oil, and other fuel products on a long-term, fixed-price basis to its clients. To win business from its competitors, the firm negotiated fixed-price contracts for as long as 10 years into the future. Of course, entering into these contracts put MG at high risk. In particular, if oil prices rose, then the firm would have to buy at the higher price and deliver it to its customers at a loss.

To hedge this risk, one of its many strategies was to purchase futures contracts on the NYMEX. Since there was a considerable maturity mismatch, the idea was to rollover the futures contracts into new ones as the old ones expired. MG was confident that these rollovers would not be a problem. However, as the number of fixed-price agreements that it entered into with its customers increased, the size of its futures positions grew so large that it exceeded limits on the number of contracts it was allowed to purchase at NYMEX. Moreover, the basis risk at the rollover dates was substantial, with reports suggesting that the firm was losing about $30 million with each successive rollover. At the same time, the price of oil began to slip, causing large losses on the futures positions. Because of the timing mismatch between the hedging costs and revenues received from customers, cash difficulties almost brought the firm to collapse. The problem reached its peak when a margin call of $200 million was issued by NYMEX in late 1993.

Cross Hedging

When **direct hedges** are placed (e.g., a corn position hedged in corn futures), basis risk can be eliminated if the hedge is lifted at the expiration of the futures contract. If no futures contracts exist with settlement dates equal to the hedging horizon, then futures with mismatched maturities must be used, and basis risk will be present.

When firms want to hedge against price movements in a commodity for which there is no futures contract, they can use futures contracts on related commodities whose price movements closely correlate with the price to be hedged. Hedges may have either an asset mismatch or a maturity mismatch. Indeed, if there were futures contracts for every asset and date that all traders desired, each market would be extremely illiquid. A hedge that is established with a mismatched maturity, a mismatched asset, or both is referred to as a **cross hedge.** When cross hedging, the trader has to establish the appropriate number of futures contracts to trade, so as to minimize the risk in the hedged position.

Cross Hedging with Maturity Mismatches

So far we have considered hedge positions in which the number of futures contracts is fully determined by the spot position. This hedge is effective if a $1 change in the spot price is exactly offset by a $1 change in the futures price. This assumption is valid when there is no maturity mismatch. However, when there is a maturity mismatch, hedging effectiveness can be improved. To see this, assume that the hedging period is $[0, t]$ and that the futures contract settles at date T, with $T > t$. From the cost-of-carry relationship, we know that

$$F_T(t) = S(t) + C(t, T) - k(t, T)$$

Here $C(t, T)$ is the accumulated carry charge from date t to T, which includes the interest expense and storage charges, and $k(t, T)$ is the accumulated convenience yield over the period $[t, T]$. If we assume that interest charges are known and that storage costs and convenience yields are proportional to the spot price and remain constant over time, then, as shown in Chapter 2, the futures price at any date t is related to the spot price by

$$F_T(t) = S(t) \ e^{(r+u-\kappa)(T-t)} \tag{3.5}$$

Note that the change in futures price for each \$1 change in the spot price, $S(t)$, is $e^{(r+u-\kappa)(T-t)}$ dollars. Since the change in futures price to a \$1 spot price change differs from 1, there is no reason a short hedge is best set up by selling a number of futures equal to the spot position.

To make matters specific, assume that b futures contracts were sold against the spot commodity at date 0. Then at date t, the anticipated cash flow would be

$$A(t) = S(t) - b[F_T(t) - F_T(0)] \tag{3.6}$$

Substituting equation (3.5) into (3.6), we obtain

$$A(t) = S(t) - b[S(t)e^{(r+u-\kappa)(T-t)} - F_T(0)]$$
$$= S(t)[1 - b \ e^{(r+u-\kappa)(T-t)}] + bF_T(0)$$

Now consider a very specific hedge ratio, $b = b^*$, where

$$b^* = e^{-(r+u-\kappa)(T-t)} \tag{3.7}$$

Then the coefficient of $S(t)$ is zero and

$$A(t) = b^*F_T(0)$$

Viewed from time 0, $b^*F_T(0)$ is certain. Note that if the holding period coincides with the settlement date $(t = T)$, then there is no maturity mismatch, $b^* = 1$, and all risk is eliminated. At the other extreme, if the hedging period is extremely short, then over the infinitesimal period, the optimal hedge ratio is $b^* = e^{-(r+u-\kappa)T}$. For intermediate periods, $0 < t < T$, b^* falls between this number and 1. The important point here is the fact that the number of futures contracts to sell should differ from that determined by the cash position alone.

EXAMPLE 3.7   **Maturity Mismatch in a Silver Hedge**

A photographic paper manufacturer must purchase silver at the end of January. It is currently June. The firm wants to hedge against increases in silver by going long futures. The nearest futures contract that expires beyond January is the March contract; thus, the firm must use a cross hedge that has a two-month mismatch. The current March futures price is \$5.90. The interest rate is 12 percent per year, and storage costs are negligible. The appropriate hedge ratio is b^*, where $b^* = e^{-(r-\kappa)(T-t)}$ and κ is the convenience yield in January. The firm believes that while silver futures should normally be close to full carry, a higher convenience yield may materialize in January. This prediction is further confirmed when the implied convenience yield for silver over the January–March period, extracted from the term structure of futures prices, yields an estimate of $\kappa = 3$ percent per year. Under the scenario that the convenience yield, κ, is 3 percent in January, $b^* = e^{-(r-\kappa)(T-t)} = 0.985$. Further, since each futures contract on the CBOT covers 1,000 troy ounces and 50,000 troy ounces are required, the firm requires about 49 contracts.

If the convenience yield is 3 percent when the hedge is lifted, then the hedge will be almost perfect. The firm can gauge the risk of this long hedge by specifying different realized convenience yields in January and investigating the resulting hedging risk. Exhibit 3.2 shows the effective hedging costs for a variety of spot prices in January, under the assumption that in January convenience yields have increased to 10 percent. The analysis in Exhibit 3.2 indicates that even if the convenience yield increases above what had been anticipated, the hedge remains very effective.

EXAMPLE 3.8   A firm holds a large inventory of silver. It is known that an important announcement to be made in the next 48 hours could have an adverse affect on silver prices. To hedge price risk over this short time period, the firm plans to sell futures contracts. The appropriate hedge ratio is given by $b^* = e^{-(r+u-\kappa)T}$. With interest rates at 12 percent per year, a convenience yield that has been robust at 3 percent, and negligible storage charges, the hedge ratio, using a contract with three months to settlement, is $b^* = e^{-(0.12-0.03)0.25} = 0.977$.

EXHIBIT 3.2   Effective Purchase Costs Under a Long Hedge

	Spot Prices						
	5.60	5.70	5.80	5.90	6.00	6.10	6.20
Projected futures price for January	5.618	5.719	5.819	5.919	6.020	6.120	6.221
Projected profit from futures	−0.281	−0.181	−0.081	0.019	0.1200	0.220	0.321
Dollar profit from 49 futures contracts (in thousands)	−13.78	−8.867	−3.95	0.965	5.882	10.798	15.714
Cost of purchasing in January (in thousands)	280	285	290	295	300	305	310
Effective purchase price (dollars per ounce)	5.875	5.877	5.879	5.881	5.882	5.884	5.886

Risk-Minimizing Hedge Positions

Example 3.7 illustrates that for a mismatched maturity, a hedge ratio of $b = 1$ may not reduce risk to a minimum. The sale of $b* = e^{-(r+u-\kappa)(T-t)}$ futures for each "unit" of spot reduced risk further. This raises the question as to what the best hedge ratio is. To answer this question, we first need a very precise measure of risk so that we can compare different strategies. In this section we assume that the goal is to reduce risk as much as possible and that the measure of risk is given by the variance of anticipated cash flows when the hedge is lifted.

Once again consider a hedge involving the sale of b futures against the spot commodity. The anticipated cash flow at date t is

$$A(t) = S(t) - bF_T(t) + bF_T(0)$$

Viewed from time 0, the first two terms are uncertain. The variance of cash flows is given by[2]

$$\text{Var}_0[A(t)] = \text{Var}_0[S(t) - bF_T(t)]$$
$$= \text{Var}_0[S(t)] + b^2\text{Var}_0[F_T(t)] - 2b\,\text{Cov}_0[S(t), F_T(t)]$$

The idea is to choose the number of futures contracts to sell, b, such that the risk, as measured by variance, is reduced to the minimum. Exhibit 3.3 shows the variance of cash flows for different b values, under the assumption that the variance and

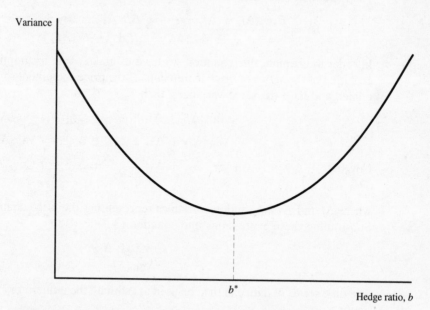

EXHIBIT 3.3   Variance of Cash Flows for Different Hedge Ratios

---

[2] The variance equation is $\text{Var}(aX + bY) = a^2\text{Var}(X) + b^2\text{Var}(Y) + 2ab\,\text{Cov}(X, Y)$. Here, $a = 1$, $X = S(t)$, and $Y = F_T(t)$.

covariance terms are given. To obtain the minimum risk position, it can be shown that b should be chosen as follows.

$$b = b* = \frac{\text{Cov}_0[F_T(t), S(t)]}{\text{Var}_0[F_T(t)]} \tag{3.8}$$

The optimal hedge ratio depends on the covariance between the spot and futures prices, relative to the variance of futures price changes.

Estimating the Minimum-Risk Hedge Position

Let $\{s_1, s_2, s_3, \ldots\}$ and $\{f_1, f_2, f_3, \ldots\}$ represent the closing daily prices of the spot and futures prices. Using these time series, we would like to estimate the terms in equation (3.8). Let $\Delta f_k = f_k - f_{k-1}$ and $\Delta s_k = s_k - s_{k-1}$ denote the price increments on the kth day. Viewed from date 0, since f_0 and s_0 are known,

$$\text{Var}_0\{f_t\} = \text{Var}_0\{f_t - f_0\} = \text{Var}_0\{\Delta f_1 + \Delta f_2 + \cdots + \Delta f_t\}$$

$$\text{Var}_0\{s_t\} = \text{Var}_0\{s_t - s_0\} = \text{Var}_0\{\Delta s_1 + \Delta s_2 + \cdots + \Delta s_t\}$$

$$\text{Cov}_0\{f_t, s_t\} = \text{Cov}_0\{f_t - f_0, s_t - s_0\}$$
$$= \text{Cov}_0\{\Delta f_1 + \Delta f_2 + \cdots + \Delta f_t, \Delta s_1 + \Delta s_2 + \cdots + \Delta s_t\}$$

Then equation (3.8) can be rewritten as

$$b* = \frac{\text{Cov}_0\{\Delta f_1 + \Delta f_2 + \cdots + \Delta f_t, \Delta s_1 + \Delta s_2 + \cdots + \Delta s_t\}}{\text{Var}_0\{\Delta f_1 + \Delta f_2 + \cdots + \Delta f_t\}} \tag{3.9}$$

In order to estimate this equation we have to make some assumptions about the evolution of the series of price increments. If the price increment series are uncorrelated and have the same variances, then

$$\text{Var}_0\{\Delta f_1 + \Delta f_2 + \cdots + \Delta f_t\} = t \, \text{Var}_0\{\Delta f\} \tag{3.10}$$

$$\text{Var}_0\{\Delta s_1 + \Delta s_2 + \cdots + \Delta s_t\} = t \, \text{Var}_0\{\Delta s\} \tag{3.11}$$

$$\text{Cov}_0\{\Delta f_1 + \Delta f_2 + \cdots + \Delta f_t, \Delta s_1 + \Delta s_2 + \cdots + \Delta s_t\} = t \, \text{Cov}_0\{\Delta f, \Delta s\} \tag{3.12}$$

where Δf and Δs are random variables representing the price change in any day. Substituting these expressions into equation (3.9) leads to

$$b* = \frac{\text{Cov}_0\{\Delta f, \Delta s\}}{\text{Var}_0\{\Delta f\}} \tag{3.13}$$

The time series of data can then be used to estimate the numerator and the denominator.

Actually, the time series of futures prices typically used in the regression analysis corresponds to the prices of the near series futures contract. The reason for this is that the variance we want to minimize is just the variance that exists at the time the futures contract is lifted. In most cases, the futures contract is chosen such that the delivery date is just after the hedge is lifted. Thus the hedge ratio should be based on analyzing the sensitivity of prices to near-term contracts. As a result, the time series of futures prices used in the analysis should correspond to the nearest-maturing futures contract. When the contract enters its delivery month, then the new closest-to-maturity futures contract should be used. The analysis is best described by an example.

EXAMPLE 3.9   Suppose a firm is holding 10,000 troy ounces of gold.[3] The spot price of gold is $360.0 an ounce, so the firm's position is worth $3.6 million. The firm fears that the price of gold will drop, and it wants to hedge its inventory. Actually, the gold will be sold at the beginning of January to another firm. According to the contract, the price to be paid will be determined by the International Monetary Market (IMM) price in Chicago at that time. This price is reported in the *Wall Street Journal* as the Handy & Harman base price. The current date is October 15. The firm decides to hedge with the gold futures contract that trades at COMEX. The closest futures contract with delivery date beyond the scheduled holding period is the February contract, so the firm decides to sell a certain number of these futures contracts. Since each contract controls 100 troy ounces, a simple naive hedge would require the sale of 100 futures.

To calculate the effective hedge ratio, we use the weekly spot prices of the IMM and the corresponding nearest-month futures prices of COMEX contracts between September 4, 1992, and October 15, 1993. This provides 59 data points. Exhibit 3.4 plots the spot and futures prices over this time interval. We begin the

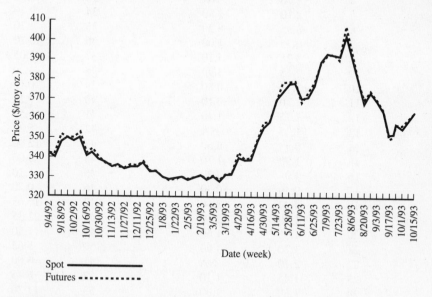

EXHIBIT 3.4   Spot and Futures Prices

---

[3] Thanks to Mikiyoshi Hayami, Hiroki Kadomo, and Sumihiro Takeda for allowing me to use their case study, which they developed in my "Options and Futures" class.

analysis by first computing the weekly changes of both the spot and futures prices. For weeks in which the nearest contract changed, the price change in the futures price obviously cannot be usefully interpreted, so those data points are dropped. This reduces the data set to 51 weekly changes. The data set was then split into an in-sample (or calibrating) set and an out-of-sample (or validation) set. For the moment we shall focus on the in-sample set of $n = 26$ data points from September 4, 1992, to March 26, 1993, shown in panel a of Exhibit 3.5. The remaining data are shown in panel b. Estimators of the numerator and denominator in equation (3.13) are given by

$$\text{Cov}_0\{\Delta f, \Delta s\} = \frac{1}{n-1} \sum_{i=1}^{n} [\Delta f_1 - \overline{\Delta f}][\Delta s_i - \overline{\Delta s}]$$

$$\text{Var}_0\{\Delta f\} = \frac{1}{n-1} \sum_{i=1}^{n} [\Delta f_i - \overline{\Delta f}]^2$$

EXHIBIT 3.5 Price Information on Gold and Gold Futures

Week	IMM Gold Spot Price Change (Δs)	COMEX Gold Futures Price Change (Δf)	Week	IMM Gold Spot Price Change (Δs)	COMEX Gold Futures Price Change (Δf)
1	−2.05	−0.80	30	7.40	NA
2	7.20	10.10	31	−2.66	−3.40
3	2.5	−2.0	32	0.35	1.30
4	−1.70	NA	33	7.05	7.30
5	2.10	1.80	34	9.40	9.70
6	−8.35	−8.20	35	3.20	0.20
7	0.75	1.00	36	10.70	10.90
8	−3.25	−4.10	37	5.05	9.60
9	−2.15	−3.90	38	4.20	0.40
10	−2.70	−0.80	39	0.15	0.20
11	1.70	−0.10	40	−7.25	NA
12	−1.75	−1.30	41	0.55	5.00
13	1.25	NA	42	5.20	5.60
14	−0.5	−0.60	43	12.00	8.60
15	1.90	1.70	44	5.00	5.60
16	−4.0	−4.30	45	−1.10	0.60
17	0.30	−0.30	46	−0.70	−2.90
18	−4.20	−3.60	47	10.45	17.00
19	−1.40	−2.50	48	−22.35	NA
20	1.05	1.60	49	−11.80	−7.30
21	1.70	1.60	50	5.65	3.90
22	−2.70	NA	51	−4.00	−4.30
23	1.45	1.10	52	−6.45	−5.00
24	1.60	1.00	53	−11.30	−14.60
25	−3.20	−1.90	54	0.35	0.40
26	2.15	1.30	55	5.75	6.40
27	−2.75	−1.90	56	−3.60	NA
28	4.65	3.80	57	4.50	4.60
29	1.05	0.20	58	6.10	4.70

where $\overline{\Delta f}$ and $\overline{\Delta s}$ are the sample averages. For our data we obtain $\text{Cov}_0\{\Delta f, \Delta s\} = 9.7842$ and $\text{Var}_0\{\Delta f\} = 11.182$. Hence, the estimate of the hedge ratio from equation (3.13) is $b^* = 0.875$. A hedge consisting of the sale of 87 futures would be the estimated minimum-variance risk strategy.

Clearly, the estimated minimum hedge ratio depends on the particular data set. This raises issues of how much historical data to use and how frequently data should be obtained (weekly, daily, on the hour, etc.). Obviously, to be useful the estimators should be stable over time. That is, using different data sets should not give dramatically different answers. We shall return to this issue shortly.

Regression Models for Minimum-Variance Hedging

The estimate of the hedge ratio, b^*, can also be obtained by regressing the daily spot price changes against the daily futures price changes and identifying the least squares estimate of the slope. Specifically, consider the model obtained by regressing daily changes in futures prices against daily changes in spot prices:

$$\Delta S(t) = \alpha + \beta \Delta F_T(t) + \epsilon(t) \tag{3.14}$$

If the error terms, $\{\epsilon(t), t = 1, 2, \ldots\}$, have zero means and the same variances and are uncorrelated, then the estimated slope of this regression equation is the appropriate estimator for the hedge ratio. That is,

$$\text{Hedge ratio} = \beta \tag{3.15}$$

EXAMPLE 3.10   A regression analysis using the above data provided the following results.

Regression Statistics	
R^2	0.8314
Standard error	1.344
Observations	26

Source	df	Sum of Squares	Mean Square	F	Significance
Regression	1	213.91	213.91	118.35	0.00
Residual	24	43.38	1.807		
Total	25	257.29			

Variable	Coef.	Standard Error	t-Stat.	p Value	Lower 95%	Upper 95%
Intercept	0.135	0.266	0.508	0.61	−0.41	0.68
ΔF	0.875	0.080	10.89	0.00	0.71	1.04

Note that the estimate of the slope, $\Delta f = 0.875$, is exactly the same as what we had earlier. The regression analysis, however, gives us additional information. For example, it provides a confidence interval for the hedge ratio. In particular, we are 95 percent confident that the true hedge ratio is somewhere between 0.71 and 1.04.

Effectiveness of Hedging

In order to measure the effectiveness of the hedge, we first need to establish the risk of an unhedged position, which is captured by the variance of the price of the commodity underlying the futures contract. Let σ_s^2 represent the variance of the weekly price changes. Now, consider the variability of the price changes of the optimally hedged position. While the futures contracts explain some of the variability, some randomness still exists. This variability, the basis error, is accounted for by the error term in the regression equation, denoted by σ_ϵ^2. The ratio $\sigma_\epsilon^2/\sigma_s^2$ can range from 0 to 1. When it is 0, there is no basis error and a perfect hedge can be constructed. When the ratio is 1, none of the risk can be hedged away. The effectiveness of the hedge is captured by ρ^2, where

$$\rho^2 = 1 - \sigma_\epsilon^2/\sigma_s^2 \tag{3.16}$$

In practice, historical data is used to estimate σ_ϵ^2, σ_s^2, and ρ^2. It turns out that in the regression analysis of spot against futures price changes, the R^2 measure is the estimate of ρ^2.

EXAMPLE 3.11   The R^2 of the above regression is 0.831. This means that the hedge can account for just over 83 percent of the total variability of spot price changes. Equivalently, of the total unhedged sum of squares, 257.29, about 83 percent (or 213.91) can be explained by the futures price changes. The total variance of the unhedged position, s^2(unhedged), is just the sample variance of the spot price changes. This is computed by dividing the total sum of squared deviations by the number of observations less 1. That is, s^2(unhedged) $= \sum_{i=1}^{n} (\Delta s_i - \overline{\Delta s})^2/(n-1)$. Computing this number yields s^2(unhedged) $= 257.29/25 = 10.292$. Hence, s(unhedged) $= \sqrt{10.292} = \$3.208$ per troy ounce.

The standard deviations of the unhedged and hedged positions provide important information. We can be about 95 percent confident that the weekly change in value of our unhedged position is within 2 (more precisely, 1.96) standard deviations. For the unhedged position we can be about 95 percent confident that the weekly change in our portfolio value is within the interval $\pm\$6.28$ per ounce. Recall that in our problem we are hedging 10,000 troy ounces. Hence, the change in the unhedged weekly portfolio value would be less than $\pm\$62,800$.

In contrast, the variability of the residuals captures the uncertainty that is left unexplained after the regression analysis. Let s(hedged) denote this variability. From the analysis of variance table in Example 3.10 we have s^2(hedged) $= 1.807$. Hence s(hedged) $= \sqrt{1.807} = \$1.344$ per troy ounce. The resulting 95 percent confidence interval for potential weekly changes in the hedged position is

±$26,350. The effectiveness of the hedge is shown by the dramatic narrowing of the interval.

Holding the length of the estimation period constant, it would appear that using more frequent data, such as daily data, would provide better estimates than using less frequent data, such as weekly data. Indeed, based on equations (3.10) and (3.12), we could use daily variance and covariance changes to obtain weekly or monthly estimates. Unfortunately, from a practical perspective, there are some problems when using data that are collected very frequently. First, transaction prices usually occur at the bid or the ask price. As the time increments become shorter, the contribution to price variability made by the random movement between bid and ask prices increases, and this distorts the true measure of price variability. Second, if short periods are used, it becomes harder to make sure that the futures and spot prices are current. In particular, if the futures and spot commodity are not traded at the same frequency, then the two prices may not reflect the same infomation. Because of the bid-ask spread and lack of simultaneous market prices, the error terms in the regression equation can display serial correlation which increases as the time increments get smaller. Finally, in some markets there are effects due to the day of the week. For example, the change of prices over a weekend may be different from the change in prices over any day. Also, Monday's return may be quite different from other business days. Seasonal factors can affect the variances of daily price changes. As a result of these factors, using daily data may not be advantageous over using weekly data. Indeed, when we used daily data to construct the hedge ratio for the above problem, the value of R^2 dropped to about 0.40.

Ex Ante Hedge Ratios Versus Ex Post Hedging Results

In Example 3.11, the hedge ratio was constructed using historical data, and then the effectiveness of the hedge was established using the same data. In practice, the hedge ratio will be computed using historical data and will then be applied to a current situation. Hopefully, the relationships will remain fairly stable and the hedge will be effective. However, the hedge is not likely to be as effective as measured by R^2, because some unanticipated changes in the structure are likely to occur. Indeed, evaluating the hedge in sample as we have done is quite likely to overstate the actual hedging effectiveness because effectiveness is measured on the same set of data from which the regression equation was derived. In practice, of course, we would estimate the hedge ratio using the most recent data and then implement the hedge. The effectiveness of the hedge would then be determined as uncertainly reveals itself. To validate the real usefulness of the hedge, we therefore should examine how well the model performs when given new data. Since we split our data set into two parts, we can evaluate how well our hedge established from data collected over the first 29 weeks would work on the second data set.

EXAMPLE 3.12 **Validating the Usefulness of the Estimated Hedge Ratio**

Panel *b* in Exhibit 3.5 shows the 25 out-of-sample validation points, starting from September 4, 1992, to March 26 1993. Over this period gold prices were extremely volatile, and the total sum of squares of weekly price changes was 1060.9 (compared to 257.29 in the first data set).

First we compute the total variation in the out-of-sample data. The unhedged variance, s^2(unhedged-out), is given by $1060.9/24 = 44.204$. The standard deviation s(unhedged-out) = $\sqrt{44.204} = 6.648$. The great volatility over this time period is reflected in a large 95 percent confidence interval of $\pm\$13.03$ per week per troy ounce. This gives a weekly range in the unhedged position of $130,300 (compare this to the in-sample unhedged interval).

Now we have to compute the basis error associated with the hedge. To do this we use our regression equation to predict the spot price change given the futures price change. The difference between this value and the actual spot price change that materializes is the residual error, or basis error. The sum of all the squared basis errors for each of the weeks can be computed. For this data set the value is 155.43.[4] That is, of the total sum of squares of 1060.9, 905.47 can be explained by the change in futures price, and only 155.43 units remain unexplained. The out-of-sample r^2 value is therefore 0.8534. Surprisingly, the hedge worked better out of sample than in sample. The standard deviation of the basis errors is s(hedged-out) = 2.493. A 95 percent confidence interval yields $\pm\$4.887$ per troy ounce, or $\pm\$48,800$. This confidence interval is much less than half the unhedged position. It certainly appears that the hedge has been effective.

Now that the model has been validated, it makes sense to rerun the regression analysis using all the data. The final estimated hedge ratio turns out to be 0.84, with an R^2 value of 0.86.

If the hedge ratio computed using the second data set alone is quite different from that obtained from the first data set, then the hedge ratio is unstable and one must proceed with caution. Oftentimes the assumptions of the regression model are being violated, or the estimates are highly sensitive to just a few data points. Researchers have shown that this method works quite well for many consumption commodities, but the level of autocorrelation should be closely monitored. Specifically, if the residuals in the regression analysis display certain time-varying patterns, then more sophisticated estimation procedures must be used.[5]

---

[4] Actually, once the weekly basis errors are computed, we could add up consecutive four-week basis errors to get a monthly basis error. The standard deviation of these errors would give a more appropriate measure of the dollar variability for the hedge if held for a one-month period. Of course, as the holding period for the hedge gets longer, more data is required in order to maintain a sufficiently large number of residuals for the standard deviation calculation.

[5] One test for autocorrelation is the Durban-Watson statistic, which is usually reported as part of the regression output.

The above procedure yields reasonable estimates if the relationship between the price changes of spot and futures remains stable over time. While this assumption seems to be well satisfied by many consumption commodities, it has been found to be lacking for several financial assets. For example, the price changes of stocks are often serially correlated, and their variances are not constant but rather fluctuate according to their prices. For such securities, the relationship between the rates of change of prices and rates of change in futures may be more stable. In such cases, it might be preferable to run a rate-of-change regression:

$$\Delta s_t / s_t = \alpha_0 + \alpha_1 \Delta f_t / f_t = \epsilon_t \tag{3.17}$$

Recall that the hedge ratio is intended to capture the sensitivity of the changes in the spot price to changes in the futures price when the hedge is lifted. In equation (3.17), the slope α_1 is capturing the percentage change in the spot relative to a percentage change in the futures. To back out the appropriate hedge ratio, then, we multiply the estimate of α_1 by the ratio of the current spot price relative to the current futures price. That is,

$$\text{Hedge ratio} = \frac{s_0}{f_0} \alpha_1 \tag{3.18}$$

Notice that the hedge ratio varies according to the spot and futures prices. As a result, over the holding period the hedge may need to be adjusted as the spot-to-futures ratio changes.

Cross Hedging with Asset Mismatches

Let $P(t)$ be the spot price of commodity P at time t. No futures contracts exist for this commodity. Let $S(t)$ be the spot price of commodity S. Futures contracts trade on this commodity, and the price movements of P are highly correlated to those of S. Consider a trader who holds an inventory of P and is concerned that prices will fall. To hedge this risk the trader sells b futures on S. The anticipated cash flow at the sales date t is $A(t)$, where

$$A(t) = P(t) - b[F_T(t) - F_T(0)]$$

Viewed from time 0, the first two terms are uncertain. Hence

$$\text{Var}_0[A(t)] = \text{Var}_0[P(t) - bF_T(t)]$$
$$= \text{Var}_0[P(t)] + b^2 \text{Var}_0[F_T(t)] - 2b\,\text{Cov}_0[P(t), F_T(t)]$$

It can be shown that this variance reaches a minimum when $b = b^*$, where

$$b^* = \frac{\text{Cov}_0[F_T(t), P(t)]}{\text{Var}_0[F_T(t)]} \tag{3.19}$$

Now consider the case where there is no maturity mismatch (i.e., $t = T$). In this case $F_T(T) = S(T)$ and

$$b^* = \frac{\text{Cov}_0[S(T), P(T)]}{\text{Var}_0[S(T)]} \qquad (3.20)$$

The easiest way to estimate b^* is to estimate the slope of the following regression equation:

$$\Delta P(t) = \alpha + \beta \Delta S(t) + \epsilon(t) \qquad (3.21)$$

If the error terms are uncorrelated and have mean 0, then the estimate of the slope is the estimate of b^*. Note, that since there is no maturity mismatch, the relationship of interest is between the price changes of the two assets. As a result, the regression analysis does not require futures data.

If there is a maturity mismatch as well, we can estimate the value of b^* with a regression analysis where $\Delta P(t)$ is the dependent variable and $\Delta F_T(t)$ the independent variable. That is,

$$\Delta P(t) = \alpha + \beta \Delta F_T(t) + \epsilon(t) \qquad (3.22)$$

The estimate of the slope is the estimate of b^*.

As a matter of fact, Example 3.11, involving hedging with gold futures, could be viewed as a cross hedge with a maturity mismatch if the underlying gold was not deliverable against the COMEX futures contract. In many cases no effective cross hedges exist. For example, a mango farmer will not be able to find a traded futures contract that provides an effective hedge. Even a commodity such as barley has weekly price changes that are not very well correlated with products such as wheat, soybeans, or corn. Indeed, a multiple regression analysis of the changes in barley prices against changes in the prices of many of the grains fails to produce highly significant predictors. U.S. barley users will thus find it difficult to hedge the price risk of barley. Although barley futures are traded at the Winnipeg futures exchange in Canada, such contracts are not that liquid, and using them introduces foreign exchange risk into the analysis. As a result, opportunities still exist for exchanges to introduce new contracts that are useful in that they expand the set of commodities that permit price risks to be better managed. Finally, cross hedges can be constructed in which more than one futures contract is used. For example, a portfolio of corporate bonds could be hedged using futures on Treasury securities and futures on stock indices.

Other Approaches to Establishing Hedge Ratios

There are other analytical, as opposed to statistical, methods for setting up hedge ratios that minimize risk. For example, when the commodity underlying the futures contract is an interest-sensitive asset or a portfolio of common stocks, specialized procedures exist. We shall defer discussion of these procedures to future chapters. In addition, we have investigated only static hedging schemes. These are schemes where the hedge is set up at date 0 and not revised over time in response to the release of new information. Dynamic hedging strategies will be described in future chapters.

The Rationale for Hedging by Corporations

Most firms have no particular expertise in predicting interest rates, exchange rate movements, commodity prices, and so on. At first glance it appears quite obvious that such firms should hedge these risks so as to be able to focus on their main activities. By hedging unwanted risks, they avoid surprises. While such a rationale may be true in many cases, a more careful case for hedging should be made on grounds other than risk aversion.

There are various reasons firms may choose to hedge. In the design of any particular hedge for a firm, it is important to evaluate what the firm wants to accomplish by hedging.

The overall objective of the firm is to maximize its value. At a conceptual level, the value of the firm, V_0, is given by the present value of all future expected cash flows. That is,

$$V_0 = \sum_{i=0}^{n} \frac{E\{CF_i\}}{(1 + \rho)^i} \tag{3.23}$$

where $E\{CF_i\}$ is the expected net cash flow in period i and ρ is the appropriate discount rate for the cash flow. The use of derivative products to manage financial risk is justified if the value of the firm can be increased by either increasing expected net cash flows or decreasing the discount rate.

Since individuals are risk-averse, at first glance one might suspect that they would want managers of the firm to reduce financial price risks by hedging. However, this is not the case. For individual shareholders, risks such as interest rate risk, commodity price risk, and foreign exchange risks are diversifiable. That is, these risks can be eliminated by holding well-diversified portfolios. Therefore, hedging by itself will not increase the value of the firm by reducing the discount rate for cash flows. Risk aversion can be used as a rationale for hedging only if the owners of the firm do not hold diversified portfolios. This may well be the case for closely held corporations. In the context of equation (3.23), for hedging to be beneficial to shareholders of a widely held firm, it must be the case that it somehow increases the expected net cash flows.

Of course, hedging is simply one of the firm's financial policies. The question is, how can any financial policy affect the real cash flows of the firm? In a famous proposition, Miller and Modigliani showed that in a world with no transaction costs and no taxes, a firm with a given investment policy could not increase its value by changing its financial policy. That is, under their assumptions, financial policies are irrelevant. The proposition is built on the premise that anything a firm can do in financial markets, its shareholders can do on their own accounts. So if it is advantageous for the firm to hedge using futures contracts, then individual shareholders could just as easily hedge. This being the case, there is no reason for investors to pay premiums for shares to be hedged when they can do it at no cost.

The Miller-Modigliani proposition implies that if hedging activities are to be relevant, in the sense that they have an impact on the value of the firm, then it must be the case that financial policies affect transaction costs, taxes, or the investment decisions of the firm. In addition, the proposition assumes that individual shareholders have complete information about the firm and hence are able to make decisions about whether to hedge risks as they materialize. We now look at how these features lead to motives for hedging.

Hedging and Taxes

The tax schedule is a convex function, illustrated in Exhibit 3.6. Consider a firm that has a certain pretax income of $\$x$. The taxable income on that is shown in Exhibit 3.6 as t_x. Now consider a second firm that has a probability of 0.5 of generating pretax income of $x - y$ and a probability of 0.5 of having pretax income of $x + y$. The tax is either t_{x-y} or t_{x+y}, and the expected tax is therefore $(t_{x-y} + t_{x+y})/2 = t_x^y$. Note that because of the convexity of the tax code, $t_x^y > t_x$. The greater the convexity, and the greater the uncertainty of the income, here captured by y, the greater the difference in expected taxes. The example shows that firms may want to reduce the uncertainty of their revenues by hedging so as to reduce expected taxes.

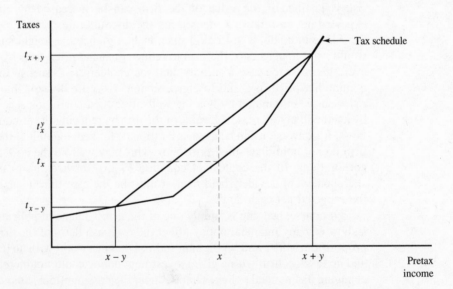

EXHIBIT 3.6   The Convex Nature of the Tax Schedule

Transaction Costs and Financial Distress

By hedging, the firm can reduce the likelihood of outcomes that head it into financial distress. The costs of distress include direct legal, accounting, and reorganization fees as well as indirect costs such as lost business and higher contracting costs with customers, employees, and suppliers. If the unhedged firm has a high probability of entering financially distressed states, and if the costs of being in financial distress are very high, then the benefits of hedging will be high.

Transaction Costs and Contract Sizes

Futures contracts are quite large and are often sized to meet the needs of firms rather than individual investors. Firms may be able to transact at wholesale prices. That is, a firm may be able to reduce transaction costs and commissions by establishing relationships with brokerage firms or even by setting up its own trading firm. As a result, the firm may be better equipped to manage the hedging activities.

Asymmetry of Information

Of course, firms may have more information than shareholders concerning specific risks. For example, in order to hedge commodity risks, the individual shareholders need to know the timing and sizes of the commitments. For strategic reasons, the firm may not want to publicize these commitments for its competitors to learn. As a result, the firm is in a better position to hedge than individual shareholders.

Conflicts of Interest Between Managers and Owners

Managers of a firm may choose to hedge and reduce risk because they are looking after their own interests, not necessarily those of the owners. In particular, managers may be adverse to risk since bad outcomes could mean loss of their jobs. Hence managers may be more likely to hedge, even if it is not in the best interest of the owners. Usually the owners are the shareholders, who are unable to monitor all the actions of the managers and therefore give them some authority to take actions on their behalf.

Hedging and Competitors

In some circumstances, the use of futures contracts can create more risk, not less. For example, consider a fairly competitive industry in which prices of raw materials fluctuate up and down but are typically passed on to the consumers in the form of higher or lower prices. In such an industry, the profit margin remains stable despite large price fluctuations.

Assume that in this market, a particular firm decides to hedge the prices of its raw materials by purchasing futures. If prices rise, then the price of outputs tends to rise as the firm's competitors pass on the increased costs. In this case the long hedger obtains larger profits. However, if prices of raw materials decrease, the hedger loses on the position. Moreover, since the price of finished goods is lower, relative to the competition, profits are lower.

In this example, the firms in the industry had a built-in hedge provided by the fact that all changes in costs could be passed on to the consumers. A firm that hedges the inputs destroys this natural hedge and actually ends up with more volatile net cash flows. Of course, if the output prices are fixed, as is the case in many long-term supply arrangements, or if not all the changes in costs are passed on to the consumers, then no natural hedge exists, and appropriate hedging strategies can be designed to reduce risk.

Conclusion

This chapter has been concerned with the design of short and long hedges. In particular, we investigated perfect hedges and cross hedges that had maturity and/or product mismatches. We also investigated how minimum-variance hedges could be constructed. The methodology used to establish the optimal hedge ratio in this chapter is a statistical approach and is somewhat generic in that it can be applied to many consumption commodities as well as a few financial assets. However, in some cases, such as hedging bond or stock portfolios, specialized methods are available. Finally, we discussed why firms hedge.

References

For additional examples of hedging applications, refer to the publications of the CBOT and other exchanges. Also, many examples are discussed in *Risk* magazine. The article by Nance, Smith, and Smithson provides some empirical tests of factors that affect firms' decisions to hedge.

Block, S., and T. Gallagher. "The Use of Interest Rate Futures and Options by Corporate Financial Managers." *Financial Management* 15 (1989): 73–78.

Chicago Board of Trade. *Introduction to Hedging.* Chicago: CBOT, 1987.

Chicago Board of Trade. *Commodity Trading Manual.* Chicago: CBOT, 1989.

Duffie, D. *Futures Markets.* Englewood Cliffs, N.J.: Prentice-Hall, 1989.

Ederington, L. "The Hedging Performance of the New Futures Market." *Journal of Finance* 34 (March 1979): 157–70.

Kolb, R. *Understanding Futures Markets.* Miami: Kolb, 1991.

Gramatikos, T., and A. Saunders. "Stability and the Hedging Performance of Foreign Currency Futures." *Journal of Futures Markets* 3 (1983): 295–305.

Miller, S., and D. Luke. "Alternative Techniques for Crosshedging Wholesale Beef Prices." *Journal of Futures Markets* 2 (1982): 121–29.

Modigliani, F., and M. Miller. "The Cost of Capital, Corporate Finance and the Theory of Investment." *American Economic Review* (June 1958): 261–97.

Nance, D., C. Smith, and C. Smithson. "On the Determinants of Corporate Hedging." *Journal of Finance* (March 1993): 267–84.

Siegel, D., and D. Siegel. *Futures Markets.* New York: Dryden Press, 1990.

Smith, C., and R. Stulz. "The Determinants of Firms' Hedging Policies." *Journal of Financial and Quantitative Analysis* 20 (1985): 391–405.

Witt, H., T. Schroeder, and M. Hayenga. "Comparison of Analytical Approaches for Estimating Hedge Ratios for Agricultural Commodities." *Journal of Futures Markets* 7 (April 1987): 135–46.

Exercises

1. A photographic paper manufacturer has estimated that the firm will require 50,000 troy ounces of silver during December and January. The firm is concerned that prices of silver will rise and would like to hedge against that risk. The current date is July 1. The CBOT's December silver futures contract is trading at $5.80 per troy ounce. Each contract controls 1000 troy ounces.
   a. Establish the position the manufacturer should take.
   b. Assume that in the middle of November, silver is selling at $7.80 per troy ounce and the December futures contract is at $8.10. At this time the firm purchases silver in the spot market. Compare the net cost of purchasing the silver for the hedged and unhedged positions.

2. The CME is the world's largest futures trading center for nonstorable commodities, one of which is live cattle futures. In November, a cattle producer buys cattle with the intent to feed them for sale in April. To cover all production costs and guarantee a profit, the producer will need to sell the cattle at $65 per hundred weight (100 pounds, or cwt). The current April live cattle futures price is $70/cwt and the basis is −$3.
   a. Set up a short hedge position for this cattle producer, and analyze it assuming that the futures price at the beginning of April, when the contract is bought back, is at $65 and the basis has narrowed by $1.
   b. Repeat Exercise 2a, computing the realized profit if the futures price in April is $72 and the basis has remained unchanged.

3. A farmer who has planted soybeans for November harvest estimates that to profit he has to sell his soybeans for $5.45 per bushel (bu). In May, cash soybeans are $5.45/bu and the November futures price is $5.75/bu.
   a. Provide a reason for the November futures price being higher than the current spot price.
   b. The farmer decides to hedge. By November the cash price has declined to $4.80/bu and the November futures price is $5.10/bu. At this point the

farmer lifts the hedge and sells the soybeans. What effective price did the farmer receive for the soybeans?

c. Compute the basis in May and in November, and establish whether the basis narrowed or widened. Did the basis move in a favorable direction for the farmer? Explain.

4. A wheat exporter receives an order in late July for 50,000 bushels of wheat to be shipped in March of the following year. The exporter does not have the wheat in inventory and needs to purchase it before the shipping date. To lock into a price, the exporter decides to hedge using the March futures contract (which controls 50,000 bushels). The current futures price is $2.90/bu, and the spot price is $2.70/bu.

a. Set up a strategy for the exporter, and analyze it under the assumption that at the time of lifting the hedge, the basis had widened by $0.15/bu and the futures price was $2.98/bu.

b. Repeat Exercise 4a, assuming that the basis had narrowed by $0.15/bu. How does a widening or narrowing basis affect the results?

5. T. Knudsen Sorghum, Inc., expects to harvest 1 million cwt sorghum in late September. The cash flows of the firm are tied solely to this product. The firm is investigating alternative ways of laying off this risk by selling futures contracts. Unfortunately, there are no liquid futures contracts on sorghum, so the firm has to look at related products. Sorghum resembles corn, both in its cultivation and in its end uses. Specifically, both products are used either as livestock food or in a variety of processed foods for humans. Both products require the same warm temperatures and rainfall distribution. As a result, the demand and price relationships for these two products should be similar. The firm decides to investigate whether a cross hedge could be effective. The following data on the price of sorghum and on the futures price of the nearest-to-maturity futures contract on corn were collected over the July–September period.

Day	Sorghum Price	Corn Futures Price	Day	Sorghum Price	Corn Futures Price
1	4.39	2.415	15	4.29	2.390
2	4.27	2.360	16	4.33	2.3575
3	4.28	2.3525	17	4.39	2.40
4	4.32	2.3725	18	4.45	2.4125
5	4.29	2.3525	19	4.41	2.41
6	4.37	2.4125	20	4.38	2.3925
7	4.41	2.4300	21	4.41	2.41
8	4.39	2.4175	22	4.36	2.365
9	4.38	2.405	23	4.48	2.3875
10	4.39	2.425	24	4.55	2.4075
11	4.39	2.440	25	4.50	2.3775
12	4.34	2.435	26	4.50	2.3875
13	4.37	2.445	27	4.45	2.3650
14	4.30	2.4125	28	4.48	2.38

Day	Sorghum Price	Corn Futures Price	Day	Sorghum Price	Corn Futures Price
29	4.46	2.3655	40	4.33	2.3675
30	4.48	2.3775	41	4.27	2.33
31	4.51	2.3675	42	4.28	2.345
32	4.50	2.3725	43	4.32	2.3575
33	4.50	2.3675	44	4.30	2.35
34	4.41	2.33	45	4.37	2.3875
35	4.45	2.34	46	4.32	2.3675
36	4.43	2.3175	47	4.38	2.3875
37*	4.37	2.2975	48	4.35	2.3850
38	4.30	2.3375	49	4.46	2.4375
39	4.36	2.3525	50	4.37	2.4425

* On day 37, the nearest futures contract changed; hence, the change in futures price from day 36 to day 37 is not defined.

a. Using the data for days 1–25, run an appropriate regression between daily sorghum price changes and daily changes in the corn futures contract. Provide a report on this regression and establish the hedge ratio. Based on an in-sample analysis, how effective will the hedge be?

b. Using the hedge ratio in Exercise 5a, compute the daily error terms out of sample, and establish the effectiveness of the hedge out of sample.

c. Compare the unhedged position with the cross hedge, and draw conclusions for the firm.

6. Prepare a case study of a hedging problem of your own choice, following the instructions below.

a. Describe the scenario. Set up a story and suggest the futures contracts that might be considered.

b. Collect the data. Collect your own data and perform the appropriate statistical analyses. Sources for data include the *Wall Street Journal* and the statistical annuals of the various futures exchanges. You probably will need spot prices as well as futures prices.

c. Analyze the data. Estimate the risk-minimizing hedge and evaluate its effectiveness in sample and out of sample. Make sure the assumptions of regression analyses hold. Provide an appendix with relevant computer output.

d. Recommend a hedge. State very precisely the hedge that you recommend and how it will meet the risk management objectives laid out in your scenario in Exercise 6a.

e. Turn in an executive summary report, with your recommendations, an appendix listing the relevant data, and so on.

PART TWO

Option Markets

In the next three chapters, we investigate the market for stock option contracts. In order to understand how options can be used as risk management instruments, we first need to understand how these contracts trade in an organized market. In Chapter 4 we describe listed call and put stock options and present the basic terminology used in this market. The prices of these standardized contracts are determined in a competitive marketplace; we discuss some of the factors that determine their prices.

Chapter 5 analyzes investment positions constructed by meshing puts and calls with their underlying securities. Options can be used to produce payouts that best reflect the expectations that an investor has for the future prospects of a security. For example, consider an investor who believes that a news announcement to be released will have major ramifications on the price of a particular company's stock. Unfortunately, the trader does not know whether the announcement will be good or bad, so is uncertain whether to buy the security or sell it. We shall see that by using options, the investor can construct a position that will obtain profits if the news announcement results in a large price move, either positive or negative. Chapter 5 discusses a variety of option strategies that can be used to produce distinctive future payouts that fully reflect the beliefs held by a trader.

Chapter 6 is concerned with the relationships that must exist between options on a given stock. If these pricing relationships do not exist, then riskless arbitrage opportunities will be available. That is, strategies can be established that require no initial outlays yet guarantee nonnegative payoffs in the future. In Chapter 6 we use simple arbitrage arguments to obtain several relationships that link the prices of various option contracts.

CHAPTER 4

Stock Option Contracts

Options are financial instruments that can be used to achieve a variety of investment objectives. For example, we shall see that ownership of a call (put) option allows an investor to profit from an increase (decrease) in the price of a security for a fraction of the price of the security. Furthermore, since losses are limited by the size of the initial investment, the holder of the call is protected against large losses that stock ownership may involve.

Options also allow shareholders to transfer unwanted risk associated with stock ownership to speculators willing to bear it. The necessity for transferring this risk generally reflects the shareholders' reluctance to sustain large losses. Option writers are investors who accept these risks. They are enticed into selling options by the size of the premium that compensates them for these risks. The size of the premium is related to the size of possible losses, the time of coverage, and other factors to be discussed. Option writers may be in a better situation to sustain such losses. For example, they may be able to pool these risks with other risks in such a way that, in aggregate, the potential losses in their portfolios are more manageable.

In order to understand how options add another dimension to portfolio risk management, it is first necessary to understand how these contracts trade in an organized market. In this chapter we describe listed call and put stock options and present the basic terminology used in this market. The prices of these standardized contracts are determined in a competitive marketplace, and we discuss some of the factors that determine their prices. Appendix 4A describes the option exchanges and illustrates how option contracts are actually traded.

The primary objectives of this chapter are the following:

- To present the basic terminology used in the market for stock option contracts;

- To describe listed call and put stock options; and

- To discuss some of the factors that determine the prices of options.

Call Options

An American call option is a contract that gives the owner the right to purchase a given number of shares of a specific security at a specific price at any point in time prior to a predetermined date.[1] Usually the number of shares per contract is 100. To completely characterize a call contract, it is necessary to know the following:

1. The name of the underlying security,
2. The specified purchase price or strike price, and
3. The duration of the contract or time to expiration.

Strike Prices

Strike prices are available at values surrounding the current stock price. Usually the prices are spaced at $2.50 intervals for stocks priced below $25, $5 intervals for stocks priced between $25 and $200, and $10 intervals for stocks priced above $200. As the stock price changes, new contracts are introduced in a systematic way, to be discussed later.

Call options with strike prices less than the stock price are termed in the money. Options with strike prices equal to the stock price are called at the money. Finally, calls with strike prices exceeding the stock price are said to be out of the money.

Expiration Dates

At any point in time, each underlying stock has option contracts available with several different expiration dates. The option with the closest expiration date is called the **near series;** the second one is called the **middle series;** and the option with the longest time to expiration is called the **far series.** Stock options usually expire on the Saturday following the third Friday in their stated month. When the near series expires, a new far series is introduced.

Until 1984 each underlying stock had option contracts available with three expiration dates. For example, a stock may have had January, April, and July options. When the January options expired, new nine-month October options were introduced. This contract belonged to the January/April/July/October series. Two other possible expiration cycles for an option existed. These were the February/May/August/November cycle and the March/June/September/December cycle. The three particular expiration months of contracts that traded at any point in time depended, of course, on the actual time of the year.

---

[1] In this chapter all options we discuss are of the American variety. European options are similar to American contracts, with the exception that they cannot be exercised prior to the expiration date. The terminology of these contracts is unfortunate in that it has no geographic meaning. Most stock option contracts traded throughout the world are American. However, a few contracts traded in the United States and Europe are of the European variety.

EXHIBIT 4.1   Option Contracts Available for January
Cycle Series

End of Current Month	Option Contracts Available
January	February, March, April, July
February	March, April, July, October
March	April, May, July, October
April	May, June, July, October
May	June, July, October, January
June	July, August, October, January
July	August, September, October, January
August	September, October, January, April
September	October, November, January, April
October	November, December, January, April
November	December, January, April, July
December	January, February, April, July

These expiration date rules applied until late 1984. In an effort to bring additional liquidity into the stock option market, the option exchanges instigated a program whereby stocks could trade an additional near-term contract. As a result, some stocks have four expiration dates. Each has the nearest two months and the next two months of its normal 3–6–9-month cycle trading at one time. Exhibit 4.1 illustrates the option contracts that are available at the end of each possible month for a January cycle option.

EXAMPLE 4.1   Consider a stock that has an option contract expiring in January. After the expiration date, February and March contracts will trade, as well as the usual April and July contracts.

Creation of Options with New Strike Prices

As already mentioned, when one option expires, a new series is introduced with strike prices surrounding the current stock price. As the stock price changes in value, new strike prices are added. In particular, if a stock price closes above (below) the highest (lowest) existing strike price for a certain number of days (usually two), a new strike price is created. Newly created contracts usually have a time to expiration exceeding 30 days. This often means that new near-term contracts in the series are not introduced.

As a result of this method of introducing new strike prices, securities that have experienced significant price fluctuations over the past several months could have a large number of different strike prices available. The most actively traded option

EXHIBIT 4.2   Selected Calls on
XYZ

Strike	April	July	October
25	√	✕	✕
30	√	√	✕
35	√	√	✕
40	√	√	√
45	√	√	√
50	√	√	√

contracts, however, tend to be those contracts trading near the money and with the closest expiration date.

EXAMPLE 4.2   Exhibit 4.2 shows the class of selected call options on XYZ that were available on February 1, when the stock price was 40. The 40 strike price options are at the money, the 45s are out of the money, the 30s and 35s are in the money, and the 20s and 25s are said to be deep in the money. The April 35, 40, and 45 options will probably be the most liquid options at this time.

Prices of Options

The price of a call option is determined in a competitive marketplace. The largest exchange is the Chicago Board Options Exchange (CBOE). Other exchanges in the United States include the American, Philadelphia, Pacific, and New York Stock Exchanges.

Exhibit 4.3 illustrates option price information as reported in the *Wall Street Journal*. The newspaper reports information on only the 1400 most active stock options. The name of the underlying security is presented first, with the closing stock price underneath. The second column indicates the strike price. The expiration months are followed by call and put volume and price information. Option prices are reported on a per share basis, so the actual price is obtained by multiplying the quoted price by the number of shares per contract (usually 100). Option prices under $3 trade in sixteenths of a point, while those over $3 trade in eighths of a point. The 40 most active stock option contracts are highlighted at the top of the page, and volume and open interest summaries by option exchange are also reported.

Long-Term Equity Anticipation Securities

A section on the option quotation page of the *Wall Street Journal* is devoted to long-term equity anticipation securities, usually referred to as LEAPS. These contracts were created by the CBOE in October 1990 and now exist on all option

LISTED OPTIONS QUOTATIONS

Option/Strike		Exp.	Call Vol.	Call Last	Put Vol.	Put Last
24 3/8	25	Jun	2093	1 1/2	1170	2
24 3/8	25	Sep	69	2 1/2	...	...
24 3/8	30	Sep	58	1	...	...
Elecim	35	Jul	...	...	40	3/4
Emplca	7 1/2	May	450	1 1/8	...	...
8 1/2	7 1/2	Jul	45	1 3/4	5	3/4
8 1/2	10	Jul	50	11/16	...	...
8 1/2	10	Oct	41	1 1/4	...	...
EnglCp	35	May	35	4	...	...
Ensrch	15	May	30	2 3/4	...	...
17 5/8	15	Nov	50	3 3/4	...	...
17 5/8	17 1/2	Nov	67	2	...	...
EnzoBi	10	May	144	7/8	...	...
10 1/2	10	Jun	100	1	...	...
10 1/2	10	Jul	85	1 9/16	...	...
10 1/2	12 1/2	May	70	3/16	...	...
10 1/2	12 1/2	Jun	80	3/8	...	...
10 1/2	12 1/2	Jul	60	5/8	...	...
10 1/2	12 1/2	Oct	110	1	...	...
Epitpe	17 1/2	May	50	3/16	75	1 1/4
EqtCos	22 1/2	May	5	1 11/16	50	3/16
24 1/8	25	May	...	...	45	1 3/8
Exbyte	12 1/2	May	14	7/16	170	5/8
12 1/4	12 1/2	Jun	53	13/16	...	...
Exide	25	Aug	...	...	192	3/16
37 5/8	30	Aug	...	...	192	1 1/16
Exxon	65	Jul	183	6 1/4	20	3/16
70 7/8	65	Oct	12	6 7/8	35	1/2
70 7/8	70	May	647	1 1/4	62	5/8
76 3/4	80	May	79	1 9/16	...	...
76 3/4	85	May	210	3/4	...	...
HlywdE	40	Jul	...	...	50	7 1/4
HlwdPk	12 1/2	Jun	40	5/8	...	...
HmeDp	40	May	807	2 1/4	170	9/16
41 3/8	40	Jun	18	2 5/8	29	3/4
41 3/8	40	Aug	12	3 5/8	53	1 3/8
41 3/8	40	Nov	713	4 1/2	35	1 7/8
41 3/8	45	May	233	3/16	33	3 3/4
41 3/8	45	Jun	38	9/16	...	...
41 3/8	45	Aug	158	1 1/4	...	...
Homstk	15	May	70	2 1/8	...	...
17	15	Jul	35	2 7/16	...	...
17	17 1/2	May	66	7/16	15	13/16
17	17 1/2	Jul	56	1 1/8	38	1 3/16
17	17 1/2	Oct	30	1 1/2	42	1 11/16
17	20	May	133	1/8	...	...
17	20	Jul	175	3/8	...	...
17	20	Oct	89	3/4	...	...
Honwll	40	May	105	1/2	...	...
38 5/8	40	Aug	35	2 1/4	20	3
38 5/8	45	Aug	...	...	40	6 1/4
HK Tel	15	Jul	...	...	100	1/8
Houshl	45	Jul	...	...	29	1 1/8
Humana	17 1/2	May	30	2 9/16	3	5/16
20	17 1/2	Nov	...	...	30	1 1/8
20	20	May	174	7/8	70	5/8
20	20	Jun	4569	1 1/8	43	7/8
20	20	Aug	27	2	10	1 1/2
Madge	25	May	105	4 1/2	4	3/8
29 1/2	30	May	60	1 3/8	5	2 5/8
29 1/2	30	Jun	77	2 1/2	...	...
29 1/2	30	Nov	32	4 1/2	...	...
MagmaC	20	May	26	1/16	...	...
Magntk	15	Sep	230	1 3/8	...	...
Malinck	40	Oct	55	13/16	...	...
Marion	20	Jun	20	4 5/8	1020	3/8
24 3/8	22 1/2	May	225	2	695	1/2
24 3/8	22 1/2	Jun	31	2	...	...
24 3/8	25	May	468	3/16	50	1 5/8
24 3/8	25	Jun	470	7/16	620	1 7/8
24 3/8	25	Sep	...	...	90	1 5/8
24 3/8	25	Dec	...	...	110	1 3/4
MartnM	55	Sep	215	4 1/2	...	...
Marvel	15	Oct	61	2 1/4	...	...
15 5/8	17 1/2	Jul	25	9/16	...	...
Maxim	35	May	38	2 3/8	...	...
35 7/8	40	Aug	138	2 3/8	...	...
Maxtor	5	May	86	7/16	...	...
5 3/16	5	Jul	30	15/16	20	11/16
MayDS	35	Sep	60	2 1/2	...	...
Maytag	17 1/2	May	30	5/16	...	...
17 5/8	17 1/2	Jul	32	13/16	5	11/16
17 5/8	20	Oct	30	5/16	...	...
Mc Don	35	May	50	5/8	...	...
35 1/8	35	Sep	25	2	...	...
35 1/8	40	Dec	26	3/4	...	...
Mc D D	40	May	555	22 3/8	...	...
43 3/4	55	May	83	1/4	2	11 1/4
P N C	25	May	183	1/2	3	1/2
25 1/8	25	Aug	55	1 1/4	14	1 7/16
P P G	40	May	302	7/16	...	...
PacCre	60	May	100	4 3/8	10	1 3/4
63	65	May	91	1 7/8	...	...
PallCp	25	Sep	112	1 1/4	...	...
ParmTc	45	May	368	1 5/8	344	1 5/8
ParkPar	22 1/2	Sep	20	1 9/16	50	1 7/8
Pegsus	10	May	32	2 1/2	...	...
Penney	40	May	...	...	50	3/16
42 7/8	40	Aug	...	...	59	15/16
42 7/8	40	Nov	180	4 7/8	11	1 7/16
42 7/8	45	May	444	5/16	49	2 3/16
42 7/8	45	Jun	335	1	10	2 1/2
42 7/8	45	Aug	30	1 1/2	...	...
Pennz	50	Jul	100	1 1/2	...	...
Peopsft	50	May	...	...	30	2 9/16
PepBys	30	Oct	60	1 1/2	...	...
Pepsi	35	Jul	29	7 1/8	...	...
42	40	May	783	2 1/4	263	1/4
42	40	Jun	52	2 1/2	60	1/2
42	40	Oct	121	3 5/8	26	1
42	45	Oct	124	1 1/16	100	3 1/2
PerSptv	5	Sep	115	4 1/4	...	...
9 1/4	7 1/2	Sep	180	2 11/16	3	3/4
9 1/4	7 1/2	Dec	30	3 1/8	...	...
9 1/4	10	Jun	69	5/8	...	...
9 1/4	12 1/2	Jun	40	3/16	...	...

MOST ACTIVE CONTRACTS

Option/Strike				Vol	Exch	Last		Net Chg	a-Close	Open Int
TelMex	May	30	p	7,284	XC	13/16	−	3/16	30 3/8	19,676
Gentch	Jul	50		4,991	XC	11/16	−	4 1/16	48	7,322
I B M	May	90	p	4,634	CB	1 1/8	+	1/2	92 1/8	17,320
Humana	Jun	20		4,569	CB	1 1/8	+	1/8	20	245
I B M	May	95		4,147	CB	1	−	1 1/16	92 1/8	16,960
Grace	May	50		3,841	AM	3 1/8	−	1	52 5/8	5,304
Chryslr	May	45		3,836	CB	7/16	−	3/8	42 1/2	24,775
Gentch	Oct	50		3,367	XC	1 1/4	−	4 1/8	48	200
Intel	May	105		3,089	AM	2 7/8	+	11/16	104 1/8	8,481
I B M	May	85	p	3,072	CB	1/4	+	1/8	92 1/8	10,965
Firstar	Jun	25		3,000	XC	4 1/4		...	28 3/4	...
Gentch	Jul	45	p	2,974	XC	5/16	−	1 7/16	48	4,683
Gentch	Jul	40	p	2,856	XC	1/8	−	1/2	48	2,578
Gentch	Jul	55		2,713	XC	3/16	−	1 15/16	48	7,953
Intel	May	100		2,689	AM	5 3/4	+	1 1/8	104 1/8	9,254
I B M	May	90		2,509	CB	3 1/8	−	2 1/4	92 1/8	15,003
I B M	May	100		2,394	CB	1/4	−	3/8	92 1/8	9,773
QuakrO	May	40		2,386	PB	1 3/16	+	1/2	36 5/8	15,097
I B M	May	95	p	2,119	CB	3 7/8	+	1 1/2	92 1/8	8,207
EleArt	Jun	25		2,093	CB	1 1/2	+	5/16	24 3/8	1,506
Micsft	Jul	80	p	1,925	PC	3	−	3/8	82 1/8	529
Dig Eq	May	35	p	1,875	XC	1/16	−	1/16	44 3/4	3,386
Micsft	May	80	p	1,871	PC	1 1/8	−	5/16	82 1/8	3,438
Micsft	May	80		1,831	PC	3 5/8	+	1/4	82 1/8	6,135
Gentch	Oct	45	p	1,803	XC	5/8	−	1 5/8	48	617
Intel	May	10		1,762	AM	1 1/8	+	1/4	104 1/8	842
Intel	May	100	p	1,762	AM	1 5/16	−	5/8	104 1/8	2,455
Chevrn	Jun	50		1,759	AM	13/16	+	7/16	48 7/8	3,207
Intel	May	90		1,739	AM	14 3/8	+	1 5/8	104 1/8	13,099
QuakrO	Jun	40		1,704	PB	1 13/16	+	5/16	36 5/8	1,273
Gentch	May	55		1,695	XC	1/16	−	5/16	48	2,772
Chryslr	Jun	45		1,675	CB	1 1/8	−	1/4	42 1/2	5,721
Motrla	May	55		1,574	AM	2 3/8	−	1/2	56 3/8	12,296
G M	May	45		1,548	CB	7/8		...	45 1/4	9,477
Corng	Nov	35		1,544	CB	2 5/8	+	7/8	34 1/8	124
I B M	Jul	100		1,460	CB	1 5/8	−	3/4	92 1/8	4,044
Motrla	Jul	60		1,421	AM	2		...	56 3/8	9,812
Micsft	May	85		1,408	PC	1 1/4	+	1/16	82 1/8	2,373
Chryslr	Jul	45		1,389	CB	1 11/16	−	7/16	42 1/2	21,430
Hewlet	May	70		1,348	CB	7/16	−	3/16	64 1/4	914

VOLUME & OPEN INTEREST SUMMARIES
Includes all equity and index contracts

CHICAGO BOARD			
Call Vol:	237,979	Open Int:	5,828,479
Put Vol:	214,566	Open Int:	4,354,644
AMERICAN			
Call Vol:	99,194	Open Int:	3,302,571
Put Vol:	50,271	Open Int:	1,776,558
PACIFIC			
Call Vol:	59,225	Open Int:	1,337,469
Put Vol:	34,886	Open Int:	751,156
PHILADELPHIA			
Call Vol:	38,850	Open Int:	1,601,063
Put Vol:	12,852	Open Int:	914,142
NEW YORK			
Call Vol:	2,863	Open Int:	828,840
Put Vol:	1,161	Open Int:	429,445
TOTAL			
Call Vol:	438,111	Open Int:	12,898,422
Put Vol:	313,736	Open Int:	8,225,945

LEAPS — LONG TERM OPTIONS

Option/Strike		Exp.	Call Vol.	Call Last	Put Vol.	Put Last
AMD	35	Jan 97	55	8 3/4	5	5
35 1/4	40	Jan 97	55	6 1/2	...	...
AT&T	45	Jan 97	100	9 1/2	...	...
50 3/8	50	Jan 96	119	3 5/8	21	2
50 3/8	55	Jan 96	169	1 3/8	20	4 3/4
50 3/8	55	Jan 97	50	3 7/8	...	...
AbtLab	40	Jan 96	50	2 1/2	2	2 7/16
AmExp	30	Jan 97	70	8	25	1 1/2
AmHess	45	Jan 96	150	9 1/2	...	...
Amgen	35	Jan 97	...	...	100	5/16
Amoco	55	Jan 96	100	12 7/8	...	...
AppleC	40	Jan 96	55	4 7/8	...	...
BarickG	25	Jan 96	42	2 7/8	...	...
24 5/8	30	Jan 96	31	1 1/8	200	5 5/8
BayNtw	45	Jan 96	151	2 1/2	...	...
BkBost	25	Jan 96	50	9 1/2	...	...
33 7/8	30	Jan 96	1045	6 1/4	3	1 3/8
BorInt	10	Jan 97	1155	3 3/8	...	...
Centocr	15	Jan 96	5	2 1/8	50	2 5/8
Chevrn	50	Jan 96	76	2 1/2	...	...
92 1/8	90	Jan 96	205	9 5/8	82	4
92 1/8	90	Jan 97	72	14 1/4	33	6 1/8
92 1/8	100	Jan 96	396	4 3/4	31	10
92 1/8	100	Jan 97	110	9 7/8	24	11 3/8
Intel	50	Jan 96	5	56 1/2	217	1/8
104 1/8	65	Jan 96	18	42	100	1/4
104 1/8	65	Jan 97	6	46 5/8	50	1
104 1/8	80	Jan 96	127	28 3/4	31	1 1/4
104 1/8	80	Jan 97	93	35 1/4	158	2 15/16
104 1/8	90	Jan 96	62	20 1/4	107	2 15/16
104 1/8	100	Jan 96	370	14 1/2	70	6 1/2
104 1/8	100	Jan 97	93	23 1/8	22	8 3/8
104 1/8	120	Jan 96	402	5 3/4	12	17 3/8
104 1/8	120	Jan 97	198	13 1/4	8	18 1/2
K mart	12 1/2	Jan 96	66	2 1/4	1000	11/16
MCI	25	Jan 96	40	13/16	...	...
MerLyn	40	Jan 97	...	...	190	2 5/8
Merck	35	Jan 96	48	8 7/8	...	...
43 1/8	40	Jan 96	61	4 7/8	30	1
43 1/8	45	Jan 96	51	2 1/4	...	...
30 3/8	50	Jan 96	666	1/2	...	...
30 3/8	55	Jan 96	1570	5/16	...	...
30 3/8	55	Jan 96	1710	3/8	...	...
30 3/8	60	Jan 96	2000	3/16	...	...
30 3/8	65	Jan 96	100	1/8	...	...
30 3/8	65	Jan 96	50	1/8	...	...
30 3/8	65	Jan 97	505	15/16	...	...
TexInd	90	Jan 96	2	22 1/4	100	4
ToyRU	20	Jan 97	51	7 3/4	...	...
24 5/8	25	Jan 97	8	4 7/8	55	2 1/4
UAL	100	Jan 96	70	25 1/8	...	...
UCarb	30	Jan 97	42	6 1/8	40	2 7/16
UHltCr	35	Jan 96	...	...	253	3 3/8
US Surg	20	Jan 96	...	...	40	1 5/16
22 1/2	30	Jan 96	2	3/4	50	7 7/8
USXMar	15	Jan 96	53	4 1/4	...	...
19 1/8	20	Jan 96	50	1 1/8	12	1 3/4
19 1/8	20	Jan 97	42	2 1/8	40	2
UnCarb	20	Jan 96	41	12 3/8	...	...

EXHIBIT 4.3 Option Price Quotations from the *Wall Street Journal*

Source: Reprinted by permission of the Wall Street Journal © 1995 Dow Jones & Company, Inc. All Rights Reserved Worldwide.

exchanges. Essentially, LEAPS are options with maturities as long as two or three years. The *Wall Street Journal* publishes information on the most active LEAPS. Since they were introduced, volume has steadily increased. In 1992 more than 1.5 million LEAPS contracts were sold, and in 1993 volume expanded by about 50 percent. Currently, such contracts account for about 6 percent of CBOE equity option volume. While this market accounts for only a fraction of the total options market, the growth of LEAPS has been rapid and significant, especially since the volume of short-term equity options has not increased since 1990, a year in which over 48 million contracts were traded.

Exhibit 4.4 shows the closing prices, in dollars, of selected call options on XYZ. The prices are recorded on a per share basis. Thus, the actual price per contract is obtained by multiplying the price by the number of shares per contract, which in this case is 100. The actual price of an April 35 call contract, for example, is $700.

The Intrinsic Value and Time Premiums of Call Options

The value of an American option depends on many factors, including the price of the underlying security, S; the strike price, X; and the time remaining to expiration, T. Let C be the call option price. Oftentimes, to make matters specific, we shall write the call price as a function of these parameters. That is, $C = C(S, X, T)$.

The intrinsic value of a call option is defined as the difference between the stock price and the strike price or zero, whichever is greatest.

$$\text{Intrinsic value} = \text{Max}(S - X, 0)$$

All in-the-money call options have positive intrinsic value. Options trading at their intrinsic value are said to be trading at parity. Theoretically, an option should never trade below parity. If it did, an investor wanting to purchase the stock would find it cheaper to buy the stock by purchasing the option and exercising it immediately. For example, with XYZ trading at $40, the value of all 35 options should exceed the intrinsic value of $5.

PROPERTY 4.1

The price of a call option should equal or exceed its intrinsic value.

$$C(S, X, T) \geq \text{Max}(S - X, 0)$$

At expiration, the option holder has the choice of buying the stock for the strike price or allowing the option to expire. The option should be exercised if it is in the money. If it is out of the money, the option is worthless.

EXHIBIT 4.4 Call Option Prices on XYZ
Stock Price = $40,
Time to Expiration of
April Series = 12 Weeks

Strike	April	July	October
25	15.06	—	—
30	10.88	12.12	—
35	7.00	8.62	—
40	4.00	5.75	7.38
45	2.00	3.69	5.39
50	0.88	2.38	3.75

EXHIBIT 4.5 Time Premiums of XYZ Call Options
Stock Price = $40,
Time to Expiration of
April Series = 12 Weeks

Strike	April	July	October
25	0.06	—	—
30	0.88	2.12	—
35	2.00	3.62	—
40	4.00	5.75	7.38
45	2.00	3.69	5.39
50	0.88	2.38	3.75

PROPERTY 4.2

At the expiration date, the value of an option equals its intrinsic value.

$$C(S, X, 0) = \text{Max}(S - X, 0)$$

The difference between the observed call price and its intrinsic value is called the **time premium.** If the time premium is zero, the call is trading at parity. Exhibit 4.5 illustrates the time premiums of the XYZ call options. Note that all options are trading above parity.

Since an option with a longer time to expiration has all the characteristics of an option with a shorter expiration but lasts longer, it should carry a higher price. The time premium reflects this value.

PROPERTY 4.3

The value of call options with the same strike price increases as the time to expiration increases.

$$C(S, X, T_1) \le C(S, X, T_2) \quad \text{if } T_1 \le T_2$$

The call value can be represented as the sum of two components:

$$\text{Call premium} = \text{Intrinsic value} + \text{Time premium}$$

As the expiration date nears, the time premium shrinks to zero. Prior to expiration, the size of the time premium depends on the time remaining to expiration and on the intrinsic value. From Exhibit 4.5 it can be seen that the time premiums of at-the-money options are relatively larger than time premiums of in-the-money or out-of-the-money options. This phenomenon will be discussed in more detail in later chapters.

Call Option Transactions

A call buyer's opening transaction consists of the initial call purchase. Since the time premium shrinks as the expiration date approaches, call buyers hope that this decay is more than offset by an increase in the intrinsic value. At any time, the call holder can do one of three things:

1. Exercise the call by paying the strike price in return for shares,
2. Cancel the position by selling the call option at the current market price, or
3. Hold onto the call and take no immediate action.

Exercising Call Options

If an option is exercised and the acquired stock is immediately sold at market price, then ignoring commission costs, the option holder will profit only from the intrinsic value.

EXAMPLE 4.3 Suppose an investor owns an April 40 call option on a stock that is priced at $42. By exercising the call option, the investor pays $40 for a stock whose market value is $42. If the stock is sold at its market value of $42, then ignoring commission costs, the net profit to the option holder will be $2 less the initial cost of the option.

PROPERTY 4.4

By exercising a call option, the investor forfeits the time premium.

Rather than exercising the call option, the investor could have canceled the position by selling the option at its current market price. In this way, the time premium would not be forfeited.

Although it appears that early exercise of a call option is not a sound strategy, there are circumstances in which it is appropriate. These include the following situations:

1. If the investor wants to own the stock and the option is trading at parity, exercising the call rather than selling the option and buying the stock may be advantageous, once transaction costs are considered.
2. Immediately before an ex-dividend date, the holder of a deep-in-the-money call option may find it profitable to exercise the call early, especially if the dividend paid on the stock is sufficiently large.

> **PROPERTY 4.5**
>
> For a stock that pays no dividends, no incentive exists to exercise the call option early. The option holder will either sell the call or hold onto it.

The optimal timing of exercising options and the impact of dividends on the exercise policy are discussed more fully in Chapter 6.

Selling Call Options

For every opening transaction involving an option purchase, there is an opening transaction involving an option sale. The seller (or writer) of an option is obliged to deliver 100 shares of the underlying stock for the agreed strike price in the event that the option is exercised. The writer of the call receives the call premium for this obligation. The writer anticipates that the stock price will decline in value or increase at a rate slower than the decrease in the time value of the option.

Unlike the call purchaser, who has a voluntary right to exercise the call, the writer has a legal obligation to deliver 100 shares at the strike price in the event that the option is exercised.

EXAMPLE 4.4   An XYZ April 45 call option initially sold for a premium of $2. In March, with the stock price at 52, the option is exercised. The writer, in this case, is obligated to deliver 100 shares of the security for $45 per share.

At any time the writer of a call option can do one of two things:

1. Close out the position by buying the call back at the current market price, or
2. Do nothing.

The call writer should be particularly aware of conditions that will encourage the buyer to exercise the call. As discussed, exercise can occur if the call trades at parity and an ex-dividend date is near.

The maximum loss an option buyer can experience is limited to the initial investment. However, the maximum loss in selling call options is unlimited. To guarantee that the writer can meet obligations, brokerage firms require certain margin requirements to be met. These requirements may be stricter than the minimum set of requirements set by law. In addition, the initial call premiums taken in are held by the brokerage firm as collateral.

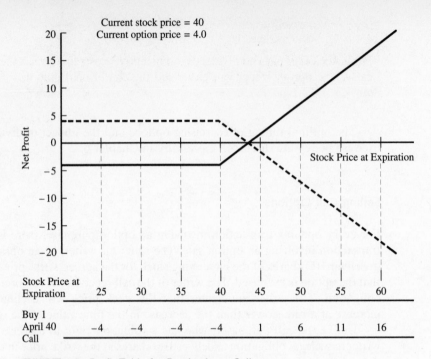

EXHIBIT 4.6   Profit Table for Purchasing a Call

Stock Price at Expiration	25	30	35	40	45	50	55	60
Buy 1 April 40 Call	−4	−4	−4	−4	1	6	11	16

Profit Diagrams for Call Options

The profit obtained by holding a call option to expiration depends on the stock price at expiration. The solid line in Exhibit 4.6 illustrates the potential profit of an April 40 call option initially purchased for $4 and held to expiration.

The profit from selling the call is the mirror image of the profit from buying the call and is represented by the dashed line in Exhibit 4.6. The profit functions clearly illustrate that the profit (loss) of the buyer equals the loss (profit) of the writer. Notwithstanding commission costs, options are zero sum games.

Put Options

A put option is a contract that gives the owner the right to sell a given number of shares of a specified security at a specified strike price at any point in time prior to a specified date. The writer of a put is legally obliged to accept delivery of the shares for the strike price in the event that the put holder exercises the option.

Prices of Put Options

Exhibit 4.4 illustrated the prices of all call options available on XYZ when the stock price was $40. Exhibit 4.7 shows the prices of all put options on a per share basis. Note that the available strike prices and times to expiration are the same as for the call options. A holder of an April 45 put option has the right to sell 100 shares of XYZ at $45 per share, regardless of the market value of the security. The ability to do this extends to the third Friday in April.

A buyer may purchase a put in anticipation of a stock price decline. The buyer need not own the underlying security. If it is owned, then the put provides insurance against stock price declines below the strike. This is more fully explained in Chapter 5.

The put options with strike 40 are trading at the money. Since their strike price equals the stock price, their full premium is a time premium. Put options have intrinsic value if the strike price is higher than the stock price. For example, the 45 put options have intrinsic value, since the put holder could buy 100 shares of XYZ at the market price of $40 per share and then "put" the shares onto the option seller for the strike price of $45 per share. Thus, for put options, the intrinsic value is given by the following equation:

$$\text{Intrinsic value} = \text{Max}(X - S, 0)$$

Options with positive intrinsic value are called in-the-money options. Thus, the 45 and 50 strike-price options are in the money. Exhibit 4.8 illustrates the dollar time premiums of the put prices in Exhibit 4.7. Note that the April 50 put option is trading at parity.

As with call options, if put options traded below parity, arbitrage opportunities would exist. For example, if the 45 put were priced below the parity value of $5, say at $3, then an arbitrager would buy the put and the stock for an initial investment (excluding transaction costs) of $43. By exercising the put immediately, the investor would obtain a $2 profit.

EXHIBIT 4.7 Selected Put Option Prices
Stock Price = $40,
Time to Expiration of
April Series = 12 Weeks

Strike	April	July	October
25	0.06	—	—
30	0.25	0.75	—
35	1.00	1.95	—
40	3.00	3.88	4.50
45	5.88	6.62	7.12
50	10.00	10.06	10.25

EXHIBIT 4.8 Time Premium of Put Options
Stock Price = $40,
Time to Expiration of
April Series = 12 Weeks

Strike	April	July	October
25	0.06	—	—
30	0.25	0.75	—
35	1.00	1.95	—
40	3.00	3.88	4.50
45	0.88	1.62	2.12
50	0.00	0.06	0.25

Put Option Transactions

At any time, a put holder, like a call holder, can either exercise or cancel the position or do nothing. If the put holder exercises the contract, then any positive time premium is lost. However, the holder of an in-the-money put option may decide to exercise even though several months may remain to expiration. By not exercising the option, the investor is foregoing receipt of the high strike price, on which interest could be earned. Example 4.5 illustrates that put holders may correctly exercise their right prior to expiration.

EXAMPLE 4.5   The owner of the three-month XYZ 50 put option and 100 shares of XYZ may exercise early. The stock is at $1, and the put option is at its parity value of $49. No further dividends are due prior to expiration. The interest rate is 8 percent.

By exercising early, the investor receives $5000 immediately. This money will generate $100 in interest over the three-month period. By delaying exercising, the investor is delaying receipt of these funds and hence sacrificing potential interest income.

If the underlying security pays a dividend, there may be incentives to wait until after the ex-dividend date before exercising the put option. For example, consider a trader who owns a put on a stock. The ex-dividend day is one day away. On the ex-dividend day, the stock price is expected to decline, pushing the put deeper into the money. As a result, the trader may decide to delay exercising in order to capture the benefits of the depreciation.

PROPERTY 4.6

1. For stocks paying no dividends, early exercise of calls is not optimal, but early exercise of puts may be optimal.
2. For stocks paying dividends, early exercise of calls and puts may be appropriate. As dividend sizes increase, early exercise of call options becomes more likely and early exercise of put options before the last ex-dividend date becomes less likely.

The decision to exercise a call or put option early depends on trade-offs between dividend and interest income and is discussed in more detail in Chapter 6.

Profit Functions for Put Options

The profit from holding a put option to expiration is represented graphically by the solid line in Exhibit 4.9. The initial cost is $3, and it is assumed that the put is held to maturity. The profit from the sale of a put option is the mirror image and is indicated by the dashed line.

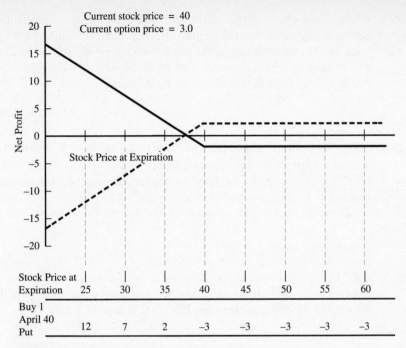

Stock Price at Expiration	25	30	35	40	45	50	55	60
Buy 1 April 40 Put	12	7	2	–3	–3	–3	–3	–3

EXHIBIT 4.9   Profit Table for Purchasing a Put

The relationship between put and call prices, together with the effects of dividends and interest rates, will be explored in Chapter 6.

Adjustment of Option Contracts for Stock Splits and Stock Dividends

Listed call options are not adjusted for cash dividends. However, strike price adjustments are made if the stock splits or if stock dividends occur.

EXAMPLE 4.6   Suppose a stock declares a two-for-one split. If the stock has been trading at $60, then after the split the price is $30. A call option with strike 50 would, in this case, split into two call options with strike 25 each. A 55 call option would split into two 27.5 strike-priced calls.

If the split ratio is not an integer, the adjustment is more complex. For example, consider a three-for-two split. In this case, not only would the strike price be adjusted, but also the number of shares per contract.

EXAMPLE 4.7   When a three-for-two split occurs, new strike prices are established by dividing the old strike price by 1.5 and rounding off to the nearest eighth of a point. If the strike price was 85, then the new strike price will be near 85/1.5, or 56 2/3. The investor now holds one option contract with strike 56 5/8. If the option is exercised, 150 shares (rather than 100 shares) will be delivered.

EXAMPLE 4.8   XYZ Corporation "spins off" its subsidiary, ABC Inc., by distributing to its stockholders 1.5 shares of ABC for every share of XYZ stock. In this case, outstanding XYZ options might be adjusted to require delivery of 100 shares of XYZ plus 150 shares of ABC stock. Alternatively, the strike prices of XYZ might be reduced by the value, on a per share basis, of the distributed property.

EXAMPLE 4.9   XYZ is acquired by a corporation in a cash merger. Each holder of XYZ stock receives $50 per share. In this case, XYZ options might be adjusted to call for the delivery of $5000 in cash rather than 100 shares of XYZ.

The Determinants of Option Value

We have seen that the stock price, strike price, time to expiration, and dividend policy are factors that influence option prices. There are only two other primary determinants of option prices, namely, the volatility of the underlying stock price and interest rates. In future chapters the exact relationship of option prices to each of these variables will be analyzed. Nonetheless, we have already seen that American option prices increase as time to expiration increases and as the stock price moves deeper into the money. Moreover, we have seen that as dividend size increases, early exercise of call options becomes more likely and early exercise of puts before the ex-dividend date becomes less likely. In this section we provide intuitive explanations of the impact of volatility and interest rates on option prices.

The Role of Volatility

The volatility of a stock is a measure of its potential dispersion over future possible stock prices. A stock with high volatility has a high degree of dispersion in future values and could thus increase or decrease by significant amounts. In contrast, a stock with no volatility is riskless since future prices are certain.

As volatility increases, call prices also increase. To see this, note that buying a call option provides an alternative to purchasing stock in anticipation of capturing gains from the stock price advance. As volatility increases, the future dispersion of possible stock prices expands. While this increases the likelihood of large profits from the stock, it also increases the chances of large losses. However, the call holders will obtain all the benefits from expanded dispersion without the drawbacks. Specifically, by owning in-the-money call options, call holders can participate dollar for dollar in favorable outcomes. If unfavorable outcomes occur, however, call holders merely do not exercise their contracts. Consequently, call holders will prefer more volatility to less. As a result, the higher the volatility of the stock over the lifetime of the call option, the higher its value relative to the stock.

Note that the same argument holds true for put options. The greater the dispersion of future potential stock prices, the greater the chance the stock price will end up in the money (below the strike). Since it is not necessary for put holders to exercise their options, their losses are limited if the stock price appreciates. Thus, put premiums should expand as volatility increases.

The Role of Interest Rates

As interest rates increase, call prices also increase. To see this, recall that buying a call option provides an alternative to purchasing stock in anticipation of capturing gains from an increasing stock price. As interest rates rise, the cost of carrying the underlying security rises, and the call option will appear more attractive vis-à-vis the stock.

For an alternative way to illustrate the impact of interest rates on option prices, consider an investor who buys the call option and invests sufficient funds (at the riskless rate) to ensure that at expiration, the account will have grown to the strike price. The effective strike price at expiration is really the present value of the strike. As interest rates increase, this effective strike price decreases. Hence, an increasing interest rate has the same impact on option prices as a decreasing strike price.

This simple analysis has assumed that interest rates do not affect the stock price. Clearly, if interest rate increases reduced the volatility of the stock, for example, the analysis would be more complex. Note, too, that with rising interest rates, the effective strike prices are reduced, and hence put premiums fall. Thus, put prices will move in an opposite direction to call prices when interest rates change.

Exhibit 4.10 illustrates the direction in which option premiums will move as each variable increases.

EXHIBIT 4.10   Effects of Increase in Variables on Option Premiums

Variable	Call Premium	Put Premium
Stock price	Increases	Decreases
Strike price	Decreases	Increases
Time to expiration	Increases	Increases
Dividend	Decreases	Increases
Stock volatility	Increases	Increases
Interest rates	Increase	Decrease

Conclusion

Standardized exchange-traded stock option contracts are introduced into the marketplace in a well-defined way. At any point in time, a variety of option contracts that differ in strike price and time to maturity can trade. Option prices are set so that in-the-money contracts are more valuable than out-of-the-money contracts, and the far series contracts are more valuable than the near series. Although the strike price and expiration date are key ingredients in determining the price of an option, we have seen that volatility, interest rates, and dividends are factors that also must be considered.

Options are highly leveraged financial instruments that allow speculators to participate in the stock market without owning stock and allow shareholders to hedge against unwanted risk. Options can be bought or sold. The maximum loss associated with the purchase of an option is the initial investment. On the other hand, the sale of an option can expose the writer to unlimited losses. The purchase of an option provides the investor with a right. In contrast, an option writer is obligated to fulfill the terms of the option contract if it is exercised.

The terms of a stock option are not adjusted for cash dividends, but they are adjusted for stock dividends and stock splits. Any adjustment is designed to be as fair as possible to both the buyer and the seller.

Options are zero sum games. That is, ignoring transaction costs, the profit (loss) obtained by the buyer of an option is equal to the loss (profit) incurred by the seller. In the next few chapters we shall see that the primary economic role of options is to provide a financial mechanism for transferring risk among investors.

References

There are numerous books and brochures that define put and call stock options and describe the institutional structure of the option markets. The Options Clearing Corporation and the option exchanges publish many booklets that describe the risks and rewards of trading options. These pamphlets can be obtained directly from the exchanges or through a stockbroker.

Bookstaber, R. *Option Pricing and Investment Strategies*. Chicago: Probus, 1987.

Chance, D. *An Introduction to Options and Futures Markets*. Hinsdale; Ill.: Dryden Press, 1989.

Cox, J. C., and M. Rubinstein. *Option Markets*. Englewood Cliffs, N.J.: Prentice-Hall, 1985.

Hull, J. *Introduction to Futures and Options Markets*. Englewood Cliffs, N.J.: Prentice-Hall, 1991.

Kolb, R. *Options: An Introduction*. Miami: Kolb, 1993.

McMillan, L. G. *Options as a Strategic Investment*. New York: New York Institute of Finance, 1986.

Exercises

1. Below are selected option prices for General Motors taken from the *Wall Street Journal* on September 16, 1993. The stock closed at 47 1/4.

Strike	Expiration Date	Calls (Vol.)	Call (Price)	Puts (Vol.)	Puts (Price)
35	September	35	12 1/4	—	—
40	September	735	7 3/8	—	—
40	October	34	6 1/8	—	—
40	December	545	8	108	9/16
45	September	686	2 1/4	379	1/16
50	September	—	—	58	3 3/4
50	October	180	5/8	16	3 1/8
50	December	548	1 5/8	10	4 1/4

   a. Which call options are in the money, and which contracts are out of the money?
   b. Which put options are in the money, and which are out of the money?
   c. Compute the time premiums of all contracts. Provide an explanation for any negative time premiums.
   d. Ignoring transaction costs, what would be the dollar cost of purchasing three call options with strike 45 and expiration in September?
   e. Look at the September 40 call and the October 40 call. If you could trade at these prices, what strategy would you put into place?
   f. Explain why the prices in Exercise 1e appear distorted—that is, explain why implementing the strategy in 1e is not likely to work.

2. A three-month call option with strike price $50 is currently trading at $5. The stock price is $50. An investor has $5000 to invest and is considering buying 100 shares or 10 options.
   a. For both strategies, compute the three-month return on investment if at the expiration date the stock price is $40, $50, or $60.
   b. Repeat Exercise 2a for a put option with strike price $50, priced at $5.
   c. On the basis of 2a and 2b, can you conclude that options are highly leveraged financial instruments?

3. Mr. Vestor knows that his certificate of deposit matures in two months; when his cash is released, he will invest in the stock market. However, he would like to buy stock now because he feels a rally is imminent. Would you recommend that Mr. Vestor buy call or put options in the interim? What type of contracts (strike price and maturity) would you recommend?

4. XYZ trades at $50. The $45 put option trades at 1 1/2, and the $50 put option trades at $3.
   a. Compute the profit (and return) from buying the $45 put if the stock price at expiration is $40 and $45.

   b. Repeat Exercise 4a assuming the $50 put is purchased.
   c. Does the out-of-the-money put option offer a higher reward (and higher risk) potential?

5. XYZ is trading at $50. Ms. Vestor believes it would be a good buy at $45. Rather than place a limit order to buy at $45, she decides to sell a $50 put option that is currently trading at $5. Discuss the benefits of this strategy by considering what happens if at the expiration date the stock trades above $50 and below $50.

6. Consider the following information: The price of XYZ = $50. The price of ABC = $50. XYZ April 50 call = $3. ABC April 50 call = $5. On the basis of this information alone, can an investor determine which option contract is overpriced? If not, what other factors should be considered?

7. XYZ is selling at $50, and a four-month call option with strike 45 is selling at $9.
   a. What is the maximum profit obtained if the call option is sold? Under what conditions would this profit be obtained?
   b. Mr. Vestor sold the call option. What loss is incurred if the stock is trading at $62 at the expiration date?
   c. What is the minimum loss that will be incurred if after two months, with the stock trading at $63, Mr. Vestor decides to cut his losses by buying back the call?

8. A call option with strike 30 and time to expiration of two months trades at $6. Another call on the same stock has strike 30 and time to expiration of three months and trades at $4. Construct a strategy that guarantees profit.

9. A put option with strike 30 and time to expiration of two months trades at $6. Another put on the same stock has strike 30 and time to expiration of three months and trades at $4. Can you construct a strategy that guarantees profit? If so, what is this strategy?

10. A dont option is an option that you pay for only if you do not exercise the option by expiration. Do you think the premium of a dont call option would be higher or lower than the premium for a regular American call option? Justify your answer.

11. A trading-range call option can be exercised for the strike price, if the underlying stock price stays within a given range of prices. Would such an option be more or less valuable than an American call option? Explain your answer.

12. An investor with $5500 is bullish on XYZ. XYZ trades at $55. One possible investment is to buy 100 shares. An alternative is to buy one call option with a strike of 55 (assume the premium is $5) and invest the remaining $5000 in bonds for six months at 10 percent. Compare the two investments, assuming that the stock pays no dividends.

13. An XYZ April 50 call option is bought for $5. At expiration the stock is selling at $60. If the call is sold, the commission will be $25. If the call is exercised and the stock is then sold, there will be a commission when the stock is bought

and again when it is sold. Assuming a commission for each transaction of $65, compare the two strategies of selling versus exercising. On the basis of this analysis, explain how commission costs affect option strategies.

14. A European option is identical to an American option except that it can be exercised only at the expiration date.

    a. Would you suspect a European call option to be worth more or less than its American counterpart? Explain.

    b. Would you expect a European put option to be worth more or less than its American counterpart? Explain.

15. Provide an intuitive explanation for the fact that put premiums drop when interest rates rise.

APPENDIX 4A

Executing Option Orders

The option exchanges attempt to provide a continuous, competitive, and fair market environment for the purchase and sale of options. They determine the underlying securities on which options are traded, and they enforce rules applicable to the handling of accounts and execution of buy and sell orders. Specific information about exchange functions is readily available in rule books of the various exchanges and in publications put out by brokerage firms.

This appendix discusses the process of executing option orders through the option exchange. In addition, it investigates the central role of the Options Clearing Corporation (OCC) and discusses the process of assigning exercise notices to investors with short positions.

Placing Option Orders

To place an order with a broker, the investor must specify the name of the underlying security, the type of option (put or call), the number of contracts to buy or sell, the strike price, the expiration month, and the type of order. The type of order provides the broker with instructions on the price the customer is prepared to pay and the time for which the order is in effect. As with futures contracts, the types of orders that can be placed include market orders, limit orders, and stop orders, among others.

EXAMPLE 4A.1 The current price of XYZ is $50. A limit order to buy one April call option with strike 50 for $4 is placed with the broker. The order is a day order. If the option price is still above $4 by the end of the day, the order is canceled.

Execution of Orders

After receiving an order from a customer, the broker will direct it to the appropriate exchange. A broker who represents the firm on the floor of the exchange will attempt to execute the order in a fashion consistent with the rules of the exchange. At the CBOE, for example, trading is done by a system of open outcry. In this system, offers to buy and sell options on a particular stock are made to all traders present in a specified area. The broker may trade with three types of traders:

1. **Market makers** trade for their own accounts. Their activity on the floor of the exchange enhances liquidity and tightens the spread between bid and ask quotes. Market makers are required to maintain bid and ask prices for each contract. The exchange sets limits for the spread between them. For options priced less than $0.50, the spread must be less than $0.25. For options priced less than $10, the spread must be less than $0.50. For options priced less than $20, the spread must be less than $0.75. Finally, for all other cases, the spread must be less than $1.

2. **Order book officials** are exchange employees who can accept only public orders. They cannot trade for their own accounts. Their job is to see that public limit orders are executed as soon as their threshold prices have been attained. Limit orders are all entered into a computer and are executed as soon as the limit price is reached. The information on all outstanding limit orders is available to all traders.

3. **Other brokers** trade on behalf of their clients and their firms' accounts. They trade on the floor with other floor brokers or with market makers.

Once an oral agreement is reached between two floor traders, the transaction is reported to the Options Clearing Corporation (OCC) and back to the original broker. Within a few minutes of placing an order, the customer will learn of the trade.

The Options Clearing Corporation

Once a price is negotiated between two brokers on the floor of the exchange, the two cease to deal with each other. Instead, they deal with the OCC, which guarantees that all option obligations are met by breaking up every trade and becoming the seller for every buyer and buyer for every seller. Thus, all traders look to the OCC to maintain its side of the bargain, rather than to other traders.

Since the number of contracts purchased by the OCC equals the number sold, its net position is always zero. However, its position is not completely free of risk. To see this, assume that a particular investor exercises a call option. In this case the OCC is obliged to deliver 100 shares of the stock for the strike price. To accomplish this the OCC will, in effect, exercise one of its call options. If the investor to whom the exercise notice is assigned delivers the shares, the OCC covers its obligation. However, if the assigned writer fails to deliver the securities, the OCC must still fulfill its obligation.

To protect itself against the risk of default by sellers of options, the OCC requires that its member firms guarantee the obligations of all their particular customers. Toward this goal, the OCC requires that all member firms whose clients have short positions provide the OCC with collateral. These accounts are balanced daily. The clearing members, in turn, must ensure that their customers have sufficient funds to meet their potential obligations. They achieve this by requiring that their clients provide collateral for all their written positions. The exact amount of collateral required depends on the transaction and is discussed in Chapter 5.

The breaking up of all trades by the OCC provides option traders with additional benefits. Since all members are, in essence, trading against the OCC, they can easily cancel their positions. For example, a writer who sells a call option (to the OCC) can cancel the position by buying an option (at market-determined prices). In essence, this action results in a cancellation of the original transaction. Without the OCC, individual sellers would have to negotiate with individual buyers to establish a price at which both parties would settle.

Exercising Option Contracts

Although most buyers and sellers of options close out their positions by an offsetting sale or purchase, there are occasions when a contract will be exercised. To exercise an option, the owner must instruct his or her broker to give exercise instructions to OCC. To ensure that an option is exercised on a particular day, this notice must be tendered before a particular time (which may vary across brokerage firms). The broker passes the exercise instructions to the OCC.

On the next business day, the OCC randomly assigns the exercise notice to a clearing member who has an account that contains a written option in the relevant security. The brokerage firm to which the notice is assigned then randomly allocates the assignment to a customer who has a written position. Once an exercise notice has been assigned to a writer, the writer can no longer effect an offsetting closing transaction, but must instead purchase (if the exercise notice is a put) or sell (if the notice is a call) the underlying securities for the strike price. Settlement between brokers on exercised options occurs on the fifth business day after exercise. Each broker involved in an exercise settles with his or her own customer.

CHAPTER 5

Option Strategies

Chapter 4 was concerned with the basic terminology and properties of options. This chapter discusses categorizing and analyzing investment positions constructed by meshing puts and calls with their underlying securities. Options can be used to produce payouts that best reflect the expectations that an investor has for the future prospects of a security. As an example, consider an investor who believes that a news announcement will soon be released that will have major ramifications on the price of the stock of a particular company. Since it is not known whether the announcement will be good or bad, the investor is uncertain whether to buy or sell the security. We shall see that, by using options, a position can be constructed so that profits will be obtained if the news announcement results in large price moves, whether positive or negative.

As a second example, consider an investor who attempts to "time" the market. Without options, such an investor attempts to smooth out the fluctuations of portfolio value by buying and selling securities. Anticipating short-term declines in stock price, an investor may choose to sell a security even if the long-term prospects appear good. Timing strategies, however, can result in large transaction costs. With options, the investor can hedge the anticipated short-term decline without selling the stock. In fact, with options available, investors can choose precisely the degree of risk they want to bear. Unwanted risk associated with some aspects of stock ownership can be transferred to others who are willing to accept it.

In this chapter we consider a variety of option strategies that produce distinctive future payouts. For the most part, we ignore commissions, margin requirements, and dividends. We shall also assume that positions are maintained unchanged to the expiration date and that no premature exercising occurs.

The primary objectives of this chapter are the following:

- To analyze almost any position containing several option contracts on a single underlying security;

- To recognize the strategic role of options in investment management; and

- To identify the most popular stock option strategies currently in use.

EXHIBIT 5.1 Call and Put Option Prices
Stock Price = $40, Time to Expiration of Near Series = 12 Weeks

| | Calls | | | | Puts | | |
| | Near | Middle | Far | | Near | Middle | Far |
Strike	(April)	(July)	(October)	Strike	(April)	(July)	(October)
25	15.06	—	—	25	0.06	—	—
30	10.88	12.12	—	30	0.25	0.75	—
35	7.00	8.62	—	35	1.00	1.95	—
40	4.00	5.75	7.38	40	3.00	3.88	4.50
45	2.00	3.69	5.39	45	5.88	6.62	7.12
50	0.88	2.38	3.75	50	10.00	10.06	10.25

Option Positions

There are four types of option positions:

1. **Naked positions** involve the purchase or sale of a single security, for example, the purchase or sale of a stock or a call or a put.
2. **Hedge positions** consist of the underlying stock together with options that provide partial or full protection from unfavorable outcomes.
3. **Spread options** consist of a long position in one option and a short position in another option on the same underlying security.
4. **Combinations** consist of portfolios containing either long or short positions in call and put options on the same security.

Exhibit 5.1 shows the price data we will use to illustrate all the strategies discussed in this chapter.

Naked Positions

Naked Positions in the Stock

Exhibit 5.2 illustrates the profit diagram for holding the stock for three months. Increases in stock price offer profits, whereas decreases in stock price offer losses.

Exhibit 5.3 illustrates the profit diagram for selling the stock short. The short seller, anticipating stock declines, intends to return the securities by purchasing them in the future at lower prices. Since the investor is liable for all dividends paid on the stock while it is outstanding, if the investor is to profit, the price declines must be significantly greater than the dividends. For the privilege of borrowing stock, the broker requires the investor to deposit collateral into a special margin account. Specifically, 50 percent of the short sale value must be deposited in cash or in interest-bearing securities with the broker. Furthermore, the proceeds of the

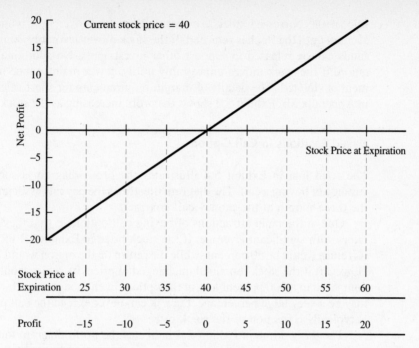

EXHIBIT 5.2 Profit Table for Purchasing Stock

Stock Price at Expiration	25	30	35	40	45	50	55	60
Profit	−15	−10	−5	0	5	10	15	20

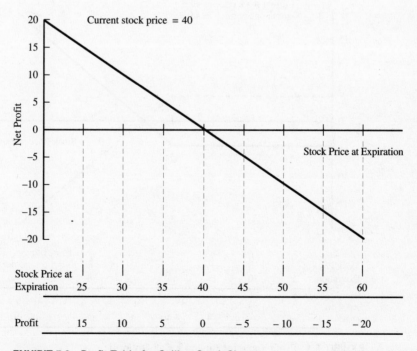

EXHIBIT 5.3 Profit Table for Selling Stock Short

Stock Price at Expiration	25	30	35	40	45	50	55	60
Profit	15	10	5	0	− 5	− 10	− 15	− 20

sale of the borrowed stock are retained by the broker in a noninterest-bearing account until the stock is returned. If the stock moves favorably, some of the margin funds can be released to support other investments. No additional margin is required if the stock moves unfavorably until a lower maintenance margin requirement is violated. The details of margin requirements for short sales are discussed in Appendix 5B. Exhibit 5.3 shows the profit increasing as the stock price declines.

Naked Positions in Call Options

The solid line in Exhibit 5.4 illustrates the profit diagram associated with the strategy of buying a call. The diagram illustrates the payouts associated with buying the three-month at-the-money call contract.

One of the main attractions of buying call options is that they provide speculators with significant leverage. If the stock price in Exhibit 5.4 increased by $20, its return would be 50 percent, while the return on the option would be 400 percent. However, if the stock remained unchanged in price, its return would be 0 percent, compared to a 100 percent loss in the option. Even though the return on the option may be a very large percentage, the risk can never exceed the call premium, which is typically a fraction of the stock price.

The dashed line in Exhibit 5.4 indicates the profit diagram for the sale of the call. The naked call writer assumes the prospect of unlimited risk in return for a

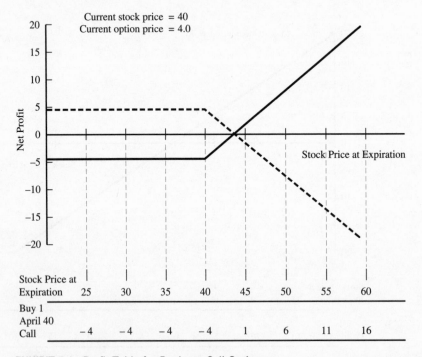

Stock Price at Expiration	25	30	35	40	45	50	55	60
Buy 1 April 40 Call	−4	−4	−4	−4	1	6	11	16

Current stock price = 40
Current option price = 4.0

EXHIBIT 5.4 Profit Table for Buying a Call Option

limited profit. Thus, this strategy is unsuitable for some investors. In Exhibit 5.4, the naked call writer will profit only if the stock price remains below $44.

Recall that call writers have an obligation to deliver shares in the event that they are exercised. In order to ensure that the investor is able to deliver the underlying security, the broker will require the call writer to deposit collateral into a margin account. The exact margin requirements are discussed in Appendix 5B.

Naked Positions in Put Options

The solid line in Exhibit 5.5 illustrates the profit diagram associated with the strategy of buying a put option and holding it to expiration. The diagram illustrates the payouts associated with buying the three-month at-the-money put contract.

Like call options, put options are highly leveraged financial instruments. From Exhibit 5.5 we can see that if the stock dropped to $25 (for a net loss of 37 percent), the return on the put would be 400 percent. As with call options, the maximum loss is limited to the put premium, which usually is a small fraction of the security price. The dashed line in Exhibit 5.5 indicates the profit function for the sale of a put. Here the maximum profit equals the put premium, while the downside loss is limited only by the fact that the stock cannot drop below zero.

Some investors who actually want to acquire stock will write naked puts. The motivation for this is illustrated by Example 5.1.

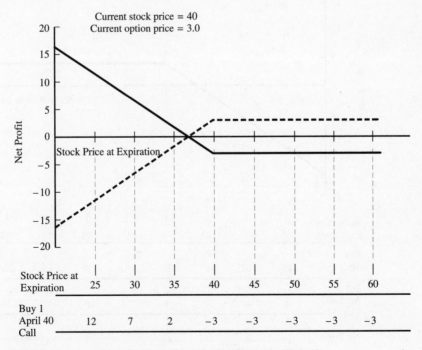

Stock Price at Expiration	25	30	35	40	45	50	55	60
Buy 1 April 40 Call	12	7	2	−3	−3	−3	−3	−3

EXHIBIT 5.5 Profit Table for Buying a Put Option

EXAMPLE 5.1   An investor feels that XYZ would be a good buy at $36. With the stock priced at $40, the investor decides to place an open buy order with a limit price of $36. Three months later XYZ has drifted down to $37, but no lower. If the price rises rapidly, the investor will not participate in the rally, since the stock will not be owned.

Rather than place an open order at $36, the investor could have written a 40 put for $4. If XYZ is below $40 at expiration, the put will be exercised and the investor will be forced to pay $40 per share for the stock. Since $4 was received from the sale of the put, the net cost of the stock is $36.

The advantage of writing a put over placing an open buy order is that the strategy generates income when the stock price does not fall to the purchase level.

Hedge Positions

Hedging Stock with Call Options

A **covered hedge position** (often referred to as a **covered write position**) consists of a portfolio in which a call is written against every 100 shares held. Exhibit 5.6 shows the profit diagram of a portfolio in which a three-month at-the-money call option is written against the stock.

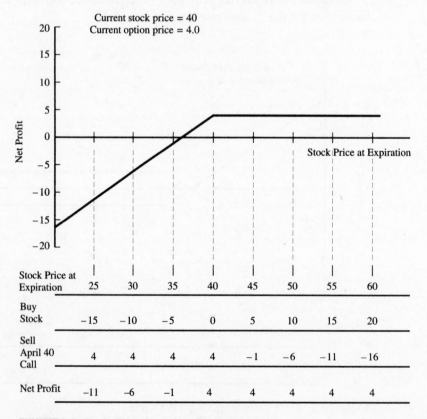

Stock Price at Expiration	25	30	35	40	45	50	55	60
Buy Stock	−15	−10	−5	0	5	10	15	20
Sell April 40 Call	4	4	4	4	−1	−6	−11	−16
Net Profit	−11	−6	−1	4	4	4	4	4

EXHIBIT 5.6   Profit Table for a Covered Call Option

The solid line in Exhibit 5.7 illustrates the profit diagram for a covered hedge position in which the April 35 calls are sold against the stock. The dashed line illustrates the position involving the sale of the April 40s (shown in Exhibit 5.6). Note that by selling the 35s rather than the 40s, the investor sacrifices upside potential for downside protection. Specifically, the new position can make a maximum of only $2 (as opposed to $4). However, the position loses money only if the stock price falls below $33 (as opposed to $36). The choice between these two positions depends on the investor's beliefs about future prices and attitude toward risk and reward.

The option premium acts as partial compensation for potential declines in the underlying stock price; this appeals to stockholders who believe that over the short term, the stock price will be flat at best. Instead of selling the stock with the intention of buying it back in the future, such stockholders can sell calls against their stock. Indeed, this strategy outperforms stock ownership if the stock price falls, remains the same, or even rises slightly.

The investor can establish a partially covered hedge position by writing calls for only part of the stock in the portfolio. The ratio of calls written to stock held is called the **hedge ratio.** Exhibit 5.8 illustrates a 1 : 2 hedge with at-the-money call options. The dashed line indicates the profit for a naked position in two stocks. Note

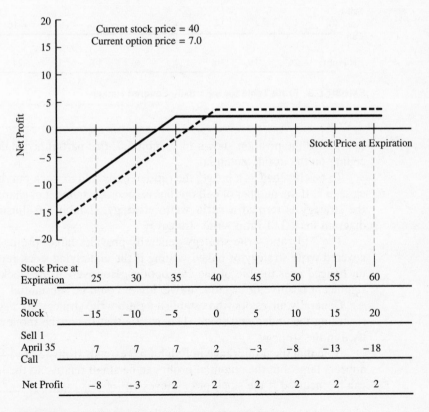

Stock Price at Expiration	25	30	35	40	45	50	55	60
Buy Stock	−15	−10	−5	0	5	10	15	20
Sell 1 April 35 Call	7	7	7	2	−3	−8	−13	−18
Net Profit	−8	−3	2	2	2	2	2	2

EXHIBIT 5.7   Profit Table for a Covered Call Position

EXHIBIT 5.8 Profit Table for a Partially Covered Hedge

Stock Price at Expiration	25	30	35	40	45	50	55	60
Buy 2 Stocks	−30	−20	−10	0	10	20	30	40
Sell 1 April 40 Call	4	4	4	4	−1	−6	−11	−16
Net Profit	−26	−16	−6	4	9	14	19	24

that unlike the position shown in Exhibit 5.7, this partial hedge does not place a ceiling on the upside potential.

To be classified as a hedge, the ratio of calls sold to stock purchased should be close to 1. If the number of call options exceeds the number of shares of stock held, the strategy is termed a **ratio write strategy**. Exhibit 5.9 illustrates the profit diagram for a 2 : 1 ratio write strategy.

The 2 : 1 ratio write strategy generally provides larger profits than either the covered write strategy or naked writing if the underlying stock remains relatively unchanged over the life of the call options. However, if the stock price makes a significant positive or negative move, losses could be substantial.

Generally, investors who establish a ratio write strategy are neutral in outlook regarding the underlying stock. This means that the at-the-money call is usually used in the strategy.

Note that the profit range in Exhibit 5.9 extends from $32 to $48. This interval appears large, but the potential profit can be small relative to the large losses that can be incurred if the stock price moves out of this range.

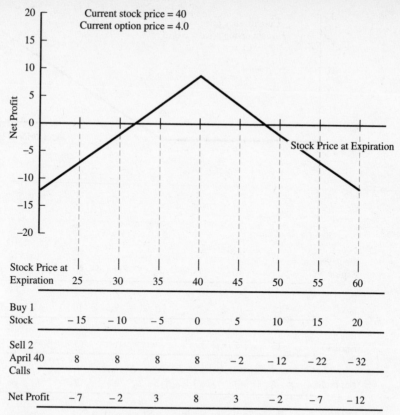

Stock Price at Expiration	25	30	35	40	45	50	55	60
Buy 1 Stock	− 15	− 10	− 5	0	5	10	15	20
Sell 2 April 40 Calls	8	8	8	8	− 2	− 12	− 22	− 32
Net Profit	− 7	− 2	3	8	3	− 2	− 7	− 12

EXHIBIT 5.9 Profit Table for a 2 : 1 Ratio Write Strategy

Hedging Stock with Put Options

Exhibit 5.10 shows the profit diagram of a long position in the stock and a put option. Note from the profit table that losses in the stock price below the strike are offset by increases in the put price. The put acts as an insurance policy providing price protection against stock declines below the strike. Note that this payout looks very similar to the payout of a call option. We shall have more to say about this in Chapter 6.

The solid line in Exhibit 5.11 illustrates the payouts achieved by hedging the stock by purchasing an April 35 put option. The dashed line shows the profit from Exhibit 5.10 for comparison.

By paying $3, the investor buying the 40 put purchases protection against all price declines below $40. By paying $1, the investor buying the 35 put purchases protection against price declines below $35. By purchasing the cheaper put, the investor is bearing more downside risk. However, this risk is compensated by higher rewards should the stock price rise.

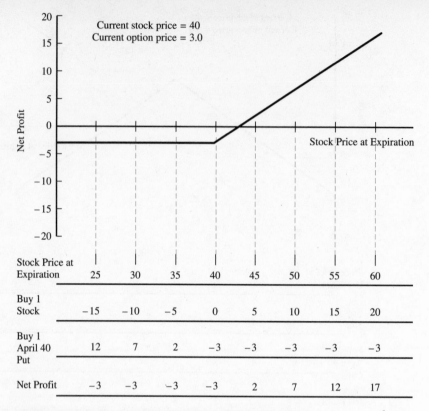

Stock Price at Expiration	25	30	35	40	45	50	55	60
Buy 1 Stock	−15	−10	−5	0	5	10	15	20
Buy 1 April 40 Put	12	7	2	−3	−3	−3	−3	−3
Net Profit	−3	−3	−3	−3	2	7	12	17

EXHIBIT 5.10 Profit Table for Hedging a Stock with a Put

The put contract can be viewed as an insurance policy on the stock price. For a higher premium, the investor can obtain an insurance policy that provides better protection against price declines.

As with call options, the ratio of puts purchased to shares owned need not be equal to 1. The solid line in Exhibit 5.12 illustrates a profit diagram for a position with hedge ratios of 1 : 2. That is, one put is purchased for every two shares owned.

Exhibit 5.12 compares three strategies: a hedge ratio of 1 : 2, the unhedged strategy of purchasing two shares, and the fully hedged strategy of purchasing two puts with the two shares. Note that the unhedged strategy produces the best results if the stock price appreciates significantly and the worst results if the stock price drops significantly. The fully insured position, on the other hand, performs the best, relatively, when the stock price drops significantly and the worst when the price appreciates. Although the partially hedged position does not truncate the downside risk below the strike price, it offers more upside potential than the fully insured hedge.

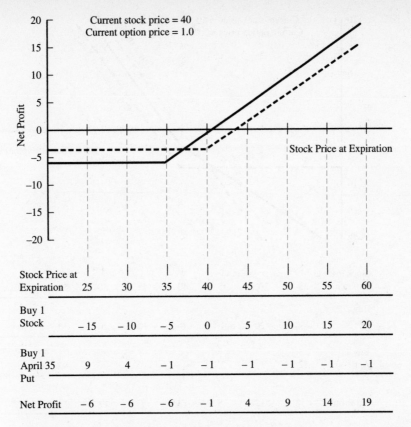

Stock Price at Expiration	25	30	35	40	45	50	55	60
Buy 1 Stock	−15	−10	−5	0	5	10	15	20
Buy 1 April 35 Put	9	4	−1	−1	−1	−1	−1	−1
Net Profit	−6	−6	−6	−1	4	9	14	19

EXHIBIT 5.11   Profit Table for Hedging a Stock with a Put

Spreads

Simple spread positions are termed bullish (bearish) if the spread benefits from stock price increase (decrease). Spread positions can be categorized into three types: vertical, horizontal, and diagonal.

Vertical Spreads

A **vertical spread** involves the simultaneous purchase and sale of options identical in all aspects except for the strike price. These spreads are often called **price spreads**.

Vertical bullish call spreads involve the sale of the option with the higher exercise price and the purchase of the option with the lower exercise price. The solid line in Exhibit 5.13 illustrates the profit diagram of a bullish call spread

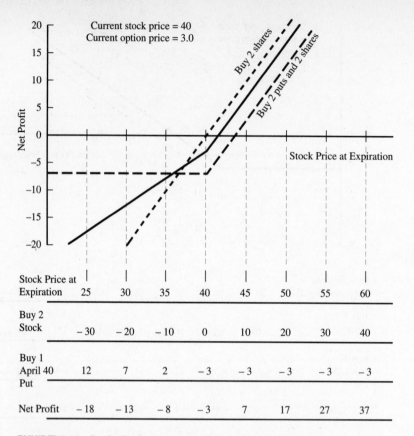

Current stock price = 40
Current option price = 3.0

Buy 2 shares

Buy 2 puts and 2 shares

Net Profit

Stock Price at Expiration

Stock Price at Expiration	25	30	35	40	45	50	55	60
Buy 2 Stock	– 30	– 20	– 10	0	10	20	30	40
Buy 1 April 40 Put	12	7	2	– 3	– 3	– 3	– 3	– 3
Net Profit	– 18	– 13	– 8	– 3	7	17	27	37

EXHIBIT 5.12   Profit Table for Buying One Put for Two Stocks

obtained by purchasing the April 35 call and simultaneously selling the April 45 call option.

Bullish call spreads tend to be profitable if the underlying stock moves up in price. The spread has limited profit potential and limited risk. In general, since the in-the-money contract is purchased and an out-of-the-money contract is sold, the initial investment for the position is positive. For example, the initial investment for the bullish call spread in Exhibit 5.13 is $5. The position always has a maximum profit if, at expiration, the stock price equals or exceeds the out-of-the-money strike price.

The maximum profit potential is obtained by computing the difference between the strike prices and subtracting the cost of the position. In this case the difference in strike prices is $10, the cost of the position is $5, and the maximum profit is $5. To compute the breakeven point for this spread, the investor simply adds the net cost of the spread to the lower strike price. In Exhibit 5.13, the breakeven point is $40.

The strike prices selected for a bullish call spread depend on the investor's beliefs concerning the stock price. A very bullish investor will select a very deep

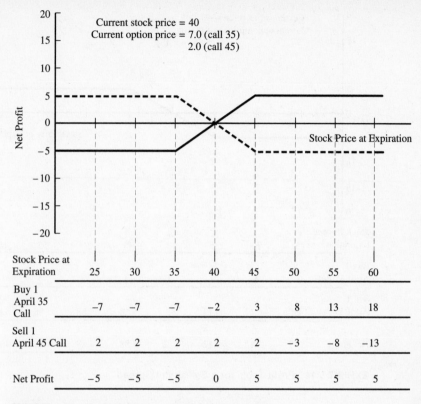

Current stock price = 40
Current option price = 7.0 (call 35)
2.0 (call 45)

Stock Price at Expiration	25	30	35	40	45	50	55	60
Buy 1 April 35 Call	−7	−7	−7	−2	3	8	13	18
Sell 1 April 45 Call	2	2	2	2	2	−3	−8	−13
Net Profit	−5	−5	−5	0	5	5	5	5

EXHIBIT 5.13 Profit Table for a Bullish Call Spread

out-of-the-money option, while a more conservative (less bullish) strategy is to select adjacent contracts. Of course, an extremely bullish investor may not be interested in selling any deep out-of-the-money contracts. That is, such an investor may prefer to hold a naked call.

A bearish call spread involves the purchase of the higher strike option and the simultaneous sale of the lower strike. For example, a bearish call spread could be established by buying the 45s and selling the 35s. Its payouts are indicated in Exhibit 5.13 by the dashed line.

Bullish vertical put spreads are constructed by selling puts with high strikes and buying puts with low strikes. Exhibit 5.14 illustrates the profit diagram of a bullish put spread that is obtained by purchasing the April 35 puts and selling the April 45 puts.

Horizontal Spreads

A **horizontal spread** (or **time** or **calendar spread**) involves the simultaneous purchase and sale of options identical in all aspects except time to expiration. The principle behind a calendar spread is that the time premium of the near-term option

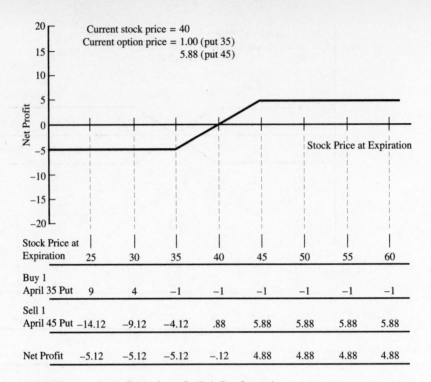

Stock Price at Expiration	25	30	35	40	45	50	55	60
Buy 1 April 35 Put	9	4	−1	−1	−1	−1	−1	−1
Sell 1 April 45 Put	−14.12	−9.12	−4.12	.88	5.88	5.88	5.88	5.88
Net Profit	−5.12	−5.12	−5.12	−.12	4.88	4.88	4.88	4.88

EXHIBIT 5.14   Profit Table for a Bullish Put Spread

will decay faster than the time premium of the long-term contract. While the initial price difference between two options with the same strike but different expiration dates may be modest, at expiration the price disparity should have grown, assuming little change in the price of the underlying stock.

For example, consider the time spread set up by buying the July 40 call options for $12.12 and selling the April 40 for $10.88. The net cost of the position is $1.34. If the stock price remains unchanged, at the April expiration date the April call will be worth its intrinsic value of $10, while the July call will be worth more. If the July 40 call is worth more than $11.34, the net profit will be positive if it is sold. In order to obtain a profit function at the April expiration date, however, one would have to be able to value the July 30 contract in April. In Chapter 10 we shall investigate how to plot the profit functions of options positions when some (or all) of the options still carry a time premium.

Diagonal Spreads

Exhibit 5.15 presents all the prices of all the call options available on the security. Vertical spreads get their name from the fact that options selected come from the same column. Horizontal spreads are so named because the options selected come

EXHIBIT 5.15 Call Option
Prices—Stock
Price = 40

Strike	April	July	October
25	15.06	—	—
30	10.88	12.12	—
35	7.00	8.62	—
40	4.00	5.75	7.38
45	2.0	3.69	5.39
50	0.88	2.38	3.75

from the same row. A diagonal spread involves the simultaneous purchase and sale of options that differ in both strike and time to maturity. For example, consider the purchase of a July 35 call option and the sale of an April 45 call contract. This position constitutes a diagonal spread.

Butterfly Strike-Price Spreads

A **butterfly strike spread** is established when two middle strike options are purchased (written) and two options, one on either side, are sold (bought). For example, consider a position consisting of buying two April 40 call options and selling the April 35 and April 45 contracts. Exhibit 5.16 illustrates the profit diagram.

Note that the payouts take the shape of a butterfly; hence the name. The sale of the butterfly involves the sale of two April 40 options together with the purchase of call options at April 45 and April 35.

Like the 2 : 1 ratio write call strategy illustrated in Exhibit 5.9, the sale of the butterfly spread produces maximum profits if the stock price remains unchanged. Note, however, that the maximum profit of the butterfly is $4, compared to $8 in the 2 : 1 ratio write strategy.

Moreover, the profit interval of the butterfly sale extends from $36 to $44, compared to $32 to $48 for the ratio write. Compensating for the reduced upside potential, however, the sale of the butterfly creates a limit of only $1 on the downside. This is in contrast to the ratio write strategy, in which losses are unlimited.

Butterfly Time Spreads

Butterfly time spreads can be established by purchasing (selling) two options in the middle series and selling (buying) a near and far series option. All options have the same strike.

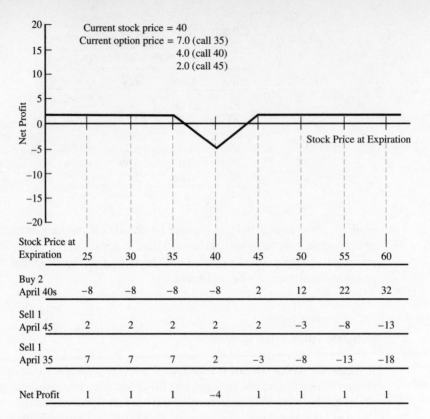

Stock Price at Expiration	25	30	35	40	45	50	55	60
Buy 2 April 40s	−8	−8	−8	−8	2	12	22	32
Sell 1 April 45	2	2	2	2	2	−3	−8	−13
Sell 1 April 35	7	7	7	2	−3	−8	−13	−18
Net Profit	1	1	1	−4	1	1	1	1

EXHIBIT 5.16   Profit Table for a Butterfly Strike-Price Spread

Combinations

Combinations consist of the simultaneous purchase (or sale) of put and call options.

Straddles

A **straddle** consists of the simultaneous purchase of a call option and a put option, with the same strike price and time to expiration. Exhibit 5.17 illustrates the profit diagram for buying the April 40 call and the April 40 put. The breakeven points are $33 and $47.

Straddles are popular strategies to implement on securities that are highly volatile or are takeover candidates. Selling straddles involves more risk, since volatility can create large losses on both sides. To reduce the risk of large losses, a straddle seller may buy a put with a lower strike and a call with a higher strike. The resulting position looks similar to a butterfly spread.

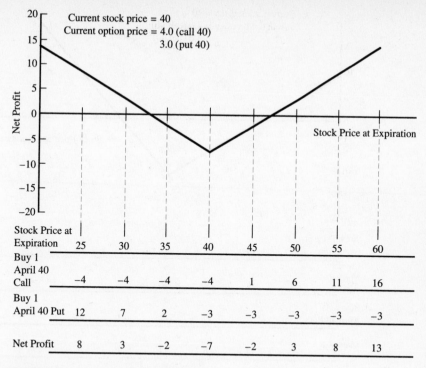

Stock Price at Expiration	25	30	35	40	45	50	55	60
Buy 1 April 40 Call	−4	−4	−4	−4	1	6	11	16
Buy 1 April 40 Put	12	7	2	−3	−3	−3	−3	−3
Net Profit	8	3	−2	−7	−2	3	8	13

EXHIBIT 5.17   Profit Table for a Straddle

Strips and Straps

A purchased **strip** consists of a long position in a call and put, together with an extra put. A **strap** consists of buying two calls and buying one put. Exhibit 5.18 illustrates the payouts of a strap consisting of buying two April 40 calls and one April 40 put.

Strangles

Consider the strategy of buying a call option with a strike price above the current stock price and a put option with a strike price below the current stock price, for example, buying the April 45 call option and the April 35 put option. Exhibit 5.19 illustrates the payouts. This position is referred to as a **strangle**. A strangle is similar to a straddle in that profits can be obtained only if the stock price moves up or down significantly. Note that the strangle profits if the stock price moves above $48 or falls below $32. In general, the stock price will have to move further than

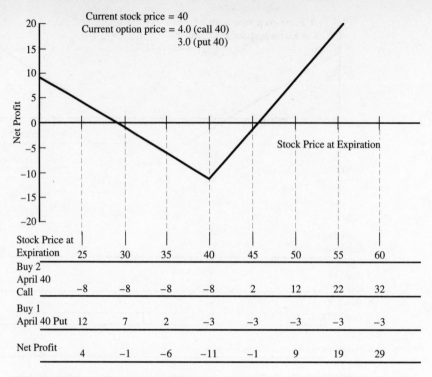

Current stock price = 40
Current option price = 4.0 (call 40)
3.0 (put 40)

Stock Price at Expiration	25	30	35	40	45	50	55	60
Buy 2 April 40 Call	−8	−8	−8	−8	2	12	22	32
Buy 1 April 40 Put	12	7	2	−3	−3	−3	−3	−3
Net Profit	4	−1	−6	−11	−1	9	19	29

EXHIBIT 5.18 Profit Table for a Strap

in a straddle for profits to be obtained. The strangle, however, has the advantage of having smaller maximum losses if the stock price does not move (compare Exhibit 5.19 with Exhibit 5.17).

Other Combinations

The number of ways options may be meshed around a particular stock is endless. To illustrate, consider call spread strategies in which the ratio of calls bought to calls sold is restricted to ratios of 1 : 2, 1 : 3, 2 : 3, 3 : 4, and 4 : 5. With just these six ratios, if six strike prices and three series are available, the number of different call spread combinations is $2 \times 6 \times \binom{6}{2} \times \binom{3}{2} = 1080$. If put options were also available, then 1080 put spreads could be constructed. The number of combinations would then be even larger (2276). This implies that there are over 4000 different spread positions that can be established using only one or two strike prices. If three strike prices (e.g., butterfly spreads) are considered, then the number of positions mushrooms further.

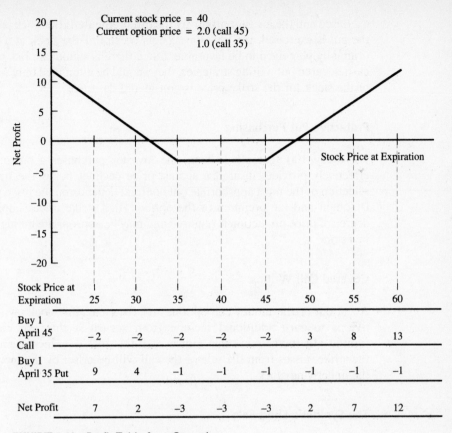

Stock Price at Expiration	25	30	35	40	45	50	55	60
Buy 1 April 45 Call	−2	−2	−2	−2	−2	3	8	13
Buy 1 April 35 Put	9	4	−1	−1	−1	−1	−1	−1
Net Profit	7	2	−3	−3	−3	2	7	12

EXHIBIT 5.19 Profit Table for a Strangle

The Most Popular Stock Option Strategies

Buy Call Options/Buy T-Bills

Rather than purchasing the stock, a less risky strategy may be to place a small fraction of funds in call options and the remainder in T-bills. If the stock does appreciate, the investor will benefit by selling the option. If the stock does not appreciate, the premium on the call is lost but the holdings in T-bills cushion this loss.

Cash-Secured Put Writing

Consider an investor who believes the current stock price is quite favorable. Rather than buying the stock, the investor sells an at- or out-of-the-money put option and deposits the exercise price in escrow. If the stock appreciates in value, the put is not exercised and the investor profits by the full premium. If the stock falls in value and the put is exercised, the investor accepts receipt of the stock at a price that was originally perceived to be favorable. Since there is significant risk associated with cash-secured put writing strategies, they should be attempted only when possession of the stock for the strike price is considered desirable.

Protective Put Purchasing

For every 100 shares held long, the investor purchases a put option. The put effectively provides insurance against price declines below the strike price. The selection of the most appropriate put contract depends on the price protection that is sought and the premium of the option. High strike prices imply that a great degree of price protection is required and may be appropriate for highly risk-averse investors.

Covered Call Writing

At- or out-of-the-money call options are written against stock owned. The objective is to earn additional income from securities that are not expected to significantly increase in value. However, if the stock does increase in value beyond the strike, losses from the sale of the call will be offset by the increased value of the underlying stock.

The Synthetic Short Sale

Rather than sell a stock short, an investor may consider buying a put and selling a call. The resultant position is referred to as a **synthetic short sale** because the profit function looks similar to the profit function associated with a short sale. The advantage of synthetic short sales over selling the stock short involves margin requirements and dividend payments. Specifically, margin requirements for the synthetic short sale are smaller, and the investor is not responsible for dividend payments to the stock lender.

Conclusion

Profit diagrams provide an extremely useful tool for comparing risks and rewards among hedging alternatives. Although we have not included margin requirements, commissions, and dividends in the analysis, such adjustments are possible. It should be recognized, however, that the profit diagrams do not tell a complete story. First, they assume that positions are maintained unchanged over time. Second, the profit diagram ignores the likelihood of early exercise. Consider, for example, the sale of a straddle. If the price of the underlying stock increases above the call strike and then decreases below the put strike, large losses can result. When the stock price increases, the in-the-money call may be exercised, in which case the straddle writer must deliver expensive stock for the strike. Then if the stock price decreases below the strike price of the put, the "cheap" stock may be put on the straddle writer for the higher strike price.

This chapter has not provided a comprehensive treatment of the topic of selecting, monitoring, and revising hedge positions. Rather, it has attempted to provide an overview of the various strategies and to illustrate some of the immense number of distinct payout patterns that the meshing of options provides. The use of stock options enables investors to design positions that reflect their preferences and outlooks for the underlying security.

References

The Options Clearing Corporation and the option exchanges publish many booklets that discuss the risks and rewards of specific option strategies and provide numerous examples. One limitation of our discussion in this chapter is that the analysis is static. In reality, option positions can be adjusted periodically as new information filters into the market. McMillan's textbook provides some insight into some dynamic strategies.

Several stock and option market computer simulation/education games allow the investor to build and analyze stock option strategies and to adjust them periodically as price changes occur, as time to expiration nears, or as dividend dates approach. These games are especially useful for those investors who are genuinely interested in learning real-world constraints without having to invest real dollars.

Blue Chip Software. *Millionaire*. Chicago: Britannica Learning Corporation.

McMillan, L. G. *Options as a Strategic Investment*. New York: New York Institute of Finance, 1980.

Options and Futures Trading Simulator. Rubinstein, M., and G. Gennotte, 1992.

Options Laboratory. Fort Collins, Colo: Mantic Software Corporation, 1994.

Ritchken P., H. Salkin, and G. Getts. *Portfolio Management: A Computer Simulation for Stock and Options*. Reading, Mass.: Addison-Wesley, 1989.

Exercises

1. XYZ trades at $50. The stock pays no dividends. The call prices are as follows:

Strike	July	October	January
45	7	9	11
50	4	6	8
55	1	3	5

a. Mr. Vestor owns 100 shares of XYZ but wants to improve the yield on the stock by earning option premium income. Mr. Vestor, however, is anxious not to have XYZ called away from him and believes that by September the prospects of the firm will begin to improve. Of all options available, which strike price/maturity combination should he write?

  b. If he sold one July 50 contract, how far can the stock advance before the strategy loses money relative to not selling options?

  c. If Mr. Vestor sells the XYZ October 50 option, over what price range (at the expiration date) will this strategy yield greater profits than holding onto the stock alone?

2. Ms. Vestor bought 100 shares of XYZ at $40 a share. It currently trades at $60. A July 60 call option trades at $6. Discuss the consequences of selling this option.

3. Mr. Vestor owns 200 shares of XYZ, purchased at $20 per share. Compare the strategy of writing one call at $15 and one call at $25 with that of writing two calls at $20. The current option prices are as follows:

Strike	Call Price
15	8
20	5
25	3

4. XYZ stock is currently $53 a share. Ms. Vestor is unwilling to pay this price. Given that a put option with strike price of $50 trades at $2 a share, construct a strategy whereby the stock could effectively be purchased for less than $50. What is the disadvantage of this strategy?

5. Mr. Vestor owns 100 shares of XYZ, which were purchased when the stock was $52. The stock currently trades at $60. A 60 put option trades for $4.

  a. Under what conditions (if any) should Mr. Vestor buy the put?

  b. Construct the payoff function for Mr. Vestor's net position at the expiration date if he buys the 60 put option.

6. XYZ trades at $47, and the following options are available:

Strike	Call Price	Put Price
40	7 3/4	1 1/2
45	2	1 3/4
50	1 1/2	7 3/4

  a. Construct the payoff function for the XYZ $45 straddle.

  b. Under what conditions would you buy the straddle? When would you sell the straddle?

  c. Consider the $45 strike-price straddle. Plot the profit function at expiration. Compare the straddle to the straddle in Exercise 6a and state the assumptions under which an investor might find one preferable to the other.

  d. Assume the $45 straddle is bought. After two weeks, with the stock at $49, the call price has increased by $2. The investor believes the stock price will not increase further and so decides to sell the call. This strategy is referred to as "lifting a leg." Discuss the advantages and disadvantages of lifting a leg.

7. XYZ trades at $80. Under what conditions would it be desirable to sell the stock short? What alternative option strategy would yield a profit function similar to the strategy of selling the stock short?

8. XYZ trades at $65. A January 60 put sells for $2 and a January 70 call for $3. Ms. Vestor buys the 60 put and sells the 70 call. Plot the profit function and discuss the pros and cons of the strategy.

9. Show that the breakeven point for a bullish call spread is obtained by adding the net cost of the spread to the lower strike price.

10. "Covered call strategies are fantastic! First you collect a lot of money for simply agreeing to sell your stock at a higher price than you paid. Your second source of profit could be cash dividends, due to you as owner of the stock. The third source of income could be the increase in price of the shares, from what you paid to the agreed selling price." Discuss this sales tactic.

APPENDIX 5A

Commission Charges for Options

Since 1975, commissions for options have been negotiable. Exhibit 5A.1 presents commission rates that may be somewhat representative of full-service brokerage houses. The rates, of course, vary significantly among firms. Large discounts can be obtained through discount brokers.

The typical round-trip commission for an option that is in the money at expiration is $50. This can be a significant percentage of the purchase price of the option. Although the commission charges are a high percentage of the option price, when a comparison is made with the commission charges incurred by buying and selling the stock itself, in absolute terms the option commissions are much less.

EXHIBIT 5A.1 Commission Charges

Option Price	Numbers of Contracts			
	1	5	10	50
1/8	$10	$10	$25	$125
1/2	$10	$25	$40	$200
1	$25	$45	$80	$300
2	$25	$50	$98	$325
5	$25	$80	$120	$450
10	$25	$100	$180	$700

APPENDIX 5B

Margin Requirements for Stocks and Options

If stocks are sold short or if options are written naked, the broker will demand some form of collateral to guarantee performance in the event of unfavorable market movements. Such transactions are conducted in margin accounts. From a margin account, an investor can also buy securities that are financed by a loan from the broker. This appendix investigates margin accounts and the rules imposed on such accounts by the Federal Reserve Board, the NYSE, and the option exchanges. The rules change from time to time, and it is unlikely that the rules that follow are current. The purpose of this appendix is merely to illustrate the types of rules that are used to establish margin reserves so as to minimize default experience. The current set of rules can be obtained from the exchanges.

Margin Accounts

There are basically two types of brokerage accounts, cash and margin. In a **cash account** the investor pays for the security in full, while in a **margin account** the investor need only deposit a fraction of the transaction, the remainder being borrowed from the brokerage firm. The purchased security is kept by the firm as collateral against the loan. Interest charges on the loan continue until the investor sells the security.

Initial Margin Requirements

The minimum allowable initial deposit that an investor must make to purchase a security in a margin account is established by the Board of Governors of the Federal Reserve Board and is binding on all brokers. Most brokerage firms set their initial margin requirements above the minimum requirements. At the present time, investors must deposit at least half the cost of the transaction. This fraction, referred to as the **margin percentage,** has remained the same since 1974. If the margin percentage were 100 percent, all purchases would have to be paid for in full. The lower the fraction, the greater the possible leverage investors can obtain. Prior to the stock market crash of 1929, the margin percentage was about 10 percent. Many brokers encouraged their customers to establish highly leveraged positions, since commission charges were based on the size of the full transactions. The low margin percentage was one reason for the collapse of the stock market.

Margin accounts are not only used for purchasing securities. All short sales are conducted from such accounts. When an investor sells a security short, the stockbroker borrows the security from a third party so delivery can be made. To protect the brokerage firm, a margin deposit from the investor selling the security short is required. In addition, the broker retains the proceeds of the short sales in a noninterest-bearing account. The initial margin requirement for short sales is 50 percent of the transaction price.

Rather than deposit cash into the margin account, the investor can deposit marginable securities with a loan value equal to the required cash deposit. Regulation T of the Federal Reserve System specifies which securities can be used as marginable securities. Virtually all stocks traded on the major exchanges and many over-the-counter stocks qualify, as well as a large number of corporate and government bonds. The loan value of marginable securities is computed by multiplying the market value of the securities by the **loan value percentage** (100 percent less the margin percentage). Currently the loan value percentage for stocks is 50 percent.

In addition to the initial margin equity requirements specified by the Federal Reserve, the NYSE requires a minimum initial equity in the margin account. Specifically, at the initiation of any new transaction, the investor must have equity of at least $2000 or its equivalent in marginable securities in the margin account.

EXAMPLE 5B.1   An investor buys 100 shares of XYZ on margin. The current price of XYZ is $80. The initial margin requirement calls for deposit of $4000 in the margin account or a deposit of marginable securities worth $8000. If the investor sold 100 shares of XYZ short, a deposit of $4000 or a deposit of marginable securities worth $8000 into the account would be required. In addition, the $8000 generated by the sale would be held by the firm in a noninterest-bearing account.

Restricted Margin Accounts

A margin account becomes restricted when the equity in the account falls below the Regulation T margin requirement. Such a situation occurs if the market moves against the investor's position of if interest charges, service fees, or dividend charges on short sales push the margin debit above its limit.

EXAMPLE 5B.2   An investor purhases 100 shares of XYZ on margin. The original margin debit is $4000. Suppose the stock price declines over time to $70. Assume that the margin debit has increased to $4200, where the $200 represents the interest charge on the loan. The margin equity is currenty $7000 − $4200 = $2800. Since the margin equity is below the original margin requirement of $4000, the account is restricted.

Maintenance Margin Requirements for Purchasing Securities Long

When a margin account becomes restricted, the investor does not necessarily have to supply more funds or marginable securities to bring the account up to the initial margin requirements. However, if the market movements continue to be unfavorable, eventually the broker will require more collateral. The NYSE requires that the equity in the margin account be at least 25 percent of the market value of the securities held in account or $2000, whichever is greater. If the condition is violated, a maintenance margin call is issued requesting that additional cash or marginable securities be placed in the account.

EXAMPLE 5B.3   An investor buys 100 shares of XYZ at $80 by depositing $4000 to comply with the Regulation T requirement and borrowing $4000 from the broker. The stock price immediately drops to $60. Twenty-five percent of $6000 is $1500. The margin equity is $6000 − $4000 = $2000. Since the account satisfies the NYSE requirement, no additional margin is required. If the stock drops to $52, however, 25 percent of the market value is $1300. The margin equity is $5200 − $4000 = $1200. In this case the broker will issue a maintenance margin call for $100. (Actually, since the $2000 lower bound is violated, additional funds will be required.)

An investor can meet a margin call by depositing cash equal to the maintenance call or by depositing marginable securities with a market value equal to 4/3 of the call. In Example 5B.3, rather than deposit $100, the investor could deposit marginable securities with a market value of $400/3 = $133.33. Note that in this case the new market value of the account is $5200 + $400/3 = $5333. Twenty-five percent of this value is $1333. The margin equity, on the other hand, is $5200 + $400/3 − $4000 = $1333. Hence, the maintenance margin condition is met.

An investor can determine the stock price at which a maintenance margin call will be issued by multiplying the initial margin debit by 4/3. In Example 5B.2, no maintenance margin call is issued unless the stock price declines to $40 × 4/3 = $53.33. If the investor does not respond to a maintenance call, the broker will sell sufficient securities in the account to meet the call.

Maintenance Margin Requirements for Selling Securities Short

The maintenance margin requirement for a short sale depends on the stock price. A typical schedule is summarized below:

Stock Price	Maintenance Margin
Below $2.50	$2.50 per share
$2.50–$5.00	100% of market value
$5.00–$16.75	$5 per share
Above $16.75	30% of market value

EXAMPLE 5B.4

1. An investor sells 100 shares of XYZ short at $60 per share. The initial margin deposit of $3000 together with the $6000 received from the sale establishes the credit balance. The current equity in the account is $3000, and maintenance margin is 30 percent of $6000, which is $1800. The market price increases to $75, so the market value of the security is now $7500. The credit balance remains at $9000, but the margin equity drops to $9000 − $7500 = $1500. The maintenance margin is 30 percent of $7500, which is $2250. Hence, no maintenance margin call is issued. However, if the price increased to $80, the margin equity would be $1000 and maintenance margin would be at 30 percent of $8000, or $2400. In this case the account would be undermargined by $1400.

2. Consider the short sale of 1000 shares of a stock priced at $10. The initial margin deposit of $5000 together with the $10,000 from the sale establishes the credit balance. The current equity is $5000 and the maintenance margin is $5 per share (i.e., $5000). Thus, the maintenance margin requirement is just met. If the stock price increases by $1, the current equity is reduced by $1000 to $4000, while the maintenance margin remains at $5 per share. Hence, a maintenance margin call for $1000 would be issued.

Margin Requirements for Options

No option contracts can be purchased on margin. Therefore, the term "margin" in options transaction refers to the collateral brokers receive from option writers to ensure that they will fulfill their obligations in the event of exercise.

Investors who sell options typically deposit cash or securities in excess of the margin requirements so their investment strategies are not disturbed by frequent margin calls. In the following section we summarize the typical structure of margin requirements for a few stock option positions.

Margin Requirements for Covered Call Writing and Cash-Secured Put Writing Strategies

When an investor sells call options against an appropriate number of shares held long, no margin is required. Indeed, the covered option can be written from either the cash or margin account. Similarly, if an investor deposits cash equal to the aggregate strike price of the put option or equivalent collateral, the written put requires no additional margin.

Margin Requirements for Selling Naked Options

The naked sale of options must be conducted in a margin account that has a minimum of $2000 equity at the time of the transaction. The investor must deposit and maintain a margin equal to 20 percent of the market value of the underlying security plus the option premium less the amount by which the option is out of the money. The proceeds from the sale can be applied toward the margin. The minimum margin for each uncovered stock option, however, must exceed 100 percent of the premium plus 10 percent of the market value of the underlying security.

EXAMPLE 5B.5   An investor sells one June 40 call option at $5. The market price of XYZ is $36. The margin requirement is determined as follows:

20% of $3600	$720
+ Option premium	+500
− Amount out of the money	−400
= Margin required	$820
10% of market value	$360
+ Call premium	500
= Minimum margin	$860

Hence, $860 of margin is required. In order for the investor to sell the option, the margin account must have a minimum of $2000 equity.

CHAPTER 6

Arbitrage Relationships for Call and Put Options

A **risk-free arbitrage opportunity** arises when an investment is identified that requires no initial outlays yet guarantees nonnegative payoffs in the future. Such opportunities do not last long, as astute investors soon alter the demand and supply factors, causing prices to adjust so that these opportunities are closed off. In this chapter we consider **static trading strategies**—once the position is chosen, we make no adjustments. We use simple arbitrage arguments to obtain some basic boundary conditions for call and put options. The beauty of the pricing relationships derives from the fact that they require no assumptions on the statistical process driving security prices. Also, no severe assumptions are made concerning the risk behavior of investors. The simple requirement is that investors like more money than less.

This chapter also investigates conditions under which it is more appropriate to exercise options than to sell them. The final section explores some fundamental pricing relationships that exist between put and call options.

The primary objectives of this chapter are the following:

- To derive boundary prices for call and put options from arbitrage arguments;
- To explain when exercising options is not appropriate; and
- To describe pricing relationships between put and call options.

Notation

Throughout this chapter we use the following notation. The current time is $t = 0$. The option expires at date T, where T is expressed in years. The time to the jth ex-dividend date is t_j, and the size of dividend declared at ex-dividend date t_j is d_j ($j = 1, 2, 3$). We are interested only in ex-dividend dates prior to expiration. In most cases, the number of dates in the interval is less than three. Throughout this chapter we assume that the risk-free rate, r, is constant. Let $B(s, t)$ be the price at time s of a riskless pure discount bond of face value \$1 that matures at time t. Then

$$B(s, t) = 1\, e^{-r(t-s)} \tag{6.1}$$

Note that from equation (6.1), with $s = 0$,

$$B(0, t) = e^{-rt} \qquad (6.2)$$

Clearly, discount bond prices decrease with maturity. That is, for $t > s$,

$$B(0, t) < B(0, s) < 1 \qquad (6.3)$$

If \$1 is invested in the risk-free asset (bank) at time s, this amount of money will grow continuously at rate r, and at time t the value will be $e^{r(t-s)}$. Let $G(s, t) = e^{r(t-s)}$ represent the growth. Clearly, $G(s, t) = 1/B(s, t)$.

Finally, as discussed in Chapter 4, a call option that can be exercised only at the expiration date (and not before) is called a European option. An American option must have a value at least as great as a European option, since the former has all the properties of the latter plus the early exercise feature. This characteristic is used in deriving several properties in this chapter.

Riskless Arbitrage and the Law of One Price

This chapter frequently uses the argument that there are no riskless arbitrage opportunities. Below we provide some illustrative examples.

EXAMPLE 6.1   **An Illustration of Riskless Arbitrage Opportunities**

Consider the following alternative investments:

1. For \$70, an investor can buy (sell) a share of A, which, at the end of the period, will either appreciate to \$120 or depreciate to \$60, depending on whether the economy booms or not.

2. For \$$b$, an investor can buy (sell) a share of B that will either appreciate to \$100 or depreciate to \$50, depending on the same economic factors.

What is the maximum price b can take? To answer this question, we assume that investors prefer more wealth to less and that they can borrow or lend funds at a riskless rate of $r = 11$ percent. Finally, we assume that the time period, T, is 1 year.

First, consider a portfolio consisting of one share of A and a short position of one share in B. The payouts of this portfolio are shown below:

$$\$70 - b \;\diagdown\!\!\!\diagup\; \begin{array}{l} \$120 - \$100 = \$20 \\ \$60 - \;\;\$50 = \$10 \end{array}$$

Clearly, all investors would prefer the final dollar payout of this portfolio to a certain payout of $10. To avoid a possible "free lunch," the present value of this portfolio must exceed the present value of $10. That is, $(\$70 - b) > 10\, e^{-rT} = \$9$, or $b < \$61$.

If, for example, $b = \$64$, then a free lunch would exist. Specifically, an investor could establish a zero-initial-investment position by selling one share of B for $64, borrowing $6, and using the total proceeds to purchase one share of A. The $6 debt would grow to $6\, e^{rT} = \$6.70$ in one year. The final payouts of this strategy are shown below:

$$\$0 \;\diagdown\!\!\!\diagup\; \begin{array}{l} \$120 - \$100 - \$6.70 = \$13.30 \\ \$60 - \;\;\$50 - \$6.70 = \;\;\$3.30 \end{array}$$

To avoid this free lunch, the price of a share of B must satisfy $b < \$61$.

The Law of One Price

3. Assume that a third investment, C, provides the following payouts:

To avoid riskless arbitrage, C must equal $70. To see this, note that this investment has identical payouts to A. If C exceeded $70, investors would buy A and sell C to lock into profits. Conversely, if C were lower than $70, investors would buy C and sell A to lock into profits.

The law of one price states that if two securities produce identical payouts in all future states, then to avoid riskless arbitrage, their current prices must be the same. We have used this law in establishing the cost-of-carry model for futures in Chapter 2 and will use it frequently in this and later chapters.

Call Pricing Relationships

In this section we establish bounds on call options and investigate conditions under which it may be optimal to exercise a call option.

Bounding Call Option Prices

Property 6.1 provides a bound for the price of a call option when the underlying stock pays no dividends over the lifetime of the option.

PROPERTY 6.1

If there are no dividends prior to expiration, then to prevent arbitrage opportunities, the call price should never fall below the maximum of zero or the stock price minus the present value of the strike. That is,

$$C_0 \geq \text{Max}[0, S_0 - XB(0, T)] \tag{6.4}$$

Proof.   Consider two portfolios, A and B. A contains one European call option and X pure discount bonds with a face value of \$1 each and maturity T. B contains a long position in the stock.

Exhibit 6.1 illustrates the prices of the two portfolios at the expiration date of the option. Note that the future value of portfolio A is never lower than the future value of portfolio B.

If an investor bought portfolio A and sold portfolio B, then at the expiration date the combined portfolio, P, would have value $V_p(T)$, given by $V_p(T) = V_A(T) - V_B(T)$, where $V_A(T)$ and $V_B(T)$ define the values of the portfolios A and B at time T.

If the call option expired in the money, then $V_A(T) = V_B(T)$, and hence $V_p(T) = 0$. However, if the call expired worthless, then $V_p(T) = V_A(T) - V_B(T) \geq 0$. The portfolio P thus can never lose money and has a chance of making money.

Now consider the initial cost of the portfolio, $V_p(0)$. Since this portfolio has a nonnegative terminal value, it must be worth a nonnegative amount now. Hence

$$V_p(0) = V_A(0) - V_B(0) \geq 0$$

Equivalently,

$$V_A(0) \geq V_B(0)$$

That is,

$$C_0 + XB(0, T) \geq S_0$$

or

$$C_0 \geq S_0 - XB(0, T)$$

EXHIBIT 6.1 Arbitrage Portfolio: Bounding Call Prices

Portfolio	Current Value	Value at Time T	
		$S_T < X$	$S_T \geq X$
A	$C_0 + XB(0, T)$	$0 + X$	$(S_T - X) + X$
B	S_0	S_T	S_T
		$V_A(T) > V_B(T)$	$V_A(T) = V_B(T)$

Since a European call option must be worth no less than $S_0 - XB(0, T)$, so must an American option. Of course, since call options offer the holder the right to purchase securities at a particular price, this right must have some value. Hence, $C_0 \geq 0$, from which we have the following result: $C_0 \geq \text{Max}[0, S_0 - XB(0, T)]$.

EXAMPLE 6.2   Consider a stock currently priced at $55, with a three-month $50 strike-price call available. Assume that no dividends occur prior to expiration and the riskless rate, r, is 12 percent. The lower bound on the price is given by the following:

$$C_0 \geq \text{Max}[0, S_0 - XB(0, T)] = \text{Max}[0, 55 - 50\, e^{-0.12(3/12)}] = \$6.48$$

We now establish bounds on the call price when the underlying security pays a dividend.

PROPERTY 6.2

If a stock pays a single dividend of size d_1 at time t_1, then to prevent riskless arbitrage, the call price should never fall below

$$\text{Max}(C_1, C_2, C_3)$$

where $C_1 = \text{Max}[0, S_0 - X]$

$C_2 = \text{Max}[0, S_0 - XB(0, t_1)]$ (6.5)

$C_3 = \text{Max}[0, S_0 - d_1 B(0, t_1) - XB(0, T)]$

Proof.   Each item (C_1, C_2, and C_3) is the value of a call option under a specific strategy.

Strategy 1: Exercise the Call Option Immediately   We know that the call price can never fall below its intrinsic value, C_1. If it did, an optimal strategy would be to exercise immediately.

Strategy 2: Exercise the Call Option Just Prior to the Ex-Dividend Date   Assume the option is exercised just prior to the ex-dividend date. Then, by using the same argument used to prove Property 6.1, we see that the call price must exceed the stock price less the present value of the strike.

Strategy 3: Exercise the Call Option at Expiration   If the dividend is sacrificed and the option held to expiration, the call value must exceed C_3.

We shall prove the result for strategy 3. Consider two portfolios, A and B. A contains d_1 bonds that pay out $\$d_1$ at time t_1 and X bonds that pay out $\$X$ at time T. In addition, a call option is held. All dividends received at time t_1 are invested in the risk-free asset. Portfolio B contains a long position in the stock. Exhibit 6.2

EXHIBIT 6.2 Arbitrage Portfolio: Bounding Call Prices with Dividends

Portfolio	Current Value	Terminal Value	
		$S_T < X$	$S_T \geq X$
A	$C_0 + XB(0, T) + d_1 B(0, t_1)$	$X + d_1 G(t_1, T)$	$S_T + d_1 G(t_1, T)$
B	S_0	$S_T + d_1 G(t_1, T)$	$S_T + d_1 G(t_1, T)$
		$V_A(T) \geq V_B(T)$	$V_A(T) = V_B(T)$

illustrates the payoffs that occur if strategy 3, exercising the call at the expiration date, is followed.

Note that in portfolio A, the d_1 dollars received at time t_1 are reinvested in the riskless security and thus grow to $d_1 G(t_1, T)$ at expiration.

Since $V_A(T) \geq V_B(T)$, it must follow that to prevent arbitrage opportunities, $V_A(0) \geq V_B(0)$. Hence, $C_0 \geq C_3$.

Since at the current time the optimal strategy is unknown, the actual call value should exceed the payoffs obtained under all three strategies. Hence, $C_0 \geq \text{Max}(C_1, C_2, C_3)$, and since $C_2 \geq C_1$, we have $C_0 \geq \text{Max}(C_2, C_3)$.

EXAMPLE 6.3 Reconsider Example 6.2, but now assume that a dividend of $5 is paid after one month. The lower bound on the call price is given by $\text{Max}(C_1, C_2, C_3)$, where

$$C_1 = \text{Max}(0, S_0 - X) = \text{Max}(0, 55 - 50) = \$5$$

$$C_2 = \text{Max}[0, S_0 - Xe^{-rt_1}] = \text{Max}(0, 55 - 49.5) = \$5.50$$

$$C_3 = \text{Max}[0, S_0 - d_1 e^{-rt_1} - Xe^{-rT}] = \text{Max}(0, 55 - 4.95 - 48.52) = \$1.53$$

Hence, $C_0 \geq \$5.50$. Note that the effect of dividends has been to lower the lower bound of the call option.

EXAMPLE 6.4 An April 50 call option on stock XYZ, which is currently priced at $66.25, trades at $16.75. The current interest rate is 8.30 percent. A dividend of $0.75 is due, with the ex-dividend date being 58 days away. The time to expiration is 136 days. To avoid riskless arbitrage opportunities, a lower bound on the call price is

$$C_0 \geq S_0 - B(0, T)X - B(0, t_1)d_1$$

Now
$$S_0 = 66.25$$

$$B(0, T)X = e^{-0.083(136/365)} \, 50 = \$48.477$$

$$B(0, t_1)d_1 = e^{-0.083(58/365)} \, 0.75 = \$0.740$$

Hence
$$C_0 \geq \$17.03$$

Since the actual price is $16.75, an arbitrage opportunity exists. Specifically, since the call is underpriced, the investor should buy the call, short one share of stock, invest $48.477 for time T, and invest $0.740 for time t_1 at the riskless rate. The cash flows at time zero and at time T are given in Exhibit 6.3.

EXHIBIT 6.3   Cash Flows Illustrating Arbitrage

	Initial Cash Flow	Cash Flow at Time T	
		$S(T) < 50$	$S(T) > 50$
Sell stock.	+$66.25	$-S(T)$	$-S(T)$
Buy call.	-$16.75	0	$S(T) - 50$
Invest at risk-free rate for time T.	-$48.477	50	50
Invest at risk-free rate for time t_1 (used to pay dividend at t_1).	-$0.740		
	+$0.28	$V(T) = 50 - S(T) \geq 0$	$V(T) = 0$

Note that if the dividend is uncertain but bounds on its value can be established such that $d_{min} < d_1 < d_{max}$, then a lower bound on the call value can be obtained by using d_{max}.

Note also that if there are two or more dividends prior to expiration, then lower bounds can be obtained by simple extensions to Property 6.2. For example, if two certain dividends d_1 and d_2 occur, then $C_0 \geq \text{Max}(C_1, C_2, C_3, C_4)$, where

$$C_1 = \text{Max}(0, S_0 - X)$$

$$C_2 = \text{Max}[0, S_0 - XB(0, t_1)]$$

$$C_3 = \text{Max}[0, S_0 - d_1 B(0, t_1) - XB(0, t_2)]$$

$$C_4 = \text{Max}[0, S_0 - d_1 B(0, t_1) - d_2 B(0, t_2) - XB(0, T)]$$

Optimal Exercise Policy for Call Options

Property 6.2 established bounds on the call prices by considering the effect of specific exercise strategies: namely, exercising immediately, exercising just prior to an ex-dividend date, or exercising at expiration. However, other exercising times are possible. In this section we show that if exercising is ever appropriate for call options, it should be done at expiration or immediately prior to an ex-dividend date.

PROPERTY 6.3

The early exercise of a call option on a stock that pays no dividends prior to expiration is never optimal. For such a stock, the price of an American call option equals the price of an otherwise identical European call.

Proof.   To prove this result we must show that for a stock that pays no dividends over the lifetime of the option, the value of a call option unexercised is always equal to or greater than the value of the option exercised.

Let t_p be any time point prior to expiration. From Property 6.1, we know that the lower bound on the call price at time t_p is the stock price, $S(t_p)$, less the present value of the strike, $XB(t_p, T)$. Hence, $C(t_p) \geq \text{Max}[0, S(t_p) - XB(t_p, T)]$. Note that the right-hand side of the equation exceeds the intrinsic value of the option, $S(t_p) - X$. Hence, early exercise is not optimal.

From Property 6.3 we see that early exercise of an American call option on a stock that pays no dividends over the lifetime of the option is never appropriate. Therefore, the value of the right to exercise the option prior to expiration must be zero. Thus, an American call option must have the same value as a European call.

PROPERTY 6.4

If a stock pays dividends over the lifetime of the option, then the American call option may be worth more than a European call option.

Proof.   Just prior to an ex-dividend date there may be an incentive to exercise early. To see this, consider an extreme case in which a firm pays all its assets as cash dividends. Clearly, any in-the-money call options should be exercised prior to the ex-dividend date, since after the date the call value will be zero. Note that the value of a European option before the ex-dividend date would be zero, whereas the American option would have positive value.

PROPERTY 6.5

The exercise of a call option is optimal only at expiration, or possibly at the instant prior to an ex-dividend date.

Proof.   Exercising call options is appropriate only if the value of the call unexercised falls below the intrinsic value. Property 6.5 says that the only times the value of the unexercised call may equal or fall below its intrinsic value are immediately prior to an ex-dividend date and at expiration. To prove this Property let t_p be any possible exercise date. We have already seen that if t_p is set such that there are no more dividends prior to expiration, early exercise is not appropriate. If t_p is set before the ex-dividend date t_1, early exercise is again not appropriate. To see this, recall that the lower bound of a call price at time t_p is given by $C \geq \text{Max}(C_1, C_2, C_3)$, where $C_1 = \text{Max}[0, S(t_p) - X]$ is the intrinsic value and $C_2 = \text{Max}[0, S(t_p) - XB(t_p, t_1)]$ is the bound obtained by delaying exercise to immediately prior to the ex-dividend date. For this case C_2 exceeds C_1. Moreover, for $t_p < t_1$, C_2 can never be equal to its intrinsic value. At time t_1 the lower bound can be attained and early exercise may be optimal.

Dividend and Income Yield Analysis for Call Options

Property 6.5 states that if early exercise occurs, it should be just prior to an ex-dividend date. The decision to exercise involves a trade-off between dividend income and interest income.

To illustrate this more precisely, consider a stock that pays a single dividend prior to expiration. Just prior to the ex-dividend date, the value of an in-the-money call, if exercised, is its intrinsic value, $S(t_1) - X$. Just after the ex-dividend date, the stock price falls to $S(t_1) - d_1$. Since there are no more dividends prior to expiration, from Property 6.1 we have

$$C(t_1) \geq [S(t_1) - d_1] - XB(t_1, T) \tag{6.6}$$

Hence, early exercise will not be optimal if

$$[S(t_1) - d_1] - XB(t_1, T) \geq S(t_1) - X \tag{6.7}$$

or equivalently if

$$d_1 \leq X[1 - B(t_1, T)] \tag{6.8}$$

The right-hand side of equation (6.8) equals the present value of the interest generated from the strike price over the time period $[t_1, T]$, viewed from time t_1. The equation states that if the dividend is less than the present value of this interest, then early exercise is not optimal. This leads to Property 6.6.

PROPERTY 6.6

1. For a single ex-dividend prior to expiration, early exercise of the American call is not optimal if the size of the dividend is less than the present value of interest earned on the strike from the ex-dividend date to expiration.
2. For multiple dividends prior to expiration, an American call will never be exercised early if, at each ex-dividend date, the present value of all future dividends is less than the present value of interest earned on the strike, from the ex-dividend date to expiration.

EXAMPLE 6.5 In Example 6.3 we had

$$C_0 \geq \text{Max}(C_1, C_2, C_3)$$
$$= \text{Max}(5, 5.50, 1.55) = \$5.50$$

Early exercise of this option will not be appropriate if the size of the dividend ($d_1 = \$5$) is lower than the forgone interest, f, which is given by

$$f = X(1 - e^{-r(T-t_1)}) = 50[1 - e^{-0.12(2/12)}] = 0.99$$

Since $d_1 > f$, premature exercise may be appropriate.

Note if there are no dividends, d_1 is zero. Then equation (6.8) is satisfied, and premature exercising is not optimal. Moreover, from equation (6.8), the option should not be exercised if the strike price exceeds the value X^*, where

$$X^* = d_1/[1 - B(t_1, T)] \tag{6.9}$$

If equation (6.8) is satisfied early, exercise of the option is never optimal. If the equation is not satisfied, then early exercise may be optimal. Of course, the benefit from exercising is that the intrinsic value is received prior to the stock price dropping by the size of the dividend. This benefit is partially offset by the loss of the time premium on the option. If at the ex-dividend date the stock price is sufficiently high, then the time premium is very small, and if equation (6.8) does not hold, early exercise is quite likely. We defer further details of this point to Chapter 9, where explicit models for the time premium are established, and rules are established for the precise timing of exercise.

Put Pricing Relationships

In this section we derive some arbitrage restrictions for American put options. Unlike American call options, American put options can be exercised early even if the underlying stock pays no dividends. Before considering early exercise policies, we first establish some pricing bounds.

Bounding Put Option Prices

As with Property 6.2 for calls, we shall first obtain some put pricing bounds by considering specific exercise strategies for put options.

PROPERTY 6.7

Consider a stock that pays a certain dividend d_1 at time t_1. An American put option must satisfy the following:

$$P_0 \geq \text{Max}(P_1, P_2)$$

where $\qquad P_1 = \text{Max}(0, X - S_0)$

$$P_2 = \text{Max}[0, (X + d_1)B(0, t_1) - S_0] \tag{6.10}$$

Proof.   To obtain these bounds, we consider two strategies. The first strategy is to exercise immediately; the second strategy is to exercise just after the ex-dividend date. Other strategies, such as exercising just before the ex-dividend date or exercising at expiration, lead to weaker bounds.

Strategy 1: Exercise Immediately   Since a put option gives the holder the right (but not the obligation) to sell stock at the strike price, the put option must have nonnegative value. Further, if exercised immediately, its intrinsic value is obtained with the loss of a possible time premium. Hence, $P_0 \geq P_1$.

Strategy 2: Exercise Just After the Ex-dividend Date, t_1   Now consider the strategy of exercising the put option just after the ex-dividend date, t_1. Then $P_0 \geq P_2$. To see this, consider two portfolios, A and B, where A consists of the put and B consists of a short position in the stock together with $(X + d_1)$ bonds that mature at time t_1. Exhibit 6.4 shows their values at time t_1, given that the put is exercised. To avoid risk-free arbitrage opportunities, it must follow that the current value of portfolio A exceeds that of B. That is,

$$P_0 \geq (d_1 + X)B(0, t_1) - S_0 = P_2$$

Hence, $$P_0 \geq P_2$$

Strategy 3: Exercise the Put Option at Expiration   If the option is exercised only at expiration, a weaker bound is obtained. To see this, consider two portfolios, A and B, where A consists of the put and B consists of a short position in the stock together with X bonds that mature at time T and d_1 bonds that mature at time t_1. Exhibit 6.5 shows their values at time T.

Note that the dividend payment that is due (because of the short sale of the stock) can be met by the d_1 bonds that mature at the appropriate time. Since portfolio A dominates portfolio B, it must follow that its current price, $V_A(0)$, is no lower than $V_B(0)$. That is,

$$P_0 \geq XB(0, T) + d_1B(0, t_1) - S_0$$

Note that this right-hand value is less than P_2.

We leave it as an exercise to show that the strategy of exercising the put prior to the ex-dividend date also leads to weaker bounds. Intuitively, we see that exercising the put prior to an ex-dividend date is not sensible, since immediately after the ex-dividend date the stock price will be lower.

EXAMPLE 6.6   Consider a stock priced at $55, with a three-month put option with strike 60 available. Assume the riskless rate, r, is 12 percent and a dividend of size $2 is due in one month. Then, we have

$$P_0 \geq \text{Max}(P_1, P_2)$$

$$P_1 = \text{Max}(0, X - S_0) = \text{Max}(0, 60 - 55) = 5$$

$$P_2 = \text{Max}[0, (X + d_1)B(0, t_1) - S_0] = \text{Max}[0, 62\, e^{-0.12(1/12)} - 55] = 6.383$$

EXHIBIT 6.4   Arbitrage Portfolio: Bounding Put Prices

Portfolio	Current Value	Value at Time t_1	
		$S(t_1) \le X$	$S(t_1) > X$
A	P_0	$X - S(t_1)$	0
B	$(d_1 + X)B(0, t_1) - S_0$	$X - S(t_1)$	$X - S(t_1)$
		$V_A(T) = V_B(T)$	$V_A(T) > V_B(T)$

EXAMPLE 6.7   An April 15 put on XYZ, currently trading at $11.50, is selling for 3 1/2. The time to expiration is 107 days and the ex-dividend date is in 57 days. The size of the dividend is $0.60. The current borrowing and lending rate is 9.0 percent.

From the above analysis, we know that a lower bound on the put price is given by

$$P_0 \ge (X + d_1)B(0, t_1) - S_0$$

$$= (\$15 + \$0.60)(e^{-0.09(57/365)}) - \$11.50$$

$$= \$15.382 - \$11.50$$

$$= \$3.88$$

Since the actual put price is $3.50, this condition is violated, and risk-free arbitrage is possible. Specifically, the put should be purchased, and portfolio B (see Exhibit 6.4) should be sold. In this case, selling portfolio B implies buying the stock and borrowing the present value of the strike and dividend [i.e., $(X + d_1)B(0, t_1) = \$15.382$]. The cash inflow upon initiation is ($3.88 - $3.50) = $0.38, and a nonnegative terminal cash flow is guaranteed.

Optimal Exercise Policy for Put Options

Unlike the case with call options, it may be optimal to exercise put options prior to expiration. To see this, consider a stock whose value falls to zero. In this case the put holder should exercise the option immediately. This follows, since if the investor delays action, the interest received from the strike price is lost. This leads to Property 6.8.

EXHIBIT 6.5   Arbitrage Portfolio: Bounding Put Prices

Portfolio	Current Value	Value at Expiration	
		$S_T \le X$	$S_T > X$
A	P_0	$X - S_T$	0
B	$XB(0, T) + d_1 B(0, t_1) - S_0$	$X - S_T$	$X - S_T$
		$V_A(T) = V_B(T)$	$V_A(T) > V_B(T)$

> ### PROPERTY 6.8
>
> Early exercise of in-the-money put options may be optimal.

Immediately after an ex-dividend date, the holder of an in-the-money put option who also owns the stock may exercise the option. This is especially likely if the put is deep in the money and no more dividends are to be paid prior to expiration. By not exercising the option, the holder forgoes the interest that could be obtained from investing the strike price. Just prior to an ex-dividend date, early exercise of a put option is never optimal. Since dividends cause the stock price to drop further, investors will always prefer to delay exercise until just after the ex-dividend date.

Since early exercise of American put options is a real possibility, these contracts are more valuable than their European counterparts. Moreover, because American put options can be more valuable exercised than not exercised, it must follow that on occasion European put options could have values less than their intrinsic values. In other words, it is possible for European put options to command a negative time premium. This fact will be reconsidered later.

> ### PROPERTY 6.9
>
> Immediate exercise of a put on a dividend-paying stock is not optimal if the size of the dividend exceeds the interest income on the strike from the current date to the ex-dividend date.

Proof.   Recall that in the absence of dividend payments, early exercise of a put may be optimal because interest income can be earned on the proceeds. Deferring exercise implies that interest income is being forgone. For a dividend-paying stock, delaying exercise also forgoes interest income. However, by exercising early the investor does not profit from the discrete downward jump in the stock price that occurs at the ex-dividend date. If the interest earned on the strike from now until the ex-dividend date is smaller than the size of the dividend, then clearly it is beneficial to wait.

For a dividend-paying stock, we can obtain a bound on the put price by considering the strategy of delaying exercise until just after the ex-dividend date. Specifically, viewed from time t where $t < t_1$, we have, from Property 6.7,

$$P(t) \geq (X + d_1)B(t, t_1) - S(t_1)$$

Clearly, immediate exercise at time t is not optimal if

$$X - S(t) \leq (X + d_1)B(t, t_1) - S(t_1)$$

which upon simplification reduces to

$$d_1 B(t, t_1) \geq X[1 - B(t, t_1)]$$

or
$$d_1 \geq X[e^{r(t_1-t)} - 1]$$

The right-hand side of this equation represents the interest income generated by the strike price from date t to t_1. Note that as t tends to t_1, the right-hand side of this equation tends to zero, and the condition will eventually be satisfied. Let t^* be chosen such that

$$d_1 = X[e^{r(t_1-t^*)} - 1] \tag{6.11}$$

Then, over the interval $[t^*, t_1]$ early exercise of an American put will never be optimal.

If the current time t falls in the interval $[t^*, t_1]$, then early exercise, prior to t_1, is not optimal. If the current time t falls outside this interval, that is, if $t < t^*$, then early exercise may be optimal. Indeed, if the stock price is sufficiently low or if interest rates are sufficiently high, early exercise is a distinct possibility.

The above result generalizes to the case where multiple dividends occur prior to expiration. In this case the interval $[t^*, t_1]$ will be wider than the interval obtained by ignoring all but the first ex-dividend date, because the effect of the additional dividends provides increased incentive to delaying exercise.

A direct implication of this property is that the probability of exercise decreases as the size of the dividend increases.

Strike-Price Relationships for Call and Put Options

Property 6.10 provides the relationships between options with different strike prices.

PROPERTY 6.10

Let C_1, C_2, and $C_3(P_1, P_2, P_3)$ represent the cost of three call (put) options that are identical in all aspects except strike prices. Let $X_1 \leq X_2 \leq X_3$ be the three strike prices, and, for simplicity, let $X_3 - X_2 = X_2 - X_1$. Then, to prevent riskless arbitrage strategies from being established, the option prices must satisfy the following conditions:

$$C_2 \leq (C_1 + C_3)/2 \tag{6.12}$$

and
$$P_2 \leq (P_1 + P_3)/2$$

Proof.   Consider portfolio A, containing two call options with strike X_2, and portfolio B, containing one call option with strike X_1 and one call option with strike X_3. Assuming the portfolios are held to expiration, Exhibit 6.6 illustrates the profits.

EXHIBIT 6.6 Arbitrage Portfolio: Strike-Price Relationships for Call Options

Portfolio	Current Value	$S_T \le X_1$	$X_1 < S_T \le X_2$	$X_2 < S_T \le X_3$	$S_T > X_3$
A	$2C_2$	0	0	$2(S_T - X_2)$	$2(S_T - X_2)$
B	$C_1 + C_3$	0	$(S_T - X_1)$	$(S_T - X_1)$	$(S_T - X_1) + (S_T - X_3)$
		$V_A(T) = V_B(T)$	$V_B(T) \ge V_A(T)$	$V_B(T) \ge V_A(T)$	$V_A(T) = V_B(T)$

Since the future value of portfolio B is always at least as valuable as portfolio A, it must follow that the current value of B, $V_B(0)$, is no less than that of A, $V_A(0)$. That is, $V_B(0) \ge V_A(0)$. Hence, $C_1 + C_3 \ge 2C_2$, from which the result follows.

If $C_2 > (C_1 + C_3)/2$, then an investor would sell portfolio A and buy portfolio B. The initial amount of money received would be $2C_2 - C_1 - C_3$. If the portfolio were held to expiration, additional arbitrage profits might become available. If, however, the X_2 options were exercised prior to expiration, when the stock was at $S*$, the amount owed could be obtained by exercising both the X_1 and X_3 calls. Hence, regardless of what price occurs in the future, riskless arbitrage strategies become available unless the middle strike call is valued at less than the average of its neighboring strikes.

A similar result holds for put options.

EXAMPLE 6.8 Consider the following option contracts:

Strike	Price
40	4
45	C_0
50	0.88

The upper bound for the 45 call option contract should be

$$C_0 \le \frac{(4 + 0.88)}{2} = 2.44$$

Property 6.10 can be generalized. Specifically, option prices are convex in the exercise price. That is, if $X_1 < X_2 < X_3$, then

$$C(X_2) \le \lambda C(X_1) + (1 - \lambda)C(X_3)$$

$$P(X_2) \le \lambda P(X_1) + (1 - \lambda)P(X_3)$$

where
$$\lambda = (X_3 - X_2)/(X_3 - X_1)$$

Put-Call Parity Relationships

In this section we develop pricing relationships between put and call options.

European Put-Call Parity: No Dividends

> **PROPERTY 6.11**
>
> With no dividends prior to expiration, a European put should be priced as a European call plus the present value of the strike price less the stock price. That is,
>
> $$P_0^E = C_0^E + XB(0, T) - S_0 \qquad (6.13)$$
>
> where the superscript E emphasizes the fact that the options are European.

Proof.   Under the assumption of no dividends and no premature exercising, consider portfolios A and B, where A consists of the stock and European put and B consists of the European call with X pure discount bonds of face value \$1 that mature at the expiration date. Exhibit 6.7 compares their future values.

To avoid riskless arbitrage opportunities, it must follow that the current values of the two portfolios are the same. That is,

$$P_0^E + S_0 = C_0^E + XB(0, T)$$

or $$P_0^E = C_0^E + XB(0, T) - S_0$$

This relationship is called the **European put-call parity equation.**

EXAMPLE 6.9   Given that the price of a stock is \$55, the price of a three-month 60 call is \$2, and the riskless rate is 12 percent, we can derive the price for a three-month 60 put option. Specifically, since

$$P_0^E = C_0^E + XB(0, T) - S_0$$

EXHIBIT 6.7   Arbitrage Portfolio: Put-Call Parity

Portfolio	Current Value	Terminal Value $S_T \leq X$	$S_T > X$
A	$P_0^E + S_0$	X	S_T
B	$C_0^E + XB(0, T)$	X	S_T
		$V_A(T) = V_B(T)$	$V_A(T) = V_B(T)$

we have

$$P_0^E = \$2 + \$60\, e^{-0.12(3/12)} - \$55$$

$$= \$2 + \$58.23 - \$55$$

$$= \$5.23$$

European Put-Call Parity Equations with Dividends

> ### PROPERTY 6.12
>
> Under the assumption of a single dividend of size d_1 at time t_1, the value of a European put option is given by
>
> $$P_0^E = C_0^E + XB(0, T) + d_1 B(0, t_1) - S_0 \qquad (6.14)$$

Proof.   Consider a stock that pays dividend d_1 at time t_1. Portfolio A contains the stock and put option. Portfolio B contains the call and X pure discount bonds of face value \$1 that mature at the expiration date, along with d_1 pure discount bonds that mature at time t_1. Exhibit 6.8 illustrates the terminal values under the assumption that all dividends or payouts are reinvested at the riskless rate.

Since the terminal values of the two portfolios are the same regardless of the future stock price, it must follow that to avoid riskless arbitrage opportunities, the current portfolio values must be the same. Hence,

$$P_0^E + S_0 = C_0^E + XB(0, T) + d_1 B(0, t_1)$$

and therefore

$$P_0^E = C_0^E + XB(0, T) + d_1 B(0, t_1) - S_0$$

The put-call parity equation not only values a European put option in terms of stocks, calls, and bonds but also provides a mechanism for replicating a put option. That is, a portfolio containing one call option, X pure discount bonds maturing at time T, d_1 pure discount bonds maturing at time t_1, and a short position in the stock completely replicates the payouts of a put option.

EXHIBIT 6.8   Arbitrage Portfolio-Put-Call Parity with Dividends

Portfolio	Current Value	Terminal Value $S_T < X$	$S_T \geq X$
A	$P_0^E + S_0$	$X + d_1 G(t_1, T)$	$S_T + d_1 G(t_1, T)$
B	$C_0^E + XB(0, T) + d_1 B(0, t_1)$	$X + d_1 G(t_1, T)$	$S_T + d_1 G(t_1, T)$
		$V_A(T) = V_B(T)$	$V_A(T) = V_B(T)$

Indirect Purchasing of Puts: A Synthetic Put

From put-call parity,

$$P_0^E = C_0^E + XB(0, T) - S_0$$

Hence, a portfolio consisting of a European call option together with X pure discount bonds and a short position in the stock produces the same payout as a European put. This portfolio is called a **synthetic put.**

Indirect Purchasing of Stock: A Synthetic Stock

From put-call parity,

$$S_0 = XB(0, T) + C_0^E - P_0^E$$

Hence, rather than buy the stock directly, one can buy it "indirectly" by purchasing X discount bonds maturing at time T, buying a call option, and selling a European put.

Indirect Purchasing of Calls: A Synthetic Call

Since

$$P_0^E = C_0^E + XB(0, T) - S_0$$

we have

$$C_0^E = S_0 + P_0^E - XB(0, T)$$

Thus, a call option can be replicated by buying the stock and put options and borrowing the present value of the strike.

American Put-Call Parity Relationships: No Dividends

PROPERTY 6.13

With no dividends prior to expiration, the value of an American put option is related to the American call price by

$$P_0 \geq C_0 + XB(0, T) - S_0 \qquad (6.15)$$

Proof.   Property 6.13 follows directly from Property 6.9 and the recognition that American puts are more valuable than European put options (that is, $P_0 \geq P_0^E$).
    Note from equation (6.15) that since $C_0^E = C_0 \geq 0$, we have

$$P_0^E \geq XB(0, T) - S_0$$

That is, a European put should always be priced no lower than the present value of the strike price less the stock price. Note that this lower bound is less than the intrinsic value, $X - S_0$. European put options can have negative time premiums.

> ### PROPERTY 6.14
>
> With no dividends prior to expiration, the value of an American put option is restricted by
>
> $$P_0 \le C_0 - S_0 + X \qquad (6.16)$$

Proof. Consider portfolio A, which contains a call and X invested in the riskless asset, and portfolio B, which contains a put option together with the stock. Exhibit 6.9 shows the cash flows of the two portfolios. Since the value of portfolio B depends on whether the put is exercised prematurely, both cases must be considered.

If the put is exercised early, the stock is delivered in receipt for $X. Note that in this case, the value of the bonds alone in portfolio A exceeds the value of portfolio B. If the put is held to expiration, then portfolio A will be more valuable than portfolio B, regardless of the future stock price. Clearly, to avoid risk-free arbitrage opportunities, the current value of portfolio A must be no smaller than the value of portfolio B. Hence,

$$C_0 + X \ge P_0 + S_0$$

from which the result follows.

EXAMPLE 6.10   Using the data for Example 6.9, we have

$$P_0 \le C_0 + X - S_0 = \$2 + \$60 - \$55 = \$7$$

and

$$P_0 \le P_0^{\text{E}} = \$5.23$$

Hence, $\$5.23 \le P_0 \le \$7$.

Other Pricing Relationship Properties

In this section we state several additional properties and leave the proofs as exercises.

EXHIBIT 6.9   Arbitrage Portfolio for Put-Call Parity

Portfolio	Current Value	Value at t if the Put Is Exercised	Terminal Value $S_T < X$	$S_T \ge X$
A	$C_0 + X$	$C_t + XG(0, t)$	$XG(0, T)$	$(S_T - X) + XG(0, T)$
B	$P_0 + S_0$	X	X	S_T
		$V_A(t) > V_B(t)$	$V_A(T) > V_B(T)$	$V_A(T) > V_B(T)$

PROPERTY 6.15

1. The difference between the prices of two otherwise identical European calls (puts) cannot exceed the present value of the difference between their strike prices.

$$C^E(X_1) - C^E(X_2) \leq (X_2 - X_1)B(0, T)$$

$$P^E(X_1) - P^E(X_2) \leq (X_2 - X_1)B(0, T)$$

2. The difference between the prices of two otherwise identical American calls (puts) cannot exceed the difference between their strike prices.

$$C(X_1) - C(X_2) \leq (X_2 - X_1)$$

$$P(X_1) - P(X_2) \leq (X_2 - X_1)$$

PROPERTY 6.16

The difference in prices between two American calls and two American puts is bounded below as follows:

$$[C(X_1) - C(X_2)] - [P(X_1) - P(X_2)] \geq [X_1 - X_2]B(0, T)$$

This relationship is called the **box spread lower boundary condition.**

PROPERTY 6.17

Option prices are homogeneous of degree one in the stock price and strike price. That is,

$$C(\lambda S, \lambda X, T) = \lambda C(S, X, T)$$

$$P(\lambda S, \lambda X, T) = \lambda P(S, X, T)$$

A direct corollary of this property is that all options can be standardized to options with a strike price of $1. This is accomplished by taking $\lambda = 1/X$.

EXAMPLE 6.11   Assume a stock is priced at $110. A call option trades with strike at $100. If the stock splits into two shares of $55 each, then the terms of the option contract has to be modified. For this property, an appropriate adjustment would be to exchange the original call option with two options each controlling one new share at a strike price of $50 per share. The value of these two options would equal the value of the original single contract.

> **PROPERTY 6.18**
>
> A portfolio of options is never worth less than an option on a portfolio. Specifically,
>
> $$C\left(\sum_i \lambda_i S_i, X, T\right) \le \sum_i \lambda_i C(S_i, X, T)$$
>
> $$P\left(\sum_i \lambda_i S_i, X, T\right) \le \sum_i \lambda_i P(S_i, X, T)$$

Property 6.18 states that a put option that provides protection against adverse moves in the portfolio value is less costly than a portfolio of put options that insures each component stock against loss. Of course, the terminal payouts of these two strategies are different, with the portfolio of options providing higher payouts in certain states. These higher payouts are reflected in the higher cost of the strategy.

Conclusion

In this chapter we used arbitrage arguments to derive bounds on option prices. In addition, we explored the relationship between put and call options and investigated conditions under which these contracts should not be exercised. Other bounds can be derived. The important point, however, is that option prices are constrained to move together in certain ways. As soon as the relative prices deviate, riskless arbitrage possibilities exist.

Several empirical studies have been conducted to test the results in this chapter. Some of this empirical research is discussed in future chapters. However, the results have shown that the bounds do hold. More precisely, only rarely are the relationships violated, and when they are, profits from implementing the appropriate strategies are insignificant, especially when trading costs are considered.

References

This chapter draws very heavily on Merton's article, published in 1973. The beauty of these arbitrage arguments stems from the fact that they require only that investors prefer more wealth to less. If additional assumptions are placed on investor preferences, tighter bounds on option prices can be derived. Examples of such approaches include Parrakis and Ryan, Ritchken, Ritchken and Kuo, and Levy. Jarrow and Rudd provide a comprehensive treatment of bounds for cases when dividends are uncertain and interest rates are random. Cox and Rubinstein also provide a rigorous treatment of this subject. Empirical tests of these bounds are discussed by Gould and Galai, Klemkosky and Resnick, and Stoll and in the survey by Galai.

Cox, J. C., and M. Rubinstein. *Option Markets.* Englewood Cliffs, N.J.: Prentice-Hall, 1985.

Galai, D. "Empirical Tests of Boundary Conditions for CBOE Options." *Journal of Financial Economics* 6 (June–September 1978): 187–211.

_____. "A Survey of Empirical Tests of Option Pricing Models." In *Option Pricing,* edited by M. Brenner. Lexington, Mass.: Lexington Books, 1983, 45–80.

Gould, J., and D. Galai. "Transaction Costs and the Relationship Between Put and Call Prices." *Journal of Financial Economics* 1 (June 1974): 105–29.

Jarrow, R., and A. Rudd. *Option Pricing.* Homewood, Ill.: Irwin, 1983.

Klemkosky, R., and B. Resnick. "Put-Call Parity and Market Efficiency." *Journal of Finance* 34 (December 1979): 1141–55.

Levy, H. "Upper and Lower Bounds of Put and Call Option Value: Stochastic Dominance Approach." *Journal of Finance* 1985: 1197–1217.

Merton, R. "Theory of Rational Option Pricing." *Bell Journal of Economics and Management Science* 4 (Spring 1973): 141–84.

Perrakis, S, and P. Ryan. "Option Pricing Bounds in Discrete Time." *Journal of Finance* 1984: 519–25.

Ritchken, P. "On Option Pricing Bounds." *Journal of Finance* 1985 : 1219–33.

Ritchken, P., and S. Kuo. "Option Pricing Bounds with Finite Revision Opportunities." *Journal of Finance* 1988: 301–308.

Stoll, H. "The Relationship between Put and Call Option Prices." *Journal of Finance* 31 (May 1969): 319–32.

Exercises

1. Consider the two investments below:

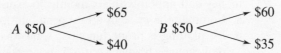

   a. Construct a riskless arbitrage portfolio.
   b. In an efficient market, what would happen to the prices of *A* and *B*?

2. XYZ trades at $50. Bonds with a face value of $1 currently trade at 90 cents. Assuming the bonds mature at the expiration date of the option, compute the lower bound price of an at-the-money call option.

3. XYZ is currently trading at $50. It is about to declare a 50-cent dividend. An at-the-money three-month call option is trading at 70 cents. The riskless rate is 10 percent.
   a. Compute the lower bound on the option price.
   b. Construct a strategy that yields riskless arbitrage opportunities.
   c. How large must the dividend be before the investor would have to consider the possibility of early exercise?

4. Explain why call options will be exercised (if at all) just prior to an ex-dividend date while put options will not be exercised at this time.

5. XYZ pays no dividends and trades at $50. The riskless rate, r, is 10 percent. What is the lowest price at which a six-month put with a strike price of $55 should be sold? If the put traded below this value, what can be done to lock into a guaranteed profit?

6. The six-month call prices on XYZ, which currently trades at $50, are shown below. XYZ pays no dividends. Construct a portfolio that will produce riskless profits.

Strike	Call Price
45	5.20
50	4.50
55	3.00
60	0.50

7. The call price on a six-month XYZ 50 call option is $6 and the riskless rate is 10 percent.
   a. Compute the lower bound on a six-month 50 put option if the stock price is $52.
   b. If the underlying stock declares a dividend of $1 two months prior to expiration, would the lower bound increase, decrease, or remain the same? Explain.

8. XYZ trades at $60. The market price of an XYZ January 50 put is 1/16. The market price of the January 50 call is $11. Consider the strategy of buying the stock and put option and selling the call. Compute the initial investment, and explain why a profit equal to the strike price less the initial investment is guaranteed.

9. XYZ trades at $30, the riskless rate of return is 12 percent, and an at-the-money call option with six months to expiration is trading at $4.
   a. Compute the price of a European put option.
   b. By plotting a profit function, show that the payouts of a stock can be replicated by buying a portfolio containing the six-month at-the-money call and a short position in the put and borrowing funds at the riskless rate. How much needs to be borrowed?

10. Using arbitrage arguments alone, show that an American call option cannot be valued more than a stock.

11. Explain why a European put option could have a negative time premium while an American put option could not.

12. Prove Property 6.15.

PART THREE

Pricing Derivatives

Part 3 is concerned with the pricing and risk management of option contracts. To accomplish this we need to be able to characterize the evolution of uncertainty in stock prices over time. Unless we understand how price uncertainty evolves, we cannot manage risk in positions containing options. In Chapter 7 we therefore study the behavior of stock prices over time. Any reasonable model of price behavior should incorporate properties that we expect of stock prices in efficient financial markets. The chapter highlights the geometric Wiener process. This representation of price behavior is the prototypical model used in analytical studies in the stock and options markets. All models that represent the behavior of prices over time are characterized by a set of parameters that require estimation. In this chapter we review a few simple methods for estimating the parameters using historical data. Of course, since all models are mathematical abstractions, their ultimate effectiveness will depend on empirical evidence. The final section investigates empirical tests that lend support for alternative stock price processes.

In Chapter 6 we obtained pricing relationships among options by considering specific static investment strategies. For example, we showed that the cash flows of a European put option could be duplicated by a portfolio containing a European call option, pure discount bonds, and a short position in the stock. The strategy of replicating the payouts of the put was static since there was no need to rebalance or readjust the replicating portfolio prior to expiration. In Chapter 8 we extend this analysis to dynamic strategies. In particular, we show that in some circumstances, a strategy involving the frequent trading of stocks and bonds can be devised to produce the same cash flows as an option. The exact trading scheme that is followed will depend on the particular path that stock prices take. However, regardless of how uncertainty reveals itself (i.e., regardless of the path of prices), the payout of the option can be duplicated. As a result, once this trading scheme is identified, by the law of one price, the cost of the option should equal the initial cost of the particular replicating portfolio.

Chapter 8 is extremely important. Not only does it illustrate how fair option prices are determined, but in the process of doing this, it illustrates specific strategies that can be initiated to capture riskless profits if the price deviates from its fair price. In this regard, the chapter is similar to Chapter 6, in which riskless profits could be generated by implementing simple trading strategies whenever certain pricing relationships were violated.

Chapter 9 considers the Black-Scholes option pricing model. This model can be viewed as a special limiting case of the binomial model developed in Chapter 8. Black-Scholes is the benchmark model used in option markets. Since the pricing formula has an elegant analytical form, the importance of key parameters can easily be investigated.

Chapter 10 focuses on the use of the Black-Scholes model for hedging and risk management of optioned positions, and it provides a variety of measures of risk for monitoring positions that contain options.

Perhaps the single most important point in Part 3 is that the pricing process and risk management issues are intertwined. That is, risk management issues can be thoroughly addressed only if a pricing mechanism is available.

CHAPTER 7

The Stochastic Process of Stock Prices

In order to obtain exact option prices, we must make more assumptions than we made in Chapter 6. In particular, we need to be able to characterize the evolution of the underlying security over time. If the underlying element is a stock, we need to make some assumptions about its behavior over time. If it is an interest rate, we need to model the behavior of interest rates over time. In this chapter we investigate plausible approaches for modeling the uncertainty of stock prices that pay no dividends. In later chapters we shall investigate models for representing the behavior of dividend-paying stocks, stock indices, futures, foreign exchange rates, bond prices and interest rates.

Models of the behavior of stock prices should incorporate several properties that stocks possess in efficient financial markets. Here we focus on the geometric Wiener process, the prototypical pricing model used in analytical studies of the stock and options markets. All models of prices over time require estimates of some key parameters. We illustrate how to estimate parameters of the geometric Wiener process using historical data. Empirical tests of this mathematical model lend support for the geometric Wiener process. The final part of the chapter investigates a simple model that approximates a geometric Wiener process. This model, called a binomial lattice, will be extremely useful in many of the following chapters.

The primary objectives of this chapter are the following:

- To identify the key factors that affect stock price changes;
- To explain the geometric Wiener process for representing prices; and
- To introduce the binomial lattice model for representing prices.

Efficient Markets

The stock market provides an arena in which participants with similar investment goals and with access to the same information actively search for mispriced securities. The keen competition among the participants ensures that new information regarding securities is rapidly absorbed and reflected in prices. If security prices fully reflect all available information, the market is said to be **efficient.** If the market were not efficient, then some information might not be rapidly used in the setting of prices. In this case, astute investors might be able to use particular information to identify predictable cycles in stock prices, then derive trading strategies yielding abnormal rates of return. Unfortunately, as soon as these strategies became apparent to investors, the information would soon be more efficiently used and abnormal profits would soon be eliminated.

In an efficient market, the process of determining prices is said to be a **fair game.** A fair game describes a process in which there is no way to use currently available information to earn a return above normal. This does not imply that returns are independent through time. For example, consider a company that increases its debt and risk over successive periods. Since the expected returns will tend to increase over time, to compensate for the increased risk, the actual observed returns should also tend to increase. In this case, one might observe a correlation in the sequence of historical returns. However, in an efficient market this information could not be used to earn abnormal excess returns.

There are three forms of market efficiency. **Weak form efficiency** describes a market in which historical prices are efficiently impounded into the current price by market participants. **Semistrong efficiency** describes a market in which all publicly available information is efficiently digested by the participants. Finally, **strong form efficiency** describes a market in which not even those participants with privileged information can obtain above-fair-market returns.

Tests of weak form efficiency involve establishing whether or not the past price or past sequence of returns can be used to predict future returns in such a way as to generate abnormal returns. Most of the early tests were tests of the random walk model, a restrictive version of the fair game model. According to this model, successive returns are statistically independent and identically distributed. The independence assumption implies that historical returns cannot provide useful information on future returns, since these returns are assumed to remain unchanged over time.

Researchers have conducted statistical autocorrelation and run tests to examine whether stock price returns are independent. Empirical tests for daily, weekly, and monthly stock price changes largely support this idea.

The Stochastic Process of Stock Prices

Processes whose outcomes are influenced by random effects through time are called **stochastic processes.** In characterizing any process, it is first necessary to specify a time set, T^*. If observations are recorded continuously during this interval, the process is called a **continuous process.** If observations are made periodically, then T^* consists of a sequence of times and the process is referred to as a **discrete process.** We first consider a discrete process where the time interval, say $[0, T]$, is partitioned into n time increments of width Δt and prices are observed at the end of each increment. Then T^* is defined as $T^* = \{0, 1, 2, \ldots, n\}$ and the collection of prices observed at those points in time constitutes the stochastic process. Let $\{S_t, t \in T^*\}$ represent this collection. Note that as the partition of the interval $[0, T]$ increases, the number of observations increases and the discrete process converges onto a continuous process.

To make matters specific, consider the sequence of price relatives. The **price relative** is the price at the end of the period divided by the price at the beginning of the period. Let $R_t = S_t/S_{t-1}$ be the price relative over the tth time increment, which is of width Δt. Then, given that the original stock price is S_0, future stock prices can be represented as follows:

$$S_1 = S_0 R_1$$
$$S_2 = S_1 R_2 = S_0 R_1 R_2 \qquad (7.1)$$
$$S_n = S_0 R_1 R_2 \ldots R_n$$

Let $r_i = \ln(R_i)$ be the logarithmic return over the ith time increment, and assume that the distribution of logarithmic returns is independent of the stock price. This implies, for example, that a 10 percent or greater logarithmic return over a time increment is as likely for a stock priced at \$10 as it is for a stock priced at \$100. In addition, assume that the logarithmic returns are independent of each other. If the sequence of returns were not independent, then the history of the returns would provide useful information about future logarithmic returns, and this might be inconsistent with a weak-form-efficient market.

The basic principles of investment are based on an analysis of expected reward and risk. The stock has a positive expected return. If no surprises occur, then the actual return over the period might equal this expected value. Of course, unanticipated shocks do occur, and they may affect the price. Let α represent the expected value of the logarithmic returns over one year. For example, if $\alpha = 20$ percent, we expect the logarithmic return over one year to be 20 percent. The expected return over a six-month period would be 10 percent, and over a period of length Δt years would be 20 Δt percent.

Like the expected reward, the uncertainty in the logarithmic return should increase as the holding period increases. For example, the logarithmic return over one day is likely to be much less variable than the return over one year. New information about the stock is unpredictable and may cause the actual logarithmic return to deviate from its expected value. The magnitude of this discrepancy is captured by the standard deviation per unit of time. A standard deviation of $\sigma = 30$ percent per year means that while $\alpha = 20$ percent is expected, fairly large deviations from this value are possible. Indeed, for the normal distribution, about 2 standard deviations around the mean capture over 90 percent of the possible outcomes. Hence, in one year, we should be confident that the logarithmic return is 20 percent $\pm$ 60 percent. A return outside this interval would be considered rare. In finance, the standard deviation is referred to as the **volatility.**

The volatility of returns expands over time. For example, the volatility over a time period of two years will be much larger than the volatility over one year. Most models of stock price behavior assume that volatility expands with the square root of the time period. Hence, if the volatility of returns is 30 percent per year, the volatility over a period of Δt years is 30% $\times \sqrt{\Delta t}$.

We also make an assumption concerning the actual distribution of the logarithmic return. Since the return over a time period is influenced by many unanticipated events, it is not unreasonable to appeal to the central limit theorem and hypothesize that the distribution of returns is normal.

In summary, then, most models of stock price behavior assume that the logarithmic returns in successive periods of width Δt years are independent normal random variable with mean $\alpha \Delta t$, linear in the time increment, and standard deviation $\sigma \sqrt{\Delta t}$, which grows with the square root of the time increment.

Let Z represent the normal random variable, with mean zero and standard deviation 1. To standardize any normal random variable, we subtract the mean and divide by the standard deviation. Hence, we obtain

$$Z = \frac{r - \alpha \Delta t}{\sigma \sqrt{\Delta t}}$$

The logarithmic returns are then

$$r = \alpha \Delta t + \sigma \sqrt{\Delta t} \, Z \tag{7.2}$$

EXAMPLE 7.1   A nondividend-paying stock has logarithmic returns over six-month increments that are normally distributed. The expected logarithmic return is 20 percent per year ($\alpha = 0.20$), and the volatility is 30 percent per year ($\sigma = 0.30$). This implies that over a six-month period the expected logarithmic return is 10 percent and the volatility is $0.30\sqrt{0.5} = 0.212$. The probability of the logarithmic return exceeding 18 percent over six months can be computed by standardizing the random variable as follows:

$$P(r > 0.18) = P\left(Z > \frac{0.18 - 0.10}{0.212}\right) = P(Z > 0.377)$$

Using standard normal tables (see Appendix 8A), we find this probability is 0.35.

Since the logarithmic return is a normal random variable, it could be any number, positive or negative. Now consider the price relative, $R = e^r$. Exponentiating any number, positive or negative, leads to a positive value. Hence, while the distribution of the logarithmic return is normal, the distribution of the price relative is not. The shape of the statistical distribution of the price relative, implied by the fact that its natural logarithm has a normal distribution, is shown in Exhibit 7.1. The statistical distribution is called the **lognormal distribution.** The expected value and variance of the price relative over any time increment Δt can be shown to be

$$E(R) = e^{\alpha \Delta t + \sigma^2 \Delta t/2} \tag{7.3}$$

$$\text{Var}(R) = E(R)^2 (e^{\sigma^2 \Delta t} - 1) \tag{7.4}$$

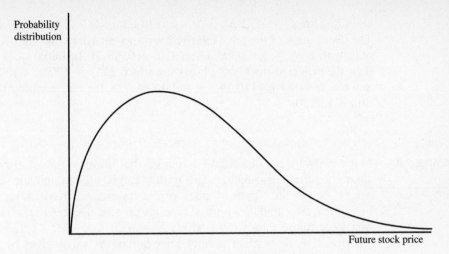

Probability distribution

Future stock price

EXHIBIT 7.1   Lognormal Distribution of Price Relatives

EXAMPLE 7.2   In Example 7.1, $\alpha = 0.20$ and $\sigma = 0.30$. The distribution of the price relative over a six-month period ($\Delta t = 0.5$) is lognormal. The expected value and variance are given by

$$E(R) = e^{[0.20 + (0.30)^2/2]0.5} = 1.1303$$

$$\text{Var}(R) = E(R)^2(e^{(0.30)^2/2} - 1) = 0.0588$$

The Geometric Wiener Process

A stock follows a geometric Wiener process if, as viewed from date 0, the distribution of logarithmic returns over any period of length T years is normally distributed with mean, αT, proportional to the time period and volatility, $\sigma \sqrt{T}$, proportional to the square root of the holding period. Equivalently, the price relative over period T, $R(T)$ say, is lognormal, with mean and variance given by

$$E[R(T)] = e^{(\alpha + \sigma^2/2)T} \tag{7.5}$$

$$\text{Var}[R(T)] = E[R(T)]^2(e^{\sigma^2 T} - 1) \tag{7.6}$$

Since $R(T) = S(T)/S_0$, we have $S(T) = R(T)S_0$, and

$$E[S(T)] = S_0\, e^{(\alpha + \sigma^2/2)T} \tag{7.7}$$

$$\text{Var}[S(T)] = E[S(T)]^2[e^{\sigma^2 T} - 1] \tag{7.8}$$

EXAMPLE 7.3   If a stock price follows a geometric Wiener process, then viewed from time zero, the logarithmic returns at all successive dates, Δt years apart, are drawings from lognormal distributions, with expectations and variances given by equations (7.5) and (7.6) for $T = \Delta t, 2\Delta t, 3\Delta t, \ldots$. In Example 7.2, $\alpha = 0.20$ and $\sigma = 0.30$. The distribution of the price relative over a six-month period ($\Delta t = 0.5$) is lognormal, with $E(R) = 1.1303$ and $\text{Var}(R) = 0.0588$. If the initial stock price is $100, then the expected stock price in six months is $E(S) = 100 \times 1.1303 = \$113.03$, and the variance is $(110.54)^2 \times 0.0588 = 718.48$. The resulting standard deviation is $26.80.

EXAMPLE 7.4   Many software packages have a routine that draws variables at random from a standard normal distribution. This routine can be used to simulate successive stock prices. To obtain a path of stock prices, take S_0 as given. Over the first time increment, Δt, simulate a normal random variable. Denote the variable by Z_1. The first logarithmic return is r_1, where $r_1 = \alpha\,\Delta t + \sigma\sqrt{\Delta t}\,Z_1$. Then compute the price relative, $R_1 = e^{r_1}$. The stock price at date Δt is then given by $S_1 = S_0 R_1$. To compute the stock price at date $2\Delta t$, use the random number generator to compute Z_2, and repeat the procedure taking the initial stock price as S_1. The entire path of prices over n successive periods of width Δt yields a typical path.

Estimation of the Parameters of a Geometric Wiener Process

If stock prices follow a geometric Wiener process, and if price information is collected at discrete points in time (e.g., daily), then the parameters α and σ^2 can be readily estimated.

EXAMPLE 7.5   Exhibit 7.2 shows daily closing prices of a nondividend-paying stock over a period of 10 consecutive days. The $n = 9$ logarithmic returns are computed by $r_t = \ln(S_t/S_{t-1})$. Assuming that the daily logarithmic returns are independent and come

EXHIBIT 7.2   Computation of Logarithmic Price Relatives

Day	Price	Price Relative	Logarithmic Price Relative
1	$30.00	—	
2	31.00	1.033	0.0328
3	31.50	1.016	0.0159
4	30.00	0.952	−0.0492
5	32.00	1.066	0.0645
6	34.00	1.062	0.0606
7	32.00	0.941	−0.0606
8	32.50	1.015	0.0155
9	32.50	1.000	0.0000
10	31.25	0.9615	−0.0392

from the same statistical distribution, then the daily logarithmic mean and variance can be estimated by the following:

$$\hat{\alpha} = \sum_{i=1}^{n} r_i/9 = 0.0044777$$

$$\hat{\sigma}^2 = \sum_{i=1}^{n} (r_i - \hat{\alpha})^2/(n - 1) = 0.00210638$$

The value $\hat{\sigma}$ is the estimate of the daily logarithmic volatility. The annual variance is given by

$$\hat{\sigma}_A^2 = (0.00210638)365 = 0.7688$$

$$\hat{\sigma}_A = \sqrt{0.7688} = 0.876$$

In annualizing the variance we multiplied the daily variance by 365. Actually, several researchers suggest annualizing the variance by multiplying by the number of business days (260) in the year. The reason for this is the lack of price volatility over the weekends. Thus, a better estimate for σ_A^2 is given by $\hat{\sigma}_A^2 = (0.00210638)$ $260 = 0.5476$ or $\hat{\sigma}_A = 0.740$.

The Behavior of Logarithmic Returns Versus Simple Returns

Again, our representation of the logarithmic returns for a stock over a period of width Δt is given by equation (7.2):

$$r = \alpha \, \Delta t + \sigma \sqrt{\Delta t} \, Z$$

Over the ith time increment, the logarithmic return is $r_i = \ln(S_{i+1}/S_i)$. Substituting this expression into equation (7.2), we obtain

$$\ln(S_{i+1}/S_i) = \ln(S_{i+1}) - \ln(S_i) = \alpha \, \Delta t + \sigma \sqrt{\Delta t} \, Z \qquad (7.9)$$

Let $\Delta\ln(S_i)$ represent the difference in logarithms of prices. Then

$$\Delta\ln(S_i) = \alpha \, \Delta t + \sigma \sqrt{\Delta t} \, Z = \alpha \, \Delta t + \sigma \sqrt{\Delta t} \, Z \qquad (7.10)$$

Equation (7.10) states that over a time increment of Δt, the change in logarithms of prices has a normal distribution. Mathematicians have shown that if the change in the logarithm of prices follows the above process, then a representation exists for the simple return over the time increment Δt. Specifically, if the time increment Δt is very small, then the simple return, defined as $\Delta S_i/S_i$, where $\Delta S_i = S_{i+1} - S_i$ is normal with a mean of $\mu \, \Delta t$ and a volatility of $\sigma \sqrt{\Delta t}$. The value of μ is given by

$$\mu = \alpha + \sigma^2/2 \qquad (7.11)$$

That is,

$$\Delta S_i/S_i = \mu \, \Delta t + \sigma \sqrt{\Delta t} \, Z \qquad (7.12)$$

To avoid confusion over terminology regarding means, whenever we refer to α, we shall emphasize that it is the mean of the *continuously* compounded returns, while μ will be referred to just as the expected return.

EXAMPLE 7.6 Suppose the expected return from a stock currently priced at $50 is 14 precent per year and the standard deviation is 20 percent per year. If time is measured in years, then $\mu = 0.14$ and $\sigma = 0.20$. If $\Delta t = 0.01$, then $\Delta s/s$ is approximately a normal random variable with mean $\mu \, \Delta t = 0.14(0.01) = 0.0014$ and standard deviation $0.2\sqrt{0.01} = 0.02$. Hence, the change in stock price, Δs, over Δt is a normal random variable with mean $S\mu \, \Delta t = \$0.07$ and standard deviation $\$50(0.02) = \$1$. Note that the change in stock price over the second time increment would also be normal. However, the mean and variance would now depend on the actual level of the stock price at time Δt. While proportional returns in successive periods are independent normal random variables, actual price changes are not. This property seems reasonable. For example, a price change of $10 is more likely for a stock priced at $100 than for a stock priced at $11.

EXAMPLE 7.7 Consider a stock currently priced at $10 with an expected return of 20 percent per year ($\mu = 0.20$) and a volatility of 30 percent per year ($\sigma = 0.30$). The expected stock price in one year's time, $E[S(T)]$, and the variance, $Var[S(T)]$, are given by

$$E[S(T)] = 10 \, e^{0.20} = 12.21$$

$$Var[S(T)] = 100 \, e^{0.4}(e^{0.09} - 1) = 14.049$$

The logarithmic rate of return is normally distributed, with mean $\alpha = \mu - \sigma^2/2 = 0.20 - 0.09/2 = 0.155$ (15.5%) and volatility 0.3 (30%).

A Continuous Time Representation of a Geometric Wiener Process

It is common practice to label $\sqrt{\Delta t} \, Z$ as Δw. Δw is a normal random variable with mean zero and standard deviation $\sqrt{\Delta t}$, and it is called a standard Wiener increment. Equation (7.12) is then written as

$$\Delta S/S = \mu \, \Delta t + \sigma \, \Delta w \tag{7.13}$$

and the limiting equation, obtained as the partition Δt is refined, is expressed as

$$dS/S = \mu \, dt + \sigma \, dw \tag{7.14}$$

Empirical Evidence of Stock Return Behavior

As long as returns over small time increments are independent and identically distributed random variables, the central limit theorem can be invoked to conclude that daily returns should be normal. The observed distribution of daily returns, however, yields a higher frequency of observations near the mean and in the tails than would be expected for a normal distribution. Skewness and kurtosis are measures that relate the shape of a distribution to a normal distribution. If random variable x has mean μ and variance σ^2, these two measures are

$$\text{skew}(x) = \frac{m_3}{\sigma_x^3} \tag{7.15}$$

$$\text{kurtosis}(x) = \frac{m_4}{\sigma_x^4} \tag{7.16}$$

where $m_3 = E[(x - \mu)^3]$ is the third central moment and $m_4 = E[(x - \mu)^4]$ is the fourth central moment.

The skewness of a normal distribution is 0, while its kurtosis is 3. Empirical evidence of daily logarithmic returns shows the skewness values to be near zero, but the kurtosis values exceed 3. This higher value means that the shape of the distribution in Exhibit 7.3 is more "humped" in the middle and has "fatter" tails than a normal distribution.

The observed distribution of daily returns indicates that the usual central limit theorem does not apply here. Mandelbrot pointed out that if the individual effects making up price change did not have finite variance but were still independent, then the limiting distribution would belong to the stable family of distributions, of which the normal distribution is a special case. Since the symmetric nonnormal members of the stable class have the shape properties observed in daily returns, this theory appeared to have promise. While initial empirical tests provided some support for this theory, recent studies have provided evidence not consistent with this hypothesis.

Stable distributions are by definition **stable** or **invariant** under addition. This means that if daily logarithmic returns are drawings from a stable distribution, then weekly and monthly returns have distributions of the same type. In practice, however, the shape of the distribution of returns changes as the holding period

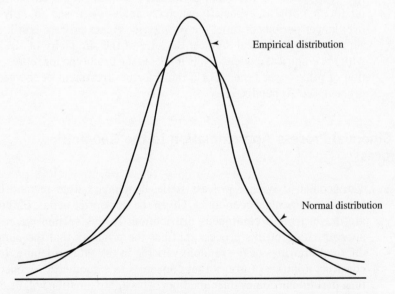

EXHIBIT 7.3 Comparison of Empirical Distribution of Logarithmic Returns with a Normal Distribution

expands. This is inconsistent with Mandelbrot's hypothesis. Actually, if weekly or monthly data are used, the logarithmic returns appear to be more normally distributed than the daily data.

An alternative explanation for the shape of the distribution of daily returns is provided by the **mixture-of-distributions hypothesis.** This theory is based on the observation that on less eventful days prices evolve slowly and on more eventful days prices may evolve faster with heavy trading. Specifically, suppose that each day a random series of events take place, each of which generates information important to the pricing of the security. After each event, the prices adjust as traders rebalance their portfolios in response to the information. The actual price change and trading value observed are related to the information content generated by the event.

The total return and volume recorded in a day represent the cumulation of price changes and volumes that occur as a result of all the information events in the day. Let $n(t)$ be the number of information events on day t. Let $r(t)$ be the logarithmic return on day t. Then, assuming $n(t)$ is large, by the central limit theorem, and conditional on $n(t) = n$, $r(t)$ should be normal with mean an and variance bn, where a and b are positive constants.

The conditioning variable $n(t)$ is referred to as a **directing** or **mixing variable.** It could be deterministic or stochastic, and stationary or seasonal. Assume the directing random variable has mean μ, variance σ^2, and third and fourth central moments m_3 and m_4. With this information, we can obtain the first four moments for the unconditional random variable, $r(t)$. Given these moments, it can also be shown that the daily logarithmic return is more peaked and has fatter tails than the normal distribution.

A variety of models have been developed with different assumptions regarding the distribution of the mixing variable. Overall, empirical studies support the mixture hypothesis, especially when the analysis is based on daily data. However, over longer periods of time, the geometric Wiener process is still reasonably well supported by empirical studies. Because of the simplicity of the model, together with the empirical evidence, this model is the prototype for representing the evolution of prices over time. (For a more formal treatment of the geometric Wiener process, see Appendix 7A.)

A Simple Binomial Process Approximation to the Geometric Wiener Process

The geometric Wiener process is the benchmark used in modeling stock price behavior in financial economics. Given the stock price at date 0, future stock prices are drawn from a continuous distribution. In this section we consider a simple approximation of this process that has the property that the number of possible different drawings of the random variable in the future is finite. In particular, we construct a lattice of prices that converges to a geometric Wiener process as the time partition becomes finer and finer. This approximation will be extremely useful for modeling the evolution of uncertainty in stock and option prices.

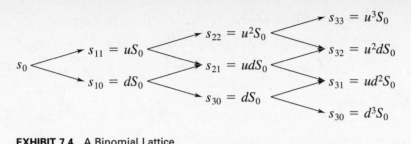

EXHIBIT 7.4   A Binomial Lattice

Assume that prices can be represented as a geometric Wiener process of the form

$$ds/s = \mu \, dt + \sigma \, dw \quad \text{with} \quad s(0) = s_0$$

where s_0 is the stock price at time $t = 0$.

In order to approximate the evolution by a discrete process, we partition the time interval $[0, T]$ into n time increments each of width Δt. Assume that in each time increment the price can rise or fall by given percentages. Specifically, let R_i be characterized by

$$R_i = \begin{cases} u & \text{with probability } p \\ d & \text{with probability } q \ (q = 1 - p) \end{cases}$$

Let s_{nj} represent the stock price after n periods, given that j upward movements (upmoves, u) and $n - j$ downward movements (downmoves, d) have occurred. Exhibit 7.4 illustrates the stock price behavior for $n = 3$.

After n periods, the stock price has $n + 1$ possible values, given by

$$s_{nj} = u^j d^{n-j} s_0 \quad \text{for } j = 0, 1, 2, 3, \ldots, n \tag{7.17}$$

The probability that the stock price in the nth period, S_n, takes on the value s_{nj} is merely the probability that in n periods (trials) there are j upmoves (successes) and $(n - j)$ downmoves (failures). This probability is given by the binomial probability law. Hence, we have

$$P(S_n = s_{nj}) = \binom{n}{j} p^j q^{n-j} \quad \text{for } j = 0, 1, 2, 3, \ldots, n \tag{7.18}$$

EXAMPLE 7.8   Assume that $S_0 = \$50$. In each time increment the stock price can appreciate by 10 percent ($u = 1.1$), with probability 0.6, or depreciate to 90.909 percent ($d = 1/u$) of its value, with probability 0.4. That lattice of possible stock prices after two periods is shown below.

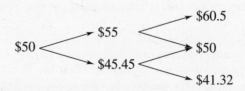

The probabilities of being in the three possible states are

$$P(S_2 = 60.5) = P(S_2 = s_{22}) = P(S_2 = u^2 d^0 S_0) = \binom{2}{0}(0.6)^2(0.4)^0 = 0.36$$

$$P(S_2 = 50.00) = P(S_2 = s_{21}) = P(S_2 = u^1 d^1 S_0) = \binom{2}{1}(0.6)(0.4) = 0.48$$

and

$$P(S_2 = 41.32) = P(S_2 = s_{20}) = P(S_2 = u^0 d^2 S_0) = \binom{2}{0}(0.6)^0(0.4)^2 = 0.16$$

The idea behind a binomial approximation is to choose the up and down parameters, u and d, and the probability, p, in such a way that the prices on the lattice serve as good proxies for the true lognormally distributed prices. As the width of each time increment Δt decreases, the number of states at date T increases, and the approximation should improve. For example, if a geometric Wiener process is to be approximated over a one-year period, using a two-period lattice with a six-month time partition will mean the terminal lognormal distribution is determined by only 3 points. This is hardly likely to be a reasonable approximation. However, if 100 partitions are used, then the lattice will lead to 101 different points, which could provide a better approximation. Of course, as the partition is refined, the jump values u and d, and their probabilities p and $1 - p$, must be adjusted. Hopefully, a mechanism for computing u, d, and p can be established such that as the partition is refined, the approximating lattice of prices becomes indistinguishable from the true geometric Wiener process. That is, the probabilities of reaching the end points of the lattice serve as good proxies for the probabilities for a lognormal distribution.

Mathematicians have shown that the binomial lattice will converge to a geometric Wiener process if values for the upmove and downmove parameters, u and d, and the probability, p, can be obtained, such that in each small time increment, Δt, the expected stock price change and the variance of the stock price change over the binomial lattice match the expected stock price change and variance given by the true underlying continuous process. In particular, it can be shown that if the parameters are chosen as

$$d = e^{-\sigma\sqrt{\Delta t}} \tag{7.19}$$

$$u = e^{\sigma\sqrt{\Delta t}} \tag{7.20}$$

$$p = \frac{e^{\mu \Delta t} - d}{u - d} \tag{7.21}$$

then, with the partition Δt suitably small, the binomial process can be used to approximate the geometric Wiener process. (See Appendix 7B for a derivation of these formulas.) That is, realizations from the binomial lattice will serve as excellent proxies as realizations from the true process.

EXAMPLE 7.9   Assume that the stock price process follows a geometric Wiener process with mean $\mu = 20$ percent per year and volatility $\sigma = 30$ percent per year. The initial price is \$100. This process can be approximated by a binomial process as follows. Assume that $\Delta t = 7/365$. Then from equations (7.19) through (7.21), we have

$$u = 1.04242$$

$$d = 0.95930$$

$$p = 0.54616$$

Under this approximation, after seven days the stock can with probability 0.5461616 increase to $104.24 or decrease with probability 0.4538384 to $95.93. The possible approximating binomial lattice for the first two weeks is shown below.

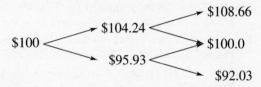

The annual expected return and volatility of this process will be exactly 20 percent and 30 percent, respectively. Moreover, the shape of the binomial distribution of stock prices after 52 binomial jumps will closely approximate the true lognormal distribution after one year.

As the partition of the one-year time interval increases, the approximation improves. For example, if $\Delta t = 1/365$, a better approximation to the original process is obtained. From a practical point of view, the convergence of the process is quite rapid, and little improvement in the approximation is obtained beyond 100 partitions.

Conclusion

In this chapter we have investigated the stochastic process of stock prices. There is good reason to suspect that in an efficient market, stock prices might follow a geometric Wiener process. Indeed, this process is the benchmark used to model stock price behavior. This process has the desirable property that stock prices cannot go negative. In addition, the volatility of returns does not depend on the level of the stock price. This process can very easily be approximated by a simple binomial lattice. Empirical evidence suggests that over the short term (e.g., days) logarithmic returns may not be exactly normal, but that over longer time intervals the approximation is more reasonable. The mixture-of-distributions hypothesis may provide explanations for the deviations from a lognormal distribution that are observed; nonetheless, as a first-order approximation, the geometric Wiener process is not too severe an assumption.

References

Most of these references are concerned with empirical tests to establish the distribution of stock returns. For a good introduction to stochastic processes see Karlin and Taylor.

Blattberg, R., and N. Gonedes. "A Comparison of the Stable and Student Distributions as Statistical Models for Stock Prices." *Journal of Business* (April 1974): 244–80.

Cheng, P., and M. Deets. "Portfolio Returns and the Random Walk Theory." *Journal of Finance* 26(1) (March 1971): 11–30.

Fama, E. "Behavior of Stock Market Prices." *Journal of Business* (January 1965): 34–105.

Garman, M., and M. Klass. "On the Estimation of Security Price Volatilities from Historical Data." *Journal of Business* 53 (1980): 67–78.

Harris, L. "Transaction Data Tests of the Mixture of Distribution Hypothesis." *Journal of Financial and Quantitative Analysis* 22 (1987): 127–42.

———. "Cross Security Tests of the Mixture of Distributions Hypothesis." *Journal of Financial and Quantitative Analysis* 21 (1986): 39–46.

Hsu, D. A., R. Miller, and D. Wichern. "On the Stable Paretian Behavior of Stock Market Prices." *Journal of the American Statistical Association* 69 (1974): 108–13.

Karlin, S., and H. Taylor. *A First Course in Stochastic Processes*. New York: Academic Press, 1975.

Kon, S. "Models of Stock Returns: A Comparison." *Journal of Finance* 39 (1984): 147–65.

Lo, A., and C. MacKinlay. "Stock Market Prices Do Not Follow Random Walks: Evidence from a Simple Specification Test." *Review of Financial Studies* 1 (1988): 41–66.

Malliaris, A. G. *Stochastic Methods in Economics and Finance*. New York: North-Holland, 1981.

Mandelbrot, B. "The Variation of Certain Speculative Prices." *Journal of Business* (October 1963): 394–419.

Merton, R. C. "On Estimating the Expected Return on the Market." *Journal of Financial Economics* 8 (1980): 323–61.

Nelson, D., and K. Ramaswamy. "Simple Binomial Processes as Diffusion Approximations in Financial Models." *Review of Financial Studies* 3 (1990): 393–430.

Oldfield, G. S., Jr., R. J. Rogalski, and R. A. Jarrow. "An Autoregressive Jump Process for Common Stock Returns." *Journal of Financial Economics* 5 (1977): 389–418.

Osborne, M. "Brownian Motion in the Stock Market." *Operational Research* (March–April 1959): 145–73.

Westerfield, R. "The Distribution of Common Stock Price Changes: An Application of Transactions Time and Subordinated Stochastic Models." *Journal of Finance and Quantitative Analysis* 12 (1977): 743–65.

Exercises

1. Explain what it would mean if you identified a stock which had historical return patterns that could be used to predict future returns.

2. The initial stock price is $s_0 = 100$. Prices are approximated by a lattice with $u = 1.2$, $d = 0.8$, and $p = 0.6$.
   a. Compute the lattice of prices over three periods.
   b. Compute the probability that after three periods, the price exceeds $140.

3. A stock price follows a geometric Wiener process. The average of the logarithmic returns is 10 percent per year ($\alpha = 0.10$) and the volatility is 20 percent per year ($\sigma = 0.20$).

a. Compute the average logarithmic return and the volatility over six months.

b. Compute the probability that the logarithmic return exceeds 5 percent over six months.

c. Compute the probability that the logarithmic return exceeds 7 percent over six months.

4. A stock price follows a geometric Wiener process. Specifically,

$$\Delta s/s = \mu \, \Delta t + \sigma \, \Delta w$$

where $\mu = 20$ percent and $\sigma = 30$ percent per year. Assume that the time increment is one day.

a. Compute the expected dollar change in the stock price given $s_0 = \$100$.

b. Compute the variance of the dollar change in stock price.

c. Assume the actual price change the first day is \$1 ($s_1 = \$101$). Compute the expected stock price change the second day, and compute its variance.

d. Why are the distributions of stock price changes different?

5. A stock follows a geometric Wiener process. The expected return is 20 percent per year and its volatility is 30 percent per year. The current price is $s_0 = \$50$. The change in the stock price is given by

$$\Delta s = \mu s \, \Delta t + \sigma s \, \Delta w$$

or

$$\Delta s = \mu s \, \Delta t + \sigma s \sqrt{\Delta t} \, \tilde{Z}$$

where Z is a standard normal random variable and Δt is the time increment. Now, assume that you want to simulate the stock price over three consecutive days. (Then $\Delta t = 1/365$.) In order to do this you need three random drawings from a standard normal distribution. Assume they are $Z_1 = 1.52$, $Z_2 = -0.25$, and $Z_3 = 0.58$. Using these numbers, establish the price of the stock at the end of each of the three days.

6. A stock follows a geometric Wiener process. Its expected instantaneous return is 20 percent per year and its volatility is 30 percent per year. The current stock price is \$50.

a. Compute the expected stock price at the end of one day.

b. Compute the standard deviation at the end of the day.

c. Construct a 90 percent confidence interval for the logarithmic return after one day.

d. Construct a 90 percent confidence interval for the stock price after one day.

7. a. For the stock in Exercise 6, construct a two period binomial lattice approximation. Each period should correspond to one week. On the lattice, identify the probability of an upmove.

b. Using the lattice, compute the logarithmic returns over two weeks in each of the three final states. Identify the probability of each occurrence, and compute the expected logarithmic return and the variance of logarithmic returns.

c. The true logarithmic return over two weeks is normal. Identify the true mean and true variance, and compare the results to those obtained in Exercise 7b.

APPENDIX 7A

A Primer on Stochastic Calculus

An increasing number of articles in financial economics use continuous time mathematics to value financial claims. This appendix presents a nontechnical treatment of this subject and provides several examples of its applications in finance. The primary purpose is to present the rules of stochastic calculus in such a way that readers of technical papers will be able to follow the literature without being intimidated by the mathematics.

To understand the economic implications of continuous trading, it is necessary to specify the properties of the time series of price changes in this environment. In the first section we briefly restate properties of Wiener processes, discuss Ito processes, and then turn to stochastic calculus. Ito's lemma is presented, together with rules of differentiation. These rules collapse to simple rules of differentiation when uncertainty is removed. Several examples are presented to reinforce the concepts.

A Standard Wiener Process

A stochastic process $\{w(t), t \geq 0\}$ is a standard Wiener process if

1. $w(0) = 0$
2. $\{w(t), t \geq 0\}$ has stationary and independent increments.
3. For every $t > 0$, $w(t)$ is normally distributed with mean zero and variance t.

Let Δw be the change in the value of $w(t)$ over a period of length Δt. Then the expected change in value, $E(\Delta w)$, is zero, while the variance, $\text{Var}(\Delta w)$, is equal to the time increment, Δt. Since the variance is given by

$$\text{Var}(\Delta w) = E[(\Delta w)^2] - [E(\Delta w)]^2$$

it follows that the second moment, $E[(\Delta w)^2]$, equals Δt.

The standard Wiener process has the property that all higher moments are of a magnitude smaller than Δt. That is,

$$E[(\Delta w)^n] = o[(\Delta t)^2] \quad \text{for } n > 2$$

where $o[(\Delta t)^2]$ means the term is of smaller order than its argument.

In the Wiener process, no matter how small the time partition is, the properties of the process are still maintained. Furthermore, it can be shown that in the limit, as Δt tends to dt and Δw becomes dw, the second and higher moments of the change, dw, can be viewed as deterministic in the sense that the probabilities of deviations from their means are negligible compared to their means. Indeed, only the first two moments play a meaningful role in characterizing the statistical evolution of the process, and for all practical purposes we can write

$$dw^2 = dt$$

$$dw^n = 0 \qquad n > 2$$

$$dt^2 = 0$$

$$dw\,dt = 0$$

Ito Processes

A stochastic process $\{x(t),\ t > 0\}$ is an Ito process if the random variable dx can be represented as

$$dx = \mu(x, t)\,dt + \sigma(x, t)\,dw$$

where $\mu(x, t)$ is the expected change in x at time t and $\sigma(x, t)\,dw$ reflects the uncertain term. For example, x could represent the stock price. The geometric Wiener process would be a special case with

$$\mu(x, t) = \mu x$$
$$\sigma(x, t) = \sigma x$$

Consider a function defined on this type of process. For example, we may be interested in valuing a contingent claim whose value depends on the stock price x and on the current time t. Let $F(x, t)$ represent the value of the claim. We assume that this function is a twice continuously differentiable function of x and a once continuously differentiable function of t.

If $x(t)$ is a deterministic function, then the differential dF is the limit of ΔF, where

$$\Delta F = F(x + \Delta x, t + \Delta t) - F(x, t)$$

and by Taylor's series we have

$$\Delta F = F_X\,\Delta x + F_t\,\Delta t + o(\Delta t)$$

where subscripts denote partial derivatives $\left(\text{for example, } F_X = \dfrac{\partial F}{\partial x}\right)$. In the limit we obtain

$$dF = F_X\,dx + F_t\,dt \qquad\qquad (7A.1)$$

When $x(t)$ is not certain but instead follows an Ito process, the above differential rule cannot be applied. Ito's lemma is just the stochastic calculus equivalent of this differential rule. In the next section we state the lemma, provide a brief sketch of the proof, and then develop some rules for stochastic calculus.

Ito's Lemma

If $F(x, t)$ is a twice continuously differentiable function of x and once continuously differentiable function of t, then the total differential of F is given by

$$dF = F_X \, dx + F_t \, dt + \frac{1}{2}\sigma^2(x, t)F_{XX} \, dt \tag{7A.2}$$

where $dx = \mu(x, t) \, dt + \sigma(x, t) \, dw$

Proof.   Using Taylor's series, we have

$$\Delta F = F_X \, \Delta x + F_t \, \Delta t + \frac{1}{2} F_{XX}(\Delta x)^2 + F_{Xt} \, \Delta x \, \Delta t + \frac{1}{2} F_{tt}(\Delta t)^2 + o(\Delta t^2) \tag{7A.3}$$

Now, from properties of the Wiener process we have

$$
\begin{aligned}
(\Delta x)^2 &= [\mu(x, t) \, \Delta t + \sigma(x, t) \, \Delta w]^2 \\
&= \mu^2(x, t)(\Delta t)^2 + \sigma^2(x, t)(\Delta w)^2 + 2\mu(x, t)\sigma(x, t) \, \Delta w \, \Delta t \tag{7A.4} \\
&= \sigma^2(x, t) \, \Delta t + o(\Delta t)
\end{aligned}
$$

$$
\begin{aligned}
\Delta x \, \Delta t &= [\mu(x, t) \, \Delta t + \sigma(x, t) \, \Delta w] \, \Delta t \\
&= o(\Delta t) \tag{7A.5}
\end{aligned}
$$

Substituting equations (7A.4) and (7A.5) into (7A.3) and rearranging, we obtain in the limit

$$dF = F_X \, dx + F_t \, dt + \frac{1}{2}\sigma^2(x, t)F_{XX} \, dt$$

Substituting for dx, we obtain

$$dF = \left\{ F_X\mu(x, t) + F_t + \frac{1}{2}\sigma^2(x, t)F_{XX} \right\} dt + F_X\sigma(x, t) \, dw \tag{7A.6}$$

Note that equation (7A.6) contains an additional term compared to equation (7A.1). This term arises because with the Ito process, not all "second-order" effects in the Taylor expansion can be ignored.

In order to become familiar with Ito's lemma, consider the following examples.

EXAMPLE 7A.1   Let $F(x, t) = e^x$ and $dx = \alpha \, dt + \sigma \, dw$. Then $F_X = e^x$, $F_{XX} = e^x$, $F_t = 0$, and from Ito's lemma

$$dF = F_X \, dx + \left(F_t + \frac{1}{2}\sigma^2 F_{XX} \right) dt$$

Substituting, we obtain

$$dF = e^x(\alpha + \sigma^2/2) \, dt + e^x \sigma \, dw$$

or

$$\frac{dF}{F} = (\alpha + \sigma^2/2) \, dt + \sigma \, dw$$

We conclude that if x follows a Wiener process with mean α and variance σ^2, then $F = \exp^x$ follows a geometric Wiener process with drift $\mu = \alpha + \sigma^2/2$.

For example, x could represent the continuous (or logarithmic) rate of return. In this case, if it is normal with drift α, then the expected price relative is lognormal with drift term $\alpha + \sigma^2/2$.

EXAMPLE 7A.2 Let $F(x, t) = \ln(x)$, where $dx = \mu x \, dt + \sigma x \, dw$, be a geometric Wiener process. Then $F_X = 1/x$, $F_{XX} = -1/x^2$, $F_t = 0$. Substituting into Ito's lemma yields

$$dF = (\mu - \sigma^2/2) \, dt + \sigma \, dw$$

Thus, $\ln(x)$ follows a Wiener process with drift $\alpha = \mu - \sigma^2/2$ and volatility σ. This example shows that if stock prices follow a geometric Wiener process, then the logarithm of the stock price follows a Wiener process. Notice that the change in the logarithmic price is $\ln\{(x(t)/x(0)\}$. Thus, the logarithmic return over the period $[0, t]$ is normal with mean $\alpha = (\mu - \sigma^2/2)t$ and variance $\sigma^2 t$.

EXAMPLE 7A.3 Let $F(x, t) = e^{-rt}x$ and $dx = \mu x \, dt + \sigma x \, dw$. Then $F_X = e^{-rt}$, $F_{XX} = 0$, $F_t = r \, e^{-rt}x$, and

$$dF = e^{-rt} \, dx - r \, e^{-rt}x \, dt$$

$$dF = e^{-rt}[\mu x \, dt + \sigma x \, dw] - r \, e^{-rt}x \, dt$$

Hence

$$\frac{dF}{F} = (\mu - r) \, dt + \sigma \, dw$$

Generalized Ito's Lemma

Ito's lemma can be generalized to take into account valuation of claims on correlated Ito processes. Below we provide the results for two correlated Ito processes. If $F(x_1, x_2, t)$ is a twice continuously differentiable function of x_1 and x_2 and a once continuously differentiable function of t, then the total differential of F is given by

$$dF = F_1 \, dx_1 + F_2 \, dx_2 + F_t \, dt + \frac{1}{2}[\sigma_1^2 F_{11} \, dt + \sigma_2^2 F_{22} \, dt + 2\rho\sigma_1\sigma_2 F_{12}] \, dt$$

$$F_1 \equiv \frac{\partial F}{\partial x_1}, \qquad F_{11} \equiv \frac{\partial^2 F}{\partial x_1^2}, \qquad F_2 \equiv \frac{\partial F}{\partial x_2},$$

$$F_{22} \equiv \frac{\partial^2 F}{\partial x_2^2}, \quad \text{and} \quad F_{12} \equiv \frac{\partial^2 F}{\partial x_1 \, \partial x_2} \tag{7A.7}$$

$$dx_i = \mu_i(x_i, t) + \sigma_i(x_i, t) \, dw_i \qquad i = 1, 2$$

$$\text{Cov}(dw_1, dw_2) = \rho \, dt$$

EXAMPLE 7A.4 Let $F(x_1, x_2, t) = x_1 x_2 t$ where $dx_1 = \mu_1 \, dt + \sigma_1 \, dw_1$ and $dx_2 = \mu_2 \, dt + \sigma_2 \, dw_2$. Applying equation (7A.7), we obtain

$$dF = tx_2 \, dx_1 + tx_1 \, dx_2 + x_1 x_2 \, dt + \frac{1}{2}(0 + 0 + 2\rho\sigma_1\sigma_2 t)$$

$$= tx_2(\mu_1 \, dt + \sigma_1 \, dw_1) + tx_1(\mu_2 \, dt + \sigma_2 \, dw_2) + \rho\sigma_1\sigma_2 t \, dt$$

$$= (t\mu_1 x_2 + x_1 x_2 + \rho\sigma_1\sigma_2 t + tx_1\mu_2) \, dt + t\sigma_1 x_2 \, dw_1 + t\sigma_2 x_1 \, dw_2$$

EXAMPLE 7A.5 Let $dy/y = \mu \, dt + \sigma \, dw$ and $dx/x = r \, dt$. Now consider the stochastic process describing the variable $F(x, y) = x/y$.

$$F_X = 1/y, \; F_{XX} = 0, \qquad F_{XY} = -1/y^2, \qquad F_Y = -x/y^2, \qquad F_{YY} = 2x/y^3$$

From Ito's rule,

$$dF = F_X \, dx + F_Y \, dy + F_t \, dt + \frac{1}{2}[\sigma_x^2 F_{xx} \, dt + \sigma_y^2 F_{YY} \, dt + 2\rho\sigma_x\sigma_Y F_{xY}] \, dt$$

$$= \frac{1}{y} \, dx - \frac{x}{y^2} \, dy + \frac{1}{2}\sigma^2 y^2 \frac{2x}{y^3} \, dt$$

Hence

$$\frac{dF}{F} = \frac{dx}{x} - \frac{dy}{y} + \sigma^2 \, dt$$

APPENDIX 7B

The Binomial Approximation to the Geometric Wiener Process

If the true stochastic process is a geometric Wiener process, then from equation (7.18), the expected value of the stock price after time Δt is given by $S\,e^{\mu \Delta t}$, while the variance is given by $S^2\,e^{2\mu \Delta t}[e^{\sigma^2 \Delta t} - 1]$. The parameters u, d, and p for the approximating binomial process must be chosen such that the expected value and variance match these two numbers.

For the geometric binomial random walk model, in a period of Δt, the stock price either increases to uS (with probability p) or decreases to dS (with probability $1 - p$). The expected stock price at time Δt is given by

$$puS + (1 - p)\,dS$$

Hence, our first requirement is

$$puS + (1 - p)\,dS = S\,e^{\mu \Delta t} \tag{7B.1}$$

The variance of any random variable X is given by $E(X^2) - [E(X)]^2$. Hence, the variance of the approximating binomial stock price at time t is given by

$$[pu^2 S^2 + (1 - p)\,d^2 S^2] - [puS + (1 - p)\,dS]^2$$

Our second constraint is

$$[pu^2 S^2 + (1 - p)\,d^2 S^2] - [puS + (1 - p)\,dS]^2 = S^2\,e^{2\mu \Delta t}(e^{\sigma^2 \Delta t} - 1) \tag{7B.2}$$

As a final constraint, we add the condition that in each time increment Δt, the downmove value, d, is given by

$$d = 1/u \tag{7B.3}$$

Given equations (7B.1), (7B.2), and (7B.3), a unique solution exists for u, d, and p. Rather than solve these equations, note that if the time increment Δt is very small, the variance of the stock price return $\Delta s/s$ is approximately $\sigma^2\,\Delta t$.[1] That is, for a small time increment Δt,

---

[1] To see why this is true, expand the exponential terms. It is well known that $\exp^x$ can be written as $e^x = 1 + x + x^2/2 + x^3/6 + \dots$. Hence, $e^{\sigma^2 \Delta t} = 1 + \sigma^2\,\Delta t + o(\Delta t)$, and $e^{2\mu \Delta t} = 1 + 2\mu\,\Delta t + o(\Delta t)$. Substituting these expressions into the variance expression yields $S^2[1 + 2\mu\,\Delta t + o(\Delta t)][\sigma^2\,\Delta t + o(\Delta t)] = S^2\sigma^2\,\Delta t + o(\Delta t)$. **177**

$$S^2 \, e^{2\mu \Delta t}(e^{\sigma^2 \Delta t} - 1) \approx S^2 \sigma^2 \, \Delta t$$

The constraints for u, d, and p can then be written as

$$pu + (1 - p)d = e^{\mu \Delta t}$$
$$pu^2 + (1 - p)d^2 - e^{2\mu \Delta t} = \sigma^2 \, \Delta t$$

and

$$d = 1/u$$

The solutions to these equations are given by

$$p = \frac{e^{\mu \Delta t} - d}{u - d}$$

$$u = e^{\sigma \sqrt{\Delta t}}$$

$$d = e^{-\sigma \sqrt{\Delta t}}$$

It can be shown that with the partition suitably small, not only are the means and variances of the discrete geometric binomial process equal to the means and variances of the geometric Wiener stock price process, but the actual distribution of the stock price at time T is indistinguishable from a lognormal distribution.

CHAPTER 8

The Binomial Option Pricing Model

In Chapter 6 we considered simple trading strategies where the payouts of one security were exactly matched by the payouts of a portfolio containing other securities. For example, the cash flows of a European put option can be duplicated by a portfolio containing a European call option, pure discount bonds, and a short position in the stock (Property 6.9). The strategy of replicating the payouts of the put is static since there is no need to rebalance or readjust the replicating portfolio prior to expiration.

In some circumstances, to ensure that the portfolio duplicates the cash flows of a particular option, it is necessary to make periodic adjustments. A **dynamic replicating strategy** is set in place to produce cash flows identical to those of a particular "targeted" security. If trading opportunities are restricted to discrete time points, then the trading strategy is said to be a **discrete time trading strategy.** For example, trading can be restricted to one time each day. In contrast, a **continuous trading strategy** allows continual trading in markets. In this chapter we shall investigate specific trading strategies involving stocks and bonds that replicate the payout of an option.

The primary objectives of this chapter are the following:

- To investigate specific dynamic trading strategies that produce payouts equivalent to those of an option;
- To describe the binomial option pricing model; and
- To introduce the Black-Scholes pricing model.

Dynamic Self-Financing Trading Strategies

The trading strategies we shall consider have two major restrictions. First, the strategy can use only information available at the current time. Second, the trading strategy must be **self-financing.** That is, the only adjustments that can be made to the composition of a portfolio are those that leave its total value unchanged. For example, if additional shares are to be purchased, the funds for these shares must be obtained by borrowing. Similarly, if shares are sold, then the funds either must be used to reduce outstanding loans or must be invested at the riskless rate. No external funds can be injected into the trading strategy, nor can funds be removed from the trading strategy over the time period.

One goal of this chapter is to identify a trading strategy involving stocks and bonds that produces the same cash flows as a European call option. If this can be accomplished, then by the law of one price, the cost of the option should equal the initial cost of the particular portfolio that duplicates the option's payouts, when the self-financing strategy is followed.

The trading strategy that we adopt will depend on how the underlying stock price moves through time. To simplify the analysis, we first assume that the time interval to expiration of the option, $[0, T]$ say, is partitioned into n equal time increments and that the movement of the stock price over these time increments can be represented by a binomial lattice. Each of the n time points represents a trading opportunity, where portfolios can be readjusted. From Chapter 7 we know that as the partition of the interval $[0, T]$ becomes finer, then, by suitably controlling the binomial up and down parameters, u and d, as well as the probability, p, of the upjumps, the distribution of the stock prices over any finite interval becomes indistinguishable from a geometric Wiener process. Thus, as the partition becomes finer, more realism is brought to bear on the problem.

With stock prices and trading opportunities restricted to points on a binomial lattice, we can establish an arbitrage-free price for an option. The **binomial option pricing model,** which accomplishes this, is the main topic of this chapter. As the partition of the binomial process that approximates the underlying geometric Wiener stock process becomes finer and finer, the option prices produced by the binomial option pricing model begin to converge. The limiting price obtained when trading opportunities are continuous is the Black-Scholes price, named after Professors Fisher Black and Myron Scholes. The Black-Scholes price is the benchmark used in most theoretical and practical studies in stock option markets and is investigated here and in Chapter 9.

The binomial option pricing model yields a fair price, one that precludes riskless arbitrage opportunities. In other words, if the option traded at any other price, then trading strategies could be constructed that would result in riskless arbitrage—free profits. The models presented in this chapter not only produce these fair prices, but as a side product, they also provide the relevant dynamic trading strategies that exploit any mispricings. If the assumptions of the model are correct, and if the market is efficient, then observed option prices must equal their computed fair values.

Background to Binomial Option Pricing

The first two examples highlight the key concepts used in this chapter.

EXAMPLE 8.1 Consider a stock currently priced at $100 and assume that there is one period to go to expiration. Assume that in this period the stock can either rise to 120 or fall to 80. A call option with strike 100 is available. Money can be borrowed or lent at 10

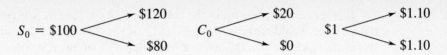

$S_0 = \$100$ $\nearrow \$120$ $\searrow \$80$ C_0 $\nearrow \$20$ $\searrow \$0$ $\$1$ $\nearrow \$1.10$ $\searrow \$1.10$

EXHIBIT 8.1   Valuation of a Call Option

percent and the stock and call can be bought or sold at the given prices. Exhibit 8.1 illustrates the information (C_0 is the call price). With this information, what is the value of the call? To answer this question we could follow the usual valuation procedure. Specifically, first compute the expected cash flows associated with the investment. Second, discount these cash flows at the appropriate risk-adjusted rate. At first glance this valuation problem appears difficult to address because we are not given the probability, p, of the stock price moving up and hence cannot compute the expected cash flow. In addition, the appropriate discount rate is not given. To establish this rate, we need to understand more about the preferences of investors in the economy, or at least to have some notion of how adding a call option to a well-diversified portfolio affects its overall risk.

We now present a somewhat surprising result. The value of the call in Exhibit 8.1 can be computed without explicitly knowing p, and without explicitly knowing the true discount rate for investments of equivalent risk to the option. Indeed, given the information above, the fair price of the option must be $13.64. If the market sets the price of the call option at any other value, a riskless arbitrage opportunity exists.

To see why the call option has to be priced at $13.64, consider a portfolio containing one stock and a short position in two calls. The initial value of this position, V_0, is

$$V_0 = \$100 - 2C_0$$

If the stock price rises, the portfolio value, V_1, will be given by

$$V_1 = \$120 - 2(\$20) = \$80$$

and if the stock price falls, the portfolio value will be given by

$$V_1 = \$80 - 2(\$0) = 80$$

Hence, regardless of what occurs in the future, the terminal value of this portfolio is $80.

Now consider placing $72.73 into the riskless asset (bank). At the end of the period, this wealth would have grown to $72.73(1.10) = \$80$.

We thus have two riskless alternatives. Either we can buy one stock and sell two calls, or we can put $72.73 in the bank. To avoid riskless arbitrage opportunities, the current values of these portfolios must be equal. Hence, $V_0 = \$100 - 2C_0 = \$72.73$, or $C_0 = \$13.64$.

If, for example, the cost of the call were $12.64, then by selling the portfolio, the investor would receive $100 − 2($12.64) = $74.73. By investing $72.73 of this in the riskless asset, the investor would have $2 left over. At the expiration date the value of the riskless asset would be $72.73(1.10) = $80, and the value of the portfolio would also be $80. Thus, regardless of what occurred in the future, the $80 received from the riskless asset would always be sufficiently large to cover the value of the portfolio. Hence, regardless of what occurred, the investor would make $2 without requiring any initial investment.

Since many arbitragers would attempt this strategy, the price of the option would soon rise to $13.64. With the option at this value, no free lunch would exist.

EXAMPLE 8.2   **Illustration of a Self-Financing Dynamic Trading Strategy**

Assume that securities A and B have price paths over time as shown below.

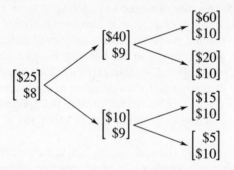

In the first period, A can increase from $25 to $40 or decline to $10. Given an upmove in the first period, A can move to $60 or $20 in the second period. Given a downmove in the first period, A can move from $10 to either $15 or $5. In contrast, B increases by $1 in each period regardless of state.

Now suppose that a third security, C, offers guaranteed payouts in the second period, depending on which state occurs. Specifically, the security offers $10 in the lowest state, $20 in the second state, $30 in the third, and $40 in the highest state.

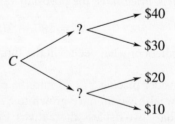

The question is, how can we establish a fair value for C?

We shall construct a **self-financing dynamic trading strategy** involving A and B that duplicates the cash flows of C. Then, to prevent riskless arbitrage, the price of C must equal the price of the dynamic trading strategy. Let $N_A(t)$ and $N_B(t)$ be the number of shares of A and B purchased by the strategy in each period t, where $t = 0, 1, 2$. Exhibit 8.2 shows the acutal dynamic trading strategy to be followed. The way in which these numbers are computed will be discussed later. For the moment, let us investigate how the strategy works.

At time 0, the cost of establishing this portfolio, $V(0)$ say, is given by

$$V(0) = N_A(0)\, S_A(0) + N_B(0)\, S_B(0)$$

$$= 0.6(\$25) + 0.9444(\$8) = \$22.56$$

Assume that an upmove occurs. Then the portfolio value appreciates to

$$V(1) = 0.6(\$40) + 0.9444(\$9) = \$32.50$$

At this point the strategy requires 0.25 shares of A and 2.5 shares of B. The cost of this portfolio is

$$0.25(\$40) + 2.5(\$9) = \$32.50$$

According to our self-financing restriction, the necessary portfolio adjustments can be made. Specifically, additional shares of B can be purchased, the funds coming from the sale of shares of A.

Note that if a downmove had occurred, the value of the original portfolio would be

$$V(1) = 0.6(\$10) + 0.9444(\$9) = \$14.50$$

The new portfolio at this vertex consists of 1 share of A and 0.5 shares of B. This new portfolio cost is

$$1(\$10) + 0.5(\$9) = \$14.50$$

Thus, the additional 0.4 shares of A that are required can be purchased using funds obtained by reducing the holdings in B from 0.9444 to 0.5.

We now turn our attention to the terminal payouts in the second period. Given an initial upmove in the first period, the payout is

$$0.25(\$60) + 2.5(\$10) = \$40 \text{ for an upmove}$$

or

$$0.25(\$20) + 2.5(\$10) = \$30 \text{ for a downmove}$$

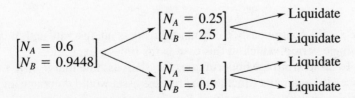

EXHIBIT 8.2   The Dynamic Trading Strategy

Similarly, given an initial downmove, the terminal payouts are either

$$(\$15) + 0.5(\$10) = \$20 \text{ for an upmove}$$

or

$$1(\$5) + 0.5(\$10) = \$10 \text{ for a downmove}$$

The above self-financing dynamic trading strategy replicates the payouts of C. The current value of the trading strategy is \$22.56. Hence, to avoid riskless arbitrage the value of C should also be \$22.56.

Both examples required the construction of a particular dynamic trading strategy that replicated the payouts of the underlying security. Next we examine how these trading strategies are actually established.

The Single-Period Binomial Model

Consider a stock currently priced at S_0. We assume that at the end of the period, which coincides with the expiration date, the stock price, $\tilde{S}_1$, can either increase to s_{11} or decrease to s_{10}. The price movements can be represented as follows:

$$S_0 \begin{array}{c} \nearrow S_{11} = uS_0 \\ \searrow S_{10} = dS_0 \end{array}$$

where $u > d$.

The current value of a call option with strike X is C_0. At expiration the call value, $\tilde{C}_1$, will be c_{11} or c_{10}, where

$$c_{11} = \text{Max}(s_{11} - X, 0)$$
$$c_{10} = \text{Max}(s_{10} - X, 0)$$

$$C_0 \begin{array}{c} \nearrow C_{11} \\ \searrow C_{10} \end{array}$$

In addition, we assume that a riskless investment of \$1 grows to \$$R$ at the end of the period, where

$$R = e^{r\Delta t}$$

Here r is the continuously compounded riskless interest rate and Δt is the length of the single period, which in this case is the time to expiration.

To avoid arbitrage opportunities, we shall assume that $d < R < u$. Clearly, if R exceeded u, an investment in the riskless asset would dominate an investment in the risky security. Conversely, if R were lower than d, no investor would purchase the riskless asset.

Replicating the Payoffs of a Call Option

Consider a portfolio containing H shares of stock that are partially financed by borrowing B dollars at the riskless rate. The current value of the portfolio, V_0, is

$$V_0 = HS_0 - B$$

At the expiration date the portfolio can take on the following values:

$$V_0 \begin{cases} V_{11} = Hs_{11} - RB \\ V_{10} = Hs_{10} - RB \end{cases}$$

We select the number of shares H and dollars borrowed B such that the terminal values V_{11} and V_{10} are exactly equal to the call values c_{11} and c_{10}. That is, we require

$$Hs_{11} - RB = c_{11}$$

$$Hs_{10} - RB = c_{10}$$

Since there are two equations and two unknowns, a unique solution for H and B can be obtained:

$$H^* = \frac{(c_{11} - c_{10})}{(s_{11} - s_{10})}$$

and

$$B^* = \frac{(c_{11}s_{10} - c_{10}s_{11})}{(s_{11} - s_{10})R}$$

A portfolio containing H^* shares partially financed by borrowing B^* dollars produces the same payoffs as the call option at the expiration. Hence, to avoid riskless arbitrage opportunities, the initial portfolio value must be equal to the price of the call. That is,

$$C^* = H^*S_0 - B^* \tag{8.1}$$

EXAMPLE 8.3   Assume that a stock is currently valued at $50. A one-period call option with strike price 50 is to be valued. The stock can either increase 10 percent to $55 or decrease 10 percent to $45. The riskless rate is 4.875 percent. The stock prices can be represented by

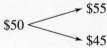

The call prices are

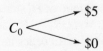

and the borrowed funds B grow to $B\,e^r = B\,e^{0.04875} = 1.05B$.

$$B \begin{cases} \nearrow 1.05B \\ \searrow 1.05B \end{cases}$$

From the information, we have $u = 1.1$, $d = 0.9$, and $R = 1.05$; and $S_{11} = \$55$, $S_{10} = \$45$, $C_{11} = \$5$, and $C_{10} = \$0$. Hence,

$$H^* = \frac{(5 - 0)}{(55 - 45)} = 0.5$$

and

$$B^* = \frac{5(\$45) - 0(\$55)}{1.05(\$55 - \$45)} = \$21.43$$

A portfolio containing 0.5 shares held long, partially financed by borrowing $21.40, is the replicating portfolio. Its current value, V_0, is

$$V_0 = H^*S_0 - B^* = \$3.57$$

After one period this portfolio will either increase to V_{11} or decrease to V_{10}:

$$V_{11} = H^*s_{11} - RB^* = \$5$$
$$V_{10} = H^*s_{10} - RB^* = \$0$$

To avoid riskless arbitrage opportunities between the call and the replicating portfolio, it must follow that

$$C_0^* = H^*S_0 - B^* = \$3.57$$

Assume the actual market price of the call option is $2.57. An astute investor will buy the call and sell the replicating portfolio. The net income from this transaction is $1. At expiration, gains (losses) in the replicating portfolio will be exactly offset by losses (gains) in the call, the investor will have earned $1 with no risk and no initial investment.

One-Period Model for Put Options

The same procedure can be used for put options. Let P_0 be the price of the put option with strike X, and let p_{11} and p_{10} represent the terminal prices.

$$P_0 \begin{cases} \nearrow P_{11} = \text{Max}(X - s_{11}, 0) \\ \searrow P_{10} = \text{Max}(X - s_{10}, 0) \end{cases}$$

Consider a portfolio of H_p shares and B_p dollars borrowed. Let V_0 be the current value, that is, $V_0 = H_p S_0 - B_p$, and let V_{11} and V_{10} be the two possible terminal values of the portfolio. In order for the portfolio to replicate the payoffs of the put, we must have

$$H_p^* = \frac{(P_{11} - P_{10})}{(s_{11} - s_{10})}$$

and

$$B_p^* = \frac{(P_{11}s_{10} - P_{10}s_{11})}{(s_{11} - s_{10})R}$$

To avoid riskless arbitrage opportunities, it must follow that

$$P_0 = H_p^* S_0 - B_p^* \tag{8.2}$$

EXAMPLE 8.4   As in Example 8.3, $S_0 = \$50$, $u = 1.1$, $d = 0.9$, and $R = 1.05$. Assume that a put option is traded with strike $X = \$50$. We can price the put as follows:

$$P_0 \left\langle \begin{array}{l} \nearrow P_{11} = \$0 \\ \searrow P_{10} = \$5 \end{array} \right.$$

and

$$H_p^* = \frac{(0 - 5)}{(55 - 45)} = -0.5$$

So

$$B_p^* = \frac{0(\$45) - 5(\$55)}{(\$55 - \$45)1.05} = -\$26.19$$

That is, the put option can be replicated by selling 0.5 shares and lending $26.20. Hence,

$$P_0 = H_p^* S_0 - B_p^* = -0.5(\$50) + \$26.19 = \$1.19$$

The put price could have been derived using the put-call parity relationship instead. That is,

$$P_0 = X e^{-rT} + C_0 - S_0$$

where $X e^{-rT}$ is the present value of the strike over the period to the expiration date. In our example $T = \$1$ and the discount factor is $1/1.05$. Hence, we have

$$P_0 = \frac{\$50}{1.05} + \$3.57 - \$50 = \$1.19$$

But this value is precisely what we had before.

Properties of Binomial Option Prices

1.   The fair price of a call option does not depend on investor preferences. The price is obtained by simply recognizing that if the call were not priced at this value, riskless arbitrage profits could be obtained. These profits would soon disappear

because astute investors would continue to exploit these opportunities until the set of prices adjusted. Since this price is the correct price in all types of economies, it must also hold true in particular economies. For example, the same price must exist in economies consisting solely of risk-averse, risk-seeking, or risk-neutral investors.

2.   The fair price does not depend on the probability of an upward or downward movement. (In Example 8.3, the fair value of the call is $3.60, regardless of whether the probability of an upmove is 0.95 or 0.05.)

3.   In view of the fact that probabilities appear unimportant, it must follow that expectations do not enter the analysis. In Example 8.3, the fair value of a call is $3.60, regardless of whether the expectation is high or low. However, variances cannot be ignored. The variance is a measure of spread, and this was clearly an important consideration. As u and d change, the call price changes.

4.   The call pricing equation, $C_0 = H^*S_0 - B^*$, can be simplified further. By substituting the values of H^* and B^* into the equation, we obtain

$$C_0 = \left[\frac{(c_{11} - c_{10})}{(s_{11} - s_{10})} \right] S_0 - \left[\frac{(c_{11}s_{10} - c_{10}s_{11})}{R(s_{11} - s_{10})} \right]$$

By rearranging the terms, we can express C_0 in terms of its future values c_{11} and c_{10}. That is,

$$C_0 = \left[\frac{RS_0 - s_{10}}{R(s_{11} - s_{10})} \right] c_{11} - \left[\frac{(s_{11} - RS_0)}{R(s_{11} - s_{10})} \right] c_{10}$$

Finally, we substitute $s_{10} = dS_0$ and $s_{11} = uS_0$ into the expression to obtain

$$C_0 = \frac{\left[\dfrac{(R - d)}{(u - d)} \right] c_{11} + \left[\dfrac{(u - R)}{(u - d)} \right] c_{10}}{R}$$

or

$$C_0 = \frac{[\theta c_{11} + (1 - \theta)c_{10}]}{R} \tag{8.3}$$

where

$$\theta = \frac{(R - d)}{(u - d)} \tag{8.4}$$

Thus, the call price can be viewed as the expected terminal value of the terminal call price, discounted at the riskless rate of return, where the probability of an upmove is given by θ. An interpretation of θ is provided in the next section.

5.   The value of a call depends solely on u, d, R, X, and S_0. No assumptions are made about the stock price behavior relative to other security prices, nor are any security equilibrium conditions imposed. Thus, market factors such as covariance terms and beta values are not relevant.

Call Prices in a Risk-Neutral Economy

In a risk-neutral economy, decision makers base their decisions solely on expectations without regard to the shape of the probability distribution of outcomes. Measures of uncertainty, captured by the standard deviation (or volatility), and the nature of higher moments do not influence decisions. As a result, investors are indifferent between a gamble G that has an expected return $E(G)$ and a certain riskless return that guarantees a payout of $E(G)$. Since investors are not compensated according to the size of risk, the prices of all securities will be set to yield the same riskless rate. That is,

$$B_1 = RB_0 \tag{8.5}$$

$$E(S_1) = RS_0 \tag{8.6}$$

$$E(C_1) = RC_0 \tag{8.7}$$

Now, in this economy, the expected stock and call prices on the binomial lattice are

$$E(S_1) = ps_{11} + (1 - p)s_{10} \tag{8.8}$$

$$E(C_1) = pc_{11} + (1 - p)c_{10} \tag{8.9}$$

where p is the probability of the stock price moving up. Hence, from equations (8.6) and (8.8),

$$RS_0 = ps_{11} + (1 - p)s_{10} \tag{8.10}$$

or, equivalently,

$$RS_0 = puS_0 + (1 - p)\, dS_0 \tag{8.11}$$

Solving the expression for p, we obtain

$$p = \frac{(R - d)}{(u - d)} = \theta \tag{8.12}$$

Furthermore, from equations (8.7) and (8.9),

$$RC_0 = pc_{11} + (1 - p)c_{10}$$

and hence

$$C_0 = \frac{[\theta c_{11} + (1 - \theta)c_{10}]}{R} \tag{8.13}$$

But this is the general call pricing equation we obtained in equation (8.3). This equation states that the call price can be computed as the expected terminal payout discounted at the risk-free rate, where the probability of an upmove is the risk-neutral probability, θ. That is,

$$C_0 = E_0(C_1)/R \tag{8.14}$$

This result implies that the call can be priced as if it were trading in a risk-neutral economy. The result motivates the following general risk-neutral valuation argument for establishing call prices: If somehow we knew that the fair value did not depend on preferences, then, to value an option we could assume a risk-neutral economy, derive the equilibrium call price in this economy (by simply computing the present value of the expected terminal call price, and discounting at the riskless rate). The resulting call price obtained in this economy is also the fair value for our risk-averse economy.

More on Risk-Neutral Valuation

To value a risky claim, normally we perform a present value calculation involving two steps. First, we replace uncertain future cash flows by their expected values and treat them as given. Second, we discount these future expected values, typically at some constant rate that reflects the nondiversifiable risk.

In contrast, we can establish the value of an option on a binomial lattice by readjusting the probability distribution to reallocate risk, allowing the appropriate discount rate to be the riskless rate. The redistribution of probability mass, in this case, involves replacing the true probability of an upmove by the risk-neutral probability θ. This redistribution of probability, together with the use of the riskless discount rate, results in the option price being set at its fair value, the fair value representing the price at which investors would be prepared to pay for bearing equivalent risks. This process is referred to as **risk-neutral valuation.** The name is a bit misleading since the prices obtained are fair prices in a risk-averse economy. They are not prices which would exist only if investors were neutral to risk. The risk-neutral valuation equation can be used only if we can establish an appropriate mechanism for redistributing the probability distribution. Such a redistribution can always be obtained if a self-financing dynamic trading strategy can be constructed to replicate the payouts of the call.

The Risk-Free Hedge

Since $C_0 = H^*S_0 - B^*$, it follows that the amount borrowed, B^*, is $H^*S_0 - C$. Equivalently, a long position of H^* shares of stock and a short position in the call must produce a return equivalent to that of an investment in the riskless asset. Consider the problem in Example 8.3 again. We shall construct a portfolio containing a long position of 0.5 shares (H^* shares) and a short position of 1 call option. The current value of this portfolio is

$$V_0 = 0.5S_0 - C_0 = \$21.43$$

The terminal value of this portfolio is either V_{11} or V_{10}, where

$$V_{11} = 0.5s_{11} - c_{11} = 0.5(\$55) - \$5 = \$22.50$$

or

$$V_{10} = 0.5s_{10} - c_{10} = 0.5(\$45) - \$10 = \$22.50$$

Hence, regardless of what stock price occurs in the future, the portfolio value is known ($22.50). If the initial investment ($21.43) were placed in the riskless asset, the terminal value would be

$$B_1 = RB = (1.05)(\$21.43) = \$22.50$$

Thus, a bond may be replicated by buying H^* shares and selling 1 call. The ratio of shares bought per call sold, H^*, is often called the **hedge ratio.**

The Two-Period Binomial Model

We now extend the one-period model to a two-period model where an opportunity exists to revise the position at the beginning of each period. The stock price movements are represented as follows:

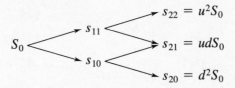

As before, we assume that in each period the stock price rises by factor u or decreases by factor d. We now consider the pricing of a call contract with two periods to go prior to expiration. The call price movements can be represented as follows:

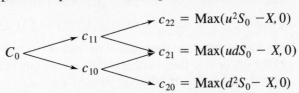

With one period to go to expiration, the stock price is either at s_{11} or s_{10} (node 1, 1 or 1, 0). If the stock price is at s_{11}, then, faced with a one-period problem, we can obtain the theoretical fair call value c_{11}. Similarly, if the stock price is at s_{10}, we can obtain the theoretical call value c_{10}.

EXAMPLE 8.5   Consider a stock currently priced at $45.45. Assume that in each period the stock can appreciate or depreciate by 10 percent. As before, assume $R = 1.05$ per period and consider a call option with strike $X = \$40$. Then $u = 1.1$, $d = 0.9$, and the stock prices can be represented as follows:

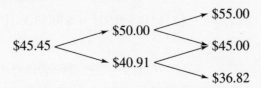

1. Assume that the stock price goes to $50. Then in the last period we have

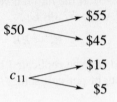

In this case, $H^* = (15 - 5)/(55 - 45) = 1$, $B^* = 15(\$45) - 5(\$55)/[\$10(1.05)] = \$38.10$, and $c_{11}^* = H^* s_{11} - B^* = 1(\$50) - \$38.10 = \$11.90$. Thus, at the beginning of the first period, if the stock price is $50 and the call price is not $11.90, riskless arbitrage opportunities exist.

2. Assume that the stock price in the first period is $40.91.

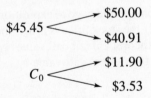

Now	$H^* = (5 - 0)/(45 - 36.82) = 0.61$
and	$B^* = (\$36.81)(5)/(\$8.18)(1.05) = \$21.43$
Thus	$c_{10}^* = (0.61)(\$40.91) - \$21.43 = \$3.53$

If we knew with certainty that at the end of the first period the call price would be either c_{11}^* or c_{10}^*, then to obtain the current fair value we could reapply the one-period model. Specifically, we would have

$$
\$45.45 \nearrow \begin{array}{l} \$50.00 \\ \$40.91 \end{array}
$$

$$
C_0 \nearrow \begin{array}{l} \$11.90 \\ \$3.53 \end{array}
$$

Hence, the replicating portfolio consists of

$$H^* = (11.90 - 3.53)/(50 - 40.91) = 0.92$$

and

$$B^* = [\$11.90(\$40.91) - \$50(\$3.53)]/[\$9.09(\$1.05)] = \$32.51$$

and hence

$$C_0^* = H^* S_0 - B^* = (\$0.92)(\$45.45) - \$32.51 = \$9.30$$

Exhibit 8.3 summarizes all the calculations.

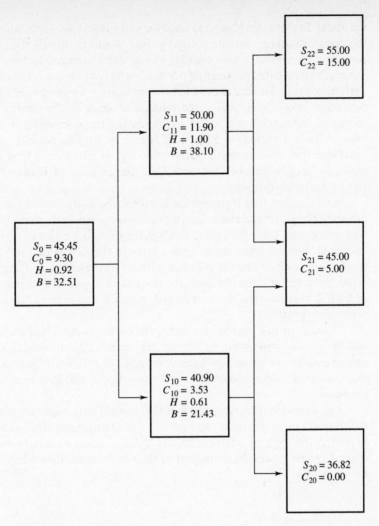

$S_{22} = 55.00$
$C_{22} = 15.00$

$S_{11} = 50.00$
$C_{11} = 11.90$
$H = 1.00$
$B = 38.10$

$S_0 = 45.45$
$C_0 = 9.30$
$H = 0.92$
$B = 32.51$

$S_{21} = 45.00$
$C_{21} = 5.00$

$S_{10} = 40.90$
$C_{10} = 3.53$
$H = 0.61$
$B = 21.43$

$S_{20} = 36.82$
$C_{20} = 0.00$

EXHIBIT 8.3   Summary Calculations for the Two-Period Binomial Option Model

Assume that the market price of the call option is $10.30. According to our analysis, the option is overpriced by $1. The arbitrager will sell the call and purchase the replicating portfolio. Specifically, the arbitrager will sell one call option and borrow $32.51 to raise a total of $42.81. Then the arbitrager will purchase 0.92 shares of the stock for $41.81. The remaining $1 could be put in the bank. Regardless of what occurs in the future, this position will not lose money and could make additional profits. To see this, assume that the stock price rises to $50. In this case, the replicating portfolio increases in value to $11.90. If the call price equals its theoretical value of $11.90, the portfolio can be sold and the proceeds used to cover the call. If the call value is less than $11.90, then additional profits can be made by liquidating the entire position. However, by the same logic, if the call price exceeds the value of the replicating portfolio, liquidation could result in net losses. In this case, however, since the call value is above its fair value of $11.90, the optimal strategy for the second period would be to sell the call and buy the replicating portfolio, which consists of one share financed by borrowing $38. The value of this required replicating portfolio is $11.90, which is the exact value of the current position. Hence, to establish the replication we need only adjust the portfolio composition. Specifically, the amount of stock in the replicating portfolio is increased from 0.92 to 1 share by increasing the borrowing from $32.30 (plus interest for one period) to $38.10 (plus interest for one period).

Once this is accomplished, the arbitrager is guaranteed that at expiration no losses (or profits) will be obtained. Thus, the original $1 is obtained without any risk or initial investment.

We have seen that if the option is overpriced at the end of the first period, the arbitrager must extend the strategy to the expiration date, when the option prices will come into line. However, this strategy could be thwarted if the option is exercised. For example, if the option price in the first period is $12.90, the arbitrager cannot close out the position without loss. However, if the option is exercised, the investor must purchase the stock for $50 and deliver it at the strike price of $40. In this case the net cost is $10, which is less than the $11.90 value of the replicating portfolio.

Thus, if for one reason or another the option is exercised early, the arbitrager will benefit and will obtain additional riskless arbitrage profits. Of course, with the option trading at a value above the strike price of $10, early exercise is not optimal, and the investor who tendered the exercise notice would have been better off selling the option.

This example illustrates the fact that even if call prices do not adjust to their theoretical fair values until expiration, a self-financing strategy can still be devised to protect the original arbitrage profits. If other investors behave irrationally or the market option prices do not adjust to their fair values, then additional profits can be generated.

Rewriting the Two-Period Option Pricing Model

We have seen that the call price, C_0, can be written as

$$C_0 = \frac{[\theta c_{11} + (1 - \theta)c_{10}]}{R}$$

where $\theta = (R - d)/(u - d)$, and $R = e^{r\Delta t}$.

Moreover, $$c_{11} = \frac{[\theta c_{22} + (1 - \theta)c_{21}]}{R}$$

and

$$c_{10} = \frac{[\theta c_{21} + (1 - \theta)c_{20}]}{R}$$

Substituting c_{11} and c_{10} into the expression for C_0, we obtain

$$C_0 = \frac{[\theta^2 c_{22} + 2\theta(1 - \theta)c_{21} + (1 - \theta)^2 c_{20}]}{R^2}$$

which can be rewritten as

$$C_0 = \left[\sum_{j=0}^{2} \binom{2}{j} c_{2j} p_{2j}\right] \Big/ R^2 \tag{8.15}$$

where $\quad p_{2j} = P(S_2 = s_{2j}) = \binom{2}{j}\theta^2(1 - \theta)^{2-j} \quad$ for $j = 0, 1, 2$
and

$$c_{2j} = \text{Max}(S_0 u^j d^{2-j} - X, 0) \quad \text{for } j = 0, 1, 2$$

Equation (8.15) states the call price can be derived as the present value of the expected terminal value of the option in a risk-neutral economy. That is,

$$C_0 = E_0(C_2)/R^2 \tag{8.16}$$

The *n*-Period Binomial Option Pricing Model

The two-period model generalizes to n periods. Assume that the time to expiration is broken down into n periods, each of width Δt.

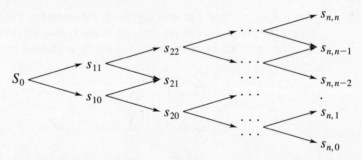

After n periods the stock price, S_n, takes on one of the values $s_{n,j}$ for $j = 0, 1, 2, \ldots, n$. The index j refers to the number of upward price movements that have occurred over the previous n periods. Since in each period the stock price increases by factor u or decreases by factor d, we have

$$s_{nj} = u^j d^{n-j} S_0 \tag{8.17}$$

and

$$p_{nj} = P(S_n = s_{nj}) = \binom{n}{j}\theta^j(1 - \theta)^{n-j} \quad \text{for } j = 0, 1, 2, \ldots, n$$

where $\theta = (R - d)/(u - d)$ and $R = e^{r\Delta r}$.

The value of the call for each state is known at expiration. That is,

$$c_{nj} = \text{Max}(s_{nj} - X, 0)$$
$$= \text{Max}(u^j d^{n-j} S_0 - X, 0) \tag{8.18}$$

Let k be the minimum number of upward stock price movements necessary for the option to terminate in the money. Then the probability that the call expires in the money is

$$P(S_n > X) = \sum_{j=k}^{n} \binom{n}{j}\theta^j(1 - \theta)^{n-j}$$

and

$$c_{nj} = 0 \qquad \text{for } j = 0, 1, 2, \ldots, k - 1$$

$$c_{nj} = s_{nj} - X \quad \text{for } j = k, k + 1, \ldots, n$$

Given the terminal option values, the fair values in period $(n - 1)$ can be computed. Specifically, we have

$$C_{n-1, j} = [\theta c_{n, j+1} + (1 - \theta)c_{n, j}]/R \quad \text{for } j = 0, 1, 2, \ldots, n - 1$$

This process can be repeated recursively throughout the lattice until the fair value C_0 is obtained.

As with the two-period model, the n-period call option price can be written as the present value of the terminal payout, assuming a risk-neutral economy. Thus,

$$C_0 = \frac{E_0(C_n)}{R^n} \tag{8.19}$$

where $R = e^{r\Delta t}$ and the expectation is taken under the assumption that in each period the probability of an upmove is the risk-neutral probability θ.

The expected price of the call is easily evaluated as

$$E(C_n) = \sum_{j=0}^{n} c_{nj} p_{nj}$$

$$= \sum_{j=0}^{k-1} c_{nj} p_{nj} + \sum_{j=k}^{n} c_{nj} p_{nj}$$

$$= 0 + \sum_{j=k}^{n} (s_{nj} - X) p_{nj}$$

$$= \sum_{j=k}^{n} \binom{n}{j}\theta^j(1 - \theta)^{n-j} u^j d^{n-j} S_0 - X \sum_{j=k}^{n} \binom{n}{j}\theta^j(1 - \theta)^{n-j}$$

Finally, using equation (8.19) and rewriting the above equation, we obtain

$$C_0 = H^*S_0 - B^* \tag{8.20}$$

where

$$H^* = \sum_{j=k}^{n} \binom{n}{j}(u\theta)^j(d(1 - \theta))^{n-j}/R^n \tag{8.21}$$

$$B^* = X \sum_{j=k}^{n} \binom{n}{j}\theta^j(1 - \theta)^{n-j}/R^n \tag{8.22}$$

and

$$\theta = (R - d)/(u - d)$$

This is the **n-period binomial option pricing equation.**

Selecting the Up and Down Parameters for the Binomial Lattice

In Chapter 7 we saw that by suitably selecting the up and down parameters, as well as the probability of an upmove, p, the binomial process could be made to converge onto a geometric Wiener process.[1] Specifically, if the true underlying process is

$$dS/S = \mu \, dt + \sigma \, dw(t)$$

then the binomial approximating process is obtained by choosing the up, down, and probability values as

$$u = e^{\sigma\sqrt{\Delta t}} \tag{8.23}$$

$$d = e^{-\sigma\sqrt{\Delta t}} \tag{8.24}$$

$$p = (e^{\mu \Delta t} - d)/(u - d) \tag{8.25}$$

In the binomial model we shall select the u and d values as in equations (8.23) and (8.24). The probability of an upmove is given by

$$\theta = (R - d)/(u - d)$$

where R is the one-period rate given by $R = e^{\Delta t}$. Given that the probability of an upmove is θ rather than p, we see that the process on the lattice converges to a geometric Wiener process of the form

$$dS/S = r \, dt + \sigma \, dw(t) \tag{8.26}$$

This is called the **risk-neutralized stochastic process.** For option valuation purposes we pretend that the underlying stock has an instantaneous mean equal to the risk-free rate r rather than μ. Equation (8.26) implies that at time T, the risk-neutralized stock price has a lognormal distribution with mean $S(0)e^{rT}$. That is, the stock is expected to grow at the same rate as a riskless investment. The value of a European option computed on the lattice, C_0 say, is just the expected terminal value of the option, computed under this risk-neutralized process, discounted at the riskless rate of return.

EXAMPLE 8.6   Pricing a Call Option Using a Four-Period Binomial Approximation

Consider a one-year at-the-money American call option on a nondividend-paying stock. The stock price is $100, the risk-free rate is 10 percent, and the annual volatility is 39.72 percent. Using four partitions, $n = 4$, and $T = 1$ yields

---

[1] Readers who skipped Chapter 7 need to know that when we select u, d, and p as indicated and use a fine partition (i.e., Δt is "small"), the distribution of the logarithm of returns should be very close to normal. Moreover, this approximation improves as Δt gets smaller. Empirical evidence suggests that the logarithm of daily or weekly returns for common stocks can be well approximated by a normal distribution. Hence, choosing u, d, and p as outlined makes sense. For further details see Chapter 7.

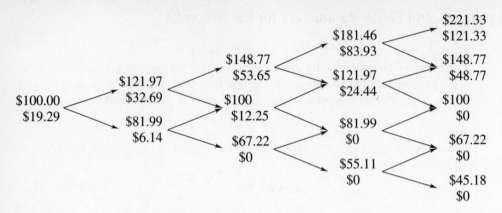

EXHIBIT 8.4   Pricing a Four-Period European Call

$\Delta t = 0.25$ and

$$u = e^{\sigma\sqrt{\Delta t}} = 1.2197$$

$$d = e^{-\sigma\sqrt{\Delta t}} = 0.8199$$

$$\theta = \frac{e^{r\Delta t} - d}{u - d} = 0.51379$$

Exhibit 8.4 shows the binomial tree. At each node the stock price is indicated together with the option price.

For a nondividend-paying stock, early exercise of a call is never optimal. Hence, the value exercised is always below the value unexercised. As the partition Δt becomes finer, the underlying price converges to the risk-neutralized process in equation (8.26) and the call price converges to its true fair value.

EXAMPLE 8.7   **Pricing a Put Option Using a Four-Period Binomial Approximation**

Consider a one-year at-the-money European put option on the same stock as in Example 8.6. Following the backward recursion from the terminal period yields the put prices indicated below the stock prices in Exhibit 8.5. Note that the option price can fall below the intrinsic value, since early exercise is not permitted. Specifically, when the option is deep in the money, early exercise may be advantageous since the strike price can be obtained early and can be used to generate interest income. Note that at node (3, 0), the value of the put is $42.42 while the intrinsic value is $100 - \$55.11 = \$44.89$. Hence, at this node there is a "negative time premium." The put is deep-in-the-money and if the contract were American, it would be exercised.

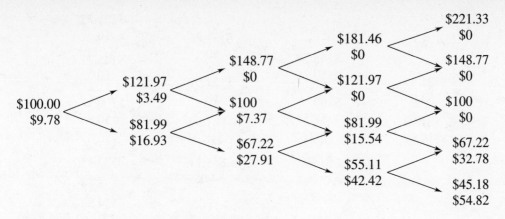

EXHIBIT 8.5   Pricing a Four-Period European Put

Pricing American Put Options on a Binomial Lattice

If the put option in Example 8.7 were American, then clearly its price could never fall below its intrinsic value. In this case the backward recursion algorithm has to be modified.

Consider vertex (i, j), and assume that all the put prices in period $i + 1$ have been obtained. (Initially, i is set at the next-to-last period, and the put prices at the terminating dates are given by their intrinsic values.) Then we define the value of the put unexercised as P_{ij}^{GO}, where

$$P_{ij}^{GO} = [\theta P_{i+1,j+1} + (1 - \theta)P_{i+1,j}]/R \qquad (8.27)$$

The intrinsic value of the option at vertex (i,j) is P_{ij}^{STOP}, where

$$P_{ij}^{STOP} = \text{Max}[X - s_{ij}, 0] \qquad (8.28)$$

If P_{ij}^{STOP} exceeds P_{ij}^{GO}, then clearly the optimal strategy is to exercise the option rather than continuing to hold it for one more period. Hence, the value of the put at vertex (i,j) is just the maximum of these two values. That is,

$$P_{ij} = \text{Max}[P_{ij}^{GO}, P_{ij}^{STOP}] \qquad (8.29)$$

Clearly, if it is optimal to exercise the put at vertex (i, j) then it must be optimal to exercise the put at all vertices in period i with a lower j index (i.e., at lower stock prices). The highest stock price at which it is optimal to exercise the option early in period i is called the **boundary price** for period i.

EXAMPLE 8.8   Pricing an American Put Option

Exhibit 8.6 shows the prices of the American put for the four-period problem in Example 8.7.

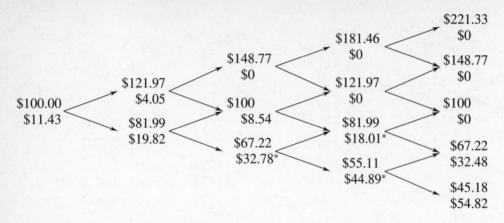

EXHIBIT 8.6   Pricing a Four-Period American Put

At nodes marked by asterisks, early exercise is appropriate. The exercise boundary for a nondividend-paying stock will increase toward the strike price as expiration gets closer.

The Limiting Form of the Binomial Model

As the partition Δt in the lattices get smaller and smaller, the price of the European call option converges to the expected terminal value discounted at the riskless rate of return, where the expectation is taken with respect to the risk-neutralized process in equation (8.26). That is,

$$C_0 = \tilde{E}_0[\text{Max}(S(T) - X, 0)]e^{-rT} \tag{8.30}$$

It can be shown that if the binomial lattice parameters u and d are chosen as indicated in equations (8.23) to (8.25), then as Δt becomes smaller, the prices from the binomial option pricing model converge to the following formula:

$$C_0 = H^*S_0 - B^* \tag{8.31}$$

where $H^* = N(d_1)$

   $B^* = X\,e^{-rT}N(d_2)$

and where $d_1 = [\ln(S_0/X) + (r + \sigma^2/2)T]/\sigma\sqrt{T}$

   $d_2 = d_1 - \sigma\sqrt{T}$

and $N(x)$ is the probability that a standard normal random variable (usually represented by Z) is less than x. Tables for computing $N(x)$ for different values of x are included in Appendix 8A.

The formula in equation (8.31) is the Black-Scholes equation for a call option on a nondividend-paying stock. By defining alternative forms for u, d, and θ (as the partition Δt goes to zero), we obtain different limiting forms for the underlying stochastic process and can establish different option pricing models. The Black-Scholes model, however, is the benchmark model used in option pricing studies. Chapter 9 studies this model in more depth.

EXAMPLE 8.9   Pricing a European Call Option Using the Black-Scholes Model

Consider the theoretical price of a three-month call option on a stock priced at $50. The strike price is $45, the riskless rate is 6 percent, and the volatility is 20 percent per year. Hence, $S(0) = \$50$, $X = 45$, $T = 0.25$, $\sigma = 0.20$, and $r = 6$ percent. The Black-Scholes call price can be computed as follows. First,

$$d_1 = \frac{\ln(S(0)/X) + (r + \sigma^2/2)T}{\sigma\sqrt{T}}$$

$$= \frac{\ln(\$50/\$45) + (0.06 + (0.20)^2/2)0.25}{0.20\sqrt{0.25}} = 1.25$$

$$d_2 = d_1 - \sigma\sqrt{T} = 1.15$$

Then, using standard normal tables, we find that $N(d_1) = 0.8944$ and $N(d_2) = 0.8749$, and we obtain

$$H^* = N(d_1) = 0.8944$$

$$B^* = X\,e^{-rT}N(d_2) = \$45\,e^{(-0.06)(0.25)}\,(0.8749) = \$38.78$$

$$C_0 = H^*S_0 - B^* = \$50(0.8944) - \$38.78 = \$5.94$$

The binomial lattice procedure is not necessary for a European call option since an analytical model is available. Moreover, if the underlying stock pays no dividends, then the early exercise feature is not valuable and the analytical model can still be used. The binomial lattice procedure is therefore particularly useful for pricing American puts. In addition, the binomial procedure can be easily modified to price American call and puts on dividend paying stocks and on a variety of other securities. Such extensions are considered in Chapter 15.

Conclusion

This chapter has investigated a pricing model for options. By suitably controlling the up and down parameters of the model, together with the probability value, we can make the underlying binomial process converge into a variety of different processes. If the parameters are chosen such that the limiting process is a geometric Wiener process, then the limiting European option pricing model is the Black-Scholes model. (This important model is discussed in more detail in Chapter 9.)

The binomial option pricing model illustrates the risk-neutral valuation concept, which is a key concept in option pricing. Normally, when a risky claim is to be valued, two steps are necessary. First, uncertain future cash flows are replaced by their expected values. Second, these future expected values are discounted at some rate that reflects nondiversifiable risk. For valuing option contracts, the two-step procedure is modified. First, the probability distribution for the cash flows is readjusted in a particular way, and the expectation is computed. Second, the expected value is discounted at the riskless rate. This process, referred to as risk-neutral valuation, produces a fair price, which is valid in a risk-averse economy. Risk-neutral valuation is an appropriate valuation mechanism if a self-financing trading strategy can be constructed to replicate the payouts of the option. In the binomial framework, the redistribution of the probability distribution took the form of computing the risk-neutral probability value, θ. Since θ is fully determined by the volatility, σ, the riskless rate, r, and the partition size, Δt, the expected return, μ, never enters directly into the analysis.

Most important, this chapter has provided insight into the creation of dynamic trading strategies and their use for valuation. The binomial model not only gives us a price for an option—it also gives us a trading mechanism that is useful for managing risk.

References

The binomial model for option pricing was developed by Cox, Ross, and Rubinstein and Rendleman and Bartter. This entire chapter draws heavily from these two articles.

Cox, J., S. Ross, and M. Rubinstein. "Option Pricing: A Simplified Approach." *Journal of Financial Economics* 7 (1979): 229–63.

Rendleman, R., and B. Bartter. "Two State Option Pricing." *Journal of Finance* 34 (1979): 1093–1110.

Exercises

1. a. Price a call option using the one-period binomial model with $s_0 = 85$, $X = 80$, $u = 1.5$, $d = 0.5$, and $R = 1.1$.
   b. Construct the replicating portfolio.
   c. Show that the call price equals the expected terminal call price discounted at the riskless rate.

2. a. Price a call option using the two-period binomial model with $s_0 = 85$, $X = 80$, $u = 1.5$, $d = 0.5$, and $R = 1.1$.
   b. Construct the replicating portfolio at time 0 and after one period, assuming the price moves up.
   c. Price a two-period European put option with strike 80 using the information in Exercise 2a.

3. A stock price follows a geometric Wiener process with a volatility of 40 percent per year. The riskless interest rate is 8 percent per year. Consider a binomial approximation to the risk-neutralized process, with $\Delta t = 0.5$ years. The initial stock price is $100.

   a. Compute the up and down parameters as well as the probability of an upmove.

   b. Use the lattice to price an at-the-money one-year European call option.

   c. Use the Black-Scholes formula to compute the price of the European call option.

   d. Compare the price of the option as computed in Exercises 3b and 3c. Explain how the price obtained in Exercise 3b could be improved upon.

   e. With your answer to Exercise 3c, use put-call parity to compute the fair price of an at-the-money European put.

4. Consider a two-period binomial model with $s_0 = 10$, $u = 1.12$, $d = 1/u$, and $R = 1.08$. A firm offers a contract called a square, which provides the holder with a payout after two periods equal to the greater of the square of the stock price less $100 or $0.

   a. Construct a dynamic trading strategy that replicates a square.

   b. What is the fair price of a square?

5. Consider a stock that can increase ($u = 1.5$), decrease ($d = 0.5$), or remain unchanged. Assume that a riskless asset exists. The exact payouts of the stock and riskless bond are shown below.

$$
\begin{array}{ccc}
& \nearrow \ \$15 & & \nearrow \ \$1 \\
\$10 \rightarrow \$10 & & \$0.8 \rightarrow \$1 \\
& \searrow \ \$ \ 5 & & \searrow \ \$1
\end{array}
$$

Given these two securities, can you obtain an unambiguous price for a one-period at-the-money call? Explain why the usual arbitrage argument works or fails.

6. Develop a spreadsheet program that will compute the call price and replicating portfolio at each node of a three-period binomial lattice.

7. Compute the price of a two-year at-the-money call option if the interest rates are 6 percent per year, continuously compounded; the volatility is zero; and the initial stock price is $100.

8. Consider a one-period binomial model with $s_0 = 10$, $u = 1.5$, $d = 0.5$, and $R = 1.1$.

   a. Compute the price of a security (called an upper) that pays $1 in the up state and $0 in the down state.

   b. Compute the price of a security (called a downer) that pays $1 in the down state and $0 in the up state.

   c. Consider a portfolio of one upper and one downer. What is its value today?

   d. Consider a portfolio of 15 uppers and 10 downers. Show that this portfolio replicates the stock.

   e. Use the price of an upper and downer to immediately price a claim that pays $25 in the up state and loses $10 in the down state.

9. Exercise 8 showed that given the price of an upper and a downer, we can easily value any claim. Consider a two-period lattice with $s_0 = 10$, $u = 1.5$, $d = 0.5$, and $R = 1.1$.

a. Compute the price of a security that pays out $1 if an up-up move occurs and zero otherwise.

b. Compute the price of a security that pays out $1 if the middle state is reached in the second period and $0 otherwise.

c. Compute the price of a security that pays $1 if a down-down move occurs and zero otherwise.

d. Use the prices of these three claims to immediately price a security that pays $20 in the up-up state, $16 in the middle state, and $100 in the down-down state.

APPENDIX 8A

Cumulative Normal Table

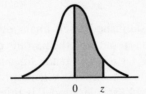

EXHIBIT 8A.1 Normal Curve Areas

z	.00	.01	.02	.03	.04	.05	.06	.07	.08	.09
0.0	.0000	.0040	.0080	.0120	.0160	.0199	.0239	.0279	.0319	.0359
0.1	.0398	.0438	.0478	.0517	.0557	.0596	.0636	.0675	.0714	.0753
0.2	.0793	.0832	.0871	.0910	.0948	.0987	.1026	.1064	.1103	.1141
0.3	.1179	.1217	.1255	.1293	.1331	.1368	.1406	.1443	.1480	.1517
0.4	.1554	.1591	.1628	.1664	.1700	.1736	.1772	.1808	.1844	.1879
0.5	.1915	.1950	.1985	.2019	.2054	.2088	.2123	.2157	.2190	.2224
0.6	.2257	.2291	.2324	.2357	.2389	.2422	.2454	.2486	.2517	.2549
0.7	.2580	.2611	.2642	.2673	.2704	.2734	.2764	.2794	.2823	.2852
0.8	.2881	.2910	.2939	.2967	.2995	.3023	.3051	.3078	.3106	.3133
0.9	.3159	.3186	.3212	.3238	.3264	.3289	.3315	.3340	.3365	.3389
1.0	.3413	.3438	.3461	.3485	.3508	.3531	.3554	.3577	.3599	.3621
1.1	.3643	.3665	.3686	.3708	.3729	.3749	.3770	.3790	.3810	.3830
1.2	.3849	.3869	.3888	.3907	.3925	.3944	.3962	.3980	.3997	.4015
1.3	.4032	.4049	.4066	.4082	.4099	.4115	.4131	.4147	.4162	.4177
1.4	.4192	.4207	.4222	.4236	.4251	.4265	.4279	.4292	.4306	.4319
1.5	.4332	.4345	.4357	.4370	.4382	.4394	.4406	.4418	.4429	.4441
1.6	.4452	.4463	.4474	.4484	.4495	.4505	.4515	.4525	.4535	.4545
1.7	.4554	.4564	.4573	.4582	.4591	.4599	.4608	.4616	.4625	.4633
1.8	.4641	.4649	.4656	.4664	.4671	.4678	.4686	.4693	.4699	.4706
1.9	.4713	.4719	.4726	.4732	.4738	.4744	.4750	.4756	.4761	.4767
2.0	.4772	.4778	.4783	.4788	.4793	.4798	.4803	.4808	.4812	.4817
2.1	.4821	.4826	.4830	.4834	.4838	.4842	.4846	.4850	.4854	.4857
2.2	.4861	.4864	.4868	.4871	.4875	.4878	.4881	.4884	.4887	.4890
2.3	.4893	.4896	.4898	.4901	.4904	.4906	.4909	.4911	.4913	.4916
2.4	.4918	.4920	.4922	.4925	.4927	.4929	.4931	.4932	.4934	.4936
2.5	.4938	.4940	.4941	.4943	.4945	.4946	.4948	.4949	.4951	.4952
2.6	.4953	.4955	.4956	.4957	.4959	.4960	.4961	.4962	.4963	.4964
2.7	.4965	.4966	.4967	.4968	.4969	.4970	.4971	.4972	.4973	.4974
2.8	.4974	.4975	.4976	.4977	.4977	.4978	.4979	.4979	.4980	.4981
2.9	.4981	.4982	.4982	.4983	.4984	.4984	.4985	.4985	.4986	.4986
3.0	.4987	.4987	.4987	.4988	.4988	.4989	.4989	.4989	.4990	.4990

Source: Abridged from Table I of A. Hald, *Statistical Tables and Formulas* (New York: John Wiley & Sons, Inc.), 1952. Reproduced by permission of A. Hald and the publisher, John Wiley & Sons, Inc.

CHAPTER 9

The Black-Scholes Model

In Chapter 8 we established a self-financing dynamic trading strategy, involving stock and bonds, that replicated the payouts of an option on a binomial lattice. As the partition of the lattice was made finer and finer, the underlying stock price process converged to a geometric Wiener process and the option pricing equation converged to the Black-Scholes model. In this chapter we discuss the Black-Scholes model in more detail. Since this equation has an elegant analytical form, the importance of key parameters can easily be investigated. The sensitivity of option prices to parameters is explored and estimates for the inputs are described.

The primary objectives of this chapter are the following:

· To explain the Black-Scholes model of option pricing;

· To discuss the application of option pricing models in the market; and

· To discuss empirical evidence that supports the Black-Scholes model.

The Option Pricing Line

Throughout the chapter we assume that the stock, bond, and option markets are frictionless. That is, we ignore transaction costs, margin requirements, and taxes; all shares are infinitely divisible; and trading can take place continuously. We also assume that all investors can borrow or lend at a constant known risk-free rate, r, and the stock price follows a geometric Wiener process with a known volatility, σ. The stock pays no dividends prior to the expiration date, T. Finally, we assume that each option controls one unit of the underlying stock.

Suppose that we had a formula to relate the call price to the underlying stock price, the strike price, the expiration date, and other factors. Such a formula would indicate, among other things, how much an option value changes when the stock price changes by a small amount within a short time. Suppose the option increases by 50 cents when the stock goes up $1 and decreases by 50 cents when the stock goes down $1. Then a hedged position could be created by purchasing 0.5 shares of stock and selling 1 option. Over a small time increment such a position will be close to riskless. For small moves in the stock, losses on one side will be mostly offset by gains on the other.

Exhibit 9.1 shows a hypothetical option price line. The current stock price is S_0, and the current call price is C_0. The slope of the line is H. The slope indicates

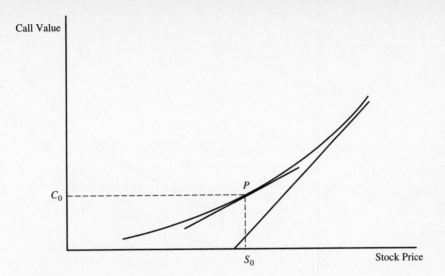

EXHIBIT 9.1   The Option Pricing Line

the sensitivity of the call price to small instantaneous changes in the stock price. As indicated, for deep-out-of-the-money calls, prices are insensitive to stock price changes, whereas for deep-in-the-money calls, the price changes almost dollar for dollar with the stock price.

In Exhibit 9.1 the slope, H, equals 0.5, and the appropriate hedge position consists of purchasing $H = 0.5$ shares and selling 1 option. As the stock price changes, and as the option approaches maturity, the number of shares of stock needed to maintain a close-to-riskless hedge changes. Of course, the hedge is really free of risk only if the stock price change over the time increment is small. Moreover, after an arbitrary time interval, Δt, the hedge will need to be adjusted even if the stock price remains the same. To illustrate this point, consider a perfect hedge established at time t when the stock price is $S(t)$ and the call price is $C(t)$ (point P in Exhibit 9.2). At time $t + \Delta t$, the call price corresponds to a point on a new option line.

If the stock price has changed by Δs, the call price is given by point Q in Exhibit 9.2. The actual change in option price is represented by the distance QR. The line RT represents the change in value of H shares of stock. The distance QT thus represents the net change in the value of the instantaneous hedge over the period Δt. Note that the size of this value will depend on ΔS and Δt. If the stock price process is a diffusion process, then as Δt tends to zero, the hedge position becomes free of risk. However, over finite periods, the hedge is not free of risk. To maintain a close-to-riskless hedge, then, continual changes in the stock position are necessary over all time increments.

We assume the investor has the ability to continuously adjust the number of shares purchased against an option that is sold, in response to stock price changes and the passage of time, without incurring transaction costs; this is called the **continuous trading assumption.** In the trading strategy that we consider, if additional shares need to be purchased then financing is obtained by borrowing funds

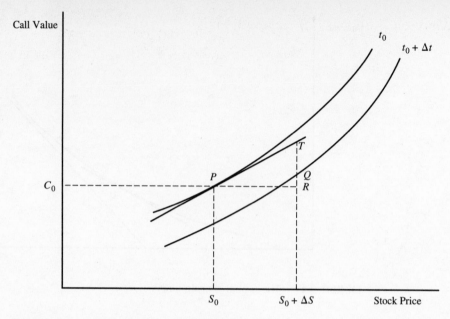

EXHIBIT 9.2   Maintaining a Hedge Position

at the riskless rate. Similarly, if shares need to be liquidated, then the proceeds from the sale are invested at the riskless rate. Such a trading strategy, which prohibits the external addition or removal of funds from the strategy over the time horizon, is referred to as a **self-financing strategy.** By following a particular continuous self-financing trading strategy, we can maintain a hedge position as a close-to-riskless position, which should return an amount equal to the short-term interest rate on close-to-riskless securities. This single principle is sufficient to provide a unique option formula. Only one formula for the value of the option has the property that the return on a continually hedged position of option and stock equals the riskless interest rate. This is the Black-Scholes formula,[1] given by

$$C(t) = H^*S(t) - B^* \qquad (9.1)$$

where
$$H^* = N(d_1) \qquad (9.2)$$

$$B^* = X e^{-r(T-t)} N(d_2) \qquad (9.3)$$

and
$$d_1 = \frac{\ln(S(t)/X) + (r + \sigma^2/2)(T - t)}{\sigma \sqrt{T - t}}$$

$$d_2 = d_1 - \sigma \sqrt{T - t}$$

$N(d_1)$ is the cumulative normal distribution function below d_1. Equivalently, it represents the area to the left of d_1 in standard normal tables.

---

[1] Appendix 9A provides a heuristic development of the formula developed by Black and Scholes.

More on the Black-Scholes Equation

The Black-Scholes equation shows that at any time t a call can be viewed as having the same value as H^* shares of stock partially financed by borrowing B^* dollars. To derive an intuitive understanding of the equation, consider the price of the call option in a world of perfect certainty. Given certainty, the terminal call price, $C(T)$, is a positive number, $S(T) - X$. (If the option expired worthless, no one would buy it.) In a world of certainty, the return on all assets would be the riskless rate. Hence

$$S(T) = S(t) \, e^{r(T-t)}$$

and

$$C(T) = S(t) \, e^{r(T-t)} - X$$

Hence, the current call price is $C(T) \, e^{-r(T-t)}$, which is

$$C(t) = S(t) - X \, e^{-r(T-t)}$$

This expression differs from equation (9.1) by the standard normal terms. These terms can be viewed as probability adjustments that must be made to reflect the uncertainty in the terminal stock price.

We have seen that whenever a risk-free hedge can be established, the risk-neutral valuation argument is valid. That is, for valuation purposes, we can pretend the economy is risk-neutral and we can compute the call price as

$$C(t) = e^{-r(T-t)} \, E_t\{\text{Max}(S(T) - X, 0)\} \tag{9.4}$$

where the expectation is taken with respect to the lognormal probability distribution of stock prices that would exist in a risk-neutral economy. Computing the expectation leads to the Black-Scholes model. The first term of the Black-Scholes model is the discounted expected value of the terminal stock, given that the option expires in the money, times the probability that it does expire in the money. The second term is the discounted strike price times the probability that the option will be exercised.

EXAMPLE 9.1   Given that $t = 0$, $S(0) = \$50$, $X = 45$, $T = 3$ months (0.25 year), $\sigma = 0.20$, and $r = 6$ percent, then

$$d_1 = \frac{\ln(S(t)/X) + (r + \sigma^2/2)(T - t)}{\sigma \sqrt{T - t}}$$

$$= \frac{\ln(50/45) + (0.06 + 0.20/2/2)0.25}{0.20(0.25)^{1/2}} = 1.2536$$

$$d_2 = d_1 - \sigma \sqrt{T - t} = 1.1536$$

Using standard normal tables, we find $N(d_1) = 0.8944$ and $N(d_2) = 0.8749$. $N(d_2)$ can be interpreted as the risk-neutralized probability that the option will be exercised. Now

$$H^* = N(d_1) = 0.8944 \quad \text{and} \quad B^* = X \, e^{-rT} N(d_2) = 45 \, e^{-0.06(0.25)} \, (0.8749)$$
$$= \$38.7843$$

Finally,

$$C(0) = H*S(0) - B* = \$50(0.8944) - \$38.784 = \$5.94$$

The initial replicating portfolio for the call consists of a leveraged position in the stock where $H* = 0.8944$ shares were purchased, partially financed by borrowing $B* = \$38.784$. If the assumptions of the model hold true, then there exists a dynamic trading strategy, initially consisting of holding 0.8944 shares of stock partially financed by borrowing \$38.784, that produces cash flows identical to the call option.

Say that the market price of the option is above the theoretical Black-Scholes value. Then, under the Black-Scholes assumption, riskless arbitrage profits could be obtained by selling the call and purchasing the cheaper replicating strategy. Since the payoff of this strategy could be used to pay off the obligations on the call, the investor will have created a free lunch. In an efficient market, these free lunches are soon closed off and option prices equate to their theoretical values.

Put Pricing

If the option is European, then, assuming the stock pays no dividends, the put-call parity relationship can be used to establish the Black-Scholes put price. At time $t = 0$,

$$P^E(0) = C^E(0) - S(0) + X\, e^{-rT}$$

Given the Black-Scholes value for $C^E(0)$, the put price can be determined as

$$P^E(0) = X\, e^{-rT}N(-d_2) - S(0)N(-d_1) \tag{9.5}$$

Properties of the Black-Scholes Price

Exhibit 9.3 illustrates the sensitivity of the near, middle, and far call and put option prices to the stock price. The exhibit clearly shows that as option contracts move into the money, their values increase. Moreover, as time to expiration increases, the price also increases. In all cases, the call time premium is positive. Deep-in-the-money American put options trade at parity. As discussed in Chapter 4, European-style puts may trade below parity.

Exhibit 9.4 illustrates the sensitivity of option prices to interest rates. As interest rates increase, call prices increase and put prices decrease. The reasons behind these results were discussed in Chapter 4. Option prices increase as volatility increases, as illustrated in Exhibit 9.5.

Exhibit 9.6 shows the decay in the time premium of an at-the-money call option, assuming the stock price remains unchanged to expiration. As expiration nears, the time premium drops off. Time premiums of call options on non-dividend-paying stocks are always nonnegative. However, as discussed, time premiums on European puts can become negative.

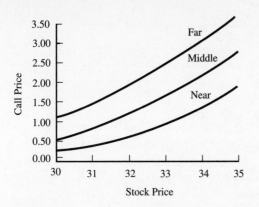

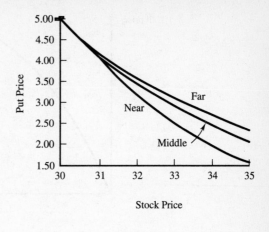

EXHIBIT 9.3   Sensitivity of Options to Stock Prices

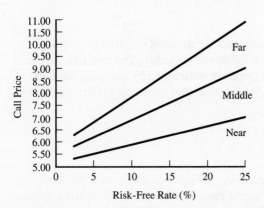

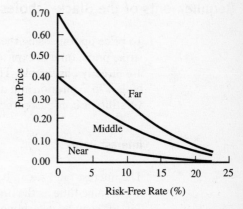

EXHIBIT 9.4   Sensitivity of Options to Interest Rates

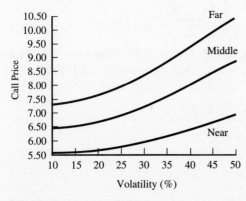

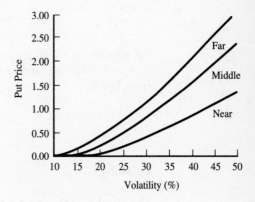

EXHIBIT 9.5   Sensitivity of Options to Volatility

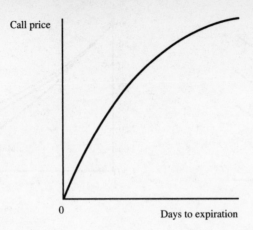

EXHIBIT 9.6   Time Decay of an At-the-Money Call Option

Requirements of the Black-Scholes Model

To price options using the Black-Scholes model, we need to know the stock price, strike price, time to expiration, interest rates, and volatility. The first two variables are directly observable. The time to expiration is obtained by counting the number of days to expiration and dividing by 365. Methods for estimating interest rates and volatility are discussed below.

Interest Rates

The interest rate, r, can be determined using the price of a Treasury bill maturing at the same time as the option. The current price of a Treasury bill with face value $10,000 can be determined using information from the *Wall Street Journal*. Let B be the bid discount and A the asked discount for the T-bill with maturity n days. The price of the T-bill, B_0, is

$$B_0 = \$10,000 \left\{ 1 - 0.01 \left(\frac{A + B}{2} \right) \left(\frac{n}{360} \right) \right\}$$

An investment of B_0 today results in a certain return of $10,000 in n days. Let $T = n/365$ be the time to expiration in years. Then we have $B_0 = \$10,000\, e^{-rT}$, from which

$$r = \frac{\ln(\$10,000/B_0)}{T}$$

Volatility

The Black-Scholes model requires the volatility of logarithmic returns, σ, to remain constant over time. Specifically, the model requires the underlying statistical process driving stock prices to have the following representation:

$$\frac{ds}{s} = \mu(s, t)\, dt + \sigma\, dw \tag{9.6}$$

Let $\{S_t \mid t = 0, 1, 2, \ldots, n\}$ represent a sequence of stock prices collected over n periods, and let $\{r_t \mid t = 1, 2, \ldots, n\}$ represent the sequence of logarithmic returns.

$$r_t = \ln(R_t) = \ln(S_t/S_{t-1}) \quad \text{for} \quad t = 1, 2, 3, \ldots, n \tag{9.7}$$

If we assume that the expected return, $\mu(s, t)$, remains the same (i.e., $\mu(s, t) = \mu$), then logarithmic returns can be considered a simple random sample from a normal distribution, with a constant mean and a variance of σ^2. Let $\bar{r}$ and s^2 be estimators of the mean and variance per period. Then

$$\bar{r} = \frac{\sum_{t=1}^{n} r_t}{n} \tag{9.8}$$

$$s^2 = \frac{\sum_{t=1}^{n} (r_t - \bar{r})^2}{n - 1} \tag{9.9}$$

The estimate of the variance, s^2, is then annualized to obtain an estimate for σ^2. For example, if stock prices are observed weekly, then we have $\hat{\sigma}^2 = 52s^2$, where $\hat{\sigma}^2$ is the annualized estimator for σ^2. The estimator for the volatility, σ, is then given by $\hat{\sigma} = \sqrt{\hat{\sigma}^2}$.

EXAMPLE 9.2   Consider a stock XYZ whose closing prices at the beginning of each of the past 20 weeks are shown in Exhibit 9.7. We obtain the following values:

$$\bar{r} = 0.0144954$$

$$s = 0.04476$$

and the annualized volatility is $\hat{\sigma} = \sqrt{52}s = 0.32$.

Other Estimators of Volatility

The disadvantage of the estimation procedure described above is that it requires all the logarithmic returns to come from the same distribution. In particular, we assumed that the average logarithmic return remained constant over time and that it could be estimated by the arithmetic mean, $\bar{r}$. If the drift term is not constant, then the average, $\bar{r}$, may not be a good estimate of the future expectation. Since the Black-Scholes model is still valid if the drift term changes over time, it seems advantageous to obtain an estimator of σ that does not assume the drift term is constant.

Let $\{r_t \mid t = 1, 2, \ldots, n\}$ be a sequence of logarithmic returns drawn from independent normal distributions with the same variances but different means.

EXHIBIT 9.7 Computation of Logarithmic Returns

Week	Price ($)	Weekly Price Relative	Logarithmic Return
1	20.50	—	—
2	21.00	1.042	0.02409
3	22.00	0.9545	0.0465
4	22.125	1.0056	0.00566
5	23.25	1.0508	0.04959
6	23.50	1.010	0.01069
7	21.25	0.9042	−0.10064
8	20.50	0.9647	−0.035932
9	20.75	1.0122	0.01212
10	20.825	1.0036	0.003607
11	21.75	1.0444	0.04345
12	24.25	1.1149	0.1088
13	26.375	1.0876	0.08399
14	26.375	1	0
15	27.25	1.033	0.0326
16	28.00	1.027	0.02715
17	27.00	0.9642	−0.03636
18	26.25	0.972	−0.02817
19	26.50	1.00952	0.009478
20	27.00	1.0188	0.0186

Recall that we had as our estimator of σ^2 the equation

$$s^2 = \frac{1}{n-1} \sum_{t=1}^{n} (r_t - \bar{r})^2$$

$$= \frac{1}{n-1} \left[\sum_{t=1}^{n} r_t^2 - n\bar{r}^2 \right]$$

Fortunately, with weekly logarithmic returns, the $n\bar{r}^2/(n-1)$ term does not contribute significantly to s^2. One reason for this is that both expectation and variance are proportional to the time period. For small time intervals, the contribution of the mean squared term is negligible. Hence,

$$s^2 = \frac{1}{n-1} \sum_{t=1}^{n} r_t^2$$

Although this estimator is not an unbiased estimator of σ^2, it avoids the requirement of estimating μ.

EXAMPLE 9.3 In Example 9.2, the value $n\bar{r}^2/(n-1)$ is 0.000222. This value is about 13 percent of the sample variance. If it is ignored, the estimate of the annual volatility is 0.31.

In practice, the volatility of a stock may not remain the same over time. Hence, it is important to establish the periodicity of data (daily or weekly, for example) and the number of historical values to use. The most common method is to use daily intervals over a period of about 20 weeks. Since option prices are sensitive to volatility, significant efforts have been made to devise better estimating procedures. These methods include the use of daily high, low, open, and close prices.[2] Other methods use time series models that revise the estimate based on historical values by taking into account economic variables, such as inflation and market/industrial sector factors. Indeed, volatilities of different stocks tend to be highly correlated with each other. This suggests that a common market-volatility factor may explain a large percentage of the variability of individual stocks. In addition, extreme volatilities of stocks in a particular industry tend to regress toward the mean values for their industry. As a result, extremely volatile stocks should have their forecasts dampened slightly, while low-volatility stocks should have their forecasts enhanced a bit. Volatilities that shift in response to stock prices, market forces, and other variables are inconsistent with the basic assumptions on volatility in the Black-Scholes model. Nonetheless, very practical results can be obtained by using the model in conjunction with volatilities that are frequently revised by more sophisticated methods than analysis of historical variability.

Implicit Volatility

If the assumptions of the Black-Scholes model held true and all the parameters were known, the market price of a call option on a nondividend-paying stock would equal the Black-Scholes price. When volatility is unknown, however, different investors estimate it differently and disagree over the theoretical price. But since call prices are observable, an investor could take the price as given and use the Black-Scholes equation to obtain the volatility that equates the theoretical price to the observed price.

Unfortunately, no explicit equation for σ^2 can be obtained from the Black-Scholes model, and numerical search procedures must be used. The method is quite simple. Conceptually, we guess a value for σ, put it into the Black-Scholes equation, and compute the fair value. If this value equals the actual market price, the guess is correct. If the computed call price is too large (small), then a smaller (larger) value for σ should be tried. The value of σ that equates the market and theoretical price is called the **implicit volatility.** It can be viewed as the current best consensus estimate by the market's participants regarding future volatility over the time period to expiration.

---

[2] Rather than using closing prices, Parkinson used daily high and low values to estimate volatility. Garman and Klass improved this procedure by including more information, including the opening and closing prices. Unfortunately, their estimators are developed under the assumption that stock prices follow a geometric Wiener process, and they may not be robust. Implicit volatilities may provide the best estimators.

If the assumptions of the model were true, then the implied volatilities computed from options on the same stock but with different strikes should all be identical. In practice, different options on the same stock may yield different implicit volatilities. If the volatility changes over time, options with the same strike but different maturities should have different implicit volatilities. Options with the same maturity but different strikes may also have different implicit volatilities. This may be especially true for stocks that pay dividends and for some deep-in-the-money contracts where early exercise may be appropriate; in such cases the market's opinion on the volatility reflects only the time to the next ex-dividend date. A more important reason implicit volatilities differ is that there are measurement errors in the stock and option prices. Specifically, the closing prices of options may not represent the actual prices that could be obtained. This measurement error is discussed in more detail later in this chapter. Of course, if the assumptions of the Black-Scholes model are violated, there is no real reason for different options on the same stock to have the same implied volatility. In this case it is possible that the implied volatility is not a reasonable estimator of the future volatility of the stock over the period to the expiration date.

Let σ_i^* represent the implicit volatility of an option belonging to a given strike and maturity class. The simplest method of deriving a single forecast of implicit volatility is to compute the average implicit volatility, $\overline{\sigma}^*$, across all m contracts. That is,

$$\overline{\sigma}^* = \sum_{i=1}^{m} \sigma_i^*/m$$

The simple averaging process gives equal weight to all option prices. However, since option prices are not equally sensitive to volatility, it appears reasonable to give extra weight to those contracts that are most sensitive to the volatility parameter—the at-the-money contracts. Let w_i be the weight assigned to the ith contract. Then

$$\overline{\sigma}^* = \sum_{i=1}^{m} w_i\, \sigma_i^*$$

where $\sum_{i=1}^{m} w_i = 1$. Although many different weighting schemes have been proposed, perhaps the best scheme is to use the at-the-money contract.[3]

The use of implied volatility computed from a Black-Scholes model is so pervasive that prices are often quoted in implied volatility form. A quoted volatility of 30 percent for an option on a nondividend-paying stock translates into a dollar price computed by the Black-Scholes model, using $\sigma = 0.30$.

Early empirical evidence confirmed that forecasts of future volatility based on implicit volatility were generally better than predictions based on simple historical estimates of volatilities computed using weekly data.

---

[3] An alternative weighting scheme is based on the sensitivity of the call to volatility, $\partial C/\partial \sigma$. The weights are taken to be proportional to this sensitivity measure. An alternative weighting scheme is based on the elasticity of variance. Beckers, however, has shown that the implicit volatility of the option nearest the money is as good as any other predictor.

Of course, if all traders used the Black-Scholes model to price contracts, and if they all agreed on the volatility, then they would all agree on the price and there would be little incentive for speculators to trade. If traders disagreed on the volatility of the stock, however, they would disagree on the option price, and there would be more opportunities for traders to speculate. Trading in options is therefore enhanced if investors have different assessments of what the future volatility will be.

Applications of Option Pricing Models

There are four primary areas in which option pricing models are useful.

To Guide Transactions

The most obvious application is to provide a decision aid to investors who are establishing stock option/hedge positions. Such investors attempt to buy under-priced options and/or sell overpriced contracts. Theoretical pricing models can be used to establish which contracts are not fairly priced. The Black-Scholes model is so popular that it is often included as a hardware function in hand-held financial calculators. The use of option pricing models to guide transactions is discussed in more detail in the next section.

To Construct Synthetic Prices

If no option prices are available for a particular option at a particular point in time, a model can be used to estimate the price that would have been established by the market had trading occurred. Such prices are established by dealers who issue options privately. The models are also useful for valuing financial arrangements that have optionlike terms in them. Such applications of option pricing will be discussed in later chapters.

To Study Market Behavior

A frequently studied aspect of market behavior is efficiency. An unavoidable step in such studies is specifying a model of price determination. With an option pricing model at hand, market efficiency tests can be conducted. The resulting tests are actually joint tests of the market itself and of the pricing model used to study the market. In order to study the functioning of the option markets, a model such as the Black-Scholes model is necessary. If observed option prices diverge systematically from their theoretical prices, then either the market is inefficient or the model is not well specified. Empirical tests of the Black-Scholes model and efficiency are discussed later in this chapter.

To Obtain Implicit Parameters

Option prices can contain useful information. Call premiums tend to expand in some periods and shrink in others. The size of these premiums depends primarily on interest rates and volatility expectations over the period. By analyzing option premiums, one can obtain useful information about how investors in aggregate perceive the future of the market. For example, if call option premiums expand, the reason may be that there is a consensus among investors that future volatility in the stock market will exceed historical volatility.

Option Strategies and Option Pricing

In Chapter 5 we introduced several option strategies and analyzed them by investigating their profit functions at expiration. With an option pricing model available, we can accomplish further analyses on positions.

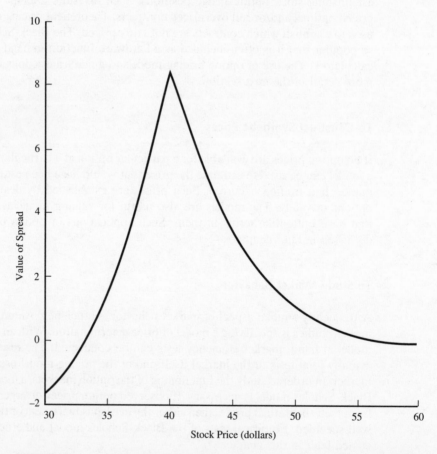

EXHIBIT 9.8   A Horizontal Call Spread at the Maturity Date of the Near Option

Buy and Sell Decisions

An investor purchasing (selling) an option would like to buy (sell) an underpriced (overvalued) contract. By using an option pricing model, the investor can establish a benchmark on prices. When observed prices deviate significantly from their theoretical prices, this signals some event. On the one hand, it could be an investment opportunity; on the other hand, it could reflect a change in the market's consensus opinion on the future volatility of the stock.

Profit Functions and Strategy Evaluation

With an option pricing formula in hand, we can plot profit functions prior to the expiration date. This is especially important for positions involving options with different maturities. For example, consider a horizontal call spread. When the near option expires, the far option still has a time premium. Using an option pricing model, we can compute time premiums for different stock prices. Exhibit 9.8 illustrates the payout of a horizontal call spread evaluated at the expiration date of the near series. The options traded have a strike of $40.

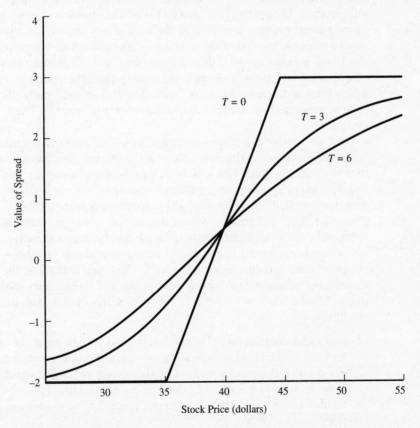

EXHIBIT 9.9   A Vertical Call Spread with *T* Months to Maturity

Option pricing models also allow investors to investigate how the profit function of any position evolves over time. Exhibit 9.9, for example, illustrates how the profit function of a vertical call spread evolves over time. This is accomplished by plotting the profit function at three points in time. The strike prices of the options in the spread are $35 and $45. As expiration nears, the profit function converges onto the piecewise linear graph. Note that the convergence rate increases as time to expiration decreases.

Empirical Evidence

The ultimate success of any model is based on empirical tests. The first test of prices of listed stock options was conducted by Galai in 1977. Using data from the first seven months of trading on the CBOE, Galai set up a trading rule and tested it to determine whether abnormal profits could be generated. If abnormal profits could have been obtained, he would have concluded that the market was inefficient and use of the Black-Scholes model could therefore lead to abnormal profits. If the model did not yield abnormal profits, he would have concluded that either the Black-Scholes model was correct and the market was efficient or the model was misspecified. The trading rule used by Galai was a feasible strategy in that decisions based on information available at the end of any day were implemented at the closing prices at the end of the next day. If an option was overpriced (according to the Black-Scholes model), the call was sold and the hedge ratio of shares was purchased. Conversely, if the call was underpriced, the option was bought and the hedge ratio of shares sold short. With positions revised daily, the net abnormal returns generated by the trading strategy (after transaction costs were included) disappeared.

An alternative experimental design, based on comparing actual option prices with theoretical prices that were computed using weighted average implied volatilities as estimates in the Black-Scholes equation, has also been considered. Chiras and Manaster, for example, consider a trading scheme in which they buy options with low implied volatility and sell options with high volatility. Their strategy generated abnormal profits. When transaction costs are included, however, the abnormal profits are significantly reduced. MacBeth and Mervill compared actual option prices to theoretical prices and were able to identify common characteristics of option contracts that were mispriced. They concluded that the Black-Scholes formula overvalues out-of-the-money options and undervalues in-the-money contracts. Similar studies by other investigators have led to the following general conclusions:

1. The Black-Scholes model is extremely good for pricing at-the-money options, especially when time to expiration exceeds two months and no dividends occur.
2. For deep-in-the-money and out-of-the-money contracts, significant deviations between market prices and model prices can occur.
3. Contracts with less than two weeks remaining to expiration are often mispriced.

4. Options on stocks with extremely low or extremely high volatility are often mispriced.

The biases reported in the empirical studies are, however, not consistent over time. For example, while the strike-price bias from Black-Scholes values is significant, its direction may change from period to period. A plot of the implied volatilities against the strike price often yields a U-shaped curve that is referred to as the **volatility smile.** If the Black-Scholes model were correct, then of course this plot would yield a straight flat line.

Most empirical tests conducted prior to 1980 used closing prices of options. These closing prices can be very misleading; on occasion, they indicate that arbitrage opportunities based on the pricing relationship described in Chapter 4 are available. The errors in using closing prices are caused by liquidity problems, nonsimultaneity of stock and option closing prices, and the bid-ask spread.

Nonsimultaneity of Stock and Option Prices

Most option trading takes place in near-the-money short-term contracts. Low liquidity in far-from-the-money contracts increases the likelihood that the last option trade occurred some time before trading ceased in the stock. This means that the reported option price need not reflect the actual price at which an option could be bought or sold for when the stock stopped trading at the end of the day.

The Bid-Ask Spread

Investors who purchase (sell) options will probably get the ask (bid) price quoted in the trading pit. By looking at the closing price, the investor does not know if the trade took place at the bid, at the ask, or in between. For example, if the spread is 1/2 and the closing price is 3, then if the last transaction took place at the bid (ask), the bid-ask spread is 3 to 3 1/2 (2 1/2 to 3). Hence, given a closing price of 3, the bid-ask spread creates uncertainty in prices between 2 1/2 and 3 1/2. This spread is 33 percent of the closing price.

To overcome these difficulties, Rubinstein used the CBOE's own record of all reported trades and quotes over a two-year period. This database provided a time-stamped record to the nearest second of option trade prices and quotes, together with the stock prices. Rubinstein found the quality of these data to be extremely high, primarily because of the CBOE's computerized error-checking procedures. Using nonparametric statistical tests, Rubinstein compared several option pricing model results to observed prices and concluded that (1) out-of-the-money options with short expirations were relatively overpriced, (2) a strike bias existed but its direction changed according to the time period, and (3) no model provided results consistently superior to the Black-Scholes model. Rubinstein suggested that a combination of these model prices could produce better results and that biases observed in any period could be correlated with macroeconomic variables such as the level of stock market prices, volatilities, and interest rates.

The strike-price and time-to-expiration biases displayed by the Black-Scholes model can be explained to a certain degree by the nontreatment of dividends. In fact, Whaley and Sterk found that for options on stocks paying exactly one dividend during the term of the option, strike-price and time-to-expiration biases could be removed by applying option models that took dividends into account.[4] Geske and Roll argue that some of the volatility biases recorded for the Black-Scholes model are attributable not to model misspecifications but rather to the errors induced by estimation methods for the volatility.

The overall conclusions, however, are that the Black-Scholes model for European options and the binomial lattice model for American options provide extremely good fits to actual data and that these pricing models do serve as useful valuation tools.

Conclusion

This chapter has taken a close look at the Black-Scholes model. The requirements for pricing an option were carefully investigated. All the inputs are directly observable except the volatility, which has to be estimated. If the assumptions of the model are upheld, then given the option price, the Black-Scholes model can be inverted to reveal the implied volatility. Actually, if the assumptions of the model are true, then the implied volatilities computed from options on the same stock but with different strikes should all be identical. Of course, if the assumptions of the model are not upheld, then it is possible that the implied volatility is not a reasonable estimator of the future volatility of the stock over the period to the expiration date. Since the basic assumption—that the volatility is known to all traders and is constant over time—is violated, it becomes an empirical issue as to whether the implied volatility is a better predictor of future volatility than other estimators based on historical data. Early evidence suggested that the implied volatility was a better estimator than others that were based on historical data. Recently, this issue has become a bit more controversial. However, there is still good evidence that implied volatility estimators are preferable to simple historical estimates.

Option pricing models have several important applications. They can be used to guide transactions, to establish synthetic or theoretical prices in illiquid markets, to study market behavior, and to obtain implicit parameters, and they are particularly useful for evaluating risk-management strategies. Overall, there is reasonably strong empirical support for the Black-Scholes model. Perhaps there is room for some improvement. However, for the most part, the model appears to perform extremely well.

---

[4] In Chapter 15 we investigate option models where the underlying asset pays dividends.

In this chapter we considered the Black-Scholes model only for pricing European options on nondividend-paying stocks. Actually, since the binomial model contains the Black-Scholes model as a special case, the binomial model can be used to price American claims. In future chapters we investigate models for pricing claims when the underlying security pays dividends. Finally, the Black-Scholes model is not the only simple analytical model; alternative models have been developed under different assumptions on the underlying stochastic process.

References

Beck, T. "Black-Scholes Revisited: Some Important Details." *Financial Review* 28 (1993): 77–90.

Beckers, S. "The Constant Elasticity of Variance Model and Its Implications for Option Pricing." *Journal of Finance* 35 (June 1980): 661–73.

———. "Standard Deviations Implied in Option Prices as Predictors of Future Stock Price Variability." *Journal of Banking and Finance* 5 (September 1981): 363–82.

Bhattacharya, M. "Empirical Properties of the Black-Scholes Formula Under Ideal Conditions." *Journal of Financial and Quantitative Analysis* 15 (December 1980): 1081–95.

Black, F. "Fact and Fantasy in the Use of Options." *Financial Analysis Journal* 27 (May 1972): 399–418.

———. "How We Came Up with the Option Formula." *Journal of Portfolio Management* 15 (1989): 4–8.

Black, F., and M. Scholes. "The Valuation of Option Contracts and a Test of Market Efficiency." *Journal of Finance* 27 (May 1972): 399–418.

———. "The Pricing of Options and Corporate Liabilities." *Journal of Political Economy* (May 1973): 637–59.

Blomeyer, E., and R. Kelmkosky. "Tests of Market Efficiency for American Call Options." In *Option Pricing*, edited by M. Brenner. Lexington, Mass.: Heath, 1983, pp. 101–21.

Bookstaber, R. "Observed Option Mispricing and the Nonsimultaneity of Stock and Option Quotations." *Journal of Business* 54 (January 1981): 141–55.

Boyle, P., and A. L. Ananthanarayanan. "The Impact of Variance Estimation in Option Valuation Models." *Journal of Financial Economics* 5 (December 1977): 375–88.

Chiras, D., and S. Manaster. "The Information Content of Option Prices and a Test of Market Efficiency." *Journal of Financial Economics* 6 (June–September 1978): 213–34.

Cox, J., and S. Ross. "The Valuation of Options for Alternative Stochastic Processes." *Journal of Financial Economics* 3 (January–March 1976): 145–66.

Cox, J., and M. Rubinstein. *Option Markets*. Englewood Cliffs, N.J.: Prentice-Hall, 1985.

Figlewski, S. "Option Arbitrage in Imperfect Markets." *Journal of Finance* 44 (1989): 1289–1311.

Finnerty, J. "The CBOE and Market Efficiency." *Journal of Financial and Quantitative Analysis* 13 (March 1978): 29–38.

Galai, D. "Tests of Market Efficiency of the Chicago Board Option Exchange." *Journal of Business* 50 (April 1977): 167–97.

————. "Empirical Tests of Boundary Conditions for CBOE Options." *Journal of Financial Economics* 6 (June–September 1978): 187–211.

————. "A Convexity Test for Traded Options." *Quarterly Review of Economics and Business* 19 (Summer 1979): 83–90.

————. "A Survey of Empirical Tests of Option Pricing Models." In *Option Pricing,* edited by M. Brenner. Lexington, Mass.: Heath, 1983, pp. 45–80.

Garman, M., and M. Klass. "On the Estimation of Security Price Volatilities from Historical Data." *Journal of Business* 53 (January 1980): 67–78.

Geske, R., and R. Roll. "On Valuing American Call Options with the Black-Scholes Formula." *Journal of Finance* 39 (June 1984): 443–55.

Gould, J., and D. Galai. "Transactions Costs and the Relationship Betwen Put and Call Prices." *Journal of Financial Economics* 1 (June 1974): 105–29.

Ho, T., and R. Macris. "Dealer Bid-Ask Quotes and Transaction Prices: An Empirical Study of Some AMEX Options." *Journal of Finance* 39 (March 1984): 23–45.

Jarrow, R., and A. Rudd. *Option Pricing.* Homewood, Ill.: Irwin, 1983.

Klemkosky, R., and B. Resnick. "Put-Call Parity and Market Efficiency." *Journal of Finance* 34 (December 1979): 1141–55.

Kolb, R. *Options: An Introduction,* 2d ed. Miami: Kolb, 1994.

Latane, H., and R. Rendleman. "Standard Deviations of Stock Price Ratios Implied in Option Prices." *Journal of Finance* 31 (May 1976): 369–82.

Lo, A., and J. Wang. "Implementing Option Models When Asset Returns are Predictable." MIT Sloan School of Management, Working Paper No. 3593-93-EFA, 1993.

MacBeth, J., and L. Merville. "An Empirical Examination of the Black-Scholes Call Option Pricing Model." *Journal of Finance* 34 (December 1979): 1173–86.

Manaster, S., and R. Rendleman, Jr. "Option Prices as Predictors of Equilibrium Stock Prices." *Journal of Finance* 37 (September 1982): 1043–58.

Parkinson, M. "The Extreme Value Method for Estimating the Variances of the Rate of Return." *Journal of Business* 53 (January 1980): 61–65.

Phillips, S., and C. Smith. "Trading Costs for Listed Options: The Implications for Market Efficiency." *Journal of Financial Economics* 8 (June 1980): 179–201.

Rogalski, R. "Variances of Option Prices in Theory and Evidence." *Journal of Portfolio Management* 4 (Winter 1978): 43–51.

Rubinstein, M. "The Valuation of Uncertain Income Streams and the Pricing of Options." *Bell Journal of Economics* 7 (Autumn 1976): 407–25.

————. "Nonparametric Tests of Alternative Option Pricing Models." *Journal of Finance* 40 (June 1985): 455–80.

Schmalensee, R., and R. Trippi. "Common Stock Volatility Expectations Implied by Option Premia." *Journal of Finance* 33 (March 1978): 129–47.

Scholes, M. "Taxes and the Pricing of Options." *Journal of Finance* 31 (May 1976): 319–32.

Smith, C., Jr. "Option Pricing: A Review." *Journal of Financial Economics* 3 (January–March 1976): 3–51.

Sterk, W. "Tests of Two Models for Valuing Call Options on Stocks with Dividends." *Journal of Finance* 37 (December 1982): 1229–38.

_____ . "Comparative Performance of the Black-Scholes and Roll-Geske-Whaley Option Pricing Models." *Journal of Financial and Quantitative Analysis* 18 (September 1983): 345–54.

Whaley, R. "Valuation of American Call Options on Dividend Paying Stocks: Emprical Tests." *Journal of Financial Economics* 10 (March 1982): 29–58.

Exercises

1. A stock is priced at $30. The volatility of the stock is 25 percent per year and the interest rate is 7 percent.
   a. Price a three-month European call option with a strike price of $35.
   b. Use put-call parity to price the European put.

2. A stock is currently priced at $50. Interest rates are 6 percent per year. The prices of three different options, all with 60 days to expiration are shown below.

Strike ($)	Call Price ($)	Implied Volatility
40	10.60	0.38
50	2.67	0.30
60	0.29	0.32

   If options were priced by the Black-Scholes model, the implied volatility of all these contracts would be the same. However, they are not.
   a. Which of the three implied volatilities would you use as an estimate for the true volatility?
   b. If somehow you know the true volatility is 0.29, what can you say about the call options?

3. The daily closing prices of a nondividend-paying stock are shown below.

Day	Price ($)	Day	Price ($)
1	20.00	9	24.50
2	20.25	10	23.75
3	21.50	11	23.50
4	22.25	12	25.75
5	22.25	13	25.75
6	23.30	14	26.50
7	22.25	15	27.00
8	23.75	16	28.00

   a. Compute the 15 daily logarithmic returns, and use them to compute the mean and variance.

b. Annualize the variance, based on 260 business days in the year. Compute the annualized volatility.

c. Comment on the value of this estimate if it is used in the Black-Scholes model. What other estimators could be considered?

4. "If the implied volatilities for European options, when plotted against the strike price, do not fall on a line parallel to the x axis, then the Black-Scholes model cannot be correct. Moreover, if there is a systematic pattern in this plot, then it indicates a consistent bias in the Black-Scholes model." Comment on this statement.

5. If all traders had the same opinions on volatilities, then the liquidity in the option market would be reduced. It is the heterogeneity of beliefs about volatility that gives the market liquidity. Discuss.

6. "The price of an option depends on the total volatility of the stock." "The price of a security depends on the total amount of nondiversifiable risk inherent in the stock." Are these two statements inconsistent? Should option prices depend only on the level of nondiversifiable risk? If not, explain.

APPENDIX 9A

A Heuristic Development of the Black-Scholes Equation[5]

In Chapter 8, dynamic trading strategies in discrete time periods were established such that the option payout was replicated over an approximating binomial process. In this chapter, we do not have an approximating stock price process, nor do we assume that trading can occur only at certain times. Rather, we assume the price process follows a geometric Wiener process and trading occurs continuously over the time increment $[0, T]$. Specifically, we assume that the stock price dynamic is given by

$$ds = \mu s\, dt + \sigma s\, dw \tag{9A.1}$$

Let the call option price be C. The call price depends critically on the stock price, S, and upon the time, t. Suppressing the additional parameters, we can write $C = C(S, t)$. We now use Ito's lemma to obtain

$$dC = C_s\, dS + C_t\, dt + 1/2(\sigma S)^2 C_{ss}\, dt \tag{9A.2}$$

Substituting equation (9A.1) into equation (9A.2), we have

$$dC = C_s(\mu S\, dt + \sigma S\, dw) + C_t\, dt + 1/2\sigma^2 S^2 C_{ss}\, dt$$

or

$$dC = [C_s \mu S + C_t + 1/2\sigma^2 S^2 C_{ss}]\, dt + \sigma S C_s\, dw \tag{9A.3}$$

If in the time increment $[t, t + \Delta t]$ the stock moves by Δs, then the call option change is given by Δc, where Δc, from equation (9A.3), is given by

$$\Delta c = [C_s \mu S + C_t + 1/2\sigma^2 S^2 C_{ss}]\, \Delta t + \sigma S C_s\, \Delta w \tag{9A.4}$$

The approach followed by Black and Scholes is to establish a portfolio of H shares long and 1 option short such that the portfolio is riskless. Let the current value of this portfolio be $V(t)$. Then

$$V(t) = HS(t) - C(t) \tag{9A.5}$$

---

[5] For a more precise proof of the Black-Scholes model, see Beck or Jarrow and Rudd.

The changes in value of this portfolio in time Δt is given by ΔV, where $\Delta V = H \Delta s - \Delta c$.[6] Substituting for Δs and Δc, we obtain

$$\Delta V = H[\mu S \, \Delta t + \sigma S \, \Delta w - [C_s \mu S + C_t + 1/2\sigma^2 S^2 C_{ss}] \, \Delta t - \sigma S C_s \, \Delta w$$

$$= [H\mu S - C_s \mu S - C_t - 1/2\sigma^2 S^2 C_{ss}] \, \Delta t + [HS\sigma - S\sigma C_s] \, \Delta w$$

The above change consists of a deterministic portion plus a stochastic portion. The stochastic portion disappears only if the coefficient $[HS\sigma - S\sigma C_s]$ equals zero, and this is the case if H is chosen to be equal to the slope of the option pricing line (that is, $H = C_s$). With $H = C_s$, we have

$$\Delta V = [-C_t - 1/2\sigma^2 S^2 C_{ss}] \, \Delta t \tag{9A.6}$$

Since the change in this portfolio value is riskless, it should earn the same rate of return as the riskless security. That is,

$$\Delta V = rV(t) \, \Delta t \tag{9A.7}$$

Substituting equation (9A.5) into equation (9A.7) yields

$$\Delta V = [rS(t)C_s - rC(t)] \, \Delta t \tag{9A.8}$$

Equating equations (9A.6) and (9A.8), we obtain

$$\frac{\sigma^2}{2} S^2 C_{ss} + rSC_s + C_t = rC \tag{9A.9}$$

This partial differential equation, together with the following call option boundary conditions, fully characterizes the call price:

$$C(S(T), T) = \text{Max}[0, S(T) - X]$$

Specifically, the solution to this partial differential equation is the Black-Scholes option price.

---

[6] The development is not precise because over the time increment the portfolio composition may change. Taking this change into consideration and using the self-financing condition, we could develop a more comprehensive proof. However, the heuristic development does lead to the right result.

CHAPTER 10

Risk Management with Options

In this chapter we take a closer look at the use of the Black-Scholes model for managing the risk of positions that contain options. The Black-Scholes analysis produces more than just a fair price for an option. It also provides information the trader uses to manage the risk of the position. The goal of this chapter is to investigate the basic risk management measures for options. These measures capture the sensitivity of option prices to changes in key variables such as the underlying stock price, time to expiration, volatility, and interest rate. An understanding of these measures is absolutely essential for any option trader. We provide examples of how traders can use these measures to curtail the overall risks of positions containing multiple option contracts.

The primary objectives of this chapter are the following:

• To explain how option prices change in response to changes in key variables; and

• To show how to use such information to manage the risk of portfolios that contain options.

The Delta Value and Delta Hedging

The delta value, Δ, measures the sensitivity of the option price to small instantaneous changes in the stock price. That is, $\Delta = \partial C / \partial S$. For the Black-Scholes call option, the formula for Δ is given by $\Delta = N(d_1)$. The delta value for European puts is $N(d_1) - 1$.

At-the-money call (put) options have delta values close to 0.5 (-0.5). Exhibit 10.1 shows the sensitivity of delta values of options to the stock price. If the delta value of a call is 0.3, then the short position in the option will lose \$0.30 if the stock price increases by \$1. Equivalently, if the short position bought 0.3 shares, then the position would be immunized against instantaneous local changes in the price.

Unfortunately, since the delta value depends on the stock price and time to expiration, it does not remain constant, and the immunized position will soon be exposed to risk. To maintain the hedge, the trader must continually adjust the position in the stock such that the number of shares bought always equals the delta value.

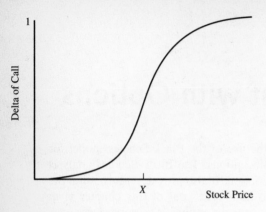

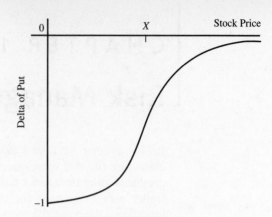

EXHIBIT 10.1   Delta Values

EXAMPLE 10.1   Delta Hedging

A stock is priced at $50. Its volatility is 38 percent per year. Interest rates are 5 percent per year. A five-week at-the-money European call option is priced at $2.47. The delta value of the option is 0.5625. To construct a delta hedge requires purchasing Δ shares of stock. Consider an investor who has sold 10,000 call options.[1] To immunize this position against a small instantaneous change in the stock price, the investor needs to purchase 5,625 shares of the stock. Assume all these shares are financed by borrowing at the risk-free rate.

The trader adjusts the hedge position each week. If the price goes down, the delta value decreases, shares are sold, and the proceeds are used to reduce the size of the outstanding loan. If prices increase, the delta value increase, and additional shares must be purchased to maintain the delta-neutral strategy. If the underlying security performs well, the delta value will eventually increase in value toward 1, while if the underlying security does poorly, then the delta value declines to zero. Exhibit 10.2 illustrates how the delta hedging strategy evolved over the five weeks prior to expiration.

At four weeks, the stock price increased by 50 cents, and the delta value changed by 0.0103. This implied that 103 additional shares had to be purchased to maintain the delta-neutral position. All purchases are financed by borrowing. The last column shows the total funds that are owed. In this example, the option expired in the money, and the total number of shares held by the trader increased from 5,625 to 10,000. The trader receives $50 per share for these stocks. This leaves a net obligation of $13,985. Offsetting this loss, of course, is the premium taken in from the sale of the 10,000 options. This revenue is $24,700, which, if invested at the riskless rate over the five weeks, would grow to $24,819. Hence, the delta hedging scheme leads to a profit of $10,834.

---

[1] We assume that each call option controls one share, not 100 shares.

EXHIBIT 10.2   Delta Hedging with Weekly Revisions

Time to Expiration (Weeks)	Stock Price ($)	Delta	Change in Delta	Shares Purchased or Sold	Cost of Shares ($)	Cumulative Cost ($)
5	50.00	0.5625	—	5,625	281,250.00	281,250
4	50.50	0.5728	0.0103	103	5,201.50	286,722
3	51.25	0.6361	0.0633	633	32,441.25	319,439
2	51.00	0.6289	−0.0072	−72	−3,672.00	316,074
1	52.25	0.8108	0.1819	1,819	95,042.75	411,421
0	54.00	1	0.1892	1,892	102,168.00	513,985

The actual profit or loss on this strategy depends on the path of prices over time, as well as on the frequency of revisions. If the frequency of revision is increased, then the outcome from the delta-neutral hedging scheme becomes more predictable. That is, as the revision frequency is increased, the performance of the hedge improves. In theory, if continuous revisions had been made, then the net profits from selling the option and following the delta hedging strategy should be zero.

The Gamma Value

The delta value changes in response to the stock price and to the passage of time. If the value is extremely sensitive to the underlying stock price or time to expiration, then frequent portfolio revisions will be necessary to maintain an effective delta hedge.

The gamma value is a measure of the rate of change of the delta value. If an option has a small gamma value, the option's delta value is relatively stable and thus can hedge a large price change in the underlying stock better than if the option had a large gamma value. The gamma value is also referred to as the curvature, since it measures the curvature of the option price with respect to the stock price. Formally, the gamma of a call option, γ, is the second partial derivative with respect to the stock price. That is, $\gamma = \dfrac{\partial^2 C}{\partial S^2}$. For a call option the gamma value can be computed as

$$\gamma = \frac{n(d_1)}{S\sigma\sqrt{T}}$$

where $n(d_1) = e^{-d_1^2/2}/\sqrt{2\pi}$

$$d_1 = [\ln(S_0/X) + (r + \sigma^2/2)T]/\sigma\sqrt{T}$$

and T is the time remaining to expiration. The gamma values for European puts are the same as those for calls.

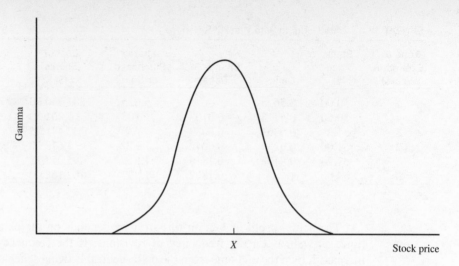

EXHIBIT 10.3   Variation of Gamma with Stock Price

EXAMPLE 10.2   A stock is priced at $50. The volatility of the stock is 30 percent, and interest rates are 5 percent. A three-month at-the-money European call option trades at $3.27. The delta value is 0.5625, and the gamma value is 0.0529. If the stock changes price by 1 cent, the change in the option price should be ($0.5625)(0.01) = $0.005625. The new delta value will not be $0.5625 but will be $0.5625 + ($0.0529)(0.01) = $0.563029.

The gamma value can increase dramatically as the time to expiration decreases. Gamma values are largest for at-the-money options and smallest for deep-in-the-money and deep-out-of-the-money options. Exhibit 10.3 shows the behavior of γ values for options as the stock price changes.

The Theta Value

The theta value measures the dollar change in the option price per unit decrease in the time to expiration, assuming the stock price remains unchanged. The theta value for call options on nondividend stocks is always negative. This is because as time to maturity decreases, the option becomes less valuable. Stock options with large negative theta values can lose their time premium rapidly. The value changes the most as maturity approaches. Thetas can be viewed as the income stream to an option seller, provided the stock price remains the same. Put options usually have negative thetas as well. However, deep-in-the-money European puts could have positive thetas. The sensitivity of the call theta for different stock prices is illustrated in Exhibit 10.4.

The theta value, θ, can be computed from the Black-Scholes model. Specifically, for a European call and put the equations are

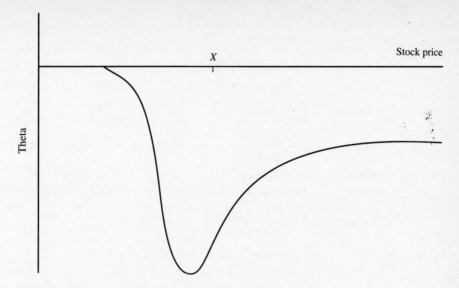

EXHIBIT 10.4   Variation of Theta with Stock Price

$$\theta_c = -\frac{\partial C}{\partial T} = -\frac{S(0)n(d_1)\sigma}{2\sqrt{T}} - rX\,e^{-rT}N(d_2)$$

$$\theta_p = -\frac{\partial P}{\partial T} = -\frac{S(0)n(d_1)\sigma}{2\sqrt{T}} + rX\,e^{-rT}N(-d_2)$$

EXAMPLE 10.3   Reconsider our stock priced at $50. The volatility of the stock is 30 percent and interest rates are 5 percent. A three-month at-the-money European call option trades at $3.27. The theta value of this option is $-$7.196 per year. If this number is divided by 52, the resulting number ($0.1384) represents the expected drop in the price of the option if the stock price remains unchanged for one week.

The Vega Value

The vega is a measure of the sensitivity of the option to the volatility. Vega measures the dollar change in the value of the option when the underlying volatility changes by 1 percent. Under the Black-Scholes model, vega, v, is given by

$$v = \frac{\partial C}{\partial \sigma} = S\sqrt{T}\,n(d_1)$$

where $n(d_1) = e^{-d_1^2/2}/\sqrt{2\pi}$

European puts with the same terms have the same vega values. A change in volatility will have the greatest total dollar effect on at-the-money options and the greatest percentage effect on out-of-the-money options.

EXHIBIT 10.5   Formulas for the Black-Scholes Delta, Gamma, Theta, Vega, and Rho Values

	European Call	European Put
Delta	$N(d_1)$	$N(d_1) - 1$
Gamma	$\dfrac{n(d_1)}{S\sigma\sqrt{T}}$	$\dfrac{n(d_1)}{S\sigma\sqrt{T}}$
Theta	$-\dfrac{S(0)n(d_1)\sigma}{2\sqrt{T}} - rX\,e^{-rT}\,N(d_2)$	$-\dfrac{S(0)n(d_1)\sigma}{2\sqrt{T}} + rX\,e^{-rT}\,N(-d_2)$
Vega	$S(0)\sqrt{T}\,n(d_1)$	$S(0)\sqrt{T}\,n(d_1)$
Rho	$XT\,e^{-rT}\,N(d_2)$	$-XT\,e^{-rT}\,N(-d_2)$

where
$$n(d_1) = \frac{1}{\sqrt{2\pi}}\,e^{-d_1{}^2/2}$$

$$d_1 = [\ln(S(0)/X) + (r + \sigma^2/2)T]/\sigma\sqrt{T}$$
$$d_2 = d - r\sqrt{T}$$

and $N(d_1)$ is the cumulative normal distribution function.

EXAMPLE 10.4   Reconsider our stock priced at $50, with volatility of 30 percent and interest rates at 5 percent. A three-month at-the-money call option is priced at $3.27 and has a vega value of $9.7833. This implies that if the volatility increases from 0.30 to 0.31, the price will change by ($9.7833)(0.01) = $0.097833.

The vega value can be viewed as a volatility hedge ratio. A trader with an opinion on volatility can choose a position that increases in value if the opinion is correct. For example, if the trader believes the implied volatility is low and is about to increase, then a position with a positive vega value can be established. Like delta, the vega approximation is valid only for short ranges of volatility estimates. Vega changes with the stock price and with time to expiration and is maximized for options that are near the money.

The Rho Value

The sensitivity of an option's theoretical value to a change in interest rates is referred to as the rho value and is usually quite small for options with maturities less than a year. This is evidenced in Exhibit 9.4, where the diagrams of option prices against interest rates produce slopes which, for small interest rate changes, are quite flat. Rho values for calls are positive and for puts are negative.

EXAMPLE 10.5   Reconsider our stock priced at $50. The volatility of the stock is 30 percent and interest rates are 5 percent. A three-month at-the-money European call option trades at $3.27. The rho of this option is 6.129. This implies that if interest rates increase from 5 percent to 6 percent, the option price will change by ($6.129)(0.01) = $0.06129.

Exhibit 10.5 summarizes the formulas for delta, gamma, theta, vega, and rho values for Black-Scholes–priced European calls and puts.

EXHIBIT 10.6   Option Prices

Strike	Near Call Series (T = 0.25)	Middle Call Series (T = 0.5)	Far Call Series (T = 1)	Near Put Series (T = 0.25)	Middle Put Series (T = 0.5)	Far Put Series (T = 1)
$30	$11.09	$12.42	$14.54	$0.64	$1.53	$2.90
40	4.65	6.68	9.63	4.05	5.50	7.30
50	1.57	3.37	6.29	10.83	11.90	13.30
70	0.13	1.65	2.73	29.09	19.87	28.65
80	0.034	0.39	1.82	38.84	38.02	37.16

Example 10.6 illustrates these sensitivity measures.

EXHIBIT 10.7   Delta Values

Strike	Near Call Series (T = 0.25)	Middle Call Series (T = 0.5)	Far Call Series (T = 1)	Near Put Series (T = 0.25)	Middle Put Series (T = 0.5)	Far Put Series (T = 1)
$30	0.8922	0.8441	0.8178	−0.1078	−0.1559	−0.1822
40	0.5761	0.6070	0.6495	−0.4239	−0.3930	−0.3505
50	0.2678	0.3813	0.4914	−0.7322	−0.6187	−0.5086
70	0.0327	0.2204	0.2632	−0.9673	−0.7796	−0.7368
80	0.0099	0.0654	0.1905	−0.9901	−0.9346	−0.8095

EXAMPLE 10.6   Exhibit 10.6 shows the prices of selected European options on a stock. The stock price is $40, its volatility is 55 percent, and interest rates are 6 percent. Note that the prices of the 80 puts do not increase with the expiration date. This occurs because the option is deep in the money, and the trader would like to exercise the contract but has to wait until the expiration date. Exhibit 10.7 lists the delta values of the options. The delta value of the near series 40 call option is 0.5761, which means that if the stock price moves immediately up by $1, the call will increase by 57.61 cents. Note that the delta values for out-of-the-money options are small. For example, the delta value for the 70 near series option is 0.0327, or 3.27 cents. Delta

EXHIBIT 10.8   Gamma Values

Strike	Near Call Series (T = 0.25)	Middle Call Series (T = 0.5)	Far Call Series (T = 1)	Near Put Series (T = 0.25)	Middle Put Series (T = 0.5)	Far Put Series (T = 1)
$30	0.0169	0.0154	0.0120	0.0169	0.0154	0.0120
40	0.0356	0.0247	0.0168	0.0356	0.0247	0.0168
50	0.0299	0.0245	0.0181	0.0299	0.0245	0.0181
70	0.0066	0.0191	0.0148	0.0066	0.0191	0.0148
80	0.0024	0.0082	0.0124	0.0024	0.0082	0.0124

EXHIBIT 10.9 Theta Values

Strike	Near Call Series (T = 0.25)	Middle Call Series (T = 0.5)	Far Call Series (T = 1)	Near Put Series (T = 0.25)	Middle Put Series (T = 0.5)	Far Put Series (T = 1)
$30	−5.55	−5.00	−3.99	−3.78	−3.26	−2.30
40	−9.72	−7.04	−5.06	−7.36	−4.71	−2.80
50	−7.79	−6.64	−5.19	−4.84	−3.73	−2.36
70	−1.68	−5.04	−4.06	2.46	−1.55	−0.10
80	−0.61	−2.12	−3.34	4.12	2.54	1.18

values also depend on maturity. In particular, as maturity approaches, the delta values should converge to either zero or 1, depending on whether the option is out of the money or in the money, respectively.

Delta values for put options are negative and are also listed in Exhibit 10.7. The delta value of the 40 near series put is −0.4239, which means the put will decline by 42.39 cents if the stock moves up by $1.

Exhibit 10.8 shows the gamma values for the options. The gamma value of the near series 40 call option is 0.03566. This means that for every $1 change in the stock price, the delta value will change by 3.56 cents. Loosely speaking, this implies that if the stock moved by $2, the change in the call option would be 57.61 cents for the first $1 change (from the delta value) and 57.61 + 3.56 = 61.17 cents for the second dollar. Similarly, if the stock price declined by $2, the option would decline 57.61 cents for the first dollar and 57.61 − 3.56 = 54.05 cents for the second dollar.

Gamma values are the largest for options at the money and smallest for deep-in-the-money and deep-out-of-the-money options. Note that the gamma values for puts equal those for calls.

Exhibit 10.9 shows the theta values for the options, reported as annual cash flows. The theta value for the near series 40 call option is −$9.7203. This means that if the stock price remained unchanged for one week, the price of the call option would decrease by ($9.7203)(1/52) = 18.69 cents. Note that the theta values reach their minimum for options at-the-money. That is, if stock prices remain unchanged, those call sellers who sold at-the-money options will benefit the most. This follows because at-the-money options are expected to have the largest time premium.

EXHIBIT 10.10 Vega Values

Strike	Near Call Series (T = 0.25)	Middle Call Series (T = 0.5)	Far Call Series (T = 1)	Near Put Series (T = 0.25)	Middle Put Series (T = 0.5)	Far Put Series (T = 1)
$30	3.71	6.77	10.57	3.71	6.77	10.57
40	7.83	10.87	14.82	7.83	10.87	14.82
50	6.59	10.78	15.95	6.59	10.78	15.95
70	1.46	8.38	13.05	1.46	8.38	13.05
80	0.53	3.60	10.87	0.53	3.60	10.87

EXHIBIT 10.11 Rho Values

Strike	Near Call Series ($T = 0.25$)	Middle Call Series ($T = 0.5$)	Far Call Series ($T = 1$)	Near Put Series ($T = 0.25$)	Middle Put Series ($T = 0.5$)	Far Put Series ($T = 1$)
$30	6.15	8.80	16.35	−1.24	−3.88	−10.18
40	4.60	8.80	16.35	−5.25	−10.61	−21.32
50	2.28	5.94	13.36	−10.01	−18.32	−33.73
70	2.95	3.58	7.80	−16.94	−25.31	−58.12
80	0.09	1.12	5.79	−19.61	−37.70	−69.54

Note from Exhibit 10.9 that all the call options have negative thetas. Positive thetas may occur for European put options because long-term deep-in-the-money options may be less valuable than shorter-term European puts. Indeed, if the theta value is positive, then the longer put may be less valuable than the nearer put with the same strike. Of course, if the options were American, the theta values would be negative.

Exhibit 10.10 shows the vega values for the options. The vega value for the near-term 40 call option is 7.83. This means that if the volatility increased by 1 percent from 55 percent to 56 percent, the option value would increase from $4.65 to $4.65 + ($7.83)0.01 = $4.7283. The largest vega values arise for the at-the-money options. The vega values increase with maturity.

Exhibit 10.11 shows the rho values for the options. The near-term 40 call option has a rho value of 4.60. This means that if interest rates increase from 6 percent to 7 percent, the option price will increase from $4.65 to $4.65 + ($4.60)0.10 = $5.11.

Position Deltas, Gammas, Thetas, Vegas, and Rhos

Consider an investor who currently holds a call spread, a straddle, or a covered position. To make matters specific, assume the position contains n_1 calls of one type, n_2 calls of another type, and m_1 and m_2 puts with different strike prices and/or expiration dates. The value of the position, V_0, is given by

$$V_0 = n_1 c_1 + n_2 c_2 + m_1 p_1 + m_2 p_2$$

where c_1 and c_2 are the cost of the two different calls and p_1 and p_2 are the costs of the two puts. The delta, gamma, theta, vega, and rho values for this position are given by

$$\Delta = n_1 \Delta_{c_1} + n_2 \Delta_{c_2} + m_1 \Delta_{p_1} + m_2 \Delta_{p_2}$$

$$\gamma = n_1 \gamma_{c_1} + n_2 \gamma_{c_2} + m_1 \gamma_{p_1} + m_2 \gamma_{p_2}$$

$$\theta = n_1 \theta_{c_1} + n_2 \theta_{c_2} + m_1 \theta_{p_1} + m_2 \theta_{p_2}$$

$$\nu = n_1 \nu_{c_1} + n_2 \nu_{c_2} + m_1 \nu_{p_1} + m_2 \nu_{p_2}$$

$$\rho = n_1 \rho_{c_1} + n_2 \rho_{c_2} + m_1 \rho_{p_1} + m_2 \rho_{p_2}$$

Stock option positions can be created to have very particular position delta, gamma, theta, vega, and rho values that reflect the decision maker's preferences. If an investor is bullish, a high-delta portfolio may be appropriate. If an investor is neutral about a stock and constructs a position by selling calls against stock held, then a portfolio with a large negative theta, almost zero delta, and a low gamma value would be desirable.

A position with a zero delta value and a low-absolute-value gamma will be better immunized than one with a larger gamma. Equivalently, a position with a low-absolute-value gamma should require less frequent portfolio revisions to keep the position delta-constant than a position with a higher-absolute-value gamma.

Regardless of the goals of an investor, the very fact that the sensitivity of optioned positions to stock price, time, volatility, and interest rates can be captured is useful.

Volatility Trading

Some traders believe that the market is efficient with respect to prices but inefficient with respect to volatility. In such a market, information about future volatility could be used in designing successful trading rules. Trading rules that exploit opinions on volatility are referred to as **volatility trading rules.**

One strategy for implementing a volatility trading rule is based on the vega value. Recall that vega measures the sensitivity of option prices to changes in volatility. A trader who thinks that volatility will increase above the current levels implied by the market should invest in a positive-vega position. Since all options have positive vegas, the investor should purchase calls and puts. If the trader also believes the stock is currently underpriced (overpriced), then clearly the best strategy is to purchase call (put) options. However, if the investor has no information on the direction of future price movement, then a risk-neutral position, with a zero delta value, may be desirable.

EXAMPLE 10.7   A Vega-Delta Trading Strategy

The current information on three-month at-the-money European call and put options is shown in Exhibit 10.12. The current option prices are set at their Black-Scholes values. Suppose a trader has established Δ^* to be the target position delta and ν^* to be the target position vega. To initiate a strategy that meets the target, the trader must purchase N_c calls and N_p puts, where N_c and N_p are chosen such that

$$\Delta_c N_c + \Delta_p N_p = \Delta^*$$

$$\nu_c N_c + \nu_p N_p = \nu^*$$

For European options, $\Delta_p = \Delta_c - 1$ and $\nu_c = \nu_p$. Hence

$$\Delta_c N_c + (\Delta_c - 1)N_p = \Delta^*$$
$$N_c + \qquad\qquad N_p = \nu^*/\nu_c$$

EXHIBIT 10.12 Option Information

	Call	Put
Price	$3.27	$2.65
Delta	0.5625	−0.4375
Gamma	0.0529	0.0529
Vega	9.7833	9.7833

Solving for N_c and N_p yields

$$N_c = \Delta^* - (\Delta_c - 1)v^*/v_c$$

$$N_p = v^*/v_c - N_c$$

For the case where the investor has no information on the direction of the stock price, $\Delta^* = 0$. In this case the solution simplifies to

$$N_c = (1 - \Delta_c)v^*/v_c$$

$$N_p = -\frac{\Delta_c}{\Delta_p}N_c$$

If the trader set the target vega value at 1.2 times the current call vega value, then the actual number of calls to buy is $N_c = (1 - 0.5625)1.2 = 0.525$, and the number of puts to buy is $N_p = -[(0.5625)/(-0.4375)]0.525 = 0.675$. A trader who purchases 525 calls and 675 puts has created a position that has a delta value of zero but will profit if volatility expands.

Clearly, if additional constraints were imposed on the desired gamma, theta, or rho of the position, then additional option contracts would be needed.

In Chapter 15 we shall consider a more direct way of placing bets on volatilities. In particular, we shall consider option contracts written on volatility indices.

Of course, these types of trading strategies meet their target restrictions only over small time increments, and continual revisions are necessary to maintain the risk profile. Before implementing any delta hedging or volatility trading scheme, the trader should perform computer simulations to establish the viability of such a strategy. This is especially important when portfolio revisions can be accomplished only at discrete points in time and when transaction costs are incurred.

The Relationship Between Delta, Gamma, and Theta

We have seen that the Black-Scholes equation is the solution to the following partial differential equation (equation (9A.9)):

$$\frac{\sigma^2}{2}S^2C_{ss} + rSC_s + C_t - rC = 0$$

We can rewrite this equation in terms of the risk management measures. In particular,

$$\frac{\sigma^2}{2}S^2\gamma + rS\,\Delta + \theta - rC = 0$$

The above equation shows the relationship between delta, gamma, and theta. If the position is delta-neutral, then the relationship reduces to

$$\frac{\sigma^2}{2}S^2\gamma + \theta = rC$$

The equation shows that a position with a large positive gamma value must necessarily have an offsetting large negative theta value. A position with a zero delta value and close-to-zero gamma value must have a theta value close to zero.

Hedging Option Positions with Other Options

So far we have not considered the effects of market imperfections. For example, in our delta hedging example, the goal was to replicate the payout of a call option by creating a synthetic call consisting of buying Δ shares of stock using borrowed funds and adjusting this delta value over time. Of course, in practice, there are transaction costs. In addition, the exact value of the volatility is not known, and imprecise estimates have to be used. Finally, the analysis assumes that shares can be traded at all prices. However, if the market experiences shocks, it may not be possible to trade at all stock prices. As a result, the value of the synthetic call option may deviate substantially from its theoretical value. That is, the hedge may not be very effective. While measures like the gamma value may provide some indications of the ability of the synthetic to duplicate the option, in fast-moving markets, traders may not be able to implement their trades fast enough to ensure the duplication is maintained over time.

Figlewski has conducted extensive simulations of the delta hedging scheme in the presence of market imperfections. He shows that the profits and/or losses from initiating a delta hedging strategy can be substantial. While the present value of expected costs asssociated with establishing and maintaining a synthetic call may be close to the Black-Scholes price, the actual variability around this amount is extremely large, even for traders who can transact at very low cost. When option prices match the Black-Scholes model, one of several conclusions can be drawn. Perhaps the risk associated with creating and maintaining a synthetic option is diversifiable. If this is the case, then in a portfolio context only the expectation matters, and the fair price of an option will be the Black-Scholes price. An alternative explanation could be that there are more efficient ways of hedging an option than using the delta hedge. This is discussed next.

When establishing a hedge, the optimal instrument is one that provides cash flows equal but opposite to the existing exposure. If a firm sells an at-the-money call, the best hedge would be to buy an identical at-the-money call (hopefully at a price cheaper than the firm received for the call it sold). If such a call is not available, the next-best strategy would be to purchase a call option with almost identical features. For example, perhaps an out-of-the-money call can be purchased. While the overall position will be exposed to some risk, as computed by delta, gamma, theta, vega, and so on, this risk will be fairly insensitive to changes along any dimension. Since a stock can be viewed as a call option with zero strike, if a stock is used to hedge it has properties that may be far away from the underlying exposure. As a result, the overall position may be quite sensitive to certain changes, and it is not surprising that to maintain the effectiveness of the hedge, frequent revisions in the stock position may be necessary.

EXAMPLE 10.8 Consider the set of call options in Exhibit 10.6. Assume a near-term 30 call was sold. The firm decides to hedge this option by buying a 40 call option in the same series. The overall strike price spread has the following risk profile.

	Sell 30 Call	Buy 40 Call	Overall Position
Cash flow	$11.09	−$4.65	$6.44
Delta	0.8922	0.5761	−0.3161
Gamma	0.0169	0.0356	0.0187
Theta	−5.55	−9.72	−4.17
Vega	3.71	7.83	4.12
Rho	6.15	4.60	1.55

From the risk profile, we see that the position is exposed to losses if the price remains unchanged or increases. The position can of course be made delta-neutral if additional 40 call options are purchased.

A delta-neutral position could be set up by buying $0.8922/0.5761 = 1.548$ 40 calls for each 30 call sold. Hence, if 100 calls with strike 30 were sold, then 155 calls with strike 40 would provide a delta-neutral hedge. Since the hedging instrument (the 40s) is "closer" to the underlying instrument that needs to be hedged than a synthetic call, based on using stock financed by borrowing, the former hedge will be more effective. In particular, if a large increase in price occurred, hedging the sale of 30s by buying 40s should be less risky then hedging the sale of the 30s by buying the appropriate amount of stock.

EXAMPLE 10.9 A market maker's position is given below.

Type	Call	Call	Put
Strike	$30	$50	$50
Expiration	0.25	0.25	0.5
Quantity	100	−200	100
Option price	$11.09	$1.57	$11.90
Delta	0.8922	0.2678	−0.6187
Gamma	0.0169	0.0299	0.0245
Theta	−5.55	−7.79	−3.73

The value of the portfolio is given by

$$V_0 = \$11.09(100) - \$1.57(200) + \$11.90(100) = \$1985$$

$$\Delta = 0.8922(100) - 0.2678(200) - 0.6187(100) = -26.21$$

$$\gamma = 0.0169(100) - 0.0299(200) + 0.0245(100) = -1.84$$

$$\theta = -5.55(100) + 7.79(200) - 3.73(100) = -149$$

The portfolio delta value of -26.21 says that this position is equivalent to holding a short position in 26.21 shares. The trader wants to set up a delta-neutral position and is considering using the call option with strike 40 in either the near-term or middle series. The price information and related risk measures are given in Exhibits 10.6 to 10.10 and are summarized below.

Type	Call	Call
Strike	$40	$40
Expiration	0.25	0.5
Option price	$4.65	$6.68
Delta	0.5761	0.6070
Gamma	0.0356	0.0247
Theta	−9.72	−7.04

First, consider the use of the near series option. If $26.21/0.5761 \approx 45$ options were bought, then the trader's overall delta position would be almost zero. If the middle series were used, then $26.21/0.6070 \approx 43$ options would be needed. A comparison of the resulting positions is shown below.

Type	Position with Near Series Call	Position with Middle Series Call
Delta	−0.28	−0.11
Gamma	−0.238	−0.778
Theta	−586.4	−451.72

By buying 45 near series calls, the trader can establish a position that is almost delta-neutral and has a small gamma value; if the stock price remains unchanged for one day, the position is expected to lose less than $2. In this example, there is not too much difference between the two hedging alternatives. However, it is possible to construct a position for the trader that is both delta-neutral and gamma-neutral. This can be accomplished by using both options in a hedging strategy. In particular, let n_1 and n_2 be the number of options to trade in each of the two series. We require

$$0.5761n_1 + 0.6070n_2 = 26.21$$

$$0.0356n_1 + 0.0247n_2 = 1.84$$

Solving these two equations yields $n_1 = 63.62 \approx 63$ and $n_2 = -17.2027 \approx -17$. The overall hedged position has a delta value of 0.23, a gamma value of -0.017, and a theta value of -641.

Share Equivalents and the Delta Value

According to the Black-Scholes equation, at any point in time a call option is equivalent to a portfolio containing H shares of stock, some of which are financed by borrowing B dollars. Under the conditions of the model, call options are redundant in the sense that their payoff patterns can always be replicated by a dynamic trading strategy which involves continual adjustments of the amount of leverage in a particular portfolio. The current number of shares (H) in this unique replicating portfolio is referred to as the **share equivalents.** Under the Black-Scholes assumptions, the analysis of risk and reward opportunities for call options at this time is equivalent to the analysis of the risk and reward of the replicating leveraged portfolio.

EXAMPLE 10.10 A stock is priced at $50. Its volatility is 20 percent. The risk-free rate is 6 percent. A three-month option with strike 45 is priced by the Black-Scholes model. In particular, from Example 9.1 we have $H^* = N(d_1) = 0.742$ and $B^* = \$29.48$. The call price is $C(0) = H^*S(0) - B^* = (0.742)\$50 - \$29.48 = \$7.62$.

Analyzing the instantaneous risk and reward of this call option is equivalent to analyzing the risks and rewards of a leveraged position consisting of 0.742 shares partially financed by borrowing $29.48.

The Role of Leverage in Risk Management

In order to analyze the risk and reward of option positions, we first must investigate how risks and rewards of leveraged stock positions can be analyzed.

Consider an investor with current wealth W_0 who borrows an additional Q_0 dollars at the risk-free rate R_F and invests the total proceeds in a risky portfolio that provides a total return of R_P. The return on this leveraged portfolio is R_Q, where

$$R_Q = [(Q_0 + W_0)R_P - Q_0 R_F]/W_0$$

$$= \lambda R_P + (1 - \lambda)R_F$$

where λ = (total funds invested)/(total funds invested borrowing).

That is,

$$\lambda = (Q_0 + W_0)/W_0$$

This is called the **leverage.** The expected return and variance of the leveraged portfolio, Q, are given by

$$E(R_Q) = \lambda E(R_P) + (1 - \lambda)R_F \tag{10.1}$$

$$\text{Var}(R_Q) = \text{Var}[\lambda R_P + (1 - \lambda)R_F)] = \lambda^2 \text{Var}(R_P) \tag{10.2}$$

The beta value of the leveraged position is related to the beta value of the unleveraged position by

$$\beta_Q = \lambda \beta_P \tag{10.3}$$

Note that if funds are borrowed, the leverage ratio, a, exceeds 1, and hence the beta value and expected return exceed the values of the unleveraged portfolio. On the other hand, if funds are lent (Q_0 is negative), then risk (as measured by variance or beta value) and reward (as measured by expectation) of the leveraged portfolio fall below the values of the unleveraged portfolio.

EXAMPLE 10.11 Consider a stock priced at $100. Its beta value is 1.2, its expected return is 12 percent, and its volatility is 30 percent. An investor buys the stock by putting down $75 and borrowing $25 at 8 percent ($Q_0 = \$25$, $W_0 = \$75$). Hence, $\lambda = \$100/\$75 = 1.33$. From equations (10.1) through (10.3) we have

$$E(R_Q) = 1.33(0.12) - (0.33)(0.08) = 0.133$$

$$Var(R_Q) = 1.33^2(0.30)^2 = 0.16$$

Taking the square root of this number gives the volatility of this leveraged position as 39.9 percent. The beta value of the position is

$$\beta_Q = (1.33)(1.2) = 1.6$$

Note that if $50 were borrowed, then the leverage ratio would be 2 and the beta value would be 2.4. On the other hand, if the investor has $125 and lends $25 at the risk-free rate, then $W_0 = 125$, $Q_0 = -25$, and $\lambda = 100/125 = 0.75$. In this case the leverage ratio is less than 1 and the beta value is

$$\beta_Q = 0.75(1.2) = 0.9$$

Leverage Ratios and Elasticity of Call Options

Since a call option is equivalent to a portfolio of H shares partially financed by borrowing B dollars, the total funds invested is $HS(0)$, and the amount of borrowed funds is B. Hence the leverage ratio λ is given by

$$\lambda = \frac{HS(0)}{HS(0) - B} = \frac{HS(0)}{C(0)} \tag{10.4}$$

The elasticity of a call option, e, measures the percentage change in the call value for a percentage change in the stock value:

$$e = \frac{\Delta C/C}{\Delta S/S} = \frac{\Delta C}{\Delta S} \frac{S(0)}{C(0)}$$

Now, $\Delta C/\Delta S$ is the change in the call price per unit change in the stock price and is given by the delta value. Hence, the above equation reduces to

$$e = \frac{HS(0)}{C(0)} \tag{10.5}$$

The elasticity of a call option is just the leverage ratio of the replicating portfolio. The higher the elasticity (leverage), the greater the risk of the option.

EXAMPLE 10.12 In Example 10.10 we had $S(0) = \$50$, $H = 0.742$, $B = \$29.48$, and $C(0) = \$7.62$. The elasticity of the call is

$$e = \frac{(0.742)50}{7.62} = 4.87\%$$

Hence, for each percentage change in stock price, the call price changes by 4.87 percent. The elasticity, or leverage value, for call options increases as the stock price decreases. Thus, calls deep out of the money are more risky (higher leveraged) than calls at or in the money.

Instantaneous Measures of Risk and Reward for Options

Since a call option can be replicated by a unique leveraged portfolio, it follows that the instantaneous return on a call, r_c, must equal the instantaneous return on the replicating portfolio. Hence

$$r_c = \lambda r_s + (1 - \lambda)r_f$$

where r_s is the instantaneous return on the stock and r_f is the instantaneous risk-free rate.

The instantaneous expected return on the call, μ_c, variance, σ_c^2, and call beta, β_c, can be computed using equations (10.1) through (10.3) to obtain

$$\mu_c = \lambda \mu_s + (1 - \lambda)r_f \tag{10.6}$$

$$\sigma_c^2 = \lambda^2 \sigma_s^2 \tag{10.7}$$

$$\beta_c = \lambda \beta_s \tag{10.8}$$

where μ_s, σ_s^2, and β_s are the instantaneous expected return, variance, and beta value for the stock.

EXAMPLE 10.13 Reconsider our three-month call option with strike 45. [$S(0) = \$50$, $C(0) = \$7.62$, $H = 0.742$, $B = \$29.48$, and the leverage ratio $\lambda = 4.87$.] The volatility of the stock is 20 percent and the riskless rate of return is 6 percent. Assume the beta value of the stock is 1.2 and the expected instantaneous return is 15 percent. Then

$$\beta_c = \lambda \beta_s = 4.87(1.2) = 5.84$$

$$\mu_c = \lambda \mu_s + (1 - \lambda)r_f = (4.87)(0.15) - (3.87)0.06 = 0.4983, \quad \text{or} \quad 49.83\%$$

$$\sigma_c = \lambda \sigma_s = (4.87)(0.20) = 0.974, \quad \text{or} \quad 97.4\%$$

Note that since the replicating portfolio value changes as time passes and the stock price changes, the instantaneous beta value, expected return, and standard deviation of the call price change. Thus, the values computed above hold true only over small time intervals and only if the stock price changes are small.

Risk and Rewards of Portfolios Containing Options

The risks and rewards of a portfolio containing options can be computed by translating all call options into their equivalent leveraged stock positions. For example, the risk and reward of a covered call writing strategy can be analyzed by converting the sale of a call option to its equivalent leveraged stock position. The "buy one stock, sell one call" position is thus equivalent to a portfolio of $(1 - H)$ shares of the stock and the purchase of B bonds. In this case, since the leverage ratio, a, is less than 1, the risk of the position is less than the risk of buying 1 share of stock.

EXAMPLE 10.14   Risk and Reward of a Covered Call Position

Reconsider Example 10.13, in which we had $S(0) = \$50$, $C(0) = \$7.62$, $H = 0.742$, and $B = \$29.48$. Now consider a portfolio containing a long position in the stock and a written call. The short position in the call is equivalent to a portfolio consisting of selling 0.742 shares and lending \$29.48. Using share equivalents, at this time the portfolio is equivalent to a long position in $(1 - H)$ shares and lending B dollars at the risk-free rate.

The equivalent portfolio consists of $(1 - 0.742) = 0.258$ shares held long and an investment of \$29.48 in the bank. The current value of the portfolio is

$$W_0 = 0.258(\$50) + \$29.48 = \$42.38$$

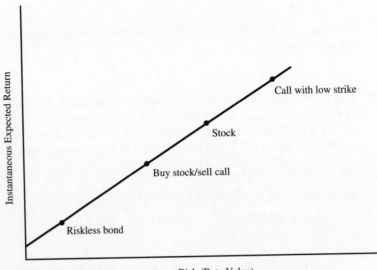

EXHIBIT 10.13   Risk-Reward Relationships for Options

and the amount borrowed at the riskless rate is $Q_0 = -\$29.48$. Hence, the leverage ratio, given by $\lambda = (Q_0 + W_0)/W_0$, is $\lambda = (42.38 - 29.48)/42.38 = 0.304$. The instantaneous beta value for this position is $\beta_Q = \lambda\beta_S = 0.304(1.2) = 0.365$. Moreover, from equations (10.6) and (10.7), the instantaneous expected return, μ_Q, and variance of return, σ_Q^2, can be computed. Specifically, $\mu_Q = 0.304(0.15) + 0.696(0.06) = 0.0874$ or 8.74 percent, and $\sigma_Q = (0.304)(0.20) = 0.0608$, or 6.08 percent. To compensate for the risk involved in this position, its expected return exceeds the risk-free rate of 6 percent.

By translating portfolios containing options into equivalent leveraged stock positions, we can compute the relationship between a portfolio's expected return and its beta value. Exhibit 10.13 illustrates the relationship for a few call option strategies.

Conclusion

The development of a pricing model is extremely important. The model gives guidelines for establishing whether prices are fair or not and also provides a mechanism for developing strategies for hedging. Indeed, without something like the Black-Scholes model, it would not be possible to establish immunized (hedged) positions. In this chapter we introduced the basic risk management measures. We also discussed applications, such as volatility trading, in which the delta, gamma, theta, and vega values of a position are adjusted to reflect the preferences of the investor.

In this chapter we have been concerned with sensitivity measures for European options. The same concepts hold true for American claims, but in many cases, analytical solutions are not available for these risk measures and numerical procedures have to be used.

References

Cox and Rubinstein's textbook has a very detailed discussion of the risk measures. The example on vega hedges is taken from Shimko.

Cox, J., and M. Rubinstein. *Option Markets*. Englewood Cliffs, N.J.: Prentice-Hall, 1985.

Figlewski, S. "Option Arbitrage in Imperfect Markets." *Journal of Finance* 44(1989): 1289–1311.

Kolb, R. *Options: An Introduction*, 2d ed. Miami: Kolb, 1994.

Shimko, D. "Volatility Trading Strategies." Technical Memorandum, School of Business Administration, University of Southern California, Los Angeles, 1989.

Exercises

1. A stock is priced at $30. The volatility of the stock is 25 percent per year and the interest rate is 7 percent. A three-month European call option with a strike price of $35 trades at its Black-Scholes price of $0.28.
   a. Use put-call parity to price the European put.
   b. The delta value of the call is 0.1515. Compute the share equivalents and the leverage.
   c. Compute the delta value of the put. Compute the share equivalent and leverage for the put option.
   d. A trader sells 100 of the European call options. How many stocks should the trader hold so that the position is locally immunized?
   e. The gamma of the call option is 0.0625. Interpret this value. In particular, assume that immediately after the trader set up the delta hedge in Exercise 1d, the stock price increased by $2. Without recomputing the new Black-Scholes option price, estimate the new value of the immunized portfolio.

2. A stock is priced at $48. Its volatility is 36 percent per year and interest rates are 7 percent per year. The following information is available on a one-year European option with strikes of 45.

	Call	Put
Price	$9.88	$3.84
Delta	0.71	−0.29
Gamma	0.0198	0.0198
Theta	−4.65	−1.71
Vega	16.43	16.43
Rho	24.20	−17.75

   a. Compute the dollar cost of a call option (assuming it controls 100 shares of stock).
   b. Assume a trader sold 50 call options. Assume the stock price remained unchanged for one week. Estimate the total dollar profit the position shows.
   c. Assume a trader purchased 50 put options. The stock volatility then increased from 36 percent to 40 percent. Estimate the increase in the value of the position.
   d. Assume a trader sold 200 call options and then interest rates declined from 7 percent to 6.5 percent. Estimate the dollar gain in the position.
   e. For the call option, identify the initial replicating portfolio (i.e., the share equivalents and borrowing).
   f. Compute the leverage of the call option and the elasticity of the call. Interpret the result.
   g. If the beta value of the stock is 1.30, estimate the instantaneous beta value of the call and the instantaneous volatility.

3. Repeat Exercise 2, but instead of solving the questions for a call, solve for the put option.

4. Information on three-month at-the-money European options on a stock that has a volatility of 30 percent are shown below. The current stock price is $20.

	Call	Put
Price	$1.37	$1.02
Delta	0.576	−0.424
Gamma	0.1306	0.1306
Theta	−3.06	−1.68
Vega	3.92	3.92
Rho	2.54	−2.37

A trader wants to establish a position that will make money if the volatility expands. The trader is delta-neutral but sets a target vega value of 4.04.

a. Establish a position that fully reflects the trader's view.

b. Contrast this position with a straddle. In particular, identify the delta value of the straddle and the vega value of the straddle, and draw conclusions from these.

c. What is the gamma value of a straddle?

d. An investor buys one call and sells one put. Compute the delta value of this position.

e. An investor buys one stock and sells one call. Compute the delta of this position as well as the share equivalents, net borrowing, and leverage.

5. In Exercise 4 we considered only an at-the-money call and put. Assume the following information is available on a call with strike 25.

	Call
Price	$0.13
Delta	0.0925
Gamma	0.0574
Theta	−1.16
Vega	1.72
Rho	0.45

a. Compute the delta and gamma values of a position consisting of a straddle together with the sale of the out-of-the-money call. How can you interpret the delta value?

6. A stock is trading at 22 1/4. Its volatility is 24 percent per year and interest rates are constant at 4 percent per year. A firm sells 10,000 European call options with strike 20 that expire in 35 days and simultaneously delta hedges, revising the position weekly. The initial price of the call option is $2.78. Below

are the stock prices at the beginning of each week, together with the delta values. Compute the net profit or loss from the delta hedge.

Days to Expiration	Stock Price	Delta Value
35	22 1/4	0.7855
28	22 1/8	0.794
21	21	0.6875
14	23 3/8	0.9512
7	22	0.9225
0	22	1.0

7. How does the value of the share equivalents change as the call option moves from being out of the money to being in the money? How does the value of the share equivalents of the put option change?

APPENDIX 10A

Computing the Greeks for American Options

In this section we describe how risk management measures can be computed for American options. Since analytical solutions are not available, we use the binomial lattice procedure to generate the values.

As befoe let s_{ij} represent the stock price in period i given that j upmoves have occurred. Exhibit 10A.1 shows the usual two-period lattice.

Here $\quad s_{ij} = s_0 u^j d^{i-j} \qquad j = 0, 1, 2, \ldots, i$
$$i = 1, 2, \ldots, n$$

To compute the delta value we need to know the change in the option price if the stock price changes a little. In a numerical differentiation method, the delta value can be approximated by constructing two new trees. The first starts at $s_0 + h$, while the second starts at $s_0 - h$, where h represents a small change in the stock price. The two resulting call values, $c(s_0 + h)$ and $c(s_0 - h)$, can be used to estimate Δ. Specifically,

$$\Delta = \frac{c(s_0 + h) - c(s_0 - h)}{2h}$$

Similarly, the gamma value can be estimated by

$$\gamma = \frac{\left[\dfrac{c(s_0 + h) - c(s_0)}{h} \right] - \left[\dfrac{c(s_0) - c(s_0 - h)}{h} \right]}{h}$$

Here, the first term in the numerator is the delta value for an upmove, while the second term is the delta value for a downmove. The numerator thus gives the change in the delta value for a stock price change of h. The ratio gives the rate of change of the delta value, which is the gamma value.

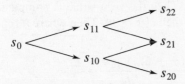

EXHIBIT 10A.1   The Two-Period Lattice

251

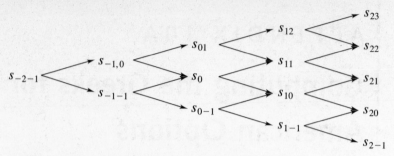

EXHIBIT 10A.2   The Extended Binomial Lattice

An alternative method is to calculate Δ by using an extended binomial lattice as shown in Exhibit 10A.2. The extended lattice consists of the original lattice together with two additional periods that are tacked onto the front end. Using the usual backward recursion on the extended lattice, we can obtain option prices at all nodes. We now approximate the delta value by

$$\Delta = \frac{c(s_{01}) - c(s_{0-1})}{s_{01} - s_{0-1}}$$

and the gamma value can be estimated by

$$\gamma = \frac{\left[\dfrac{c(s_{01}) - c(s_0)}{s_{01} - s_0}\right] - \left[\dfrac{c(s_0) - c(s_{0-1})}{s_0 - s_{0-1}}\right]}{s_{01} - s_0}$$

Using the extended tree is not only computationally faster than rerunning the binomial lattice for small changes in the initial stock price, but is shown by Pelsser and Vorst to be more precise.

Given the estimates of delta and gamma, theta can be calculated using the Black-Scholes's differential equation. Alternatively, the value of θ can be estimated by comparing $c(s_{-2-1})$ and $c(s_0)$. The difference in prices represent the loss of time premium given that the stock price over the two time increments is unchanged. Hence

$$\theta = \frac{c(s_{-2-1}) - c(s_0)}{2\,\Delta t}$$

where Δt is the width of the time increment.

For the remaining Greeks, namely the vega and rho, numerical differentiation methods must be used. In particular let $c(\sigma)$ be the call price computed on the usual lattice based on a volatility of σ. Then the vega value is computed by using two lattices to compute $c(\sigma - h)$ and then $c(\sigma + h)$. Then where h represents a small change in volatility

$$\nu = \frac{c(\sigma + h) - c(\sigma - h)}{2h}$$

Similarly, ρ is computed by using two option prices on two different lattices, the first taking the interest rate to be $r - h$, the second taking the interest rate to be $r + h$. Then,

$$\rho = \frac{c(r + h) - c(r - h)}{2h}$$

Reference

Pelsser, A., and T. Vorst. "The Binomial Model and the Greeks." *The Journal of Derivatives* 1 (Spring 1994): 45–49.

PART FOUR

The Wide Variety

of Derivative

Contracts

Up until now, we have considered derivative contracts that require delivery of a specific financial asset or consumption commodity. For the case of options, we have emphasized option contracts on stocks. Of course the underlying could be any financial asset or consumption commodity. In Chapter 11 we provide a broad overview of a variety of derivative contracts, including options on financial assets (such as bonds, foreign currency, futures, and even other options); options on indices (such as stock market and interest rate yields); options on economic indicators (such as GNP, inflation, or health care costs); and options on accrued statistics (such as a minimum price or an average end-of-week price). In addition, we investigate contracts that involve a commitment or an option to exchange one product for another at a given future date. Such contracts are called exchange agreements or exchange options. Ordinary forward and option contracts can be viewed as special cases of these contracts, if one of the commodities is a predetermined quantity of cash. We also study multiple exchange agreements involving commodity swaps.

In Chapters 12 through 14 we look in more detail at some specific markets. In Chapter 12 we investigate option contracts on futures and forwards. Options on futures are traded on most U.S. futures exchanges, while options on forwards are mainly encountered in over-the-counter markets. We closely investigate pricing relationships for European- and American-style contracts. We shall see that options on futures have properties that are similar but not identical to options on stocks. In addition, options on forwards have different properties than options on futures; the former are easier to analyze.

In Chapter 13 we focus on the financial innovations provided by stock index futures and options. Indeed, stock index options now account for over 50 percent of equity option volume. We identify how these markets can be used to modify the risk-reward relationships of a stock portfolio. We discuss some of the technological advances that make these innovations possible. We review stock markets in the United States and detail how individual securities and portfolios of securities are traded, provide several examples of stock index futures and options and discuss the difference between these contracts and the other types of contracts that we have encountered so far. Finally, we describe application of these contracts in portfolio risk management.

In Chapter 14 we examine foreign exchange derivatives. A brief overview of the interbank and organized exchange markets is followed by a discussion of forward, futures, and foreign currency options. We present examples of a few foreign currency contracts, together with some strategies for managing foreign currency risk. We also explain some arbitrage relationships unique to foreign currencies.

In Chapter 15 we return to the pricing of option contracts. We extend the Black-Scholes analysis to include the pricing of contracts when the underlying pays dividends. We apply the resulting models to the pricing of options on futures, stock indices, and foreign currencies.

In Chapter 16 we investigate the world of exotic derivative contracts, the majority of which are traded in the over-the-counter market. Financial engineers design specific contracts to meet the needs of specific situations. Here we look at the more successful exotic option contracts that have been designed. Of course, many of the successful contracts can hardly be considered exotic, since they have become quite common, are easily priced, and are readily available through most investment banks.

In Chapter 17 we discuss the variety of contingencies that are built into corporate securities. First we review the vast array of corporate bonds. Unlike government securities, corporate bonds are not standardized, and each bond issue must be considered separately. In our discussion of corporate bonds, we emphasize the variety of option features encountered in many contracts. These include callable, puttable, extendable, and conversion options. Next we examine the risk structure of corporate bonds in more detail and develop a simple model of the required risk premium on corporate discount bonds. In addition to valuing a discount corporate bond issue, we investigate pricing a subordinated debt issue, coupon bonds, convertible bonds, and some foreign currency bonds.

CHAPTER 11

The Wide Variety
of Derivative Contracts

In the first part of this chapter we investigate option contracts on financial assets such as bonds, foreign currency, futures, and even other options.

Derivative contracts also exist on underlying entities that are not commodities. For example, derivative contracts can be based on stock market and interest rate indices. When such contracts are exercised, the underlying "commodity" is not exchanged for a predetermined price. Rather, settlement is conducted in cash. This chapter provides several examples of cash-settled contracts that have direct applications in managing portfolio and interest rate risk.

We also investigate cash-settled contracts based on indices that are not directly related to investments (for example, economic indicators such as unemployment, GNP, inflation, or health care costs). Other indices are based on statistics computed from a time series of prices (for example, the payout of a contract might depend on the average end-of-week price that is collected through a given time interval).

Contracts that involve a commitment or an option to exchange one product for another at a given future date are called **exchange agreements** or **exchange options.** Forward (option) contracts are special cases of exchange rate agreements (exchange options), if one of the commodities is a certain amount of money. However, exchange agreements generally involve two distinct commodities, both with uncertain prices. Contracts that involve the periodic exchange of the two commodities before a predetermined expiration date are called **multiple exchange agreements** or **commodity swap contracts.** This chapter provides numerous examples of such contracts.

The primary objectives of this chapter are the following:

- To illustrate the wide variety of derivative contracts;
- To motivate the reader to further study this area; and
- To introduce the topics covered in Chapters 12–17.

Contracts on Financial Assets and Consumption Commodities

We have considered forward and futures contracts in which the underlying asset is a consumption commodity. Of course, option contracts can also be designed on these commodities. Indeed, options and futures can be written on almost any consumption commodity or financial asset. For example, options can exist on metals, such as copper; on debt instruments, such as government bonds; on foreign exchange; and even on futures.

Options and Futures on Bonds

A long position in either a futures or forward contract on a bond has a commitment to purchase the underlying bond for a predetermined price in some predetermined future period. Such contracts allow traders to lock into specific borrowing or lending rates in the future. Let $FO_T(0)$ represent the forward price for delivery of a discount bond that has maturity M at the delivery date T. The face value of the bond is \$1. Let $P(T, T + M)$ represent the actual price of the M-period bond at date T. The terminal payout of this forward contract is $Q(T)$, where

$$Q(T) = P(T, T + M) - FO_T(0) \tag{11.1}$$

A call option with strike X on this bond has a terminal value of $C(T)$, where

$$C(T) = \text{Max}[P(T, T + M) - X, 0] \tag{11.2}$$

Such an option is referred to as a **price-based option** since the exercise price is expressed in terms of the price of the underlying security. If a call written on a coupon bond is exercised, payment of the strike price, together with accrued interest up to the settlement date, is required in return for that particular coupon bond. In addition to options on *specific* debt instruments, options requiring the delivery of securities with certain properties are also available. Such options require the call writer to deliver any bond issue that satisfies the required criteria at the delivery date. For example, a contract may require the deliverable bond to have a particular maturity (measured from the exercise date) and coupon. In this case, more than one issue might be used to satisfy delivery. An example of such a **fixed-deliverable contract** is a nine-month option on a three-month government discount bond. If the option is exercised, the deliverable bond must be a bond with a maturity of three months.

EXAMPLE 11.1   A manager expects to receive a significant amount of funds in three months. Current long-term interest rates are high, and the manager expects them to decline. The manager wants to lock into the prevailing high rate and is considering buying a three-month call option on a 12 percent U.S. Treasury bond, due August 2013, with a principal value of \$100,000. Such an option provides insurance against unanticipated interest rate declines that would push the bond price above the strike price.

Markets in interest rate derivatives are very active. Indeed, the most active futures contracts that trade in the world are government bond futures contracts. We will examine these markets in much more detail in future chapters.

Options and Futures on Foreign Currencies

Let $S(t)$ be the dollar price of 1 unit of foreign currency at date t, and let $FO_T(t)$ be the forward price at date t for delivery of 1 unit of foreign currency at date T. Investors can lock into an exchange rate by buying forward contracts. For example, consider an investor who believes the British pound will appreciate dramatically against the dollar. The exchange rate at time t is $S(t) = \$1.46$. The forward exchange rate for delivery at time T is $FO_T(t) = 1.490$. By buying the forward contract the investor is obligated to purchase at time T one pound for $\$1.49$. Conversely, firms may sell forward contracts to hedge against unanticipated declines in foreign currency. Such strategies lock into an exchange rate from the foreign to the local currency.

EXAMPLE 11.2   A U.S. firm has a British subsidiary. The cash flows produced by the subsidiary are in pounds and are subject to exchange rate risk. If the pound depreciates relative to the dollar, the profits produced by the subsidiary may be eroded. To hedge against this event, the parent company would like to lock into a future exchange rate from pounds to dollars. By selling a forward contract at 1.490, the firm is committed to selling one pound for $\$1.49$.

A call option on a foreign currency gives the holder the right to buy a certain quantity of the currency for a given price in dollars, namely, the strike price. This right exists up to the expiration date. At expiration the value of the call option is given by

$$C(T) = \text{Max}[S(T) - X, 0]$$

Active forward, futures, and option markets in foreign currencies will be discussed in more detail in Chapter 14.

Options on Futures

An option on a futures contract allows the holder to enter into a position with a futures price equal to the exercise price of the option. Upon exercise, then, a futures call (put) option holder acquires a long (short) futures position with a futures price equal to the exercise price. At the close of the day's trading the futures contract is marked to the market. At this time, the option holder is free to withdraw in cash the difference between the futures price and the exercise price. Thus, exercising a futures option is equivalent to receiving in cash the exercisable value or intrinsic value of the option.

Like stock options, futures options are completely characterized by the name of the underlying futures contract together with its delivery month, the strike price of the option, and the maturity of the option. Of course, the maturity date of the option must precede the settlement date of the futures contract. In many cases the option expires on a specific date in the month preceding the delivery month. For example, an option on the March futures contract may expire in February. Such an option contract is referred to as a March option because its exercise would result in a position in a March futures contract. There are exceptions to this rule; indeed, a series of option contracts on the March futures contract may trade with maturity dates in December, January, and February.

EXAMPLE 11.3   **Options on CBOT Corn Futures**

An investor has a September call option with a strike price of 200 cents per bushel on a corn futures contract at the Chicago Board of Trade (CBOT). Recall that the corn futures contract is based on 5000 bushels. Suppose the current futures price of corn is 210 cents per bushel. If the option is exercised the investor will receive 10×5000 cents or $500, plus a long position in a futures contract to buy 5000 bushels of corn in September. The futures position can be closed out at no cost. Of course, as with other options, it may be more appropriate to sell rather than exercise the contract.

Options on CME Gold Futures

The Chicago Mercantile Exchange (CME) trades call and put options on its gold futures contracts. The option contracts expire on the second Friday of the month prior to delivery. Thus, an April gold futures option will expire on the second Friday of March. Strike prices surrounding the current gold futures price will exist. A put option on a gold futures contract has a strike price of $370. The current gold future price is $360. By exercising the put, the holder will assume a short position in the futures contract, together with $10. (This transaction is actually accomplished by establishing the futures position at the strike price and then immediately marking to market.)

A commercial user of gold wants to avoid the risk of a gold price increase in the next several months. To achieve this goal, the company purchases gold futures call options. If gold prices increase, the profit on the calls will offset the higher price the user will have to pay to acquire the gold. If gold prices decline, however, all that is lost is the full premium of the call option. In this case, the gold can be bought at the low market price.

In Chapter 12 we will investigate option contracts on futures and on forwards, comparing these contracts to options on commodities.

Options on Options

Since an option is a financial asset, options can exist on them. Such contracts are called **compound options.** In the over-the-counter market, call and put options can be purchased on calls. Similarly, markets exist for call and put options on puts. Compound options are particularly important for situations where there are multiple contingencies. This is best illustrated by an example.

EXAMPLE 11.4   Consider a U.S. manufacturer who submits to the Japanese government a sealed bid for the sale of a large turnkey plant. The foreign bidder not only must deal with the uncertainty of winning the bid but also must contend with exchange rate risk. If the foreign currency in which the bid is denominated depreciates significantly against the dollar, then the profitability of the bid may be eroded away. To offset this risk, the bidder could use a variety of risk management instruments.

1. If a forward contract is sold and the bid is won, the hedge replaces foreign currency risk with less volatile basis risk. However, if the bid is lost, the bidder has no foreign currency to offset the commitment in the forward contract, and significant losses could occur. As a result, the bidder may prefer a conditional forward contract that essentially has an escape clause.

2. Foreign currency options provide an alternative hedging mechanism for this case. If the bid is won, the bidder, having purchased a put, has limited the exchange rate risk. On the other hand, if the bid is lost, the bidder is left with an unwanted speculative position in the foreign currency.

3. Another alternative is to purchase a **compound put option.** Upon initiation, this contract grants the holder the right to purchase a put option in the future at prices that are agreed upon today. The future date is set soon after the bid uncertainty is resolved. If the manufacturer wins the bid, and if exchange rates have moved adversely, then the bidder will exercise this option and receive the put, which provides the appropriate protection.

Compound puts are extremely efficient contracts for hedging risks that are contingent on projects being awarded.

The over-the-counter market for compound options is fairly large. Compound options are also encountered in corporate finance. Indeed, future chapters discuss compound options in several different situations; we will examine how to price compound options and will use the resulting model to solve a variety of interesting problems.

Cash-Settled Futures and Options

The instrument underlying an option or futures contract need not be a traded commodity. In this section we consider contracts where the underlying instrument is an index. An index is a statistical measure designed to show changes in the level of some underlying process. Stock market, interest rate, and economic indices are a few examples. Of course, indices may have nothing to do with market prices or economic performance. For example, indices based on batting averages of professional baseball players serve to summarize each player's overall effectiveness.

Let $I(t)$ be the level of the index at date t. We assume that the index is well defined. That is, its construction is well understood. Further, we assume that its level cannot be manipulated by the actions of any individual. Finally, we assume that at all dates the index fully reflects all known information.

A forward contract on an index is a side bet on the future level of the index. At the delivery date, T, the short position is committed to deliver the *cash value* of the index, $I(T)$ dollars, for the predetermined forward price, $FO_T(0)$. In many cases the cash value is defined to be equal to the index level multiplied by a predetermined constant called a **multiplier.** The cash flow for the long position is given by $CF(T)$, where

$$CF(T) = [I(T) - FO_T(0)]M \tag{11.3}$$

where M is the multiplier. A futures contract is similar, but the contract is marked to market daily.

A call (put) option on an index is a cash-settled contract that provides the holder with the option to call away (put) the cash value of the index in exchange for payment (receipt) of the strike price. This right terminates at the predetermined expiration date. The terminal call and put prices are

$$C(T) = \text{Max}[I(T) - X, 0]M \tag{11.4}$$

$$P(T) = \text{Max}[X - I(T), 0]M \tag{11.5}$$

The following section illustrates cash-settled contracts that exist in organized and over-the-counter markets.

Stock Index Futures and Options

There are many stock indices that attempt to capture the overall movement in the stock markets of individual countries. Perhaps the best-known index is the Dow Jones Industrial Average, which attempts to capture the movements of industrial stocks in the United States. Unfortunately, no cash-settled contracts are based on this index. Futures contracts do trade on the Standard and Poor's 500 Index (S & P 500). This index is highly correlated with the Dow Jones Industrial Average. The value of the S & P 500 is determined according to the market value of all outstanding stocks of 500 firms, most of which trade on the New York Stock Exchange (NYSE). Indeed, the market value of this index equals approximately 80 percent of the value of all stocks listed on the NYSE. Many other stock index futures contracts exist, but the S & P 500 is by far the most liquid stock index futures contract. (Chapter 13 provides more discussion on stock index derviatives.) Example 11.5 illustrates its use.

EXAMPLE 11.5   The S & P 500 Stock Index Futures Contract

In 1982 the CME introduced the S & P 500 stock index futures contract. In 1993 the S & P accounted for over two-thirds of all stock index futures trading. The multiplier for the contract is 500. For example, if the futures price is $300, the dollar price is 500 × $300, or $150,000. The last day of trading is the Thursday prior to the third Friday of the contract month. Settlement is by cash and is based on the Special Opening Quotation on Friday morning of the S & P 500 stock price index.

Portfolio Immunization with Stock Index Futures

A firm holds $10 million in a well-diversified stock portfolio. A regression analysis of the returns on this portfolio against the returns on the S & P 500 Index shows that the beta value is 1.2. That is, for every 1 percent advance in the index, the expected advance in the portfolio is 1.2 percent.

Anticipating a falling market, the firm decides to sell S & P 500 futures to compensate for the portfolio losses. The current S & P 500 Index is 300. Since the multiplier of the futures contract is 500, the dollar value that each contract controls is $300 × 500 or $150,000. If the beta value were 1 then the appropriate number of S & P futures contracts to sell would be $10,000,000/$150,000 or 66.66 contracts.

However, since the portfolio is more sensitive than the index to market changes, additional futures should be sold. In particular, the beta value is used as the appropriate hedge ratio. The number of futures contracts to be sold is 66.66 × 1.2 = 79.999. Hence, the sale of 80 futures contracts should immunize the portfolio from a deteriorating market.

A stock index call option provides the owner with the right to purchase, for a predetermined price, an amount of dollars equal to the index value multiplied by a given multiplier. The index value is determined by the closing price on the exercise date. This right exists up to a specific expiration date.

For example, consider a trader who purchases a June 150 call option when the market index is 151. A few weeks later the index closes at 161. If the investor exercises the call, the net payout will be ($161 − $150) multiplied by the given dollar multiplier.

The S & P 100 Stock Index Options Contract
The S & P 100 Option, known by its ticker symbol OEX, was introduced in 1983. Average daily volume in the first year was over 51,000 contracts. By 1984, volume had quintupled to over 250,000 contracts per day, making it the most liquid option contract traded in the United States. The trading unit of each index option is the level of the S & P 100 Index multiplied by 100. The contract is American-style and trades on the Chicago Board Options Exchange (CBOE).

Portfolio Insurance with Put Options
Assume the current value of a portfolio is $160,000 and the S & P 100 Index level is 80. At-the-money put options are to be purchased to protect the portfolio. The exercise price of each option is $80 × 100 or $8,000. The purchase of 20 put options represents an aggregate exercise price of $160,000, which equals the value of the portfolio.

If the beta value of the portfolio, computed with respect to the S & P 100 market index on which the option trades, is 1, the portfolio value is expected to appreciate or depreciate at the same rate as the market index. In this case, the purchase of 20 put options will provide an appropriate insurance against market declines. However, the hedge is not perfect, since the portfolio may decline more or less than the overall market. Indeed, it is possible for the actual portfolio to depreciate rapidly while the index remains stable. In this case the protective puts would not produce offsetting profits. On the other hand, if the investor had picked superior stocks, profits could be realized in a declining market from the protective puts, even though no losses were incurred on the portfolio.

If the beta value is greater than 1, then the rate of decline of the portfolio is expected to be greater than the rate of decline of the market index. In this case, to obtain insulation against market declines, the portfolio manager must purchase more put options. For example, if the beta value is 1.5, then 30 (rather than 20) options would be appropriate. The purchase of put options to protect a stock portfolio from declining below a certain floor value is a simple **static portfolio insurance strategy.**

Interest Rate Index Derivatives

An interest rate can be viewed as an index. For example, an index of short-term interest rate yields could be established by selecting a certain number of government bond dealers each day and taking the average of their quoted asking rates for 90-day Treasury bills.

There are several very important interest rate indices. These include the rates on selected Treasury securities that differ according to their maturities. For example, the yields on 2-, 5-, and 10-year Treasury notes are often tracked, as are the yields on longer-term Treasury bonds. Other important interest rates are the daily federal funds rate (the rate banks with excess reserves can charge for lending overnight) and the three-month London interbank offered rate or **LIBOR rate** (the interest rate on short-term loans between large banks quoted over the international market centered in London). The LIBOR is commonly used as a benchmark for short-term interest rates.

Let $y(0)$ represent a specific interest rate that prevails at date 0 and let $y(T)$ be the rate at the settlement date, T. A forward rate agreement entered into at date 0, at a forward rate of $f_T(0)$, is a cash-settled contract that pays out an amount based on a quantity $Q(T)$ determined at date T and given by

$$Q(T) = [y(T) - f_T(0)]M \tag{11.6}$$

where M is a predetermined multiplier. Forward rate agreements (FRAs) are actively traded in the over-the-counter market; they will be discussed in more detail in Chapter 21.

Options on interest rates, or **yield options**, are cash-settled contracts based on an underlying value (called a **composite**) that is calculated using interest rate yields. Almost all exchange-traded interest rate options are European-style contracts. This eliminates the risk of early exercise. The terminal payout of a call option on a yield index that is set at $y(T)$ at expiration is

$$C(T) = \text{Max}[y(T) - X, 0]M \tag{11.7}$$

where X is the strike and M is the predetermined multiplier.

EXAMPLE 11.6   **CBOE Yield Options**

The CBOE trades a short-term rate option (the IRX option) based on the yield of the most recently auctioned 13-week T-bill. The multiplier for this contract is 10. The exchange also trades a long-term rate option (the LTX option) based on the average yield to maturity of the two most recently auctioned 7- and 10-year Treasury notes and 30-year Treasury bonds. These six rates are averaged, and this average multiplied by 10 forms the index on which the long-term option trades. The index is updated throughout the trading day.

To illustrate how the interest rate call option works, consider an investor who anticipates a rise in short-term interest rates. Such an investor could purchase an IRX call option. With T-bill rates at 8.75 percent, the short-term composite is 87.50. A three-month IRX option with strike 87.50 is available and sells for $1 (total cost is $100). At the expiration date, T-bill rates are 9 percent, the index is at 90, and the call price is 2.5 ($250).

In Example 11.6, the long positions in FRAs and call yield options benefit from interest rate increases. There are several interest rate contracts that have payouts that depend on the complement of an interest rate. That is, payouts depend on the value of $\bar{y}(T) = 1 - y(T)$, where $y(T)$ is a yield index. In this case, long positions in forward or futures contracts and call option holders will benefit from interest rate declines.

Consider a trader who enters into a long position in a forward contract at date 0 that is based on the complement of the three-month yield at date T. Let $\bar{f}_T(0)$ represent the forward price for this contract ($\bar{f}_T(0) = 1 - f_T(0)$). Clearly, as the settlement date approaches, the forward price index will converge to the complement of the actual three-month rate, $\bar{y}(T)$. The payout the long position receives at the expiration date is

$$Q(T) = [\bar{y}(T) - \bar{f}_T(0)]M \qquad (11.8)$$

where M is the appropriate multiplier. Substituting for $\bar{y}(T)$ and $\bar{f}_T(0)$ into equation (11.8) yields

$$Q(T) = [f_T(0) - y(T)]M \qquad (11.9)$$

That is, the long position profits if yields are lower at date T than the contracted yield $f_T(0)$.

EXAMPLE 11.7   **Eurodollar Futures at the CME**

Eurodollar futures and futures option contracts, which trade at the CME, are very important contracts based on interest rate complements. The underlying index for these contracts is the complement of a three-month LIBOR rate observed at the delivery date, T.

Locking in a Borrowing Rate with Eurodollar Futures

In December a firm knows that it will need to borrow $1 million for 90 days, beginning in March, when the Eurodollar (ED) futures contract settles. The interest payment for the loan will be based on the three-month LIBOR rate at the time the $1 million is due. Management fears that LIBOR rates will increase and would like to lock into a rate today. By selling a June Eurodollar futures contract, the firm locks into a fixed rate equal to the implied LIBOR rate. To see this, let $\pi(T)$ be the profit in June from selling the futures contract. Then

$$\begin{aligned} \pi(T) &= -[\bar{y}(T) - \bar{f}_T(t)](\$1{,}000{,}000) \\ &= -[f_T(t) - y(T)](\$1{,}000{,}000) \\ &= [y(T) - f_T(t)](\$1{,}000{,}000) \end{aligned}$$

The net cash flow at time T for the loan is then

$$[y(T) - f_T(t)](\$1{,}000{,}000) - y(T)(\$1{,}000{,}000) = -f_T(t)(\$1{,}000{,}000)$$

That is, by entering a short position the firm is locking into the implied three-month LIBOR rate $f_T(t)$.

Transforming Variable to Fixed-Rate Loans

The preceding example readily extends to multiperiod problems. Consider a firm that borrows $10 million in December. Payments on the variable-rate loan are linked to quarterly LIBOR; in particular, the loan rate is the three-month LIBOR rate. The loan requires three quarterly interest payments, with the balloon payment of $10 million due in one year. The interest payment dates correspond to the settlement dates of successive ED futures. Assume the current LIBOR rate is 8 percent, and March, June, and September ED futures prices are 91.75, 91.50, and 91.40 respectively. The implied LIBOR rates are therefore 8.25, 8.75, and 8.60 percent. By selling 10 March, June, and September ED futures, the firm can lock into these implied LIBOR rates.

To confirm this, assume that in March the LIBOR rate is 9 percent. The March futures contract settles at 91, giving the firm a profit of $-10(0.0825 - 0.09)$ $(90/360)(\$1{,}000{,}000) = \$18{,}750$. The interest payment is $0.09(90/360)$ $(\$10{,}000{,}000) = \$225{,}000$. The net expense therefore is $206,250, which is $[\$206{,}250/\$10{,}000{,}000](360/90) = 8.25$ percent. This is the implied rate. By selling a *strip* of ED futures, the firm can essentially transform a variable-rate loan into a series of fixed-rate loans.

Note that with the index price convention, Eurodollar futures prices move linearly with the bank discount yield. Specially, regardless of the level of the interest rate, a 1 percent change in yield causes a $2,500 [$1,000,000(1/100) $\times$ (90/360)] change in price. This is in contrast to futures contracts on bonds, where the price movement is linear in bond prices. We shall have much more to say about this in Chapter 22.

Cash-Settled Contracts on Economic Indices

The cash-settled contracts we have considered so far are based on stock market and interest yield indices. As discussed, contracts can also be developed on economic indicators such as the consumer price index, inflation, or unemployment. In Example 11.8 we illustrate how derivative contracts can be designed as hedging instruments in rather innovative ways. We describe a contract with payouts linked to insurance costs in the health care industry. In 1992 the CBOT designed four contracts based on insurance for group health care, personal automobile collision damage, homeowners property damage, and commercial property damage. These insurance contracts were designed to track the underwriting experience of these different businesses. All of them follow the same design format; we focus here on the health insurance futures.

EXAMPLE 11.8   **Health Care Insurance Futures**

The CBOT's group health insurance futures contract was designed to assist firms in managing the risk of their health care costs. The futures contract price reflects the market's expectations of changes in health care costs. At expiration the futures price will be set at the level of the health insurance index. The underlying index tracks the cost of claims, standardized by premium levels, for a pool of insurance policies. This ratio provides a benchmark for changing health care costs. The policies used in these calculations come from plans that meet certain requirements (for example, group size, covered benefits, deductibles, and coinsurance are curtailed, as well as the duration of the policies). Insurers who contribute information to the pool have to report information on premiums and paid claims on policies at the end of each month, up to the third month after the policy expires. A profile of the pool's aggregate policy characteristics is made public.

Once the pool is formed, trading of a cash-settled futures contract based on the performance of that pool can begin. Consider a pool formed in January. Futures contracts with expiration dates in June, September, December, and the following March will trade. The prices of these contracts will fluctuate in accordance with the changing prospects for profit on the pooled policies. The June contract will settle against premiums reported from January to March and claims paid from January to the end of June, provided service was rendered in the first quarter.

Suppose that premiums for policies over the first quarter total $50 million and that claims received over the first two quarters for heath care performed in the first quarter equal $35 million. Then the final settlement price for the June contract is based on the profit ratio of ($50,000,000 − $35,000,000)/$50,000,000. The final settlement price is given by this profit ratio multiplied by a fixed multiplier of $100,000. For this problem the settlement price is $30,000.

In theory, the settlement price could be negative if claims paid out exceeded premiums generated. The futures price of the June contract prior to June will reflect the expectations of the underlying profitability of the underwriting business for the first quarter and will converge to the index level in June. Similarly, the September (December) contract prices reflect the expectations that the underlying policies will generate premiums in excess of claims during the second (third) quarter.

Suppose an insurance company sells a September futures contract in January at a price of $33,000 and holds the position until some time in July, at which time the price is $30,000. Ignoring marking-to-market effects, the profit would be $3,000. This profit would offset the unanticipated increase in costs of claims that have occurred over the period.

Derivatives on Indices Computed from Time Series

The settlement prices of some cash-settled contracts are based on a statistic computed on a time series of prices. To make matters specific, let $S_0, S_1, S_2, \ldots, S_n$ be the sequence of observed prices of the underlying asset observed over the life of the option, with S_0 being the price at date 0 and S_n being the price at the expiration date. The payout of a simple call option at date n is given by C_n, where

$$C_n = \text{Max}[S_n - X, 0]$$

Here X is the strike price of the option. Note that this payout depends only on the final stock price and not on its path. That is, the final price of the option is independent of the path taken by the stock in reaching its final value. Cash-settled options could have terminal values that depend on more than just the last price. For example, an average-rate call option is a cash-settled contract with terminal value given by C_n, where

$$C_n = \text{Max}[\bar{A} - X, 0] \tag{11.10}$$

where $\quad \bar{A} = \sum_{i=1}^{n} S_i/n$

Options with payouts depending on the average have become increasingly popular. There are many reasons why traders may desire option contracts based on the average. For example, many traders want to cap the total expense of ongoing transactions over finite time horizons. Rather than capping the cost of each individual transaction using European options, they may prefer average-rate options, which pay out if aggregate expenses are above some limiting threshold.

EXAMPLE 11.9 **An Average-Rate Contract**

1. Consider a builder who has just won a contract to build multiunit homes. The builder knows that a stream of lumber purchases will be necessary over the fixed time horizon and would like to purchase a contract to provide protection against the total cost of lumber exceeding a planned threshold value. Since the lumber purchases are made frequently over the lifetime of the project, the price protection required is more likely linked to the average price over the period than to any individual end-of-period prices.

2.   Consider a muncipality that has a fixed budget for purchasing heating oil for the winter months and is concerned that expenses over this period could exceed the budget. To hedge against this event, it purchases call options based on the average price of oil over the winter period. The number of contracts purchased depends on the total usage of heating oil.

3.   Examples 1 and 2 involve trading average-rate options in the over-the-counter market. Average-rate contracts also exist in organized markets. For example, the CBOT trades a futures contract that has a terminal value linked to the arithmetic average of 30 consecutive days of daily interest levels of the federal funds rate. This contract is called the 30-day interest rate futures contract.

The arithmetic mean is just one of many statistics that can be computed. For example, option contracts can be based on percentiles of the previous n-period prices or the variances or range of previous prices. A quite common option encountered in the over-the-counter market is a cash-settled contract based on the minimum of all the n prices. In particular, the terminal payout is based on the final price less the lowest price that occurred in the data collection period. We shall have more to say about these types of path-dependent contracts in Chapter 16.

In principle, cash-settled contracts could be created on almost any underlying index. In practice, however, the success of a cash-settled contract depends on several factors. Most important is the identification of a clientele of hedgers who would be interested in laying off some of this risk. The way the index is computed is also important. If the index is updated only infrequently and if there is an asymmetry of information regarding the implicit level of the index between the periodic updates, traders may be reluctant to enter contracts unless they have access to this information. In other words, if the index is updated frequently and is based on all known information, then the contract has a higher chance of being successful. Of course, the market must attract liquidity by ensuring that speculators and arbitragers can operate between markets. For stock index and interest rate index contracts, arbitrage activities between the derivative contracts and the underlying portfolios of stocks or bonds can easily be accomodated. When there is no commodity that comes close to the underlying index, arbitrage activities between the "spot" and derivative products are less clear, and, all other factors being equal, the product is less likely to be successful.

Single-Commodity Exchange Agreements and Exchange Options

The types of forward and futures contracts we have discussed involve a commitment to exchange a *fixed amount of dollars* for a given quantity of an underlying asset or its cash value. Similarly, for the case of options, exercise has required the exchange of a *predetermined amount of dollars*, namely the strike price, in return for the underlying commodity or for the cash value of the commodity. Several contracts exist in which the committed value or the strike price is not certain. For example, consider a firm that enters into a forward contract that requires it to deliver a certain quantity of a commodity, such as oil, and in return receive a certain quantity of a second commodity, gold say. The actual value of this contract at the delivery date, $Q(T)$, will of course depend on the market prices of the two assets. In particular,

$$Q(T) = S_1(T) - S_2(T) \tag{11.11}$$

where $S_1(T)$ and $S_2(T)$ are the market prices of the two assets to be exchanged.

A commodity exchange call option is similar to the forward contract except that rather than an obligation to exchange, it gives the holder the right to exchange one commodity for another. At the expiration date T, the value of such an option is

$$C(T) = \text{Max}[0, S_1(T) - S_2(T)] \tag{11.12}$$

Note that if the commodity S_2 is a fixed quantity of dollars, then these two contracts reduce to forward contracts and standard option contracts. Exchange agreements are very common in the over-the-counter market. In many commodity exchange contracts, the underlying commodity is exchangeable for a particular quantity of foreign currency. Since the exchange rates are not certain, the contract can be viewed as an exchange contract. Finally, the majority of contracts are settled by cash, with the loser paying the winner the cash value of the contract.

Multiple Exchange Rate Agreements

Consider a firm that enters into an exchange agreement with a counterparty whereby two specific commodities are to be exchanged on a periodic basis. Let t_1, t_2, t_3, . . . , t_n represent the exchange dates. Actually, in most cases, rather than having a physical exchange at each of these dates, the contract is cash-settled. Specifically, at each date the market prices of the two commodities are recorded; the loser then pays the winner the difference.

EXAMPLE 11.10 Consider a two-year exchange agreement that requires the long position to deliver one unit of oil in exchange for one unit of gold at the end of every six months. That is, four exchanges are to be made. The exact dates and the mechanism for establishing the market prices are well specified. The prices for single units of the two commodities at the exchange date are shown below.

Date (Month)	Oil Price ($)	Gold Price ($)	Difference ($)
6	10,500	11,500	+1,000
12	10,200	10,400	+200
18	10,100	9,800	−300
24	10,400	9,900	−500

The long position in this contract receives two payments and is obligated to make two payments. If the firm that is long in this contract is an oil company that is exchanging its output, then the resulting set of cash flows will be linked to gold prices rather than oil prices.

Now consider the special case when the firm exchanges one underlying commodity (oil) for a predetermined amount of cash at each exchange date. In this case, the oil manufacturer has completely eliminated the price risk of oil and has in effect established a constant price for its output. The counterparty, on the other hand, has exchanged certain cash flows for cash flows that are linked to the price of the commodity.

Interest Rate Swaps

A very important class of commodity swaps is the interest rate swap. Interest rate swaps emerged in the early 1980s. The growth of the market has been spectacular. Indeed, no other market has grown as rapidly as the swap market. In 1993 the notional principal of interest rate swaps exceeded $2 trillion. Today interest rate swaps play a central role in almost all debt management activities for individual firms. We shall devote more attention to these contracts in future chapters. Here we provide a brief outline of the basic interest rate swap.

An **interest rate swap** is a customized commodity exchange agreement between two parties to make periodic payments to each other according to well-defined rules. In the simplest of interest rate swaps, one party periodically pays a cash flow determined by a fixed interest rate and receives a cash flow determined by a floating interest rate.

There are four major components to a swap: the notional principal amount, the interest rates for each party, the frequency of cash exchanges, and the duration of the swap. A typical swap in swap jargon might be "$20 m, two year, pay fixed, receive variable, semi." Translated, this swap would be for $20 million in notional principal, where one party makes a fixed-interest-rate payment every six months based on $20 million, and the counterparty makes a variable-rate payment every six months based on $20 million.

The variable-rate payment is based on a specific short-term interest rate index such as six-month LIBOR. The time period specified by the variable-rate index usually coincides with the frequency of swap payments. For example, a swap that is fixed versus six-month LIBOR would have semiannual payments, whereas a swap against three-month T-bill rates would usually have quarterly payments. Of course, there can be exceptions to this rule. For example, the variable-rate payment could be linked to the average of all T-bill auction rates during the time period between settlements.

Most interest rate swaps have payment dates in arrears. That is, the net cash flow between parties is established at the beginning of the period but is actually paid out at the end of the period.

The fixed rate for a generic swap is usually quoted as some spread over benchmark U.S. Treasuries. For example, a quote of "20 over" for a 5-year swap implies that the fixed rate will be set at the 5-year Treasury yield that exists at the time of pricing plus 20 basis points. Usually, swap spreads are quoted against the 2-, 3-, 5-, 7-, and 10-year benchmark maturities. The yield used for other swaps (such as a 4-year swap) is then obtained by averaging the surrounding yields (the 3- and 5-year yields).

EXAMPLE 11.11 Consider a $20 million, two-year, pay fixed, receive variable, semi swap, where the fixed rate is 25 basis points above the two-year Treasury rate and the variable rate is six-month LIBOR. The current Treasury rate is 7.5 percent. This implies that the fixed rate is 7.75 percent. The fixed payer will pay according to the six-month LIBOR rates determined at dates 0, 6 months, 1 year, and 1.5 years.

Treasury rates are quoted with semiannual compounding and are based on a 365-day year, while six-month LIBOR rates are annualized based on a 360-day year. In any specific interest rate swap, the necessary adjustments must be to ensure consistency. In this example, we assume the payouts are based on a 365-day year, and all the quoted LIBOR rates have been adjusted by (365/360). Say the initial LIBOR rate at date 0 is $L_0 = 8\%$ and that the three successive rates are $L_1 = 8.5\%$, $L_2 = 8.4\%$, and $L_3 = 7.5\%$. Then the variable-rate payer is responsible for the following payments:

$800,000 in 6 months

$850,000 in 1 year

$840,000 in 1 year 6 months

$750,000 in 2 years

The cash flows that take place from the fixed-rate to the variable-rate payer are summarized below.

Receive

	800	850	840	750
	775	775	775	775

Pay

The payments at each date are netted out, with the losing party paying the difference. The net difference checks received or written by the fixed-rate payer are

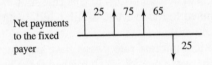

EXAMPLE 11.12   Consider a bank with significant short-term deposits that are repriced every six months at LIBOR less 25 basis points. The bank has a major portfolio mismatch problem because its customers borrow for long maturities. To avoid this maturity mismatch the firm has offered variable-rate loans that are repriced every six months. However, the majority of borrowers still prefer long-term fixed-rate loans, and the bank's strategy has not solved the interest rate exposure problem.

Suppose the bank enters into a swap arrangement. This is a $100 million, 5-year swap where the bank pays a fixed interest rate of 10 percent semiannually, while the counterparty pays the bank the six-month LIBOR rate. The effective result is to transform the floating-rate liabilities into an effective fixed-rate liability of 9.75 percent.

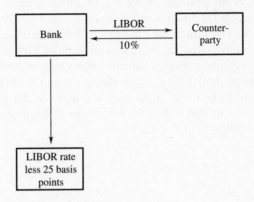

The Wide Variety of Interest Rate Swaps

The "plain vanilla" fixed-for-variable interest rate swap that we have just discussed has given way to hundreds of variants, all designed to serve specific needs.

Specific contingencies may be built into the swap contract. For example, perhaps the initiation date can be delayed, or the final settlement date adjusted, at the discretion of one of the counterparties. Option contracts also exist on swaps. Such contracts provide the holder with the right to initiate a particular swap as the fixed-rate payer, where the fixed rate is predetermined. The counterparty in this case is the dealer who provided the option.

You-Design-It, You-Name-It Contracts

The types of derivative contracts that can be designed are endless. An enormous market exists in customizing over-the-counter contracts to meet the very specific risk management needs of corporations. In Chapter 16 we shall discuss a variety of exotic contracts that have become important risk management tools for firms facing specific needs. The firm needs to understand the nature of the risk that must be managed and then to establish a risk management strategy. The resulting solution should meet the risk management needs in the most cost-effective way. If this involves working with an investment banker and designing a new product that transfers the risk the firm wants to lay off more efficiently than any other alternative, then this new product should be considered. Of course, understanding how and why this product creates value for the firm is crucial. In future chapters we shall return to this issue.

Conclusion

This chapter has illustrated a wide variety of derivative contracts. The details of specific contracts were not provided; rather, we provided a broad overview of selected derivative products.

The remaining chapters in Part 4 provide more details about some types of contracts introduced in this chapter. In particular, we shall investigate stock index derivatives, foreign currency contracts, and a host of exotic options, as well as the many derivative features that are found in corporate securities. Since interest rate contracts are so important, we separate these and study the basics of these contracts in Part 5. See the references in the following chapters for material on topics mentioned in this chapter.

Exercises

1. An investor expects funds to become available for investment in a specific coupon bond in three months. The investor is concerned that interest rates will drop in the interim and would like to cap the total cost. What type of contract would you recommend? Explain.

2. A firm makes a sale for which it will receive 125,000 deutsche marks in one month. The firm is concerned about exchange rates and would like to convert this currency into dollars. The firm could hedge this risk using futures, forwards, or options. Discuss three possible strategies that might be appropriate, and compare them.

3. The spot exchange rate for deutsche marks is $0.3920. The futures price for delivery in six weeks is $0.3950. A 40 put option is at $0.0144 and a 40 call option is at $0.0120. After four weeks the spot exchange rate is $0.3540, the futures price is $0.3559, the put is at $0.0447, and the call is at $0.0001.
   a. If the investor had sold a futures contract, what profit or loss would have occurred?
   b. What is the profit on the purchase of a put?
   c. What would the profit be if a call had been sold?

4. Explain why options on futures may have some advantages over options on commodities.

5. A company puts in a bid for a project whose costs are linked to the price of copper. The company may win the bid, but because copper prices are increasing dramatically, its profit margin may be eroded. Explain why a compound option may be helpful in this situation.

6. A firm holds a well-diversified stock portfolio that has a beta value of 1.5. The firm is concerned that in the next month prices may decline. To avoid this risk the firm decides to sell futures contracts on the S & P 500 Index. The portfolio value is $100 million, the S & P 500 Index is at 330, and the multiplier is 500. How many futures should be sold?

7. Cash-settled contracts are often linked to interest rates. Explain how a CBOE yield option could be used to speculate on a declining interest yield.

8. Do you think the health care insurance futures contract will be successful? Explain your answer.

9. Create your own option contract on an economic index. Explain why you think it is important, and provide an example where a hedger may find it useful.

10. A dont option is an option that you pay for only if you do not exercise it at the expiration date. What do you think of this contract? Do you think it will be more or less expensive than an ordinary option?

11. An oil company has fixed debt obligations. Its revenues are linked to the price of oil. To reduce the likelihood of not meeting its obligations, it is considering a variable-for-fixed swap, where it will be the variable payer making payments according to the price of a barrel of oil. Explain how this swap may be helpful.

CHAPTER 12

Options on Futures, Forwards, and Consumption Commodities

In this chapter we discuss option contracts on futures and forwards. Most U.S. futures exchanges trade in options on futures, while options on forwards are mainly encountered in over-the-counter markets. In addition, in some countries option contracts are available on metals and agricultural commodities. In the United States, organized option markets on consumption commodities are not permitted, but such contracts are encountered in the over-the-counter market. We closely investigate pricing relationships for European- and American-style contracts. We shall see that options on futures have properties similar but not identical to those of options on commodities; options on forwards also have different properties than options on futures.

Throughout this chapter we assume interest rates are certain; that being the case, forward prices and futures prices are the same. We defer discussion of option contracts on interest-rate-sensitive forward and futures contracts to Chapters 20 to 24.

The primary objectives of this chapter are the following:

- To investigate option contracts on futures and forwards;

- To determine pricing relationships for European- and American-style contracts; and

- To analyze the differences between options on forwards and options on futures.

Options on Futures and Options on Forwards

Although options on futures have been in existence in Europe for some time, they have only recently become available in America. In 1982 the Commodity Futures Trading Commission allowed each commodity exchange to trade options on one of its futures contracts, and eight exchanges introduced options. These contracts were based on gold, heating oil, sugar, T-bonds, and three stock market indices. Options on futures now trade on every major futures exchange. The underlying spot commodities include financial assets such as bonds, Eurodollars, and stock indices; foreign currencies such as British pounds and German marks; precious metals such as gold and silver; livestock commodities such as hogs and cattle; and agricultural commodities such as corn and soybeans.

As discussed in Chapter 11, futures options are similar to stock options. Calls give the holder the right to buy, and puts give the right to sell. Futures options differ from stock options in that the underlying security is a futures contract. Upon exercise, the option holder obtains a position in the futures contract.

An option on a forward contract requires the delivery of an underlying forward contract with a forward price equal to the exercise price. Exercising a call forward option results in a long position in a forward contract with the forward price equal to the strike price. Exercising a put forward option results in a short position in the underlying forward contract at the strike price. Unlike futures options, forward options are not traded on organized exchanges. They are, however, encountered in over-the-counter markets.

EXAMPLE 12.1   An investor owns a call option with strike $360 and an expiration date in September. The underlying contract is a forward contract on gold with a delivery date in December. The forward price in July is $370. By exercising the forward option, the investor receives a forward contract with forward price $360. If an offsetting position is taken in the forward market, the investor will lock into a $10 profit in September. Note that if the contract is a call option on the futures, then the $10 profit is realized in July.

Pricing Relationships for Options on Futures and Forwards

In this section we develop some pricing relationships for options on futures and forwards. As in Chapter 6, we assume perfect markets with no transaction costs, unrestricted short sales, continuous trading opportunities, and a short-term riskless rate of interest that is constant through time. For short-term contracts on most commodities, the last assumption may not be too severe. However, for futures options written on long-term debt instrument futures contracts, such as U.S. T-bond and T-note futures, this assumption may be too restrictive. Pricing of such contracts is discussed in Parts 5 and 6. With the interest rate certainty assumption, forward prices must equal futures prices. However, this does not imply that options on forward contracts have the same value as options on futures.

Our final assumption concerns the underlying forward or futures contract. For simplicity we assume the contract has no delivery options and that delivery takes place at a particular time T. The option on the futures (or forward) contract has expiration date t ($t \leq T$).

Exercise Values

PROPERTY 12.1

1. The value of a call option on a futures contract at the expiration date is given by $CFU(t)$, where

$$CFU(t) = \text{Max}[F_T(t) - X, 0] \qquad (12.1)$$

2. The value of a call option on a forward contract at expiration date t is given by $CFO(t)$, where

$$CFO(t) = \text{Max}[FO_T(t) - X, 0]B(t, T) \qquad (12.2)$$

Proof. If the futures option is exercised at the expiration date t, a long position in the underlying futures is obtained at a price of X. If the actual futures price is $F_T(t)$, then, due to the marking-to-market feature, the difference can be immediately obtained. Equation (12.1) follows.

If the option on the forward contract is exercised, a forward position is entered into at the strike price. If the trader immediately offsets this position by selling forward, a profit equal to the difference between the forward and strike prices is guaranteed at the settlement of the forward contract. That is, the amount $FO_T(t) - X$ can be received only at the settlement date T. Equation (12.2) follows.

Note that if the option's expiration date t coincided with the futures settlement date T, then the terminal value of the two contracts would be identical. Moreover, since the futures price at settlement equals the spot price, Property 12.2 follows.

PROPERTY 12.2

Assume the expiration date of the option coincides with the settlement date. Then a European option on the commodity is equivalent to a European option on a forward contract and to a European option on the futures contract. That is,

$$C^E(0) = CF^E(0) = CFU^E(0)$$

Put-Call Parity Relationships

We now investigate the relationships that must exist between European calls and puts on futures contracts and on forward contracts.

PROPERTY 12.3

1. The relationship between a European put and call on a futures contract is

$$PFU^E(0) = CFU^E(0) + [X - F_T(0)]B(0, t) \qquad (12.3)$$

2. The relationship between a European put and call on a forward contract is

$$PFO^E(0) = CFO^E(0) + [X - FO_T(0)]B(0, T) \qquad (12.4)$$

Proof.   To see this, consider two portfolios. Portfolio A contains a European put on a futures contract, a borrowed amount equal to the present value of the option's exercise price [i.e., $XB(0, t)$ dollars], and a long position in the futures contract. Portfolio B contains a call option on the futures contract, partially financed by borrowing the present value of the futures price. Exhibit 12.1 shows the cash flows of the two portfolios. Since the cash flows of portfolios A and B are identical, to prevent riskless arbitrage their current values must be equal. That is,

$$PFU^E(0) - XB(0, t) = CFU^E(0) - F_T(0)B(0, t)$$

from which the result follows.

The proof of put-call parity for forward options is similar except that T-period bonds are used rather than the t-period bonds.

In Chapter 6 the put-call parity condition in equation (6.13) stated that the value of the European put equaled the value of a European call plus the present value of the strike less the current stock price. Here, in contrast, put-call parity holds with respect to the present value of the futures price rather than the futures price itself.

Early Exercise Values of Options on Forward and Futures Contracts

If the expiration date of a European option coincides with the futures settlement date, then the price of the futures option equals the price of the forward option. However, the prices of two American contracts may differ. Property 12.4 shows

EXHIBIT 12.1   Arbitrage Portfolio for Property 12.3

Portfolio	Initial Value	Cash Flow at Time t $F_T(t) \leq X$	Cash Flow at Time t $F_T(t) > X$
A	$PFU^E(0) - XB(0, t)$	$X - F_T(t) - X + F_T(t) - F_T(0)$	$-X + F_T(t) - F_T(0)$
B	$CFU^E(0) - F_T(0)B(0, t)$	$-F_T(0)$	$F_T(t) - X - F_T(0)$

that the early exercise feature for options on forwards is not valuable, while Property 12.5 shows that the early exercise feature for options on futures is valuable.

PROPERTY 12.4

1. American call options on forward contracts have the same value as European call options on forward contracts.
2. American put options on forward contracts have the same value as European put options on forward contracts.

Proof.   In general, American call options are more valuable than European call options if the underlying pays out some dividend that could be captured by early exercise. Since the underlying forward contract has no cash disbursements prior to the settlement day, it is not very surprising that early exercise of a call option on a forward is never appropriate. To see this more formally, consider a portfolio A containing an option on a forward contract with strike X and expiration t. The settlement date is time T. Also consider a portfolio B consisting of the purchase of $[FO_T(0) - X]$ pure discount bonds and a forward contract. The values of these portfolios at time 0 and at time t are shown in Exhibit 12.2. Since A dominates B, the current value of portfolio A must exceed that of B. Specifically, $CFO(0) \geq [FO_T(0) - X]B(0, T)$.

Now, if the option is exercised immediately, the value $[FO_T(0) - X]$ is obtained only at time T. The value of this strategy at time 0 is $[FO_T(0) - X]B(0, T)$. Hence, early exercise is never optimal. Similar results hold for puts.

We now turn attention to American options on futures contracts.

PROPERTY 12.5

1. Early exercise of American call options on futures may be optimal.
2. Early exercise of American put options on futures may be optimal.

EXHIBIT 12.2   Arbitrage Portfolio for Property 12.4

Portfolio	Initial Value	Cash Flow at Time t $FO_T(t) \leq X$	Cash Flow at Time t $FO_T(t) > X$
A	$CFO(0)$	0	$[FO_T(t) - X]B(t, T)$
B	$[FO_T(t) - X]B(0, T)$	$[FO_T(t) - X]B(t, T) +$ $[FO_T(t) - FO_T(0)]B(t, T)$ $V_a(t) > V_b(t)$	$[FO_T(t) - X]B(t, T) +$ $[FO_T(t) - FO_T(0)]B(t, T)$ $V_a(t) = V_b(t)$

Before we prove this result, recall that buying a call option requires an initial cash outlay. In contrast, buying a futures contract requires only a good faith deposit, which can be satisfied by posting Treasury securities that generate interest. Now, as a call moves deeper and deeper into the money, it behaves more and more like the underlying security. While the investment characteristics of the deep-in-the-money call are similar to the futures contract itself, there are some advantages to owning the futures. In particular, since the futures contract is marked to market daily, the cash generated can earn interest. In contrast, the option requires a substantial commitment of funds, which are tied up. As a result, deep-in-the-money calls held in a portfolio could be replaced by futures, which would not alter the return structure yet would release funds to earn additional interest.

A second explanation for early exercise is obtained by recognizing that for a commodity providing no yield, the futures price can be written as $F_T(0) = S(0)e^{hT}$, where $h = (r + u)$. Ceteris paribus, the futures price should decline as settlement nears. In fact, the behavior of the futures price is similar to that of a stock price that pays out a continuous dividend yield. This decline will affect the futures option in the same way that a continuous dividend yield would affect a stock option. As we have seen, if a stock pays out a dividend then early exercise of an American option may be optimal. The exact point at which the option should be exercised is described more fully in Chapter 15.

When the option's expiration date equals the settlement date, then the American-style option on the futures contract will be more valuable than an equivalent American-style forward contract.

PROPERTY 12.6

1. The put-call parity relationship for American options on forward contracts is given by

$$CFO(0) - PFO(0) = [FO_T(0) - X]B(0, T) \qquad (12.5)$$

2. The put-call parity relationship for American futures options is given by

$$F_T(0)B(0, T) - X \le CFU(0) - PFU(0) \le F_T(0) - XB(0, T) \quad (12.6)$$

Proof.   Since the early exercise feature for options on forwards is not valuable, equation (12.5) follows immediately from Property 12.3. To establish the lower bound in equation (12.6), consider a portfolio containing a long position in one call, a short position in one put, a forward contract with delivery date t, and N bonds with maturity t. The value of the portfolio is shown in Exhibit 12.3.

Assume the number of bonds sold short, N, is given by $N = F_T(0) - X/B(0, t)$. Then the initial value of this portfolio is $V(0)$, where

$$V(0) = CFU(0) - PFU(0) - F_T(0)B(0, t) + X$$

EXHIBIT 12.3 Arbitrage Portfolio for Property 12.6

Position	Initial Value	Value at Date s	Terminal Value $F_T(t) \le X$	Terminal Value $F_T(t) > X$
Buy call	$CFU(0)$	$CFU(s)$	0	$X - F_T(t)$
Sell forward	—	$-[F_T(s) - F_T(0)]B(s,t)$	$-[F_T(t) - F_T(0)]$	$-[F_T(t) - F_T(0)]$
Sell put	$-PFU(0)$	$-(X - F_T(s))$	$-(X - F_T(t))$	0
Sell N bonds	$-NB(0,t)$	$-NB(s,t)$	$-N$	$-N$

If the position is held until expiration, regardless of what happens the terminal value is $V(t)$, where

$$V(t) = X(1/B(0,t) - 1) \ge 0$$

Since the option sold is an American option, it is possible that at some time s, where $0 \le s \le t$, the contract will be exercised. In this case the value of the portfolio is $V(s)$, which upon simplification yields

$$V(s) = CFU(s) + F_T(s)[1 - B(s,t)] + X[e^{rs} - 1]$$

Each of these three terms is positive, so $V(s) \ge 0$. Hence, to avoid riskless arbitrage, $V(0) \ge 0$, from which the lower bound is obtained.

To establish the upper bound for equation (12.6), consider a portfolio containing long positions in a put, a forward with settlement date t, N bonds with maturity t, and a short position in a call. Exhibit 12.4 shows the value of this portfolio. Assume the number of bonds purchased is $N = F_T(0)/B(0,t) - X$. If the position is held to expiration, the value at date t is given by

$$V(t) = F_T(t)(1/B(0,t) - 1) \ge 0$$

Since the option sold is an American option, it is possible that at time s, where $0 \le s \le t$, the contract will be exercised. In this case the value at date s reduces to

$$V(s) = PFU(s) + F_T(s)[e^{r(t-s)} - 1] + X[1 - e^{-rs}]$$

All three terms are positive, so $V(s) \ge 0$. Hence, to avoid riskless arbitrage, the initial value should be nonnegative. Now, the initial value is given by

$$V(0) = PFU(0) + F_T(0) - XB(0,t) - CFU(0) \ge 0$$

from which the result follows.

EXHIBIT 12.4 Arbitrage Portfolio for Property 12.6

Position	Initial Value	Value at Date s	Terminal Value $F_T(t) \le X$	Terminal Value $F_T(t) > X$
Buy put	$PFU(0)$	$PFU(s)$	$X - F_T(t)$	0
Long $1/B(0,t)$ forwards	—	$\dfrac{[F_T(S) - F_T(0)]B(s,t)}{B(0,t)}$	$\dfrac{[F_T(t) - F_T(0)]}{B(0,t)}$	$\dfrac{[F_T(s) - F_T(0)]}{B(0,t)}$
Buy N bonds	$NB(0,t)$	$-NB(s,t)$	N	N
Sell call	$-CFU(0)$	$-[F_T(s) - X]$	0	$-[F_T(s) - X]$

Options on Consumption Commodities

So far we have considered options on stocks, forwards, and futures. In this section, we examine some of the difficulties in establishing pricing relationships for options on consumption commodities that carry a convenience yield.

Early Exercise of American Commodity Options

As discussed in Chapter 2, the convenience yield for a commodity can be viewed as a nonobservable dividend stream. If the dividend stream is sufficiently large, early exercise of an American call option could be optimal. The problem of determining whether to exercise the option early is made more complex because the dividend stream is not directly observable.

If a futures contract trades on the commodity, implied convenience yields can easily be obtained. Specifically, from equation (2.18), the average annualized implied convenience yield over the period $[0, T]$ is given by

$$\kappa^* = [\ln(S(0)/F_T(0)) + (r + u)T]/T$$

If the option maturity coincides with the futures maturity, κ^* is just the dividend yield forgone by not exercising the option.

With no futures contracts available, the implied convenience yield cannot readily be extracted; hence, the rate of "dividend loss" forgone by not exercising the option is more difficult to access. By exercising a commodity call option early, the investor is able to capture the convenience yield (dividend) of the underlying commodity. The fact that the convenience yield is not directly observable makes the timing of early exercise a bit more difficult. Models for establishing when to exercise such contracts will be discussed in Chapter 15. Nonetheless, we can conclude that American options on commodities that have convenience yields are similar to American options on dividend-paying stocks. This leads to Property 12.7.

PROPERTY 12.7

The early exercise feature of options on commodities that possess convenience yields is valuable.

Comparison of Prices of Options on Spots, Forwards, and Futures

When the option's expiration date coincides with the settlement date, European options on the spot price, futures options, and forward options all have the same value. If the contracts are American, forward options have values that equal their European counterparts. Commodity call options and futures options could have higher values reflecting the fact that early exercise may be optimal. If the underlying asset carrys a low convenience yield, early exercise of the commodity option is unlikely. In this case, futures call options will be priced higher than commodity call options. (The reverse is true for puts.) Finally, for commodities with high convenience yields, futures prices may fall below spot prices, and the value of the early exercise feature of the call option on the commodity may exceed that of the futures option.

Options on Cash Markets and Futures Markets

Options on futures serve functions similar to options on the spot commodity. Options on cash instruments and futures currently coexist. For example, there are options on stock indices and stock index futures, Treasury bonds and Treasury bond futures, foreign currency and foreign currency futures. In some cases, the market participants clearly prefer one option market over the other. In other instances, the preferences are not so clear.

In some markets there are several benefits to trading options on futures rather than options on the cash instrument. First, cash markets are often fragmented, over-the-counter, bid-and-offer markets that are dominated by major dealers, with little direct public participation. Quotes on prices may be difficult to obtain or may vary among dealers, and transaction costs may be high; therefore option premiums may be inflated. In contrast, futures trading takes place in centralized markets, where buyers and sellers meet in a freely competitive auction. During the day there are continuous price disclosures. Thus, option premiums are less likely to be distorted because of the uncertainty of not knowing the market price at any point in time.

Second, futures options may overcome liquidity problems that are associated with shortages of the spot asset. Traders in options require the underlying market to be liquid. If the deliverable supply of the commodity is limited, option writers may become concerned about obtaining the commodity for delivery. This uncertainty is reflected in the premiums of options. That is, option prices will reflect a liquidity or convenience yield factor. Futures markets, on the other hand, do not have problems with limited supplies of contracts.

Third, futures options may be attractive because of their utility in implementing certain strategies. Selling a commodity short may be significantly more difficult than selling a futures contract. Thus, more strategies are available when the underlying commodity is a futures contract. In addition, futures floor traders find it easier and cheaper to hedge their positions with futures options that trade at the same exchange than to establish option positions using contracts that trade on the floor of a different exchange.

And fourth, futures options are popular because of their limited capital requirements. To exercise a stock option, the exerciser must have sufficient capital to cover the strike price. In contrast, to exercise an options contract on a futures, the exerciser need only post futures margin. (This difference is relevant only for traders with limited capital.)

The exchange that first brings a new product to market is usually at an advantage—if the product is successful, liquidity develops, making it extremely difficult for a second exchange to compete. In cases where there are only slight differences in the start-up times of the various products, technical and operational features of the markets may make one product more desirable than another. For example, options on stock indices (such as the S & P 100 Index) are much more liquid than options on stock index futures (S & P 500 futures options). One reason is that the stock index option contracts are much smaller than the futures option contracts, and this attracts more retail interest. Moreover, stock index options can be sold by registered stockbrokers, but stock option futures can be sold only by representatives registered with the Commodity Futures Trading Commission (CFTC). In contrast, options on Treasury bond futures have attracted more business than options on the actual Treasury bonds. The main reason for this is the innovative design of the Treasury futures and option futures contracts. These contracts will be described in future chapters.

Liquidity and existing markets greatly influence the success of any new product. In the case of a commodity like gold or silver, an option on the physical would involve establishing mechanisms for ensuring quality at delivery. Consequently, no active option market has developed for such commodities. While an option contract on a gold/silver index was introduced, the main option market has developed on gold and silver futures contracts.

Conclusion

This chapter has investigated some properties of options on futures, on forwards, and on consumption commodities that contain convenience yields. A great variety of futures options trade on organized futures exchanges. In contrast, most trading of commodity options and forward options takes place in over-the-counter markets. The basic pricing relationships and differences between these contracts were identified using very simple arbitrage arguments.

In Chapter 15 additional assumptions will be made that permit theoretical prices of these contracts to be established. These models also permit the trader to identify exactly when to exercise American claims.

References

Bailey, W. "An Empirical Investigation of the Market for Comex Gold Futures Options." *Journal of Finance* 22 (December 1987): 1187–94.

Black, F. "The Pricing of Commodity Contracts." *Journal of Financial Economics* 3 (March 1976): 167–79.

Brenner, M., G. Courtadon, and M. Subrahmanyam. "Options on the Spot and Options on Futures." *Journal of Finance* 40 (December 1985): 1303–17.

Ramaswamy, K., and S. Sundaresan. "The Valuation of Options on Futures Contracts." *Journal of Finance* 40 (December 1985): 1319–40.

Wolf, A. "Fundamentals of Commodity Options on Futures." *Journal of Futures Markets* 2 (1982): 391–408.

Exercises

1. A trader owns a call option with strike $400 and an expiration date in June. The underlying contract is a forward contract on gold with a delivery date three months later, in September.
   a. Explain what happens if the trader exercises the call option in June.
   b. Assume that in June the forward price of a September gold contract is $420. Interest rates are 5 percent per year, continuously compounded. What is the exercise value of the option?

2. Repeat Exercise 1, but this time assume the contract is a call option on a futures.

3. The price of a European call futures option is $3. The strike price equals the futures price. Compute the fair price of a European put option.

4. The price of a European call futures option is $13. The strike price is $100. The futures price is $90. Interest rates are 5 percent per year, continuously compounded. The option expires in two months, and the futures settles in six months. Compute the price of a European put option on the futures.

5. Repeat Exercise 4, assuming the options are on forward contracts. If the contracts were American options on forwards, would the prices be the same?

6. Provide a simple intuitive explanation for why an option on a futures contract may be exercised early.

7. The price of an American call futures option is $13. The strike is $100, and the futures price is $90. Interest rates are 5 percent per year, continuously compounded. The option expires in two months, and the futures settles in six months. Compute bounds for the price of an American put option on the futures.

8. Explain why it may be optimal to exercise a call option on copper prior to the expiration date.

CHAPTER 13

Stock Index Derivatives

In the last two decades stock markets have undergone dramatic change. In 1975, American households held 70 percent of the equities outstanding. Since then, volume has increased tenfold, and households now account for less than 25 percent of equities outstanding. In the interim, equity holdings have become increasingly more concentrated within a few groups of institutional investors, especially pension funds and mutual funds. Today, institutional investors dominate daily trading, accounting for about 80 percent of average daily volume on the New York Stock Exchange (NYSE). The growth of large institutional investors' influence has been accompanied by an expanding assortment of equity derivative products, particularly those designed to efficiently transfer portfolio risk among participants. These products include stock index futures, stock index options, and futures options. By the mid-1980s the value of the securities underlying the daily traded volume in stock index futures and options had outstripped the daily value of stock trading on the NYSE. Also, the volume of trade in just a few stock index option contracts exceeded the volume of all stock options. Trading strategies involving these products have significantly altered the nature of the stock market. Program trading, stock index arbitrage, portfolio insurance, synthetic equities, and other derivative strategies are now used constantly by brokers and market makers and their institutional clients.

The growth of stock index derivatives markets has been facilitated by dramatic advances in security trading technologies and by deregulation. Multiple orders can be executed quickly and safely in multiple markets. The quality of information is higher, and the speed at which it is disseminated has also been enhanced. Linkages between prices of derivative products and prices of their underlying assets have therefore become more precise. In addition, deregulation has reduced commission charges to pennies per share. As a result, the analysis of fairly complex investment strategies has become possible.

Advances in trading technologies and telecommunications have led to further innovations. Large institutions that wish to avoid brokerage fees can trade electronically with other large investors without an intermediary, and without the stock passing through the exchange. Indeed, a significant volume of stock transactions is regularly traded through off-exchange systems. As a result of these changes, traditional organized markets could suffer, and in the future more trading could be conducted away from organized exchanges. This has raised substantial questions regarding the regulatory aspects of these markets and the rules relating to quotation and transaction reporting. In addition, the very nature of organized markets in the future is in doubt. They could very well consist of elaborate systems of computers networked together and located all over the world, with no centralized geographical location.

This chapter focuses on the financial innovations provided by stock index futures and options. In particular, we identify why these markets are useful and how they can be used to modify the risk-reward relationships of a stock portfolio. Since many of these innovations would not be possible without technological advances, where necessary we provide an appropriate discussion of their influence. First we review stock markets in the United States and detail how individual securities and portfolios of securities are traded. Then we discuss indices and the use of stock index derivatives, using several examples of stock index futures and options and pointing out the differences between these contracts and the other contracts we have encountered so far. We describe applications of these contracts to problems of portfolio risk management. Here we consider derivatives based on U.S. stock market indices; in Chapter 16 we shall discuss contracts based on foreign stock market indices.

The primary objectives of this chapter are the following:

- To describe how securities and portfolios are traded; and
- To describe the use of stock index futures and options in portfolio risk management.

Stock Markets in the United States

There are several major stock exchanges in the United States. The New York Stock Exchange (NYSE) is the largest and accounts for about 80 percent of the total stock exchange–traded volume. The second-largest exchange is the American Stock Exchange (AMEX). All other exchanges in the United States are regional—they list firms located in their geographical areas. Examples include the Midwest, Pacific, and Philadelphia stock exchanges.

In 1975, average daily volume on the NYSE was under 20 million shares per day. Since then, volume has increased tenfold. Institutional investors frequently trade blocks of over 10,000 shares in a single transaction. Indeed, such transactions account for over half of all trading on the NYSE.

Exchanges will list only those stocks that meet certain requirements. The NYSE has fairly selective criteria that preclude small firms from being considered. AMEX has less stringent listing standards, and the standards of the regional exchanges are still lower. The stocks of firms that do not meet the criteria are traded in the over-the-counter (OTC) market. This market is primarily conducted through the National Association of Securities Dealers Automated Quotation System (NASDAQ). This computerized system allows dealers to post their bid and ask prices in stocks in which they make markets. The trader can examine all the quotes for a particular security, then call the dealer with the best quote and execute the trade. It is possible for a particular stock to trade in more than one exchange. Since

1975 centralized reporting of transactions and a centralized quotation system have been mandated; these enhance competition among market makers. To further enhance competition, in 1978 the Intermarket Trading System was implemented to link prices quoted on the NYSE, AMEX, Boston, Cincinnati, Midwest, Pacific, and Philadelphia exchanges. This system ensures that quotes in all markets are competitive.

Modern investment theory suggests that in the absence of special information, investors should hold fully diversified portfolios rather than bear the risk of holding positions in a limited number of securities. This being the case, it is sensible to trade portfolios when an investor either needs cash or has cash to invest. Mutual funds are natural vehicles for achieving this. Indeed, since their introduction in the 1970s there has been a steady growth in the number and size of these funds. A common surrogate often used for the market portfolio is the Standard and Poor's 500 (S & P 500) stock index. This index represents about 70 percent of the value of all U.S.-traded common stock. Mutual funds that "track" the S & P 500 purchase all 500 stocks in the same proportion as their weights in the index. Each investor in the fund shares proportionately in income and capital gains and losses. Since management expenses are very small (typically less than 0.4 percent of assets), this type of fund provides a convenient way for small investors to purchase diversified portfolios.

Managers of index funds must reinvest all dividends in the same proportions as their weights in the index. Such investors need methods for simultaneously trading in large lists of stocks to reallocate assets. Portfolio trading refers to the trading of a list of stocks in a single transaction or pursuant to a single order. In the next section we investigate how individual and multiple orders can be executed.

Equity Trading and Portfolio Trading

Trades in single stocks can currently be executed in several ways, depending on the size of the order. Small trades, less than 30,000 shares, can be executed by a stockbroker, who enters the order with the specialist for the stock on the appropriate exchange. An alternative way for trading smaller orders is to use the designated order turnaround (DOT) system. This computerized system allows brokerage firms to transmit small client orders directly to the specialist without using a floor broker, and it virtually guarantees execution of orders within a few minutes. The DOT system was developed for the NYSE. Similar systems exist at other exchanges. Not only do they provide automatic routing of orders, but they also provide automated reporting.

Medium-sized orders are normally executed by stockbrokers in concert with floor traders, through specialists. Large orders, termed **block orders,** are traded by brokers who typically agree on a single price for a client's block trade either by finding another client for the other side of the trade or by taking the trade into their own account. The trade is often "crossed" on the exchange floor. In crossing, the broker is required to take any orders with better terms for the client than the agreed price when the order is executed on the floor. However, crossing is not necessary, and large traders may negotiate directly with each other. Indeed, because of advances in trading technologies and telecommunications, large institutions can avoid brokerage fees by trading electronically with other large investors, by passing the exchange. Block traders are typically employed by large brokerage firms and are often said to operate in the "fourth market" or "upstairs markets"; the name derives from the fact that transactions are negotiated from offices off the floor of the exchange.

In the mid-1970s, stocks began to be traded not only individually but also in packages or "programs." The NYSE statistics define a **program trade** as any order for a portfolio of 15 or more stocks. **Portfolio trading,** as the name implies, is the trading of a portfolio of stocks in a single transaction or pursuant to a single order. Portfolio trades can typically be accomplished in two ways. First, each stock in the list could be executed through normal means at the best possible price. This strategy can be very expensive because each stock in the list is traded separately. In principle, the cost of trading a large number of different stocks in a single portfolio ought to be less than the sum of the costs of trading each of the stocks separately. The transaction costs include commission charges and the market impact costs associated with the bid-ask spread. These transactions can be easily accomplished electronically through the DOT system. Brokers can load their portfolio lists into computers, which, on command, send the orders for the various stocks to the DOT terminals at the various specialist posts. Alternatively, brokers may carry preprinted order tickets to the specialist posts.

Automated trading systems, such as the DOT system, have helped portfolio trading, but the cost is still high because the portfolio has to be broken up into individual securities. Thus, investors who want to buy the S & P 500 must buy 500 individual securities in given amounts, while investors who want to sell the S & P 500 portfolio have to liquidate 500 separate positions.

There are alternative ways of trading diversified portfolios. A broker may guarantee to buy a portfolio at a price no less than the price calculated on the basis of the closing prices of each of the stocks in the portfolio. As part of the agreement, the commission charges are specified. Some portfolio trading contracts include incentives for the broker to obtain better prices. For example, the investor can share the profits if the broker gets prices better than the bid prices.

When entering into a portfolio trading agreement with a broker, the client may specify the list of issues included in the portfolio. Such a contract, referred to as a **disclosed contract,** can hurt a portfolio seller. If prices are based on closing prices that day, the broker has an incentive to make sure that the closing prices are at the bid side rather than the ask side. The stocks acquired by the broker at these prices can then be sold the next day at higher prices. To overcome this "moral hazard" problem, the client can insist on providing only a general description of the list of securities to be sold. (For example, the contract may specify the percentage of over-the-counter stocks or the number of securities in the S & P 500). Such contracts are referred to as **blind agreements.** Although blind agreements eliminate the moral hazard issue, the dealer has less information and bears more risk and is therefore more likely to charge a larger commission.

Although the speed and general efficiency of trading portfolios have improved, the cost of accomplishing these trades is still quite high because portfolio orders usually have to be unbundled into single orders.

Managing Market Price Risk with Derivatives

Diversification can reduce portfolio risk to levels proportional to the risk inherent in the market as a whole, but it cannot reduce risk below market-related levels. Managers of well-diversified portfolios must either contend with this market risk or "time" the market. The latter strategy involves selecting times to enter and withdraw from the stock market and can result in large transaction costs.

In recent years, some investors have modified the buy-and-hold strategy as they have become more aware of the effects shorter-term market risks have on their longer-term investment goals. Protection against falling prices can be obtained by purchasing put options on individual securities. However, this strategy can provide more protection than desired. Some investors may be willing to bear nonmarket-related risks of some securities, or they may have already reduced them to acceptable levels through diversification. Such investors may require only hedges against market-related risks.

Portfolio managers may desire contracts that insure their particular portfolios against price declines below particular levels. A tailor-designed contract can be built around the composition of a particular portfolio. However, for a well-diversified portfolio, the correlation of the returns with those of a broad-based market index, such as the S & P 500, would be high. If derivative contracts based on the index were available, then investors could use them to hedge market risks of their individual portfolios.

Stock Index Futures and Options

Stock index futures began trading in 1982, when the Kansas City Board of Trade introduced the Value Line Stock Index, the first futures contract based on the stock index. In the same year, the Chicago Mercantile Exchange (CME) introduced futures on the S & P 500 Index, and the New York Futures Exchange introduced a futures contract on the NYSE Composite Index. Two years later, the CBOT introduced futures contracts on the Major Market Index (MMI). Stock index futures were very well received, and by 1987 daily volume exceeded 150,000 contracts, with open interest at about 100,000 contracts. After the stock market crash of 1987, however, the popularity of these contracts diminished, and their annual volume subsided from about 24 million contracts to less than half that number.

Index options began trading in March 1983, when the Chicago Board Options Exchange (CBOE) introduced options on the S & P 100 Index. The AMEX followed with an option contract on the MMI, and the NYSE introduced options on its Composite Index. Volume on the S & P 100 Index was so great that after

18 months the option pit in which it traded became the world's biggest trading arena after the NYSE. After one year of trading, index options accounted for over 50 percent of the total volume of all options traded, and daily volume in the options amounted to over $4 billion in the underlying stock.

Before illustrating how stock index derivatives can be used to manage the risk of portfolios, it is first necessary to understand how stock market indices are constructed.

Indices

Each stock in an index is assigned a relative weight. There are three common weighting schemes: the market-value-weighted index, the price-weighted index, and the equally weighted index. To illustrate these weighting schemes, consider an index made up of three stocks, A, B, and C, whose prices in the initial (or base) period and some future period t are shown in Exhibit 13.1, which also indicates the number of shares outstanding.

Market-Value-Weighted Index   The market-value-weighted index at time t is obtained by computing the ratio of the market value of all outstanding shares that make up the index at time t to the value at the initial period and multiplying by an initial index value.

EXAMPLE 13.1   Let $MV(t)$ be the market value of all outstanding shares at time t, and let $I(t)$ be the index value at time t. Then we have

$$MV(0) = \$150(50) + \$40(100) + \$10(500) = \$16,500$$

$$MV(t) = \$150(50) + \$80(100) + \$30(500) = \$30,500$$

Assuming $I(0) = 100$, we have

$$I(t) = \left[\frac{MV(t)}{MV(0)}\right]I(0) = \left(\frac{\$30,500}{\$16,500}\right) \times 100 = 184.85$$

Note that stock splits have no effect on the index. However, adjustments to the formula are necessary to reflect capitalization changes over time.

Price-Weighted Index   A price-weighted index reflects the change in the *average* price of the stocks that make up the index.

EXHIBIT 13.1   Composition of a Three-Stock Index

Stock	Initial Price ($)	Price at Date t ($)	Shares Outstanding
A	150	150	50
B	40	80	100
C	10	30	500

EXAMPLE 13.2   The average stock price at the initial period and at date t are

$$\bar{S}(0) = \frac{(\$150 + \$40 + \$10)}{3} = \$66.667$$

$$\bar{S}(t) = \frac{(\$150 + \$80 + \$30)}{3} = \$86.67$$

Assuming an initial index of 100, we have

$$I(t) = [\bar{S}(t)/\bar{S}(0)]\, I(0) = [\$86.67/\$66.67]100 = 130$$

The base value, $I(0)$, of the price-weighted index has to be adjusted from time to time to reflect specific events. For example, consider what happens if a $2:1$ split in stock A occurs. Without the split, the index is $I(t) = 130$. In light of the split, we have

$$\bar{S}(t) = \frac{(\$75 + \$80 + \$30)}{3} = \$61.67$$

Without adjusting the index, we would obtain

$$I(t) = \left(\frac{61.67}{66.67}\right)100 = 92.45$$

To prevent stock splits from jolting the index value, we adjust the base value, $I(0)$, from 100 to a new value, which is set so that the new index value equals the old value. That is, $I(0)$ is chosen such that

$$130 = \left(\frac{61.67}{66.67}\right)I(0)$$

Hence

$$I(0) = 140.6$$

The base value is also adjusted when stocks in the index are changed. These changes may occur when companies go bankrupt, lose market share, or are taken over. If left unchanged, the dated index would not represent the group it was initially intended to represent.

Equally Weighted Index   In an equally weighted index, an equal dollar amount is invested in each stock in the index.

EXAMPLE 13.3   Assume $1000 is invested in each stock in our example. Then 6.667 shares of A, 5 shares of B, and 100 shares of C could be purchased. The investment in the base period would be $3000. In time period t, the portfolio value would be $6000. The new index in this case is

$$I(t) = \left[\frac{MV(t)}{MV(0)}\right]I(0) = 200$$

Using Indices in Portfolio Management

Value-weighted indices are appropriate benchmarks for index funds that attempt to invest "in the market"; price-weighted indices are appropriate benchmarks for investors who allocate wealth across stocks in ratios corresponding to their prices; and equally weighted indices are appropriate benchmarks for investors who allocate equal funds to all stocks in the portfolio.

EXAMPLE 13.4

1. The Dow Jones Industrial Average is a price-weighted average of 30 blue-chip stocks, all of which are traded on the NYSE. The average is calculated by adding the closing prices of the 30 component stocks and then dividing by a specific divisor that maintains the continuity of the index when stocks split or when a particular company is replaced in the index. While the Dow is one of the best-known indicators, it does not serve as the basis for any derivative contract.

2. The S&P 100 Index is a market-weighted index that consists of 100 blue-chip firms (92 industrial, 5 financial, 2 transportation, and 1 utility). The 12 largest firms in the index account for over 50 percent of the total market value of the S & P 100.

3. The S&P 500 Index is a market-weighted index composed of 500 stocks, mostly NYSE-listed companies, with a few AMEX and over-the-counter (OTC) stocks included as well. The market value of this index equals approximately 80 percent of the value of all stocks listed on the NYSE.

4. The MMI is a price-weighted index that includes 20 blue-chip stocks, of which 17 are in the Dow Jones Industrial Average. As such, this index is highly correlated to the Dow Jones Index.

Exhibit 13.2 shows some indices on which derivatives are traded. All but the MMI are market-value-weighted indices.

Long-term options on the S&P 500, S&P 100, and the MMI also exist. Most foreign option markets trade index options on indices, especially on their local broad-based country index.

EXHIBIT 13.2   Broad-Based Stock Market Indices on Which Options Trade

Index	Option Exchange	Type*	Futures Exchange	Futures Options	Description
S & P 100	CBOE	A	—	—	100 stocks
S & P 500	CBOE	E	CME	Yes	500 stocks
NYSE Composite Index	NYSE	A	NYFE	Yes	All NYSE stocks
Major Market Index	AMEX	E	CBOT	Yes	20 blue-chip stocks
S & P Midcap 400	AMEX	E	CME	Yes	400 mid-sized stocks

*A = American; E = European.

In addition, option contracts trade on narrow-based (market sector) indices, such as computer technology and institutional, pharmaceutical, and biotechnology indices. The computer technology index, for example, is based on 30 computer stocks, and the options that trade at the AMEX are American. In contrast, the Institutional Index consists of 75 stocks held widely by institutions. The options on this index are European.

Stock Index Options

Stock index option trading accounts for over half the volume of all stock option contracts traded. Exhibit 13.3 shows the closing prices of several index option contracts as they appear in the *Wall Street Journal*. As with equity options, the minimum premium quotation is 1/16 point for premiums of less than 3 points and 1/8 point for premiums of 3 points or greater.

EXAMPLE 13.5   **The S & P 100 Option Contract**

The S & P 100 Option, known by its ticker symbol OEX, is the most liquid option contract traded in the United States. The trading unit of each index option is the level of the S & P 100 Index multiplied by 100. The holder of an in-the-money call or put who exercises the option receives a cash amount equal to the difference between the closing dollar value of the index on the exercise date and the aggregate exercise price of the option. This American-style contract trades on the CBOE.

The S & P 100 Index option accounts for over 80 percent of the index options market. Since the multiplier is only 100, small investors have been important participants. Indeed, about 70 percent of orders, accounting for about 20 percent of contract volume, were for 10 contracts or less. The S & P 100 closely tracks other indices. For example, it has shown 0.97 correlation with the S & P 500 Index and 0.95 with the Dow. Each point in the index is equivalent to about a 7- or 8-point move in the Dow.

On some days in 1984, OEX traders struggled to execute three-quarters of a million contracts a day while maintaining timely, accurate quotes and records of sales. Heavy volume, much of it in small orders, created a blizzard of paper that clogged the flow of orders through the pit. To overcome this problem, the CBOE introduced a retail automatic execution system that provides split-second "fills" at the best bid and ask prices. Market and limit orders can be handled for up to 10 contracts. Currently, this automated system handles about 100,000 contracts per day.

The OEX pit has also been a proving ground for other innovations. For example, hand-held terminals are used to report last sales. Information is punched in and sent by radio to the pit and reformatted for the trade reporting system. More than 20 percent of all OEX orders are reported from these terminals. Ultimately, these terminals could be used by market makers to report trade data, to record trades for clearing firms, and to track open positions.

INDEX OPTIONS TRADING

Monday, May 1, 1995
Volume, last, net change and open interest for all contracts. Volume figures are unofficial. Open interest reflects previous trading day. p-Put c-Call

CHICAGO

Strike	Vol.	Last	Net Chg.	Open Int.
CB MEXICO INDEX(MEX)				
Jun 60c	45	14⅛	− ½	509
May 65c	45	9⅛	+ ⅜	1,540
May 70c	11	4½	− 1⅜	217
May 70p	38	1¼	...	1,430
Jun 70p	10	2⅜⁄₁₆	+ 3⁄₁₆	1,403
Sep 70p	2	4½	+ ¼	780
May 75c	20	2	− ⅝	368
May 75p	12	3⅜	+ ¼	1,373
Jun 75c	34	3⅞	+ ⅛	703
Sep 75c	10	7½	− 2	750
May 80c	10	¾	− 15⁄₁₆	386
Jun 80c	2	2	− 3⅛	272
Sep 80c	4	5	− 3	710
May 85c	15	5⁄₁₆	− ⅛	201
Jun 85c	10	15⁄₁₆	− ¼	274
Jun 90c	200	1⁄₁₆	− ⅛	535
Sep 100c	10	⅞	− 5⁄₁₆	90
Sep 125c	10	¼	...	...
Call vol. 426	Open int. 15,336			
Put vol. 72	Open int. 18,595			

S & P 100 INDEX(OEX)				
May 415c	195	1⁄₁₆	...	1,883
Jun 415p	37	⅜	− 3⁄₁₆	80
May 420c	10	1⁄₁₆	− 1⁄₁₆	11,820
Jun 420p	20	1⅛	+ 1⁄₁₆	3,994
Aug 420p	3	1¼	− ⅜	4
May 425p	302	⅛	...	4,654
May 430c	272	58¼	...	1,305
May 430p	591	1⁄₁₆	− 1⁄₁₆	12,053
Jun 430p	89	½	− 1⁄₁₆	3,247
Jul 430p	11	1⅛	− 1⁄₁₆	1,743
Aug 430p	10	1⅝	− ⅛	19
May 435c	62	3⁄₁₆	...	11,802
May 435p	95	⅛	+ ⅛	2,184
Jul 435p	10	1¼	...	1,011
May 440c	71	48½	− ¼	4,435
May 440p	551	3⁄₁₆	...	18,165
Jun 440c	2	48⅜	+ ⅛	2,554
Jun 440p	97	⅝	+ 1⁄₁₆	8,967
Jul 440p	60	1½	...	2,531
Aug 440p	4	2¼	− ⅛	29
May 445c	600	43¼	− 1½	2,938
May 445p	666	¼	...	20,950
Jun 445p	120	13⁄₁₆	...	7,464
May 450c	186	38¾	+ 1¼	7,420
May 450p	1,341	7⁄₁₆	...	37,834
Jun 450c	14	38⅜	− 2⅞	3,384
Jun 450p	937	1	...	11,946
Jul 450p	487	2	− ⅛	3,696
Aug 450p	2	3	− ¼	47
May 455c	100	33⅝	− ⅜	3,866
May 455p	4,826	11⁄₁₆	+ ⅜	33,554
Jun 455c	75	35¼	+ 1½	846
May 455p	424	1¼	− ⅛	3,221
Jul 455c	3	39	+ 2½	54
Jul 455p	135	2½	+ ½	90
May 460c	172	29	...	13,735
May 460p	4,432	9⁄₁₆	+ ⅛	35,522
Jun 460c	30	30⅜	+ ¾	14,803
Jun 460p	1,787	1⅞	+ ⅛	8,721
Jul 460p	1,013	3	+ ⅛	18,960

	Vol.	Last	Net Chg.	Open Int.
Aug 460c	3	35	+ 3⅛	109
Aug 460p	1	3¾	+ ⅛	266
May 465c	715	23¾	− 1	15,083
May 465p	5,458	¾	+ 1⁄₁₆	42,123
Jun 465c	5	26	− ½	2,879
Jun 465p	787	2⁄₁₆	+ ⅛	10,351
Jul 465c	1	29	− 1	3,030
Jul 465p	26	3½	...	4,090
May 470c	2,832	18¾	− 1¼	34,554
May 470p	10,077	1¹⁄₁₆	+ ⅛	62,018
Jun 470c	958	21	...	9,398
Jun 470p	1,784	2¹¹⁄₁₆	+ ¼	13,956
Jul 470p	153	4⅜	+ ¼	8,264
Aug 470c	100	26½	+ 2½	7,371
May 470p	46	5½	+ ⅛	7,597
May 475c	1,166	13⅞	− 1⅝	39,978
May 475p	9,074	1½	+ ⅛	56,916
Jun 475c	76	17½	+ ¼	8,360
Jun 475p	1,759	3½	+ ⅜	11,948
Jul 475c	1	20⅝	+ 15⁄₈	3,778
Jul 475p	47	5⅝	− ½	2,897
May 480c	4,717	9⁷⁄₁₆	− 1⅛	35,760
May 480p	14,971	2⅜	+ 3⁄₁₆	47,689
Jun 480c	551	13¼	− ¾	20,089
Jun 480p	1,814	4⅝	+ ⅜	13,839
Jul 480p	154	6⅝	+ ¼	2,693
Aug 480p	8	7⅞	+ ⅜	359
May 485c	16,225	6⅛	− 1⅛	30,144
May 485p	21,855	3¾	+ 3⁄₁₆	27,044
May 485c	1,100	9⅞	− ¾	7,634
Jun 485p	2,024	6¼	+ ½	4,422
Jul 485c	45	13¼	− ¼	6,619
Jul 485p	323	8⅛	+ ⅞	718
May 490c	17,534	3¼	− ⅞	29,660
May 490p	11,434	6⅛	+ ¾	7,298
May 490c	1,020	6⅜	− ¾	8,238
May 490p	1,421	8⅝	+ ¼	1,324
Jul 490c	246	9⅞	− ⅝	11,366
Jul 490p	481	9¾	+ ⅝	359
Aug 490p	15	11	...	39
May 495c	8,805	1¹¹⁄₁₆	− ½	29,444
May 495p	330	9⅝	+ ⅛	334
Jun 495c	806	4	− ⅝	4,760
Jun 495p	105	11	− ½	66
Jul 495c	191	7¼	− 1⁄₁₆	6,243
May 500c	2,865	⅞	− 3⁄₁₆	18,729
May 500p	288	13¼	− ½	25
May 500c	887	2⁷⁄₁₆	− 5⁄₁₆	15,003
Jul 500c	103	5¼	− ...	2,982
Jul 500p	20	15⅜	+ ...	28
Aug 500c	6	6⅛	− ½	272
May 505c	752	1⁄₁₆	− 3⁄₁₆	13,985
May 505p	385	15¹¹⁄₁₆	− 5⁄₁₆	5,180
Jul 505c	11	3¾	− ¼	1,399
Jul 505p	1	18⅜	...	2
Aug 505c	205	3¼	+ ¼	225
Jun 515p	3	½	...	...
Jun 515p	3	28	...	...
Call vol. 64,622	Open Int. 454,487			
Put vol. 102,776	Open Int. 590,441			

S & P 500 INDEX-AM(SPX)				
May 375c	85	139¼	+ 30	...
May 375p	85	1⁄₁₆	...	410
May 420p	12	¼	+ ⅛	4,458
Jun 450c	550	65¾	+ ¼	10,978
May 450p	503	¾	− ⅛	39,717
May 455c	3	⅝	...	1,132
May 465p	50	⅞	− ...	3,614
May 465c	500	51	+ 1⅞	7,226
Jun 465p	500	2	− ...	14,661
May 470p	525	¾	− 5⁄₁₆	20,553
May 475c	3	39⅞⁄₁₆	− ...	1,612
May 475p	856	1¼	+ ⅛	12,086
Jun 475p	551	41½	− ⅜	13,010
Jun 475c	2,321	2⅛	− 1⁄₁₆	30,140
Jul 475p	2,854	1⅞	− ⅝	20
May 480p	180	1¼	− 1⁄₁₆	15,479
Jun 480p	1	36½	+ ¼	6,243
May 480p	2,058	13¹⁄₁₆	− 5⁄₁₆	18,925
Jul 480p	10	2¼	− ½	739
May 485p	1,334	7⁄₁₆	...	25,773
May 485c	1	33	+ 2⅛	10,004
Jun 485p	206	17¹⁄₁₆	− 1⁄₁₆	26,205

AMERICAN

AM MEXICO INDEX(MXY)				
Jun 100c	1	2¼	− ⅛	41
Jun 105c	30	1¾	+ ⅛	45
Call vol. 21	Open Int. 3,750			
Put vol. 0	Open Int. 4,362			

BIOTECH(BTK)				
May 80c	5	2¾	+ ¾	30
Call vol. 5	Open Int. 1,487			
Put vol. 0	Open Int. 1,251			

HONG KONG INDEX(HKO)				
Jun 160p	7	4⅞	− ¼	677
Jul 160p	1	6	− ...	...
May 165c	20	4	+ ¼	45
May 170c	10	1⅞	− 15⁄₁₆	320
May 170p	10	7	+ ¾	30
May 175c	10	15⁄₁₆	− 1¹³⁄₁₆	225
Call vol. 20	Open Int. 2,109			
Put vol. 38	Open Int. 2,914			

INSTITUTIONAL-AM(XII)				
Jun 400p	45	1⅜	+ ...	55
May 505p	100	1	− 2⅞	140
May 520c	25	6⅜	+ 1¼	240
Jun 530c	25	4½	+ 2¹⁄₁₆	...
Jun 535p	50	13¾	+ ⅜	225
Jun 535p	50	14½	− 2	150
Call vol. 25	Open Int. 27,473			
Put vol. 265	Open Int. 7,860			

JAPAN INDEX(JPN)				
May 165p	50	1⅛	− 3⁄₁₆	2,708
May 170c	1	2⅞	− ¾	965
May 170p	6	2¾	+ ⅛	166
May 170c	1	4⅞	− ¼	1,072
Jun 170p	25	4⅜	+ ⅛	53
May 175c	3	½	− ½	215
Jun 185c	20	½	− 1⁄₁₆	523
Jun 190c	35	¼	− 1⁄₁₆	366
Call vol. 501	Open Int. 34,397			
Put vol. 381	Open Int. 27,833			

MAJOR MARKET(XMI)				
May 400p	150	7⁄₁₆	− ...	1,103
Jul 405p	600	1⅛	− 3⁄₁₆	250
May 410p	50	3⁄₁₆	− 3⁄₁₆	311

PHILADELPHIA

GOLD/SILVER(XAU)				
Jul 105p	20	1⅜	+ ½	6
May 110c	10	10⅛	+ 1⅛	83
May 110p	325	⅝	− ⅜	905
May 115c	26	5⅝	+ ⅜	4,248
May 115p	39	2	− ⅜	703
Jun 115c	12	8	+ ¼	72
Jun 115p	2	3⅜	− ⅜	85
May 120c	89	2⅝	+ 13⁄₁₆	822
May 120p	55	3⅞	− ⅞	594
May 120c	15	5	+ ⅜	1,940
May 120p	55	6⅜	+ ⅛	1,712
Jun 125c	65	1⅜	+ ⅛	263
Jun 125p	17	6½	− 1⅛	373
May 125c	28	3⅜	+ ⅜	660
May 130c	71	5⅜	+ ¼	1,044
May 130c	15	1⅜	− ⅜	1,099
May 135c	38	5⁄₁₆	− ¼	41
Jul 135c	5	2½	+ ¼	5,469
Jun 145c	2	7⁄₁₆	− 2¹⁄₁₆	...
Call vol. 421	Open int. 21,098			
Put vol. 460	Open int. 6,119			

OTC INDEX(XOC)				
May 565p	569	1⁄₁₆	...	450
May 605p	100	¼	− 9⁄₁₆	300
Jun 615p	6	1⅜	− 7⅛	6
May 640p	10	9	+ ...	515
May 645p	30	1⅜	− ⅜	53
May 660p	40	5	+ ¾	549
May 665c	10	17¼	+ 9¼	122
May 665p	1	5⅜	− 1⅞	15

	Vol.	Last	Net Chg.	Open Int.
Jun 680p	5	19	− 6½	2
May 685c	11	3⅜	− ⅞	52
May 685p	15	14	− 2½	103
May 690c	20	3	− ⅜	1,050
May 690p	3	17⅜	− 14⅛	...
May 690p	3	27	− ...	...
May 695c	68	11⁄₁₆	− ⅛	60
May 700c	178	13⅜	+ 13⅞⁄₁₆	20
May 705c	20	3⅜	− ⅛	390
May 715c	20	⅛	...	...
Call vol. 200	Open Int. 2,445			
Put vol. 754	Open Int. 3,062			

PHLX KBW BANK(BKX)				
May 285p	50	3⅜	+ ⅛	1,528
Jun 290c	50	8¼	− 1¼	202
Call vol. 50	Open Int. 7,338			
Put vol. 50	Open Int. 12,886			

UTILITY INDEX(UTY)				
Jun 230c	10	9⅛	+ ⅛	78
May 235p	194	1¼	− 2	43
May 240c	5	1⅜	− ¼	300
May 240c	1	2½	− 1¼	48
Call vol. 26	Open Int. 2,206			
Put vol. 194	Open Int. 1,397			

VALUE LINE(VLE)				
May 465c	30	5⁄₁₆	− 11⁄₁₆	30
May 470p	30	½	− ⅞	51
May 490p	5	3½	− ⅛	83
May 500p	18	8¼	+ 1	45
Call vol. 0	Open Int. 5,198			
Put vol. 83	Open Int. 5,691			

NEW YORK

NYSE INDEX new(NYA)				
Jul 260p	1	1¼	− ...	...
Jun 270p	5	1⅞	− ⅛	107
May 275p	2	1¾	− ...	263
Jun 275c	10	5⅜	+ 1⅛	135
May 280p	18	4½	− ...	11
Jul 280p	1	5¾	− ...	...
Call vol. 10	Open Int. 729			
Put vol. 27	Open Int. 1,074			

LEAPS-LONG TERM

HONG KONG INDEX — AM				
Jan 96 15p	50	⅞	− 1⁄₁₆	1454
Jan 96 20c	40	5	− ...	1394
Call vol. 50	Open Int. 2,084			
Put vol. 50	Open Int. 2,607			

S & P 100 INDEX — CB				
Dec 95 35p	20	⅛	− 1⁄₁₆	12515
Dec 95 37½p	20	¼	− ...	20524
Dec 95 40p	105	¼	− ...	43874
Dec 95 45c	2	43¼	+ ½	2553
Dec 95 45p	353	11⁄₁₆	− ...	33908
Dec 97 45p	10	2¾⁄₁₆	− ...	559
Dec 95 47½c	2	3⅛	+ ⅛	7844
Dec 97 47½p	56	15⁄₁₆	− ...	5945
Dec 97 47½p	10	3⅜	− ¼	441
Dec 95 50p	307	2⁵⁄₁₆	− 1⁄₁₆	955
Dec 97 50p	10	4	− ...	5469
Call vol. 31	Open Int. 35,813			
Put vol. 3,024	Open Int. 195,093			

S & P 500 INDEX — CB				
Dec 95 40p	12	3⁄₁₆	− ...	7437
Dec 95 45p	10	7⁄₁₆	− ⅛	34029
Dec 95 50p	64	11⁄₈	− ...	17893
Dec 95 52½p	72	1⅞	− ...	1945
Call vol. 0	Open Int. 8,741			
Put vol. 402	Open Int. 167,708			

EXHIBIT 13.3 Selected Stock Index Option Price Information from the *Wall Street Journal*

Index options trade like stock options. Strike prices are expressed in dollars and are fixed at levels surrounding the current level of the underlying index. Additional contracts are introduced as index prices rise or decline. Like stock options, most index options expire on the Saturday following the third Friday of the expiration month. When initially introduced, index options were assigned three-, six-, and nine-month expiration dates. From the beginning, however, investor interest concentrated in the nearby expiration months. Option contracts with monthly expirations up to a maximum of four months now trade at any time.

EXAMPLE 13.6   **Flexible Exchange Options at the CBOE**

Institutional investors often wish to reduce their exposure to a decline in stock values. For example, a manager may believe that although owning equities is a sound long-term strategy, over the next year equity exposure is not wise. Selling stock and repurchasing later is inappropriate because of the bid-ask spreads, commission costs, and the fact that the large transactions required may move the market itself. Some managers may conclude that trading the S & P 100 and the S & P 500 stock index options may be appropriate. However, other managers may want more customized contracts. For example, a specific manager may want a two-year European put option with a settlement date corresponding to the close date at the end of the year. Such a contract could be obtained from an investment bank in the OTC market. Alternatively, such an order could be brought to the "flex pit" of the CBOE.

Market participants who use the flex pits are able to select any strike price and maturity up to 5 years and can request the contract be American or European. Once the contract is established, price negotiations are scheduled to last at least 10 minutes so that all interested parties have sufficient time to establish prices at which they would be prepared to do business. In particular, market makers compete for orders in a modified open-outcry system. Quote and last sales information for flex options are made available. As with ordinary options, flex trades are cleared, settled, and guaranteed through the Options Clearing Corporation. The CBOE introduced this product to recover market share from the OTC market. The hope was that institutions would be attracted to this market because of the reduction in counterparty risk. Since the primary users of this market are institutions, the minimum deal size is based off $10 million of stock equity.

Stock Index Futures and Futures Options

Futures contracts based on stock indices are known as **stock index futures contracts.** A stock index futures contract is a legal commitment to deliver or receive the dollar value of the index at a predetermined future date at a predetermined cost.

Exhibit 13.4 shows price information on stock index futures as reported in the *Wall Street Journal*. Of the stock index contracts shown, the S & P 500 futures contract is the most active.

INDEX

S&P 500 INDEX (CME) $500 times index

	Open	High	Low	Settle	Chg	High	Low	Open Interest
June	516.55	517.25	514.70	515.30	− 1.45	517.25	449.50	193,084
Sept	520.55	520.80	519.40	519.65	− 1.45	521.60	456.30	15,176
Dec			....	524.00	− 1.55	526.00	474.50	4,263
Mr96	530.20	530.20	530.20	528.85	− 1.55	531.00	511.00	1,091

Est vol 64,976; vol Fri 74,028; open int 213,619, +3,865.
Indx prelim High 515.60; Low 513.42; Close 514.25 −.46

S&P MIDCAP 400 (CME) $500 times index

June	186.40	186.50	185.75	185.95	− .55	187.50	165.50	9,390

Est vol 283; vol Fri 1,049; open int 9,436, − 58
The index: High 185.80; Low 185.14; Close 185.21 −.61

NIKKEI 225 STOCK AVERAGE (CME)−$5 times index

June	16855.	16875.	16830.	16860.	+ 5	22050.	15510.	32,312
Sept		....		16935.	+ 5	20625.	15700.	107

Est vol 500; vol Fri 1,084; open int 32,475, −213.
The index: High 16838.61; Low 16700.17; Close 16811.46 +4.71

GSCI (CME)−$250 times nearby index

June	183.50	184.50	183.50	184.10	+ 1.90	184.50	172.00	12,918
Aug			....	180.50	+ 1.30	180.50	172.30	119

Est vol 470; vol Fri 425; open int 13,037, +86.
The index: High 186.22; Low 183.61; Close 185.31 + 1.68

CAC-40 STOCK INDEX (MATIF)−FFr 200 per index pt
NOT AVAILABLE

FT−SE 100 INDEX (LIFFE)−£25 per index point

June	3223.0	3245.0	3218.0	3237.0	+ 16.0	3255.0	2960.	70,476
Sept	3263.5	3263.5	3263.5	3259.0	+ 15.0	3263.5	3005.	1,839
Dec		....	....	3287.5	+ 14.5	....	....	180

Est vol 6,051; vol Fri 10,620; open int 72,495, −2.

ALL ORDINARIES SHARE PRICE INDEX (SFE)
A$25 times index

June	2071.	2081.	2067.	2070.	− 3.0	2200.	1861.	70,743
Sept	2105.	2105.	2105.	2096.	− 3.0	2114.	1882.	6,346
Dec		....	....	2114.	− 3.0	2128.	1913.	1,720
Mr96		....	....	2142.	− 3.0	2150.	1950.	618

Est vol 4,758; vol Fri 7,201; open int 79,427, +789.
The index: High 2050.2; Low 2037.7; Close 2039.6 −10.6

EXHIBIT 13.4   Stock Index Futures Price Information from the *Wall Street Journal*

Source: Reprinted by permission of the Wall Street Journal © 1995 Dow Jones & Company, Inc. All Rights Reserved Worldwide.

EXAMPLE 13.7   **The CME's S & P 500 Futures and Futures Options Contracts**

The S & P 500 stock index futures contract accounts for over two-thirds of all stock index futures trading. Options on these futures also trade. The multiplier for the contract is 500. For example, if the futures price is $300.50, the dollar price is 500 × $300.50, or $150,250. The minimum trading price change for the contract is $0.05, so a tick up or down has a dollar value of $25 per contract ($500 × $0.05). The contract months are March, June, September, and December. The last day of trading is the Thursday prior to the third Friday of the contract month. Settlement is by cash and is based on the Special Opening Quotation on Friday morning of the S & P 500 stock price index.

Option contracts trade on the futures contract. Option contracts are listed for all 12 calendar months. At any point, there will be options available for trading that expire in the next three calendar months, plus two further quarterly expirations. The underlying instrument for the three monthly option expirations within a quarter is the quarter-end futures contract. For example, if you exercise a January, February, or March option, you receive a position in the March futures. The quarter-end options expire at the same time as the futures contracts. The interim options expire on the third Friday of their month.

Risk Management with Stock Index Derivatives

The uses of futures and options to hedge or insure against losses have been discussed in previous chapters. Therefore, in this section we provide only a few illustrative examples.

Protecting Diversified Portfolios from Market Downturns

In Chapter 11 we considered the situation of an owner of a well-diversified portfolio who anticipated a short-term decline in the stock market. Liquidation of the portfolio for the short term is not realistic because of high transaction costs, dividend income, and tax consequences. Without financial hedging devices, the owner may have to bear the risk of a short-term declining market. With stock index derivatives available, the investor can hedge against market-related risk by selling stock index futures or can insure against downside losses by purchasing put index options. The effectiveness of these strategies depends on the degree of correlation between the index and the portfolio. In a worst-case situation, the portfolio value could depreciate while the market index appreciates. However, this event is unlikely if the stock index on which the option trades is highly correlated with the portfolio.

The purchase of put options to protect a stock portfolio from declining below a certain floor value is a simple **static portfolio insurance** strategy. Later in this chapter we shall investigate dynamic trading strategies where synthetic option contracts are created that provide ongoing protection against portfolio declines below a predetermined floor. Typically, such strategies involve dividing the portfolio between stocks and bonds. If the value of the stock portfolio increases, less insurance is required, so riskless assets are sold and more risky securities are purchased. If stock prices decline, however, the position in the stock portfolio is decreased and the funds obtained are used to increase the quantity of riskless bonds. The trading strategy is set up such that regardless of what occurs over a fixed time horizon, the investor is always assured of obtaining a predetermined floor or better. The merits of these dynamic strategies will be explored later in this chapter. However, the purchase of index puts against a portfolio is a static portfolio insurance scheme that offers the advantage that once initiated, protection is guaranteed over the lifetime of the option.

EXAMPLE 13.8   Adjusting the Beta Value of a Portfolio

Consider a portfolio manager who owns three stocks.

Stock	No. of Shares Owned	Stock Price ($)	Beta
A	1 million	40	1.2
B	2 million	20	1.3
C	2 million	10	1.1

The values of the investments are shown below.

Stock	Value of Investment ($)	Fraction of Wealth
A	40 million	0.4
B	40 million	0.4
C	20 million	0.2

The beta value of the portfolio is $\beta_p = 0.4(1.2) + 0.4(1.3) + 0.2(1.1) = 1.22$.

Assume the manager is concerned about future market developments and wishes to reduce the risk associated with this portfolio. The manager believes market uncertainties will clarify over the next few months and does not want to liquidate the portfolio and purchase government bonds. Rather, he decides to reduce the beta value using stock index futures.

Recall that the beta value of the portfolio captures the sensitivity of expected returns to the underlying index. Assume for the moment that the S&P 500 was used to compute the beta values. The analysis indicates that for every 1 percent change in the S & P 500 Index, the portfolio is expected to appreciate by 1.22 percent. Assume the S & P 500 Index is at 300. That is, each contract controls $300 \times 500 = \$150,000$. With no maturity mismatch and a beta value of 1, the minimum-variance hedge is therefore to sell $\$100,000,000/\$150,000 = 666.66$ futures. Since the beta value is 1.22, additional futures should be sold—a total of $666.6 \times 1.22 = 813.3$ futures need to be sold.

If the beta values of the stocks were based on an index other than the S & P 500, additional adjustments would have to be made. For example, assume the stock betas were computed against some index, I. A regression analysis relating the weekly percentage changes in index I to the weekly percentage changes in the S & P 500 yielded a slope of $\beta_{I, S\&P} = 0.8$. This means that for every 1 percent change in the S & P 500, index I is expected to change by 0.8 percent. The modified hedge ratio of 813.3 now has to be adjusted to $813.3 \times 0.8 = 651$ contracts. In general, then, with no maturity mismatch, the hedge ratio is given by $\beta_{pI} \times \beta_{I, S\&P}$ where β_{pI} is the beta value of the stock portfolio with respect to index I.

A primary advantage of selling futures to reduce the beta value over a period of time, rather than selling stocks and buying bonds, is the ease with which the former transaction can be made. The transaction costs involved in buying and later selling a futures contract may be about $14. This implies a charge of $9,114 for the above transaction. In contrast, the round-trip cost of selling $100 million worth of stock and purchasing it back at a future date may be 0.1 percent of the value of the portfolio, or $100,000. Unless the futures contracts are significantly mispriced, the commission charges certainly favor the futures strategy.

EXAMPLE 13.9   **The Role of Index Options in Small Portfolios**

Stock market index derivatives are not only useful for hedging large, diversified portfolios. Suppose an investor feels comfortable with picking stocks but is unsure of market timing and direction. The risk components of the small portfolio can be unbundled into market and nonmarket components, thus allowing hedging against market risk. The investor can lay off market risk associated with market declines by buying protective put options. As an extreme example, consider a portfolio containing only one security. Assume that only 20 percent of the total risk of the stock can be accounted for by market forces. Assume the beta value of the security is 1.2. The significant amount of nonmarket risk is not of concern to the investor because she believes the company is positioned to perform well. However, since the investor is concerned about the overall direction of the market, she may decide to buy protective puts on the market index.

EXAMPLE 13.10   Narrow-Based Index Options in Small Portfolios

Some investors are comfortable ranking companies within a given industry but are unwilling to predict the future direction of the industry as a whole. With industry options available, insurance against poor industry performance can be obtained, and the investor may be able to profit from his or her ability in picking stocks. Consider an investor who believes that company XYZ should outperform other companies in the transportation sector but is unsure how the transportation sector as a whole will perform. By buying the stock together with put options on the S & P Transportation Index, the investor can partially hedge industry-related risks. The number of puts to purchase can be determined by establishing the sensitivity of rates of return on XYZ relative to rates of return on the index. This sensitivity can be obtained by regressing the returns on XYZ against the returns on the index and estimating the slope.

EXAMPLE 13.11   Time Spreads with Put Options

Consider an investor who buys a June XYZ 80 put and sells a March 80 put on the same index. On Monday the option is exercised. The closing price is $72, which means the investor must pay $800. The investor learns about the exercise notice on Tuesday and decides to offset the loss by exercising the June XYZ 80 put. However, since the closing price on Tuesday was $76, the investor will receive only $400 and sustain a net loss of $400. Rather than exercise the put and lose the time premium, a superior strategy would have been to sell the put early on Tuesday.

EXAMPLE 13.12   Intermarket Spreading with Futures

The broad-based market indices are highly correlated with each other. However, if the returns on one index are regressed against the returns on another, the resulting slope could be significantly different from 1. For example, if the S & P 500 is used as the base index and the NYSE Index is regressed against it, a beta estimate of, say, 1.23 could be obtained. This implies that the NYSE could rise approximately 23 percent more than the S & P 500 Index in a bull market. An investor who perceives a bullish market could buy the "high-beta" futures contract and sell the "low-beta" futures in anticipation of the spread widening in favor of the high-beta index. Conversely, in a declining market, the low-beta futures could be bought and the high-beta futures sold in anticipation of the spread narrowing.

Pricing Relationships for Index Derivatives

"Holding the stock index" means buying all the securities that make up the index in their correct proportions and reinvesting all dividends into the stocks of the index, also in appropriate proportions. The price of a stock index derivative clearly is linked to the underlying index.

Below we investigate how stock index futures and options are affected by the dividends. To simplify the discussion, we consider contracts on a price-weighted index, $I(t)$, which is computed by taking the average of the prices of two stocks, A and B, and multiplying the resulting value by a multiplier, m. That is,

$$I(t) = [S_A(t) + S_B(t)]m/2$$

Assume stock A pays a dividend of d_A at time t_A. Similarly, B pays d_B at time t_B.

Pricing Bounds for Stock Index Options

Consider a portfolio P_1, containing $m/2$ shares of A and $m/2$ shares of B that are partially financed by borrowing $m/2 \times d_A$ pure discount bonds that pay out at time t_A, $m/2 \times d_B$ pure discount bonds that pay out at time t_B, and X pure discount bonds that pay out at time T. In addition, consider a portfolio P_2 that contains a European option on the index. The initial and terminal values of the two portfolios are shown in Exhibit 13.5. Note that the dividends can be used to pay off the loans on the d_A bonds of maturity t_A and d_B bonds of maturity t_B, leaving a portfolio value for P_1 equal to the index value at time T less the strike X. Since the cash flows of portfolio P_2 dominate those of P_1, to prevent risk-free profits the initial value of portfolio P_2 must exceed that of P_1. That is,

$$C_0 \geq I(0) - XB(0, T) - \frac{m}{2} d_A B(0, t_A) - \frac{m}{2} d_B B(0, t_B)$$

The above equation shows that the pricing relationships for index options must take into consideration the timing and size of the cash flows of the securities that make up the index.

Property 6.5 states that early exercise of American index options may be optimal. As usual, early exercise may be optimal if the dividend captured exceeds the forgone interest on the strike. This is most likely to occur when dividend yields are high relative to interest rates and when the option is deep in the money.

EXHIBIT 13.5   Arbitrage Bounds for Call Index Options

		Terminal Value	
Portfolio	Initial Value	$I(T) < X$	$I(T) > X$
P_1	$\dfrac{m}{2} S_A(0) + \dfrac{m}{2} S_B(0) - XB(0, T)$	$I(T) - X$	$I(T) - X$
	$-d_A \dfrac{m}{2} B(0, t_A) - d_B \dfrac{m}{2} B(0, t_B)$		
P_2	C_0	0	$I(T) - X$

Empirical Tests for Boundary Conditions of Index Derivatives

There is overwhelming empirical support for the stock option boundary conditions established in Chapter 6. Our discussion of differences between stock and index options, however, makes clear that index options may not satisfy the same bounds. For example, an American call index option price need not exceed the intrinsic value of the option. To see this, note that if the index option were less than its intrinsic value, then purchasing the call and immediately exercising it would not be riskless since the relevant index value is the value of the index at the close. In order to come close to obtaining risk-free arbitrage profits, the investor who purchased the call would have to sell the index. As discussed, this would require selling short several stocks in a proxy portfolio, which could be difficult.

Evnine and Rudd have conducted empirical tests to establish whether index options do satisfy the stock option boundary conditions. Using data collected over a two-month period starting in June 1984, they showed that on over 2 percent of occasions the call asking price was less than the intrinsic value. Moreover, both the European and American put-call parity relationships (with dividend adjustments) were violated sometimes. Although they acknowledge some concern about the prices they used in their analysis, the researchers concluded that the violations of the boundary conditions were significant. More recently, Chance has performed similar tests for the S & P 100 Index options. He shows that a simple put-call parity condition is violated, and like Evnine and Rudd, he attributes this to the fact that the necessary arbitrage cannot be executed at sufficiently low cost.

Stock Index Futures Pricing, Stock Index Arbitrage, and Program Trading

Consider a futures contract with delivery date T that trades on an index and settles in cash. In order to apply the cost-of-carry model to this problem, we consider the strategy of purchasing the index with borrowed funds and selling the futures contract. Unfortunately, the index cannot be bought. However, it is possible to buy $m/2$ shares of stock A and $m/2$ shares of stock B. If this is done, the price of the portfolio should perfectly correlate with the index. However, while the index does not pay dividends, the underlying portfolio does. These dividends will be used to reduce the cost of carry and hence will affect the price of the futures contract.

EXHIBIT 13.6   The Cost-of-Carry Model for Futures

Strategy	Initial Value	Final Value
Borrow $I(0)$ dollars.	$-I(0)$	$-I(0) \, e^{rT}$
Buy $m/2$ shares of A.	$\dfrac{m}{2} S_A(0)$	$\dfrac{m}{2} S_A(T) + \dfrac{m}{2} d_A \, e^{r(T-t_A)}$
Buy $m/2$ shares of B.	$\dfrac{m}{2} S_B(0)$	$\dfrac{m}{2} S_B(T) + \dfrac{m}{2} d_B \, e^{r(T-t_B)}$
Sell futures contract.	0	$F_T(0) - I(T)$

Exhibit 13.6 summarizes the transactions associated with this strategy. It is assumed that at time t_A stock A pays a dividend of size d_A and at time t_B stock B pays a dividend of size d_B. All dividends are invested at the riskless rate until time T. To avoid riskless arbitrage the value at time T of this strategy must be nonpositive. That is, $V(T) \leq 0$. Therefore we have

$$F_T(0) - I(T) + \left[\frac{m}{2} S_A(T) + \frac{m}{2} S_B(T) \right] + \frac{m}{2} [d_A \, e^{r(T-t_A)}$$
$$+ d_B \, e^{r(T-t_B)}] - I(0) \, e^{rT} \leq 0$$

or

$$F_T(0) \leq I(0) e^{rT} - \frac{m}{2} [d_A \, e^{r(T-t_A)} + d_B \, e^{r(T-t_B)}] \qquad (13.1)$$

If the futures price exceeds the right-hand side of equation (13.1), an arbitrage opportunity exists. If the futures price is not at full carry, then a reverse cash-and-carry strategy can be created to capture riskless returns. Specifically, the futures contract is purchased and $m/2$ shares of both stock A and stock B are sold short, with the proceeds invested at the riskless rate. Since the investor is responsible for the dividend payments, payments are made from the riskless investment. The cash flows from this strategy are shown in Exhibit 13.7. The initial value of the portfolio is \$0. Hence, to avoid riskless profits, $V(T) \leq \$0$, which implies

$$F_T(0) \geq I(0) \, e^{rT} - \frac{m}{2} [d_A \, e^{r(T-t_A)} + d_B \, e^{r(T-t_B)}] \qquad (13.2)$$

EXHIBIT 13.7   The Reverse Cash-and-Carry Model for Futures

Strategy	Initial Value	Final Value
Sell $m/2$ shares of A.	$-\dfrac{m}{2} S_A(0)$	$-\dfrac{m}{2} S_A(T) - \dfrac{m}{2} d_A \, e^{r(T-t_A)}$
Invest proceeds in bonds.	$\dfrac{m}{2} S_A(0)$	$\dfrac{m}{2} S_A(0) \, e^{rT}$
Sell $m/2$ shares of A.	$-\dfrac{m}{2} S_B(0)$	$-\dfrac{m}{2} S_B(T) - \dfrac{m}{2} d_B \, e^{r(T-t_B)}$
Invest proceeds in bonds.	$\dfrac{m}{2} S_B(0)$	$\dfrac{m}{2} S_B(0) \, e^{rT}$
Buy forward contract.	0	$I(T) - F_T(0)$

Equations (13.1) and (13.2) imply that a futures contract on an index, which corresponds to traded securities, should be at full carry.

EXAMPLE 13.13 **Stock Index Arbitrage with a Price-Weighted Index**

A stock index is computed as the price-weighted average of two stocks, A and B. A futures contract trades on the index. The contract settles in 60 days. Current interest rates are 10 percent. The following information is available.

	A	B
Price	$100	$200
Dividend	$1.50	$2.00
Time to dividend	10 days	15 days

The index price $I(0)$ is computed as $I(0) = (\$100 + \$200)/2 = \$150$. To compute the theoretical futures price, we first compute the total carry charge for purchasing the stocks underlying the index with borrowed funds. The initial investment is $300. The amount owed in 60 days is

$$\$300 \, e^{0.10(60/365)} - \$1.50 \, e^{0.10(50/365)} - \$2.00 \, e^{0.10(45/365)} = \$301.42$$

The futures price is expressed in units related to the actual index price. In this example the index value is half the total value of the stock prices in the index. Hence, the theoretical futures price is 150.71.

If the actual futures price were 153.71, an index arbitrage opportunity would become available. In particular, the arbitrager would sell two overpriced futures contracts and initiate the program trade for the two underlying assets. The funds for the purchase of the assets would be obtained by borrowing. The sequence of events is shown below.

	Cash Market	**Futures Market**
Day 0	Borrow $300 and buy A and B.	Sell two overpriced futures at futures price of $153.71.
Day 10	Receive dividend. Invest it for 50 days at 10%.	
Day 15	Receive dividend. Invest it for 45 days at 10%.	
Day 60	Sell A and B for $S_A(T) + S_B(T)$ and repay the net amount owed, which is $301.42.	At settlement, futures price is $[S_A(T) + S_B(T)]/2$. Profit on the sale of two futures contracts is $\$307.42 - [S_A(T) + S_B(T)]$.
	Profit $= S_A(T) + S_B(T) - \$301.42$	Profit $= \$307.42 - [S_A(T) + S_B(T)]$

Total profit is therefore $\$307.42 - \$301.42 = \$6$, which is captured regardless of the future index level.

EXAMPLE 13.14   Stock Index Arbitrage with a Value-Weighted Index

Consider the PR3 index. It is a value-weighted index of three stocks, A, B, and C. The current information on the stocks is shown below.

Stock	A	B	C
Price	$40	$35	$25
Shares outstanding	1 million	2 million	2 million
Market value	$40 million	$70 million	$50 million
Dividend	$0.50	$0.50	—
Time to dividend	10 days	12 days	—

Given the market values, the composition of the index is $40/160 = 4/16$ in stock A, $70/160 = 7/16$ in B, and $50/160=5/16$ in C. The current index is 400. Consider a futures contract on this index. The multiplier of the contract is 500. Therefore, the contract controls $400 \times 500 = \$200,000$. Of this amount, $(4/16)200,000 = \$50,000$ is in A, $(7/16)200,000 = \$87,500$ is in B, and the remaining $(5/16)200,000 = \$62,500$ in C. The initial replicating portfolio consists of $\$50,000/\$40 = 1,250$ shares of A, $\$87,500/\$35 = 2,500$ shares of B, and $\$62,500/\$25 = 2,500$ shares of C.

Assume the futures contract settles in 30 days and interest rates are 10 percent. The calculations for the theoretical futures price are shown below.

Stock	A	B	C
Borrowed funds	$50,000	$87,500	$62,500
Number of shares bought	1,250	2,500	2,500
Dividend income received and reinvested at			
10 percent until settlement date	$628.43	$1,256.18	—

The amount owed after 30 days is $\$200,000\, e^{-0.10(30/365)} = \$201,650.61$. The net amount owed, after adjusting for dividends, is therefore $\$201,650.61 - \$1,884.61 = \$199,766$. The theoretical futures price is therefore $\$199,766/\$500 = \$399.53$.

The stock index arbitrage strategy just described ensures that futures prices do not deviate too far from the implied net cost of carry. However, in the analysis we made several simplifying assumptions. First, we assumed that transaction costs could be ignored. While computer entry systems such as DOT have made the trading of portfolios more efficient, stock index arbitragers estimate the total round-trip costs to be at least 0.5 percent of the portfolio value. Second, the assumption that index prices and replicating portfolio prices are exactly equal is not precise. Third, the size and timing of all dividends on all stocks in the index were assumed to be known with certainty. This assumption may be valid for some short-term contracts, but any uncertainty in dividends will affect the arbitrage scheme. Fourth, the reverse cash-and-carry strategy requires selling short stocks in the index. Such a strategy implicitly assumes that the proceeds of the sales from selling stock short would be immediately available for investment at the riskless rate. In fact, margin is required for short sales, and these funds may not be available to the investor. Moreover, short selling all stocks in the index may be difficult or may take some time. Specifically, stocks can be sold short only after an uptick in the stock price. Finally, certain rules, such as circuit breakers, can impede arbitrage.

Because of these real-world considerations, the futures price on an index may not be at full net carry. Indeed, there are price bands within which no riskless arbitrage strategies exist. Only when the futures price moves outside this range does it become possible for traders to initiate cash-and-carry or reverse cash-and-carry arbitrage. These features must be considered when implementing systems that actually monitor the stock index futures–stock portfolio relationship.

EXAMPLE 13.15   The Dividend Stream for S&P 500 Index

Constructing a dividend yield for a stock index is quite cumbersome, since all dividends on all stocks must be considered. In Example 13.14 we assumed the exact amount and timing of the dividends were known. In practice, these quantities may be well predicted, but they are not known with certainty. Exhibit 13.8 shows a typical distribution of dividend payments made over a year.

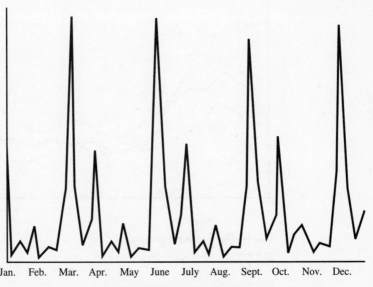

Typical Distribution of Dividend Payments

EXHIBIT 13.8   Typical Distribution of Dividend Payments

Dividends tend to cluster in certain periods, namely, March, June, September, and December. Several financial services report dividend yields on a weekly basis for the major stock market indices. For well-diversified, broad-based indices, the dividend stream is more continuous than for individual stocks. In recent history, the average dividend yield on S&P 500 stocks has ranged from 3 to 5 percent. Because of the extreme variability of dividends over time, the theoretical futures price could sometimes be above the spot index price, while at other times it could be below the spot index price.

If we approximate the actual dividend stream by a continuous dividend stream, and if the current interest rate is much larger than the average dividend yield, we see that early exercise of all but the most deep-in-the-money options is quite unlikely. This suggests that for the most part, the early exercise feature of the American call option may not be very valuable, and the contract could be closely approximated by a European call index option on a "stock" paying out a continuous dividend. Exact option pricing models on stock market indices are deferred to future chapters.

For futures prices, the cost-of-carry model, modified for real-world imperfections such as transaction charges, works extremely well. Exhibit 13.9 shows the

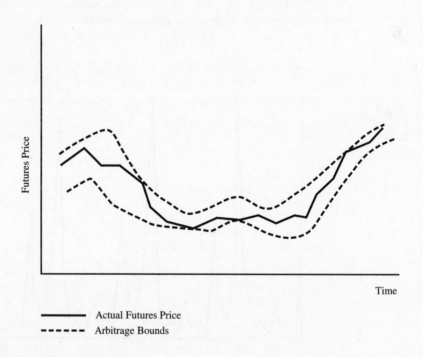

EXHIBIT 13.9   Price Bands for Futures

futures prices and spot prices. Around the futures prices are theoretical price bounds generated using the cost-of-carry model. If the actual futures price drifts out the theoretical band, arbitrage between the two markets is possible. Note that the actual futures price almost never deviates outside the band.

Differences Between Contracts on Stocks and Contracts on Stock Indices

Contracts on an index are quite similar to contracts on an individual stock. There are, however, several differences that are significant enough to cause strategies, arbitrage boundary relationships, and pricing mechanisms to differ. In this section the major differences are discussed.

The Underlying Asset

A stock index is not a traded security. To "hold" the stock index means to buy all the securities in the index in their correct proportions and to reinvest all dividends into the stocks of the index, also in appropriate proportions. If transaction costs could be ignored, borrowing and lending rates were equal and remained constant over time, the exact dividend timing and size of payouts on all stocks were known, and short selling could be initiated with no margin requirements, then indices could be well replicated. But since it is virtually impossible to establish a portfolio that exactly reproduces the price of an index, such as the S&P 100, proxy portfolios are constructed that closely follow the underlying index. These portfolios typically contain only the most highly liquid stocks included in the index. The weights of the stocks in the portfolio are chosen so that the proxy portfolio tracks the index quite closely. Nonetheless, since exact duplication of the index prices is not possible, the arbitrage arguments that lead to bounds on stock index option prices, and the cost-of-carry model for futures, may not be as precise as for ordinary stock options and storable commodity futures. The risk involved with particular strategies can be greater with index options than with stock options. Covered call writing strategies, for example, are not precise with index options. Call writers who hold a proxy portfolio must bear the risk that the index value will expand more rapidly than the portfolio value. Similarly, put holders who purchase protection for their proxy portfolios run the risk that their portfolios will depreciate faster than the index.

Cash Settlement

When index options are exercised, no underlying securities are delivered. Instead, settlements are made in cash. The size of the payment is the difference between the exercise price of the option and the value of the index on the day of exercise, multiplied by the multiplier. This settlement process introduces two types of risk that are not present with stock options.

Exercise Risk   Unlike stock options, when an option holder exercises an index option, the exact amount received remains uncertain until the closing price of the index becomes available. If the closing price is lower (higher) than the strike price of the exercised option, the call (put) holder is obliged to pay the writer. To reduce the likelihood of this occurring, if an index option is to be exercised, the order should be delayed as long as possible. The latest time of day at which exercise notice for index options can be made, the **cutoff time,** is usually set by the brokerage firm; it may be earlier than the cutoff time for stock options.

Timing Risk   The amount of cash received when an option holder exercises a contract is determined at the close of the market on the exercise day. The writer will not learn that assignment has been made until the next business day at the earliest. The time between exercise and notice of assignment poses no risk for covered call writers if the underlying asset is to be delivered. However, in the case of an index option, the writer is obliged to pay a fixed amount. If the investor held a perfectly matched portfolio and the security prices remained unchanged over the lag time, then it would theoretically be possible to liquidate the portfolio and use the proceeds to cover the fixed obligation. In practice, stock prices will have changed, and liquidation of the portfolio may not cover the obligation. The risk caused by this delay is termed **timing risk.** Timing risk limits the ability to reduce risk exposure by holding the underlying stock positions.

For European index options, both exercise and timing risks are greatly reduced. Since most hedgers are concerned about adverse market movements over finite horizons, they may not find the early exercise feature desirable in a contract. Indeed, it is not surprising that many index options that are traded are of the European variety.

Margin Requirements

Margin requirements for index options are similar to those for stock options. All option purchases must be paid in full. Margin requirements for naked written positions on indices are are also similar to those for stock options. Narrow market-based index options usually require more margin. Since covered call writing is not precise and is therefore more risky than with stock options, additional margin is required. Although certain index option spreads may qualify for a reduced margin, the requirements are generally higher than for stock option spreads.

Reporting Problems with Indices and Nonsynchronous Trading

Although the index value is reported throughout the trading day, the reported level may not provide the most recent information. For example, if trading is interrupted in some stocks used in the index, the index information will be based on the most recently reported levels of all trading securities and the last reported price for those stocks not trading. Trading of index derivatives may be halted if trading is interrupted in a large portion of the index value. In this case holders of options may be prohibited from exercising their right, and special arrangements may be introduced if the interruptions persist through the expiration date.

If markets were efficient, the true returns on any stock market index would be uncorrelated. In practice, the reported index returns are correlated. The serial correlation arises because securities in the index trade at discrete times. The reported prices are based on last trade information, which can be quite different from the quoted bid-ask prices that are currently available. This is especially true for stocks that have not traded recently. Due to this nonsynchronous trading, the reported return on any day incorporates a part of the true return for the previous day as well as information based on the return for the current day. Indeed, it can be shown that the reported index returns follow a moving average of true returns. The upshot of this is that actual prices and reported prices can deviate significantly. This fact has to be taken into account in the pricing of the contract. The price of the derivative should be set relative to a portfolio of traded securities, and the prices of these traded securities may differ from the reported index.

Dynamic Portfolio Insurance with Stock Index Futures*

In this section we consider a dynamic trading portfolio insurance mechanism that guarantees a return that exceeds a prespecified floor, while at the same time allowing the portfolio to participate in any market rallies. In setting up a portfolio insurance program, several factors must be considered. First, the floor level must be determined, as well as the time horizon of the insurance. The higher the floor and the longer the time horizon, the costlier the program. Second, the mechanism for insuring must be established. In general, there are two different mechanisms: **static strategies,** which can be put into place with a single order, and **dynamic strategies,** which require portfolio updating in response to price movements over time. The static strategy of purchasing index put options against a diversified stock portfolio is one of the simplest static portfolio insurance strategies. Not only are no subsequent trading adjustments necessary, but the cost of the program is fully determined by the premium of the put option. Unfortunately, the most liquid options are short-term at-the-money contracts, and most portfolio insurance programs are designed with longer holding periods in mind. In addition, the floor levels, or strike prices that the portfolio manager may desire, may not correspond to those offered by listed options on exchanges. As a result, dynamic trading schemes that attempt to replicate or synthetically create payouts with properties similar to put options may be desirable. Indeed, synthetic securities having payouts similar to put options were first marketed by Leland, O'Brien, Rubinstein Associates in the early 1980s. Prior to the crash of 1987, these strategies had become quite popular, and over $60 billion worth of stock was protected. In this section we investigate these trading schemes and examine the implications of the marketing of these portfolio insurance strategies as synthetic securities.

---

* This section provides advanced material and is optional reading for students.

The return pattern of any insured program should satisfy two properties. First, the probability of experiencing any losses below the floor should be zero. Second, the return on any profitable position should be a predictable percentage of the rate of return that would have been earned by investing all funds without taking insurance.

If no option contracts with the appropriate terms are available, then the contract has to be created synthetically. Under the assumptions of the Black-Scholes model, the put option can be replicated by a continuous trading strategy involving the underlying bonds and stock. The theory assumes that it is possible to buy and sell continuously at all prices. Since the portfolio involves multiple securities, rapidly adjusting the composition of the underlying portfolio can be difficult. Hence, most applications of portfolio insurance are based on trading in stock index futures such as the S & P 500 contract.

A Model of Portfolio Insurance

Without loss of generality, assume an investor starts off with a wealth of $1 and wants to invest in a fully diversified mutual fund. To simplify the analysis we assume that this risky mutual fund pays no dividends and that futures on this fund exist. The possible evolution of the $1 investment over the three time periods is shown below.

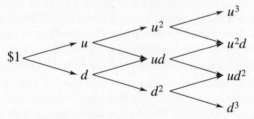

Recall that under interest rate certainty, the futures price equals the forward price. Let $R = e^{r\Delta t}$, where Δt is the length of each period. The prices of futures contracts that expire in three periods are shown below.

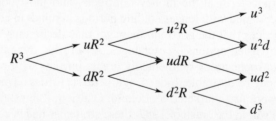

The investor wants to establish a floor of K of wealth after three periods. Assume $d^3 \leq K < R^3$. Clearly, if $K < d^3$ then no insurance is necessary, and if $K > R^3$ then the strategy would completely dominate the riskless investment and could not be guaranteed.

The trader places $(1 - h_0)$ dollars in the risky fund and leaves it there for three periods. The remaining h_0 dollars will be actively managed to ensure the floor constraint is met. Indeed, h_0 can be viewed as the cost of portfolio insurance. The idea is to find the strategy that minimizes this cost. For the moment assume h_0 is given. The idea behind the strategy is to invest h_0 in the riskless asset and to sell futures contracts against the fund. If the fund deteriorates in value, then the futures position will be increased (to cover losses on the passive portfolio). If, on the other hand, the fund increases in value, futures positions will be liquidated (so as to be able to fully participate in the market rally).

To begin, the trader invests the h_0 dollars in the riskless portfolio and sells n_0 futures. The value of the active portfolio after one period is

$$V_0 = h_0 \begin{cases} V_{11} = h_0R - n_0[uR^2 - R^3] \\ V_{10} = h_0R - n_0[dR^2 - R^3] \end{cases}$$

The active portfolio strategy has the property that additional funds are never required. At each node in the lattice, money can be removed from the active portfolio, but under no circumstances can money be added. Assume $h_{11} \leq V_{11}$ and $h_{10} \leq V_{10}$ are the dollars that are available for investment in the second period.

Consider the strategy if an upmove occurs. Let n_{11} represent the number of futures sold. The portfolio value over the next time period changes as follows.

$$h_{11} \begin{cases} V_{22} = h_{11}R - n_{11}[u^2R - uR^2] \\ V_{21}^+ = h_{11}R - n_{11}[udR - uR^2] \end{cases}$$

If the first move is a downmove, let h_{10} dollars represent the money available for investment and assume n_{10} futures are sold. In this case we have

$$h_{10} \begin{cases} V_{21} = h_{10}R - n_{10}[udR - dR^2] \\ V_{20} = h_{10}R - n_{10}[d^2R - dR^2] \end{cases}$$

Note that an upmove followed by a downmove results in a different portfolio value (V_{21}^+) than a downmove followed by an upmove (V_{21}^-). The amount of funds available for investment if the value of the fund is at node (2, 1) is represented by h_{21}, where $h_{21} \leq \text{Min}[V_{21}^+, V_{21}^-]$.[1] If these funds are invested in the riskless asset, and if n_{21} futures are sold, the payouts in the third period are

$$h_{21} \begin{cases} h_{21}R - n_{21}[u^2R - udR] \\ h_{21}R - n_{21}[ud^2 - d^2R] \end{cases}$$

Similar strategies exist at the other nodes. The sequence of investments at each node for the active portfolio is summarized below.

---

[1] If this constraint is not present, then the number of nodes in the lattice doubles with each additional period. For a 20-period problem we would end up with 2^{20} or 1,048,576 nodes.

$$h_0 \begin{cases} h_0 R - n_0[uR^2 - R^3] \geq h_{11} \begin{cases} h_{11}R - n_{11}[u^2R - uR^2] \geq h_{22} \begin{cases} h_{22}R - n_{22}[u^3 - u^2R] \\ h_{22}R - n_{22}[u^2d - u^2R] \end{cases} \\ h_{11}R - n_{11}[udR - uR^2] \\ h_{10}R - n_{10}[udR - dR^2] \end{cases} \geq h_{21} \begin{cases} h_{21}R - n_{21}[u^2R - udR] \\ h_{21}R - n_{21}[ud^2 - d^2R] \\ h_{21}R - n_{21}[ud^2 - d^2R] \end{cases} \\ h_0 R - n_0[dR^2 - R^3] \geq h_{10} \begin{cases} h_{10}R - n_{10}[d^2R - dR^2] \geq h_{20} \begin{cases} h_{20}R - n_{20}[d^3 - d^2R] \end{cases} \end{cases} \end{cases}$$

The idea, then, is to choose an investment strategy such that regardless of the final node that is reached, the total wealth exceeds the floor. At the same time, we would like to allocate the smallest possible amount into the active portfolio so that the passive portfolio can participate in market rallies. To find this strategy, we solve the following linear programming problem:

$$\text{Min } h_0$$

subject to

$$h_{11} \leq h_0 R - n_0[uR^2 - R^3]$$

$$h_{10} \leq h_0 R - n_0[dR^2 - R^3]$$

$$h_{22} \leq h_{11} R - n_{11}[u^2R - uR^2]$$

$$h_{21} \leq h_{11} R - n_{11}[udR - uR^2]$$

$$h_{21} \leq h_{10} R - n_{10}[udR - dR^2]$$

$$h_{20} \leq h_{10} R - n_{10}[d^2R - dR^2]$$

and

$$(1 - h_0)u^3 \ \ + h_{22} R - n_{22}[u^3 - u^2R] \ \ \geq K$$

$$(1 - h_0)u^2d + h_{22} R - n_{22}[u^2d - u^2R] \ \geq K$$

$$(1 - h_0)u^2d + h_{21} R - n_{21}[u^2d - udR] \geq K$$

$$(1 - h_0)ud^2 + h_{21} R - n_{21}[ud^2 - udR] \ \geq K$$

$$(1 - h_0)ud^2 + h_{20} R - n_{20}[ud^2 - d^2R] \ \geq K$$

$$(1 - h_0)d^3 \ \ + h_{20} R - n_{20}[d^3 - d^2R] \ \ \geq K$$

Here the decision variables are the investment funds and the number of futures to sell at each node. The first set of constraints states that at each node you cannot invest more funds than you have. Such constraints occur at all nodes except the initial node and the nodes in the final period. The second set of constraints states that at each terminal node, the wealth level should exceed the floor. The effective cost of this insurance is h_0 dollars, and the objective is to find the minimum-cost program.

Options and Synthetic Options for Portfolio Insurance

Prior to the stock market crash of October 1978, portfolio insurance was more commonly implemented through dynamic hedging than through put options. As discussed earlier, the main reason for using synthetic puts was the fact that the time horizons of portfolio insurance could be customized to the clients' needs as well as the nature of the floors (strike prices).

Portfolio insurance may be appropriate for pension plans that are required to fund fixed liabilities out of future funds. Prior to the 1987 crash, this technique was being used by portfolio managers who wanted to protect themselves against poor short-term performance. In this application, as portfolio values rose, managers readjusted their floor price upward in an attempt to lock in profits. In essence, put options with low strike prices were canceled and more expensive puts with higher strikes were created.

If portfolio insurance were provided by ordinary put options, sellers would have to be found for all buyers. Prices would adjust to balance supply and demand. In contrast, with synthetic portfolio insurance, no option price directly equates demand with supply. The cost of modifying the floor levels of a dynamic trading scheme is not directly observable. Of course, the implicit cost depends on the usual factors that drive option premiums. The major difference between using traded put options and using synthetic options is that with traded options the cost of insurance is always made explicit.

Users of portfolio insurance therefore pay for the put through their commitment to a dynamic hedging strategy. This is not a problem as long as portfolio insurance is relatively small. By 1987, however, about $100 billion worth of portfolio insurance programs was in force, representing about 3 percent of market capitalization. At this level some practitioners felt that if a market drop occurred, the magnitude of required trading could trigger a market meltdown. This fear increased as many trading strategies continued to rachet up their floors in response to increased levels in the market. By raising the floor, the trading strategy causes more stock to be sold when prices fall than would be the case if the strike price had not been increased.

Stock Index Futures and the October 1987 Crash

Blame for the stock market crash of 1987 has been directed at stock index arbitrage, program trading, and portfolio insurance.

After the crash many studies investigated possible market reforms, including circuit breakers, price limits, higher margin requirements, transaction taxes, and restricted access to computerized order submission systems. The goal of these studies was to identify mechanisms that would decrease market volatility and prevent panic. Since the crash, a number of exchanges have adopted new policies. For example, the NYSE, the AMEX, and the CME now halt trading for one hour if the Dow falls by 250 points. If it falls an additional 150 points, the exchanges halt trading for two more hours.

Stock Index Arbitrage   Suppose an opinion developed that the stock market level was too high. To act on this opinion, investors could sell their securities or sell stock index futures. Since the futures markets are extremely liquid and offer lower trading costs, a majority of traders may find it desirable to sell index futures rather than liquidate large portfolios. The demand for selling futures would drive futures prices down relative to the stock market. If this occurred, index arbitragers would soon observe that the stock market was overvalued relative to the futures, and eventually they would initiate the reverse cash-and-carry index arbitrage strategy. Their activity would drive stock market prices down and force the linkages between the two markets to be reestablished.

Some market observers see index arbitrage strategies leading to selling stocks, but their conclusion that these activities forced prices down is false. In reality, index arbitrage is only a response to a rapid decline in futures prices. This theory of trading has been confirmed by empirical studies that provide evidence that movements in stock index futures tend to lead movements in the spot indices. This is true even after nonsynchronous trading has been taken into account. It is doubtful, then, that stock index arbitrage contributed to the crash of 1987.

Program Trading   Program trading has also been blamed for the crash, but this explanation is very weak. Since program trading is a mechanism by which orders can be executed, it cannot explain why a preponderence of sales orders were submitted. At best, program trading may reduce trading costs and hence allow investors to act on new information more readily than in the past.

Portfolio Insurance   As discussed, the portfolio insurance strategy replicates a put option by a dynamic trading strategy that effectively buys stocks when prices are rising and sells stock when prices are falling. Prior to the crash of 1987, the market had steadily been increasing. Many managers with insured portfolios may have held onto overvalued stocks, believing that their downside risk was minimal. Indeed, many investors continued to hold or build up equity positions under the belief that as the market increased, they could increase the floor on their insurance policies. When bad news eventually caused prices to drop, all portfolio insurance programs triggered sales of stock index futures. The surge in sell orders caused the S & P 500 Index to drop dramatically. Indeed, since trades could not be conducted at all prices through which the index moved, many portfolio insurance schemes could not initiate their replicating trades. As a result, the insurance schemes were not particularly effective, and a lot of clients who thought their portfolios were insured found out that their funds were essentially unprotected. Of course, those funds that had insured against losses by purchasing put options did not suffer from this problem.

Portfolio insurance may have caused prices to be bid up higher than they should have been prior to the crash. In hindsight, we can say that portfolio managers may have underestimated the implicit cost of portfolio insurance and overestimated the actual risk protection it provided.

Conclusion

This chapter has investigated the mechanisms for trading portfolios of common stock and for hedging market- and industry-related risks using index options and futures. Index options and futures have cash settlements. Since the underlying index is not a traded security, hedging strategies may be imprecise, and pricing relationships may differ somewhat from pricing of contracts where the underlying instrument is a single traded security.

Stock index option trading accounts for over half the volume of all stock option contracts traded. Together with stock index futures, index options have been very successful financial innovations. This chapter has provided several examples of the use of these contracts. Portfolio trading, stock index arbitrage, and portfolio insurance schemes were discussed. Specific models for pricing index option contracts are discussed in Chapter 15.

References

The Options Clearing Corporation and the option and futures exchanges publish booklets describing their specific contracts and illustrating alternative investment strategies.

Billingsley, R., and D. Chance. "The Pricing and Performance of Stock Index Futures Spreads." *Journal of Futures Markets* 8 (1988): 303–18.

Brennan, M., and E. Schwartz. "Arbitrage in Stock Index Futures." *Journal of Business* 63 (1990): S7–S31.

Chance, D. "Parity Tests of Index Options." *Advances in Futures and Options Research* 2 (1987): 47–64.

Chicago Mercantile Exchange. "Using S & P 500 Stock Index Options and Futures." 1987.

Cornell, B., and K. French. "Taxes and the Pricing of Stock Index Futures." *Journal of Finance* 38 (1983): 675–94.

Evnine, J., and A. Rudd. "Index Options: The Early Evidence." *Journal of Finance* 40(3) (July 1985): 743–56.

Fabozzi, F., G. Gastineau, and S. Wunsch. "Introduction to Options on Stock Indexes and Stock Index Futures Contracts." In *Stock Index Futures,* edited by F. Fabozzi and G. Kipnis. Homewood, Ill.: Dow Jones-Irwin, 1984.

Fabozzi, F., G. Gastineau, and A. Madansky. "Options on Stock Indexes and Stock Index Futures: Pricing Determinants, Role in Risk Management, and Option Evaluation." In *Stock Index Futures,* edited by F. Fabozzi and G. Kipnis. Homewood, Ill.: Dow Jones-Irwin, 1984.

Gould, F. "Stock Index Futures: The Arbitrage Cycle and Portfolio Insurance." *Financial Analysts Journal* 44 (1988): 48–62.

Harvey, C., and R. Whaley. "Dividends and S & P 100 Index Option Valuation." *Journal of Futures Markets* 12 (1992): 123–38.

Hill, J., and F. Jones. "Equity Trading, Portfolio Trading, Portfolio Insurance, Computer Trading and All That." *Financial Analysts Journal* 44 (1988): 29–38.

MacKinlay, A., and K. Ramaswamy. "Index Futures Arbitrage and the Behavior of Stock Index Futures Prices." *Review of Financial Studies* 1 (1988): 137–58.

Neal, R. "Is Program Trading Destabilizing?" *Journal of Derivatives* 1 (Winter 1993): 64–77.

Ronn, A., and E. Ronn. "The Box Spread Arbitrage Conditions: Theory, Tests, and Investment Strategies." *Review of Financial Studies* 2 (1989): 91–108.

Sofianos, G. "Index Arbitrage Profitability." *Journal of Derivatives* 1 (Fall 1993): 3–20.

Stoll, H., and R. Whaley. "Program Trading and Expiration Effects." *Financial Analysts Journal* 43 (1987): 16–28.

———. "Futures and Options on Stock Indices: Economic Purpose, Arbitrage, and Market Structure." *Review of Futures Markets* 7 (1988): 224–48.

———. "The Dynamics of Stock Index and Stock Index Futures Returns." *Journal of Financial and Quantitative Analysis* 25 (1990): 441–68.

Exercises

1. An investor manages a portfolio composed of 20 major oil and gas company stocks. The dividend yield on the portfolio is 5 percent. Current money market yields are 9 percent. The portfolio manager believes that over the next few months oil and gas prices will decline and prices of these stocks will not advance. The investor believes that this industry will stabilize and that there will be significant long-term growth. The manager therefore does not want to sell securities but would like to enhance the short-term return. Establish a strategy using an oil index option contract that will achieve a higher return without trading stocks. How should the manager determine the number of contracts to be purchased or sold?

2. An investor has significant investments in a money fund. The investor believes that the market will bottom out in about two months and then some excellent buying opportunities will occur. Assuming the investor will buy stocks selected from the S & P 100 Index, construct an option strategy that is consistent with these beliefs.

3. An investor has been aggressively buying shares of computer companies that produce certain printing devices. Recently, however, there have been rumors that the industry could face reduced profits because of new products introduced by foreign competition. How can computer stock index options be useful in offsetting this industry-specific risk?

4. Index options have affected the liquidity of the stock option market. Investors who previously traded stock options have replaced their strategies with index option strategies. Provide several reasons for this occurrence.

5. The greatest activity in index options is always focused on the near series. Index options with time to maturity exceeding four months are not actively traded. Offer several reasons why strategies using index options are short-term.

6. Can arbitrage arguments like those developed in Chapter 4 be used to obtain bounds on index option prices? What problems, if any, are caused by the fact that the underlying stocks pay out dividends?

7. Why is it important for an arbitrager to know how the index of a particular indicator is developed? How will an arbitrager attempt to profit from "mispriced" index options?

8. An option to buy 100 shares of a specific fully diversified mutual fund is not the same as an index option. Explain the differences. If options on particular mutual funds were available, could the arbitrage arguments of Chapter 4 be applied, or would special restrictions prevent their application?

9. A portfolio of call options is different from an option on a portfolio. Explain the differences.

10. If you could introduce two new index option contracts, which two would you introduce? Explain why these contracts would be useful in the current economy. Specify the underlying index.

11. Consider the SR3 Index, a value-weighted index of three stocks, A, B, and C. The current information on the stocks is shown below.

Stock	A	B	C
Price	$35	$35	$35
Shares outstanding	1 million	2 million	3 million
Dividend	$0.50	$0.50	—
Time to dividend	10 days	12 days	—

a. The current index is $400. Consider a futures contract on this index. The multiplier of the contract is 500. Establish the replicating portfolio.

b. Assume the futures contract settles in 30 days and interest rates are 10 percent. Compute the theoretical futures price.

12. If a call option on the S & P 100 Index was overpriced according to the American put-call parity equation, what strategy could be adopted to obtain riskless arbitrage profits? What risks (if any) would be involved in this strategy?

CHAPTER 14

Foreign Currency Contracts

Imports and exports can account for a significant percentage of gross national product (GNP). In the United States, for example, exports account for over 10 percent of GNP, while in Britain the figure is close to 25 percent. Trades of this magnitude would not be possible without a market where investors can easily buy and sell foreign currencies. Hedging foreign exchange risk is an important activity of treasury management in international corporations and banks.

The foreign exchange market is the world's largest market. Daily turnover amounts to about $700 billion. The bulk of foreign currency transactions take place in the interbank foreign exchange market. Until 1972 the interbank market was the only channel through which foreign exchange spot and forward transactions took place. Since then, organized markets in foreign currency futures, options on foreign currencies, and options on currency futures have developed. Relative to the interbank foreign exchange market, however, the organized markets are still quite small.

This chapter begins with an overview of the interbank and organized exchange markets. Then forward, futures, and foreign currency options are discussed. Examples of a few foreign currency contracts are presented, together with some strategies for managing foreign currency risks. Some arbitrage relationships unique to foreign currencies are also explained.

The primary objectives of this chapter are the following:

- To provide a brief overview of the interbank and organized exchange markets;

- To discuss forwards, futures, and options on foreign currency; and

- To explain strategies for managing foreign currency risks.

The Exchange Rate

The exchange rate is best thought of as just the price of a commodity. The commodity just happens to be another currency. This price is referred to as the **exchange rate,** the **spot rate,** or the **cash rate.** When you buy foreign currency you are converting dollars into the commodity (foreign currency). When you sell foreign currency you are selling the commodity and converting foreign currency back into dollars.

By convention, exchange rates in the United States are quoted on a per dollar basis. This means that the exchange rate for British pounds or Japanese yen is stated as the dollar cost of one unit of foreign currency. For example, the dollar cost of one British pound could be $1.50. This means that $1.50 could be exchanged for one British pound. The exchange rate in Britain would be expressed in pounds per dollar. Clearly, the number of pounds that it takes to purchase $1 is 1/1.5 or 0.6667 British pounds.

EXAMPLE 14.1 The price of a British pound moves from $1.46 to $1.47 over the time period t to $t + 1$. Let $S(t)$ denote the spot rate of one unit of foreign currency at time t. Then $S(t) = \$1.46$ and $S(t + 1) = \$1.47$. Since it takes more dollars to buy one pound at time $t + 1$, we say the pound has appreciated in value, or the dollar has weakened.

An investor who buys foreign currency is transforming dollars into pounds. An investor who sells foreign currency is transforming foreign currency back into dollars.

The Interbank Foreign Exchange Market

The bulk of foreign exchange transactions are done over the telephone between specialized divisions of the large head offices of the major banks. These banks have rooms equipped with electronic devices that allow them to communicate with other banks around the world. The market has no regular trading hours, and currencies can be bought or sold somewhere 24 hours a day. The banks are referred to as **market makers** since they trade in the major currencies on a more or less continuous basis. When extremely large transactions occur, **foreign exchange brokers** may be employed to find takers for these deals. Unlike specialists at the major banks, these brokers do not trade on their own accounts. Rather, they specialize in large transactions.

The exchange rates quoted in financial newspapers refer to quotes made by banks to other banks for currency deals in excess of $1 million. Exhibit 14.1 shows daily exchange rates as reported in the *Wall Street Journal*. These rates are expressed as the number of units of a particular currency that exchange for $1 and the number of U.S. dollars that exchange for one unit of foreign currency.

Regional banks may not deal directly in the interbank foreign exchange market. Usually they have special arrangements with larger banks. Corporations and individuals that require foreign currency engage in such transactions through their own banks. Banks typically charge their customers higher prices for foreign currency than those quoted in the newspapers. The difference in rates partially reflects the bank's profit margin and provides compensation to the bank for holding foreign currency in denominations too small to be sold in the interbank market.

CURRENCY TRADING

EXCHANGE RATES

Monday, May 1, 1995

The New York foreign exchange selling rates below apply to trading among banks in amounts of $1 million and more, as quoted at 3 p.m. Eastern time by Bankers Trust Co., Dow Jones Telerate Inc. and other sources. Retail transactions provide fewer units of foreign currency per dollar.

Country	U.S. $ equiv.		Currency per U.S. $	
	Mon.	Fri.	Mon.	Fri.
Argentina (Peso)	1.00	1.00	1.00	1.00
Australia (Dollar)	.7298	.7283	1.3703	1.3732
Austria (Schilling)	.10218	.10255	9.79	9.75
Bahrain (Dinar)	2.6526	2.6525	.3770	.3770
Belgium (Franc)	.03492	.03495	28.63	28.61
Brazil (Real)	1.0911075	1.0887316	.92	.92
Britain (Pound)	1.6155	1.6120	.6190	.6203
30-Day Forward	1.6141	1.6102	.6196	.6210
90-Day Forward	1.6119	1.6081	.6204	.6219
180-Day Forward	1.6080	1.6044	.6219	.6233
Canada (Dollar)	.7376	.7375	1.3558	1.3560
30-Day Forward	.7363	.7352	1.3582	1.3601
90-Day Forward	.7344	.7333	1.3616	1.3638
180-Day Forward	.7323	.7311	1.3656	1.3677
Czech. Rep. (Koruna)				
Commercial rate	.0387072	.0387072	25.8350	25.8350
Chile (Peso)	.002572	.002572	388.75	388.75
China (Renminbi)	.118943	.118943	8.4074	8.4074
Colombia (Peso)	.001137	.001138	879.20	878.82
Denmark (Krone)	.1831	.1836	5.4615	5.4473
Ecuador (Sucre)				
Floating rate	.000407	.000407	2456.00	2456.00
Finland (Markka)	.23384	.23436	4.2765	4.2670
France (Franc)	.20192	.20323	4.9525	4.9205
30-Day Forward	.20164	.20224	4.9593	4.9447
90-Day Forward	.20105	.20171	4.9740	4.9576

Country	U.S. $ equiv.		Currency per U.S. $	
	Mon.	Fri.	Mon.	Fri.
Italy (Lira)	.0005993	.0005972	1668.50	1674.50
Japan (Yen)	.011976	.011876	83.50	84.20
30-Day Forward	.012032	.011920	83.11	83.90
90-Day Forward	.012130	.012017	82.44	83.22
180-Day Forward	.012283	.012165	81.41	82.21
Jordan (Dinar)	1.4472	1.4535	.6910	.6880
Kuwait (Dinar)	3.4066	3.4211	.2936	.2923
Lebanon (Pound)	.000613	.000613	1631.50	1631.50
Malaysia (Ringgit)	.4049	.4047	2.4700	2.4710
Malta (Lira)	2.8729	2.8729	.3481	.3481
Mexico (Peso)				
Floating rate	.1690617	.1690617	5.9150	5.9150
Netherland (Guilder) ..	.6423	.6443	1.5570	1.5521
New Zealand (Dollar) .	.6749	.6723	1.4818	1.4874
Norway (Krone)	.1602	.1605	6.2410	6.2310
Pakistan (Rupee)	.0324	.0324	30.83	30.83
Peru (New Sol)	.4457	.4460	2.24	2.24
Philippines (Peso)	.03839	.03839	26.05	26.05
Poland (Zloty)	.42105263	.42105263	2.37	2.37
Portugal (Escudo)	.006792	.006804	147.23	146.97
Saudi Arabia (Riyal) ...	.26663	.26663	3.7505	3.7506
Singapore (Dollar)	.7191	.7174	1.3907	1.3940
Slovak Rep. (Koruna) ..	.0343053	.0343053	29.1500	29.1500
South Africa (Rand) ...	.2764	.2764	3.6180	3.6180
South Korea (Won)	.0013117	.0013117	762.35	762.35
Spain (Peseta)	.008104	.008109	123.40	123.32
Sweden (Krona)	.1371	.1374	7.2926	7.2769
Switzerland (Franc) ...	.8726	.8737	1.1460	1.1445
30-Day Forward	.8750	.8751	1.1428	1.1427
90-Day Forward	.8790	.8789	1.1377	1.1377
180-Day Forward	.8853	.8853	1.1295	1.1296
Taiwan (Dollar)	.039377	.039368	25.40	25.40
Thailand (Baht)	.04065	.04066	24.60	24.60
Turkey (Lira)	.0000235	.0000236	42560.51	42374.01
United Arab (Dirham) .	.2723	.2723	3.6727	3.6730

EXHIBIT 14.1   Exchange Rates in the *Wall Street Journal*

Source: Reprinted by permission of the Wall Street Journal © 1995 Dow Jones & Company, Inc. All Rights Reserved.

The Cash Market and the Forward Market

The spot market is not the only foreign currency market that is maintained. For the major currencies, up to four prices will be quoted. One is the spot price. The others are the 30-day forward, 90-day forward, and 180-day forward, The 90-day forward, for example, is the rate at which a trader can contract for delivery of some foreign currency in 90 days. The major currencies traded by U.S. banks are the German mark (deutsche mark, or DM), the British pound sterling, the Canadian dollar, the Swiss franc, the Japanese yen, and the French franc. The annual turnover in currencies exceeds $600 billion. Most of this activity is focused on the spot market. Activity in the forward markets accounts for less than 30 percent of total activity.

Forward markets allow international firms to hedge foreign currency risks. For example, importers, who must pay for foreign goods in foreign currencies in the future, can eliminate risks of adverse movements in exchange rates by buying forward contracts. Similarly, exporters, who expect to receive foreign currency in the future, can sell these funds forward, thus avoiding the risk of anticipated drops in the foreign currency. In addition to forward contracts, large banks may offer their corporate customers tailor-made foreign exchange contracts. These over-the-counter contracts offer clients hedging facilities that may be more appropriate than forward contracts.

As discussed in Chapter 1, a forward contract is a binding obligation to buy or sell a particular commodity at a specific future date for a designated price.

EXAMPLE 14.2   Investors can lock into an exchange rate by buying forward contracts. Consider an investor who believes the British pound will appreciate dramatically against the dollar. The current exchange rate at time t is $S(t) = \$1.46$. Let $FO_T(t)$ be the forward price at date t for delivery of one unit of foreign currency at date T. The forward exchange rate for delivery at time T is $FO_T(t) = \$1.49$. By buying the forward contract the investor is obligated to purchase at time T one pound for $1.49.

Firms may sell forward contracts to hedge against unanticipated declines in foreign currency. Such strategies lock into an exchange rate from the foreign to the local currency.

EXAMPLE 14.3   A U.S. firm has a British subsidiary. The cash flows produced by the subsidiary are in pounds and are subject to exchange rate risk. If the pound depreciates relative to the dollar, the profits produced by the subsidiary may be eroded. To hedge against this event, the parent company would like to lock into a future exchange rate from pounds to dollars. By selling a forward contract at $1.49, the firm is committed to selling one pound for $1.49.

Most foreign exchange forward contracts do not actually require the short to sell foreign currency to the long at the agreed-upon exchange rate. Rather, the contract is settled by the losing party paying the difference between the spot and agreed-upon exchange rate in cash. As a result, no foreign currency needs to be delivered.

EXAMPLE 14.4   A firm buys a forward contract on British pounds at a price of $1.490. At the delivery date the spot exchange rate is $1.495. The short position is committed to selling one pound in exchange for $1.490. Since the market value of a pound is $1.495, the short just pays the long the difference (i.e., $0.005 for each pound in the contract).

Geographical Arbitrage

Let $S(t)$ be the price of one unit of foreign currency in U.S. dollars. For example in New York the price of one British pound might be $S(t) = \$1.68$. The New York price implies each dollar is worth $1/1.68 = 0.59$ pounds. In London, dollars are sold for pounds. Let $S^F(t)$ be the price of \$1 in pounds. Clearly, to avoid riskless arbitrage,

$$S^F(t) = 1/S(t) \qquad (14.1)$$

To avoid arbitrage, forward prices must be related in the same way. Let $FO_T^F(t)$ be the forward price of a dollar in foreign currency. Then

$$FO_T^F(t) = 1/FO_T(t) \qquad (14.2)$$

Triangular or Cross-Rate Arbitrage

Given the exchange rates between two currencies, such as dollars per pound and dollars per mark, an exchange rate between pounds and marks is implied. This implied rate is referred to as a **cross rate.** If the actual exchange rate between pounds and marks differs from the cross rate, arbitrage opportunities exist.

Because of the existence of the cross rate, the U.S. dollar has become the primary "money" used in foreign exchange markets. Cross-rate markets between many currencies are very thin, and forward cross-rate markets may not exist. For example, the bulk of foreign exchanges between British pounds and Brazilian cruzeiros involve pound-to-dollar and dollar-to-cruzeiro transactions instead of direct pound-to-cruzeiro trading. In a very liquid market (such as the dollar-medium market), transaction costs are typically lower. Of course, there are some very liquid markets that do not involve the dollar. These include the currencies of western Europe and Japan.

Let $S(t)$ be the price of one unit of foreign currency and let $M(t)$ be the price of a second currency. The cross rate between the two currencies is given by $XR(t)$, where

$$XR(t) = S(t)/M(t)$$

Here $XR(t)$ is the cost of one unit of the currency of M in units of the currency of S. For example, if S represents the price of one pound and M the price of one deutsche mark, then

$$XR(t) = \frac{\text{dollars/pound}}{\text{dollars/mark}} = \frac{\text{marks}}{\text{pound}}$$

EXAMPLE 14.5   Let $S(t) = \$1.470$ per pound and $M(t) = \$0.540$ per deutsche mark. The cross rate is $XR(t) = 1.47/0.54 = 2.722$ marks per pound.

Assume the quoted cross rate is 2.822 marks per pound. Then riskless arbitrage would be available. In particular, an astute investor would buy one pound for \$1.47 and then immediately exchange this pound for 2.822 marks. Since each mark can be sold for \$0.54, these marks could then be exchanged for $2.822 \times \$0.54 = \$1.524$. Hence, \$1.47 could be translated into \$1.524.

Interest Rate Parity, the Cost-of-Carry Model, and the Fair Forward Price

Interest rates are established according to costs of borrowing and lending for specific time periods, and they need not be the same in different currencies. Let r be the risk-free rate in the local country, and let r_F be the risk-free rate in the foreign country.

Assume an investor has K dollars to invest. If invested locally the amount grows to Ke^{rT} dollars. An alternative risk-free investment is to exchange the local currency for $K/S(0)$ units of foreign currency and invest at the foreign riskless rate. At time T the foreign investment will be worth K_F units of foreign currency, where

$$K_F = [K/S(0)] \, e^{r_F T}$$

To ensure that the return in dollars is riskless, at the end of the period proceeds from the investment must be converted back into the home currency at an exchange rate that is established at time 0. This is accomplished by selling K_F forward contracts initiated at the outset of the holding period. If $FO_T(0)$ is the forward price at time 0, then by selling K_F contracts, the foreign currency at time T can be converted at the guaranteed exchange rate to $K_F FO_T(0)$ dollars.

Clearly, to avoid riskless arbitrage, the return on these two strategies should be equal. That is,

$$K_F FO_T(0) = K \, e^{rT}$$

Substituting for K_F in the above expression, we obtain

$$[K/S(0)] \, e^{r_F T} FO_T(0) = Ke^{rT}$$

or
$$\frac{FO_T(0)}{S(0)} = e^{(r-r_F)T} \tag{14.3}$$

Equation (14.3) is referred to as the **interest rate parity condition.** It asserts that interest and exchange rates form one system. Specifically, the ratio of forward exchange rates to spot exchange rates will depend on the level of domestic and foreign riskless interest rates. If the interest rate in the domestic country is higher than in the foreign country, then forward exchange rates will be set higher than the current spot rate. Rearranging equation (14.3), we obtain

$$FO_T(0) = S(0) \, e^{(r-r_F)T} \tag{14.4}$$

Note that the forward price given here is exactly the same as the forward price computed using the cost-of-carry model, given by equation (2.14). The net cost of carry is lower than the local risk-free rate because the investment in the foreign currency generates a return of r_F.

EXAMPLE 14.6   The set of forward prices plotted against settlement dates contains information about interest rate differentials between the two countries. If the forward prices of the British pound, as reported in the *Wall Street Journal*, were increasing with the settlement date, then we could conclude that the British risk-free rate was higher than the local risk-free rate.

Futures Contracts

In 1972 the International Monetary Market (IMM) of the Chicago Mercantile Exchange (CME) began trading currency futures. Today, this exchange is the largest foreign exchange futures market. Contracts exist on a variety of currencies, including the Australian dollar, British pound, Canadian dollar, German mark, French franc, Japanese yen, and Swiss franc. All prices are quoted in dollars per unit of currency. Exhibit 14.2 summarizes the terms of a few foreign currency futures traded on the IMM.

Exhibit 14.3 shows the prices as reported in the *Wall Street Journal*.

Foreign currency futures markets similar to the IMM exist in financial centers in other countries. The London International Financial Futures Exchange (LIFFE) is the second-largest organized futures market. Other markets include the Philadelphia Exchange, the Singapore International Monetary Exchange, and several others. In 1982 the LIFFE began trading foreign currency futures in bundles identical to those sold on the IMM. In 1984 the Singapore International Monetary Exchange also began trading in a few foreign currencies contracts identical to those offered by the IMM. Indeed, these contracts can be offset at the IMM. This arrangement has effectively increased the hours of trading.

The Fair Price of a Futures Contract

Purchasing a futures contract is different from purchasing a forward contract. Suppose, for example, a trader bought a January British pound futures contract and planned to take delivery of the 62,500 pounds at the settlement date. The futures

EXHIBIT 14.2 Selected Currency Futures Contracts

Contract	Amount	Minimum Price Fluctuation per Unit of Foreign Currency	
Australian dollar	100,000	$0.0001	($10.00)
British pound	62,500	$0.0002	($12.50)
Canadian dollar	100,000	$0.0001	($10.00)
Deutsche mark	125,000	$0.0001	($12.50)
French franc	250,000	0.005 cents	($12.50)
Japanese yen	12,500,000	0.0001 cents	($12.50)
Swiss franc	125,000	$0.0001	($12.50)
European currency unit	125,000	$0.0001	($12.50)

CURRENCY

	Open	High	Low	Settle	Change	Lifetime High	Low	Open Interest
JAPAN YEN (CME)—12.5 million yen; $ per yen (.00)								
June	1.1935	1.2075	1.1915	1.2058	+ .0104	1.2625	.9915	58,642
Sept	1.2165	1.2220	1.2163	1.2206	+ .0107	1.2670	1.0175	3,375
Dec	1.2350	1.2350	1.2348	1.2359	+ .0109	1.2813	1.0300	826
Mr96	1.2505	1.2505	1.2505	1.2518	+ .0110	1.2990	1.0465	419
June	....	....	....	1.2674	+ .0111	1.3130	1.0780	132
Est vol 15,146; vol Fri 15,805; open int 63,394, +1,078.								
DEUTSCHEMARK (CME)—125,000 marks; $ per mark								
June	.7216	.7225	.7182	.7207	− .0017	.7448	.5980	63,561
Sept	.7233	.7250	.7228	.7237	− .0018	.7450	.6290	3,447
Dec	.7265	.7265	.7265	.7268	− .0018	.7480	.6580	644
Mr96	....	....	....	.7298	− .0018	.7505	.6525	137
Est vol 17,552; vol Fri 34,488; open int 67,789, +494.								
CANADIAN DOLLAR (CME)—100,000 dlrs.; $ per Can $								
June	.7360	.7366	.7344	.7357	+ .0010	.7600	.6948	44,850
Sept	.7332	.7342	.7325	.7333	+ .0011	.7438	.6920	3,192
Dec	.7318	.7325	.7310	.7315	+ .0011	.7400	.6895	2,104
Mr96	....	....	....	.7300	+ .0011	.7325	.6900	691
June	.7295	.7300	.7290	.7287	+ .0011	.7230	.6905	258
Est vol 3,317; vol Fri 4,591; open int 51,096, +900.								
BRITISH POUND (CME)—62,500 pds.; $ per pound								
June	1.6116	1.6184	1.6102	1.6136	+ .0032	1.6530	1.5330	23,058
Sept	1.6090	1.6150	1.6090	1.6100	+ .0030	1.6480	1.5410	319
Est vol 3,948; vol Fri 5,340; open int 23,439, +135.								
SWISS FRANC (CME)—125,000 francs; $ per franc								
June	.8763	8779	.8711	.8757	− .0016	.9038	.7193	27,661
Sept	.8807	.9834	.8800	.8819	− .0016	.9085	.7605	2,223
Dec	....	....	....	.8883	− .0015	.9138	.7834	528
Est vol 12,078; vol Fri 20,465; open int 30,422, −227.								
AUSTRALIAN DOLLAR (CME)—100,000 dlrs.; $ per A.$								
June	.7225	.7291	.7232	.7281	+ .0012	.7762	.7187	8,776
Est vol 657; vol Fri 537; open int 8,848, −2.								

EXHIBIT 14.3 Currency Futures Prices for Selected Contracts from the *Wall Street Journal*

Source: Reprinted by permission of the Wall Street Journal © 1995 Dow Jones & Company, Inc. All Rights Reserved Worldwide.

price was $1.50. At the delivery date, 62,000 pounds are delivered in exchange for the dollar price determined at the settlement date. Say the pound had strengthened over the period and the settlement price was $1.58. Then the long position would have to pay an additional $0.08 per pound above the $1.50. Of course, offsetting this would be the fact that futures position would have made $0.08 over the period, together with accrued interest. Moreover, the accrued interest would depend on the path of futures prices. As with other commodities, if both domestic and foreign interest rates are assumed to be constant, then forward and futures prices will be equal, and equation (14.3) is valid for futures contracts as well.

EXAMPLE 14.7 Hedging with Foreign Exchange Futures

An American firm makes a large shipment of goods to England. The firm will be paid 2 million pounds for the shipment in 60 days. The current exchange rate is $1.50 per pound. The firm is concerned that the pound will weaken. A pound futures contract on the IMM has a settlement date in 70 days. Interest rates in both Britain and the United States are 5 percent. The futures price is set at $1.50. Since each contract controls 62,500 pounds, a naive hedge would consist of 2,000,000/62,500 = 32 contracts. By selling 32 contracts, the firm is replacing foreign currency risk by basis risk.

EXAMPLE 14.8   **Cross Hedging**

An American firm is purchasing a large shipment of goods from a Dutch firm. The purchase price is 3.7 million guilder. The current exchange rate is $0.54 per guilder. At this exchange rate, the dollar cost would be $1,998,000. The firm is concerned that the guilder may strengthen in the interim, and it would like to hedge this risk using foreign currency futures. Initial studies have shown that the guilder is highly correlated with the deutsche mark. As a result, the firm decides to purchase deutsche mark futures. To establish the number of futures contracts to trade, a regression analysis is performed between the weekly change in the guilder rate and the weekly change in the nearby deutsche mark futures. The estimated slope is 0.9432, and the R^2 is 0.981. Each futures contract controls 125,000 deutsche marks. The current exchange rate is $0.6090 per deutsche mark. Hence, the commitment of 3.7 million guilder translates to $1,998,000 and hence to $1,998,000/0.6090 = 3,280,788 deutsche marks. The number of futures contracts to trade is therefore $0.9432 \times 3,280,788/125,000 \approx 25$ contracts. Before implementing this hedge, the firm conducts extensive out-of-sample tests to access the magnitude of the basis risk. If the firm suspects that the relationship between the two currencies will not remain stable over the time period, it might consider a direct hedge using a customized over-the-counter contract.

Options on Foreign Currencies and Foreign Currency Futures

As discussed in Chapter 11, a call (put) option on a foreign currency gives the holder the right to buy (sell) a certain amount of foreign currency at a given exchange rate. This right exists up to a given expiration date. Organized trading in foreign currency options takes place in many financial centers. The largest exchange is the Philadelphia Stock Exchange. Other centers includes the Toronto, Vancouver, and Montreal Stock Exchanges; the London International Financial Futures Exchange; the International Stock Exchange in the United Kingdom; and the European Options Exchange in Amsterdam.

EXAMPLE 14.9   **Options on the Philadelphia Exchange**

The Philadelphia Exchange trades options on the British pound, German mark, Japanese yen, Swiss franc, and the Canadian dollar. American-style options are traded side by side with European options. The most heavily traded contracts are the deutsche mark and Japanese yen American-style options.

Foreign interest in these contracts motivated the Philadelphia Exchange to initiate evening trading sessions (6 P.M. to 10 P.M. EST) to accommodate traders in Asia-Pacific time zones and an early morning session (4:30 A.M. to 8:30 A.M.) to accommodate European traders. As a result, this market is open 14 hours a day.

EXHIBIT 14.4 Terms of Selected Option Contracts at the Philadelphia Exchange

Currency	Contract Size	Strike-Price Intervals	Premium Quotations
German mark	62,500	1.0	Cents
Pound sterling	31,250	2.5	Cents
Swiss franc	62,500	1.0	Cents
Japanese yen	6,250,000	0.01	Hundredths of a cent

Exhibit 14.4 shows the terms of some of the option contracts traded. The strike price of each foreign currency option is the U.S. dollar price of a unit of foreign exchange. The expiration dates correspond to the delivery dates in the futures. Specifically, the expiration dates correspond to the Saturday before the third Wednesday of the contract month. Contract months are March, June, September, and December, plus the two near-term contracts. The daily volume of contracts traded on the Philadelphia Exchange has steadily increased to about 40,000 contracts per day. Exhibit 14.5 shows the prices of these options as they appear in the *Wall Street Journal*.

To understand the quotes in Exhibit 14.5, consider the British pound. Each contract is for 31,250 British pounds. From the first column we see the closing spot price, in cents per pound sterling. The second column lists the strike prices in cents

PHILADELPHIA OPTIONS

Monday, May 1, 1995

		Calls		Puts	
		Vol.	Last	Vol.	Last
Australian Dollar					**72.99**
50,000 Australian Dollar EOM-cents per unit.					
72	May	...	...	4	0.36
British Pound					**161.70**
31,250 British Pounds-cents per unit.					
155	Sep	...	...	40	2.01
157½	Jun	...	...	8	0.80
160	May	10	2.10	...	...
162½	May	5	0.70	...	...
162½	Jun	...	...	8	2.88
British Pound-GMark					**224.84**
31,250 British Pound-German Mark cross.					
222	May	8	3.40	...	...
31,250 British Pound-German mark EOM.					
218	May	...	...	8	0.10
220	May	...	...	12	0.86
224	May	8	2.68	...	...
Canadian Dollar					**73.70**
50,000 Canadian Dollars-cents per unit.					
69	May	7	4.70	...	...
70	Jun	...	...	4	0.01
73	May	7	0.87	...	...
73	Jun	10	0.98	16	0.38
74	Jun	14	0.45	...	...
78	Sep	20	0.09	...	...
French Franc					**201.84**
250,000 French Francs-10ths of a cent per unit.					
19¼	Jun	...	...	12	0.72
German Mark					**71.89**
62,500 German Marks EOM-cents per unit.					
74	May	4	0.42	...	...
76	Jun	200	0.50	...	...
62,500 German Marks-European Style.					
60½	May	30	11.28	...	...
62,500 German Marks-cents per unit.					
64	Sep	...	...	35	0.21
65	Jun	...	...	7	0.04
67	Jun	...	...	25	0.15
67	Sep	...	...	5	0.59
68	Jun	...	...	9	0.25
71	Jun	...	...	3	0.97
71½	May	5	0.94	...	...
72	Jun	60	1.35	2	1.42
72½	May	3	0.45	...	...
72½	Jun	10	1.20	...	...
73	May	40	0.33	...	...
75	Jun	7	0.53	...	...
76	May	200	0.05	...	...
Japanese Yen					**120.02**
6,250,000 Japanese Yen -100ths of a cent					
115	Jun	...	...	2	0.70
115	Sep	...	...	1	1.61
117	May	...	...	50	0.30
119	May	3	1.47	50	0.77
120	May	...	...	10	1.12
120	Sep	...	...	3	3.52
121	May	1	0.65	...	...
122	Sep	50	4.20	50	4.65
124	May	50	0.23	...	...
125	Jun	50	0.92	...	...
125	Sep	50	3.06	...	...
6,250,000 Japanese Yen EOM-100ths of a cen					
120	May	145	1.98	...	...
6,250,000 Japanese Yen-100ths of a cent per unit.					
100	Sep	...	...	30	0.08
6,250,000 Japanese Yen-European Style					
111	Sep	200	10.83	...	...
112	Sep	200	10.05	...	...
Swiss Franc					**87.34**
62,500 Swiss Francs EOM.					
86½	May	3	1.72	...	...
62,500 Swiss Francs-cents per unit.					
77	Sep	...	...	5	0.26
82	Sep	...	...	2	1.01
85	Jun	1	3.60	1	0.96
86	May	...	...	25	0.46
87	May	...	...	25	0.84
87½	May	...	...	3	1.30
87½	Jun	...	...	3	2.15
89	May	25	0.42	...	...
Call Vol 1,570			**Open Int ... 256,856**		
Put Vol 609			**Open Int ... 314,947**		

EXHIBIT 14.5 Prices of Selected Option Contracts from the *Wall Street Journal*

Source: Reprinted by permission of the Wall Street Journal © 1995 Dow Jones & Company, Inc. All Rights Reserved Worldwide.

per pound, at 2 1/2 cent intervals. The next three columns show the call premiums for the given expiration dates. These prices are also in cents per pound. The final three columns show the put prices.

Futures Options at the CME

The principal marketplace for options on foreign currency futures is the Chicago Mercantile Exchange. The volume of contracts traded on the exchange is comparable to that of the Philadelphia Exchange.

Cross-Rate Foreign Currency Futures Contracts

Suppose a trader expects the mark to strengthen against the pound. By buying futures on the mark and selling futures on the pound, the trader can lock in a future exchange rate between the pound and the mark. As long as the mark appreciates more with respect to the dollar than the pound does, profits will be made.

EXAMPLE 14.10 **Synthetic Cross-Currency Contracts**

A British manufacturer purchases equipment from a German firm for a price of 1 million marks. The payment date is set up to coincide with the last trading date of the CME's currency futures contract, in exactly three months. The manufacturer wants to hedge against mark appreciation relative to the pound. To do this the manufacturer buys three-month mark futures and sells three-month pound futures. Currently, the three-month mark futures price is $0.5760 and the pound futures is $1.4820. The number of mark futures to buy is 1,000,000/125,000 = 8 contracts. These contracts lock into a purchase price of $576,000.

The British firm wants to lock into the price in pounds. By selling a pound futures contract, the short position is locked into paying pounds and receiving dollars at an exchange rate of $1.4820 per pound. At this exchange rate $576,000 is equivalent to 388,664 pounds. Since each contract covers 62,500 pounds, the number of futures contracts to sell is 388,664/62,500 = 6.2. By taking a long position in 8 mark futures and a short position in 6.2 pound futures, the cost of 1,000,000 marks is locked into 388,664 pounds, for a cross rate of 0.3886 pounds per mark.

Actually, the British firm could have hedged this risk directly using a mark futures contract that trades in pounds on the LIFFE. This might be preferable, since the daily dollar cash flows associated with the synthetic cross hedge introduce additional complications for the British manufacturer.

Actually, foreign-settled cross-currency contracts are traded on organized exchanges in the United States. For example, in 1992 the CME began trading yen-settled deutsche mark/Japanese yen futures and options on futures. With these

DM/JY futures contracts, the currency in which prices are quoted and payment made is yen. Each contract locks in the yen price of 125,000 deutsche marks. As with all futures contracts, daily cash adjustments are made in yen.

EXAMPLE 14.11 Recently, a German firm decided to take advantage of lower interest rates in Japan by borrowing 100 million yen. The yen were immediately sold for German marks. Repayment is due in three months. The firm is concerned that the yen could strengthen relative to the mark. The current three-month DM/JY futures price is 88.32 yen per mark. The firm decides to hedge the risk by selling futures. Each contract is based on 125,000 deutsche marks. The 100 million yen translates to 100,000,000/88.32 = 1,132,246 marks. Since each contract controls 125,000 marks, the number of contracts to sell is 9.06 or 9 contracts.

Arbitrage Relationships for Foreign Currency Options

The usual arbitrage arguments of Chapter 6 yield several relationships for exchange rate call and put options. Many of the relationships used in Chapter 6 need to be modified, however; foreign currency options differ from ordinary stock options because the underlying security of a foreign currency option always provides a continuous dividend yield equal to the foreign riskless rate.

In this section we shall highlight a few pricing relationships that must hold true for foreign currency options. In order to accomplish this, let $B(t, T)$ and $B_F(t, T)$ be the prices at date t of pure discount bonds that pay one unit of domestic and foreign currency respectively at time T. We consider option contracts with strike X and maturity T.

PROPERTY 14.1 BOUNDS ON EUROPEAN OPTIONS

The price of a European call option is bounded by

$$C(0) \geq \text{Max}[S(0)e^{-r_F T} - X e^{-rt}, 0] \tag{14.5}$$

Proof.   Consider the following two portfolio strategies undertaken at time t when the price of foreign currency is $S(t)$.

Strategy 1:   Purchase portfolio A, consisting of 1 European call and X bonds with maturity T.

Strategy 2:   Purchase portfolio B, consisting of 1 foreign discount bond with maturity T.

The values of these two portfolios at time 0 and time T are shown in Exhibit 14.6. Note that strategy 1 has payouts that dominate those of strategy 2. Therefore,

EXHIBIT 14.6   Arbitrage Strategy for European Option Bounds

Portfolio	Initial Value in Domestic Currency	$S(T) < X$	$S(T) \geq X$
A: 1 call and X domestic bonds	$C(0) + XB(0, T)$	X	$S(T)$
B: 1 foreign bond	$B_F(0, T)S(0)$	$S(T)$	$S(T)$

to avoid riskless arbitrage, the initial value of portfolio A must equal or exceed that of portfolio B. That is,

$$C(0) + XB(0, T) \geq B_F(0, T)S(0)$$

from which the result follows. Note that Property 14.1 can be restated in terms of forward prices. In particular, equations (14.5) and (14.4) imply that

$$C(0) \geq [FO_T(0) - X] e^{-rT}$$

PROPERTY 14.2

An American foreign exchange call option may be exercised early.

Proof.   Property 14.2 follows from Property 14.1. The lowest price to which a European call could fall is its lower bound, given in equation (14.5). There are, however, situations where the exercise value $S(t) - X$ may exceed this value. Thus, there are cases where the unexercised value may be lower than the exercised value. Property 14.2 also follows directly from the fact that options on stocks paying continuous dividends may be optimally exercised early.

Both American and European contracts trade on the Philadelphia Stock Exchange. Since their terms are identical, price differences are solely attributable to the early exercise premium. For foreign exchange options this premium may be significant, especially for deep-in-the-money contracts.

Two other properties are summarized below. We leave the proof of these properties as an exercise.

PROPERTY 14.3 EUROPEAN PUT-CALL PARITY

The price of calls and puts are related through

$$C^E(t) = P^E(t) + S(t)B_F(t, T) - XB(t, T) \tag{14.6}$$

> **PROPERTY 14.4 PUT OPTION BOUNDS**
>
> European and American put options are bounded by
>
> $$P^E(t) \geq XB(t, T) - S(t)B_F(t, T) \qquad (14.7)$$
>
> $$P(t) \geq \text{Max}[XB(t, T) - S(t)B_F(t, T), B_F(t, T) - S(t)] \qquad (14.8)$$

We could develop additional properties of option prices, mostly along lines described in Chapter 6. In the remainder of this section we discuss a few relationships particular to foreign currency options.

EXAMPLE 14.12   Consider the Philadelphia Exchange's call option on 62,500 deutsche marks. Suppose the strike price is $0.40 per mark. This option provides the owner with the right to buy 62,500 deutsche marks for 62,500 ($0.4) = $25,000. Equivalently, this contract gives the right to sell $25,000 in exchange for 62,500 deutsche marks. This is a put option on $25,000, with a strike price of 1/$0.4 = 2.5 marks per dollar.

Example 14.12 motivates Property 14.5.

> **PROPERTY 14.5 INTERNATIONAL PUT-CALL EQUIVALENCE**
>
> The price of a foreign exchange put option in one currency equals that of a call option in the other currency at the same strike.
>
> $$C(X) = S(0)XP_F(X_F) \qquad (14.9)$$
>
> $$P(X) = S(0)XC_F(X_F) \qquad (14.10)$$
>
> where $X_F = 1/X$ is the strike price in foreign currency units.

Proof.   To see this, note that an option to buy foreign currency with local currency at an exchange rate $X has a terminal payout of $C(T)$ where

$$C(T) = \text{Max}[S(T) - X, 0]$$
$$= \text{Max}[S(T)X[1/X - 1/S(T)], 0]$$
$$= S(T)X \, \text{Max}[X_F - S_F(T), 0]$$
$$= S(T)[XP_F(T)]$$

where $P_F(T)$ is the terminal value of a foreign put option on one unit of local currency. The terminal value, $C(T)$, is therefore equivalent to the payout of X such put options. The initial value of the X options is $XP_F(0)$ in foreign currency or $[XP_F(0)]S(0)$ dollars.

PROPERTY 14.6 INTERNATIONAL OPTIONS PRICE PARITY

The spot exchange rate depends on domestic and foreign option prices and interest rates as follows.

$$S(0) = \frac{C(X) + XB(0, T)}{XC_F(X_F) + B_F(0, T)} \tag{14.11}$$

$$= \frac{P(X) + XB(0, T)}{XP_F(X_F) + B_F(0, T)} \tag{14.12}$$

Proof. To see this, we combine the interest rate parity theorem with the put-call forward parity relationship. Specifically, we have

$$FO_T(0) = S(0)B_F(0, T)/B(0, T) \tag{14.13}$$

The put-call forward relationship, as discussed in Chapter 12 (equation (12.4)), is

$$C(X) - P(X) = [FO_T(0) - X]B(0, T) \tag{14.14}$$

Substituting equation (14.13) into equation (14.14), we obtain

$$C(X) - P(X) = S(0)B_F(0, T) - XB(0, T) \tag{14.15}$$

But

$$P(X) = XS(0)C_F(X_F) \tag{14.16}$$

Substituting equation (14.16) into equation (14.15) and simplifying yields the result.

Other Currency Contracts

As markets continue to become more global, exchange rate risk and its management has become increasingly more important. Many firms look to the over-the-counter market for tailor-designed products that fit their needs. The largest interbank markets for currency contracts are centered in London and New York. These markets are massive. For example, the volume of European options traded in the interbank market is at least ten times larger than the volume of listed currency options traded on the Philadelphia Stock Exchange.

Over the last decade, an enormous number of custom-designed products have been introduced. While many have been experimental, others have flourished and over time have become more and more standardized. Indeed, some products have become so popular that standardized versions of them have been successfully introduced in organized exchanges. We shall discuss additional foreign currency contracts in Chapter 16.

Conclusion

In this chapter we have briefly discussed foreign exchange markets. The forward market in foreign exchange is extremely active. In addition, a variety of futures and option contracts exist. Here we examined some arbitrage relationships unique to foreign currencies. In Chapter 15 we will discuss specific models for pricing foreign currency options, and we will examine other foreign currency contracts in Chapter 16.

References

Benet, B. "Commodity Futures Cross Hedging of Foreign Exchange Exposure." *Journal of Futures Markets* 10 (1990): 287–306.

Biger, N., and J. Hull. "The Valuation of Currency Options." *Financial Management* (Spring 1983): 24–28.

Bodurtha, J., and G. Courtadon. "Efficiency Tests of the Foreign Currency Options Market." *Journal of Finance* 41 (March 1986): 151–62.

Chang, J., and L. Shanker. "Hedging Effectiveness of Currency Options and Currency Futures." *Journal of Futures Markets* 6 (1986): 289–305.

Chrystal, K. *A Guide to Foreign Exchange Markets*. St. Louis: Federal Reserve Bank of St. Louis, 1984, pp. 5–18.

Garman, M., and S. Kohlhagen. "Foreign Currency Option Values." *Journal of International Money and Finance* 2 (1983): 231–37.

Giddy, I. "An Integrated Theory of Exchange Rate Equilibrium." In *International Finance: Concepts and Issues*, edited by R. Kolb and G. Gay. Richmond, Va.: Robert Dame, 1982.

_____. "Foreign Exchange Options." *Journal of Futures Markets* (Summer 1983): 143–66.

_____. "The Foreign Exchange Option as a Hedging Tool." *Midland Corporate Finance Journal* 1 (Fall 1993): 32–42.

Grabbe, J. "The Pricing of Call and Put Options on Foreign Exchange." *Journal of International Money and Finance* 2 (1983): 239–53.

_____. *International Financial Markets*, 2d ed. New York: Elsevier, 1991.

Grammatikkos, T., and A. Saunders. "Stability and the Hedging Performance of Foreign Currency Futures." *Journal of Futures Markets* 3 (1983): 295–305.

Grandreau, B. "New Markets in Foreign Currency Options." *Business Review* (July–August 1984): 3–13.

Jacque, L. "Management of Foreign Exchange Risk: A Review Article." In *International Finance: Concepts and Issues*, edited by R. Kolb and G. Gay. Richmond, Va.: Robert Dame, 1982.

Kolb, R. *Understanding Futures Markets.* Glenview, Ill.: HarperCollins, 1985.

Loosigian, A. *Foreign Exchange Futures: A Guide to International Currency Trading.* Homewood, Ill.: Dow Jones-Irwin, 1981.

McFarland, J., R. Pettit, and S. Sung. "The Distribution of Foreign Exchange Price Changes: Trading Day Effects and Risk Measurement." *Journal of Finance* (June 1982): 693–716.

Shastri, K., and K. Tandon. "Arbitrage Tests of the Efficiency of the Foreign Currency Options Market." *Journal of International Money and Finance* 4 (December 1985): 455–68. University of Pittsburgh.

Sweeney, R. "Beating the Foreign Exchange Market." *Journal of Finance* 41 (March 1986): 163–82.

Westerfield, J. M. "An Examination of Foreign Exchange Risk Under Fixed and Floating Rate Regimes." *Journal of International Economics* 7 (May 1977): 181–200.

Yang, H. "A Note on Currency Option Pricing Models." *Journal of Business Finance and Accounting* 12 (Autumn 1985): 429–37.

Exercises

1. A U.S. firm has a British subsidiary. The firm is concerned about the British pound depreciating.
   a. What types of contracts and strategies should the firm consider if it wants to lock into an exchange rate? What drawbacks, if any, might this strategy entail?
   b. If the firm wanted to place a limit on exchange rate risk, what option strategies should it consider?

2. The current interest rates in the United States and Britain are 6 percent and 9 percent per year, continuously compounded. Compute the six-month and one-year forward prices given that the current exchange rate is $0.65 per pound.

3. For the data in Exercise 2, compute the lower bound of an at-the-money European call option price on the British pound for contracts expiring in six months.

4. Explain why an American call option on foreign currency may be exercised early.

5. Provide an example that illustrates Property 14.5. That is, given the price of a foreign put option, compute the price of a European call option in the United States.

6. The following prices exist for CME options on British pound futures at the beginning of February.

Strike	Feb.	March	April	Feb.	March	April
1450	2.22	2.98	—	0.004	0.76	1.64
1500	0.004	0.66	1.12	2.70	3.44	4.48
1525	0.004	0.24	0.60	5.28	5.50	6.44

The underlying contract for February and March options is the March futures contract, the price of which is $1.4722. The underlying futures contract for the April options is the June futures, which is priced at $1.4662. Each contract controls 62,500 British pounds. Option quotes are in cents per British pound.
   a. Which columns correspond to call prices, and which columns correspond to put prices?
   b. What is the actual dollar price of the March 1500 contract?
   c. Compute the intrinsic value of the March and April 1500 options.

7. Assume a U.S. firm expects a lump cash flow of 5 million British pounds in March and is concerned about exchange rate risk. The firm might hedge by
   a. Selling futures
   b. Buying at-the-money puts
   c. Selling at-the-money calls
   For each of these three cases, use the information in Exercise 6 to plot profit functions of the hedged versus unhedged cash flows. Assume the contract is held to the settlement date, at which time the 5 million pounds are received.

8. A British importer contracts to purchase a U.S. computer for $610,000. Payment is due in June, four months from now.
   a. Explain how the trader could use futures contracts that trade at the CME to hedge against a weakening pound.
   b. The June futures price is $1.4662. How many contracts should the firm enter into?
   c. Compute the effective cost of the computer if, when the hedge is lifted, the futures price equals the spot price at $1.36 per pound.

9. Using the information below, compute the fair price of a European put on the German mark.

Risk-free rate in United States	6%
Risk-free rate in Germany	8%
Time to expiration	0.5 years
Strike price	$0.7935/mark
Current exchange rate	$0.7935/mark
European call price	3.7 cents

10. Consider the following options.

Option	Pay	Receive
1	6 pounds	15 Swiss francs
2	6 pounds	10 dollars
3	10 dollars	15 Swiss francs

a. Show that to avoid riskless arbitrage, the total value of options 2 and 3 must exceed that of option 1.

b. How does this property relate to the property that an option on a portfolio of stocks is never as valuable as a portfolio of options on the individual stocks in the portfolio?

CHAPTER 15

Pricing Options on Futures, Stock Indices, and Foreign Currencies

In this chapter we first investigate procedures for pricing European options under alternative dividend policies. The procedures are not only useful for pricing options on dividend-paying stock but also can be used to price European options on stock indices, foreign currencies, and futures. Next we consider the prices of American options on dividend-paying stocks. We obtain simple bounds on option prices and then use the binomial lattice procedure to obtain numerical prices. Such models permit us to price American options on dividend-paying stocks, on foreign currencies, on stock indices, and on futures. Next we develop an exact option pricing equation for American calls on a dividend-paying stock. The model is of some interest because it illustrates the importance of compound option pricing. Finally, we present an alternative numerical procedure for efficiently pricing options.

The primary objectives of this chapter are the following:

- To investigate procedures for pricing European and American options on instruments that pay dividends;

- To develop lattice-based procedures to price American call options on stocks that pay dividends;

- To present an analytical model for pricing American options on stocks that pay dividends; and

- To use such models to price options on futures, foreign currency, stock indices, and commodities that possess a convenience yield.

Valuation of Call Options on Dividend-Paying Stocks

In this chapter we consider two types of dividend policies. The first policy assumes dividends are paid out at discrete points in time; the second policy assumes dividend yields occur continuously.

Known Dividend Payouts

The price of a stock, $S(0)$, reflects the present value of all future dividends. In particular,

$$S(0) = \sum_{i=1}^{n} d_i \, e^{-\rho t_i} \tag{15.1}$$

where d_i is the expected dividend at date t_i and ρ is the appropriate discount rate for the cash flows. The exact discount rate depends on the risk of the cash flows and is usually greater than the riskless rate, r. Now, assume that the size of the first dividend, d_1, is certain. Since there is no uncertainty about its value, its discount rate should be the riskless rate, r. Hence, equation (15.1) has to be adjusted to

$$S(0) = G(0) + d_1 \, e^{-rt_1} \tag{15.2}$$

where $G(0) = \sum_{i=2}^{n} d_i \, e^{-\rho t_i}$

reflects the present value of the remaining risky cash flows. By putting aside $d_1 \, e^{-rt_1}$ dollars in the riskless asset, the firm can guarantee that the first dividend payment will be made.

At date t, the stock price $S(t)$ is

$$S(t) = \begin{cases} G(t) + d_1 \, e^{-r(t_1-t)} & \text{for } t < t_1 \\ G(t) & \text{for } t_1 \le t < t_2 \end{cases} \tag{15.3}$$

where $G(t) = \sum_{i=2}^{n} d_i \, e^{-\rho(t_i-t)}$

Now consider a European call option that has expiration date T, where $t_1 < T < t_2$. Since the option cannot be exercised before date t_1, the holder has no claim on the first dividend. Therefore, the asset underlying the option contract is not the stock, with price $S(0)$, but the risky component of the stock, which is currently worth $G(0)$. If the risky component is assumed to follow a geometric Wiener process, then the Black-Scholes model can be used to price European options. In particular,

$$C^E(0) = G(0)N(d_1^*) - X \, e^{-rT} N(d_2^*) \tag{15.4}$$

where $d_1^* = [\ln(G(0)/X) + (r + \sigma^2/2)T]/\sigma\sqrt{T}$

$d_2^* = d_1^* - \sigma\sqrt{T}$

$G(0) = S(0) - d_1 \, e^{-rt_1}$

Note that as the magnitude of the dividend increases, the value of $G(0)$ decreases and the value of the call option declines.

EXAMPLE 15.1   **Pricing a European Call Option on a Stock**

Consider a stock priced at $100, with volatility of 30 percent per year. The risk-free rate is 10 percent. A one-year at-the-money European call option trades on the stock. A dividend of $10 is paid out in six months.

The present value of the dividend is $10\ e^{-0.05} = \$9.5123$. Hence, the capital gains component is $\$100 - \$9.5123 = \$90.4877$. The value of a one-year European call option, computed using equation (15.4), is $10.79.

Continuous-Dividend-Yield Payouts

Consider a stock that continuously pays out a dividend at a rate that is a constant proportion of the level of the stock price. Let q represent the annualized rate. If the total expected return from stock ownership, including the dividend yield, is μ, then the expected rate of price appreciation must be $\mu - q$. Hence, the dynamics for the price appreciation are

$$ds/s = (\mu - q)\ dt + \sigma\ dw$$

Of course, stocks do not pay out dividends continuously at a rate proportional to the level of the stock price. However, there are a number of applications in finance where the underlying asset can be viewed as paying out a continuous dividend yield.

EXAMPLE 15.2   1.   Consider a large, well-diversified portfolio of common stocks, all of which pay out dividends at different times. We could view q as the average dividend yield on the portfolio.

2.   Consider the price of a consumption commodity such as corn. We could view q as the convenience yield derived from maintaining an inventory.

3.   Consider the price of foreign currency. Since foreign currency is held in an interest-bearing account, we could view q as the foreign riskless rate of return.

4.   Consider the price of a building. The total return on investment equals price appreciation and rental income. In this case let q represent the net income or rental yield, expressed as a percentage of the value of the building.

For "stocks" that pay a continuous yield q, the growth rate will be reduced from what it would be if no dividends were declared. Let $S(T)$ be the stock price at date T. If no dividends have been paid out, the growth rate of the price would have been higher, and the price would be $S(T)e^{qT}$. Equivalently, the price of a dividend-paying stock at date T equals the price on an otherwise identical nondividend-paying stock if at date 0 the latter stock has a price of $G(0) = S(0)e^{-qT}$. Hence, *the price of a European call option on a dividend-paying stock currently worth $S(0)$ should be the same as the price of a European call option on a nondividend-paying stock* *currently worth* $G(0)$. Using the Black-Scholes model, we have

$$C^E(0) = G(0)N(d_1^*) - X\,e^{-rT}N(d_2^*) \qquad (15.5)$$

where $d_1^* = [\ln(G(0)/X) + (r + \sigma^2/2)T]/\sigma\sqrt{T}$

$d_2^* = d_1^* - \sigma\sqrt{T}$

$G(0) = S(0)e^{-qT}$

This model is called **Merton's continuous-dividend-yield European option pricing model.** If dividends are not constant over the life of the option, the equation is still true, but q has to be set equal to the average (annualized) dividend yield over the period to expiration.

Applications of Merton's Model

Below we provide several examples of Merton's continuous-dividend-yield option pricing model.

EXAMPLE 15.3   **Pricing a European Option on a Stock**

A stock is priced at $100. An option is to be priced with strike price $100. The time to expiration is 100 days, the volatility is 30 percent, and the riskless rate of return is 6 percent. Using equation (15.5), the following call prices were computed for dividend yields ranging from 3 to 8 percent per year. The corresponding put prices, obtained from the put-call parity equation, are also shown.

			Dividend Yield			
	3%	4%	5%	6%	7%	8%
Call price	$6.596	$6.447	$6.300	$6.156	$6.014	$5.074
Put price	5.784	5.906	6.031	6.156	6.283	6.412

EXAMPLE 15.4   **Pricing a European Option on a Stock Index**

Consider valuing a European call option on an index such as the S & P 500. The expiration date is one month, the strike price is $300, and the current level of the index is 300. The risk-free rate is 6 percent per year, and the volatility of the index is 30 percent. While the exact dividends on all the stocks in the index are not known, it is predicted that the total dividend yield over the one month to expiration is 0.35 percent. Hence, $q = 0.35\,(12)$ percent $= 4.2$ percent per year.

Given that the index follows a geometric Wiener process, the price of a European call option, using equation (15.5), is $10.47.

EXAMPLE 15.5   **Pricing a European Option on a Foreign Currency**

A foreign exchange option can be viewed as an option on a security that pays out a continuous dividend yield equal to the foreign riskless rate. If we assume both the local and the foreign riskless rates are constant over the life of the option and that exchange rates follow a geometric Wiener process, then Merton's continuous-dividend-yield option pricing model can be applied, with $G(0) = S(0)e^{-r_F T}$, where r_F is the foreign riskless rate of return and T is the expiration date of the option. For this case equation (15.5) can be rewritten as

$$C^E(0) = S(0)e^{-r_F T}N(d_1) - X e^{-rT}N(d_2) \qquad (15.6)$$

where $d_1 = [\ln\{S(0)/X\} + (r - r_F + \sigma^2/2)T]/\sigma\sqrt{T}$

$d_2 = d_1 - \sigma\sqrt{T}$

To illustrate this model, consider the theoretical price of a European call option on the British pound that trades at the Philadelphia Exchange. The time to expiration is six months. The spot price is \$1.60 per pound. An at-the-money call is to be valued. The volatility of the exchange rate is 10 percent per year. The domestic interest rate and the foreign interest rate are both equal to 8 percent. Using equation (15.6), we find that the theoretical price of the European call option is \$0.0433.

EXAMPLE 15.6   **Pricing European Commodity Options**

Consumption commodities provide a convenience yield, which, as discussed in Chapter 2, can be viewed as a nonobservable dividend stream. If the dividend stream were observable, then Merton's model would be directly applicable for valuing European options on commodities. Since the yield is not observable, additional problems emerge. For the moment, assume that futures trade on the commodity. Using these prices, the implied convenience yield can be obtained. Specifically, from equation (2.18) the average annualized implied convenience yield over the period $[0, T]$ is given by where

$$\kappa = [\ln(S(0)/F_T(0)) - (r + u)T]/T$$

If the option maturity coincides with the futures maturity, this value of y^* can be used as q in Merton's model for pricing European commodity options.

With no futures contracts available, the implied convenience yield cannot readily be extracted; hence, an additional parameter enters into the valuation equation, namely the convenience yield.[1]

---

[1] Since the convenience yield is largely influenced by preferences of investors in the economy, any resulting equation is preference-dependent.

Note too that the value of the early exercise feature of an American commodity option is not easily determined. By exercising a commodity call option early, the investor is able to capture the convenience yield (dividend) of the underlying commodity.

EXAMPLE 15.7 **The Black Model for Pricing European Options on Futures**

Recall that the futures price for a commodity can be related to the spot price by $F_T(0) = S(0)e^{(r-q)T}$. In the case of a financial asset, q is the dividend yield on the asset, whereas for a consumption commodity, q must be modified to reflect the convenience yield less the storage cost. Now, in a risk-neutral economy the expected growth rate in the price of a stock that pays continuous dividends at rate q is $r - q$. In such an economy, the expected growth rate of a futures price should be zero, because trading a futures contract requires no initial investment. This means that for pricing purposes, the value of q should be r. That is, for pricing an option on a futures, the futures price can be treated in the same way as a security paying a continuous dividend yield at rate r. Substituting $G(0) = F_T(0)e^{-rT}$ into Merton's model leads to the following model for European call options on futures:

$$CFU^E(0) = e^{-rT}[F_T(0)N(d_1^*) - XN(d_2^*)] \tag{15.7}$$

where $CFU^E(0)$ is the call option price with time T to expiration, $F_T(0)$ is the current futures price, and

$$d_1^* = [\ln(F_T(0)/X) + \sigma_F^2 T/2]/\sigma_F\sqrt{T}$$
$$d_2^* = d_1^* - \sigma_F\sqrt{T}$$
$$\sigma_F = \text{Volatility of the futures price}$$

This model was originally established by Black.

Sensitivities for Stock Index, Foreign Currency, and Futures Options

In Chapter 10, we considered the sensitivity of option prices to changes in the underlying parameters. In particular, we investigated the role of risk measures such as the delta, gamma, theta, vega, and rho. In the case of options on dividend-paying stocks, these same risk measures are applicable. The formulas for these measures are summarized for the Merton option model in Exhibit 15.1.

The following terms are used in Exhibit 15.1:

$$d_1^* = [\ln(G(0)/X) + (r + \sigma^2/2)T]/\sigma\sqrt{T}$$
$$d_2^* = d_1^* - \sigma\sqrt{T}$$

EXHIBIT 15.1   Sensitivity Measures for the Merton Model

	European Call	European Put
Delta	$e^{-qT}N(d_1^*)$	$e^{-qT}[N(d_1^*) - 1]$
Gamma	$\dfrac{n(d_1^*)}{G(0)\sigma\sqrt{T}}$	$\dfrac{n(d_1^*)}{G(0)\sigma\sqrt{T}}$
Theta	$-\dfrac{G(0)n(d_1^*)\sigma}{2\sqrt{T}} + qG(0)N(d_1^*)$ $-rX\,e^{-rT}\,N(d_2)$	$-\dfrac{G(0)n(d_1^*)\sigma}{2\sqrt{T}} - qG(0)N(-d_1^*)$ $+rX\,e^{-rT}\,N(-d_2^*)$
Vega	$G(0)\,\sqrt{T}\,n(d_1^*)$	$G(0)\,\sqrt{T}\,n(d_1^*)$
Rho	$XT\,e^{-rT}N(d_2^*)$	$-XT\,e^{-rT}N(-d_2^*)$

where $G(0) = S(0)e^{-qT}$ and $n(d_1^*) = \exp^{-d_1^{*2}/2}/\sqrt{2\pi}$ and $N(d_1^*)$ is the cumulative normal distribution function.

Price Bounds for American Call Options on Dividend-Paying Stocks

The early exercise feature of an American call option may be valuable if the underlying stock pays dividends. This is easily seen to be the case when the underlying stock pays continuous dividend payouts. By substituting for $G(0)$ into Merton's model, equation (15.5) can be rewritten as

$$C^E(0) = S(0)e^{-qT}N(d_1^*) - X\,e^{-rT}N(d_2^*) \tag{15.8}$$

where $d_1^* = [\ln(S(0)/X) + (r - q + \sigma^2/2)T]/\sigma\sqrt{T}$

$d_2^* = d_1^* - \sigma\sqrt{T}$

Note that if the stock price becomes extremely large relative to the strike, the values of $N(d_1^*)$ and $N(d_2^*)$ approach 1, and the European call approaches $S(0)e^{-qT} - X\,e^{-rT}$. This value could be lower than the intrinsic value of the option, $S(0) - X$. Hence, if q is sufficiently large, early exercise of an American option on a continuous-dividend-paying stock may be optimal. In this section we consider bounding American option prices when dividends are present, and in the next section we consider methods for establishing the fair American price.

Assume the stock pays a fixed dividend of size d_1 at time t_1. If the dividend is ignored and the Black-Scholes model is used to value the call, the resulting price will be too high. This occurs because dividends reduce the stock price at the ex-dividend date and hence reduce the probability that the terminal stock price is in the money. Let $c(s)$ be the price of an American call, and let $c^E(s)$ be the price of the option computed using the Black-Scholes equation and ignoring all dividends. Then, at date 0,

$$c(s) \le c^E(s) \tag{15.9}$$

If the option is European, then, as we have seen, the value of the claim is given by the Black-Scholes equation where the stock price $S(0)$ is replaced by $G(0)$. Let $c^E(g)$ represent the value of this European claim. Since an American call option is at least as valuable as its European counterpart, we have

$$c(s) \ge c^E(g) \tag{15.10}$$

Hence, from equations (15.9) and (15.10), the true value of the American call can be bounded by

$$c^E(g) \le c(s) \le c^E(s) \tag{15.11}$$

Actually, we can get tighter bounds than those provided by equation (15.9). We have seen that it is never optimal to exercise a call option early, except perhaps just before an ex-dividend date. Now consider an option on a stock, and as before, assume one ex-dividend date occurs prior to the expiration date at time t_1. Ex ante, investors know that the call option will be exercised either at time t_1 or at time T, if at all. Of course, viewed from time zero it is unclear at which point the option should be exercised. Indeed, the exercise time will only be resolved just prior to the ex-dividend date. If the stock price at that time is sufficiently high, and if the dividend income exceeds interest income, then early exercise may be appropriate. Viewed from time 0, then, there exists a probability, say p, that the option will be exercised at time t_1, and a probability $q = (1 - p)$ that it will be exercised (if at all) only at time T.

Now, consider a pseudo-American call option. This is an option where the buyer, at the time of purchase, has to specify the exact exercise date, in the interval $[0, T]$. Pseudo-American calls are useful concepts in that their values can be used to obtain lower bounds on option prices when dividends are paid. Given a pseudo-American call option on a dividend-paying stock, some investors will select the ex-dividend date t_1 as their exercise date, while others will select the expiration date T. The first set of investors will value the option as a European option with maturity t_1. Let $c^E(s, t_1)$ represent this value. The second set of investors will value the option as a European option on the capital gains component with maturity T. Let $c^E(g, T)$ be this value. Clearly, to avoid riskless arbitrage, the value of the pseudo-American call must equal the maximum of these values. Moreover, the true American call option must have a value that exceeds that of the pseudo-American call. This follows because the American call has all the features of the pseudo-American call, plus the additional feature that the option holder does not have to commit to any early exercise policy. Hence

$$c(s) \ge \text{Max}[c^E(s, t_1), c^E(g, T)]$$

Using prices of pseudo-American options to approximate the American price was first suggested by Black.

EXAMPLE 15.8   Consider a stock priced at $100, with volatility 30 percent per year. The risk-free rate is 10 percent. A one-year American call option trades on the stock. A dividend of $10 is paid out in six months.

The present value of the dividend is $10\ e^{-0.05} = \$9.5123$. Hence, the capital gains component is $\$100 - \$9.5123 = \$90.4877$. The value of a one-year European call option on the stock is computed as $10.79. Alternatively, using an initial stock price of $100 and a time to expiration of six months, the Black-Scholes model yields a price of $10.91. Hence, the pseudo-American call is priced as

$$\text{Max}[\$10.91, \$10.79] = \$10.91.$$

The value of the American option is at least $10.91.

Binomial Models for Pricing American Options When the Stock Pays Continuous Dividends

The binomial option pricing model can easily be modified to value American options on stocks paying continuous dividend yields. In particular, the only adjustment that needs to be made on the lattice involves the risk-neutral probability measure, θ. Recall that if the underlying asset pays no dividends and grows at a rate μ, then the approximating binomial lattice requires the true probability value of an upmove to be $(e^{\mu \Delta t} - d)/(u - d)$. To value options, we replace the true probability by the risk-neutral probability. This is accomplished by replacing μ by the capital appreciation rate that should occur in the risk-neutral economy. For stocks that pay no dividends, this value is the riskless rate, r. For stocks paying dividends continuously at the rate q, this value is $r - q$. Hence, for valuation purposes we have

$$\theta = \frac{e^{(r-q)\Delta t} - d}{u - d}$$

EXAMPLE 15.9   **Pricing Options on Futures**

We have seen that for a futures contract $q = r$. Hence, $\theta = (1 - d_F)/(u_F - d_F)$ where u_F and d_F were the upmove and downmove parameters of the underlying futures contract. This formula is consistent with the above formula, since for futures contracts $q = r$. Assume that futures prices over three periods are given below.

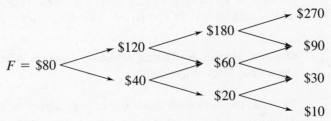

The one-period interest rate is given as 5 percent. A two-period American option with strike 80 trades on the futures contract. To value this option, note that $u_F = 1.5$, $d_F = 0.5$, and hence $\theta = (1 - d_F)/(u_F - d_F) = 0.5$. The call price lattice is now developed using backward recursion.

$$
\begin{array}{c}
CFU_0 = \$22.67
\begin{array}{c}
\nearrow \\
\searrow
\end{array}
\begin{array}{c}
CFU_{11} = \$47.62 \\
CFU_{10} = \$0
\end{array}
\begin{array}{c}
\nearrow \\
\searrow \\
\nearrow \\
\searrow
\end{array}
\begin{array}{c}
CFU_{22} = \$100 \\
CFU_{21} = \quad \$0 \\
CFU_{20} = \quad \$0
\end{array}
\end{array}
$$

Clearly, $CFU_{10} = \$0$ and $CFU_{11} = \text{Max}\{[\$100(0.5) + \$0]/1.05, \$40\} = \$47.62$. Finally, $CFU_0 = \text{Max}\{[\$47.62(0.5) + \$0]/1.05, \$0\} = \$22.67$. In this example early exercise of the futures option never occurred. For deep-in-the-money contracts early exercise may be a distinct possibility.

Note that the futures prices increased or decreased by 50 percent in each period. Recall that the futures price is linked to the spot price through the cost-of-carry relationship. If the commodity is a financial asset that does not pay dividends, we have

$$
F_0 = S_0 R^3
\begin{array}{c}
\nearrow \\
\searrow
\end{array}
\begin{array}{c}
F_{11} = u S_0 R^2 \\
F_{10} = d S_0 R^2
\end{array}
$$

where u and d are the upmove and downmove parameters for the underlying commodity. Hence, we have $F_{11} = u_F F_0 = u_F S_0 R^3 = u S_0 R^2$, from which $u_F = u/R$. Similarly, $d_F = d/R$. Substituting these expressions into the expression for θ, we obtain the usual expression, $\theta = (R - d)/(u - d)$.

EXAMPLE 15.10   **Pricing Options on Foreign Currency**

In Example 15.5 we considered the theoretical price of a European call option on the British pound that trades at the Philadelphia Exchange. The spot price was $1.60 per pound, the time to expiration was six months, and an at-the-money call was priced. The volatility of the exchange rate was 10 percent per year. The domestic interest rate and the foreign interest rate were both equal to 8 percent. The theoretical price of the European call option can be computed to be $0.0433. If the option was an American option, its price computed on a binomial lattice can be shown to be $0.0436. If foreign interest rates increased to 15 percent, the European price would be $0.0213 while the American price would be $0.0273.

Binomial Models for Pricing American Options When the Stock Pays Known Dividends

To value the option on a stock that pays a certain dividend at time $t_1 < T$, we decompose the stock price into a certain component (namely, the reserved present value of the dividend) and a risky component. Let g_0 be the risky component at time

$t = 0$. Then

$$g_0 = S_0 - k_0 \qquad (15.12)$$

where k_0 is the reserved dividend, that is, $k_0 = d_1 e^{-rt_1}$. We approximate the price dynamics of the risk component by a multiplicative random walk over a binomial lattice. In each time increment, the risky component either increases or decreases while the riskless component grows at the riskless rate. Let s_{ij} be the price of the stock in period i, state j. Then, prior to the ex-dividend date, we have

$$s_{ij} = g_{ij} + k_0 e^{r(i\Delta t)} \qquad \text{for } j = 0, 1, 2, \dots, i$$
$$\qquad \qquad \qquad \qquad \qquad \qquad \qquad \qquad \qquad (15.13)$$
where $\qquad \qquad g_{ij} = g_0 u^i d^{i-j} \qquad \text{for } j = 0, 1, 2, \dots, i$

After the ex-dividend date, the total stock price equals the risky component, that is,

$$s_{ij} = g_{ij} \qquad (15.14)$$

Given the lattice of s_{ij} values, the call option price can be computed by backward recursion. We illustrate the procedure by an example.

EXAMPLE 15.11 Consider a 96-day option with strike $75 on a stock currently priced at $100. A $2.50 dividend is due in 24 days. Interest rates are 5 percent and the stock volatility is 50 percent.

The stock price process over a four-period binomial lattice to expiration is shown below. The ex-dividend date occurs in the first period, and at that time, the price declines by $2.50. The present value of the dividend is $2.49. Hence, the current capital gains component is $97.51.

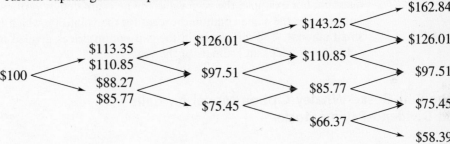

Here $\Delta t = 24/365$, $\sigma = 0.50$, and $u = e^{\sigma\sqrt{\Delta t}} = 1.13679$. Hence, $g_{11} = ug_0 = \$110.85$. Just before the dividend date, the stock price is $110.85 + $2.50 = $113.35. If the option holder exercises the option, the intrinsic value of $(113.35 - 75) = $38.35 is received. After the dividend is paid, the stock price drops to $110.85, and the option price is given by $36.58. Hence

$$c_{11} = \text{Max}[c_{11}^{\text{STOP}}, C_{11}^{\text{GO}}]$$

$$= \text{Max}[\$38.35, \$36.58] = \$38.35$$

If the stock price increases in the first period, then the optimal decision is to exercise the option and capture the dividend. If, on the other hand, the stock price falls in the first period, $g_{10} = \$85.77$ while $s_{10} = \$88.27$. Early exercise yields a $13.27 profit. The value unexercised, however, is $13.81. Hence

$$c_{10} = \text{Max}[c_{10}^{STOP}, c_{10}^{GO}] = \text{Max}[\$13.27, \$13.81] = \$13.81$$

Thus, if the stock price declines in the first period, the optimal policy is not to exercise the option. The lattice of option prices is shown below.

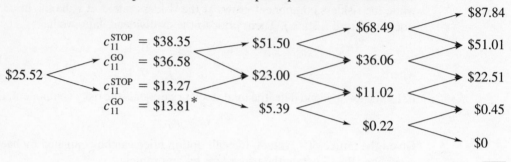

Sensitivity Measures for American Options on Dividend-Paying Stocks

Since numerical procedures are used to price American options on dividend-paying stocks, there are no simple formulas for their sensitivity measures. The delta, gamma, theta, vega, and rho values can be calculated by rerunning the option model on the lattice using the same parameter values except for the variable in question. For example, the vega value can be estimated by rerunning the binomial lattice under the same conditions except for the volatility, which is increased by a small amount. The difference in the two option prices divided by the change in volatility provides an estimate of the vega value.

The Roll-Geske-Whaley Option Model for Calls on Dividend-Paying Stocks*

As the partition of the time interval to expiration becomes finer and finer, the option price converges in value. The value that it converges to can be obtained analytically and is referred to as the **Roll-Geske-Whaley option pricing model.** This model assumes that the risky component $g(t)$ follows a geometric Wiener process.

At the instant before the ex-dividend date, the option holder recognizes that if the option is left unexercised, it will be worth $C^E(g(t_1), X, T - t)$. If it is exercised,

---

*This section provides advanced material and is optional reading for students.

the option holder will capture the intrinsic value $g(t_1) - X$, together with the dividend d_1. The call holder will exercise if

$$g(t_1) + d_1 - X > C^E(g(t_1), X, T - t_1)$$

Substituting in the Black-Scholes equation yields the following early exercise condition:

$$g(t_1) - X + d_1 > g(t_1)N(d_1) - X e^{-r(T-t_1)}N(d_2)$$

Now, for $g(t_1)$ sufficiently large, $N(d_1) \approx N(d_2) \approx 1$, and the right-hand side converges to $g(t_1) - X e^{-r(T-t_1)}$. Hence, for sufficiently large stock prices the early exercise condition will be met. Let $\overline{g}(t_1)$ be the lowest stock price for which early exercise is appropriate. That is, $\overline{g}(t_1)$ satisfies the equation

$$\overline{g}(t_1) + d_1 - X = C^E(\overline{g}(t_1), X, T - t_1) \tag{15.15}$$

If the price $g(t_1)$ is lower than $\overline{g}(t_1)$ then the European option price, $C^E(g(t_1), X, T - t_1)$, will be lower than $C^E(\overline{g}(t_1), X, T - t_1) = \overline{g}(t_1) + d_1 - X$.
Hence, for $g(t_1) < \overline{g}(t_1)$,

$$C^E(g(t_1), X, T - t_1) < \overline{g}(t_1) + d_1 - X \tag{15.16}$$

and for $g(t_1) \geq \overline{g}(t_1)$,

$$C^E(g(t_1), X, T - t_1) \geq \overline{g}(t_1) + d_1 - X \tag{15.17}$$

Now, let $C^A(\bullet)$ denote the value of the American call. From the above analysis, we see the early exercise condition at time t_1 is given by

$$C^A(g(t_1), X, T - t_1) = \begin{cases} g(t_1) + d_1 - X & \text{if } g(t_1) \geq \overline{g}(t_1) \\ C^E(g(t_1), X, T - t) & \text{if } g(t_1) < \overline{g}(t_1) \end{cases} \tag{15.18}$$

At any time before the ex-dividend date, the American option should reflect the probability that it will be exercised early. If the probability that the stock price exceeds $\overline{g}(t_1)$ at time t_1 is close to 1, then it is almost certain that the option will be exercised early. In this case the value of the option will approach the Black-Scholes valuation, with the ex-dividend date used rather than the option's contracted expiration date. Exhibit 15.2 shows the exercise policy.

Since the stock price $\overline{g}(t_1)$ that separates the exercise and nonexercise regions on the ex-dividend date is known in advance, a combination of hypothetical options can be constructed so as to perfectly match the payouts of the original American call option.

The value of an American call option on a stock that makes a single dividend payment prior to expiration can be replicated by (1) buying a European call option with strike X and maturity T, (2) buying a European call option with strike $\overline{g}(t_1)$ and maturity t_1, and (3) selling a European claim that provides the holder with the option to purchase the European call in part 1 of this strategy at time t_1 for a strike price of $\overline{g}(t_1) + d_1 - X$. The last contract in this replicating strategy is an option on an option and is referred to as a **compound option**.

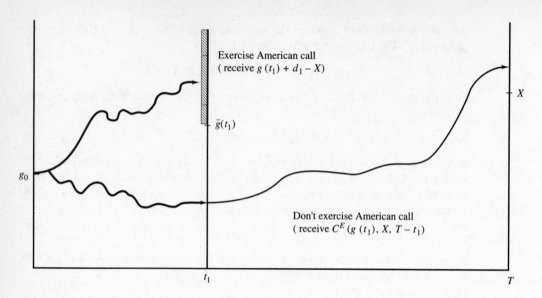

EXHIBIT 15.2   Exercise Boundaries for the American Call

The portfolio's cash flow at time t_1 depends on whether the stock price $g(t_1)$ is above or below the critical price $\bar{g}(t_1)$. If $g(t_1) < \bar{g}(t_1)$, then from equation (15.16) the value of the underlying call option ($C^E(g(t_1), X, T - t_1)$) is lower than the strike price, and the compound option expires worthless. If $g(t_1) > \bar{g}(t_1)$, then the compound option expires in the money, and its exercise value is $C^E(g(t_1), X, T - t_1) - (\bar{g}(t_1) + d_1 - X)$. Exhibit 15.3 summarizes the cash flows of the portfolio at time t_1.

Since the arbitrage portfolio in Exhibit 15.3 duplicates the boundary conditions, to avoid riskless arbitrage, the initial value of the American call must equal the value of this portfolio. That is, the initial American call value is given by

$$C(g(0), X, T) = C^E(g(0), X, T) + C^E(g(0), \bar{S}(t_1), t_1)$$
$$- CO(g(0), \bar{g}(t_1) + d_1 - X, t) \tag{15.19}$$

EXHIBIT 15.3   Replicating an American Call Option on a Dividend-Paying Stock

	Value at Date t_1	
Portfolio	$g(t_1) \le \bar{g}(t_1)$	$g(t_1) > \bar{g}(t_1)$
American call	$C^E(g(t_1), X, T - t_1)$	$\bar{g}(t_1) - X + d_1$
1. European call (strike X, maturity T)	$C^E(g(t_1), X, T - t_1)$	$C^E(g(t_1), X, T - t_1)$
2. European call (strike $\bar{g}(t_1)$, maturity t_1)	0	$g(t_1) - \bar{g}(t_1)$
3. Short position in a compound option on position 1 (strike $\bar{g}(t_1) - X + d_1$ and maturity t_1)	0	$-C^E(g(t_1), X, T - t_1) + \bar{g}(t_1) - X + d_1$

where $CO(\cdot)$ is the value of the compound option at time zero, with $C(g(0), X, T)$ representing the underlying option. If we had a formula to compute the value of the compound option, then we would have an analytical solution to the American call. The valuation formula for a compound option is presented in Appendix 15A.[2]

This modification of the Black-Scholes formula produces an American call price that is consistently lower than the incorrect procedure of using the Black-Scoles model and ignoring the dividend altogether.

The Barone-Adesi and Whaley Model

Barone-Adesi and Whaley extended a model to price American calls and puts developed by MacMillan to the case where the underlying stock pays a continuous dividend yield. The advantage of this model over the binomial lattice is that it is computationally more efficient. As a result, it is often used when theoretical option prices are required in real time or in empirical studies that require theoretical prices to be generated. The Barone-Adesi and Whaley model is described in Appendix 15B.

Dividend Policies and the Illusion of Profit Opportunities for Option Writers

Assume that on November 7, XYZ traded at $63. A January 50 call traded at $13 and a $3 dividend was due in one week. The in-the-money call was quoted for sale at near $13 for the entire week, while the price of the stock stayed near $63. On the ex-dividend date the stock dropped to $60 and the option dropped to $10.75. This seems to imply an option decline of 17.3 percent in one day, accompanying the $3 drop in stock price.

The option price sequence, however, is completely rational. Specifically, since the early exercise condition was met on November 6, all outstanding options should have been exercised. On November 7, new options written with the same strike and maturity began trading, and these prices were quoted at $10.75. Note that although such large price declines of the option can easily be forecast, they do not represent extraordinary profit opportunities for option writers. Of course, if some option holders are irrational and do not follow an optimal exercise policy, then some option sellers who were not assigned an exercise notice will be able to capture large profits.

---

[2] The compound option has already been discussed in Chapter 11 and will be encountered in future chapters. The first pricing model for a compound option model was developed by Geske.

Conclusion

This chapter has explored the problem of pricing options when the underlying stock pays continuous or discrete dividends. For European options, the analysis is quite simple. Specifically, the present value of all dividends that occur over the time to expiration is subtracted from the stock price, and the resulting price is used as the value of the underlying security in the Black-Scholes analysis. For American options, the analysis is more complex because dividends can be captured by exercising prior to the ex-dividend date. This chapter has investigated a few of the models that have been developed for this situation. Specifically, the binomial lattice option pricing model was adapted to take dividends into account. The Roll-Geske-Whaley model can be viewed as a limiting case of this model. Alternative numerical procedures are available for pricing. Perhaps the most notable is the Barone-Adesi and Whaley model, which is used extensively in theoretical and applied studies of option prices.

The incorporation of dividends is important because it permits models to be developed for pricing options on foreign currencies, stock indices, futures, and consumption commodities.

References

Barone-Adesi, G., and R. Whaley. "Efficient Analytical Approximation of American Option Values." *Journal of Finance* 42 (1987): 301–20.

Biger, N., and J. Hull. "The Valuation of Currency Options." *Financial Management* (Spring 1983): 24–28.

Black, F. "Fact and Fantasy in the Use of Options and Corporate Liabilities." *Financial Analysts Journal* 31 (1975): 36–41.

———. "The Pricing of Commodity Contracts." *Journal of Financial Economics* 3 (March 1976): 167–79.

Bodurtha, J., and G. Courtadon. "Efficiency Tests of the Foreign Currency Options Market." *Journal of Finance* 41 (March 1986): 151–62.

Brennan, M., and E. Schwartz. "The Valuation of American Put Options." *Journal of Finance* 32 (May 1977): 449–62.

———. "Finite Difference Methods and Jump Process Arising in the Pricing of Contingent Claims: A Synthesis." *Journal of Financial and Quantitative Analysis* 13 (September 1978): 461–74.

Brenner, M., G. Courtadon, and M. Subrahmanyam. "Options on the Spot and Options on Futures." *Journal of Finance* 40 (December 1985): 1303–17.

Courtadon, G. "A More Accurate Finite Difference Approximation for the Valuation of Options." *Journal of Financial and Quantitative Analysis* 17 (December 1982): 697–703.

Garman, M., and S. Kohlhagen. "Foreign Currency Option Values." *Journal of International Money and Finance* 2 (1983): 231–37.

Geske, R. "Pricing of Options with Stochastic Dividend Yield." *Journal of Finance* 33 (May 1978): 618–25.

_____. "The Valuation of Compound Options." *Journal of Financial Economics* 7 (1979): 63–81.

_____. "A Note on an Analytical Valuation Formula for Unprotected American Call Options on Stocks with Known Dividends." *Journal of Financial Economics* 7 (1979): 375–80.

Geske, R., and H. Johnson. "The American Put Valued Analytically." *Journal of Finance* 39 (1984): 1511–24.

Geske, R., and R. Roll. "On Valuing American Call Options with the Black-Scholes Formula." *Journal of Finance* 39 (June 1984): 443–55.

Geske, R., and K. Shastri. "Valuation by Approximation: A Comparison of Alternative Option Valuation Techniques." *Journal of Financial Quantitative Analysis* 20 (March 1985): 45–71.

Giddy, I. "Foreign Exchange Options." *Journal of Futures Markets* (Summer 1983): 143–66.

Grabbe, J. D. "The Pricing of Call and Put Options on Foreign Exchange." *Journal of International Money and Finance* 2 (1983): 239–53.

Kolb, R. *Options: An Introduction,* 2d ed. Miami: Kolb, 1993.

_____. *Option! Software for Options.* Miami: Kolb, 1993.

MacMillan, L. "Analytical Approximation for the American Put Option." *Advances in Futures and Options Research* 1 (1986): 119–39.

Ramaswamy, K., and S. Sundaresan. "The Valuation of Options on Futures Contracts." *Journal of Finance* 40 (December 1985): 1319–40.

Roll, R. "An Analytical Formula for Unprotected American Call Options on Stocks with Known Dividends." *Journal of Financial Economics* 5 (1977): 251–58.

Shastri, K., and K. Tandon. "Arbitrage Tests of the Efficiency of the Foreign Currency Options Market." *Journal of International Money and Finance* 4 (December 1985): 455–68. University of Pittsburgh.

Whaley, R. "Valuation of American Call Options on Dividend Paying Stocks: Empirical Tests." *Journal of Financial Economics* 10 (March 1982): 29–58.

Exercises

1. A stock is priced at $100. The volatility is 30 percent per year, and interest rates are 12 percent per year. The stock pays a dividend of $5 in two months.
   a. Ignoring the dividend, compute the price of an at-the-money European call option on the stock. The expiration date is 0.25 years away.
   b. Repeat Exercise 1a, but this time take into consideration the dividend.
   c. Use the results in Exercises 1a and 1b to establish bounds on the price of an American call option.
   d. Now treat the option as a pseudo-American call option, and compute the value of the call if the contract is exercised just prior to the ex-dividend date. Show that the bounds established in Exercise 1c can be improved upon.

2. Reconsider the stock in Exercise 1. Assume the risky part of the stock price follows a geometric Wiener process.
   a. Using a partition of $\Delta t = 1$ month, set up the lattice for the stock price process over three periods. At each node identify the value of the risky component of the stock and the value of the reserved proceeds for the dividend.
   b. Using the lattice, compute the price of a three-month American call option on the stock. Carefully identify all the nodes at which early exercise is optimal.
   c. Establish the initial replicating portfolio for the American call option.

3. The exchange rate is $0.5550 per deutsche mark. The current domestic interest rate is 9 percent. The German interest rate is 4 percent. Exchange rates have a volatility of 10 percent per year.
   a. Use the information to price a European call on the deutsche mark. The strike price is $0.60, and the time to expiration is 0.25 years.
   b. Explain why you could use the European pricing model to price an American option.

4. The exchange rate is $1.72 per British pound. The domestic interest rate is 8 percent, the British interest rate is 10 percent, and the volatility of exchange rates is 30 percent.
   a. Use a two-period binomial model to price an at-the-money European call that expires in two months.
   b. Use the two-period lattice to price an at-the-money American call that expires in two months.
   c. Use the result in Exercise 4a to price a European put option on the dollar, denominated in pounds.
   d. Is it possible to price an American put option on the dollar, denominated in pounds, without reconstructing a binomial lattice? Explain.

5. A futures contract is priced at $100. The volatility of the futures contract is 20 percent and the interest rate is 10 percent.
   a. Price a two-month at-the-money European call.
   b. Use put-call parity to price an at-the-money put option on the futures.

6. Reconsider the futures contract in Exercise 4. Using a two-period binomial lattice, price an American call with strike $110 on the futures. Identify any node where early exercise may be optimal.

7. A stock pays a continuous dividend yield of 2 percent per year. The current stock price is $100. Use Merton's model to price an at-the-money six-month European call. The interest rate is 5 percent per year and the volatility of the stock is 30 percent per year.

8. Reconsider Exercise 7. Use a two-period binomial lattice to compute the price of an at-the-money six-month American call. Is early exercise optimal at any node?

9. A stock follows a geometric binomial walk with $s_0 = \$100$, $u = 1.20$, $d = 0.8$, and $R = 1.05$.
   a. Compute a three-period lattice for the stock.

b. Establish the lattice of prices of a two-period at-the-money European call option.

c. Consider the lattice of European option prices. Now consider a one-period at-the-money compound call option written on this option. Compute the cost of the option, and indicate the replicating portfolio.

10. The futures price is $100. A 90-day European call option on the futures has a strike of $90. The volatility of the futures price is 30 percent per year, and interest rates are 4 percent per year. The price as given by Merton's model and the values of some sensitivity measures are given below.

Price	$11.874
Delta	0.7751
Gamma	0.0195
Theta	−8.32
Vega	14.45

a. Compute the initial replicating portfolio for the call option.

b. If the volatility increased by 10 percent, what would happen to the price of the option?

c. An otherwise identical American option on this futures contract is priced using a binomial lattice with 100 partitions. The theoretical value is $11.916. Estimate the value of the early exercise feature.

d. If the futures price is increased by $1, the American option price increases to $12.693. Use this information to estimate the delta value of the American call.

e. Interpret the gamma value of the European call option.

APPENDIX 15A

Geske's Compound Option Model

Geske considered the price of a compound call option with strike X_1 and maturity T_1. The underlying asset is a European call option with strike X and expiration date T where $T > T_1$. Geske showed that to avoid riskless arbitrage, the compound option must be priced as

$$C_0 = V_0 N_2(x, y; \rho) - F e^{-rT} N_2(x', y'; \rho) - X e^{-rT_1} N(x') \qquad (15A.1)$$

where $\quad x = \dfrac{\ln(V_0/V^*) + (r + \sigma^2/2)T_1}{\sigma\sqrt{T_1}}$

$$y = \dfrac{\ln(V_0/X) + (r + \sigma^2/2)T}{\sigma\sqrt{T}}$$

$$x' = x - \sigma\sqrt{T_1}$$

$$y' = y - \sigma\sqrt{T}$$

$$\rho = (T_1/T)^{1/2}$$

and V^* satisfies $\quad V^* N(z) - F e^{-r(T-T_1)} N(z - \sigma\sqrt{T_1}) - X = 0$

where $\quad z = \dfrac{\ln(V^*/X) + (r + \sigma^2/2)(T - T_1)}{\sigma\sqrt{T_1}}$

and $N_2(z_1, z_2; \rho)$ is the probability that Z_1 is less than z_1 and Z_2 is less than z_2, where Z_1 and Z_2 are standard normal random variables with correlation ρ.

APPENDIX 15B

The Barone-Adesi and Whaley Model

In the Barone-Adesi and Whaley model, the cost of carrying the underlying commodity is b, where b is a constant, proportional rate. For a nondividend-paying stock, the cost of carry is equal to the riskless rate (i.e., $b = r$), but for other commodities this may not be the case. In Merton's constant proportional dividend yield model, for example, the cost of carry is the riskless rate less the dividend yield (i.e., $b = r - q$). Like the MacMillan model, the Barone-Adesi and Whaley model approximates the option price by first approximating the exercise boundary at the current time t.

For a call option the exercise boundary at date t, above which the call is exercised, is approximated by $b(t) = s^*$, where s^* is the solution to the following equation:

$$s^* - X = C^E(s^*, t) + [1 - e^{(b-r)(T-t)}N(d_1(s^*))]s^*/q_2 \qquad (15B.1)$$

where $\quad q_2 = \{(1 - m) + [(1 - m)^2 + 4n/k]^{1/2}\}/2$

$$k = 1 - e^{-r(T-t)}$$

$$n = 2r/\sigma^2$$

$$m = 2b/\sigma^2$$

and $C^E(s, t)$ is the Merton European call price, given by

$$C^E(s, t) = S\, e^{(b-r)(T-t)}N(d_1(s)) - X\, e^{-r(T-t)}N(d_2(s))$$

where $\quad d_1(s) = [\ln(s/X) + (b + \sigma^2/2)(T - t)]/\sigma\sqrt{(T - t)}$

$$d_2(s) = d_1(s) - \sigma\sqrt{(T - t)}$$

Given the exercise boundary, the approximating call value is

$$\begin{aligned} C^A(s, t) &= C^E(s, t) + A_2(s/s^*)^{q_2} &&\text{when } s < s^* \\ C(s, t) &= s - X &&\text{when } s \geq s^* \end{aligned} \qquad (15B.2)$$

where $\quad A_2 = (s^*/q_2)[1 - e^{(b-r)(T-t)}N(d_1(s^*))]$

For the American put, the Barone-Adesi and Whaley approximation is given by first finding the exercise boundary $b(t) = s^*$ at time t, below which the option should be exercised. This point is approximated by solving the following equation:

$$X - s^* = P^E(s^*, t) - [1 - e^{(b-r)(T-t)}N(-d_1(s^*))]s^*/q_1 \qquad (15B.3)$$

where $q_1 = \{(1 - m) + [(1 - m)^2 + 4n/k]^{1/2}\}/2$

$k = 1 - e^{-r(T-t)}$

$n = 2r/\sigma^2$

$m = 2b/\sigma^2$

and $P^E(s^*, t)$ is the price of a European put option at date t with strike X and time to expiration of $T - t$. Given the boundary s^*, the American put is approximated by

$$\begin{aligned}
P^A(s, t) &= P^E(s, t) + A_1(s/s^*)^{q_1} & \text{when } s > s^* \\
&= X - s & \text{when } s < s^*
\end{aligned} \qquad (15B.4)$$

where $A_1 = (s^*/q_1)[1 - e^{-(b-r)(T-t)}N(-d_1(s^*))]$

CHAPTER 16

Exotic Options

In this chapter we discuss option contracts whose values depend on the path taken by the stock in reaching its final value. We also explore option contracts that have payouts linked to the performance of more than one asset. For example, we consider contracts that give the holder the right to purchase the best-performing of a finite number of assets for a predetermined price. Finally, we investigate a variety of exotic foreign currency contracts that decouple asset performance from exchange rate risk.

The primary objectives of this chapter are the following:

- To discuss path-dependent option contracts;
- To identify economic reasons for specific path-dependent contracts;
- To consider options with payouts linked to more than one asset; and
- To investigate exotic foreign currency contracts.

Path-Dependent Option Contracts

Let $S_0, S_1, S_2, \ldots, S_n$ be the sequence of observed prices of the underlying asset observed over the life of an option, with S_0 being the price at date 0 and S_n being the price at the expiration date. The payout of a simple call option at date n is given by C_n, where

$$C_n = \text{Max}[S_n - X, 0]$$

and X is the strike price of the option. Note that this payout depends only on the final stock price and not on the path that it took to reach its final value. That is, the final price of the option is independent of the path taken by the stock in reaching its final value. In contrast, the terminal value of a path-dependent option may well depend on the history of the price process up to its final value.

In this chapter, however, we illustrate how path-dependent options work. We shall often assume the contracts exist on a stock whose price can be represented by the two-period lattice in Exhibit 16.1. In this lattice, in each period the price increases by $1.20 ($u = 1.20$) or decreases by 20 percent ($d = 0.8333$). The initial stock price is $100 and the riskless rate per period is 10 percent. The risk-neutralized probability, θ, is given by 0.72727. The prices of an at-the-money European call and put are shown in Exhibit 16.2.

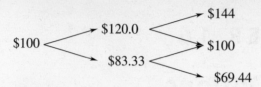

EXHIBIT 16.1   Prices of a Stock over a Two-Period Lattice

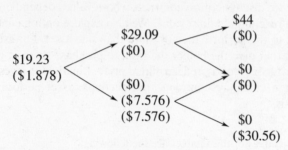

EXHIBIT 16.2   At-the-Money Call (Put) Prices

Lookback Options

A **lookback option** differs from a regular option in that the strike price is determined only at the exercise date; the strike price is determined by "looking back" over the path of prices that have occurred over the lookback period. Lookbacks differ according to how the effective strike price is determined. This is best illustrated by examples.

Lookback Options on the Minimum

The effective strike price at the expiration date of a lookback call option on the minimum is

$$X_n = \text{Min}\{S_1, S_2, \ldots, S_n\}$$

The terminal cash flow to the holder of a lookback call option on the minimum is

$$C_n = \text{Max}[0, S_n - X_n]$$

A lookback call option on the minimum price allows the holder to buy the underlying security at the minimum price that occurs over the period $[0, n]$. This period is referred to as the **lookback period.**

EXAMPLE 16.1   A small U.S. importer is negotiating a large transaction with a huge Japanese exporting firm. Since prices are negotiated in yen and payments are due upon receipt in six months, the importer is concerned about adverse movements in exchange rates over the interim. To entice the sale, the exporter grants the importer a six-month lookback option. With this contract, the importer can pay for the product at the lowest exchange rate that occurs over the granted period.

In foreign currency markets such contracts are often referred to as **most-favorable-rate options**.

Lookback Options on the Maximum

A lookback put option on the maximum allows the holder to sell the underlying instrument at the maximum price that occurred over the lookback period. The effective strike price over the lookback period is X_n, where

$$X_n = \text{Max}\{S_1, S_2, \ldots, S_n\}$$

and the terminal payout is P_n, where

$$P_n = \text{Max}\{X_n - S_n, 0\}$$

Call lookback options on the minimum and puts on the maximum almost always expire in the money. If the underlying asset pays no dividends, then the early exercise feature for the call is not valuable. As usual, early exercise of puts may be optimal.

Lookback Options on the Average

The terminal value of any lookback option is determined by first looking back over the path of prices in the lookback period and computing some statistic. In Example 16.1, the statistic was the minimum price over the time period. In theory, the statistic could have been any computable statistic. Examples include the range, the geometric mean, the arithmetic mean, and the standard deviation. If the statistic is the arithmetic mean, then

$$C_n = \text{Max}\{S_n - \bar{A}, 0\}$$
$$P_n = \text{Max}\{\bar{A} - S_n, 0\}$$

where $\bar{A} = \Sigma_{i=0}^{n} S_i/n$

Such contracts are called lookbacks on the average over the period $[0, n]$.

EXAMPLE 16.2   Consider a jeweler who purchases gold at market prices continuously throughout the year. The jeweler uses the gold in all of his products, most of which are sold over the Christmas season. The jeweler is concerned that prices of gold could steadily decline over the year, culminating in very low prices during the Christmas season. These low prices could drag down the prices of his finished products, giving him net losses. To cap the risk of this event, the jeweler purchases lookback puts on the average. If the final gold price is lower than the average price over the year (which is his effective price), then the option will pay out the difference. The number of contracts purchased should be close to the total number of units of gold the jeweler plans on purchasing throughout the year.

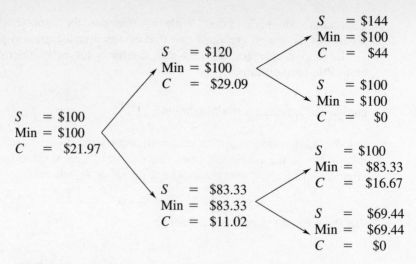

EXHIBIT 16.3   Pricing Lookback Call Options on the Minimum

EXAMPLE 16.3   **Pricing Lookback Options on the Minimum and Maximum**

Exhibit 16.3 shows the four possible paths the stock in Exhibit 16.1 could take over the two periods. The terminal value of the lookback call option on the minimum is shown in Exhibit 16.3. We can obtain the value of the option at each node in the lattice with the usual backward recursion. The results are also shown in Exhibit 16.3.

Exhibit 16.4 shows the stock prices and maximum to date at each node along each path as well as the corresponding price of the lookback put option on the

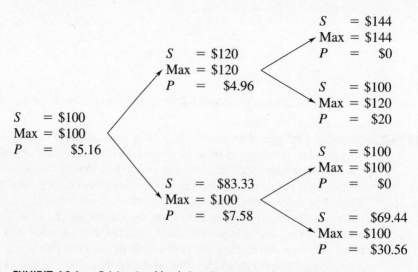

EXHIBIT 16.4   Pricing Lookback Put Options on the Maximum

maximum. Note that lookback options on the minimum and maximum are much more expensive than their ordinary at-the-money European counterparts. Note also that if a trader purchased a lookback call on the minimum and a lookback put on the maximum, then at the expiration date the payoff would be $Max\{S_i\} - Min\{S_i\}$. This corresponds to the profit of buying at the lowest price and selling at the highest price, and this strategy represents the maximum profit that could be obtained by trading in the stock over the lookback period.

EXAMPLE 16.4   **Pricing Lookback Options on the Average**

Exhibit 16.5 shows the lattice of stock prices, together with the accumulated arithmetic average to date and the prices of the lookback calls on the average. For example, consider the up-down path. If an upmove occurs, the average changes from $100 to $110 ([$100 + $120]/2) and ends up at $106.67 ([$100 + $120 + $100]/3). To compute the lookback prices, we start with their terminal values in the second period and do the usual backward recursion.

In these examples the initiation period began immediately. (That is, the lookback period was from time 0 to the second period. If the lookback period began only in the first period, then the averages at each node would be different, as would the option price.) The averages and call option prices for this case are shown in Exhibit 16.6.

Note that option prices have to be computed along all possible paths. If, for example, there were 3 periods, then 8 paths would have to be constructed. Indeed, the number of paths doubles with each additional period. Hence, if 10 periods were

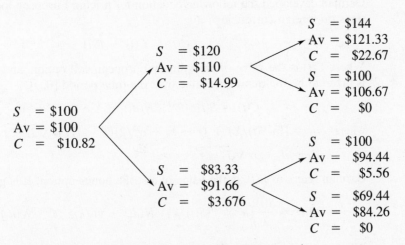

EXHIBIT 16.5   Lookback Call Options on the Average

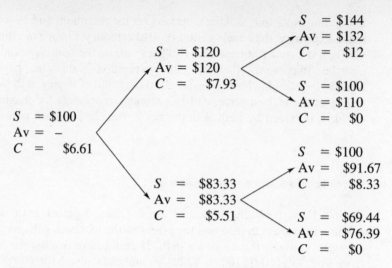

$$S = \$144$$
$$Av = \$132$$
$$C = \$12$$

$$S = \$120$$
$$Av = \$120$$
$$C = \$7.93$$

$$S = \$100$$
$$Av = \$110$$
$$C = \$0$$

$$S = \$100$$
$$Av = -$$
$$C = \$6.61$$

$$S = \$100$$
$$Av = \$91.67$$
$$C = \$8.33$$

$$S = \$83.33$$
$$Av = \$83.33$$
$$C = \$5.51$$

$$S = \$69.44$$
$$Av = \$76.39$$
$$C = \$0$$

EXHIBIT 16.6   Lookback Options on the Average with a Delayed Start

used, the number of nodes would be 2^{10}. This type of exponentially growing lattice causes computational problems, even if calculations are done on fast computers. Fortunately, in most cases, alternative methods can be used to reduce the computational complexity. Analytical solutions are often available for the case when the underlying lattice converges to a geometric Wiener process.

EXAMPLE 16.5   **The Garman Lookback Call Option on Foreign Currency**

Garman developed the following equation for pricing European lookback call options on foreign currencies:

$$LC(t) = C(t) + B(t) \tag{16.1}$$

Where $C(t)$ is the value of an ordinary European call option, and the strike price is taken to be the minimum value over the time period $[0, t]$,

$$C(t) = S(t)e^{-r_F(T-t)}N(d_1) - X e^{-r(T-t)}N(d_2) \tag{16.2}$$

where $d_1 = [\ln(S(t)/X) + (r - r_F + \sigma^2/2)(T - t)]/\sigma\sqrt{T - t}$
   $d_2 = d_1 - \sigma\sqrt{T - t}$

Garman refers to $B(t)$ as the value of a strike bonus option. It is given by

$$B(t) = \frac{S(t)}{\lambda}[e^{-r(T-t)}(S(t)/X)^{-\lambda}N(d_1) - (1/\lambda)e^{-r_F(T-t)}N(d_2) \tag{16.3}$$

where $\lambda = 2(r - r_F)/\sigma^2$
   $d_1 = [\ln(X/S(t)) + (r - r_F - \sigma^2/2)(T - t)]/\sigma\sqrt{T - t}$
   $d_2 = d_1 - 2(r - r_F)\sqrt{T - t}/\sigma$

The strike price bonus captures the notion that the the effective strike price in the future may be lower than the current minimum price X.

For the lookback option on the average, an analytical approximation to the price is given by Ritchken, Sankarasubramanian, and Vijh.

Average-Rate Options

An average-rate option is an option on the average. Average-rate call and put options have terminal values given by

$$C_n = \text{Max}[\overline{A} - X, 0]$$
$$P_n = \text{Max}[X - \overline{A}, 0]$$

where $\overline{A} = \Sigma_{i=0}^{n} S_i/n$

Options with payouts depending on the average have become increasingly popular. These contracts are often referred to as **Asian options** to distinguish them from European and American options. The terminology is somewhat confusing because average-rate options can be European or American.

There are many reasons traders may desire average-rate option contracts. For example, many traders are keen to cap the total expense of ongoing transactions over finite time horizons. Rather than capping the cost of each individual transaction using European options, they may prefer a contract that pays out if aggregate expenses are above some limiting threshold.

EXAMPLE 16.6   Consider a builder who has just won a contract to build multiunit homes. The builder knows that a stream of lumber purchases will be necessary over the fixed time horizon and would like to purchase a contract that would provide protection against the total cost of lumber exceeding a planned threshold value. Since the lumber purchases are made frequently over the lifetime of the project, the price protection required is more likely linked to the average price over the period than to any individual end-of-period price.

EXAMPLE 16.7   Pricing Average-Rate Options

Exhibit 16.7 shows the values of a two-period at-the-money European averaging option at all nodes. As the number of intervals, n, over the time period is increased, the value of the average-rate option decreases rapidly until n reaches around 15. Further increases in n do not affect the option price significantly. This behavior is similar to the reduction in portfolio variance obtained by diversifying among different stocks. The largest reductions occur when there are only one or two stocks

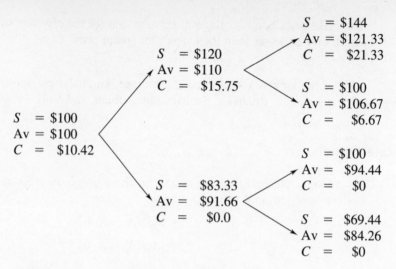

EXHIBIT 16.7   Pricing Average-Rate Options

in the portfolio. When there are more than 15 securities, the benefits of diversification are marginal. Similarly, as the number of points over which the average price is calculated reaches 15 or 20, the variance of the average (and hence the price of the averaging option) stabilizes. Under the usual Black-Scholes assumptions, Ritchken, Sankarasubramanian, and Vijh have developed analytical approximation models for the price of an average-rate option.

Volatility Options

So far we have only considered option contracts on an arithmetic average. Option contracts could exist on other statistics accumulated over time, such as the median, the range, the variance, or the standard deviation. Options on volatilities actually make considerable sense. For example, consider a trader who plans on selling regular options. The trader is concerned that over the time period, volatilities will steadily rise. Rather than attempt to establish vega-neutral positions, the trader may want to purchase a contract that pays out if the volatility over the trading period exceeds a particular threshold.

Many traders who accumulate positions in options are concerned that the volatilities on the underlying will change dramatically. Rather than establish a vega-neutral portfolio, such traders may want to hedge against massive volatility moves over a time period. For example, wide fluctuations in exchange rate volatilities may be of considerable concern to a foreign currency trader. Perhaps this trader does not want to bear the risk of an expanding exchange rate volatility. Since the trader is concerned with future volatility rather than historical volatility, perhaps a contract could be designed that has payouts conditional on the future implied volatility of a particular option contract. Alternatively, perhaps an index could be established that captures the overall volatility in a market, and this index could serve as the basis for a futures and/or options contract.

EXAMPLE 16.8   The Chicago Board Options Exchange (CBOE) Market Volatility Index (MVI) is based on the implied volatilities of the S & P 100 stock index options. The MVI provides a reliable estimate of short-term stock market volatility. The index is based on the implied volatilities of eight different option series and is updated almost continuously. Since the S & P 100 index option contract accounts for over 75 percent of the total number of index options traded in the United States, the MVI fully reflects current market conditions. Futures and options could be written against this underlying volatility index. Such volatility derivatives could be used to hedge the market volatility risk of portfolios that contain optionlike features. In addition, such contracts could provide traders with a mechanism for directly betting on the direction of the volatility.

EXAMPLE 16.9   During the trading day, a trader accumulates an enormous position in particular at-the-money call and put options. The overall delta value of the position is not that large, but the vega exposure is significant. As discussed in Chapter 10, the trader could immunize the position and make the portfolio vega-neutral. However, the trader does not want to alter the delta value of the position and is reluctant to totally rearrange the position so that it is both delta- and vega-neutral. If futures were available on the volatility itself, then the trader could sell such contracts to reduce the vega exposure. In particular, assume the vega exposure was $500. This means that if the volatility decreased from its current level of 30 percent to 29 percent, the trader would lose $500. To hedge against this event, the trader could sell futures contracts on the volatility index. Since the price of a volatility futures moves directly with the volatility, a 1 percent change in the volatility elicits a $1 change in the futures contract. Assume the futures contract had a multiplier of 100. Then the appropriate number of futures contracts to sell would be 5. Alternatively, if options traded on the volatility, then the appropriate number of options to trade could be determined once the delta value of the option was known.

Barrier Options

A **barrier option** is a contract where the payoff depends on whether or not the underlying asset reached a predefined "barrier" price during the life of the option. There are several common barrier options, which differ only in what happens if a barrier is hit.

An **immediate rebate barrier option** is one that pays out a given rebate as soon as the barrier is reached. One such contract is an **up-and-out call option,** which has a terminal payout of Max$[0, S_n - X]$ only if the stock price fails to reach a certain level, H say, over the time to expiration. If the price does reach H or higher, then the contract is automatically exercised and the holder receives a rebate of $H - X$.

EXAMPLE 16.10   **Capped Stock Index Options**

Capped stock index call (put) options on the S & P 100 and S & P 500 indices trade on the CBOE. These contracts are similar to European stock index options with the exception that they are immediately exercised whenever the closing price is 30 points or more above (below) the strike price. Based on historical data from 1987 to 1991, the holder of a four-month at-the-money capped call (put) stock index option would have just over a 40 percent chance of reaching the barrier price.

The rebate of the barrier option need not equal the intrinsic value. **Knockout options** are ordinary European options that are "knocked out" and made worthless if the barrier is reached. With a **down-and-out call option,** if the stock price falls below a critical level, H say, the option immediately expires worthless. An **up-and-out put** expires worthless if an upper price is penetrated.

Knockout options are cheaper than ordinary options and may be more desirable to traders who want to insure against adverse moves in the underlying asset only if prices are in some region.

EXAMPLE 16.11   A buyer of a stock at $100 wants protection against price declines only if the path of the stock never crosses $120. If the price does cross $120, then no downside protection is deemed necessary. Rather than buying an ordinary put, the holder chooses to buy an up-and-out put with barrier at $120.

To value barrier options on a binomial lattice, we change only the early exercise condition at each node of the usual binomial lattice. If the barrier is hit, then the rebate, if any, is immediately applied.

EXAMPLE 16.12   Consider the two-period binomial lattice in Exhibit 16.1. How do we price an at-the-money up-and-out call option with a cap of $118 and an immediate rebate? If an upmove occurs in the first period, the threshold is reached and a rebate equal to $118 − $100 is immediately paid out. The value of the contract at all nodes is shown in Exhibit 16.8.

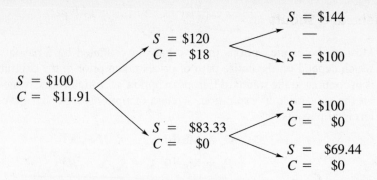

EXHIBIT 16.8   Valuing a Barrier Option

Another type of barrier option is a **knock-in option.** Such an option "knocks in" only if a barrier price is attained. A **down-and-in call option** is a call that comes into existence only when the barrier, $H(H < X)$, is reached. Similarly, an **up-and-in put** is created only if the barrier, $H(H > X)$, is reached. The rule that ignites or extinguishes a barrier option may be relatively complex. For example, a **baseball option** is a regular call option that is knocked out (worthless) if the closing price falls below a barrier on three separate occasions prior to expiration.

EXAMPLE 16.13   **Pricing a European Down-and-In Call Option**

Under the usual Black-Scholes assumptions, the value of a European down-and-in option that comes into existence only when the barrier $H(H < X)$ is reached is given by

$$C(0) = S(0)e^{-r_F T}(H/S(0))^{2\lambda}N(d_1) - X\, e^{-rT}(H/S(0))^{2\lambda-2}N(d_2) \qquad (16.4)$$

where $\lambda = [r - r_F + \sigma^2/2]/\sigma^2$

$d_1 = \ln(H^2/S(0)X) + \lambda\sigma^2 T]/\sigma\sqrt{T}$

$d_2 = d_1 - \sigma\sqrt{T}$

Here we have assumed the underlying contract is a foreign currency. If it is a commodity that pays out a yield or has a convenience yield, replace r_F by the yield.

Forward start options are options paid for in the present but received at a prespecified future date. They can be viewed as knock-in options that become ignited after a particular date. Since these options cannot be exercised over the lockout period, they are less valuable than American options, which have no lockout period.

Cliques, Ladders, and Shouts

Most of the exotic options that we have investigated have payouts at expiration which depend on the entire path of prices taken prior to the expiration date. This is in contrast to the standard European option's terminal value, which is based only on the spot price at expiration. A class of options exist that have the following terminal payouts:

$$C_n = \text{Max}[0, S_n - X, H - X]$$
$$P_n = \text{Max}[0, X - S_n, X - H]$$

where H is determined according to a particular rule. If, for example, $H = X$, then the option is an ordinary option. If $H = \text{Max}\{S_i\}$, then the call is a special type of lookback on the maximum. If H is the stock price at a single predetermined date, then it is a **one-click option.** Such a contract can be used to hedge the price at a particular date, such as year-end. If H is some predetermined level, if attained by the stock price, else X, then the option is a **one-rung ladder option.** If H is S at any contemporary moment chosen by the buyer, then the option is a **shout option.**

EXAMPLE 16.14   A trader buys a shout call option on the deutsche mark with $X = \$1.60$. Assume that at some point the exchange rate is $\$1.66$, and the holder decides to shout. The holder is guaranteed to receive ($\$1.66 - \$1.60$) times the multiplier of the contract at the expiration date. In addition, the holder is still long in what now is an ordinary call option with strike $\$1.66$.

EXAMPLE 16.15   **Pricing a Shout Option**

Consider our two-period lattice of prices in Exhibit 16.1. Assume an at-the-money (that is, $X = S_0$) call shout option was issued. The terminal value of the shout option depends on when the shout was issued; hence, the valuation procedure is more complex. We have to condition on all possible shout policies—that is, for a given shout policy, the terminal values will be known, and the usual backward valuation can proceed. The optimal value of the option corresponds to the shout policy that maximizes the value of the option over all policies.

Clearly, if the stock stayed below or at $\$100$, then the terminal value of the claim would be equal to that of an ordinary call option. Further, if the price increased every period, then the terminal value would be 44. This just leaves the up-down path. Now consider this path under the assumption that no shout was issued in the first period. Then the terminal value of the claim would be $\$0$. However, if a shout was issued, then $H = 120$ and the terminal value in the up-down node would be $\$20.0$. For this example, it is clearly optimal to issue a shout if an up move occurs in the first period. The value of the shout option at time 0 is $\$22.30$. The paths are shown in Exhibit 16.9.

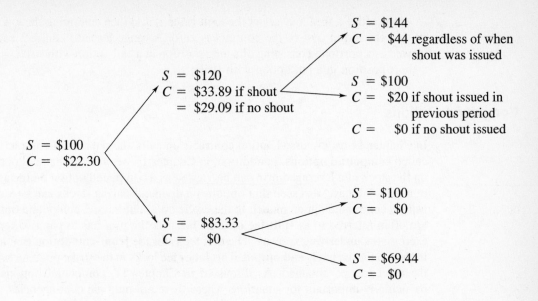

S = $120
C = $33.89 if shout
   = $29.09 if no shout

S = $144
C = $44 regardless of when
        shout was issued

S = $100
C = $20 if shout issued in
        previous period
C = $0 if no shout issued

S = $100
C = $22.30

S = $83.33
C = $0

S = $100
C = $0

S = $69.44
C = $0

EXHIBIT 16.9   Pricing a Shout Option

One click and one-rung ladders as well as one-shouts all have natural extensions to multi-click, multi-rung, and multi-shout contracts.

Range Forward and Conditional Forward Purchase Derivatives

So far, our discussion of exotics has focused on contracts that have option charac-teristics. However, there are many contracts that are similar to forward contracts. In a **range forward contract,** the buyer and bank agree on two exchange rates, s_1 and s_2. At maturity, the buyer will purchase the foreign currency at s_1 if the exchange rate is less than s_1 or at s_2 if the exchange rate is greater than s_2. The two prices s_1 and s_2 are set such that the initial value of the contract is zero.

Another variant of a forward contract is the **conditional forward purchase contract.** It is like a forward contract except that the buyer has the right to pull out of the contract by paying a penalty fee to the short prior to the settlement date.

EXAMPLE 16.16   A U.S. firm wishes to purchase British pounds in one year. The current forward rate is $1.62. A range forward contract can be entered into with $s_1 = $1.64 and $s_2 = $1.58. This contract binds the firm to purchasing at the spot rate after one year if the spot rate falls between $1.58 and $1.64. If the exchange rate is higher than $1.64, the firm pays only $1.64 per pound. However, if the exchange rate is below $1.58, the firm has to pay $1.58 per pound.

In practice a firm may select the high value s_1 and then determine the low rate so that the initial cost of the contract is zero. A range forward contract can be viewed as a portfolio consisting of a long position in a call option with strike s_1 and a short position in a put option with strike s_2.

Compound Options

In Chapter 11 we discussed option contracts on calls and puts. Such contracts are called **compound options.** In addition, in Chapter 17 we will see that call options on the stock of a leveraged firm can be viewed as a compound option on the assets of a firm. We have also seen that options on dividend-paying stocks can be valued using a compound option model. In the exotic option literature, compound options are often referred to as **split-fee options** because the user has to pay two fees to exercise the underlying security. The first fee is for the **front-end option** that locks in the fee for the **back-end option.** This latter fee locks in the strike price for which the asset can be obtained. As discussed in Chapter 11, compound options are particularly important for situations where there are multiple contingencies.

Options That Depend on More Than One Price

The terminal values of all the exotic options we have considered so far depend on the path of a single underlying commodity. Other contracts have terminal payouts or rebates contingent on information that may not be directly related to the path of prices. For example, a **poison put option** is an ordinary put option that can be exercised only if a particular event, such as a hostile takeover, occurs. A **credit risk option** is an option that pays out if some credit-related event, such as a drop in credit ratings, occurs. Finally, the payouts on some life insurance policies can be viewed as contingent claims that pay out only upon the death of the insured. In many of these problems, the pricing of the option contract is made complex because the exact maturity date of the contract is random. In addition, there is a family of exotic options with terminal values that depend on the path of more than one underlying asset. Such contracts include exchange options and options on the best-performing of two or more securities.

Exchange Options

As discussed in Chapter 11, an **exchange option** allows the holder to exchange one asset for another. The value of such an option at the expiration date, $E(T)$ say, is

$$E(T) = \text{Max}[S_2(T) - S_1(T), 0]$$

where $S_1(T)$ and $S_2(T)$ are the prices of the two assets at the expiration date. An exchange option can be viewed as a call on asset 2 with a strike price equal to the future price of asset 1, or a put on asset 1 with a strike price equal to the future value of asset 2.

EXAMPLE 16.17 A large firm tenders for shares of a smaller firm by offering one of its own shares, currently priced at $100, for one of the second firm's shares, currently priced at $80. The exchange offer is good for 60 days. Essentially, shareholders of the second firm have received an exchange option.

EXAMPLE 16.18 **Pricing Exchange Options**

Assume the prices of two assets follow a joint lognormal process with

$$dS_1/S_1 = \mu_1 \, dt + \sigma_1 \, dw_1$$

$$dS_2/S_2 = \mu_2 \, dt + \sigma_2 \, dw_2$$

where $E\{dw_1 \, dw_2\} = \rho \, dt$. Here, σ_1^2 and σ_2^2 are the variances of the logarithmic returns of the two stocks and ρ is the correlation of these logarithmic returns. Margrabe has shown that under the Black-Scholes assumptions, the fair price of an exchange option is $E(0)$, where

$$E(0) = S_2(0)N(d_1) - S_1(0)N(d_2) \tag{16.5}$$

and $d_1 = [\ln(S_2(0)/S_1(0) + \sigma^2 T/2]/\sigma\sqrt{T}$

$d_2 = d_1 - \sigma\sqrt{T}$

$\sigma^2 = \sigma_1^2 + \sigma_2^2 - 2\rho\sigma_1\sigma_2$

The above model can be used to value exchange options only if the underlying assets are traded securities and do not pay dividends.

Outperformance Options

An **outperformance call option** is a special exchange option that allows an investor to capitalize on anticipated differences in the performance of two underlying instruments or indices. The terminal payout of such an option is the return on one index minus the return on the second index (both expressed as percentages) times a fixed multiplier. The outperformance option can be viewed as an exchange option, where the underlying instruments are usually funds or indices. For example, the most common outperformance contract is the **bond-over-stock option,** which has a payout linked to the return of a bond fund less that of a stock fund, if the difference is positive.

Options on the Best of Two Risky Assets and Cash

An option on the best of two risky assets and cash has a terminal payout of $C(T)$, where

$$C(T) = \text{Max}\{S_1(T), S_2(T), X\}$$

EXAMPLE 16.19   Assume an investor requires a certain cash flow of X dollars at date T. Rather than buying X pure discount bonds, the investor purchases the above option. In this particular case $S_1(T)$ represents a diversified domestic stock fund and $S_2(T)$ represents the dollar value of a diversified foreign stock fund. In the worst case, the return on this investment is X dollars. However, the investor will participate in additional profits if the domestic return or foreign return is abnormally high.

The terminal payout of an option on the best of two risky assets and cash can be written as

$$C(T) = X + \text{Max}[\text{Max}\{S_1(T), S_2(T)\} - X, 0]$$

Hence, the initial value of this contract, $C(0)$, must equal the present value of the right-hand side. That is,

$$C(0) = X\,e^{-rT} + M(0) \tag{16.6}$$

where $M(0)$ is the value at date 0 of a call option on the maximum of two assets with strike X.

Options on the minimum of two risky assets are also encountered quite frequently. The terminal payout of such a contract is $W(T)$, where

$$W(T) = \text{Max}[0, \text{Min}\{S_1(T), S_2(T)\} - X]$$

Actually, the call on the minimum is related to the call on the maximum. The above equation can be rewritten as

$$W(T) = \text{Max}[S_1(T) - X, 0] + \text{Max}[S_2(T) - X, 0] - M(T) \tag{16.7}$$

Hence, a call on the minimum can be synthetically created by a portfolio containing long positions in the two ordinary options and a short position in the call on the maximum.

EXAMPLE 16.20   **Pricing Options on the Minimum of Two Assets**

Assume the prices of two assets follow a joint lognormal random walk, with

$$dS_1/S_1 = \mu_1\,dt + \sigma_1\,dw_1$$
$$dS_2/S_2 = \mu_2\,dt + \sigma_2\,dw_2$$

where $E\{dw_1\,dw_2\} = \rho\,dt$. As before, σ_1^2 and σ_2^2 are the variances of the logarithmic returns and ρ is the correlation of these logarithmic returns. Stulz has shown that the price of a call option on the minimum of two assets S_1 and S_2 is given by

$$W(0) = S_1 N_2(d_1,\ \gamma_1;\ v_1) + S_2 N_2(d_2,\ \gamma_2;\ v_2)$$
$$X\,e^{-rT}[1 - N_2(-d_1 + \sigma_1\sqrt{T}, d_2 + \sigma_2\sqrt{T};\ \rho)] \tag{16.8}$$

where $d_1 = [\ln(S_1/X) + (r + \sigma_1^2/2)T]/\sigma_1\sqrt{T}$
$d_2 = [\ln(S_2/X) + (r + \sigma_2^2/2)T]/\sigma_2\sqrt{T}$

$$\sigma^2 = \sigma_1^2 + \sigma_2^2 - 2\rho\sigma_1\sigma_2$$

$$v_1 = \frac{\sigma_1 - \rho\sigma_2}{\sigma\sqrt{T}}$$

$$v_2 = \frac{\sigma_2 - \rho\sigma_1}{\sigma\sqrt{T}}$$

$$\gamma_1 = [\ln(S_1/S_2) + \sigma^2 T/2]/\sigma\sqrt{T}$$

$$\gamma_2 = -\gamma_1 + \sigma\sqrt{T}$$

and $N_2(a, b; \rho)$ is the cumulative bivariate normal distribution function with correlation coefficient ρ.

Rainbow Options

Rainbow options are options on the best performer of a number of different assets. For example, an equity index fund with an international portfolio could receive the right to receive the better of Britain's FTSE-100 and Japan's TOPIX (a two-color rainbow) or the best of Germany's DAX, Britain's FTSE-100, and Japan's TOPIX (a three-color option). Pricing and hedging these contracts require knowledge not only of the variances but also of the correlations among asset returns. Hedging the correlation risk is particularly important to firms that offer these contracts.

A portfolio of call options on each of the indices in the rainbow obviously pays out more than the rainbow option. Hence, the cost of a rainbow option is less than the cost of the portfolio of regular options on the individual indices. Of course, the rainbow option will be more expensive than any individual ordinary option.

Spread Options

A **spread option** is an option in which the terminal payout is based on the difference between two prices.

EXAMPLE 16.21 A trader thinks that the yield curve is very steep and is likely to flatten. By purchasing an interest rate spread option, the trader can enter into a position that reflects this outlook. In particular, the payoff from the contract is given by Max$\{0, \Delta_{5,1}(0) - \Delta_{5,1}(T)\}K$, where K is a given multiplier and $\Delta_{5,1}(s)$ is the difference between five-year and one-year interest rates at date s. Such a contract is a put spread option with strike price given by the current spread, $\Delta_{5,1}(0)$. Pricing and hedging such contracts will be deferred to Chapter 24.

Foreign Exchange Exotics

Over the last decade many contracts have been introduced that have payouts linked to exchange rates and foreign stock market indices. In this section we consider a few of these contracts.

Recall from Chapter 15 that an ordinary foreign exchange option can be viewed as an option on a security that pays out a continuous dividend yield equal to the foreign riskless rate. If we assume that both the local and the foreign riskless rates are constant over the life of the option and that exchange rates follow a process

$$dS(t) = \mu S(t) \, dt + \sigma_S S(t) \, dw_s(t) \tag{16.9}$$

then Merton's continuous-dividend-yield option pricing model can be applied, and the European option can be priced as

$$C^E(0) = S(0)e^{-r_F T}N(d_1) - X \, e^{-rT}N(d_2) \tag{16.10}$$

where $d_1 = [\ln\{S(0)/X\} + (r - r_F + \sigma^2/2)T]/\sigma\sqrt{T}$

$d_2 = d_1 - \sigma_s\sqrt{T}$

In this section we shall assume that contracts trade on a foreign index. Let $G_F(t)$ be the value of the foreign index, in foreign currency, at date t. The dynamics of the index are given by

$$dG_F(t) = [\mu_G - \delta_G]G_F(t) \, dt + \sigma_G G_F(t) \, dw_G(t) \tag{16.11}$$

where δ_G is the continuous dividend yield on the stocks in the index and μ_G is the total instantaneous return on the portfolio of stocks that make up the index. In what follows we shall refer to the index as a foreign stock.

Foreign Stock Index Contracts Designated in Foreign Currency

Consider an investor who expects a certain foreign stock to appreciate significantly. The investor would like to purchase a call option on the foreign stock in the foreign country. The terminal payout of the contract in U.S. dollars is

$$C(T) = S(T)\text{Max}[G_F(T) - X_F, 0]$$

Here $G_F(T)$ is the price of the foreign stock in foreign currency and X_F is the strike price. The value of this European call option in the foreign country is given by the usual Black-Scholes or Merton model. Let $C_F(0)$ be the price of the option in the foreign country. In the United States the fair price of the contract would then be

$$C(0) = S(0)C_F(0) \tag{16.12}$$

where $C_F(0) = G_F(0)e^{-\delta_G T}N(d_1) - X \, e^{-rT}N(d_2)$

$d_1 = [\ln(G_F(0)/X_F) + (r - \delta_G + \sigma_G^2/2)T\}/\sigma_G\sqrt{T}$

$d_2 = d_1 - \sigma_G\sqrt{T}$

Foreign Stock Index Contracts Designated in Domestic Currency

Assume the same investor expected a certain foreign stock to appreciate significantly but was concerned about the risk of a decreasing exchange rate. The strategy of purchasing a foreign call designated in foreign currency could result in losses even though the stock price appreciated. For such an investor it is the dollar value of the foreign stock that is important, and an option on this value would be desirable. The terminal payout of this foreign equity call option struck in domestic currency is

$$C(T) = \text{Max}[G_F(T)S(T) - X, 0]$$

Here X is the strike price in U.S. dollars. Let $W(T) = G_F(T)S(T)$ be the terminal dollar value of the stock. Then

$$C(T) = \text{Max}[W(T) - X, 0]$$

If $G_F(T)$ and $S(T)$ are both lognormal, then it follows that $W(T)$ is lognormal. It is therefore not surprising to find that the valuation formula for such an option is similar to the Black-Scholes model. In particular, it can be shown that

$$C(0) = G_F(0)S(0)e^{-\delta_G T}N(d_1) - X\,e^{-rT}N(d_2) \qquad (16.13)$$

where $\quad d_1 = [\ln(G_F(0)S(0)/X) + (r - \delta_G + \sigma_W^2/2)T\}/\sigma_W\sqrt{T}$

$\qquad d_2 = d_1 - \sigma_W\sqrt{T}$

$\qquad \sigma_W^2 = \sigma_S^2 + \sigma_G^2 + 2\rho\sigma_S\sigma_G$

Foreign Stock Index Contracts with Guaranteed Exchange Rates

Consider an investor who expects a certain foreign stock to appreciate significantly. The investor anticipates investment funds to arrive in the future but is keen to participate in the perceived gain over the short term. If the investor is not concerned with exchange rate risk, then a suitable strategy may be to purchase a futures or forward contract on the foreign stock in the foreign country. Let $F(0, T)$ be the forward price at date 0 of such a contract that settles at date T in U.S. dollars. The forward price in the foreign country is given by the cost-of-carry model, namely,

$$F_F(0, T) = G_F(0)\,e^{(r_F - \delta_G)T}$$

Hence,

$$F(0, T) = 1/F_F(0, T) = G_F(0)\,e^{-(r_F - \delta_G)T} \qquad (16.14)$$

If, however, the investor is concerned about the risk of a potential drop in the exchange rate, then to hedge this risk the investor might desire a forward contract that prespecifies the exchange rate. A **guaranteed exchange rate forward contract** on a foreign stock is an agreement to receive on a certain date the stock's prevailing price in exchange for a predetermined foreign currency delivery price, with both prices converted to dollars at a predetermined exchange rate. Let

$F^*(0, T)$ be the forward price of this contract in units of the foreign currency. The terminal payout of this forward contract is

$$(G_F(T) - F^*(0, T))S^*$$

where S^* is the agreed-upon exchange rate. The fair forward price of this contract is determined as the value of $F^*(0, T)$ that makes the forward contract's value $F^*(0, T)$ at date 0 equal to 0. It can be shown that

$$F^*(0, T) = G_F(0) \, e^{(r_F - \delta_G - \sigma_{GS})T} \tag{16.15}$$

where $\sigma_{GS} = \rho \sigma_G \sigma_S$ is the instantaneous covariance between the foreign stock and exchange rates. Note that $F^*(0, T)$ is different from $F_F(0, T)$ in that the covariance term enters into the equation. In general, if this covariance term is positive, then $F^*(0, T) < F_F(0, T)$ reduced forward price has intuitive appeal. A positive covariance means that on average, when the foreign currency is expected to strengthen the stock price is expected to appreciate. As a result, an ordinary forward contract that has a delivery price specified in foreign currency and has payouts converted to dollars has a greater dollar value than a guaranteed exchange rate forward. Therefore, we would expect a lower forward delivery price if the exchange rate is guaranteed.

If the investor wants insurance against an increase in the foreign stock price, then using a **guaranteed exchange rate call option,** the terminal value is given by

$$C(T) = S^* \text{Max}[G_F(T) - X_F, 0]$$

While the terminal payout of this contract does not depend on exchange rates, the value of the contract at time 0 will depend on how exchange rates evolve jointly with the foreign stock. The fair price of this call option at date 0 is given by

$$C(0) = S^* G(0) e^{-(\delta_G + \alpha)T} N(d_1) - S^* X \, e^{-rT} N(d_2) \tag{16.16}$$

where
$$d_1 = [\ln(G_F(0)/X_F) + (r - (\delta_G + \alpha) + \sigma_G^2/2)T]/\sigma_G \sqrt{T}$$

$$d_2 = d_1 - \sigma_G \sqrt{T}$$

$$\alpha = r - r_F + \rho \sigma_S \sigma_G$$

Guaranteed exchange-traded options are often referred to as **quantos.**

Equity-Linked Foreign Exchange Contracts

Consider an investor who expects a certain foreign stock to appreciate significantly. The investor does not desire protection against losses in the equity but would like protection against exchange rates dropping below a threshold of S_L^*. A contract that accomplishes this goal is an **equity-linked foreign exchange call option.** The terminal payout of such a contract is

$$C(T) = G_F(T) \text{Max}[S(T), S_L^*]$$

$$= G_F(T)[S_L^* + \text{Max}\{S(T) - S_L^*, 0\}]$$

$$= G_F(T)S_L^* + G_F(T)\text{Max}\{S(T) - S_L^*, 0\}$$

The current value of this contract is

$$C(0) = G_F(0)S_L^* + \xi(0) \tag{16.17}$$

where $\xi(0)$ is the value at time 0 of a contract that pays out a random number of call options on the foreign currency. The number of call options is linked directly to the price of the foreign stock. It can be shown that the call price is

$$C(0) = G_F(0)S(0)e^{-\delta_F T}N(d_1) - S_L^* G_F(0)e^{-(\delta_G + \alpha)T}N(d_2) \tag{16.18}$$

where $\quad d_1 = \{\ln(S(0)/S_L^*) + (\delta_G + \alpha) + \sigma_S^2/2)T\}/\sigma_S\sqrt{T}$

$\qquad d_2 = d_1 - \sigma_S\sqrt{T}$

You-Make-It, You-Name-It Options

The variants of options available are endless. Examples of other exotics include dont options and digitals. A **dont option** is an option that the holder does not pay for unless it is *not* exercised. If the option is not exercised, then at the expiration date, the holder pays a predetermined premium. A **digital option** gives the holder a fixed constant if the price falls in some predetermined interval, and zero otherwise.

No doubt in the next decade some exotics will become so common that they will hardly be considered exotic. The average-rate option, for example, would fit into this category. At the same time, many exotics that currently are actively traded will become less desirable. As risks in the economy change, so do the needs of traders. The most successful exotic options have been those that provide clients with very precise instruments for managing very specific risk management needs. For example, the average-rate option serves a very precise need and is a much cheaper strategy for capping aggregate costs associated with ongoing purchasing activities over a given time period than other alternatives, such as purchasing a sequence of options on all interim transactions. In general, expensive options that are passive strategies are less likely to succeed among active traders. For example, lookback options on the minimum are expensive, and active traders are unlikely to use them. After all, traders believe they know the market, and indeed they are paid good salaries for that reason. Hence, they would argue that paying for a lookback option that automatically selects the best price will not take into account their knowledge. Such traders may prefer to purchase shout options since these products require active participation in deciding the time to shout. While their payouts are never as great as those of lookbacks (where it is the maximum stock price over the period), traders believe that they can get close to the same payout at a fraction of the cost. According to these active traders, lookbacks, ladder, and many barrier features are much more likely to be successful if they are incorporated into retail products such as warrants or bonds.

Investment banks are willing to work with their clients to design products that best meet their risk management needs. If risks do not grow linearly in the underlying asset, banks will create products that offset the nonlinear risk. For example, if exchange rate increases affect your business in a quadratic way and you want to hedge or cap the risk, then a payout linked to the square of the exchange rate may be in order. In this (somewhat unlikely) case, the firm may want a contract with terminal payouts Max[0, $S(T)^2 - X$]. Although such a contract does not currently exist, the pricing of such a claim, using binomial lattices (or other procedures), is possible. The role of the investment bank would be to identify, price, and market to the firm this "squared price" option. Since the square of the price can very rapidly become an enormous number, the chances are that this product will be very expensive. To reduce the cost, placing a barrier on the maximum profit may make sense. If this can be done without compromising the risk that the firm needs to hedge, then it is very effective. So now a *ba*rrier *s*quared *o*ption or BASO is born.

Conclusion

This chapter has explored a variety of exotic option contracts. Exotics are often path-dependent contracts. That is, their terminal values depend on the path of prices to that date. Lookbacks, average-rate contracts, and barrier contracts are the most common path-dependent contracts. Other contracts depend on information that may go beyond the path of prices. For example, some contracts have payouts that depend on the prices of more than one asset. Such contracts include exchange options and options on the best performer of two or more assets. A number of other exotic options exist. The main purpose of this chapter was to introduce some of the important ideas. For any exotic to be successful, it must fill a need that cannot be filled at a cheaper cost. That is, markets are made more complete with the existence of this contract.

This chapter used binomial lattices to illustrate the pricing of exotics. While the lattices do serve as conceptual aids in understanding the pricing mechanism, in practice pricing is accomplished using specialized models. In many of our examples, we have seen that the size of the problem grows exponentially in the number of periods. Each path needs to be accounted for; if 20 periods are used, the number of distinct paths is 2^{20}, which is an enormous number. In such cases specialized models are usually developed. Ritchken, for example, describes efficient procedures for pricing and hedging many types of barrier contracts.

Even if all paths do not need to be checked, the pricing of exotics can still be problematic. For example, if lattices are used to price contracts such as barrier or digital options, the convergence rate of prices can be particularly slow, and the number of partitions needed to get reasonable accuracy can be much larger than for an ordinary call option.

Investment banks that make markets in exotic products not only need to price these securities but also need to hedge them. This in turn means the sensitivity measures must be computed. The properties of the delta, gamma, theta, vega, and rho measures, for example, need to be well understood before a replicating scheme is initiated.

References

Benson, R., and N. Daniel. "Up, Over and Out." *Risk* 4 (June 1991): 17–19.

Brenner, M., and D. Galai. "Hedging Volatility in Foreign Currencies." *Journal of Derivatives* 1 (1993): 53–60.

Boyle, P., J. Evnine, and S. Gibbs. "Numerical Valuation of Mutivariate Contingent Claims." *Review of Financial Studies* 2 (1989): 241–50.

Derman, E., P. Karasinski, and J. Wecker. "Understanding Guaranteed Exchange Rate Contracts in Foreign Stock Investments." Goldman, Sachs & Co., 1990.

Dewyne, J., and P. Wilmott. "Partial to the Exotic." *Risk* 6 (March 1993): 38–43.

Dravid, A., M. Richardson, and T. Sun. "Pricing Foreign Index Contingent Claims: An Application to Nikkei Index Warrants." *Journal of Derivatives* 1(1993): 33–52.

Garman, M. "Recollection in Tranquility." *Risk* (March 1989): 16–18.

Goldman, B., H. Sosin, and M. Gatto. "Path Dependent Options: Buy at the Low, Sell at the High." *Journal of Finance* 34 (1979): 1111–27.

Gruca, E., and P. Ritchken. "Exchange Traded Foreign Warrants." *Advances in Futures and Options Research* (1993): 36–49.

Grunbichler, A., and F. Longstaff. "Valuing Options on Volatility." Working Paper, University of California at Los Angeles, 1993.

Hunter, W., and D. Stowe. "Path Dependent Options: Valuation and Applications." *Economic Review* (August 1992): 30–43.

Johnson, H. "Options on the Maximum of ZMinimum of Several Assets." *Journal of Financial and Quantitative Analysis* 22 (1987): 277–83.

Kemna, A., and A. Vorst. "A Pricing Method for Options Based on Average Asset Values." *Journal of Banking and Finance* (March 1990): 113–29.

Margrabe, W. "The Value of an Option to Exchange One Asset for Another." *Journal of Finance* 33 (March 1978): 177–86.

Reiner, E. "Quanto Mechanics." *Risk* 5 (1992): 49–53.

Ritch, D. "The Mathematical Foundations of Barrier Option Pricing Theory." *Advances in Options and Futures Research* 7 (1994): 267–311.

Ritchken, P. "Pricing and Hedging Barrier Options." *Journal of Derivatives,* forthcoming.

Ritchken, P., L. Sankarasubramanian, and A. Vijh. "The Valuation of Path Dependent Contracts on the Average." *Management Science* (November 1993): 1202–1213.

_____ . "Averaging Options for Capping Total Costs." *Financial Management* 19: 1990 35–41.

Ritchken, P., and T. Vital. "Pricing American Vulnerable Lookback Options." Working Paper, 1986.

Rubinstein, M. "Exotic Options." Research Program in Finance, Working Paper 220, University of California at Berkeley, 1991.

_____ . "Pay Now, Choose Later." *Risk* (February 1991).

_____ . "Options for the Undecided." *Risk* (April 1991).

_____ . "Two into One." *Risk* (May 1991).

_____ . "One for Another." *Risk* (July 1991).

———. "Somewhere Over the Rainbow." *Risk* (November 1991).

———. "Double Trouble." *Risk* (December 1991).

Rubinstein, M., and E. Reiner. "Breaking Down the Barriers." *Risk* (September 1991): 28–35.

———. "Unscrambling the Binary Code." *Risk* (October 1991)

Rumsey, J. "Pricing Cross Currency Options." *Journal of Futures Markets* 11 (1991): 89–93.

Rutiens, A. "Classical Replica." *Risk* 3 (1990): 33–38.

Stulz, R. "Options on the Minimum or the Maximum of Two Risky Assets." *Journal of Financial Economics* 10 (1982): 161–81.

Thomas, B. "Something to Shout About." *Risk* (May 1993): 56–58.

Whaley, R. "Derivatives on Market Volatility: Hedging Tools Long Overdue." *Journal of Derivatives* 1 (1993): 71–86.

Exercises

1. A stock is priced at $10. Construct a three-period lattice of prices, given that $u = 1.12$, $d = 1/u$, and $R = 1.08$.
   a. Use the lattice to price a three-period European call option that has a payout given by $Max[S^2 - 100, 0]$. What is the initial replicating portfolio for this contract? What is the value of the contract if it has an early exercise feature?
   b. Use the lattice to compute the price of a European put that has a terminal value given by $Max[100 - S^2, 0]$.
   c. The usual put-call parity condition is $C - P = S - Xe^{-rT}$. It is tempting to think that for this contract, $C - P = S^2 - X e^{-rT}$. Check whether this condition holds. Explain why this simple put-call parity condition does not hold.
   d. Establish the dynamic trading strategy that produces cash flows after three periods equal to the square of the stock price. What is the initial value of this replicating portfolio? Using the replicating portfolio as the underlying security, show that the put-call parity equation holds.

2. A stock is priced at $100. Construct a three-period lattice of prices, given $u = 1.5$, $d = 0.5$, $R = 1.10$.
   a. An averaging option exists that has reset dates in the first and third periods. That is, the terminal average is based on the average of the first- and third-period prices. The strike price is $100. Compute all possible paths; then, using backward recursion, compute the price of the call option.

3. Compute the price of the following down-and-in option on the pound. The current exchange rate is $1.40. The option comes into existence when the barrier of $1.35 is reached. The strike price is $1.38, the volatility is 25 percent, and the time to expiration is one year. The current interest rates in the United States and Britain are 5 and 6 percent, respectively.

4. The Nikkei 225 Stock Average Index is a price-weighted index of Japenese stocks. The CME trades a futures contract on the Nikkei 225. This cash-settled contract is valued at $5 × the futures price. At the delivery date, the futures price is taken to be equal to the level of the Nikkei index (in yen) multiplied by 5. For example, if the index is 28,000, the value of the futures contract is $140,000. Prior to the delivery date, the futures price is quoted as an implied Nikkei index level. The actual dollar value is this quoted value multiplied by 5.
   a. Explain why the usual cost-of-carry model cannot be used to price the futures contract.
   b. Assume the Nikkei index is at 24,000. Using equation (16.15), compute the theoretical dollar futures price. Assume the settlement date is one year away, the foreign risk-free rate is 5 percent, the volatility of the index is 30 percent, the volatility of exchange rates is 12 percent, and the correlation between the two is 0.5. Also take the dividend yield on the Nikkei index to be 1 percent.
   c. Assume a guaranteed exchange rate at-the-money European call option exists on the Nikkei index. Using equation (16.16), compute the fair price of the option.
5. A stock is priced at $10. Construct a lattice of prices for three periods, given that $u = 1.4$, $d = 1/u$, and $R = 1.10$.
   a. Consider a contract that pays out 10 shares if the stock exceeds $20, 5 shares if the price is between $14 and $20, and 1 share otherwise. Price this contract.
   b. Compute the price of a one-period option on the contract in Exercise 5a. Assume the strike price is $20.
6. a. "An averaging option is similar to an option on a portfolio. The averaging option provides insurance against an intertemporal portfolio of transactions rather than each on each transation. Similarly, an option on a portfolio insures the portfolio value, not each security in the portfolio." Is this statement true? Discuss.
   b. A firm purchases copper on an ongoing basis. From time to time the firm insures against an increasing copper price by buying call options on copper. Explain the benefit, if any, of using averaging options.
7. A trader is considering buying a rainbow option on the best performer of the S & P 500 Index and the FTSE 100 Index. Contrast this strategy to purchasing call options on the separate indices.
8. A trader holds a huge inventory in options. The position is delta-neutral, but it is extremely sensitive to changes in volatility. Explain how futures on the implied volatility can be used to hedge this risk. Also explain how options can be used to cap the vega risk.
9. Discuss how a rainbow volatility exchange option might work. This contract is an option on the most volatile of two or more foreign currencies.

CHAPTER 17

Corporate Securities

In the first part of this chapter we review the basics of risky debt issued by corporations. There is a vast array of corporate bonds. Unlike government securities, there are no standard corporate bonds and each issue must be considered separately. In our discussion of corporate bonds, we emphasize the types of option features encountered in many contracts. These include callable, puttable, extendible, and conversion options. Floating-rate bonds are also described. In the second part of this chapter we examine the risk structure of corporate bonds in more detail. A simple model of the required risk premium on corporate discount bonds is developed. In addition to valuing a discount corporate bond issue, we investigate pricing a subordinated debt issue, coupon bonds, convertible bonds, and some foreign currency bonds.

The primary objectives of this chapter are the following:

- To discuss corporate bonds and common options;
- To develop a model of the risk premium on corporate discount bonds; and
- To discuss relevant pricing issues associated with corporate securities.

Basics of Corporate Bonds

Bonds are issued by firms for the purpose of raising funds. In order to issue bonds, a firm must establish a legal contract with a third party called a **trustee,** who receives a fee for providing services. It is the duty of the trustee to ensure that the issuer stands by the provisions of the contract. The contract or **bond indenture** contains the restrictions and promises that back the bond. If the firm does not follow the covenants, the trustee, on behalf of the bondholders, may take legal action.

The indenture sets forth the term to maturity, face value, and coupon payments of the issue. In addition, it states whether the bond is secured or unsecured. A **secured issue** is one for which the firm pledges specific assets that may be used to pay the bondholders if the firm defaults on its payments. For example, the indenture may provide a legal right for the bondholders to receive proceeds from the sale of specific property if the firm defaults. Bonds that are backed by specific real property (land or buildings) are **mortgage bonds.** Many bond issues are unsecured.

That is, no specific assets act as collateral. Long-term unsecured issues are called **debentures,** while short-term maturities are referred to as **notes.**

If the issuing firm defaults, bondholders who have secured bonds have claims on the collateral. If these assets do not cover the full amount, the secured bond-holders join the other creditors as general or unsecured creditors. Since secured bonds receive preferential treatment, debenture holders will often require protection from the firm issuing bonds in the future. In some cases the indenture states that no secured bonds may be issued in the future unless the debentures are secured first. Alternatively, the indenture may allow the firm to issue debentures only if it first meets specific earnings conditions and subordinates the new debt to the current issues. Finally, debenture holders may require that the indenture contain restrictions on working capital and dividend policies.

The risk that the issuer will default on its obligations is called **credit risk.** The activity of the investment management process of evaluating this risk is known as **credit analysis.** Most large investment banking firms have their own credit analysis departments. Small bond investors usually rely on bond ratings published by commercial rating companies such as Moody's Investor Services and Standard and Poor's. Subscribers pay a fee for this service. Moreover, issuers of debt pay these firms to evaluate and rate their debt issues, as well as to update the rating throughout its life.

Exhibit 17.1 shows the ratings notation used by the two agencies. The highest-grade bonds, those considered to currently have almost no default risk, are AAA (Aaa) bonds. The next-highest-grade bonds in Standard and Poor's notation are AA, then A, BBB, BB, and B. C grades are also assigned. Bonds with ratings of BBB or better are referred to as **investment-grade bonds,** whereas lower-rated bonds are classified as **junk bonds.** For each rating category, Standard and Poor's may apply a + or − modifier. For example, a BBB+ rating is marginally higher than a BBB rating. Similarly, Moody's has a modifier of 1, 2, or 3. For example, Aa-1 is marginally higher than Aa-2.

Both agencies have a credit watch list that alerts subscribers when the agency is considering a change in the ratings of a particular issue. Of course, it is possible for the same issue to be ranked differently by the two agencies.

EXHIBIT 17.1   Credit Ratings

Moody's	S & P	Explanation
Aaa	AAA	Best quality
Aa	AA	High-grade
A	A	Upper medium quality
Baa	BBB	Medium quality
Ba	BB	Lower medium and speculative
B	B	Clearly speculative
Caa	CCC	Very speculative; may be in default
Ca	CC	Highly speculative; often in default
C	C	Lowest grade; very poor prospects
D	D	Debt in default; payments in arrears

The yield spread between two issues identical in all respects except for quality is referred to as the **quality yield spread.** As the ratings of an issue deteriorate, the required return for bearing the additional risk increases. Exhibit 17.2 shows the default experience for Moody's rankings.

As can be seen, the lower the rankings, the greater the default likelihood. No firm with the highest rating has ever defaulted. The reason for this is that as the condition of a firm deteriorates, the ratings are lowered. Exhibit 17.3 shows the probability defaulting in each consecutive year classified by their original ratings.

When a bond defaults, the firm is rarely liquidated. More often the firm files for protection from creditors and reorganizes under Chapter 11 of the bankruptcy code. At this time management negotiates a debt restructuring plan. The bond price will reflect some speculative value because there is a chance that interest and principal payments will be continued or the bond exchanged for some other security. If negotiations fail, the Chapter 11 filing is converted to a Chapter 13 filing, and the company is liquidated. The value of the bonds at this time will represent the present value of payments arising from the assets sold.

The bond indenture stipulates how the issuer may pay back the investors other than from scheduled coupon and principal payments. The most important alternatives are from sinking fund and call provisions. **Sinking funds** require the firm to retire a given portion of the bond issue each year. In addition to regular coupon payments, the sinking fund provides evidence of solvency of the firm and may prevent a crisis from developing at maturity. Moreover, if the firm cannot pay the cash into the sinking fund, the bondholders can demand their money back.

The sinking fund requirement can usually be fulfilled in one of two ways. The first is for the firm to purchase bonds in the open market and pay the trustee by delivering the required number of bonds. The second way is for the firm to make a cash payment to the trustee, who then will call the bonds for redemption at the

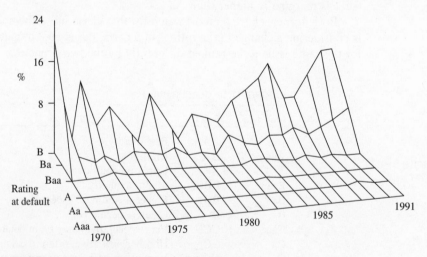

EXHIBIT 17.2   Corporate Bond Default Rates

Source: Moody's Investors Service. Reprinted with permission.

EXHIBIT 17.3 1991 Mortality Rates By Original Rating (1971–1991 Experience)

Rating		Years After Issuance							
		1 (in %)	2 (in %)	3 (in %)	4 (in %)	5 (in %)	7 (in %)	9 (in %)	10 (in %)
AAA	Yearly	0.00	0.00	0.00	0.00	0.00	0.05	0.00	0.00
	Cumulative	0.00	0.00	0.00	0.00	0.00	0.17	0.17	0.17
AA	Yearly	0.00	0.00	1.09	0.32	0.11	0.19	0.08	0.09
	Cumulative	0.00	0.00	1.09	1.41	1.52	1.71	1.79	1.87
A	Yearly	0.00	0.19	0.26	0.31	0.17	0.12	0.17	0.00
	Cumulative	0.00	0.19	0.45	0.76	0.93	1.08	1.49	1.49
BBB	Yearly	0.10	1.00	0.42	0.52	0.70	1.09	0.13	0.75
	Cumulative	0.10	1.10	1.51	2.03	2.72	3.96	4.09	4.81
BB	Yearly	0.00	0.91	3.66	1.93	2.78	4.33	0.00	2.66
	Cumulative	0.00	0.91	4.53	6.37	8.97	14.02	14.02	16.31
B	Yearly	1.72	4.67	9.16	5.61	6.64	4.24	5.07	3.58
	Cumulative	1.72	6.31	14.90	19.67	25.00	30.09	35.54	37.85
CCC	Yearly	1.55	14.84	11.74	9.23	3.82	1.54	N.A.	N.A.
	Cumulative	1.55	16.16	26.01	32.84	35.40	38.85	N.A.	N.A.

Source: From E. Altman "Revisiting the High Yield Bond Market." *Journal of Financial Management* (Summer 1992): 78–92.

sinking fund call price. The trustee selects the bonds on a lottery basis. Most sinking funds commence five to ten years after the bond's original issue date. The sinking fund provision represents an option for the firm in which the corporation can retire its debt at the sinking fund call price or at the market price, whichever is lower. Since this option works to the advantage of the firm (and hence the firm's shareholders) and to the disadvantage of the bondholders, the yield on a sinking fund bond issue should be higher than the yield on an otherwise identical straight bond.

An alternative strategy that reduces the risk created by large balloon payments is to issue **serial bonds**. A serial bond issue is divided into a series of different maturities. The issuing firm redeems each part of the series at the different dates.

Callable, Puttable, Extendible, and Conversion Features in Corporate Bonds

Many indentures have special provisions for repaying the loan. For example, the firm may retain the option to call in the bonds prior to maturity at a small premium over face value. This price is the **call price** or **redemption price** and may vary over time. It is highest in the early years of the loan and gradually decreases until it equals the face value at maturity. If interest rates decline, the firm has the option to repurchase the bonds at the call price and refinance at a lower rate. The expected gains to the firm from refunding a bond at a lower rate are equal to the expected losses the bondholders have to accept on their funds. Since bondholders recognize that the call feature will be exercised only in cases damaging to their interests, they will demand higher rates of interest (relative to otherwise identical noncallable bonds) to compensate for the additional risk borne. Almost all long-term corporate bonds and some Treasury bonds have call features.

Occasionally, a firm may issue a bond that gives the investor the option to demand early repayment at the bond's face value at a specified date prior to maturity. This bond is termed a **puttable bond.** The feature is particularly attractive since it allows the investor to withdraw funds early if interest rates rise, and it provides protection against deterioration in the credit quality of the issuing firm. Of course, the firm recognizes that a valuable feature has been granted, and this is reflected in a lowering of the required yield relative to that on a straight bond.

An **extendible bond** is a bond whose maturity and coupon payments can be extended at the option of the investor. When the new terms are established, the bondholder has the right to accept the terms or put the bond back to the issuer. Extendible bonds are often sold in an attempt to lower transaction costs associated with the alternative strategy of issuing shorter-term bonds and then rolling them over.

In addition to callable, puttable, and extendible options, other additional option features are often encountered in debt instruments. **Convertible bonds,** for example, provide the bondholder with the option to convert the bond into a particular stock. Optional foreign currency bonds allow the investor to select the currency (local or foreign) in which the principal is paid back. Oftentimes many option features are packaged together within one debt instrument. An example of this is the liquid yield option note (LYON) developed by Merrill Lynch, which is a convertible bond with both put and call features. This security is a zero-coupon convertible with a put option that provides the holder with the option to sell back the bond on its put date. Like ordinary convertibles, the bond can be converted into the issuer's common stock. Finally, the issuer retains a callable option.

Innovations in the Bond Market

Firms bring to market bonds that have innovative provisions to try to raise funds more efficiently or to better suit their needs. Since each bond must be designed to reflect the concerns of both the issuer and the investors, there are no standardized corporate bonds.

The process of designing financial instruments that best meet the goals of the firm, taking into account the situation of the firm and the demands made by investors, is referred to as **financial engineering.** In the last decade there has been a flood of new securities. Not all of them have been innovative. To be innovative a security must provide benefits either to the issuer or to a clientele of investors that would not otherwise be interested. Specifically, the security must enable an investor to realize a higher after-tax risk-adjusted rate of return or enable the issuer to realize a lower after-tax cost of funds than was possible prior to the introduction of the security. A new security that accomplishes this makes the market more efficient, or more complete. A new security that does not accomplish this provides no added value to the issuing company's shareholders.

EXAMPLE 17.1   As an example of designing a debt instrument that meets the goals of the firm, consider an oil company whose cash flows fluctuate with the market price of oil. Rather than issuing a fixed-income bond, such a firm may be better off linking its interest and/or principal payments to a well-defined oil index. Such a bond gives the firm protection against the volatility of oil prices. Specifically, should oil prices decline, causing company revenues to drag, at least the cost of servicing the debt will also decline. Another example is a multinational company that issues foreign currency bonds, where the face value is denoted in a different currency from the local currency. Such bonds may serve to hedge exchange rate risk from the revenues generated in the foreign country.

While many debt innovations are created to reallocate risk and reduce required yields, other innovations are designed to reduce transaction costs, for tax arbitrage reasons (extendible notes), or to reduce agency costs. An example of the latter is the puttable feature on extendible bonds, which provides the investor with protection against a deterioration in credit quality of the firm.

There are a huge variety of bonds, and new types continue to emerge in response to changes in economic conditions. For example, in countries with high inflation, investors will not want fixed-coupon bonds but rather bonds that give a fixed real return. In such countries, a great demand will exist for bonds with payments indexed to the rate of inflation.

Floating-Rate Notes

Index bonds are bonds whose payments are tied to some price index. A special type of index bond is a **floating-rate bond.** Such bonds have coupon payments pegged to the yield of a particular interest rate such as LIBOR or the yield on a Treasury security. The interest rate that the borrower pays is reset periodically. For example, the rate might be reset every six months to the current T-bill rate plus 100 basis points.

Floating-rate notes were innovative, since they reduced transaction costs. For example, an investor considering a strategy of rolling over short-term instruments (e.g., T-bills) may find a floating-rate note attractive since it substitutes a one-time transaction fee for the repeated transaction costs of the rollover strategy.

The value of a floating-rate note depends crucially on the coupon payment rule. Most floaters employ a coupon rule that is based on the T-bill or LIBOR rate. For example, the coupon could be defined as the six-month T-bill yield plus a premium to reflect the credit risk of the issuer.

EXAMPLE 17.2 A firm provides variable-rate financing to purchasers of its products. To provide financing to one of its largest customers, it needs to raise $20 million in new capital. To match the fluctuating interest rate received from the customer, the firm borrows at a rate that is also variable. By selling $20 million worth of floating-rate notes, the firm can better hedge interest rate risk.

EXAMPLE 17.3 The Citicorp floater has a maturity in May 2004 and pays semiannual coupons on May 1 and November 1. The coupon rate on May 1 is based on the simple average of the six-month bond-equivalent yields on T-bills auctioned October 8 through October 21 of the previous year. Similarly, the November 1 coupon is based on the average six-month bond-equivalent yield on T-bills auctioned April 7 through April 20 of the same year. The markup is 105 basis points for the first five years, 100 basis points for the next five years, and 75 basis points thereafter.

In Example 17.3, the markups at future reset dates are not the same but at least are known. In other contracts, the markups are determined at the reset dates according to spreads between certain observable yields. In most simple floating-rate notes, however, the markup, or yield spread, is constant.

There are many variations on floating-rate notes, including call features, issued by the firm, or conversion features that allow the investor to transfer to a fixed-rate note. In addition, the coupon rate may have a floor or a ceiling. Put features, whereby the holder can redeem the investment at par at particular coupon payment dates or after some predetermined date, may also be present. **Capped floaters** have caps placed on the interest rate. **Convertible floaters** permit the issuer to convert to fixed-rate debt during a fixed period. **Drop-lock floaters** automatically convert to fixed-interest-rate debt when rates fall below a stated floor. **Double drop-lock floaters** are similar except they require rates to be below the floor for two consecutive interest-setting dates. **Step-down floaters** are long-term floaters where the markup above the reference interest rate declines over time. Finally, **inverse floaters** pay interest in an inverse relationship to movements in a benchmark interest rate.

Prices of Floating-Rate Notes

Consider a firm that can borrow short-term at the six-month LIBOR rate. Rather than repeatedly borrowing short-term over the next 10 years, the firm decides to issue a $100 million 10-year floating-rate bond, where the semiannual coupon payment is linked to a rate such as six-month LIBOR. Assume there is no markup at each reset date. If we ignore default risk for the moment, then the 10-year floating-rate note should sell at par on its reset dates. The logic for this proceeds as follows. Recall that we have assumed the issuer is always able to borrow short-term at LIBOR flat. Now consider the pricing of the floating-rate note in 9 1/2 years. At that time the note would be identical to six-month LIBOR paper and would therefore sell at par. In 9 years, the interest payment in six months' time would be set at the LIBOR rate. An investor who held the floating-rate note for six months would receive the same interest as on six-month LIBOR paper and would then would be able to sell the floating-rate note at par. Therefore, in 9 years' time, holding the floating-rate note for six months would be a perfect substitute for holding six-month LIBOR paper. As a result, the floating-rate note in 9 years' time must be priced at par. Repeating this logic period by period shows that at each reset date the floating-rate note should sell at par.

Of course, the above analysis is extremely simplistic, since it does not take default risk into account. If we allow for the possibility of credit downgrades, then the strategy of combining LIBOR flat borrowing for the first six-month period, followed by semiannual rollovers at uncertain spreads over LIBOR for the next 9 1/2 years, is not a perfect substitute for a 10-year floating-rate note. Indeed, while A-rated firms may be able to borrow for six months at LIBOR flat, they are not able to issue 10-year floating-rate notes at LIBOR flat. Investors demand a risk premium to compensate for the potential risk of future downgrades in credit quality ratings. An A-rated firm would probably be able to issue the floating-rate note at a small premium above LIBOR. The exact size of this premium depends on the maturity of the bond and on the assessment of potential downgrades in the quality of the firm over the remaining time period. For an A-rated firm that could borrow short-term at LIBOR, the premium on a 10-year floater might be of the order 30 to 150 basis points.

In general, the price risk of a floating-rate note is quite small. Large deviations from par occur if reset dates are very infrequent, if the credit quality rating is changed, and if there are caps and floors on the index, as well as other option features.

More on Credit Risk and Risk Premiums

The determination of the fair market price for any corporate bond is more complex than pricing default-free fixed-income securities. First, the many option features in corporate bonds create difficulties since the stream of coupon payments is no longer certain; moreover, option pricing models are required to ascertain the values of the option features. Second, even without the option features, because of default risk, future coupons are not certain. In this section we provide more information about the nature of the risk premiums, and we investigate a very simple model for evaluating the risk premium required to compensate holders of certain corporate bonds.

The default risk premium of a bond depends on its time to maturity. For high-quality-rated firms, the probability of default lessens as time remaining to maturity decreases. For lower-grade categories of bonds, the risk of default may not increase with maturity. Indeed, as the maturity date gets closer, it may become increasingly more clear that the firm will not be able to meet its payments. Poor-quality firms may find it impossible to refinance and meet their final principal obligations. As a result of this crisis near maturity, short-term bonds of poor-credit-quality firms may command higher risk premiums than their longer-term counterparts.

Empirical studies show that default experience is highly correlated with the economic cycle. During periods of low economic output the risk premium widens, while in periods of economic prosperity the premium narrows.

A Simple Model of the Risk Structure of Bond Prices

Consider a corporation that has n shares of common stock outstanding and a single issue of discount bonds of total face value F that is due at time T. Let B_0 denote the current value of the bond issue and let E_0 be the current total value of outstanding shares. Assume the bond indenture prohibits dividend payments during the life of the bond and also prevents the firm from issuing senior debt or repurchasing shares. The current value of the firm is

$$V_0 = B_0 + E_0$$

If the firm cannot pay the face value at maturity, then the bondholders take over the company. The value of the bond at maturity is

$$B_T = \text{Min}(F, V_T)$$
$$= F - \text{Max}(F - V_T, 0)$$
$$= F - P_T$$

where P_T is the value of a put option on the firm with strike price equal to F. The payout of the bond is thus identical to the payout of a portfolio containing a riskless, default-free bond paying out F at time T and a short position in the put. Hence, by the law of one price, it must follow that

$$B_0 = F e^{-rT} - P_0 \qquad (17.1)$$

where r is the riskless interest rate, assumed to be constant. Within this framework, shareholders can be viewed as owners of the assets of the firm who have borrowed the present value of F and purchased a put. The loan is an obligation that must be met, regardless of what occurs. Without the put option, the shareholders would not have limited liability. That is, at maturity, if the value of the firm was lower than F, the shareholders would be obliged to pay the difference. Fortunately, the put option provides insurance against this event. If the shareholders cannot meet their obligations, they will exercise their in-the-money put option and deliver the firm to the bondholders. Note that the likelihood of defaulting is exactly equal to the likelihood of exercising the put. From equation (17.1), we have the result

$$\text{Bond price} = \text{Default-free bond price} - \text{Put price} \qquad (17.2)$$

or $$\text{Bond price} = \text{Default-free bond price} - \text{Default premium} \qquad (17.3)$$

Risky bonds will thus trade at a discount to default-free bonds. We can analyze the size of the risk premium by investigating the factors that influence put premiums. To do this, we make some assumptions about the stochastic behavior of the value of the firm. If, for example, the Black-Scholes assumptions hold and the assets of the firm follow a geometric Wiener process, then we have

$$P_0 = F \, e^{-rT} N(-d_1) - V_0 N(-d_2) \qquad (17.4)$$

where $d_1 = [\ln(V_0/F) + (r + \sigma^2/2)T]/\sigma\sqrt{T}$

$d_2 = d_1 - \sigma\sqrt{T}$

Substituting equation (17.3) into equation (17.1), we have

$$B_0 = F \, e^{-rT} K \qquad (17.5)$$

where $K = 1 - N(-d_1) + N(-d_2)/\omega$ and $\omega = F \, e^{-rT}/V_0$.

Here ω represents a quasi debt-to-value ratio, where the debt is the default-free discounted value of the face amount.

We can always write the price of a corporate discount bond as

$$B_0 = F \, e^{-r_B T}$$

Equating this equation with equation (17.4), we have

$$F \, e^{-r_B T} = F \, e^{-rT} K$$

from which

$$r_B = r - \ln(K)/T$$

Let the default risk premium be denoted by π. Then

$$\pi = r_B - r = -\ln(K)/T \qquad (17.6)$$

EXAMPLE 17.4   Consider a firm of value $V_0 = 30$. Assume the face value of the debt is 20 and matures in one year. The riskless rate, r, is 10 percent and the instantaneous volatility, σ, is 0.3. The value of the bond is given by $B_0 = F \, e^{-rT} - P_0$. Computing the first term yields $F \, e^{-rT} = 20 \, e^{-0.10} = 18.10$. To compute the second term, note that $a_1 = [\ln(20/30) - (0.10 - 0.0450]/0.30 = -1.535$ and $a_2 = -1.535 - 0.30 = -1.835$. Substituting these values into equation (17.3) yields $P_0 = 18.10(0.0624) - 30(0.033) = 0.13$. Given these two terms, we have $B_0 = 18.10 - 0.13 = 17.97$. (Alternatively, from equation (17.4), we have $\omega = 18.10/30 = 0.603$, $K = 1 - 0.0624 + 0.033/0.603 = 0.9923$, and $B_0 = F \, e^{-rT} K = 18.10(0.9926) = 17.97$.)

Finally, from equation (17.5) we have $r_B = \ln(20/17.97) = 10.7$ percent. Since the risk-free rate is 10 percent, the default risk premium must be $10.7\% - 10\% = 0.7\%$.

If the firm had a current value of 25, rather than 30, then the debt would be more risky. In this case $\omega = 0.724$, $K = 0.98331$, and $B_0 = 17.79$. The lower bond price reflects the greater risk.

EXHIBIT 17.4 Sensitivity Analysis of Bond Values

Variable Increases	Direction of Bond Price Change
Value of firm	Increase
Face value	Increase
Maturity	Decrease
Volatility	Decrease

EXAMPLE 17.5 **Sensitivity Analysis of Corporate Bond Values**

By taking the partial derivative of equation (17.4) we can investigate the effect of incremental changes in the important variables. As the value of the firm increases, the probability of default declines, and the put moves out of the money and its value declines, increasing the bond price. Hence, as the value of the firm increases, the bond price increases ($\partial B_0 / \partial V_0 > 0$).

As the face value of debt increases, the value of the debt increases ($\partial B_0 / \partial F > 0$) because the higher the face value, the higher the default-free portion of the bond's value. Although the bond value increases, the default premium also increases with ω. Thus, the increase in value is not the full increase in the present value of the face value.

As the time to maturity increases, the bond prices decrease ($\partial B / \partial T < 0$) because the present value of the face amount declines and the default premium increases, driving the bond price down.

The maximum payout the bondholders may receive is F. This value does not increase as the variance increases. The variance, however, does affect the default premium. As the variance increases, the value of the put also increases and the value of the bond drops ($\partial B / \partial \sigma^2 < 0$). Exhibit 17.4 summarizes the results.

Those factors that decrease the value of the bond increase the interest rate, r_B. For example, since the volatility of the firm's assets is negatively related with the bond values, it is positively related with the interest rate, r_B.

The Role of Bond Covenants

In a leveraged firm, the bondholders own straight default-free debt together with the sale of a put option on the assets of the firm. Since the value of the put increases with volatility, the bondholders will encourage shareholders not to adopt risky investments. The shareholders, on the other hand, will be keen to enhance the volatility.

Since the shareholders have voting power, the policies of the firm may be directed toward their benefit. With no restrictions, a leveraged firm could invest in risky projects to increase the share price and decrease bond prices. To protect themselves from such actions, bondholders must take certain precautions. First, bondholders may offer a price for the debt that is low enough to compensate for the most risky actions shareholders could take. If the shareholders do not adopt the most risky projects, then the bondholders will be overcompensated for the risky bond. Second, bondholders may require that stockholders write a covenant into the bond issue that restricts the kind of projects or assets the firm can acquire. Third, bondholders may request that stockholders collateralize the bonds. This minimizes uncertainty about the nature of the claim bondholders have over the company.

EXAMPLE 17.6   **Event-Risk Protected Debt**

Event-risk protected debt is debt with covenants that protect debtholders from the risk of a change in control, a leveraged recapitalization, or other specific events that could lead to a downgrade of the issuer's credit rating. These covenants generally allow investors to put the debt back to the issuer at par (or even at a premium) if the stipulated event occurs. These rights are often referred to as **poison puts.** An alternative to a poison put is for the bond covenant to specify increases in the yield of the bond if a triggering event results in a credit downgrade.

Covenants that inhibit the firm from being taken over, taking over other companies, buying stock back, paying shareholders large dividends, and selling large quantities of assets all are viewed favorably by bondholders concerned with event risk. Standard and Poor's covenant ranking system attempts to assess the degree of protection afforded by the covenants of each issue. The covenants are ranked from 1 to 5. An E1 ranking gives strong protection against virtually all anticipated events, while an E5 ranking gives virtually no protection. Very few issues are ranked E1.

Valuation of Subordinated Debt

Subordinated (or **junior**) **debt** is debt over which other (**senior**) debt takes priority. Specifically, in the event of default and subsequent liquidation, subordinated debtholders receive payment only after senior debtholders are paid.

Consider a firm with two discount bond issues with the same maturity date. Let F_S and F_j be the face value of the senior debt and junior debt, respectively. Let B_{S0} and B_{j0} be their current values, and let the market price of all the shares be E_0. The value of the firm is V_0, where $V_0 = E_0 + B_{S0} + B_{j0}$.

We shall assume that the firm cannot declare dividends until the debt is paid off. If at the maturity date the value of the firm, V_T, exceeds F_S, then the senior bondholders receive their repayment. If V_T is less than F_S, the senior bondholders receive the assets of the firm while the junior bondholders and shareholders receive nothing. If V_T exceeds $F_S + F_j$, both types of bondholders are paid off and the shareholders receive the residual value. Finally, if V_T exceeds F_S but is less than $F_S + F_j$, the junior bondholders receive the value of the firm less the senior debt, while the shareholders receive nothing. Mathematically, these conditions can be written as follows:

$$E_T = \text{Max}[0, V_T - (F_S + F_j)]$$
$$B_{ST} = \text{Min}[V_T, F_S]$$
$$B_{jT} = \text{Max}[\text{Min}(V_T - F_S, F_j), 0]$$

Exhibit 17.5 illustrates the payout values to the shareholders, senior debtholders, and junior debtholders at expiration.

As before, we can represent the payouts of the stock, senior debt, and junior debt by European options. The pricing of senior debt is unchanged. The value of the stock is also unchanged (the strike price is taken as $F = F_S + F_j$). The junior debt can be replicated by a portfolio constructed by buying a call on the firm with strike F_S and selling a call with strike $F_S + F_j$. Hence,

$$B_{j0} = C_0(F_S) - C_0(F_S + F_j) \tag{17.7}$$

where $C_0(X)$ is the value of a European call option with strike X and maturity T.

In general, the value of subordinated debt depends on the value of the firm, V_0; the size of the senior debt, F_S; the junior debt, F_j; the volatility of the firm, σ; and the riskless rate, r.

Valuation of Corporate Coupon Bonds

The value of a default-free coupon bond is equivalent to the value of a portfolio of default-free discount bonds. Consider a three-period bond that pays coupons of size k at times t_1, t_2, and t_3. In addition, the face value, F, is due at time t_3. The value of this bond is equivalent to the value of a portfolio of three discount bonds. The first discount bond has face value $k_1 = k$ and is due at time t_1. The second bond has face value $k_2 = k$ and is due at time t_2. The final bond has face value $k_3 = F + k$ due at time t_3.

Such an analysis cannot be extended to risky bonds because the portfolio of discount bonds cannot be assumed to be independent. To see this, note that at time

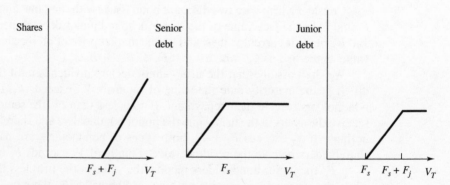

EXHIBIT 17.5   Payouts of Stock, Senior Debt, and Junior Debt

t_2 the shareholders have to determine whether to pay out k_2 or default. If they default, the final payment, k_3, will not be paid.

To understand how coupon bonds are valued, we shall start off at time t_3, then consider times t_2 and t_1 and eventually the current time, $t = 0$. At time t_3, the shareholders must determine whether it is in their interests to pay k_3 and take back possession of the firm. At this time the shareholders own a call option on the firm with strike price k_3. Let C_3 denote this call option.

At time t_2, the shareholders again have to make a decision. By paying k_2, they receive option C_3. If they do not pay k_2, they surrender the company to the debtholders. At this time the shareholders own an option with strike price k_2. Since the underlying security is option C_3, this option contract is really an option on an option and is referred to as a **compound option.** Let C_2 denote this compound option. Going back to time t_1, we can see that the shareholders are in the same situation. They own an option on the compound option C_2. By paying the coupon k_1, the shareholders are exercising their option and receiving C_2. Let C_1 denote this compound option.

Now consider time zero. The stockholders own a European compound option, C_1, that has an exercise price of k_1 and time to maturity of t_1. If it is exercised, the shareholders will receive a compound option with strike k_2 and time to expiration $t_2 - t_1$. Finally, if C_2 is exercised at time t_2, the shareholders will receive a simple European call option with strike price k_3 and time to expiration $t_3 - t_2$.

Exhibit 17.6 illustrates the decision processes. Note that by paying k_1, the shareholders receive more than an option to continue their quest for the firm for another period. At the same time, they receive a promise from the bondholders that if k_2 is met, they will receive a final option on the value of the firm. The value of the bond is not equal to the value of a portfolio of simple call options. For example, it is incorrect to assume the shareholders own a portfolio of calls of strike k_1, k_2, and k_3, with times to expiration t_1, t_2, and t_3, respectively.

Viewed in this light, we see that when a firm issues coupon bonds, the shareholders have granted the bondholders the firm but have retained a compound call option that permits them to regain control of the firm if they can continue to make their coupon payments.

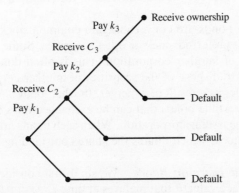

EXHIBIT 17.6   Sequence of Compound Options Owned by Shareholders

Another way of viewing the corporate bond is as follows. The spread above the Treasury rate is compensation for the implicit compound put option that noteholders have written. If the value of the firm as an ongoing concern falls below the current interest obligation, the payment will not be made and the firm will be put to the noteholders. Thus the firm's note spread will be an increasing function of the debt-equity ratio and the variance of the rate of return on total market value.

Callable Corporate Bonds

As discussed earlier, many bonds can be viewed as packages of contingent claims, together with a straight bond. A common feature on many corporate bonds is the call feature, which provides the firm with the opportunity to recall the bonds when interest rates drop sufficiently low. Let CB_0 represent the price of a callable bond. Then

$$CB_0 = B_0 - C_0$$

where B_0 is the price of an otherwise identical straight bond and C_0 is the price of the call option on the bond.

Convertible Bonds

A **convertible bond,** like a conventional bond, is an obligation of the issuing corporation. The bond provides a fixed rate of interest over its lifetime. In addition, at the discretion of the owner, it can be converted (exchanged) into a fixed number of shares of common stock. For example, the convertible bonds of XYZ pay a coupon of 8 percent and mature in 20 years. In addition, at any point in time the bond can be converted into six shares of XYZ common stock. The number of shares that can be acquired via conversion is called the **conversion ratio,** which need not be fixed over time. For example, a bond may be convertible into 10 shares during the first three years and 6 shares thereafter. In addition to surrendering the bond, some convertibles require a cash payment to convert. This additional payment may be fixed or related to the current stock price. For example, conversion of the XYZ convertible bond is accomplished by surrendering the bond and paying an additional $400 or 45 percent of the market value of the common stock, whichever is lower.

Not all convertible bonds are convertible into common stock. Instead, some may be convertible into preferred stock or other securities. Some bonds are convertible into securities of another corporation. This is often done by an issuing corporation that wants to dispose of the securities of another corporation. Many firms issue such securities as a result of a merger. In what follows, we shall discuss the more common convertible bonds that can be exchanged for a fixed number of shares of the stock of the issuing corporation. When such bonds are converted, the firm issues additional stock, which dilutes the shares outstanding.

Noncallable Convertible Discount Bonds   We shall first consider a noncallable convertible bond with face value F that matures at time T. Assume the convertible issue can be exchanged for k shares of stock. The firm has value V_0, and n shares of stock are outstanding. The stock and convertible issue are the only claims on the capital structure of the firm. Hence

$$V_0 = nS_0 + G_0$$

where G_0 is the value of the convertible issue at time 0.

Consider the value of the convertible issue at its maturity. If the value of the firm is less than the final payment, F, the bondholders take over the firm. If, on the other hand, the value of the firm is sufficiently high, they will convert. If the convertible issue is converted, the firm has to issue k shares and the postconversion stock price, S_T, will be given by

$$S_T = V_T/(n + k)$$

The value of the convertible issue exercised is therefore $kS_T = [k/n + k]V_T = \gamma V_T$, where γ is referred to as the dilution factor. If this value exceeded the face value F, then the convertible issue would be exercised. The lowest value the firm has to reach at time T in order for exercise to occur is V_T^*, where $\gamma V_T^* = F$ or $V_T^* = F/\gamma$. Hence,

$$G_T = \begin{cases} V_T & \text{if } V_T \leq F \\ F & \text{if } F < V_T < F/\gamma \\ \gamma V_T & \text{if } V_T > F/\gamma \end{cases}$$

Exhibit 17.7 illustrates the terminal value of the issue.

The final payment is seen to equal the payout of a straight bond, together with an option on the equity of the firm. The option has strike price F/γ and maturity T and is written on an underlying security having a value γV.

Assuming no dividends are paid out prior to time T, then the current value of the convertible must equal the current value of a straight bond, together with a call.

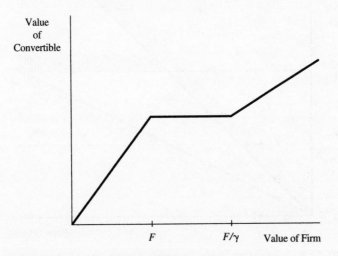

EXHIBIT 17.7   Terminal Value of Convertible Issue

Specifically,

$$G_0 = B_0 + C_0$$

where B_0 is the value of the straight bond with maturity T and C_0 is the value of the above call option at date 0. At time T, if it is in the interests of the convertible holder, the payment of F can be exchanged for γV. The premium of a convertible bond over a straight bond can then be represented by the price of a call option.

Callable Convertible Discount Bonds   In practice, almost all convertible bonds are callable. Exhibit 17.8 illustrates the boundaries for convertible bonds with call provisions. Exhibit 17.9 shows the terminal value of a convertible bond.

The call provision essentially places a ceiling on the upside potential of the convertible. Specifically, consider what would happen if the value of the firm were sufficiently high that the postconversion exercise price of the issue exceeded the call price. Without the callable feature, bondholders have no incentive to exercise their conversion option early, unless the dividends are sufficiently large. However, with the callable feature, there will always be the possibility that the firm will call the bond in at the call price; when the firm's value is high, the call price is lower than the current conversion value. When the bond may be called in at the lower price, investors bear risk by waiting. More important, however, from the firm's perspective, there is no incentive to delay in calling in the bond. By calling in the bonds that pay only the call price as opposed to converting the bond issue, the firm may have to pay a larger amount. The break-even point occurs when the value of the firm reaches K/γ, where K is the call price. Exhibit 17.9 shows the payout at the maturity date of a convertible.

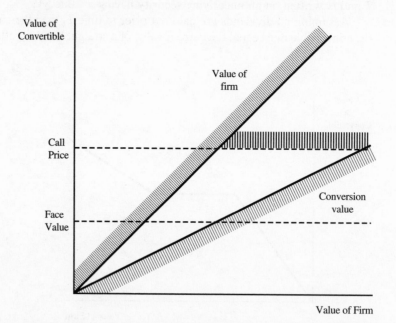

EXHIBIT 17.8   Boundaries for Convertible Bond with Call Provision

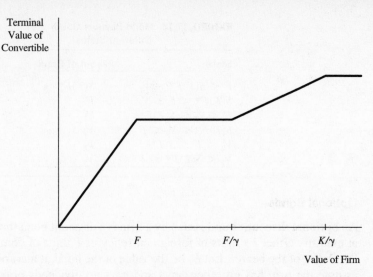

Terminal Value of Convertible

Value of Firm

F F/γ K/γ

EXHIBIT 17.9 Payout of a Callable Convertible Bond at Its Maturity Date

Corporate Securities Involving Foreign Currencies

A wide variety of corporate securities have payoff functions that include the payoff of a put or call option on the minimum or maximum of the prices of two risky assets. In this section we shall provide two examples of such claims.

Foreign Currency Bonds

A simple foreign currency discount bond is a bond whose face value is denominated in a different currency from the currency in which the common stock is traded. Consider a firm of value V_0 that has issued a discount foreign currency bond of face value F^* in foreign currency. Assume the firm has no other debt and does not declare any dividends prior to maturity at time T. Let $S(T)$ be the exchange rate at time T. The payout in domestic currency of the bond at time T is EV_T, where

$$EV_T = \text{Min}[V_T, S(T)F^*] \qquad (17.8)$$

Note that the terms in brackets in equation (17.8) are uncertain at the current time. Equation (17.8) can be trivially rewritten as

$$EV_T = \text{Max}[0, \text{Min}(V_T, S(T)F^*) - 0] \qquad (17.9)$$

That is, the final payout of the foreign currency bond can be viewed as the payout from a call option on the minimum of two values. The first risky value is the value of the firm; the second risky value is the local currency value of the face price of the bond. The strike price of this option is zero. To avoid riskless arbitrage, the current value of the foreign currency bond must equal the current value of the call option on the minimum of the two risky prices.

EXHIBIT 17.10   Bond Payouts Under Different States

State	Payout of Bond
$F < S(T)F^* \leq V_T$	$S(T)F^*$
$S(T)F^* < F \leq V_T$	F
$F < V_T \leq S(T)F^*$	V_T
$S(T)F^* < V_T \leq F$	V_T
$V_T < F \leq S(T)F^*$	V_T
$V_T < S(T)F^* \leq F$	V_T

Optional Bonds

An **optional discount bond** issued by a firm is a discount bond that promises to pay at maturity either F^* units of foreign currency or F units of domestic currency at the choice of the bearer. Let B_T be the value of the bond at maturity. As before, we assume the firm has no other debts and pays no dividends prior to maturity. At maturity, six possible states are possible. Exhibit 17.10 lists these states and gives the value of the bond in each state.

The payouts can be replicated by a portfolio consisting of a riskless discount bond of face value F; a written European put option on the value of the firm with strike F; and a European option on the minimum of two risky values, V_T and H_T. V_T is the value of the firm, and H_T is the value, in dollars, of a foreign riskless bond of face value F^* at the maturity date T. That is, $H_T = F^*S(T)$. The current value of this portfolio, W_0, can be written as

$$W_0 = B_0 + M(V, H; F, T) - P(V; F, T) \qquad (17.10)$$

where $B_0 = F e^{-rT}$ is the current value of the discount bond, $M(V, H; F, T)$ is the value of the option bond on the minimum of V and H, and $P(V; F, T)$ is the value of the put option on the value of the firm. The final value of this portfolio, W_T, is given by

$$W_T = F + \text{Max}[\text{Min}(V_T, S(T)F^*) - F, 0] - \text{Max}(F - V_T, 0)$$

Exhibit 17.11 values this portfolio in each of the six possible states. The exhibit shows that the final payouts of this portfolio are exactly equal to the payouts of the

EXHIBIT 17.11   Payouts of a Replicating Portfolio

State	Bond Value	Value of Option on Minimum	Value of Put	Portfolio Value
$F < S(T)F^* \leq V_T$	F	$S(T)F^* - F$	0	$S(T)F^*$
$S(T)F^* < F \leq V_T$	F	0	0	F
$F < V_T \leq S(T)F^*$	F	$V_T - F$	0	V_T
$S(T)F^* < V_T \leq F$	F	0	$F - V_T$	V_T
$V_T < F \leq S(T)F^*$	F	0	$F - V_T$	V_T
$V_T < S(T)F^* \leq F$	F	0	$F - V_T$	V_T

optional bond. Hence, to avoid riskless arbitrage, the current value of the optional bond, FB_0, must equal the current value of the portfolio, W_0. That is,

$$FB_0 = B_0 + M(V, H; F, T) - P(V; F, T) \qquad (17.11)$$

Specific pricing models for options on the minimum of two securities were developed in Chapter 16.

Conclusion

This chapter laid out the basics of corporate bonds. The array of corporate debt instruments is vast, and few corporate debt issues are similar. The chapter provided an option approach for the valuation of many corporate securities. Corporate discount bonds can be viewed as straight riskless debt less a risk premium, the size of which can be determined by valuing an appropriate European put. Subordinated debt, convertible bonds, coupon bonds, and foreign bonds can also be seen as a collection of options on the value of the firm. All the models shown here are quite simple in that there is only one source of uncertainty, namely the value of the firm. Recently more complex models of corporate securities have been developed that incorporate interest rate risk as a second source of uncertainty and also have more complex default rules.

References

Altman, E. "Revisiting the High Yield Bond Market." *Financial Management* 21 (Summer 1992): 78–92.

Bartter, B., and R. Rendleman, Jr. "Fee-Based Pricing of Fixed-Rate Bank Loan Commitments." *Financial Management* 8 (Spring 1979): 13–20.

Black, F., and J. Cox. "Valuing Corporate Securities: Some Effects of Bond Indenture Provisions." *Journal of Finance* 31 (May 1976): 351–68.

Black, F., and M. Scholes. "The Pricing of Options and Corporate Liabilities." *Journal of Political Economy* 81 (1973): 637–59.

Boyle, P., and E. Schwartz. "Equilibrium Prices of Guarantees Under Equity-Linked Contract." *Journal of Risk and Insurance* 44 (December 1977): 639–80.

Brennan, M., and E. Schwartz. "The Pricing of Equity-Linked Life Insurance Policies with an Asset Value Guarantee." *Journal of Financial Economics* 3 (June 1976): 195–213.

_____. "Savings Bonds, Retractable Bonds, and Callable Bonds." *Journal of Financial Economics* 5 (August 1977): 67–88.

_____. "Convertible Bonds: Valuation and Optimal Strategies for Call and Conversion." *Journal of Finance* 32 (December 1977): 1699–1716.

_____. "Corporate Income Taxes, Valuation and the Problem of Optimal Capital Structure." *Journal of Business* 51 (January 1978): 103–14.

_____. "Savings Bonds: Valuation and Optimal Redemption Strategies." In *Financial Economics: Essays in Honor of Paul Cootner,* edited by W. Sharpe and C. Cootner. Englewood Cliffs, N.J.: Prentice-Hall, 1982, pp. 202–15.

_____. "Evaluating Natural Resource Investments." *Journal of Business* 58 (1985): 135–57.

Constantinides, G. "Warrant Exercise and Bond Conversion in Competitive Markets." *Journal of Economics* 13 (September 1984): 371–97.

Constantinides, G., and R. Rosenthal. "Strategic Analysis of the Competitive Exercise of Certain Financial Options." *Journal of Economic Theory* 32 (February 1984): 128–38.

Copeland, T., and J. Weston. "A Note on the Evaluation of Cancellable Operating Leases." *Financial Management* (Summer 1982): 60–67.

Cox, J., J. Ingersoll, Jr., and S. Ross. "An Analysis of Variable Rate Loan Contracts." *Journal of Finance* 35 (May 1980): 389–404.

Cox, J., and M. Rubinstein. *Option Markets.* Englewood Cliffs, N.J.: Prentice-Hall, 1985.

De, S., and J. Kale. "Contingent Payments and Debt Contracts." *Financial Management* 22 (Summer 1993): 106–23.

Emanuel, D. "Warrant Valuation and Exercise Strategy." *Journal of Financial Economics* 12 (August 1983): 211–36.

———— "A Theoretical Model for Valuing Preferred Stock." *Journal of Finance* 38 (September 1983): 1133–55.

Finnerty, J. "Financial Engineering in Corporate Finance: An Overview." *Financial Management* (Winter 1988): 14–33.

————. "Indexed Sinking Fund Debentures: Valuation and Analysis." *Financial Management* (Summer 1993): 76–94.

Fischer, S. "Call Option Pricing When the Exercise Price Is Uncertain, and the Valuation of Index Bonds." *Journal of Finance* 33 (March 1978): 169–76.

Galai, D. "Pricing of Optional Bonds." *Journal of Banking and Finance* 7 (September 1983): 323–37.

Galai, D., and R. Masulis. "The Option Pricing Model and the Risk Factor of Stock." *Journal of Financial Economics* 3 (January-March 1976): 53–81.

Galai, D., and M. Schneller. "Pricing Warrants and the Value of the Firm." *Journal of Finance* 33 (December 1978): 1333–42.

Geske, R. "The Valuation of Corporate Liabilities as Compound Options." *Journal of Financial and Quantitative Analysis* 12 (November 1977): 541–52.

Geske, R., and H. Johnson. "The Valuation of Corporate Liabilities as Compound Options: A Correction." *Journal of Financial and Quantitative Analysis* 19 (June 1984): 231–32.

Hawkins, G. "An Analysis of Revolving Credit Agreements." *Journal of Financial Economics* 10 (March 1982): 529–82.

Ho, T., and R. Singer. "Bond Indenture Provisions and the Risk of Corporate Debt." *Journal of Financial Economics* 10 (December 1982): 375–406.

————. "The Value of Corporate Debt with Sinking-Fund Provisions." *Journal of Business* 57 (July 1984): 315–36.

Ingersoll, J., Jr. "A Contingent-Claims Valuation of Convertible Securities." *Journal of Financial Economics* 4 (May 1977): 463–78.

————. "An Examination of Corporate Call Policies on Convertible Securities." *Journal of Finance* 32 (May 1977): 463–78.

Jones, E., and S. Mason. "Valuation of Loan Guarantees." *Journal of Banking and Finance* 4 (March 1980): 89–107.

Margabe, W. "The Value of an Option to Exchange One Asset for Another." *Journal of Finance* 33 (March 1978): 177–86.

Mason, S., and S. Bhattacharya. "Risky Debt, Jump Processes, and Safety Covenants." *Journal of Financial Economics* 9 (September 1981): 281–307.

Mason, S., and R. Merton. "The Role of Contingent Claims Analysis in Corporate Finance." In *Recent Advances in Corporate Finance,* edited by E. Altman and M. Subrahmanyam. Homewood, Ill.: Dow Jones–Irwin, 1985.

McConnell, J., and J. Schallheim. "Valuation of Asset Leasing Contracts." *Journal of Financial Economics* 12 (1983): 237–61.

Merton, R. "On the Pricing of Corporate Debt: The Risk Structure of Interest Rates." *Journal of Finance* 29 (May 1974): 449–70.

———. "An Analytic Derivation of the Cost of Deposit Insurance and Loan Guarantee: An Application of Modern Option Pricing Theory." *Journal of Banking and Finance* 1 (June 1977): 3–11.

Miller, M. "Financial Innovation: The Last Twenty Years and the Next." *Journal of Financial and Quantitative Analysis* (December 1986): 459–71.

Schwartz, E. "The Valuation of Warrants: Implementing a New Approach." *Journal of Financial Economics* 4 (January 1977): 79–93.

Smith, C., Jr. "Applications of Option Pricing Analysis." In *Handbook of Financial Economics,* edited by J. Bicksler. New York: North-Holland, 1979, pp. 79–121.

———. "On the Theory of Financial Contracting: The Personal Loan Market." *Journal of Monetary Economics* 6 (July 1980): 333–57.

Smith, C., Jr., and J. Zimmerman. "Valuing Employee Stock Option Plans Using Option Pricing Models." *Journal of Accounting Research* 14 (Autumn 1976): 357–64.

Sosin, H. "On the Valuation of Federal Loan Guarantees to Corporations." *Journal of Finance* 35 (December 1980): 1209–21.

Stulz, R. "Options on the Minimum or the Maximum of Two Risky Assets: Analysis and Applications." *Journal of Financial Economics* 10 (July 1982): 161–85.

Van Horne, J. "Of Financial Innovation and Excesses." *Journal of Finance* (July 1985): 621–31.

Exercises

1. Consider a firm valued at $40 million. Assume the only debt consists of a discount bond of face value $25 million that matures in one year. The riskless rate is 8 percent, and the annual volatility rate is 0.40.
   a. Compute the value of the corporate discount bond.
   b. State the assumptions you have made.
   c. Compute the default risk premium.
2. Reconsider Exercise 1. If the face value of the debt were $20 million, what would the default risk premium be? Explain why the value differs from the risk premium in Exercise 1c.

3. A down-and-out call option must be exercised if the underlying security price drops below a certain value (that may vary over time).

   a. Using the binomial model, show with an illustration how a down-and-out option price can be computed. Explain why a down-and-out call option will never be worth more than a regular call option with the same strike and time to expiration.

   b. Based on your analysis in Exercise 3a, explain why strict bond covenants have value to bondholders.

4. "The payout of a subordinated bond is similar to the payout on a bullish European call spread." Under what circumstances, if any, is this statement true?

5. Explain why a corporate coupon bond cannot be perceived as a portfolio of discount bonds with face values that match the coupon payments.

6. Construct a three-period binomial model that values a European convertible bond. In order to establish this model, assume the income from the convertible issue is immedietely distributed to the shareholders. Assume the value of the firm is 100, $u = 1.20$, $d = 1/u$, and $R = 1.05$. The firm is an all-equity firm with 100 shares. The convertible issue can be converted into 25 shares. The interest payments on the entire issue are \$2 per period. The firm pays no dividends. What is the value of the three-period convertible issue?

7. Provide two examples that apply the concept of options on the minimum or maximum of two risky assets.

8. In some lease arrangements, the lessee has the right to buy the item for a fixed price at the expiration date of the lease. How could such an option be valued? Explain how you might estimate the parameters for the option model.

9. The management of an electric utility faces a choice between building a power plant that burns oil and one that burns either oil or coal. Although the latter plant is costlier, it offers management greater flexibility. In making the choice between the two plants, management must assess the value of this operating option. Using a contingent claims approach, discuss the issues that one may encounter in comparing these two alternatives.

10. A warranty allows the owner to obtain a rebate on an item if the item fails. This right exists over a prespecified lifetime. Can a warranty be viewed as an option? What problems, if any, are encountered when using a contingent claims approach to value a warranty?

PART FIVE

Interest Rate

Derivatives

The chapters in Part 5 discuss interest rate derivative contracts. In Chapter 18 we review bond pricing and the measurement of yields. We explore the linkages between the cash and forward markets and investigate how forward contracts on bonds can be used to eliminate unanticipated interest rate risk.

In Chapter 19 we review the factors behind bond price volatilily. The Macaulay measure of duration and modified duration are described. This latter measure describes the exposure of a bond to interest rate risk. We discuss immunization strategies based on duration matching and duration-convexity matching, along with measures of risk due to a twisting term structure. The basic measures of duration, convexity, and twist risk are helpful in characterizing risk exposures.

In Chapter 20 we provide an overview of exchange-traded futures and option contracts. In particular, we examine contracts on short-term instruments such as T-bills and Eurodollar time deposits and on medium-term T-notes and long-term T-bonds.

The liquidity benefits of standardization and the institutional features that ensure all parties perform are the main advantages of exchange-traded products. The disadvantage is that there are only a few types of contracts, which may not be appropriate for managing an investor's exposure. The investor can purchase tailor-made products designed to manage the very specific situation. In Chapter 21 we describe the "standard vanilla" interest rate swap and other "nonstandard" swaps—the nature of the products, the way in which they trade, the participants, and the pricing of these products.

CHAPTER 18

Spot and Forward Markets for Debt Instruments

In this chapter we review the basics of bond pricing and the measurement of yields over different maturities. The term structure of interest rates shows the relationships between rates of return and maturities that can be obtained in the cash market. Transactions can also be accomplished in a forward market. This market permits loans to be established in the future at interest rates that are guaranteed today. Traders can therefore use these markets to hedge against adverse interest rate moves in the interim. Forward markets are of course linked to the cash market. Indeed, the fair prices of forward contracts can be obtained by extracting information from the yield curve. In the first part of this chapter we explore the linkages between the cash and forward markets and investigate how forward contracts on bonds can be used to eliminate unanticipated interest rate risk.

Since much information can be extracted from the yield curve, its construction is important. In order to estimate the relationship, we must first review riskless securities issued by the government. The United States Treasury is the largest issuer of debt in the world, with over $3 trillion outstanding. The majority of the debt consists of marketable Treasury securities, namely, bills, notes, and bonds. Treasury securities account for over $2 trillion. The size of this market is enormous—the entire U.S. corporate bond market accounts for about $1 trillion of debt. The huge volume makes the Treasury market the most liquid market in the world. In this chapter we also investigate the repurchase agreement market and the Eurodollar market. In the final part of this chapter we return to the construction of the term structure.

The primary objectives of this chapter are the following:

- To describe construction of a yield curve from information on Treasury securities;
- To use the yield curve to compute forward prices for Treasuries; and
- To discuss the market for repurchase agreements and Eurodollars.

Default-Free Fixed-Income Securities

A **default-free fixed-income security** is a security that promises specific cash flows at future dates. These cash flows can be represented as

$$\{CF_1, CF_2, \ldots, CF_m\}$$

where $CF_t, t = 1, 2, \ldots, m$ is the cash flow in period t and m is the last period in which a flow is promised. Many fixed-income securities provide constant periodic cash flows until the last period, when a larger payment, called the balloon payment, is received. Most bonds, for example, provide constant coupon payments every six months until maturity, when the face value of the bond is received in addition to the final coupon payment. Mortgages, on the other hand, typically require monthly payments, which continue for a fixed number of years to maturity. However, in general, the size of cash flows associated with fixed-income securities could be different in each of the periods. The income stream $\{CF_1, CF_2, \ldots, CF_m\}$ of default-free fixed-income securities can be viewed as a combination of m single-payment income streams of the form

$$\{CF_1, 0, 0, \ldots, 0\}$$

$$\{0, CF_2, \ldots, 0\}$$

$$\ldots$$

$$\{0, 0, \ldots, 0, CF_m\}$$

An investor who acquires the income stream $\{CF_1, CF_2, \ldots, CF_m\}$ can be regarded as acquiring this package of m income streams. If markets exist for these simple income streams, then clearly an investor will be indifferent between separately buying each of these income streams or buying the single composite income stream, provided the costs of each strategy are the same.

Each of the single-payment income streams $\{0, \ldots, 0, CF_t, 0, \ldots, 0\}$ can be viewed as the sum of CF_t single-payment streams of the form $\{0, \ldots, 0, 1, 0, \ldots, 0\}$. Thus, the income streams

$$\{1, 0, \ldots, 0\}$$

$$\{0, 1, \ldots, 0\}$$

$$\{0, \ldots, 0, 1\}$$

form the basic building blocks for all income streams. If markets for these building blocks existed, then any investor requiring the income stream $\{CF_1, CF_2, \ldots, CF_m\}$ could buy CF_1 units of $\{1, 0, \ldots, 0\}$, CF_2 units of $\{0, 1, 0, \ldots, 0\}$, and so on.

Let $P(0, t)$ be the current price of the single-payment stream that provides a \$1 cash flow in period t. $P(0, t)$ can be viewed as a discount function that transforms \$1 to be received in t periods into current dollars. The cost, then, of establishing an income stream of $\{CF_1, CF_2, CF_3, \ldots, CF_m\}$ is $CF_1 P(0, 1) + CF_2 P(0, 2) + \ldots + CF_m P(0, m)$. Let B_0 represent the current value of this income stream,

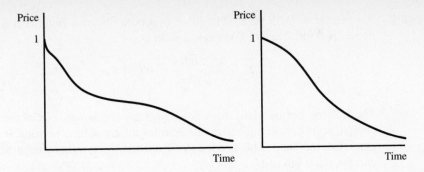

EXHIBIT 18.1   Typical Shapes of the Discount Function

that is,

$$B_0 = \sum_{t=1}^{m} CF_t P(0, t) \qquad (18.1)$$

Note that if the value of the fixed-income security that promised payouts $\{CF_1, CF_2, \ldots, CF_m\}$ did not equal B_0, then risk-free arbitrage opportunities would exist. The plot of the prices of these pure discount bonds against their maturities is called the **discount function.** Typical shapes of the discount function are shown in Exhibit 18.1. The shape of the discount function is restricted. Clearly, the price of any bond should be positive. Also, $P(0, t) < 1$, since investors are not likely to pay more than \$1 today to receive \$1 in the future. Finally, we would expect $P(0, t) < P(0, t - 1)$, since the value of \$1 to be received far in the future is worth less than the value of \$1 to be received earlier. These assumptions imply that the discount function $P(0, \cdot)$ is a decreasing function of time, bounded in the interval $(0, 1)$.

Annualizing Yields

As in the previous section, we assume the time period is split up into n trading periods. Let the time interval of each period be Δt years. We label the trading periods $0, 1, 2, \ldots, n$ and assume that pure discount bonds exist that mature on each of these trading dates. Let $P(t, T)$ be the price at time t of a bond that pays \$1 at time T. Clearly, $P(T, T) = 1$.

Let R represent the return obtained over the first period from holding a discount bond that matures at date T. Then

$$R = \frac{P(1, T) - P(0, T)}{P(0, T)}$$

EXAMPLE 18.1 Assume $\Delta t = 0.25$ years. The price of a pure discount bond that matures in one period is 0.98. The holding period yield is

$$R = \frac{1 - 0.98}{0.98} = 0.024 \quad \text{or} \quad 2.04\%$$

The holding period yield does not adjust for the length of the period. To make comparisons between investments held for different time periods, it is common to annualize the yield. This is done in one of two ways, either as simple interest or as compounded interest.

EXAMPLE 18.2 1. The annualized simple interest in Example 18.1 is given by multiplying the holding period yield by the number of periods in the year, namely, 4, so the annualized yield is $4 \times 2.04\% = 8.16\%$.

2. The compounded rate of return in Example 18.1 is given by $(1 + R)^n - 1$, where $n = 4$. This value is $(1.0204)^4 - 1 = 8.42\%$.

In Example 18.2 the compounding interval was taken to be quarterly ($\Delta t = 0.25$). In many cases the investment period could be quite small, for example, one day. In this case the compounded annualized return is $(1 + R)^{365} - 1$, where R is the one-day return. If the holding period is small, then the calculation of annualized return can be approximated by continuous compounding. Specifically, for R close to zero and n large, $(1 + R)^n \approx e^{nR}$.

EXAMPLE 18.3 An investment offers a daily rate of return of 0.00025. A $1 million investment for one day grows to $(\$1,000,000)(1.00025) = \$1,000,250$. The annual rate, approximated by continuous compounding, is $e^{365(0.00025)} - 1 = 9.554\%$.

When the continuously compounded return, y say, is expressed as an annual rate, 1 plus the return over any time period, s years say, is computed as e^{ys}. The annualized continuously compounded return in this case is $y = 0.09554$. The return for $s = 0.25$ year is $e^{(0.09554)(0.25)} - 1 = 2.417\%$.

In all calculations care must be taken that the annual interest rate used is consistent in all calculations. For example, if a security returns 10 percent over a six-month period, then the equivalent continuously compounded return is obtained by solving the equation $e^{y(0.5)} = 1.10$. Equivalently, $y = \ln(1.10)/0.5 = 19.06\%$ per year.

Yield to Maturity for Discount Bonds

Let $y_0(t)$ be the yield on a pure discount bond of maturity t. Then $y_0(t)$ satisfies the equation

$$P(0, t) = \frac{1}{(1 + y_0(t))^t} \qquad (18.2)$$

or

$$y_0(t) = P(0, t)^{-1/t} - 1 \qquad (18.3)$$

The yield is that rate of return per period that the bond will earn if held to maturity. As such it is usually referred to as the **yield to maturity.**

EXAMPLE 18.4   A one-year pure discount bond is priced at $0.90. Assume $\Delta t = 1$ year. Then the yield to maturity is given by $y_0(1) = [0.9]^{-1} - 1 = 11.11\%$.

If the partition were $\Delta t = 6$ months, then the yield to maturity would be given by $y_0(2) = [0.9]^{-1/2} - 1 = 5.41\%$ per six months. On an annualized basis this is 10.82% per year. Note that in annualizing, we just doubled the rate rather than considering the compounding effect.

If the partition were $\Delta t = 1$ day, then the yield to maturity of the one-year bond would be $y_0(365) = [0.9]^{-1/365} - 1 = 0.0002887$ per day. Multiplying by 365, we obtain the simple annualized yield of 10.537%.

Finally, consider a two-year-to-maturity discount bond with face value $1, currently priced at $0.80. With $\Delta t = 1$ year, the annualized yield to maturity for this bond is $y_0(2) = [0.80]^{-1/2} - 1 = 11.8\%$.

If continuous compounding is used, then the annualized yield to maturity is given by solving the following equation for $y(t)$:

$$P(0, t) = e^{-y(t)t\,\Delta t} \qquad (18.4)$$

or

$$y(t) = -\ln [P(0, t)]/t\, \Delta t \qquad (18.5)$$

EXAMPLE 18.5   In Example 18.4, the bond price is $0.90 and the time to maturity, $t\, \Delta t$, is one year. Hence, the annualized continuously compounded yield to maturity for this bond is $-\ln[0.9] = 10.536\%$.

EXAMPLE 18.6   An investor who has a one-period investment horizon is considering two strategies:

1. Buy a one-year discount bond and hold it to maturity.
2. Buy a two-year discount bond and sell it after one year.

The current yield to maturity on the one-year bond is 10 percent while that of the two-year bond is 12 percent. By buying the one-year bond the investor is guaranteed a one-year return of 10 percent. The investor who buys the two-year bond is uncertain of the yield that will be obtained. For example, if after one year the yield on a single-period bond is 13 percent, then the price of the bond at that time will be $1/1.13 = \$0.8849$. Since the original price of the bond was $1/(1.12)^2 = \$0.79719$, the single-period return from the second strategy would be $0.8849/0.79719 - 1$, or 11%. The actual yield obtained on the two-year bond in the first year depends critically on yields on one-year bonds after one year.

Yield to Maturity for Default-Free Coupon Bonds

As discussed earlier, the value of a default-free coupon bond is equal to the value of a particular portfolio of pure discount bonds. Specifically, equation (18.1) can be rearranged as

$$B_0 = \sum_{t=1}^{m} P(0, t)CF_t$$

Here CF_t is the total coupon payment received at time t. The yield to maturity of this coupon bond is its internal rate of return, y, a value that makes the following equation true:

$$B_0 = \sum_{t=1}^{m} \frac{CF_t}{(1 + y)^t} \tag{18.6}$$

If in equation (18.6) the cash flows occur annually, then y is the annual yield to maturity. If the bond has k cash flows per year and matures after m cash payments, then the annualized yield to maturity is y^*, where

$$B_0 = \sum_{t=1}^{m} \frac{CF_t}{(1 + y^*/k)^t} \tag{18.7}$$

EXAMPLE 18.7   Consider a bond with face value $1000 and a semiannual coupon rate of 12 percent that matures in two years. The current price of the bond is $900. Using the bond pricing equation, we have

$$\$900 = \frac{60}{(1 + y^*/2)} + \frac{60}{(1 + y^*/2)^2} + \frac{60}{(1 + y^*/2)^3} + \frac{1060}{(1 + y^*/2)^4}$$

Calculating the annualized yield to maturity, y^*, that solves this equation is somewhat complicated. Fortunately, hand-held calculators possess function keys to compute the yield to maturity given the coupon rate, the final maturity, and the present market price. For this problem the yield is 9.093 percent.

The yield to maturity computed on the basis of this market convention is called the **bond-equivalent yield**.

If continuous compounding were used, then the annualized yield to maturity for the bond in Example 18.7 would be given by solving the following equation for y:

$$B_0 = \sum_{t=1}^{m} CF_t \, e^{-yt\Delta t} \qquad (18.8)$$

where Δt is the time period between cash flows, expressed in years.

Yield to Call

The yield to maturity is based on the assumption that coupon payments will be received up to maturity, at which time the face value payment will also be made. However, this assumption may not be true. Many bonds have call provisions that allow the issuer to buy back the bond at a specific price (the call price) before maturity. The call price is usually set above the face value. In some cases a schedule of call prices exists that decreases over time. The call feature provides the borrower with flexibility, especially when interest rates decline. In such an instance, the borrower can call in the issue and refinance at lower cost. Naturally, this feature is undesirable to bondholders. In fact, any investor who buys a callable bond is buying a straight bond and then granting (writing) a call option to the issuing firm. The strike price of the option corresponds to the call price, and the time to expiration corresponds to the call date. Investors will not purchase callable bonds unless they are compensated by a higher yield for carrying the additional risk. In addition to computing the yield to maturity, investors in callable bonds often compute the yield to call by finding the interest rate that equates the current price of the bond and the assumed cash flows to the call date.

Spot and Forward Rates and Spot and Forward Prices

The continuously compounded yield to maturity, $y_0(t)$ say, is the solution to the equation

$$P(0, t) = e^{-y_0(t)t\Delta t} \quad \text{for } t = 1, 2, \ldots, n$$

These yields are called **spot rates.** The plot of these yields against maturity, namely, the yield curve, indicates how much additional yield can be obtained in exchange for each extension in maturity.

EXAMPLE 18.8   Suppose time periods are split up into six-month intervals. The annualized yields over the first four periods obtained from the yield curve are $y_0(1) = 7\%$, $y_0(2) = 8\%$, $y_0(3) = 9\%$, and $y_0(4) = 10\%$. That is, the annualized rate of return for a six-month loan is 7 percent. The prices of one-, two-, three-, and four-period discount bonds are given by

$$P(0, 1) = e^{-0.07(1)0.5} = 0.9656$$

$$P(0, 2) = e^{-0.08(2)0.5} = 0.9231$$

$$P(0, 3) = e^{-0.09(3)0.5} = 0.8737$$

$$P(0, 4) = e^{-0.10(4)0.5} = 0.8187$$

Hence, the current price of a six-month discount bond with face value $10,000 is $9,656.

The yield curve changes a little every day. Its exact shape at any point in time can be upward-sloping, downward-sloping, or humped. If the yield curve is upward-sloping, then short-term rates are below longer-term rates.

Short-term rates are usually more volatile than longer-term rates. In the early 1980s, for example, short-term interest rates reached record highs, with 90-day rates exceeding 9 percent, while almost a decade later, the same rates were under 4 percent. In contrast, long-term rates have been much more stable. Long-term rates are less volatile because they reflect what will transpire over the long haul; they tend to average out future anticipated events. In contrast, the short-term rate is influenced only by near-term events. Long-term rates would be as volatile as short-term rates if the market anticipated the shocks to the short-term rates to be permanent. Usually, however, the market believes that over the longer period, short-term rates will return to more "normal" levels.

EXAMPLE 18.9

1. In 1992 the yield curve was very steeply upward-sloping, and short-term rates had reached very low levels. Such a curve arose because the economy was weak and low inflation had pushed short-term rates down. However, long-term rates did not decline as much, possibly because investors were unconvinced that over the longer term inflation rates would be kept as low as their current levels. That is, investors did not believe that permanent changes had occurred in the economy, and they anticipated inflation rates would increase, pushing future short-term rates toward their more "normal" levels.

2. Many simple models of the term structure assume the yield curve to be flat; they focus on shocks to the curve that are parallel. Such an assumption implies that the volatilities of all rates are the same. Equivalently, shocks to the short-term rate are assumed to be permanent and hence affect all rates equally across the term structure.

The term structure of interest rates shows the relationship between yields and maturity. To better understand the theory that explains the different yields, it is first necessary to understand how investors can use forward contracts to lock into borrowing or lending rates for future time periods. These contracts permit investors to avoid the risks associated with unanticipated shifts in the yield curve. The fair prices of these contracts can be computed from information extracted from the yield curve. Theories of the term structure try to explain the relationship between these locked-in rates and actual future spot rates. For example, it may be interesting to see whether we can extract information from the term structure that will be helpful in predicting future spot interest rates.

Forward Prices of Discount Bonds

Consider an investor who anticipates purchasing an m-period discount bond at some future date t. Assume the yield curve is currently upward-sloping, as in Example 18.8. The investor could wait until date t to make the purchase but is concerned that interest rates may drop unexpectedly in the interim, forcing bond prices to rise. To avoid the risk of having to pay a higher price, the investor enters into a contract which promises to deliver the m-period bond at date t for a predetermined price. Let $F_0[t, t+m]$ represent the predetermined price of this commitment based on a bond with face value $1.

EXAMPLE 18.10   Given the information from Example 18.8, the investor knows the current price of a six-month (one-period) pure discount bond is $P(0, 1) = \$0.9656$. If the yield curve remained unchanged over a six-month period, then the investor would anticipate paying $0.9656 for each $1 face value of a six-month bond. An investor concerned that interest rates might fall over the interim might consider entering into a forward contract that commits to purchasing a six-month discount bond in six months at a predetermined price.

Let $F_0[t, T]$ be the forward price at date 0 that requires delivery at date t of a pure discount bond that matures at date T. Assume that in Example 18.10, the forward price at date 0 requiring delivery at date 1 of a pure discount bond that matures at date 2 is given by $F_0[1, 2] = 0.9560$. It is straightforward to establish whether this price is a fair price that does not permit riskless arbitrage opportunities, since the bond underlying the contract is a traded security and the cost-of-carry model for forwards can be invoked.

To apply the cost-of-carry model, consider the trader who at date 0 wants to lock into the price of a pure discount bond that will have m periods to maturity at some future date t. The underlying security, a discount bond with maturity $t + m$, is financed by borrowing funds that will be paid back at the settlement date t. At the same time the trader sells these bonds forward at a forward price of $F_0[t, t+m]$. The underlying bond cost is $P(0, t+m)$ and is funded by borrowing at the rate $y_0(t)$. Since each dollar borrowed at date 0 requires a payback of $e^{y_0(t)t\Delta t} = 1/P(0, t)$ dollars at date t, borrowing $P(0, t+m)$ dollars requires a payback of $P(0, t+m)/P(0, t)$ dollars at date t. Exhibit 18.2 shows the cash flows for this strategy. Note that the cash flows at date t are known with certainty at date 0. Since the strategy required no initial investment, to avoid riskless arbitrage the cash flows at date t cannot be positive. Note too that since the underlying commodity is a tradable security, the reverse cash-and-carry strategy will prevent the terminal cash flows from being negative. Hence, it follows that

EXHIBIT 18.2 Cash-and-Carry Strategy

Action at Date 0	Cash Flow at Date 0	Action at Date t	Cash Flow at Date t
Buy underlying bond.	$-P(0, t + m)$	Deliver bond for forward price.	$F_0[t, t + m]$ $-P(0, t + m)/P(0, t)$
Borrow $P(0, t + m)$ dollars.	$P(0, t + m)$	Pay back loan.	$F_0[t, t + m]$
Sell forward contract.	—		$-P(0, t + m)/P(0, t)$
Net cash flow	0		

$$F_0[t, t + m] - P(0, t + m)/P(0, t) = 0$$

or

$$F_0[t, t + m] = P(0, t + m)/P(0, t) \qquad (18.9)$$

Investors can use the forward market to arrange for a loan to begin at some future date at a rate determined today. This rate is referred to as the **forward rate.** Specifically, the forward rate of return locked in over the period $[t, t + m]$, $f_0[t, t + m]$ say, is given by the solution to

$$F_0[t, t + m] = e^{-f_0[t, t+m]m\Delta t} \qquad (18.10)$$

Hence,

$$f_0[t, t + m] = -\ln\{F_0[t, t + m]\}/m\Delta t \qquad (18.11)$$

The forward rate $f_0[0, 1]$ for the immediate period $[0, 1]$, is the single-period spot rate, $y_0(1)$, and is usually referred to as the spot rate.

EXAMPLE 18.11 Continuing Example 18.10, the forward price for a one-period bond to be delivered in one period is $F_0[1, 2] = P(0, 2)/P(0, 1) = 0.9560$, and the forward rate from equation (18.11) is $f_0[1, 2] = -\ln\{F_0[1, 2]\}/0.5 = 0.0900$. At time $t = 0$, a trader who purchases the forward contract can lock into a borrowing annual rate of 9 percent for the six-month period $[1, 2]$. Also, by selling the forward contract, an investor who currently owns a two-period bond can lock into a sales price for the next period.

The remaining one-period forward prices and rates, calculated using equations (18.10) and (18.11), are $F_0[2, 3] = 0.9465$ and $f_0[2, 3] = 11\%$; $F_0[3, 4] = 0.9370$ and $f_0[3, 4] = 13\%$.

Once all the one-period forward prices and forward rates are computed, multiperiod forward prices and rates can easily be established. In particular, from equation (18.10), forward prices are linked as follows:

$$F_0[t, t+m] = F_0[t, t+s]F_0[t+s, t+m] \qquad \text{for } 0 < s < m$$

Hence, $F_0[2, 4] = F_0[2, 3]F_0[3, 4] = 0.8869$.

Finally, forward rates are linked as

$$f_0[t, t+m]m\ \Delta t = f_0[t, t+s]s\ \Delta t$$

$$+ f_0[t+s, t+m](m-s)\ \Delta t \quad \text{for } 0 < s < m$$

Hence, $f_0[2, 4] = \{f_0[2, 3] + f_0[3, 4]\}/2 = 12\%$.

Forward Prices of Coupon Bonds

Consider a forward contract that requires delivery of a coupon bond at date t. Assume the coupon bond has cash flows in each of the next m periods. Let the cash flow in period k be CF_k for $k = 1, 2, \ldots, m$, where m is the maturity date of the bond. Since a coupon bond can be viewed as a portfolio of discount bonds, its price, B_0 say, can be written as

$$B_0 = \sum_{k=1}^{m} CF_k P(0, k)$$

Once the forward price of discount bonds has been derived, the forward price for a contract that requires delivery of a coupon bond can easily be established. At date t the value of the portfolio of bonds is given by

$$B_t = \sum_{k=t+1}^{m} CF_k P(t, k)$$

That is, the short position is obligated to deliver CF_{t+1} pure discount bonds that mature in period $t + 1$, CF_{t+2} bonds that mature in period $t + 2$, and so on. Since the forward price of each pure discount bond can be extracted from the term structure, the forward prices of all these cash flows are known, and the forward price for the coupon bond is given by $FB_0[t, m]$, say, where

$$FB_0[t, m] = \sum_{k=t+1}^{m} CF_k F_0[t, k] \tag{18.12}$$

EXAMPLE 18.12   Consider a forward contract on a bond. The forward contract settles in two periods. The underlying bond is currently a four-period bond with coupons of $60 and final principal of $1000. The data are provided in Example 18.11. From equation (18.12) we have

$$FB_0[2, 4] = \$60F_0[2, 3] + \$1060F_0[2, 4]$$

Now, $F_0[2, 3] = 0.9465$ and $F_0[2, 4] = 0.8869$. Substituting into the above equation yields $FB_0[2, 4] = \$996.87$.

Rather than locking into a specific rate now, the investor could wait until time t and then invest at the prevailing rate. Since future spot rates are uncertain, the actual rate obtained by waiting until time t will be different from the forward rate. The strategy of waiting not only provides different returns but also entails different risks. Using the data in Example 18.11, the investor can lock in a yield of 9 percent for period $[1, 2]$. However, if the investor expects spot rates in the future to exceed 9 percent, then waiting may be preferable. We explore this choice problem later.

Forward Rates and Bond Prices

From equations (18.9) and (18.10), we have at time $t = 0$,

$$F_0[T - 1, T] = \frac{P(0, T)}{P(0, T - 1)} = e^{-f_0[T-1, T]\Delta t} \qquad (18.13)$$

or

$$P(0, T) = P(0, T - 1) \, e^{-f_0[T-1, T]\Delta t} \qquad (18.14)$$

Similarly,

$$P(0, T - 1) = P(0, T - 2) \, e^{-f_0[T-2, T-1]\Delta t}$$

Hence,

$$P(0, T) = [P(0, T - 2) \, e^{-f_0[T-2, T-1]\Delta t}] \, e^{-f_0[T-1, T]\Delta t}$$

Using this equation recursively leads to

$$P(0, T) = e^{-\sum_{j=0}^{T-1} f_0[j, j+1]\Delta t} \qquad (18.15)$$

Equation (18.15) shows that the bond price is fully determined by the sequence of forward rates. Equivalently, by comparing equations (18.4) and (18.15), we see the yield to maturity, $y_0(T)$, is just the average of all the relevant forward rates. That is,

$$y_0(T) = \frac{\sum_{j=0}^{T-1} f_0[j, j+1]}{T} \qquad (18.16)$$

EXAMPLE 18.13   Continuing Example 18.11, we had $f_0[0, 1] = 0.07, f_0[1, 2] = 0.09$, and $f_0[2, 3] = 0.11$. If these values are substituted into equation (18.16), the yield to maturity is recovered. In particular, $y_0(3) = 9\%$ and the bond price is $P(0, 3) = \$0.8737$.

Yield Curves and Forward Rates

Given the yield-to-maturity curve, all forward rates for all future time periods can readily be obtained, and forward prices of particular bonds can also be computed. Actually, the forward rates for each future time period are the real building blocks for many interest rate risk management activities, and in future chapters we shall begin our analyses by extracting all relevant forward rates. In order to do this we need to know how to construct the yield curve. This in turn requires knowledge of the basic riskless debt securities. We now turn attention to the set of securities issued by the U.S. government.

Treasury Securities

Treasury securities are issued to finance budget deficits. The securities are issued on regular schedules and sold at auctions where the participants include the Federal Reserve (mainly the New York Fed) and primary government security dealers. Through these auctions, funds are raised for new projects or to retire existing debt.

The Primary Market

There are about 40 primary government security dealers. They act as underwriters of new debt and maintain an active and liquid market for existing issues. The dealers must meet guidelines designated by the Federal Reserve Bank. They are expected to participate in Treasury auctions and to make markets in the full range of Treasury issues. Primary dealers are required to provide the Fed with daily reports on trading activity, inventory, and financial position. Each primary dealer is expected to generate at least 1 percent of the total customer volume across all primary dealers. With these responsibilities come significant benefits. Dealers have direct access to the New York Fed's trading desk, and consequently, they have a direct pulse on the market. In addition, many institutional investors restrict their business to primary dealers. The exact nature of these auctions is described in Appendix 18A.

The Secondary Market

Once Treasury securities are issued, they trade in the most active financial markets in the world. While some Treasury issues trade on organized exchanges, almost all of the secondary market activity occurs in the over-the-counter dealer market. The 40 primary dealers transact business over the telephone, buying and selling securities for their own accounts, arranging specific transactions for their customers and other dealers, and buying debt directly from the Treasury through the regular auctions for resale to investors. The primary dealers continually provide bids and offers on outstanding Treasuries. They profit by the bid-ask spread and by possible price appreciations in their inventories. The secondary market trades more than $100 billion worth of Treasury securities per day.

Trades between dealers are often facilitated by **interdealer brokers.** Such brokers do not carry proprietary positions. Instead, they anonymously display individual dealers' bid and ask prices as well as the quantities that are available. The emphasis on confidentiality ensures the trading positions and strategies of dealers are protected. In addition to the dealers and brokers, there are about 400 **secondary dealers** in this market. These dealers do not have access to the New York Fed's trading desk, and they do not have the reporting requirements the primary dealers have. They generally hold positions and profit from favorable occurrences, as well as earning the bid-ask spread. Since these inventories are usually financed, dealers can experience losses from carrying inventory if the financing charge exceeds the interest return.

The Instruments

Debt issued by the Treasury with maturities of one year or less is issued as discounted securities called **Treasury bills** (T-bills). Securities with maturities greater than a year are coupon securities. Coupon securities with maturities less than 10 years are called **Treasury notes;** those with longer maturities are called **Treasury bonds.** In this section we shall briefly describe these instruments as well as some other contracts, including repurchase agreements and Eurodollars.

Treasury Bills: The Short-Term Instruments

Treasury bills are issued in increments of $5,000 above a minimum amount of $10,000. Over $200 billion are issued per year. T-bills are unusual in that their prices are not directly quoted. The *Wall Street Journal*, for example, ranks T-bills by maturity. The maturity date is followed by "prices" expressed in **bank discount yield form,** r_y, where

$$r_y = \frac{[F - B_0]}{F} \times \frac{360}{m} \tag{18.17}$$

Here F is the face value, B_0 is the bond price, and m is the maturity in days. The difference between the bid and asked discount yield is the profit margin of the dealer. By substituting the asked discount yield into equation (18.17), we can obtain the asked bond price, B_0. That is,

$$B_0 = F\{1 - (m/360)r_y\} \tag{18.18}$$

The final column of Exhibit 18.3 shows the annualized bond-equivalent yield, r_A, based on the asked price.

$$r_A = \{(F - B_0)/B_0\} \times \{365/m\} \tag{18.19}$$

EXAMPLE 18.14 Consider a 13-week $10,000 T-bill with an asked discount yield of 8.88 percent. The cost of this bond is

$$B_0 = F\{1 - (m/360)r_y\}$$
$$= \$10,000\{1 - (91/360)0.0888\}$$
$$= \$9,775.53$$

The annualized bond-equivalent yield is

$$r_A = \{(F - B_0)/B_0\}(365/m)$$
$$= \left[\frac{\$10,000 - \$9,775.53}{\$9,775.53}\right]\left[\frac{365}{91}\right]$$
$$= 9.21\%$$

The effective annual rate of return compounded on a daily basis is

$$\left\{\frac{\$10,000}{\$9,775.53}\right\}^{365/91} - 1 = 0.0953 \quad \text{or} \quad 9.53\%$$

and the effective annual rate of return, compounded on a continuous basis, computed using equation (18.5) is

$$\ln\left\{\frac{\$10,000}{\$9,775.53}\right\} \times \frac{365}{91} = 0.0911 \quad \text{or} \quad 9.11\%$$

TREASURY BILLS

Maturity	Days to Mat.	Bid	Asked	Chg.	Ask Yld.
May 04 '95	1	5.69	5.59	+0.01	5.67
May 11 '95	8	5.58	5.48	....	5.56
May 18 '95	15	5.65	5.55	+0.01	5.64
May 25 '95	22	5.53	5.43	−0.01	5.52
Jun 01 '95	29	5.67	5.57	+0.01	5.67
Jun 08 '95	36	5.66	5.62	....	5.73
Jun 15 '95	43	5.64	5.60	+0.02	5.72
Jun 22 '95	50	5.65	5.61	+0.01	5.73
Jun 29 '95	57	5.62	5.58	....	5.71
Jul 06 '95	64	5.65	5.63	+0.01	5.77
Jul 13 '95	71	5.66	5.64	....	5.78
Jul 20 '95	78	5.67	5.65	+0.01	5.80
Jul 27 '95	85	5.71	5.69	+0.02	5.85
Aug 03 '95	92	5.73	5.71	+0.01	5.88
Aug 10 '95	99	5.74	5.72	+0.02	5.89
Aug 17 '95	106	5.75	5.73	+0.02	5.91
Aug 24 '95	113	5.74	5.72	+0.01	5.91
Aug 31 '95	120	5.74	5.72	....	5.93
Sep 07 '95	127	5.75	5.73	....	5.95
Sep 14 '95	134	5.75	5.73	....	5.95
Sep 21 '95	141	5.76	5.74	+0.02	5.95
Sep 28 '95	148	5.72	5.70	−0.01	5.93
Oct 05 '95	155	5.78	5.76	+0.01	6.00
Oct 12 '95	162	5.79	5.77	−0.01	6.02
Oct 19 '95	169	5.82	5.80	+0.01	6.05
Oct 26 '95	176	5.82	5.80	+0.01	6.07
Nov 16 '95	197	5.86	5.84	+0.02	6.10
Dec 14 '95	225	5.86	5.84	+0.02	6.11
Jan 11 '96	253	5.88	5.86	+0.01	6.14
Feb 08 '96	281	5.89	5.87	....	6.17
Mar 07 '96	309	5.89	5.87	+0.01	6.21
Apr 04 '96	337	5.91	5.89	....	6.25
May 02 '96	365	5.94	5.92	....	6.30

EXHIBIT 18.3   Treasury Bill Prices in the *Wall Street Journal*

Repurchase Agreements Dealers purchase large quantities of Treasury securities which are then redistributed to their clients. While these transactions could be financed with their own funds, more typically dealers use the repurchase agreement market or "repo" market to obtain financing.

A **repurchase agreement** is a contract in which an investor sells a security and promises to repurchase it at a specific future date for a predetermined higher price. The most common repurchase agreements extend for one day and are called **overnight repos.** The market for overnight repos is huge, with about $100 billion outstanding. Longer-term arrangements called **term repos** exist, but the market thins out rapidly as maturities extend beyond two weeks. Repo market rates are quoted as a percentage of the security's price and are annualized based on a 360-day year.

EXAMPLE 18.15 Assume a dealer needs to finance $10 million worth of T-bills. Suppose a customer has excess funds available. The dealer agrees to deliver the T-bills to the customer in exchange for $9,998,056 and to repurchase them for $10 million the next day. The $1,944 difference is the dollar interest on financing.

The following formula is used to calculate the dollar interest on a repo transaction:

$$\text{Dollar interest} = \text{Dollar principal} \times \text{Repo rate} \times \frac{\text{Repo term}}{360}$$

If the repo rate is 7 percent, then the dollar interest is $9,998,56 × 0.07 × 1/360 = $1,944.

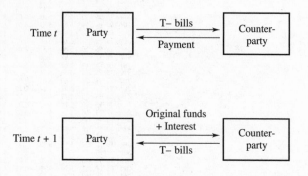

Generally, overnight repo rates are slightly lower than the rate for **federal funds,** which are reserves that depository institutions lend each other on an unsecured and traditionally overnight basis. The repo market is highly competitive and decentralized. Market participants include dealers, banks, nonfinancial corporations, pension funds, and the Federal Reserve.

Dealers profit if their inventories appreciate in value. Since these inventories are often financed at current repo rates, dealers can experience losses from carrying inventory if the financing charge exceeds the interest return. In many circumstances dealers will enter into forward contracts with clients, or they will sell T-bill futures contracts so as to better manage the risk of their inventories. The use of such contracts will be discussed later.

Eurodollars   Eurodollars are U.S. dollars on deposit outside the United States. The market for Eurodollars has grown dramatically as the dollar has become the major currency in international trade. Eurodollar (ED) deposits in major foreign banks and in foreign branches of U.S. banks are often preferred to domestic deposits because Eurodollars are not subject to the severe restrictions in place in the United States. Being more risky, Eurodollar deposits typically provide a higher rate than U.S. Treasury bills. Unlike T-bills, Eurodollar certificates of deposit (CDs) are direct obligations of the commercial banks and are not guaranteed by any government. Eurodollar deposits are most typically thought of as being U.S. dollar deposits in London. The interest rate offered on these deposits is called LIBOR, for London interbank offered rate, and is a good indicator of the cost of borrowing. Due to the credit risk of the issuing bank and political risk, LIBOR rates tend to be higher than T-bill rates, and they tend to change more rapidly than U.S. T-bill rates. The usual denomination of Eurodollar CDs is $1,000,000, and maturities are usually three to six months, although longer maturities are possible. Interest on Eurodollar deposits is simple interest based on a 360-day year and is paid at the maturity date.

EXAMPLE 18.16   Consider a three-month $1 million Eurodollar time deposit. Assume the three-month LIBOR rate is 10 percent. Then, after three months (90 days, say) the interest will be $1,000,000 \times (10/100) \times (90/360) = \$2,500$. If LIBOR were 10.01 percent, then the interest would be an additional $25. Hence, each basis point corresponds to $25.

Derivative contracts, such as options and futures, having payouts linked to interest rates or either T-bill or Eurodollar prices are available and will be discussed later.

Treasury Notes and Bonds: The Long-Term Instruments

So far we have considered only short-term contracts that pay no coupons prior to maturity. We now turn to coupon bonds issued by the Treasury. All Treasury bonds are identified by their coupon and maturity. "The ten and a half of 1999" means the Treasury bond with a 10.5 percent annual coupon rate that matures in 1999. The dollar amount of interest paid per year is 10.5 percent of the face value. In practice the coupon is paid in two equal installments, six months apart.

Quotations for Treasury notes and Treasury bonds are usually reported together, ordered by maturity. The bid and ask prices are reported in a special form. For example, a quotation of 86.12 means the price is 86 12/32 percent of face value. To actually purchase a bond, the investor must pay the asked price together with accrued interest since the last coupon payment. Accrued interest is computed by taking the size of the last coupon payment and multiplying by the ratio of the actual number of days since the last coupon payment, relative to the actual number of days in the coupon period.

Exhibit 18.4 illustrates the price quotations as they appear in the *Wall Street Journal*. Some T-bonds are callable, with the first call date coming five years before the bond matures. Recently, the number of callable Treasury securities has decreased.

Viewed from a coupon date, the yield to maturity of a Treasury bond is linked to its market price by the usual bond pricing equation

$$B_0 = \sum_{k=1}^{m} \frac{c/2}{(1 + y/2)^k} + \frac{1}{(1 + y/2)^m}$$

where y = Annual yield to maturity

c = Coupon rate

m = Number of coupon payouts remaining to maturity

If, however, the time to the first coupon date is not exactly six months, then the bond pricing equation must be modified. According to market convention the pricing equation is then given by

$$B_0 = \frac{1}{(1 + y/2)^p} \left\{ \sum_{k=1}^{m} \frac{c/2}{(1 + y/2)^{k-1}} + \frac{1}{(1 + y/2)^{m-1}} \right\} \qquad (18.20)$$

where $p = T_1/T$

T_1 = Number of days to the next coupon payment

T = Number of days from the last coupon date to the next coupon date

The price that an investor pays is the quoted price together with the accrued interest. The accrued interest at date t, $AI(t)$ say, equals the proportion of the current coupon period that has elapsed, times the coupon size. That is,

$$AI(t) = [1 - p]c/2$$

and

$$B(t) = Q(t) + AI(t)$$

where $Q(t)$ is the quoted bond price at date t.

EXAMPLE 18.17   Consider a T-bond with a 10 percent coupon which pays out 20 more coupons. The time from the last coupon date to the next, T, is 183 days. Since the last coupon was paid 83 days ago, the time to the next coupon, T_1, is 100 days. The quoted price for the bond, $Q(t)$, based on $100 face value is $104.08. In decimal form the price is 104 8/32 = $104.25. To obtain the market price, $B(t)$, the accrued interest must be

TREASURY BONDS, NOTES & BILLS

Monday, May 1, 1995

Representative Over-the-Counter quotations based on transactions of $1 million or more.

Treasury bond, note and bill quotes are as of mid-afternoon. Colons in bid-and-asked quotes represent 32nds; 101:01 means 101 1/32. Net changes in 32nds. n-Treasury note. Treasury bill quotes in hundredths, quoted on terms of a rate of discount. Days to maturity calculated from settlement date. All yields are to maturity and based on the asked quote. Latest 13-week and 26-week bills are boldfaced. For bonds callable prior to maturity, yields are computed to the earliest call date for issues quoted above par and to the maturity date for issues below par. *-When issued.

Source: Federal Reserve Bank of New York.

U.S. Treasury strips as of 3 p.m. Eastern time, also based on transactions of $1 million or more. Colons in bid-and-asked quotes represent 32nds; 101:01 means 101 1/32. Net changes in 32nds. Yields calculated on the asked quotation. ci-stripped coupon interest. bp-Treasury bond, stripped principal. np-Treasury note, stripped principal. For bonds callable prior to maturity, yields are computed to the earliest call date for issues quoted above par and to the maturity date for issues below par.

Source: Bear, Stearns & Co. via Street Software Technology Inc.

GOVT. BONDS & NOTES

Rate	Maturity Mo/Yr	Bid	Asked	Chg.	Ask Yld.
$5\frac{7}{8}$	May 95n	100:00	100:02	+ 1	3.88
$8\frac{1}{2}$	May 95n	100:02	100:04	....	4.54
$10\frac{3}{8}$	May 95	100:05	100:07	....	3.59
$11\frac{1}{4}$	May 95n	100:06	100:08	....	3.51
$12\frac{5}{8}$	May 95	100:07	100:11	....	2.12
$4\frac{1}{8}$	May 95n	99:28	99:30	+ 1	4.86
$4\frac{1}{8}$	Jun 95n	99:24	99:26	+ 1	5.23
$8\frac{7}{8}$	Jul 95n	100:18	100:20	+ 1	5.59
$4\frac{1}{4}$	Jul 95n	99:18	99:20	– 1	5.73
$4\frac{5}{8}$	Aug 95n	99:20	99:22	+ 1	5.67
$8\frac{1}{2}$	Aug 95n	100:22	100:24	– 1	5.74
$10\frac{1}{2}$	Aug 95n	101:08	101:10	– 1	5.73
$3\frac{7}{8}$	Aug 95n	99:09	99:11	....	5.89
$3\frac{7}{8}$	Sep 95n	99:03	99:05	+ 1	5.96
$8\frac{5}{8}$	Oct 95n	101:03	101:05	+ 1	5.97
$3\frac{7}{8}$	Oct 95n	98:29	98:31	+ 1	6.03
$5\frac{1}{8}$	Nov 95n	99:14	99:16	....	6.09
$8\frac{1}{2}$	Nov 95n	101:06	101:08	....	6.08
$9\frac{1}{2}$	Nov 95n	101:24	101:26	....	6.00
$11\frac{1}{2}$	Nov 95	103:00	103:04	– 1	5.48
$4\frac{1}{4}$	Nov 95n	98:29	98:31	+ 1	6.09
$4\frac{1}{4}$	Dec 95n	98:23	98:25	+ 1	6.16
$9\frac{1}{4}$	Jan 96n	102:00	102:02	....	6.21
4	Jan 96n	98:11	98:13	....	6.21
$7\frac{1}{2}$	Jan 96n	100:27	100:29	....	6.24
$4\frac{5}{8}$	Feb 96n	98:23	98:25	....	6.23
$7\frac{7}{8}$	Feb 96n	101:05	101:07	– 2	6.27
$8\frac{7}{8}$	Feb 96n	101:30	102:00	....	6.24
$4\frac{5}{8}$	Feb 96n	98:21	98:23	+ 1	6.24
$7\frac{1}{2}$	Feb 96n	100:30	101:00	+ 1	6.24
$5\frac{1}{8}$	Mar 96n	98:30	99:00	+ 1	6.27
$7\frac{3}{4}$	Mar 96n	101:07	101:09	....	6.28
$9\frac{3}{8}$	Apr 96n	102:25	102:27	– 1	6.25
$5\frac{1}{2}$	Apr 96n	99:05	99:07	....	6.32
$7\frac{5}{8}$	Apr 96n	101:07	101:09	+ 1	6.27
$4\frac{1}{4}$	May 96n	97:28	97:30	....	6.34
$7\frac{3}{8}$	May 96n	100:31	101:01	....	6.33
$5\frac{7}{8}$	May 96n	99:14	99:16	– 1	6.36
$7\frac{5}{8}$	May 96n	101:08	101:10	– 1	6.35
6	Jun 96n	99:17	99:19	– 1	6.37
$7\frac{7}{8}$	Jun 96n	101:20	101:22	+ 1	6.35
$7\frac{7}{8}$	Jul 96n	101:20	101:22	– 1	6.40
$6\frac{1}{8}$	Jul 96n	99:19	99:21	– 1	6.42
$7\frac{7}{8}$	Jul 96n	101:21	101:23	– 1	6.42
$4\frac{3}{8}$	Aug 96n	97:14	97:16	....	6.43
$6\frac{1}{4}$	Aug 96n	99:22	99:24	....	6.45
$7\frac{1}{4}$	Aug 96n	100:31	101:01	....	6.43
$6\frac{1}{2}$	Sep 96n	100:00	100:02	– 1	6.45
7	Sep 96n	100:23	100:25	– 1	6.41
8	Oct 96n	102:01	102:03	– 1	6.47
$6\frac{7}{8}$	Oct 96n	100:16	100:18	...	6.47
$4\frac{3}{8}$	Nov 96n	96:29	96:31	....	6.48
$7\frac{1}{4}$	Nov 96n	101:02	101:04	....	6.47
$6\frac{1}{2}$	Nov 96n	99:31	100:01	– 1	6.48
$7\frac{1}{4}$	Nov 96n	101:00	101:02	– 1	6.53
$6\frac{1}{8}$	Dec 96n	99:15	99:17	– 1	6.43
$7\frac{1}{2}$	Dec 96n	101:15	101:17	– 1	6.51
8	Jan 97n	102:10	102:12	....	6.50

Rate	Maturity Mo/Yr	Bid	Asked	Chg.	Ask Yld.
$11\frac{3}{4}$	Feb 01	122:28	123:00	– 3	6.87
8	May 01n	105:08	105:10	+ 1	6.91
$13\frac{1}{8}$	May 01	130:06	130:10	– 3	6.90
$7\frac{7}{8}$	Aug 01n	104:20	104:22	– 2	6.94
8	Aug 96-01	101:13	101:17	....	6.74
$13\frac{3}{8}$	Aug 01	132:12	132:16	– 2	6.92
$7\frac{1}{2}$	Nov 01n	102:23	102:25	– 2	6.96
$15\frac{3}{4}$	Nov 01	145:22	145:26	....	6.92
$14\frac{1}{4}$	Feb 02	139:02	139:06	+ 2	6.92
$7\frac{1}{2}$	May 02n	102:30	103:00	– 3	6.95
$6\frac{3}{8}$	Aug 02n	96:10	96:12	– 4	7.02
$11\frac{5}{8}$	Nov 02	126:18	126:22	– 3	7.01
$6\frac{1}{4}$	Feb 03n	95:06	95:08	– 3	7.05
$10\frac{3}{4}$	Feb 03	121:26	121:30	– 4	7.04
$10\frac{3}{4}$	May 03	122:06	122:10	– 5	7.06
$5\frac{3}{4}$	Aug 03n	91:25	91:27	– 3	7.07
$11\frac{1}{8}$	Aug 03	124:31	125:03	– 2	7.07
$11\frac{7}{8}$	Nov 03	130:05	130:09	– 5	7.09
$5\frac{7}{8}$	Feb 04n	92:06	92:08	– 2	7.07
$7\frac{1}{4}$	May 04n	101:03	101:05	– 3	7.07
$12\frac{3}{8}$	May 04	134:21	134:25	– 5	7.09
$7\frac{1}{4}$	Aug 04n	101:02	101:04	– 3	7.08
$13\frac{3}{4}$	Aug 04	144:15	144:19	– 7	7.11
$7\frac{7}{8}$	Nov 04n	105:11	105:13	– 3	7.09
$11\frac{5}{8}$	Nov 04	130:21	130:25	– 6	7.12
$7\frac{1}{2}$	Feb 05n	102:30	103:00	– 5	7.07
$8\frac{1}{4}$	May 00-05	104:05	104:09	– 4	7.22
12	May 05	134:07	134:11	– 5	7.15
$10\frac{3}{4}$	Aug 05	125:23	125:27	– 3	7.16
$9\frac{3}{8}$	Feb 06	116:18	116:22	– 5	7.13
$7\frac{5}{8}$	Feb 02-07	101:15	101:19	....	7.32
$7\frac{7}{8}$	Nov 02-07	103:21	103:25	– 1	7.22
$8\frac{3}{8}$	Aug 03-08	107:01	107:05	– 3	7.21
$8\frac{3}{4}$	Nov 03-08	109:15	109:19	– 4	7.22
$9\frac{1}{8}$	May 04-09	112:06	112:10	– 3	7.24
$10\frac{3}{8}$	Nov 04-09	121:06	121:10	– 4	7.24
$11\frac{3}{4}$	Feb 05-10	131:16	131:20	– 3	7.19
10	May 05-10	119:06	119:10	– 3	7.26
$12\frac{3}{4}$	Nov 05-10	140:01	140:05	– 4	7.24
$13\frac{7}{8}$	May 06-11	149:20	149:24	– 5	7.25
14	Nov 06-11	151:30	152:02	– 6	7.26
$10\frac{3}{8}$	Nov 07-12	124:11	124:15	....	7.35
12	Aug 08-13	138:29	139:01	– 3	7.35
$13\frac{1}{4}$	May 09-14	150:27	150:31	+ 1	7.36
$12\frac{1}{2}$	Aug 09-14	144:23	144:27	+ 3	7.37
$11\frac{3}{4}$	Nov 09-14	138:20	138:24	+ 2	7.36
$11\frac{1}{4}$	Feb 15	139:09	139:11	– 5	7.42
$10\frac{5}{8}$	Aug 15	133:03	133:05	....	7.43
$9\frac{7}{8}$	Nov 15	125:12	125:14	....	7.44
$9\frac{1}{4}$	Feb 16	118:26	118:28	– 3	7.45
$7\frac{1}{4}$	May 16	97:28	97:30	– 1	7.45
$7\frac{1}{2}$	Nov 16	100:17	100:19	– 3	7.44
$8\frac{3}{4}$	May 17	113:22	113:24	– 2	7.47
$8\frac{7}{8}$	Aug 17	115:03	115:05	– 1	7.47
$9\frac{1}{8}$	May 18	118:00	118:02	– 3	7.47
9	Nov 18	116:22	116:24	– 4	7.48
$8\frac{7}{8}$	Feb 19	115:12	115:14	– 4	7.48
$8\frac{1}{8}$	Aug 19	107:04	107:06	– 1	7.48
$8\frac{1}{2}$	Feb 20	111:13	111:15	....	7.48

EXHIBIT 18.4 Price Quotations of Selected T-Bonds and T-Notes in the *Wall Street Journal.*

Source: Reprinted by permission of the Wall Street Journal © 1995 Dow Jones & Company, Inc. All Rights Reserved Worldwide.

added. Since the last coupon was paid 83 days ago, the accrued interest per $100 face value, $AI(t)$, is given by

$$AI(t) = [83/183]5 = \$2.26775$$

The actual market price for the bond is its quoted price plus accrued interest. That is,

$$B(t) = \$104.25 + \$2.26775$$

$$= \$106.51775$$

or $106,517.75 per $100,000 face value. The yield to maturity, y, is obtained by solving the bond pricing equation.

Stripped-Coupon Bonds   Zero-coupon bonds are attractive investments for investors such as pension funds and insurance companies who have fixed obligations in the future and want to ensure that these obligations will be met regardless of future interest rates. Zero-coupon bonds permit terminal values to be locked in at known rates of return without incurring price and reinvestment risk. Given the likelihood of sizable demand for zeros by pension funds and insurance firms, it is somewhat surprising that few zeros have been issued. Indeed, apart from short-term Treasury bills, the U.S. Treasury has not issued any zeros. Moreover, very few firms have issued zeros. Prior to the Tax Equity and Responsibility Act of 1982, significant tax advantages were given to issuing zeros over coupon bonds. Yet even then hardly any zeros were issued. Today, the tax treatment of the two kinds of bonds is quite even, and zeros are still not regularly issued.

EXAMPLE 18.18   There may be good reasons for corporations not to issue zeros. De and Kale argue that if insiders of a corporation issuing debt have private information, then before revealing this information they may have incentives to issue bonds which exclude fixed-coupon payments and provide investors with no contingencies. As a result, uninformed market participants will view the issuance of such debt as an unfavorable signal. De and Kale show that debt contracts that do not provide for periodic payments cause more mispricing than debt contracts that do carry such provisions.

Although nonfinancial corporations do not sell many zeros, financial intermediaries do construct securities that resemble zero-coupon debt. Beginning in 1982, the practice of "stripping" U.S. Treasury securities developed. The first two big strippers were Merrill Lynch, which created TIGRS (Treasury investment growth receipts), and Salomon Brothers, which created CATS (certificates of accrual on Treasury receipts). These firms would purchase Treasury bonds, place them in trust, and then sell claims on the individual cash flows. If a 10-year bond with 20 semiannual coupons is stripped, the underlying bond is resold as 20 zeros, each of which trades separately in the securities market. In a perfect market, the portfolio of the individual strips has the same value as the whole bond. Differences in values could occur if tax treatments were different. Indeed, the creation of this product by Merrill Lynch and Salomon was primarily motivated by the favorable tax treatment of strips and the perception that there was an unsatisfied clientele who demanded zeros and who were prepared to pay a premium for them.

In practice, the cost of stripping and reselling the packages of zeros was quite high. First, trust accounts had to be set up. Second, buyers for the strips had to be found. Third, interest rate risk over the interim period had to be hedged. In order to reduce these costs and expedite stripping, in 1985 the U.S. Treasury declared some Treasury securities eligible to be stripped through the Federal Reserve book entry system. The resulting securities, called STRIPS (separate trading of registered interest and principal of securities), now dominate this market because it is the least costly form of stripping.

By issuing bonds that could be easily stripped, the Treasury reduced its interest costs. The reason is that the value of a strippable bond is determined by the maximum of two values, namely, the value of an otherwise identical but nonstrippable bond and the value of the strip. In 1987, the Treasury began to allow strips to be rebundled into underlying bonds. Thus, certain designated bonds can be stripped and rebundled repeatedly at essentially zero cost. Since such bonds have additional flexibilities, they must be at least as valuable and perhaps more valuable than their more rigid counterparts.

The Zero-Coupon Yield Curve The present value of \$1 due at a future date t, $P(0, t)$, can be established if the date t coincides with a payment date of a zero. Exhibit 18.5 shows the prices of STRIPS as reported in the *Wall Street Journal*.

U.S. TREASURY STRIPS

Mat.	Type	Bid	Asked	Chg.	Ask Yld.
May 95	ci	99:26	99:26	....	5.83
May 95	np	99:26	99:26	....	5.87
Aug 95	ci	98:11	98:11	....	5.87
Aug 95	np	98:10	98:10	....	5.93
Nov 95	ci	96:27	96:27	....	6.09
Nov 95	np	96:27	96:27	+ 1	6.08
Feb 96	ci	95:08	95:09	....	6.25
Feb 96	np	95:07	95:08	....	6.27
May 96	ci	93:24	93:25	+ 1	6.32
May 96	np	93:22	93:23	....	6.38
Aug 96	ci	92:13	92:14	....	6.20
Nov 96	ci	90:23	90:24	....	6.43
Nov 96	np	90:20	90:21	....	6.50
Feb 97	ci	89:06	89:08	....	6.47
May 97	ci	87:18	87:20	....	6.61
May 97	np	87:18	87:20	− 1	6.61
Aug 97	ci	86:04	86:06	....	6.61
Aug 97	np	86:01	86:02	− 1	6.66
Nov 97	ci	84:19	84:21	− 2	6.69
Nov 97	np	84:17	84:19	− 1	6.71
Feb 98	ci	83:04	83:06	− 1	6.72
Feb 98	np	83:03	83:05	− 1	6.72
May 98	ci	81:22	81:24	− 1	6.76
May 98	np	81:22	81:24	− 1	6.76
Aug 98	ci	80:07	80:10	− 1	6.78
Aug 98	np	80:06	80:09	− 2	6.80
Nov 98	ci	78:27	78:30	− 1	6.81
Nov 98	np	78:26	78:29	− 2	6.82
Feb 99	ci	77:16	77:19	− 1	6.81
Feb 99	np	77:15	77:17	− 1	6.83
May 99	ci	76:06	76:09	− 1	6.83
May 99	np	76:05	76:08	− 2	6.83
Aug 99	ci	74:30	75:01	....	6.82
Aug 99	np	74:28	74:31	− 1	6.83
Nov 99	ci	73:21	73:24	− 1	6.83
Nov 99	np	73:16	73:19	− 2	6.88
Feb 00	ci	72:12	72:15	− 1	6.84
Feb 00	np	72:07	72:10	− 2	6.88
May 00	ci	71:08	71:12	− 1	6.82

EXHIBIT 18.5 The Prices of Selected STRIPS in the *Wall Street Journal*.

Exhibit 18.6 shows the yields and prices of a few of the STRIPS. The next-to-last column shows the annualized continuously compounded rates of return. These values are computed using the equation

$$y_0(t) = -\ln[P(0, t)]/t \, \Delta t \qquad (18.21)$$

where $t \, \Delta t$ is the time in years until the bond matures. A plot of these yields is referred to as the zero-coupon yield curve. The zero-coupon yield curve computed using the prices of zeros is very useful because it permits us to determine the present value of any sequence of known cash flows. The actual discount factors for each maturity date are shown in the last column of Exhibit 18.6.

EXAMPLE 18.19 Consider a bond that provides the following cash flows:

Time (Months)	Size of Cash Flow ($)
6	300
12	600
18	1,800

From Exhibit 18.6 we see the discount factors for these three cash flows are 0.99469, 0.96687, and 0.94594. Hence, the value of this bond is $300 × 0.99469 + $600 × 0.96687 + $1,800 × 0.94594 = $2,581.22.

EXHIBIT 18.6 Computing Discount Factors from Prices of Strips

Maturity Date	Time to Maturity (Years)	Ask Price*	Ask Yield	Continuously Compounded Return	Discount Factor
Nov. 93	0.25	99.08	3.03	3.011	0.99250
Feb. 94	0.5	98.15	3.16	3.086	0.99469
May 94	0.75	97.19	3.30	3.248	0.97594
Aug. 94	1	96.22	3.40	3.369	0.96687
Feb. 95	1.5	94.19	3.76	3.705	0.94594
Aug. 95	2	92.18	3.92	3.864	0.92562
Aug. 96	3	87.22	4.44	4.380	0.87687
Aug. 97	4	82.16	4.88	4.809	0.8250
Aug. 98	5	77.18	5.15	5.082	0.7756
Aug. 00	7	68.03	5.57	5.489	0.6809
Aug. 03	10	55.03	6.06	5.944	0.5518
Aug. 08	15	37.29	6.57	6.467	0.3790
Aug. 13	20	26.10	6.79	6.676	0.2631
Aug. 22	29	15.00	6.65	6.542	0.1500

*The price after the decimal point is in 32nd. For example, 99.08 nears 99 8/32 percent of par. This gives a discount rate of 0.9925.

Source: Data taken from the *Wall Street Journal*, August 16, 1993.

If the cash flows do not occur at times at which zeros provide payouts, then the appropriate yield at which to discount the cash flow is not observable. In this case, the appropriate yield to use could be established by interpolation.[1]

Manufacturing Zero-Coupon Yield Curves from Coupon-Bearing Bonds   The true present value of any particular cash flow from a default-free bond is obtained by discounting each cash flow by its appropriate rate obtained from the zero-coupon yield curve. However, if all the cash flows of the bond are discounted at the bond's yield to maturity, then the sum of these resulting present values will equal the sum of all the true present values of cash flows.

In general, to value a sequence of cash flows, the yields to maturity for coupon bonds are not particularly useful. However, the price information provided by coupon bonds is quite useful, because it contains information on zero-coupon yields. Indeed, the price information provided by strips represents only a small sector of bond market activity, and the reported information may not fully reflect all information. That is, the reported strip information could be quite stale. The most active bonds that are traded are the most recently auctioned bonds, referred to as on-the-run Treasuries. Information on the prices of these bonds should be used in constructing the zero-coupon yield curve. There are several statistical procedures for extracting the zero-coupon yield curve from the prices of coupon bonds. Example 18.20 illustrates the simplest method, called a bootstrap method.

EXAMPLE 18.20   **The Bootstrap Method for Obtaining a Zero-Coupon Yield Curve**

Suppose the price of a one year T-bill with face value $100 is $92.311. Assume a T-bond with a coupon rate of 8 percent and a face value of $10,000 is due in two years. For simplicity, assume the coupon payments are made annually. Hence, $800 is due in one year and $10,800 is due in two years. The price of this bond is $2,682.49. Finally, assume there is a three-year T-bond that has annual coupons of 4 percent and face value of $100,000. The price of the bond is $85,242.72.

From the price of the one-year T-bill, we know the one-year discount rate is 0.92311. This implies a continuous yield to maturity of 8 percent. Now consider the two-year bond. The first cash flow should be discounted at 0.92311. The second cash flow should be discounted at $P(0, 2)$. Hence, we have

$$\$2,682.49 = \$800 \times 0.92311 + \$10,800 \times P(0, 2)$$

from which $P(0, 2) = 0.8352$ and $y_0(2) = 9.0$ percent. We now proceed to the three-year coupon bond, which pays annual coupons of $4,000. We have

$$\$85,242.72 = \$4,000 \times P(0, 1) + \$4,000 \times P(0, 2) + \$104,000 \times P(0, 3)$$

---

[1] Alternatively, a smooth function, obtained by regressing the yields to some polynomial function of time, can be established and then used to compute all yields at all time points.

Substituting for $P(0,1)$ and $P(0,2)$, we obtain

$$\$85,242.72 = \$4,000 \times 0.92311 + \$4,000 \times 0.92311 + \$104,000 \times P(0, 3)$$

from which $P(0, 3) = 0.75201$ or $y_0(3) = 9.5$ percent.

Continuing this procedure, we can generate the appropriate discount function, or zero-coupon yield curve, for increasing maturities. Of course, this procedure allows us only to compute yields for points in time where bonds pay coupons. If rates are required for dates between observed rates, then interpolation methods must be used.

Conclusion

This chapter focused on the construction of a yield curve from information provided by Treasury securities. Given the yield curve, we can compute forward prices for T-bills and T-bonds. This chapter emphasized the linkage between yields obtained from cash markets and the forward rates. In addition, we investigated the repo market and the Eurodollar market.

References

Carleton, W., and I. Cooper. "Estimation and Uses of the Term Structure of Interest Rates." *Journal of Finance* 31 (September 1976): 1067–83.

Coleman, T., L. Fischer, and R. Ibbotson. "Estimating the Term Structure of Interest Rates from Data That Include the Prices of Coupon Bonds." *Journal of Fixed Income* (September 1992): 85–116.

De, S., and J. Kale. "Contingent Payments and Debt Contracts." *Financial Management* 22 (1993): 106–22.

Fabozzi, F. *The Handbook of Fixed Income Securities,* 3rd ed. Business One, Homewood, Ill.: Irwin, 1991.

———. *Bond Markets, Analysis and Strategies,* 2nd ed., Englewood Cliffs, N.J.: Prentice-Hall, 1993.

McCulloch, J. "Measuring the Term Structure of Interest Rates." *Journal of Business* 44 (1971): 19–31.

Nelson, C., and A. Siegel. "Parsimonious Modeling of Yield Curves." *Journal of Business* 60 (October 1987): 473–89.

Shea, G. "Interest Rate Term Structure Estimation with Exponential Splines." *Journal of Finance* 40 (March 1985): 319–25.

Van Horne, J. *Financial Market Rates and Flows.* Englewood Cliffs, N. J.: Prentice-Hall, 1987.

Exercises

1. An investment requires an initial outlay of $100 and guarantees $104 back in 0.25 years.
   a. Compute the holding period return.
   b. Compute the simple annualized yield.
   c. Compute the compounded annualized yield for the investment, assuming quarterly compounding.
   d. What is the annualized continuously compounded rate of return for this investment?

2. A pure discount bond with a maturity of five years and a face value of $1000 is priced at $670.03.
   a. Compute the continuously compounded yield to maturity.
   b. Compute the yield to maturity using the bond-equivalent market convention. That is, compute the semiannualized yield to maturity, and then double it.

3. A discount bond with a face value of $1000 is currently priced at $786.60. The maturity of the bond is six years. The bond is callable in three years, however, for a price of $860.71.
   a. Compute the continuously compounded yield to maturity.
   b. Compute the continuously compounded yield to call.
   c. Comment on the potential problems with interpreting these two yield measures.

4. Suppose time periods are split up into six-month intervals. The annualized continuously compounded yields for the first four periods are

$$y_0(1) = 4\%$$

$$y_0(2) = 4\%$$

$$y_0(3) = 5\%$$

$$y_0(4) = 5\%$$

   a. Compute the pure discount bond prices.
   b. Compute the price of a forward contract that requires delivery of a one-period bond after one period.
   c. Compute the price of a forward contract that requires delivery of a two-period bond after one period.
   d. Compute the price of a forward contract that requires delivery of a coupon bond after one period. The underlying bond pays coupons of $50 in the second and third periods and returns the principal of $100 in the third period.
   e. Compute all one-period forward rates at dates 1, 2, and 3.
   f. Explain how a manager might interpret the above forward rates.

5. A Treasury bill provides a bank discount yield of 5 percent. The maturity of the bill is 90 days, and its face value is $10,000.

    a. Compute the price of the T-bill.

    b. Compute the annualized continuously compounded return for the bill.

6. The quoted price for a T-bond based on $100 face value is $104.02. The bond has a coupon of 8 percent payable semiannually. The time between coupon dates is 182 days. The last coupon was paid 140 days ago. Compute the market price of this bond.

7. The current continuously compounded yield curve is shown below.

Years to Maturity	Yield to Maturity (%)
1	4.02
2	4.50
3	5.20
4	5.40
5	6.00
10	6.05

    a. Use the yield curve to price a coupon bond that pays $300 in 3 years, $400 in 4 years, $500 in 5 years, and $1000 in 10 years.

    b. A forward contract with a settlement date of two years is written on this bond. Compute the forward price.

    c. What ramifications, if any, would there be if the contract in Exercise 7b were a futures contract?

8. An investor is considering a 90-day, $1 million Eurodollar time deposit. The three-month LIBOR rate is 7 percent. Compute the dollar interest that will be earned, and use it to compute the annualized rate of return.

APPENDIX 18A

The Treasury Auctions

About a week before each of its more than 150 auctions during the year, the Treasury would announce the amount of debt it was planning to sell. All eligible dealers would submit competitive sealed bids which specified the price they were prepared to pay and the quantity of debt. Other investors could place noncompetitive bids up to a fairly low ceiling without specifying a price. (Dealers are expected to bid competitively in each auction on behalf of their customers and for their own accounts. At most, a dealer can bid for 35 percent of the total issue.) Until recently, the Treasury sold securities through a **multiple-price, sealed-bid auction.** This is explained next.

Once all the bids were received, the Treasury would add up the quantity of noncompetitive bids and subtract that from the total debt it planned to sell. Historically, noncompetitive bids have accounted for about 10 to 25 percent of the issue. Then, starting at the highest-priced bid and moving down, the Treasury would add up the quantities of the competitive bids until it hit its total. Each bidder who won paid the stated price of its bid. Thus, each winning bidder paid a different price. All the noncompetitive bidders paid the average price of the awarded competitive bids.

The multiple-price, sealed-bid procedure is one of many possible bidding procedures. With such large amounts at stake, any improvements in the Treasury's auctioning procedure could lead to large savings. For example, a reduction of 1 basis point in the average issuing rate would trim more than $200 million from the federal deficit each year. In 1992 the Treasury decided to experiment with a **uniform-price, sealed-bid auction.** Under this procedure, with bids ranked from highest to lowest, the Treasury accepts bids up to the amount it planned to sell, but the winning bidders' prices would not vary. Instead, all winning bidders pay the same price, namely, the amount of the highest bid *not* accepted.

The main reason for changing the bidding procedure is that multiple-price, closed-bid procedures provided incentives for bidders to shade their bids toward the perceived market consensus. The higher the bid, the greater the probability of winning, but the lower the profit. All dealers attempt to guess where the security will trade after the auction, and their bids reflect their forecasts. High bids signal heightened probabilities of subsequent loss of profit. Indeed, the "winner" with the highest bid at the auction has valued the after-auction price the highest and is therefore most likely to lose profits. This is referred to as the **winner's curse;** it provides incentives for bidders not to be too aggressive in their bidding. Of course, bid shading carries with it the risk that the bid may be so low that the bidder is not awarded any securities. In selecting a bid price, bidders want to balance the gain from a lower winning bid against the risk of not winning. As a result, bidders have strong incentives to learn what others are planning to bid. Economists have shown that the more certain the consensus after-auction price is, the greater the incentives for dealers to submit bids lower than the true price they would otherwise pay. Multiple-price, sealed-bid auctions therefore encourage collusion among competing bidders, and strong incentives exist for bidders to shade their bids. Rules put in place to protect against market manipulation have been violated. For example, in 1991 Salomon Brothers was found guilty of illegal bidding practices, and the firm was temporarily barred from bidding in auctions for customer accounts; a year later, the firm settled with the government by paying $122 million to the Treasury and $68 million to the Justice Department.

In a uniform-price auction, the price paid by the winner does not depend solely on the bidder's bid. Hence, bid shading is less extreme, and the incentive to learn what other bidders plan to bid is also smaller. As a result, such auctions are less likely to be susceptible to market manipulation.

CHAPTER 19

Simple Models for Interest Rate Risk Management

In this chapter we review the factors that cause bond prices to be volatile. The Macaulay measure of duration and modified duration are described; the latter captures the exposure of a bond to interest rate risk. We present portfolio immunization strategies based on duration matching and duration-convexity matching, discussing the limitations of these approaches. We also discuss measures of risk caused by a twisting term structure. We can use the basic measures of duration, convexity, and twist risk to determine risk exposures. When derivatives are added to bond portfolios, the measures of duration and convexity change; this chapter provides measures of duration and convexity for call options.

The primary objectives of this chapter are the following:

- To describe measures of duration and convexity in regard to bond price volatility;

- To discuss the use of duration and convexity measures in immunization strategies; and

- To provide measures of duration and convexity for call options.

Sensitivity of Coupon Bond Prices

Changes in the yield curve tend to affect the price of some fixed-income securities more than others. The sensitivity of bond prices to interest rate change depends on many factors, including time to maturity, coupon size, and the risk of the bond. In this section we review the factors that influence bond pricing.

Effect of Coupon Size

Consider two coupon bonds alike in all aspects except coupon size. *A given change in yields will cause the price of the lower-coupon bond to change more in percentage terms.* The reason for this follows from the fact that higher-coupon bonds, having greater cash flows, return a higher proportion of value earlier than lower-coupon bonds. This implies that relatively less of the high-coupon bond faces the higher compounding associated with the new discount factor. Therefore, on a relative basis, less price adjustment is required for the higher-coupon bond.

EXAMPLE 19.1   Consider two four-year annual coupon bonds, both priced to yield 8 percent. The first bond has a 5 percent coupon, the second 10 percent. From the bond pricing equation, their prices are $900.63 and $1066.24, respectively. Assume interest rates change so that each bond is now priced to yield 10 percent. Then the new bond prices are

$$B_1 = \frac{\$50}{1.10} + \frac{\$50}{1.10^2} + \frac{\$50}{1.10^3} + \frac{\$1050}{1.10^4} = \$841.50$$

$$B_2 = \frac{\$100}{1.10} + \frac{\$100}{1.10^2} + \frac{\$100}{1.10^3} + \frac{\$1100}{1.10^4} = \$1000$$

In percentage terms, the 5 percent coupon bond has changed by

$$\frac{(\$900.63 - \$841.50)}{\$900.63} = 6.6\%$$

while the 10 percent coupon bond has changed by

$$\frac{(\$1066.24 - \$1000)}{\$1066.24} = 6.2\%$$

Hence, low-coupon bonds are more sensitive to yield changes than high-coupon bonds.

Bonds trading above their face value (**premium bonds**) have higher coupon rates than bonds trading below their face value (**discount bonds**); hence, all things being equal, premium bonds will be less sensitive to yield changes.

Effect of Maturity

In most cases a given change in yield will cause a longer-term bond to change more in percentage terms than a shorter-term bond. With some discount bonds, however, for a given decrease in yield, the percentage change in prices increases with maturity up to a point, then decreases with maturity.

EXAMPLE 19.2   Consider two 5 percent coupon bonds, both priced to yield 8 percent. One is a four-year bond, the second an eight-year bond. Both bonds pay interest annually. The shorter-term bond is priced at $900.63, while the longer-term bond is priced at $827.60. Assume yields rise to 10 percent. Then, from the bond pricing equation, the four-year bond will be priced at $841.50, while the eight-year bond will be priced at $733.40. In percentage terms, the decline in price of the shorter-term bond is 6.6 percent, compared to 11.4 percent for the longer-term bond.

Price-Yield Relationships

For a large decrease in yield, the percentage increase in price is greater than the percentage decrease in price for an equal increase in yield. That is, prices increase at an increasing rate as yields fall and decrease at a decreasing rate when rates rise.

EXAMPLE 19.3   Consider a four-year 8 percent bond with annual coupons sold at par ($1000) to yield 8 percent. First, assume yields fall to 6 percent. Then the bond price is

$$B_0 = \frac{\$80}{1.06} + \frac{\$80}{1.06^2} + \frac{\$80}{1.06^3} + \frac{\$1080}{1.06^4} = \$1069.30$$

This yield change causes a 6.93 percent change in bond price.

Second, assume yields rise to 10 percent. Then the bond price is

$$B_0 = \frac{\$80}{1.10} + \frac{\$80}{1.10^2} + \frac{\$80}{1.10^3} + \frac{\$1080}{1.10^4} = \$936.60$$

This yield change causes a 6.34 percent change in bond price. Thus, bond prices are more sensitive to yield decreases than to yield increases. Indeed, the smaller the initial yield to maturity, the larger the percentage change in the value of a bond for a given change in yield to maturity.

We have seen that the price sensitivity of a straight bond is affected by its coupon rate and maturity as well as the current level of yield. In general, for a given maturity, the lower the coupon rate, the greater the volatility; and for a fixed coupon, the greater the maturity, the greater the volatility. To compare bonds with different coupons and different maturities, a measure called duration is required. This is considered next.

Maturity and Duration

Since high-coupon bonds provide a larger proportion of total cash flow earlier in their life than lower-coupon bonds with the same maturity, they are effectively shorter-term instruments. As a result, the actual maturity date of the bond is not necessarily a good measure of the length of a coupon bond.

To obtain a more meaningful measure, it is helpful to first represent the bond as a portfolio of discount bonds and to measure the maturity of each cash flow.

From the bond pricing equation:

$$B_0 = \sum_{t=1}^{m} P(0, t)CF_t \qquad (19.1)$$

Let w_t be the present value contribution of the tth cash flow to the bond price. Then

$$w_t = \frac{P(0, t)CF_t}{B_0} \qquad t = 1, 2, \ldots, m \qquad (19.2)$$

The duration, $\mathbb{D}$, of a bond is just the weighted average number of periods for cash flows for this bond. That is,

$$\mathbb{D} = \sum_{t=1}^{m} tw_t = \sum_{t=1}^{m} tP(0, t)CF_t/B_0 \qquad (19.3)$$

Note that the greater the time until payments are received, the greater the duration. If the bond is a discount bond, all payment is deferred to maturity and the duration equals maturity. For bonds making periodic coupon payments, the early payments will reduce the duration away from the maturity.

Duration is affected by changes in the market yield, the coupon rate, and the time to maturity.

EXAMPLE 19.4 Consider a four-year bond paying a 9 percent coupon semiannually and priced to yield 9 percent. The cash flows every six months are shown in Exhibit 19.1, as well as the weights and duration calculation. Duration is

$$\sum_{t=1}^{8} \frac{tP(0, t)F_t}{1000} = \frac{6892}{1000} = 6.89 \text{ half years, or } 3.45 \text{ years}$$

EXHIBIT 19.1 Duration Calculations

Period	Cash Flow	$P(0, t)F_t$	$t^*P(0, t)^*F_t$
1	$ 45	$ 43.06	$ 43.06
2	45	41.21	82.42
3	45	39.43	118.30
4	45	37.74	150.94
5	45	36.11	180.55
6	45	34.56	207.33
7	45	33.07	231.47
8	1045	734.83	5878.63
Total		1000.00	6892.70

EXAMPLE 19.5   Exhibit 19.2 illustrates the sensitivity of duration to changes in yield, coupons, and maturity for a five-year bond that pays 12 percent annual coupons and yields 12 percent. For zero-coupon bonds the duration equals the maturity. For all bonds, with the exception of some bonds selling at deep discounts, duration will increase with maturity. In addition, duration increases as coupon rates decline and as yield to maturity declines. The figures in Exhibit 19.2 are therefore quite typical of the general behavior of duration.

Duration and Bond Price Sensitivity

The price of a coupon bond that pays m coupons can be written as

$$B_0 = \sum_{t=1}^{m} CF_t/(1 + y)^t$$

where y is the current market yield. Exhibit 19.3 shows the relationship between the bond price and yield.

The bond price is located at point P. The slope of the curve at P, dB/dy, can be shown to be[1]

$$\frac{dB}{dy} = -\mathbb{D}\frac{B}{(1 + y)} \tag{19.4}$$

EXHIBIT 19.2   Sensitivity of Duration to Yield, Coupon, and Maturity Change

Yield (Percent)	4	8	12	16	20
Duration	4.2	4.1	4.0	3.7	2.9

Coupon (Percent)	4	8	12	16	20
Duration	4.5	4.2	4.0	3.9	3.8

Maturity (Years)	3	5	7	10	30
Duration	2.7	4.0	5.1	6.3	9.0

---

[1] A proof of this result is provided in Appendix 19A.

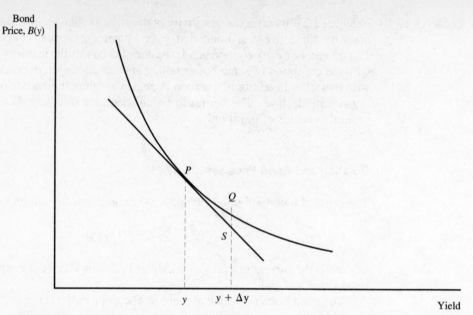

EXHIBIT 19.3   Bond Price–Yield Relationship

If we define modified duration as

$$\mathbb{D}_m = \mathbb{D}/(1 + y) \tag{19.5}$$

Then

$$\frac{dB}{dy} = -\mathbb{D}_m B \tag{19.6}$$

or

$$dB/B = -\mathbb{D}_m \, dy \tag{19.7}$$

That is, the instantaneous percentage change in bond price equals the negative of modified duration times the change in yield, provided the change in yield is very small. If a bond has a modified duration of 4, for example, then its market value will change by 4 percent when the yield per period changes by 1 percentage point. The higher the modified duration, the more exposed the bond is to interest rate changes.

EXAMPLE 19.6   Consider a four-year bond paying a 9 percent coupon semiannually and priced to yield 9 percent. The duration of the bond is 6.89 periods. The modified duration is therefore

$$\mathbb{D}_m = \mathbb{D}/(1 + y) = 6.89/1.045 = 6.593 \text{ periods or } 3.297 \text{ years}$$

For a 1-percentage-change in the annual yield to maturity, the change in the bond price is 3.297 percent.

Linear and Quadratic Approximations for the Change in a Bond Price

Assume the yield changes from y to $y + \Delta y$, where Δy is small. The bond price in Exhibit 19.3 then changes from $B(y)$ (point P) to $B(y + \Delta y)$ (point Q). For Δy sufficiently small, $B(y + \Delta y)$ can be approximated by $B'(y + \Delta y)$, where

$$B'(y + \Delta y) \approx B(y) + \frac{dB}{dy}\Delta y \qquad (19.8)$$

which is indicated by point S in Exhibit 19.3. Since $dB/dy = -\mathbb{D}_m B$, equation (19.8) can be rewritten as

$$B'(y + \Delta y) \approx B(y) - \mathbb{D}_m B(y)\,\Delta y \qquad (19.9)$$

Note that if Δy is "large," either positive or negative, then the linear, or first-order approximation, $B'(y + \Delta y)$, is always lower than the actual bond price. The error is attributable to the curvilinear or convex relationship between bond prices and yields.

To account for this convexity, we could use a second-order approximation, which takes into consideration how the slope changes as y changes. For convex relationships, the change in the slope is always increasing. For example, the slope at point Q is less negative than the slope at point P. A second-order approximation of $B(y + \Delta y)$ which takes into account the curvilinear relationship is given by[2]

$$B''(y + \Delta y) = B(y) - \mathbb{D}_m B(y)\,\Delta y + \frac{1}{2}\mathbb{C}(y)B(y)(\Delta y)^2 \qquad (19.10)$$

where $\quad \mathbb{C}(y) = \displaystyle\sum_{t=1}^{m} \frac{t(t+1)CF_t}{(1+y)^{t+2}B(y)}$ \qquad (19.11)

$\mathbb{C}(y)$ is referred to as the **convexity** of the bond. For noncallable bonds, convexity is always positive, implying that the slope of the price-yield equation is increasing (becoming less negative) as yields increase. The approximate change in the bond price for a small yield change is then given by

$$\Delta B(y) = B(y + \Delta y) - B(y) \approx -\mathbb{D}_m B(y)\Delta y + \frac{1}{2}\mathbb{C}(y)B(y)(\Delta y)^2 \qquad (19.12)$$

The quadratic approximation differs from the linear approximation by the last convexity term. Since this term is always positive, the quadratic approximation, $B''(y + \Delta y)$, will always provide higher values than the linear approximation, $B'(y + \Delta y)$.

For small changes in the yield to maturity, the linear approximation provides a good proxy for the change in bond price. That is, modified duration is a useful measure for price volatility. However, when the market perceives interest rate

---

[2] A derivation of this result is provided in Appendix 19A.

volatility to be high, then the adjustment made by the second-order approximation may be significant.

EXAMPLE 19.7 Consider a five-year bond that pays $80 in coupons semiannually (i.e., $40 per six months), has a face value of $1000, and is currently priced to yield 8 percent per year. The duration of this bond is 8.435 periods (half years), and the modified duration is $8.435/1.04 = 8.111$ periods. The convexity of the bond is 80.75 periods squared.

In this example, each period corresponds to a six-month interval. To convert the convexity measure to an annual figure, we divide by the square of the number of periods in the year. Hence, the annualized convexity in this example is $80.75/4 = 20.18$ years squared.

Exhibit 19.4 shows the actual bond price as computed by the bond pricing equation for a variety of yields to maturity and compares it to the linear and quadratic approximations.

Exhibit 19.5 provides a graphical comparison of the linear and quadratic approximations.

The following expressions may be useful for computing bond prices, duration, and convexity. The underlying bond pays a coupon of size c for the next n periods. The face value of the bond is F. The yield per period is y. For a semiannual coupon bond, the yield to maturity is therefore $2y$.

Bond price
$$B_0 = \frac{c}{y}\left\{1 - \frac{1}{(1+y)^n}\right\} + \frac{F}{(1+y)^n}$$

Modified duration
$$\mathbb{D}_m = \frac{\frac{c}{y^2}\left\{1 - \frac{1}{(1+y)^n}\right\} + \frac{n(F - c/y)}{(1+y)^{n+1}}}{B_0}$$

Convexity
$$C(y) = \frac{1}{B_0}\left[\frac{2c}{y^3}[1 - 1/(1+y)^n] - \frac{2c}{y^2}[n/(1+y)^{n+1}] + \frac{n(n+1)(F - c/y)}{(1+y)^{n+2}}\right]$$

EXHIBIT 19.4 Linear and Quadratic Approximations of the Bond Pricing Equation

Semiannual Yield to Maturity (%)	Bond Price ($)	Linear Approximation ($)	Error in Linear Approx. ($)	Quadratic Approximation ($)	Error in Quadratic Approx. ($)
2	1179.65	1162.20	17.45	1179.689	−0.039
3	1085.30	1081.10	4.20	1085.477	−0.177
4	1000.00	1000.00	0	1000.000	0
5	922.78	918.90	3.88	923.257	−0.477
6	852.79	837.80	14.99	855.248	−2.458
7	789.29	756.70	32.59	795.975	−6.685
8	731.59	675.60	55.99	745.435	−13.845

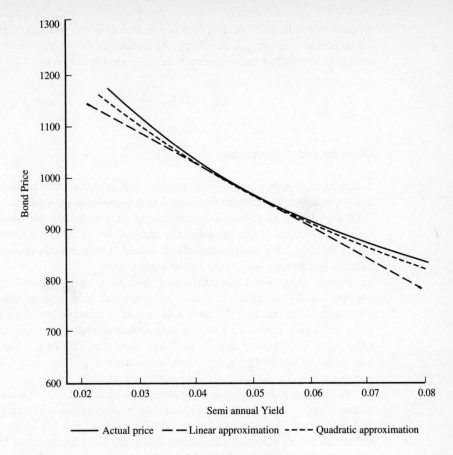

EXHIBIT 19.5   Linear and Quadratic Approximations

The bond formula is based on the fact that a coupon bond can be viewed as a combination of an annuity that pays c dollars for n periods and a discount bond that pays F dollars after n periods. The first term in the bond pricing equation is the value of the annuity. The modified duration equation is actually obtained by differentiating the bond pricing formula with respect to y and dividing by the bond price. Similarly, the convexity equation is obtained by differentiating the bond pricing equation twice with respect to y and then dividing by the bond price.

The Duration and Convexity of a Bond Portfolio

Like the beta value of an equity portfolio, the duration of a bond portfolio, $\mathbb{D}_p$, is computed as the weighted average of the durations of the individual bonds:

$$\mathbb{D}_p = \sum_{i=1}^{k} \alpha_i \mathbb{D}_i \qquad (19.13)$$

where k is the number of different bonds and α_i is the fraction of portfolio dollar value invested in bond i. Similarly, the convexity of a bond portfolio, $\mathbb{C}_p$, is the weighted average of the convexities of the individual bonds:

$$\mathbb{C}_p = \sum_{i=1}^{k} \alpha_i \mathbb{C}_i \qquad (19.14)$$

Duration and Immunization

Consider an investor whose goals require that an investment be dedicated to meet a specific liability of nominal amount F that comes due in m periods. If the investor held a portfolio of discount bonds having face value F and maturity m, then, regardless of interest rate behavior, the future value of the portfolio would cover the future liability. This dedicated portfolio is said to be **perfectly immunized** since its value is insensitive to changes in the yield curve.

Rather than use a discount bond, assume a coupon bond was held. With coupon bonds, two types of risk exist: price risk and coupon reinvestment risk. **Price risk** is the risk that the bond will be sold at a future time for a value different from what was expected. **Coupon reinvestment risk** is the risk associated with reinvesting the coupons at rates different from the yield of the bond when it was purchased. If the maturity date coincides with the holding period, then price risk is eliminated. As the maturity date increases, so does price risk.

As interest rates increase (decrease), bond prices decline (increase) while the returns from reinvested coupon receipts increase (decrease). The fact that price risk and reinvestment risk move in opposite directions and are subject to the same influences offers a way to manage interest rate risk. The choice of the appropriate coupon and maturity bond to hold over a given investment holding period is often accommodated by means of duration.

To illustrate the general idea, consider the case where the yield curve starts out flat, but immediately after the bond is purchased the yield changes to some new value and stays there. In this case, the investor is faced with both reinvestment and price risk, and after m periods, the liability may not be covered by the accrued value of the coupons and the residual price of the bond. To focus on this problem, assume the firm has a future obligation of $\$F$ to be paid out in m periods. The current value of this liability is V_0, where

$$V_0(y) = F/(1 + y)^m \qquad (19.15)$$

To meet this obligation the firm reserves V_0 dollars and uses this cash to purchase a coupon bond with maturity n. The value of this bond is

$$V_1(y) = \sum_{t=1}^{n} \frac{CF_t}{(1 + y)^t} \qquad (19.16)$$

Here, CF_t is the cash flow of the bond in period t, and, since the yield curve is flat, the yield y is the same as in equation (19.15). Moreover, by construction the number of bonds purchased is established such that $V_0(y) = V_1(y)$.

Now, assume a small shift in the yield curve occurs from y to $y + \Delta y$. The value of the liability changes from $V_0(y)$ to $V_0(y + \Delta y)$, while the value of the bond changes from $V_1(y)$ to $V_1(y + \Delta y)$. From equation (19.10) the bonds can be approximated by

$$V_0''(y + \Delta y) = V_0(y) - \mathbb{D}_m^0 V_0(y)\,\Delta y + \frac{1}{2}\mathbb{C}^0 V_0(y)(\Delta y)^2 \qquad (19.17)$$

$$V_1''(y + \Delta y) = V_1(y) - \mathbb{D}_m^1 V_1(y)\,\Delta y + \frac{1}{2}\mathbb{C}^1 V_1(y)(\Delta y)^2 \qquad (19.18)$$

For the liability to be immunized by the bond, their market values after the interest rate change should remain equal. That is,

$$V_0(y) - \mathbb{D}_m^0 V_0(y)\,\Delta y + \frac{1}{2}\mathbb{C}^0 V_0(y)(\Delta y)^2 = V_1(y) - \mathbb{D}_m^1 V_1(y)\,\Delta y + \frac{1}{2}\mathbb{C}^1 V_1(y)(\Delta y)^2$$

and since $V_0(y) = V_1(y)$, this implies

$$-\mathbb{D}_m^0\,\Delta y + \frac{1}{2}\mathbb{C}^0(\Delta y)^2 = -\mathbb{D}_m^1\,\Delta y + \frac{1}{2}\mathbb{C}^1(\Delta y)^2$$

For small interest rate changes, $(\Delta y)^2$ is insignificant and the above equation reduces to

$$\mathbb{D}_m^0 = \mathbb{D}_m^1 \qquad (19.19)$$

That is, the bond selected to immunize the liability should have the property that its duration equals the time remaining to maturity of the liability.

In summary, we have shown that if the yield curve is flat, with a small parallel shift occurring after purchase of the bond, then for the market value of the coupon bond to equal the market value of the future obligation, the duration of the bond selected should equal the holding period. Since in our example the duration of the liability is m, the target bond portfolio should also have a duration of m.

The above result is really only approximate, since the change in bond prices was captured by a first-order approximation. If the changes in yields are large, this approximation may not hold very well. If a tighter immunization is required, the convexities should be matched as well, that is, $\mathbb{C}^0 = \mathbb{C}^1$. For our particular problem, using the convexity equation, the convexity of the liability is given by

$$\mathbb{C}^0(y) = \frac{m(m + 1)F}{(1 + y)^{m+2}V_0(y)}$$

Substituting for $V_0(y)$ and simplifying leads to

$$\mathbb{C}^0(y) = \frac{m(m + 1)}{(1 + y)^2}$$

Equating the convexity of the liability to that of the bond and simplifying leads to the condition

$$m(m + 1) = \sum_{t=1}^{n} t(t + 1)CF_t/(1 + y)^t \qquad (19.20)$$

A bond having a duration of m and satisfying equation (19.20) will match the liability more precisely than an alternative bond that satisfies equation (19.19) alone.

EXAMPLE 19.8   Consider a five-year bond that pays 12 percent annual coupons and yields 12 percent. Assume the investment horizon is four years. Since the duration is four years, the bond is locally immunized. If rates fall immediately to 11 percent and stay there over the four-year period, the drop from coupon reinvestment returns will be offset exactly by increases in the price of the bond.

EXAMPLE 19.9   A $1480 liability is due in 10 periods (five years). The yield curve is currently flat at 4 percent per period (8 percent per year). With semiannual compounding the present value of this liability is $V_0(y) = \$1480/(1.04)^{10} = \$1000$.

To immunize this liability an investor is considering purchasing the appropriate number of units of a bond that pays $69.75 every period and matures in 14 periods. The current price of the bond is $1314.25, and its duration is 10 periods. Suppose $1000 (or 0.7609 units) of the bond were purchased. If the yield curve stays flat at 8 percent and all coupons are reinvested, then the value of this portfolio after five years will equal the liability of $1480.

If, on the other hand, after the investor buys the bond the yield to maturity changes from 8 percent to 10 percent and stays there, then all bond prices will drop. However, the higher returns on coupon income will partially offset this price drop. The total accumulated value from holding one bond for five years (10 periods) is given by

$$\sum_{t=1}^{10} CF(1.05)^{t-1} + \sum_{t=11}^{14} \frac{CF}{(1.05)^{t-10}} + \frac{\$1000}{(1.05)^4} = \$1947.34$$

where $CF = \$69.75$ is the coupon payout in each period. Hence, the total value of 0.7609 units of the bond is $(0.7609)(1947.34) = \$1481.7$, which is sufficient to meet the $1480 liability.

Exhibit 19.6 shows the accrued value of the portfolio for different changes in the yield curve. Note that regardless of the shift in the yield curve, price risk is offset by reinvestment risk and the accrued value from the portfolio always exceeds the liability.

Exhibit 19.7 provides information on two alternative bonds A and C.

The previous analysis is repeated for these bonds and illustrated in Exhibit 19.8. Note that the total accumulated value after five years may not be sufficient to meet the liability. For example, by holding bond C, the investor is speculating that interest rates will decrease and that the loss of reinvestment income obtained from lower yields will be more than offset by the accompanying price increase. Similarly, if bond A (low duration) is held, the investor is speculating that interest rates will increase and that the drop in price will be compensated by higher reinvestment income.

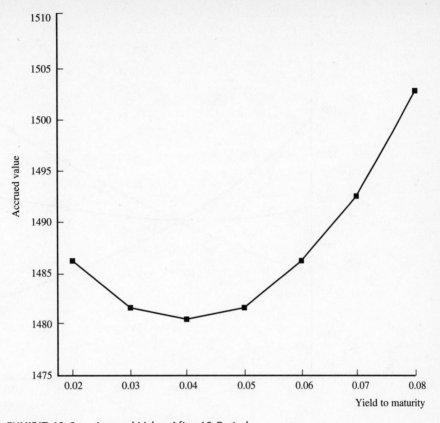

EXHIBIT 19.6   Accrued Value After 10 Periods

A portfolio of bonds A and C could be constructed to have a duration equal to the duration of the liability (10 periods) and an initial value equal to the liability ($1000). Specifically, consider purchasing 0.4574 units of bond A and 0.3143 units of bond C. The value of this portfolio, V_p, is

$$V_p = 0.4574(\$1218.99) + 0.3143(\$1407.71) = \$1000$$

Moreover, the duration of the portfolio is easily computed. The fraction of wealth

EXHIBIT 19.7   Bond Information

	Bond A	Bond B	Bond C
Bond price	$1218.994	$1314.253	$1407.71
Amount of bond	0.8203	0.7609	0.7103
Semiannual yield	4%	4%	4%
Maturity (periods)	10	14	20
Coupon	$67	$69.75	$70
Face value	$1000	$1000	$1000
Duration (periods)	7.85	10	12.71

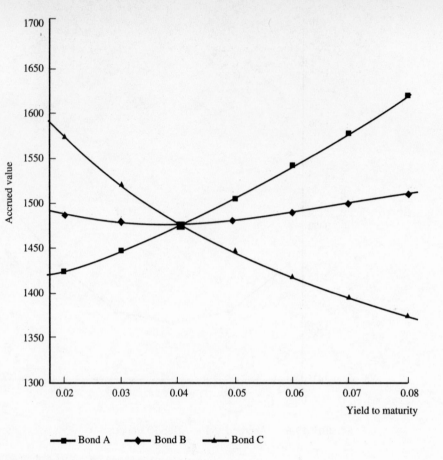

Bond A ■ Bond B ◆ Bond C ▲

EXHIBIT 19.8   Accrued Values of Different Bonds

in bond A, α_A, is given by

$$\alpha_A = \frac{0.4574(\$1218.99)}{\$1000} = 0.55756$$

Hence, the duration of the portfolio is $\mathbb{D}_P$, where

$$\mathbb{D}_P = \alpha_A \mathbb{D}_A + (1 - \alpha_A)\mathbb{D}_C$$

$$= (0.55756)(7.85) + (0.44243)(12.717) = 10 \text{ periods}$$

Exhibit 19.9 compares the accrued value of this portfolio to the value of bond B. The above analysis reveals that many portfolios of bonds could be constructed to have the same duration as the targeted liability, and hence the portfolio that immunizes the liability by duration matching is not unique. In this example the portfolio of bonds appears to be superior to bond B because the portfolio's accrued terminal value is larger for all yield shifts. The convexity of the portfolio is 131.3 compared to 101.7 for the liability.

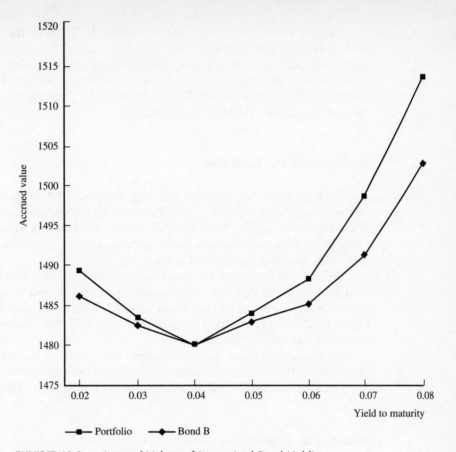

EXHIBIT 19.9   Accrued Values of Immunized Bond Holdings

Rather than match the convexity of the liability, we might conclude that among all duration-matched bond portfolios, the best portfolio is the one with the highest convexity. The appropriate portfolio of bonds that achieves maximum convexity can be obtained by solving the following linear programming problem.

$$\text{Maximize} \atop \alpha_i \qquad \sum_{i=1}^{k} \alpha_i \mathbb{C}_i$$

$$\text{subject to} \qquad \sum_{i=1}^{k} \alpha_i \mathbb{D}_i = m$$

$$\sum_{i=1}^{k} \alpha_i = 1$$

where α_i is the proportion of wealth allocated to bond i and k represents the number of candidate bonds. A duration-matched bond portfolio having maximum convexity has the property that the selected bonds usually have extreme durations and/or maturities. Such a portfolio is called a **barbell portfolio** since the cash flows reach their maximums at extreme time points.

EXAMPLE 19.10 Consider our three bonds A, B, and C. Exhibit 19.10 shows the composition of three portfolios. All portfolios have the same duration but different convexities. Portfolio 3 has convexity equal to the convexity of the liability. Exhibit 19.11 compares the total accrued values of the three portfolios. As can be seen, portfolio 3 most closely matches the cash flows of the liability. The high-convexity portfolio appears to dominate the other portfolios.

Immunization and Twist Risk

The linear programming problem following Example 19.9 produced the portfolio of bonds that was most convex, and hence most likely to produce surplus cash flows at the date of the liability. However, this analysis was based on parallel shifts in the yield curve. If interest rate shifts are not parallel, a duration-matched portfolio may have value less than the targeted liability.

The risk we neglected by assuming that yield curves shifted in parallel is referred to as **twist risk.** We now consider measures of twist risk. Exhibit 19.12 shows the cash flows of two portfolios of bonds having the same duration as the target. Portfolio A is a barbell portfolio; portfolio B is closer to a bullet portfolio. As before, the liability date is m.

While portfolio A has greater convexity than portfolio B, it is riskier. To see this, consider what happens if interest rates change in an arbitrary nonparallel way. Suppose short-term rates decline and long-term rates increase. The accrued values

EXHIBIT 19.10 Portfolio Comparisons

Bonds	Portfolio 1			Portfolio 2		
	A	B	C	A	B	C
Quantity (x_i)	0	1	0	0.5574	0	0.4426
Duration	7.85	10	12.70	7.85	10	12.70
Convexity	72.9	121.6	204.8	72.9	121.6	204.8
Portfolio duration		10			10	
Portfolio convexity		121.6			131.3	

Bonds	Portfolio 3		
	A	B	C
Quantity (x_i)	−1.14	3.04	−0.90
Duration	7.85	10	12.70
Convexity	72.9	121.6	204.8
Portfolio duration		10	
Portfolio convexity		101.7	

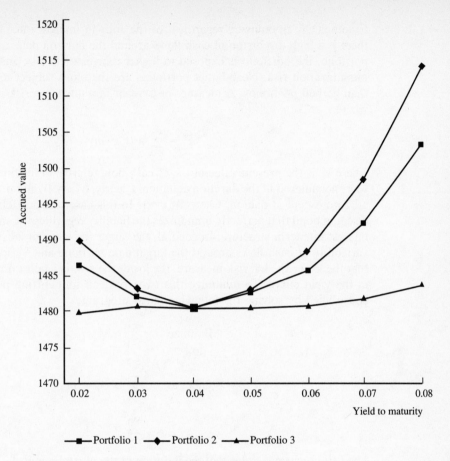

EXHIBIT 19.11   Portfolio Comparisons Versus Yield

of A and B will be lower than the target value because of lower reinvestment rates and lower bond prices. However, the loss will be greater in A than in B. First, lower reinvestment rates are experienced for longer periods with A; and second, the price risk at m is greater for the long-term bond in A than that in B. The bullet portfolio has much less exposure to a change in shape of the term structure. Indeed if the bond portfolio immunizing the liability has no reinvestment risk, then the liability

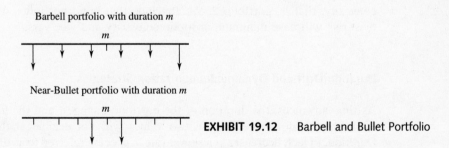

EXHIBIT 19.12   Barbell and Bullet Portfolio

is completely immunized regardless of the shift in interest rate structure. When there is a high dispersion of cash flows around the horizon date, as in the barbell portfolio, the portfolio is exposed to higher reinvestment risk and hence greater immunization risk. Near-bullet portfolios are therefore subject to less twist risk than barbell portfolios. A measure of twist or immunization risk is given by $\mathbb{M}^2$, where

$$\mathbb{M}^2 = \sum_{t=1}^{n} w_t(t - m)^2 \qquad (19.21)$$

where W_t is the present value of the tth cash flow relative to the bond price, which was encountered in the duration equation. Clearly, $\mathbb{M}^2 = 0$ only if the weights are all zero except at date m, where $W_m = 1$. In this case, the portfolio consists of a discount bond that perfectly immunizes the liability regardless of any shocks in the interest rate term structure. In general, the larger the value of $\mathbb{M}^2$, the greater the variability of cash flows around the target date m. Fong and Vasicek have shown that the lower the $\mathbb{M}^2$ risk measure, the lower the risk is against nonparallel shifts in the yield curve. To minimize this twist risk, an immunizing portfolio can be constructed by solving the following linear program:

$$\underset{\{\alpha_j\}}{\text{Minimize}} \quad \sum_{j=1}^{k} \alpha_j \mathbb{M}_j^2$$

$$\text{subject to} \quad \sum_{j=1}^{k} \alpha_j \mathbb{D}_j = m$$

$$\sum_{j=1}^{k} \alpha_j = 1$$

The first constraint states that the duration of the portfolio must be m. The second constraint forces the sum of the fraction of wealth invested in each bond to add up to one. Additional constraints, such as convexity and nonnegativity constraints, could be included.

EXAMPLE 19.11 Consider the three bond portfolios in Example 19.10. Their twist risk measures are 37.49, 52.28, and 7.17, respectively. The minimum-twist-risk portfolio is portfolio 3. The maximum-twist-risk portfolio is precisely the portfolio that maximizes convexity, that is, portfolio 2. We conclude that bond portfolios with minimum twist risk will have minimum portfolio convexity and vice versa.

Duration Drift and Dynamic Immunization Strategies

As time advances, the duration of the portfolio changes, and the holding period diminishes. Unfortunately, these two values will not decline at the same rate. Duration, in fact, decreases at a slower rate, a process referred to as **duration drift.**

Hence, a portfolio of coupon bonds with duration matching the original liability period, m, will after a certain amount of time, t say, have a duration exceeding the target value, $m - t$. This implies that to maintain an immunized position, the portfolio needs to be periodically readjusted to reset its duration to the time remaining to the liability payment.

The duration procedures described in this chapter have for the most part assumed yield curves to be flat, and shocks to the yield curve have been restricted to parallel shifts. In practice, yield curves do not behave this way. Indeed, it is unreasonable to assume that yields to maturity on different assets will change by the same amount. First, yields to maturity are complex averages of the underlying spot rates. For a given shift in the spot rate curve, the yields to maturity on different assets will change by differing amounts. Second, yields for different maturities are imperfectly correlated. If short-term rates increase by 1 percent, long-term rates typically move by less than 1 percent. Indeed, the short- and long-term rates could move in different directions, causing the yield curve to increase or decrease in steepness, for example. This twisting shape in the yield curve was not explicitly considered in the previous models. It suggests that the yield curve responds to more than one factor. Because more than one factor is causing shocks to the yield curve, we need to establish more complex duration models. Ideally, these models should be based on more realistic models of interest rate behavior. A significant body of research has been devoted to this problem, and many alternative duration measures have been constructed.

These more complex approaches, however, have not as yet been shown to produce significantly better results. The main reason for this is that the true specification of the interest rate process is not well understood.[3] Empirical studies using alternative definitions of duration have been conducted, and the conclusions are that the simple method works as well as any of the more complex alternatives.

Duration and Convexity of Options on Bonds and Callable Bonds*

For the moment, assume that we have a model for pricing call options on a bond. Let $C(y)$ be the call price. Recall that the delta value, Δ, measures the sensitivity of the call price to small changes in the underlying bond price. That is,

$$\Delta = \frac{dC}{dB} \tag{19.22}$$

Similarly, the gamma value, γ, measures the rate of change of the Δ value. That is,

$$\gamma = \frac{d\Delta}{dB} = \frac{d^2C}{dB^2} \tag{19.23}$$

The modified duration of a bond is given by

---

* This section provides advanced material and is optional reading for students.

[3] More will be said about the interest rate process in Part 6.

$$\frac{dB}{dy} = -\mathbb{D}_m B$$

and the convexity of a bond is

$$\frac{d^2B}{dy^2} = \mathbb{C}B$$

Similarly, the modified duration of a call, $\mathbb{D}_m^c$, and its convexity, $\mathbb{C}^c$, capture the sensitivity of the call to changes in interest rates:

$$\frac{dC}{dy} = -\mathbb{D}_m^c C$$

$$\frac{d^2C}{dy^2} = \mathbb{C}^c C$$

The duration of a call option is related to the duration of the bond underlying the call. To see this, note that

$$\frac{dC}{dy} = \frac{dC}{dB}\frac{dB}{dy}$$

Hence $-\mathbb{D}_m^c C = \Delta(-\mathbb{D}_m B)$

or $\mathbb{D}_m^c = \mathbb{D}_m \frac{B}{C}\Delta$ (19.24)

Similarly, the convexity of a call option is related to the convexity of the underlying bond and the gamma of the option. It can be shown that

$$\mathbb{C}_c = \frac{B}{C}\{\Delta\mathbb{C} - \mathbb{D}_m B\gamma\}$$ (19.25)

Recall that a callable bond can be viewed as a portfolio consisting of a straight bond together with a written call option on the bond. Let G represent the price of a callable bond. Then

$$G = B - C$$ (19.26)

The duration, $\mathbb{D}^G$ say, and convexity, $\mathbb{C}^G$ say, of the callable bond can then easily be computed. In particular,

$$\mathbb{D}^G = \frac{B}{G}\mathbb{D}_m(1 - \Delta)$$ (19.27)

$$\mathbb{C}^G = \frac{B}{G}\{\mathbb{C}(1 - \Delta) - B\Delta^2\gamma\}$$ (19.28)

The duration of a callable bond gives an indication of the true price sensitivity of the bond to interest rates. The value will always be lower than the duration of the straight bond but higher than the duration of the option. Similarly, the convexity of

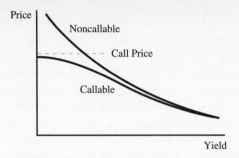

EXHIBIT 19.13   Price-Yield Relationship for a Callable Bond

the callable bond will never be greater than that of the straight bond, because the delta and gamma values will never be less than zero. A small delta and gamma value imply that the convexity is close to that of the noncallable bond. However, if delta and gamma are large, it is possible for the convexity to become negative. Negative convexity can best be illustrated graphically. Exhibit 19.13 shows the price-yield relationship for the callable bond. As rates decline, the value of the straight bond increases, as does the value of the call option. When the call is deep in the money, its price rises dollar for dollar with the bond, causing the callable bond price to converge in value.

In Part 6 we shall establish pricing models for interest rate claims. These models will then permit delta and gamma values to be computed as well as the duration and convexity measures.

Conclusion

This chapter has reviewed the basic concepts of risk management measures in the bond market. The most common measures of the sensitivity of default-free bonds to interest rate changes are captured by modified duration and convexity. The assumption here is that when shocks occur in the yield curve, they are parallel shocks. Applications of these measures were provided. In particular, we investigated how portfolio managers can use duration and convexity to immunize debt obligations.

References

This chapter draws very heavily from the presentation of duration in the textbook *Numerical Methods in Finance* by Simon Benninga; the book and its accompanying software are highly recommended. Another excellent discussion of duration is given by Dunetz and Mahoney. For a comprehensive treatment of duration, the text by Bierwag is recommended. More advanced material that discusses innovations such as key rate durations, are provided by Ho.

Benninga, S. *Numerical Methods in Finance.* Cambridge, Mass.: MIT, 1989.

Bierwag, G. O. "Immunization, Duration, and the Term Structure of Interest Rates." *Journal of Financial and Quantitative Analysis* 12 (1977): 725–41.

————. *Duration Analysis: Managing Interest Rate Risk.* Cambridge, Mass.: Ballinger.

Bierwag, G. O., I. Fooladi, and G. S. Roberts. "Designing an Immunized Portfolio: Is *M*-squared the Key?" *Journal of Banking and Finance* 17 (1993): 1147–70.

Bierwag, G. O., G. G. Kaufman, and C. Khang. "Duration and Bond Portfolio Analysis: An Overview." *Journal of Financial and Quantitative Analysis* 13 (1978): 671–85.

Bierwag, G. O., G. G. Kaufman, C. Latta, and G. S. Roberts. "Usefulness of Duration in Bond Portfolio Management: Response to Critics." *Journal of Portfolio Management* 13 (1987): 48–52.

Bierwag, G. O, G. C. Kaufman, R. Schweitzer, and A. Toevs. "The Art and Risk Management in Bond Portfolios." *Journal of Portfolio Management* (Spring 1981): 27–36.

Bierwag, G. O., G. C. Kaufman, and A. Toevs. "Single-Factor Duration Models in a General Equilibrium Framework." *Journal of Finance* 37 (1982): 325–38.

Chambers, D. R. "An Immunization Strategy for Future Contracts on Government Securities." *Journal of Future Markets* 4 (1984): 173–88.

Chambers, D. R., and W. Carleton. "A Generalized Approach to Duration." *Research in Finance* 7 (1988): 163–81.

Chua, J. "A Closed-Form Formula for Calculating Bond Duration." *Financial Analysts Journal* (May/June 1984): 76–78.

Dunetz, M., and J. Mahoney. "Using Duration and Convexity in the Analysis of Callable Bonds." *Financial Analysts Journal* (May 1988): 53–72.

Fong, H. G., and F. J. Fabozzi. *Fixed Income Portfolio Management.* Homewood, Ill.: Dow Jones–Irwin, 1985.

Fong, H. G., and O. Vasicek. "The Tradeoff Between Return and Risk in Immunized Portfolios." *Financial Analysts Journal* (September-October 1983): 73–78.

————. "Return Maximization for Immunized Portfolios." In *Innovations in Bond Portfolio Management,* edited by G. O. Bierwag, G. Kaufman, and A. Toevs. Greenwich, Conn.: JAI Press, 227–38.

Ho, T. "Key Rate Durations: Measures of Interest Rate Risks." *Journal of Fixed Income* 2 (1992): 29–44.

Ingersoll, J. E., J. Skelton, and R. L. Weil. "Duration Forty Years Later." *Journal of Financial and Quantitative Analysis* 13 (1978): 627–52.

Livingston, M. "Measuring Bond Price Volatility." *Journal of Financial and Quantitative Analysis* 14 (1979): 343–49.

Macaulay, F. R. *Some Theoretical Problems Suggested by the Movements of Interest Rates, Bond Yields, and Stock Prices in the U.S. Since 1856.* New York: National Bureau of Economic Research, 1938.

Nawalkha, S. K., and N. J. Lacey. "Closed-Form Solutions of Higher-Order Duration Measures." *Financial Analysts Journal* (November-December 1988): 82–84.

Prisman, E. Z., and M. R. Shores. "Duration Measures for Specific Term Structure Estimates and Applications to Bond Portfolio Immunization." *Journal of Banking and Finance* 12 (1988): 493–504.

Exercises

1. The term structure is flat at 8 percent. Consider an 8 percent coupon bond with semiannual payouts that matures in 10 years. If yields increased by 1 basis point ($y = 8.01\%$), what would be the effect on price? If the yield curve were flat at 9 percent and increased by 1 basis point, would the price effect be bigger or smaller? Explain.

2. A bond has two years to maturity, pays semiannual coupons, and has a face value of $1000. The coupon is 7 percent and the yield to maturity is 8 percent.
   a. Compute the price of the bond.
   b. Compute the duration and modified duration of the bond.
   c. Compute the convexity of the bond.

3. Assume the yield on the bond in Exercise 2 changes from 8 percent to 8.05 percent.
   a. Using the bond pricing equation, compute the new price of the bond, and then establish the change in the bond price.
   b. Using the linear approximation, compute the change in the bond price.
   c. Using the quadratic approximation, compute the change in the bond price.
   d. Compare your answers in Exercises 3b and 3c to that in 3a and draw conclusions.

4. Repeat Exercise 2, but this time assume the yield changes from 8 to 10 percent.

5. A discount bond is available with a maturity of six years. The annualized yield to maturity of this bond is 7 percent (computed on a semiannualized basis) and the face value is $1000.
   a. Compute the price of this bond.
   b. Compute the duration, modified duration, and convexity of this bond.

6. A trader has an obligation of $10 million due in four years. The trader decides to purchase units of the bonds in Exercises 1 and 3 and wants to choose a portfolio that has a duration equal to that of the liability. Establish the required portfolio.

7. An eight-year bond has annual coupons. The coupon is 10 percent, the face value is $1000, and the current yield curve is flat at 10 percent.
   a. Compute the duration of the bond.
   b. Assume the yield curve increased from 10 percent to 10.5 percent and remained unchanged for two years, at which time the bond was sold. Assume all coupons were reinvested. What would be the total accrued value of the account?
   c. Another coupon bond with a duration of two years was available. Assume the number of units purchased of this bond were chosen so that the initial investment was equal to the initial value of the bond in Exercise 7b. After two years, would the accrued value of the account be more insulated from an immediate parallel shift in the yield curve? Explain.

8. Assume the yield curve is flat at 10 percent ($y = 10\%$). Consider the following three bonds:

Bond	A	B	C
Maturity (years)	2	5	8
Coupon	8%	10%	12%
Face value	$1000	$1000	$1000

a. Compute the prices of the three bonds.

b. Compute the duration, modified duration, and convexity of the three bonds.

c. Use bonds A and B to construct a portfolio that has a duration of three years.

d. Use bonds A and C to construct a portfolio that has a duration of three years.

e. Which of the two portfolios constructed in Exercises 8c and 8d is more convex? If the trader wanted a duration of three years to immunize an obligation due in three years, which of the two portfolios would you recommend? Explain.

f.* Of all the portfolios of bonds A, B, and C, find the portfolio that maximizes convexity. Assume the trader is not allowed to sell bonds short. That is, solve the linear programming problem for the maximum convexity problem, but include in your constraints the fact that all the weights of the portfolio must be nonnegative.

g.* Compute the twist risk for each bond, and then identify the minimum-twist-risk portfolio that has a duration of three years. Again, in your linear programming formulation, assume the trader is concerned only with portfolio weights that are nonnegative.

h.* Compute the portfolio that maximizes twist risk, subject to the duration and nonnegativity constraints. Compare this portfolio to that obtained in Exercise 8f.

---

*These exercises are based on advanced material from this chapter.

APPENDIX 19A

Derivation of Equations (19.4) and (19.10)

Differentiating the bond pricing equation leads to

$$dB/dy = -\sum_{t=1}^{m} tCF_t/(1 + y)^{t+1} \tag{19A.1}$$

Dividing both sides by the bond price yields

$$\frac{dB}{dy}\frac{1}{B} = \frac{-\sum_{t=1}^{m} tCF_t/(1 + y)^t}{B(1 + y)} \tag{19A.2}$$

or

$$\frac{dB}{dy}\frac{1}{B} = -\mathbb{D}\frac{1}{(1 + y)} \tag{19A.3}$$

from which equation (19.4) follows.

Using Taylor's expansion, we obtain the quadratic approximation to $B(y + \Delta y)$ as

$$B''(y + \Delta y) = B(y) + \frac{dB}{dy}\Delta y + \frac{1}{2}\frac{d^2B}{dy^2}(\Delta y)^2 \tag{19A.4}$$

The second derivative, d^2B/dy^2, is obtained by differentiating equation (19A.1). This equals

$$\frac{d^2B}{dy^2} = \sum_{t=1}^{m} \frac{t(t + 1)F_t}{(1 + y)^{t+2}}$$

$$= B(y)\,\mathbb{C}_B(y)$$

Substituting this expression into equation (19A.4) yields the result, equation (19.10).

CHAPTER 20

Organized Exchange–Traded Interest Rate Contracts

In this chapter we discuss some of the more important exchange-traded futures and option contracts. We examine the use of futures and option contracts on short-term instruments such as T-bills and Eurodollar time deposits as well as on medium-term T-notes and long-term T-bonds. We address special attention to the T-bond futures contract, not only because it is one of the most heavily traded futures contracts but also because of its innovative design. Indeed, more recent contracts on 2-, 5-, and 10-year Treasury notes have adopted features similar to those of this long-term T-bond futures contract.

The primary objectives of this chapter are the following:

- To discuss exchange-traded options and futures contracts on Treasuries and Eurodollars; and

- To illustrate the use of the interest rate futures contract in managing interest rate risk.

Treasury Bill Futures

The Treasury bill futures contract traded by the International Monetary Market (IMM) at the Chicago Mercantile Exchange (CME) calls for delivery of T-bills with face value of $1 million, having 90 days to maturity. Delivery takes place on the three business days following the last day of trading. The contract expires the business day before new 13-week T-bills are issued. This permits newly issued T-bills to be delivered against the contract. Alternatively, seasoned bills with 13 weeks remaining to maturity can be delivered. Although the contract specifies delivery of a T-bill with 90 days to maturity, delivery of T-bills with 91 or 92 days will suffice, with an appropriate price adjustment.

Exhibit 20.1 illustrates price quotations as they appear in the *Wall Street Journal*. The delivery months are March, June, September, and December. The last column in each row shows the open interest. As can be seen, most of the activity is concentrated on the near-term contracts. The first four columns provide the opening price, high for the day, low for the day, and the settlement price. The change in the settlement price from the previous close is reported. The next two

FUTURES PRICES

INTEREST RATE

TREASURY BONDS (CBT)–$100,000; pts. 32nds of 100%

	Open	High	Low	Settle	Change	Lifetime High	Lifetime Low	Open Interest
June	105-10	105-13	105-02	105-07	– 4	113-15	94-27	355,167
Sept	104-26	104-29	104-19	104-23	– 5	112-15	94-10	22,084
Dec	104-10	104-12	104-08	104-10	– 5	111-23	93-27	2,921
Mr96	104-01	104-01	103-29	103-29	– 5	104-11	93-13	386
June	....	....	103-17	– 5	104-28	93-06	37

Est vol 175,000; vol Fri 387,125; op int 380,672, +3,615.

TREASURY BONDS (MCE)–$50,000; pts. 32nds of 100%

	Open	High	Low	Settle	Change	Lifetime High	Lifetime Low	Open Interest
June	105-10	105-10	105-02	105-07	– 3	105-24	95-20	14,838
Sept	104-21	104-26	104-20	104-23	– 4	105-08	98-19	100

Est vol 5,000; vol Fri 4,075; open int 15,013, +251.

TREASURY NOTES (CBT)–$100,000; pts. 32nds of 100%

	Open	High	Low	Settle	Change	Lifetime High	Lifetime Low	Open Interest
June	105-10	105-11	105-04	105-07	– 3	105-31	97-27	248,881
Sept	104-27	104-27	104-21	104-23	– 4	105-14	97-11	19,336
Dec	104-08	104-09	104-07	104-09	– 4	105-03	96-30	484

Est vol 39,134; vol Fri 91,296; open int 267,704, –142.

5 YR TREAS NOTES (CBT)–$100,000; pts. 32nds of 100%

	Open	High	Low	Settle	Change	Lifetime High	Lifetime Low	Open Interest
June	04-015	104-02	103-29	03-315	– 2.5	04-245	99-06	203,719
Sept	03-215	103-23	103-19	103-21	– 2.5	04-125	99-07	8,183

Est vol 21,500; vol Fri 57,069; open int 211,903, +1,835.

2 YR TREAS NOTES (CBT)–$200,000; pts. 32nds of 100%

	Open	High	Low	Settle	Change	Lifetime High	Lifetime Low	Open Interest
June	102-07	102-08	02-065	102-07	....	102-177	99-24	28,751

Est vol 1,050; vol Fri 4,819; open int 28,755, –727.

30-DAY FEDERAL FUNDS (CBT)–$5 million; pts. of 100%

	Open	High	Low	Settle	Change	Lifetime High	Lifetime Low	Open Interest
May	93.98	93.98	93.97	93.98	....	94.00	92.60	3,243
June	93.93	93.94	93.93	93.94	....	93.97	92.82	4,507
July	93.86	93.86	93.86	93.86	....	93.90	92.65	5,293
Aug	93.79	93.80	93.79	93.80	....	93.85	93.10	252
Sept	93.75	93.75	93.75	93.75	....	93.83	93.40	238

Est vol 1,444; vol Fri 2,920; open int 16,350, +543.

TREASURY BILLS (CME)–$1 mil.; pts. of 100%

	Open	High	Low	Settle	Chg	Discount Settle	Discount Chg	Open Interest
June	94.25	94.25	94.22	94.23	– .02	5.77	+ .02	13,220
Sept	94.05	94.05	94.01	94.02	– .04	5.98	+ .04	12,844
Dec	93.82	93.82	93.80	93.81	– .06	6.19	+ .06	11,481
Mr96	....	....	....	93.79	– .04	6.21	+ .04	208

Est vol 1,466; vol Fri 3,248; open int 37,753, +157.

MUNI BOND INDEX (CBT)–$1,000; times Bond Buyer MBI

	Open	High	Low	Settle	Chg	Lifetime High	Lifetime Low	Open Interest
June	89-03	89-07	88-24	89-06	+ 3	91-24	83-25	15,812

Est vol 3,500; vol Fri 9,428; open int 15,889, –977.
The index: Close 90-28; Yield 6.47.

EURODOLLAR (CME)–$1 million; pts of 100%

	Open	High	Low	Settle	Chg	Yield Settle	Yield Chg	Open Interest
June	93.71	93.71	93.69	93.71	....	6.29	....	476,843
Sept	93.55	93.55	93.51	93.52	– .03	6.48	+ .03	369,571
Dec	93.30	93.31	93.25	93.28	– .04	6.72	+ .04	286,978
Mr96	93.28	93.30	93.26	93.27	– .05	6.73	+ .05	227,279
June	93.16	93.17	93.14	93.15	– .04	6.85	+ .04	175,533
Sept	93.06	93.07	93.04	93.05	– .04	6.95	+ .04	151,076
Dec	92.94	92.95	92.92	92.93	– .04	7.07	+ .04	118,717
Mr97	92.93	92.95	92.92	92.93	– .03	7.07	+ .03	98,482
June	92.89	92.91	92.88	92.89	– .03	7.11	+ .03	86,639
Sept	92.86	92.88	92.86	92.86	– .03	7.14	+ .03	70,808
Dec	92.78	92.81	92.78	92.79	– .02	7.21	+ .02	60,970
Mr98	92.78	92.80	92.77	92.78	– .02	7.22	+ .02	56,469
June	92.71	92.74	92.71	92.72	– .02	7.28	+ .02	52,224
Sept	92.66	92.69	92.66	92.67	– .02	7.33	+ .02	41,648
Dec	92.58	92.61	92.58	92.59	– .02	7.41	+ .02	35,327
Mr99	92.57	92.61	92.57	92.59	– .01	7.41	+ .01	29,878
June	92.51	92.55	92.51	92.53	– .01	7.47	+ .01	23,134
Sept	92.45	92.49	92.45	92.47	– .01	7.53	+ .01	15,767
Dec	92.36	92.40	92.36	92.39	....	7.61	....	11,970
Mr00	92.36	92.40	92.36	92.39	....	7.61	....	9,552
June	92.32	92.33	92.30	92.32	+ .01	7.68	– .01	7,142
Sept	92.25	92.27	92.25	92.27	+ .01	7.73	– .01	7,346
Dec	92.17	92.20	92.17	92.19	+ .01	7.81	– .01	7,233
Mr01	....	....	92.18	+ .01	7.82	– .01	5,731
June	92.11	92.14	92.10	92.12	+ .01	7.88	– .01	6,505
Sept	92.04	92.07	92.04	92.05	+ .01	7.95	– .01	8,074
Dec	91.96	91.99	91.96	91.97	+ .01	8.03	– .01	7,277
Mr02	91.96	91.99	91.96	91.97	+ .01	8.03	– .01	4,320
June	91.85	91.92	91.85	91.91	+ .02	8.09	– .02	3,664
Sept	91.85	91.85	91.81	91.84	+ .02	8.16	– .02	2,640
Dec	....	....	91.76	+ .02	8.24	– .02	2,118

FUTURES OPTIONS PRICES

INTEREST RATE

T-BONDS (CBT)
$100,000; points and 64ths of 100%

Strike Price	Calls–Settle Jun	Calls–Settle Sep	Calls–Settle Dec	Puts–Settle Jun	Puts–Settle Sep	Puts–Settle Dec
103	2-22	....	....	0-08	....	....
104	1-34	2-20	2-48	0-20	1-39	2-28
105	0-54	....	....	0-40	....	....
106	0-24	1-22	1-53	1-10	2-39	3-30
107	0-08	....	....	1-58	....	....
108	0-03	0-45	1-10	2-51	3-60	....

Est. vol. 80,000;
Fri vol. 45,177 calls; 60,192 puts
Op. int. Fri 300,754 calls; 348,248 puts

T-NOTES (CBT)
$100,000; points and 64ths of 100%

Strike Price	Calls–Settle Jun	Calls–Settle Sep	Calls–Settle Dec	Puts–Settle Jun	Puts–Settle Sep	Puts–Settle Dec
103	2-16	2-30	....	0-03	0-49	....
104	1-25	1-52	2-02	0-12	1-07	1-48
105	0-43	1-17	1-35	0-29	1-35	....
106	0-15	0-54	1-10	1-01	2-07	....
107	0-04	0-34	....	1-54	....	....
108	0-01	0-20	....	....	....	....

Est vol 12,000 Fri 9,754 calls 20,237 puts
Op int Fri 139,194 calls 154,582 puts

5 YR TREAS NOTES (CBT)
$100,000; points and 64ths of 100%

Strike Price	Calls–Settle Jun	Calls–Settle Sep	Calls–Settle Dec	Puts–Settle Jun	Puts–Settle Sep	Puts–Settle Dec
10250	1-34	1-45	....	0-03	0-36	....
10300	1-06	1-24	....	0-07	0-47	....
10350	0-45	1-05	....	0-14	0-59	....
10400	0-25	0-53	....	0-26	1-11	....
10450	0-13	0-39	....	0-46	....	....
10500	0-05	0-28	....	1-06	1-48	....

Est vol 8,800   Fri 4,909 calls 5,877 puts
Op int Fri   103,494 calls 135,087 puts

EURODOLLAR (CME)
$ million; pts. of 100%

Strike Price	Calls–Settle May	Calls–Settle Jun	Calls–Settle Sep	Puts–Settle May	Puts–Settle Jun	Puts–Settle Sep
9325	0.46	0.47	0.38	0.00	0.01	0.12
9350	0.22	0.24	0.23	0.01	0.03	0.21
9375	0.02	0.05	0.10	0.06	0.09	0.33
9400	0.00	0.01	0.04	0.29	0.30	0.51
9425	0.00	0.00	0.02	....	0.54	0.74
9450	....	0.00	0.01	....	0.79	0.98

Est. vol. 53,173;
Fri vol. 29,054 calls; 56,000 puts
Op. Int. Fri 925,428 calls; 1,226,660 puts

LIBOR – 1 Mo. (CME)
$3 million; pts. of 100%

Strike Price	Calls–Settle May	Calls–Settle Jun	Calls–Settle	Puts–Settle May	Puts–Settle Jun	Puts–Settle ....
9350	0.40	0.35	0.31	0.00	0.01	0.05
9375	0.16	0.11	0.12	0.01	0.01	0.11
9400	....	0.02	0.03	....	....	....
9425	....	....	....	....	....	....
9450	0.00	....	....	....	....	....
9475	....	....	....	....	....	....

Est vol 26   Fri 50 calls 0 puts
Op int Fri   1,760 calls 667 puts

2 YR. MID-CURVE EURODOLLAR (CME)
$1,000,000 contract units; pts. of 100%

Strike Price	Calls–Settle Jun	Calls–Settle	Calls–Settle	Puts–Settle Jun	Puts–Settle	Puts–Settle ....
9250	0.44	....	....	0.05	....	....
9275	0.25	....	....	0.11	....	....
9300	0.12	....	....	0.23	....	....
9325	0.04	....	....	....	....	....
9350	....	....	....	....	....	....
9400	....	....	....	....	....	....

Est vol 1,050   Fri 0 calls 200 puts
Op int Fri   6,360 calls 6,510 puts

EXHIBIT 20.1   Futures Prices and Futures Options on Selected Interest Rate Contracts

Source: Reprinted by permission of the Wall Street Journal © 1995 Dow Jones & Company, Inc. All Rights Reserved Worldwide.

columns show the settlement discount and its change from the previous close. The settlement discount is $100 -$ the settlement price. Hence, the two "Change" columns have the same value with opposite signs.

Let QF represent the quoted settlement price of the T-bill futures contract. Then the implied discount, ID, is given by

$$QF = 100 - ID \tag{20.1}$$

For example, if a contract is quoted at 91.9 ($QF = 91.9$), then the implied bank discount yield on the bill is $ID = 100 - 91.9 = 9.1\%$ on an annualized (360-day) basis. Since the futures contract requires delivery of a 90-day T-bill, the bank discount yield must be deannualized by multiplying by 90/360. Specifically, the actual discount is $(9.1)(90/360) = 2.275\%$. The settlement price in dollars is then computed as $(100 - 2.275)$ percent of par or $977,250.

The minimum price fluctuation or "tick" for the futures contract is 0.01. A change of 0.01 translates into a 1-basis-point (i.e., a hundredth of 1 percent) change in the yield on a bank discount basis. The dollar price change of a tick is $(0.0001)(\$1,000,000)(90/360) = \$25$ for a 90-day contract. As the delivery date draws near, the implied discount yield will converge to the actual bank discount yield in the spot market, and the futures price will converge to the spot price of the T-bill.

EXAMPLE 20.1   Suppose the IMM index for delivery in six months is $QF = 89$. Then the implied bank discount yield is 11 percent and the dollar price of the futures contract is

$$\frac{\{100 - 11(90/360)\}}{100}\$1,000,000 = \$972,500$$

If this contract is purchased, a margin of $2,000 is required and the futures contract is marked to market. A trader purchasing this contract is locking into a purchase price of a T-bill for delivery in six months that will provide an annualized bank discount yield of 11 percent.

EXAMPLE 20.2   **Arbitrage Opportunities Between Spot and Futures Markets**

An arbitrager is faced with the following information and wants to investigate whether riskless arbitrage exists.

Yield on T-bill	8.0%
Maturity of T-bill	104 days
Face value of T-bill	$1 million
T-bill futures price	$91.90
Time to settlement	14 days
Current repo rate	7.5%

The price of the T-bill is $1,000,000[1 - (0.080)(104/360)] = \$976,888.88$. The futures price is $1,000,000 [1 - 0.0810(90/360)] = \$979,750$. If the

T-bill is financed at the repo rate of 7.5 percent, the finance charge is $976,888.88(0.075 \times 14/360) = \$2,849.25$. The total cost of purchasing and carrying over 14 days is ($976,888.88 + \$2,849.25) = \$979,738.13$. The net guaranteed profit over the 14-day period in financing a T-bill at the repo rate and selling in the futures market is $979,750 - \$979,738.13 = \$11.87$.

EXAMPLE 20.3   **Using Futures to Change Maturity**

A firm holds a six-month T-bill with a face value of $10 million. The firm realizes that it needs cash in three months and would like to reduce the maturity of its investment to three months. The following current information is available.

Maturity of T-Bill (Days)	Bank Discount Yield (%)
90	10
180	11

A T-bill futures contract with a settlement date in three months trades at $87.70. The following strategies are considered.

1. Liquidate the current position and use the proceeds to purchase a three-month T-bill.
2. Hold onto the current position and sell 10 T-bill futures.

Arbitrage considerations should limit the profitability of one strategy over the other. However, for this firm strategy 2 requires lower transaction costs and may be preferable. Ignoring transaction costs, consider strategy 1. Let $P(0, 90)$ be the value of a pure discount bond that matures in 90 days. From the bank discount yield equation we have

$$0.10 = \frac{1 - P(0, 90)}{1}(360/90)$$

from which $P(0, 90) = \$0.975$. The simple return of the first investment is therefore $(1 - 0.975)/0.975 = 2.564\%$.

Now consider strategy 2. The present value of the 180-day T-bill can be computed from its discount yield. In particular,

$$0.11 = \frac{1 - P(0,180)}{1}(360/180)$$

from which $P(0,180) = \$0.9450$. Hence, the current value of the $10 million face value portfolio is $9.45 million.[1] The quoted futures price of 87.70 gives an implied

---

[1] Note that the forward price $F_0[\$90, 180] = P(0, 180)/P(0, 90) = \$0.969231$. Hence, the forward price for delivery of a $10 million face value discount bond is $9,692,310. If the quoted future does not translate into a value reasonably close to this value, then arbitrage opportunities are available.

discount yield of 12.30. By selling 100 futures contracts at an IMM index value of 87.70, the trader is locking into a dollar price of

$$\frac{100 - 12.30(90/360)}{100}\ \$10 \text{ million} = \$9,692,500$$

This strategy implies a 90-day simple return of 2.566 percent, which is almost identical to the yield in strategy 1.

Eurodollar Futures Contracts

The Eurodollar (ED) futures contract that trades at the CME is based on a three-month LIBOR rate. Eurodollar futures contracts trade in exactly the same way as T-bill futures. Eurodollar futures contracts are extremely liquid, and the volume of contracts traded makes this market one of the largest. The major difference between this contract and the T-bill futures is that the Eurodollar contract is settled in cash. The settlement price is based on the three-month LIBOR rate at the expiration date, which is the third Monday of the delivery month. Exhibit 20.1 shows the prices of Eurodollar futures as reported in the *Wall Street Journal*. They are reported in the same way as T-bill futures. Note that trading in contracts with settlement dates exceeding two or three years is quite active. The final settlement price is determined by selecting at random 12 reference banks from a list of 20 major banks in the London Eurodollar market and identifying their quotes on three-month Eurodollar time deposits. The two highest and two lowest quotes are dropped, and the arithmetic average is computed.

Let L represent the annualized LIBOR rate in *percentage* form. The quoted futures price at the settlement date is given by

$$QF = 100 - L \qquad (20.2)$$

Prior to expiration, the quoted price

$$QF = 100 - IL \qquad (20.3)$$

Here IL is the *implied* annualized three-month LIBOR rate. As the settlement date approaches, the implied LIBOR rate converges to the actual spot LIBOR rate. The actual dollar futures price, AF, is given by

$$AF = \frac{\{100 - IL[90/360]\}}{100}(\$1,000,000)$$

or $\qquad AF = [1 - il(90/360)]\$1,000,000 \qquad (20.4)$

where il is the implied yield in decimal form ($il = IL/100$).

Note that with the index price convention used for both Treasury and Eurodollar futures, prices move linearly with the bank discount yield. Specifically, regardless of the level of the interest rate, a 1 percent change in yield causes a $2,500 ($1,000,000[1/100] $\times$ [90/360]) change in price. The typical daily gain or loss in one futures contract is in the range of $300 to $1,000. Margin requirements are typically equal to about four times the typical daily move.

In Chapter 11 we provided some examples of Eurodollar futures contracts for hedging. A few additional examples follow. More examples are provided in Chapter 21.

EXAMPLE 20.4   Locking in a Borrowing Rate with Eurodollar Futures

In January a firm knows that it will need to borrow $10 million for three months beginning on March 18, which happens to coincide with the last trading day of the March Eurodollar futures contract. A bank agrees to provide this loan at the three-month LIBOR rate on March 18.

The current three-month LIBOR rate is 8 percent. If LIBOR remained unchanged, then the interest expense would be $10,000,000 \times (0.08) \times (3/12) = $200,000 due in June. Management fears that LIBOR rates will increase and would like to lock into a rate today. Assume the current implied futures rate for March is 8.5 percent and the firm sells 10 March Eurodollar futures contracts. On March 18 the profit from this strategy, $\pi(t)$, is

$$\pi(t) = -[AF(t) - AF(0)]10$$

$$= -[(1 - il(t)) - (1 - il(0)]10,000,000 \times (3/12)$$

$$= [il(t) - il(0)](10,000,000) \times (3/12)$$

$$= [l(t) - il(0)](10,000,000) \times (3/12)$$

The last line follows from the fact that at the settlement date the implied yield converges to the actual LIBOR rate, $l(t)$. If profits are obtained ($\pi(t) > 0$), then the funds can be placed in an interest-bearing account for three months. If losses arise ($\pi(t) < 0$), the required funds have to be borrowed. Let $i(t, T)$ be the interest generated on $\pi(t)$ over the three-month period from April (date t) to June (date T). Clearly, $i(t, T)$ could be positive or negative.

The size of the payment in June is $10 million plus the interest of $l(t)($10,000,000) \times (3/12)$. The effective amount owed in June is

$$\$10,000,000 + L(t)(\$10,000,000) \times (3/12) - [\pi(t) + i(t, T)]$$

Substituting for $\pi(t)$, this expression reduces to

$$\$10,000,000 + il(0)(\$10,000,000) \times (3/12) - i(t, T)$$

Ignoring for the moment the interest expense $i(t, T)$, the hedging strategy essentially locks into a borrowing rate of $il(0)$.

Assume the three-month LIBOR on March 18 was 9 percent. Then the interest expense on the loan would be $10,000,000 \times 0.09 \times 3/12 = $225,000, and $10,225,000 would be due in June. If the hedge had been initiated, then in March the short position would have yielded a profit of $[0.090 - 0.085](\$10,000,000) \times (3/12) = $12,500. Assuming these funds are invested at the three-month LIBOR rate of 9 percent, the interest would be $i(t, T) = \$281.25$. Ignoring this amount for the moment, the funds of \$12,500 could be used to reduce the cost of borrowing to \$212,500, which is exactly the implied yield of 8.5 percent.

Note that if the additional interest amount of \$281.25 were added into the analysis, the effective cost of borrowing would change modestly to 8.49 percent. Since the interest adjustment is so minor, it is often ignored.

EXAMPLE 20.5   Creation of Synthetic Fixed-Rate Loans

Consider a bank that offers fixed-rate loans financed by rolling over successive Eurodollar time deposits. Since the rate paid is fixed while the rate earned is variable, interest rate risk is present. A natural hedge against this risk would be for the bank to replace the fixed-rate accounts with variable-rate accounts. In this case, cash flows could be precisely matched. However, if the bank's clients demanded fixed rates, the bank could convert its own stream of variable-rate loans to a stream of fixed-rate loans. This is accomplished by selling a sequence of Eurodollar futures contracts with consecutive settlement dates and locking into their implied LIBOR rates.

EXAMPLE 20.6   The TED Spread

A relatively popular futures strategy is to speculate on the gap between T-bills and Eurodollar (ED) yields using a **TED spread.** The TED spread is the difference in price between a three-month T-bill futures contract and a three month Eurodollar deposit in which the two contracts have the same delivery month. An investor thinks that due to political tensions in Europe, the LIBOR–T-bill spread will widen. By buying a TED spread, the investor hopes to profit from a widening spread.

The March Eurodollar futures price is \$92, while the T-bill futures price is \$93.41. The difference between the two is 141 basis points. Two weeks later, the Eurodollar futures is at \$91.88 while the T-bill is at \$93.45. Since the basis has expanded from 141 to 157, the profit from the TED spread is $\$(157 - 141)25 = \$400$.

Duration-Based Hedging

Assume a bond portfolio is being hedged using an interest rate futures contract. The duration of the bond portfolio is $\mathbb{D}^p$ years, and the modified duration is $\mathbb{D}_m^p$. The approximate change in the bond portfolio is given by

$$\Delta P \approx -\mathbb{D}_m^P P \Delta y$$

where P is the value of the portfolio.

We assume that the change in yield, Δy, is the same for all maturities. This implies that the yield shifts are all parallel. To a reasonable degree, the change in the futures price can be approximated by

$$\Delta F \approx -\mathbb{D}_m^F F \Delta y$$

where $\mathbb{D}_m^F$ is the modified duration of the futures contract, which is defined as the modified duration of the asset underlying the futures contract when the hedge is lifted. (In the case of a 90-day T-bill futures contract and a 90-day Eurodollar futures contract, the ordinary duration measure equals the maturity of 0.25 years.)

To offset the risk, the number of futures contracts, n, should be chosen such that any change in value of the underlying bond portfolio is offset by an opposite change in the futures position. Hence, n is chosen such that

$$\Delta P \approx n \Delta F$$

or
$$n \approx \Delta P / \Delta F = \frac{\mathbb{D}_m P \Delta y}{\mathbb{D}_m^F F \Delta y}$$

Using the fact that modified duration equals ordinary duration divided by 1 plus the yield, the above equation simplifies to

$$n \approx = \frac{\mathbb{D}^P P}{\mathbb{D}^F F} \tag{20.5}$$

where $\mathbb{D}^P$ and $\mathbb{D}^F$ are the ordinary duration measures.

EXAMPLE 20.7   A firm holds $10 million in six-month T-bills. The firm is concerned that interest rates will increase, and it would like to hedge this risk using T-bill futures. The term structure is flat at 10 percent, compounded continuously. The duration of the T-bill is $\mathbb{D}^P = 0.5$, and the duration of the futures is $\mathbb{D}^F = 0.25$.

The current T-bill price is $P = \$10,000,000 \times e^{-(0.10)0.5} = \$9,512,294$. The current T-bill futures price in dollars is $F = \$1,000,000 \times e^{-(0.10)0.25} = \$975,310$. The approximate number of futures to sell is n, where

$$n \approx \frac{\mathbb{D}^P P}{\mathbb{D}^F F} = \frac{0.5 \times \$9,512,294}{0.25 \times \$975,310} = 19.5$$

Hence, 19 or 20 futures should be sold.

The strategy in Example 20.7 is not a static hedge and must be periodically adjusted to reflect the fact that the duration of the underlying portfolio changes over time. The duration of the underlying bond decays until at the delivery date its duration is 0.25 and the hedge should consist of only a short position in 10 futures.

Options on Short-Term Interest Rate Futures

Option contracts trade on T-bill and Eurodollar futures. Strike prices bracket the futures price and are separated by 0.25 index units. A quote of 0.35 means an option price of $875. This is computed by multiplying 35 by the value of each basis point, $25. The options trade at the same times as the futures.

EXAMPLE 20.8 **Hedging Floating-Rate Liabilities: Locks, Caps, and Floors**

Consider a borrower who funds a $10 million project with a six-month variable-rate loan. The loan rate for the first three months is 9.3 percent, which is 100 basis points above the current three-month LIBOR rate. The current month is September. At the reset date in December, the financing cost for the remaining three-month period will be 100 basis points over the 90-day LIBOR rate.

The borrower is fortunate to have Eurodollar futures maturing on the reset date. The following price information is available.

December Eurodollar futures price = $91.37

Option Strike ($)	Yield (%)	Call Price ($)	Put Price ($)
90.5	9.5	0.95	0.10
91	9	0.58	0.22
91.5	8.5	0.31	0.43
92	8	0.13	0.75
92.5	7	0.04	—

Below, we consider three possible strategies the borrower could use to manage the uncertainty of the borrowing expense.

Locking in the Borrowing Cost

The simplest hedge is to sell 10 December Eurodollar futures contracts. The borrower can sell the futures for $91.37 and therefore lock into a LIBOR of 8.63 percent. Since the cost of borrowing is 100 basis points above LIBOR, the locked-in LIBOR rate is 9.63 percent. Exhibit 20.2 shows the profits or losses from the futures position contingent on the LIBOR rates in December.

Capping Borrowing Costs

Rather than selling futures, consider the strategy of buying 10 put options at $91. The total cost of these puts is $5500 ($25 \times 22 \times 10$). These puts cap the total borrowing cost for the firm at 10 percent. The cost of setting up this cap is $5500. Exhibit 20.3 shows the costs.

EXHIBIT 20.2   Establishing the Borrowing Cost

	LIBOR				
	7%	8%	9%	10%	11%
ED futures price ($)	93	92	91	90	89
Interest expense ($, in thousands)	200	225	250	275	300
Loss on futures ($, futures price change × 25)	40.75	15.75	−9.25	−34.25	−59.25
Net borrowing cost ($, in thousands)	240.75	240.75	240.75	240.75	240.75

EXHIBIT 20.3   Establishing the Borrowing Cost

	LIBOR					
	6%	7%	8%	9%	10%	11%
ED futures price ($)	94	93	92	91	90	89
Interest expense ($, in thousands)	175	200	225	250	275	300
Payout on put ($, in thousands)	0	0	0	0	25	50
Net borrowing cost ($, in thousands)	175	200	225	250	250	250

Caps and Floors on Borrowing Costs

To reduce the cost of capping the interest expense at 10 percent, the borrower decides to add to the above position by selling 10 calls at $92. This strategy brings in the premium of $3250 (13 × 25 × 10). The net interest expense is shown in Exhibit 20.4. Note that the cost of capping net interest expenses has been reduced from $5500 to $2250 at the expense of placing a floor on interest expenses. That is, if LIBOR drops below 8 percent, the benefits of lower financing charges will be offset by the obligations on the call option.

EXHIBIT 20.4   Establishing the Borrowing Cost

	LIBOR					
	6%	7%	8%	9%	10%	11%
ED futures price ($)	92	93	92	91	90	89
Interest expense ($, in thousands)	175	200	225	250	275	300
Payout on put ($)	0	0	0	0	25	50
Payout on call ($)	−50	−25	0	0	0	0
Net borrowing cost ($, in thousands)	225	225	225	250	250	250

Long-Term Interest Rate Futures Contracts

The Chicago Board of Trade (CBOT) trades futures contracts on 2-, 5-, and 10-year T-notes and on T-bonds. The T-bond futures contract is the most active futures contract traded anywhere. All these contracts require delivery of underlying securities. However, they all have the feature that a number of alternative deliverable securities will suffice. For example, the T-bond futures contract permits any one of up to 40 different T-bonds to be delivered against the contract.

Long-term bond futures are also actively traded in other countries. For example, futures contracts exist on long-term Japanese government bonds (Tokyo Stock Exchange), on French government bonds (MATIF, France), on German goverment bonds (LIFFE, England), on United Kingdom government bonds (LIFFE, England), on U.S. T-bonds (LIFFE, England), on Australian government bonds (Sydney Futures Exchange), and on Brazilian government bonds (BM&F, Brazil). In this section we focus on the CBOT's long-term Treasury futures contract.

The futures contract calls for $100,000 face value in deliverable-grade U.S. Treasury bonds during a specific delivery month. To meet delivery standards, the bond must have at least 15 years to maturity or to the first call date. The maturity is measured from the first day of the delivery month. The last day of trading the contract is 8 business days prior to end of the delivery month. The short position can choose any business day in the delivery month to deliver. Typically, there are between 20 and 40 eligible bonds that the short position can deliver against the contract. Having many eligible bonds reduces the possibility of someone or some group of traders buying all deliverable bonds and preventing others from delivering. That is, it prevents **short squeezes**.

The price quotations for T-bond futures are based on a hypothetical 8 percent semiannual coupon-bearing bond with a 20-year maturity. Given this quoted price, a well-defined mechanism exists for computing the effective futures price for all the bonds that satisfy delivery requirements. Before discussing this mechanism, consider the price quotations shown in Exhibit 20.1. From the first column it can be seen that contracts mature in March, June, September, and December. Contracts trade for maturities for as long as three years into the future. The next four columns give the opening high, low, and settlement quotations in points and thirty-seconds of a point. Each point is worth $1000 and each $1/32$ point is worth $31.25. Then the bond-equivalent yield corresponding to the settlement price and the change in that yield are reported. The final column reports the total number of outstanding contracts.

Assume the September contract settled at 101-25. This implies that the buyer is entitled to receive $100,000 face value in 20-year, 8 percent coupon bonds for a price of $\{101 + 25/32\} = 101.78125\%$ of $100,000, or $101,781.25. In general, let F^* represent the **dollar futures price** associated with the quoted price. Of course, this is a hypothetical bond, so it cannot be delivered. Given the dollar futures price, however, the dollar settlement price for any eligible bond can be established by multiplying this value by the bond's **conversion factor**. The resulting price is the effective dollar futures price for that bond. Let F_j represent this value. Then

$$F_j = F^*CF_j \qquad (20.6)$$

where CF_j is the conversion factor for bond j. The conversion factors for all eligible bonds are published by the CBOT.

The conversion factors attempt to adjust for the bond delivered so that the short position is indifferent as to which bond among all eligible bonds is delivered. Clearly, high-coupon bonds are worth more than low-coupon bonds of the same maturity. This means that conversion factors for bonds with higher coupons should be greater than for lower coupons. The sizes of the conversion factors also should take maturities into account.

The conversion factor for a particular bond is computed as the price of a $1 face value bond with a coupon rate and maturity equal to the delivered bond if it were priced to yield 8 percent, compounded semiannually. That is, the conversion factor for the bond is given by the price in equation (18.20), where the time is measured from the first day in the delivery month and maturities are rounded to the nearest quarter (i.e., T_1/T is either 0 or 1/2).

EXAMPLE 20.9 Consider the price of an 8 percent 20-year bond with semiannual coupons and a yield to maturity of 8 percent. Using the bond pricing equation, we find the price of the bond is $100. Now consider the price of a 14 percent, 15-year bond priced to yield 8 percent. The bond price is

$$B(0) = \sum_{t=1}^{40} \frac{7}{(1.04)^t} + \frac{\$100}{(1.04)^{40}} = \$159.38$$

The only difference between the two bonds is their coupons. The value of the 14 percent bonds is 1.5938 times greater than the 8 percent coupon. Hence, the conversion factor for the 14 percent coupon is 1.5938.

EXAMPLE 20.10 If a particular bond has a conversion factor of 1.5048, then the settlement price for that bond would be 1.5048 times the settlement price of the benchmark 20-year 8 percent bond. This means that for each 1-point move in the futures market, the effective futures price for this particular bond changes by 1.5048 points.

The Cheapest-to-Deliver Bond

The actual price received by the short position if bond j is delivered at the settlement date is the dollar futures price, F_j, plus the accrued interest since the last semiannual payment date. Let DP_j be the delivery price for the jth bond. Then

$$DP_j = F_j + AI_j \tag{20.7}$$

The total cost of buying bond j, B_j, consists of its quoted price in dollars, Q_j, and the accrued interest payments. That is,

$$B_j = Q_j + AI_j \tag{20.8}$$

The profit obtained from buying bond j, selling the futures contract, and using the bond to make delivery is π_j, where

$$\pi_j = DP_j - B_j$$

Substituting for DP_j and B_j in the profit equation leads to

$$\pi_j = [F_j + AI_j] - [Q_j + AI_j] = F_j - Q_j$$

or
$$\pi_j = F^*CF_j - Q_j \qquad (20.9)$$

If all bonds were priced to yield 8 percent, or equivalently, if the yield curve was flat at 8 percent, then the conversion factor system would be precise in the sense that the short position would be indifferent as to which bond was delivered, and all the π_j values would be equal. When the yield curve is not flat at 8 percent, then all bonds are not placed on an equal footing, and it becomes advantageous to deliver one bond against the contract rather than another. Clearly, the short position will select to deliver the bond that maximizes profit.

The **cheapest-to-deliver bond** is that bond that maximizes the short position's profit. Assume that at expiration the cheapest-to-deliver bond is bond i. If the profit, π_i, were positive, then an arbitrage opportunity would exist. Specifically, an astute trader would sell the futures and make immediate delivery using bond i to generate an immediate profit of size π_j. Similarly, if $\pi_i < 0$ then the investor would reverse the trade by buying the futures, taking delivery, and selling the bond, locking into arbitrage-free profits. Hence, at the expiration date, the profit from selling the futures contract and buying and delivering the cheapest-to-deliver bond must be 0. Hence,

$$Q_i = F^*CF_i$$

and the terminal dollar futures price is given by

$$F^* = Q_i/CF_i \qquad (20.10)$$

EXAMPLE 20.11　For simplicity assume the deliverable set consists of two bonds. The quoted price of a particular 14 percent bond is 103-08 or $103,250. Its effective futures price, obtained by multiplying the futures price by the conversion factor, equals $102,912. This implies a $338 cost for delivery.

The second bond, at 7 5/8 percent, is quoted at 61-26 or $61,812. Its effective futures price is $61,800. This implies a $12 cost for delivery.

To minimize losses, the short position would prefer to deliver the 7 5/8 percent bond over the 14 percent bond.

The Cost-of-Carry Model and Pricing the T-Bond Futures Contract

We now construct the fair futures price prior to the settlement date. Consider a strategy of purchasing a particular bond j in the deliverable set at date 0 and financing the charges at the term repo rate. The net amount owed at the settlement date, T days away, is

$$B_j(0)[1 + rT/360] - FV_j(0, T) \qquad (20.11)$$

where $FV_j(0, T)$ is the future value of all coupon payments received over the time period, assuming they are reinvested at the annualized term repo rate, r. Actually, viewed from time 0, $FV_j(0, T)$ is not certain because of reinvestment risk that arises from the fact that the coupons will be invested at a future repo rate which is uncertain.

We have assumed a term repo with T days to maturity is used. In practice, financing is usually accomplished by rolling over a sequence of shorter- term repos. This also introduces reinvestment risk. To some extent, this reinvestment risk is offset by the reinvestment risk associated with the future coupons. If interest rates increase, the carrying cost of the bonds increases. Offsetting this, however, is the increased income from reinvesting coupons at the higher rate. For simplicity, then, we shall ignore the reinvestment uncertainty altogether.

If at time zero the investor could guarantee a sales price at time T for the bond in excess of the amount owed, riskless arbitrage profits could be made. Indeed, to avoid riskless arbitrage, the forward price for bond j, $F_j(0)$, together with accrued interest up to date T, $AI_j(T)$, must equal the above value. That is,

$$F_j(0) + AI_j(T) = B_j(0)[1 + rT/360] - FV_j(0, T) \qquad (20.12)$$

Ignoring the differences between forward and futures contracts, to avoid riskless arbitrage, the futures price for bond j must equal $F_j(0)$, where

$$F_j(0) = B_j(0)[1 + rT/360] - FV_j(0, T) - AI_j(T) \qquad (20.13)$$

If we knew bond j would be the cheapest-to-deliver bond among all the deliverable bonds, then to avoid riskless arbitrage the dollar T-bond futures price would be

$$F^*(0) = F_j(0)/CF_j \qquad (20.14)$$

Since bond j may not be the cheapest-to-deliver bond, the calculation must be computed for all bonds. Then, to avoid riskless arbitrage, the theoretical futures price must be given by the lowest of these values. That is,

$$F^*(0) = \underset{j}{\text{Min}} \, [F_j(0)/CF_j] \qquad (20.15)$$

The Implied Repo Rate

In the above analysis, the existing repo rate was taken as given and the theoretical futures price was developed. Alternatively, the actual futures price could be taken as given and the equation solved for the implied repo rate. Specifically, from the above analysis, if bond i was the cheapest-to-deliver bond and remained the cheapest to deliver, then

$$F^*(0) = F_i(0)/CF_i$$

Substituting equation (20.13) into the above expression yields

$$F^*(0) = \frac{1}{CF_i} [B_i(0)(1 + rT/360) - FV_i(0, T) - AI_i(T)] \qquad (20.16)$$

Taking the futures price as given, equation (20.16) can be solved for the implied repo rate for bond i. Let r_i^* be this value. Then

$$r_i^* = \frac{[CF_i F_{(0)} + AI_i(T) + FV_i(0, T) - B_i(0)][360/T]}{B_i(0)} \qquad (20.17)$$

If bond i is purchased and held to the delivery date and a futures contract is sold, then the position is riskless and should provide a yield no greater than a Treasury yield for the same period. Clearly, the cheapest-to-deliver bond will be that bond that has the highest implied repo rate. If this value exceeds the Treasury rate, then arbitrage opportunities are available.

EXAMPLE 20.12 In July a $100,000 face value T-bond that pays 8 3/8 percent and is callable in 15 years is priced at 86-16. The time since the last coupon date is five months, or more precisely 151 days. A coupon is due in 31 days. The conversion factor for the bond is 1.0359.

The September futures contract trades at 81-19. The settlement date is assumed to be the first day in September, which is 36 days away. The current price of the bond is

$$B(0) = \$86,500 + (151/365)(8.375/2)1,000$$

$$= \$86,500 + \$1,732.36 = \$88,232.36$$

The total amount received at expiration consists of the futures price and the coupon together with the accrued interest. The September futures price is $81.59375 per $100 face value. The dollar price of the contract is therefore $81,593.75, and the effective futures price for this bond is ($81,593.75)1.0359 = $84,522.96. The coupon received is $4,187.5. The accrued interest is $(5/365)(8.375/2)(1,000) = \$57.36$. The total sum received is $88,767.82.[2] The implied repo rate is given by:

$$r^* = [(\$88,767.82 - \$88,232.36)/\$88,232.36](360/90)$$

$$= 0.0606882 \quad \text{or} \quad 6.068\%$$

If this bond was the cheapest to deliver, then its implied repo rate would be higher than that for other bonds in the deliverable set. Finally, arbitrage considerations ensure that this rate would not deviate from the actual term repo rate for this period.

---

[2] We have ignored the small amount of interest generated from the coupons over the five-day period.

In practice, the theoretical futures price overprices T-bond futures. Equivalently, the implied repo rate may be biased up. There are two main reasons for this. First, the above analysis assumes that the cheapest-to-deliver bond remains the cheapest to deliver. In practice, due to shifts in the yield curve, it is possible for the cheapest-to-deliver bond to change over time. The flexibility to change the deliverable bond provides the short position with additional value that is not incorporated into the above analysis. Second, in calculating the futures price, the other implicit delivery and trading restriction options were ignored.

Other Option Features in the Treasury Bond Futures Contract

As just discussed, since the conversion factors used to adjust for the bond delivered do not perfectly reflect price differences, the short position will choose to deliver the cheapest eligible bond. Moreover, since knowledge of which bond will be cheapest at maturity is uncertain at the time the contract is entered into, the option to defer selection of the deliverable bond has value. This option feature is called the **what-to-deliver** or **quality option.**

In addition to the quality option, the T-bond futures contract grants the seller important **timing options**. The short seller can select to deliver the bonds on any business day in the deliverable month. This option is referred to as the **when-to-deliver option.** Trading restrictions imposed by the exchange produce two additional delivery options. The first option, referred to as the **wild card option**, arises because the futures markets close each trading day at 2 P.M. while the short position has until 8 P.M. on each trading day in the deliverable month to declare an intent to deliver. Since bonds essentially trade in the dealer market to 8 P.M., the short position has effectively been granted a six-hour put option at the 2 P.M. prices, which allows bonds to be delivered at the 2 P.M. settlement prices. The sequence of daily wild card options continues to be granted in each business day in the delivery month until the T-bond futures contract stops trading.

The second option resulting from trading restrictions is referred to as the **end-of-month-option** and arises because the futures contract stops trading seven business days before the end of the delivery month. An important American-style put is therefore created that allows the short to deliver a bond at the closing futures price over any of the last seven days.

All these delivery options create value for the short position and mean that futures prices should be lower than values provided by traditional valuation models, which ignore these features. If we ignore the timing and trading restriction options granted to the short, the futures prices we obtain using arbitrage arguments are actually upper bounds on the true value.

Hedging Potential of the T-Bond Futures Contract

Given the complexity of the T-bond futures contract, with all its implicit options, one might wonder whether T-bond futures prices correlate highly with the prices of any specific long-term bond. After all, if the contract is going to be used as a hedge, a prerequisite is that its price movements correlate very highly with those of the underlying bond. It turns out that the correlations between bond returns and futures returns are very high. For example, the correlation between the T-bond futures and a 20-year Treasury bond typically exceeds 0.99. This is quite reassuring, and it suggests that from a hedging perspective, the impact of all the option features may be minor.

Before we examine some hedging strategies, it is useful to compare the T-bond futures contract to the Eurodollar (ED) futures contract. The face value of the ED futures contract is $1 million, compared to $100,000 for the T-bond futures. This does not mean that transacting in ED contracts involves bigger stakes. The large amount required for the ED contract stems from the fact that price volatilities and risks for short-term contracts are smaller than for longer-term T-bond futures. Specifically, the modified durations for the underlying T-bonds are substantially greater than for T-bills. The sizes of all these contracts are chosen so that the typical price changes on a single contract are economically meaningful and have similar sizes in all markets.

Basis Point Values

A **basis point value** (BPV) is simply the price change of a debt instrument given a 1-basis-point (0.1%) change in the yield of the instrument. For example, if the yield on a bond with a 20-year maturity changes from 8 percent to 8.01 percent and the resulting price changes by $70, then its BPV is $70. As yields and maturity change, the BPV changes. The greater the BPV, the greater the interest rate exposure.

Now consider the T-bond futures contract. The BPV of the futures contract is related to the BPV of the cheapest-to-deliver bond. To determine its value, first we identify the cheapest-to-deliver bond. As discussed earlier, this is accomplished by identifying the bond with the smallest basis (quoted price − adjusted futures price). The futures price closely tracks the cheapest-to-deliver bond. In particular, the change in the futures price will closely track the change in the adjusted futures price of the cheapest-to-deliver bond divided by the conversion factor. Therefore, the BPV of the futures contract will be the BPV of the cheapest-to-deliver instrument divided by the appropriate conversion factor.

If we assume that a 20-year 8 percent reference bond exists, then the BPV of the futures contract is just the BPV of the underlying reference bond. The BPV of the T-bond futures contract increases as interest rates decline. For example, a 1 percent increase when rates are 4 percent changes the futures price by $17,057; a 1 percent increase from 8 percent to 9 percent changes the price by $9,201; and a 1 percent change when rates are 16 percent changes the prices by $3,217. This is in sharp contrast to ED futures, in which each 1 percent change in rates changes prices by $2,500. That is, unlike the payout of a T-bond futures contract, the payout of a Eurodollar futures contract is linear in terms of the interest rate.

Hedging Strategies with T-Bond Futures

The objective of pure hedging is to lock in a price. Investors holding securities may sell futures to lock in a future selling price. Conversely, traders who plan on purchasing in the future may buy futures to lock in a delivery price.

There are a few different ways to establish the number of futures contracts to trade. These methods include conversion factor weighting, basis point value weighting, and regression methods. We illustrate these methods by examples.

Conversion Factor Weighting

A conversion factor of 2 means that the price sensitivity of the bond is approximately double the futures price sensitivity. In this case, two futures contracts need to be sold to immunize the price change of every $100,000 in face value of the underlying bond. If the underlying bond is the cheapest-to-deliver bond, then the futures price change tends to track the cheapest-to-deliver-bond. However, if the underlying bond is not the cheapest to deliver, then the futures price is tracking another bond. As a result, the futures position may not closely track changes in the cash position, so basis error will be greater.

EXAMPLE 20.13   A firm holds a T-bond with $5 million face value. The bond happens to be the cheapest to deliver. Management is concerned that interest rates will rise over the next 30 days. To protect the bonds from a decline in value, the firm decides to fully hedge the position by selling T-bond futures. The current information is summarized below.

Bond price	131-01
Coupon rate	12%
Conversion factor	1.3782
T-bond futures price	94-22
Short-term financing rate	8%

The current value of the T-bond is $131.03125 per $100 face value, or $6,551,562 per $5 million face value. As a first step, we need to establish the number of futures to sell. If the conversion factor were 1, then the number of contracts would be $5,000,000/$100,000 = 50. However, since the bond is 1.3782 times greater, the number of contracts to sell must be adjusted to 50 × 1.3782 = 69.

Assume interest rates increase and the bond price drops to 130-04. Furthermore, assume the futures price drops to 94-02. The change in the futures price is 20 ticks, which translates to 20 × 31.25 = $625. The profit on selling 69 futures

EXHIBIT 20.5 Comparison of Hedged and Unhedged Positions

	Day 0	Day 30
Without Futures		
Portfolio value	$6,551,562	$6,506,250
Interest	—	50,000
Net value		$6,556,250
Annualized return		0.8586%
With Futures		
Portfolio value	$6,551,562	$6,506,250
Interest	—	50,000
Futures gain		43,125
Net value		$6,599,375
Annualized return		8.75%

contracts is $43,125. Exhibit 20.5 compares the hedged portfolio to the unhedged position. Note that the interest on the bonds corresponds to the one-month interest on the 12 percent coupon bonds (1% of $5 million).

By selling futures against the bond, interest rate sensitivity is reduced. The hedged portfolio is essentially converted to the equivalent of a short-term security and should provide a yield close to the short-term financing rate.

Basis Point Value Weighting

Treasury futures can be used to alter the duration of a fixed-income portfolio. Buying (selling) futures increases (decreases) the portfolio's interest rate sensitivity. Indeed, hedging a bond portfolio by selling futures lowers the duration of the portfolio. In a completely hedged portfolio, the duration is lowered to that of a portfolio of short-term securities, and the resulting rate of return should be the short-term riskless rate. *Hedging decisions can therefore be seen as duration decisions.* In order to use futures to alter portfolio duration, it is first necessary to calculate the sensitivity of the bond being hedged to changes in yield and to measure the sensitivity of futures prices to changes in yield.

Let $B(y)$ be the value of the bond (or bond portfolio). If the yield changes by $\Delta y = 1$ basis point, then the bond price will move to $B(y + \Delta y)$. The change in bond price $\Delta B(y) = B(y + \Delta y) - B(y)$ can be computed exactly using the bond pricing equation, or it can be estimated using the linear bond pricing approximation with modified duration. Specifically,

$$\Delta B(y) \approx \mathbb{D}_m B(y) \Delta y = \mathbb{D}_m B(y)0.0001$$

Recall that this change in dollar value is called the basis point value (BPV) for the bond (bond portfolio). The greater the BPV, the greater the interest rate exposure. Now consider the T-bond futures contract. Recall that the BPV of the futures contract equals the BPV of the cheapest-to-deliver instrument divided by the appropriate conversion factor.

If every 1-basis-point change in the bond portfolio were accompanied by a 1-basis-point change in the cheapest-to-deliver bond, then an effective hedge position could be constructed by selling N^* futures, where

$$N^* = \frac{BPV_P}{BPV_F} \qquad (20.18)$$

Here BPV_P is the change in bond portfolio value and $BPV_F = BPV_i/CF_i$, i being the cheapest-to-deliver bond. However, it is possible that the yield changes in the two instruments are not of the same magnitude. Let β represent the yield change volatility of the bond portfolio relative to the cheapest-to-deliver bond. Then

$$N^* = \left(\frac{BPV_P}{BPV_F}\right)\beta \qquad (20.19)$$

We can derive β by regressing the historical changes in the yield of the bond portfolio against historical yields of the cheapest-to-deliver bond.

EXAMPLE 20.14 A portfolio manager holds a portfolio which has a duration of 5 (measured in half years). The current T-bond futures price is $85. The portfolio value is $10 million, the annualized yield to maturity is 9 percent (or $y = 4.5\%$ semiannually), and the BPV of the futures is $77. The portfolio manager wants to immunize the portfolio by selling T-bond futures.

First, the modified duration has to be computed.

$$\mathbb{D}_m = \mathbb{D}/(1 + y) = \frac{5}{1 + 0.09/2} = 4.785$$

Hence $\qquad BPV_P = \mathbb{D}_m(\$10,000,000)(0.001) = \$47,850$

A regression analysis of weekly yields of a portfolio that has a duration of 5 half years against historical yields of the cheapest-to-deliver bond provides a slope estimate, β, of 0.91. The optimal number of futures is then estimated to be $[BPV_P/BPV_F]\beta = 565$.

The hedging scheme described in Example 20.14 uses the current yields to set up the hedge ratio. As yields change over time, the hedge ratio will change and the position must be rebalanced. If a static strategy is to be set up, then perhaps the hedge ratio should be based on BPV numbers calculated around yields that are expected to arise when the hedge is lifted rather than on current yields.

Creating Synthetic Instruments and Asset Allocation

T-bond futures can be used in conjunction with individual securities or bonds to create synthetic instruments. A synthetic long-term instrument can be created by buying a T-bill and then buying additional T-bill futures to create a synthetic security with the required duration. A synthetic short-term instrument can be created by buying longer-term securities and selling futures to obtain the targeted duration.

EXAMPLE 20.15   Changing the Duration of a Portfolio

Consider a portfolio manager who holds a portfolio with a duration of 4.6. The portfolio is tied to a broad-based bond index and is not to be disrupted. The manager has a strong conviction that yields will drop significantly and therefore wants to increase the duration to about 10. The current information is summarized below.

Portfolio duration	4
Target duration	10
Bond futures price	80-12
Portfolio value	$10 million
BPV of futures	$86
Portfolio yield to maturity	9%

The first step is to compute the BPV of the portfolio. The modified duration is given by $\mathbb{D}_m = \mathbb{D}/(1 + y/2) = 4.0/(1 + 0.09/2) = 3.82775$. The BPV is then given by

$$BPV = \mathbb{D}_m \times \text{(portfolio value)} \times 0.0001 = \$3,828$$

The target portfolio duration is 10. This means the ideal BPV is

$$BPV = 10/(1 + 0.09/2) \times \$10,000,000 \times 0.0001 = \$9,569$$

This means that the BPV must be increased by $5,741. The number of futures contracts that will accomplish this is 5,741/86 = 67 contracts.

EXAMPLE 20.16   Changing Asset Allocations

This example illustrates how futures can be used for temporary asset reallocations, allowing time for research on specific purchase and sale decisions.

A portfolio is divided up with 80 percent in the stock market and 20 percent in bonds. External managers were given these funds to allocate in their funds. The current information on the portfolios is shown below.

Bond portfolio duration	5
Bond portfolio yield	8%
BPV of bond futures	$98.02
Market value of bonds	$100 million
Stock portfolio beta	1
Stock index futures price	$300.25
Stock index futures multiplier	500
Market value of stocks	$400 million

The portfolio manager ideally would like 60 percent in stocks and 40 percent in bonds, which would require selling $100 million in stocks and buying $100 million in bonds. Without disrupting this portfolio, the manager would like to synthetically create a portfolio that is 60 percent in stocks and 40 percent in bonds. To do this, the manager first computes the BPV of the additional bonds required as $5.0/(1 + 0.08/2) \times \$100{,}000{,}000 \times 0.0001 = \$48{,}077$.

Now, the number of bond futures can be established as $\$48{,}077/\$98.02 = 490$ contracts. Finally, the number of stock index futures to sell has to be determined. The stock index futures market value is 500 times the index level or $150,125. Since the beta value is 1, the number of futures contracts to sell is $\$100{,}000{,}000/\$150{,}125 = 666$ contracts.

Options on T-Bonds and Options on T-Bond Futures

A very thin market exists for exchange-traded options on specific Treasury bonds. Since the most active trading centers on the most recently auctioned T-bond issue, options on these issues are introduced as soon as the new T-bond is available. When new bond issues are introduced, options on the older issue are phased out. Prices are quoted in points and thirty-seconds of a point, with each point representing 1 percent of the principal value ($1,000). The price paid upon exercise is established by multiplying the strike by the underlying principal and adding accrued interest. For example, the settlement price of an option with strike $90 is simply $\$100{,}000(\$90/100) = \$90{,}000$, plus accrued interest. Examples 20.17 and 20.18 illustrate potential uses of T-bond options.

EXAMPLE 20.17 **Options on Bonds at the CBOE**

A manager is told that there is a high likelihood the company will receive a significant amount of funds in three months. Currently, long-term interest rates are high, and the manager expects them to decline. The manager wants to lock into the prevailing high rate. In order to do this, the manager buys a three-month $96 T-bond call option quoted at 0-20 or $625. This option is written on a 12 percent U.S. Treasury bond due August 2013, with a principal value of $100,000, currently priced at $95,000. The profit table is as follows:

T-Bond Price ($)	95	96	97	98	99
Net profit from buying 92 call ($)	−625	−625	−375	1,375	2,375

If prices do rise (interest rates drop), the option strategy will produce profits. By purchasing call options, the manager is purchasing protection against interest rate declines or future price increases.

EXAMPLE 20.18 A corporation is financing a large project by using corporate bonds. However, there is a threat that interest rates will rise before the bonds are issued, which would mean a drop in the bond price. Thus, to insure against interest rates rising above a threshold, the company buys put options on a T-bond. If interest rates do rise and the corporate bond value declines, the put will become valuable and will compensate for the loss in corporate bond value. The corporation buys a three-month June 94 put option quoted at 2-16 or $2,500. This option is written on a 12 percent U.S. T-bond due August 2013, with a principal value of $100,000, currently priced at $95,000. The profit table is as follows:

T-Bond Price ($)	91	92	93	94	95	96	97
Net profit from buying 94 put option ($)	1,500	500	−500	−1,500	−2,500	−2,500	−2,500

The quantity of puts to purchase depends on the level of protection desired.

Interest Rate or Yield Options

As discussed in Chapter 7, cash-settled option contracts exist on yield indices. Almost all exchange-traded interest rate options are European-style contracts. Note that with yield options, call prices increase with increasing yields. An alternative to buying a call yield option is to buy a debt put option. Of course, the payoff from an in-the-money call yield option is linear in the interest rate, whereas the payout of an in-the-money option on a bond is linear in the price. For examples of cash-settled yield options see Chapter 7.

Options on Futures

Options on 2-, 5-, and 10-year Treasury note futures are available, as well as options on T-bond futures and options on Eurodollar futures. The market for options on T-bond futures is more liquid than that for options on T-bonds. There are several reasons for this. First, the underlying futures markets are extremely liquid, and information on prices is readily available and centered at one location.

In contrast, the prices of individual T-bonds are not as easily available. The bond futures price is readily available from the last trade, but the actual bond price can be established only by canvassing bond dealers. Second, options on futures trade at the same locations as the futures, and the trading hours are coordinated; hedging and pricing relationships between the futures and their options are therefore quite precise. In contrast, since option markets close before the markets for T-bonds, significant price movement can take place that cannot be reflected in the option markets. This creates a risk that debt options may be exercised on the basis of price movement after the close of option trading, when writers are no longer able to close out their short positions. Third, options on futures cannot suffer from delivery squeezes. In contrast, delivery squeezes on any particular bond issue could occur.

EXAMPLE 20.19   Options on CBOT T-Bond Futures

Active option markets exist on the 2-, 5-, and 10-year T-note futures as well as on the T-bond futures contracts that trade on the CBOT. Strike prices bracket the current futures price. The interval between strike prices is 2 basis points (which corresponds to $2,000). Contracts trade on the three nearest futures contracts. The expiration date is the Friday that precedes the first notice day by at least five days. Prices are quoted in multiples of 1/64 of 1 percent of a $100,000 T-bond futures contract. Each 1/64 point is worth $15.63. The volume of trading in the options contract is about one-third the volume of trading in the underlying futures contract.

Over-the-Counter Options

T-bill and T-bond options on physical instruments are not very liquid, and large transactions cannot easily be accommodated. As a result, investors wanting to trade debt options on actual securities often do so on an over-the-counter basis. These markets are maintained by many of the large government securities dealers. In many cases, dealers will establish option contracts tailored to the needs of the institution requesting them. The dealer market is also responsible for introducing a huge array of specialized option contracts. Examples include contracts that provide payouts only if the bill-to-bond spread exceeds a particular value, contracts based on the average daily interest rate over finite time horizons, contracts based on swapping fixed for variable-based payouts, floor-ceiling agreements, and many others. These markets are discussed in Chapter 22.

Conclusion

This chapter provided an overview of interest rate futures and option products that trade in U.S. markets. The major focus of this chapter was on the T-bond futures contract. This contract and the Eurodollar futures contract are the most liquid futures contracts traded. Several examples demonstrated the use of T-bond futures in interest rate risk management.

Options also exist on interest rate indices and interest rate futures. The most active option contracts are on the T-bond and the Eurodollar futures. Several examples illustrated hedging interest rate exposure using T-bond futures. In all cases, the hedged position needs to be carefully monitored over time and adjustments need to be made.

References

This chapter draws heavily from the many first-rate publications put out by the Chicago Board of Trade. Indeed, many of the examples in this chapter were based on examples the CBOT developed. Figlewski's very good textbook emphasizes hedging applications. For some other models, see the Kolb articles.

Chicago Board of Trade. *Treasury Futures for Institutional Investors*. Chicago, 1990.

Figlewski, S. *Hedging with Financial Futures for Institutional Investors*. Cambridge, Mass.: Ballinger, 1986.

Hegde, S., and B. Branch. "An Empirical Analysis of Arbitrage Opportunities in the Treasury Bill Futures Market." *Journal of Futures Markets* 2 (1982): 407–24.

Hull, J. *Options, Futures and Other Derivative Securities*. Englewood Cliffs, N.J.: Prentice-Hall, 1993.

Kane, A., and A. Marcus. "The Quality Option in the Treasury Bond Futures Market." *Journal of Futures Markets* 4 (1984): 55–64.

Kawaller, I., and T. Koch. "Cash and Carry Trading and the Price of Treasury Bill Futures." *Journal of Futures Markets* 3 (1983): 451–72.

Kolb, R. *Interest Rate Futures: A Comprehensive Introduction*. Miami: Kolb, 1990.

Kolb, R., G. Gay, and J. Jordan. "Are There Arbitrage Opportunities in the Treasury Bond Futures Market?" *Journal of Futures Markets* 2 (1982): 217–30.

Kolb, R., and R. Chiang. "Duration, Immunization, and Hedging with Interest Rate Futures." *Journal of Financial Research* 10 (1982): 161–70.

———. "Improving Hedging Performance Using Interest Rate Futures." *Financial Management* 10 (1981): 72–79.

Kuberek, R., and N. Pefley. "Hedging Corporate Debt with U.S. Treasury Bond Futures." *Journal of Futures Markets* 3 (1983): 345–53.

Exercises

1. A firm holds a 180-day T-bill with a face value of $10 million. The firm needs cash in three months. The term structure is flat at 10 percent, continuously compounded.
   a. Compute the price of the 180-day and 90-day T-bills.
   b. Compute the forward price of a contract that requires delivery of a 90-day T-bill in 90 days. Translate the forward price in the IMM index price format.

  c. Assume the actual futures price was given by the forward price that you computed in Exercise 1b. Explain how the firm could use T-bill futures to translate its six-month maturity investment into a guaranteed three-month investment. Show all the transactions involved.

2. A firm wishes to invest $100 million in a Eurodollar time deposit for 90 days and is considering two alternatives: (1) Deposit the funds in a Eurodollar time deposit for 90 days. The rate on this deposit is 8.20 percent. (2) Deposit funds into a 180-day Eurodollar time deposit that yields 8.5 percent, and sell 100 Eurodollar futures contracts that settle in three months. The current futures price is $91.70.

  a. Compare these two strategies under the assumption that the 90-day LIBOR rate in three months will either increase by 50 basis points or decrease by 50 basis points. Provide a recommendation as to which strategy should be followed.

3. In Exercise 1, T-bill futures were used to shorten the maturity. Similarly, the second strategy in Exercise 2 used ED futures contracts to shorten the maturity. What feature of the futures contracts makes these strategies different? Explain.

4. A firm takes out a $10 million loan with the following terms. Every three months the three-month LIBOR rate is observed. This LIBOR rate determines the next quarterly interest expense: the next interest payment is the LIBOR rate plus 100 basis points. The initial LIBOR rate is 11.0 percent. The dates coincide with the IMM expiration dates of the ED futures contracts. Current prices of the ED futures are shown below.

Maturity (Months)	ED Futures Price ($)
3	89.45
6	89.34
9	89.20

  a. Explain what interest rate the firm is exposed to.
  b. If the firm believes the futures price provides a window into the future, what does it expect its future interest payments to be?
  c. The firm is concerned that LIBOR rates will increase unexpectedly and wants to hedge against this risk. Establish an appropriate hedging strategy using ED futures.

5. A firm plans to borrow 10 million for three months beginning in March, which is five months from now. The interest rate on the loan is determined by the three-month LIBOR rate at the initiation date. The firm is concerned that interest rates will expand over the next five months and wants to place a cap on the interest expense. The firm is considering using option contracts on ED futures.

  a. Should the firm purchase call options or put options?
  b. What factors should be considered when selecting a strike price?

c. Below are prices and terms of a few options. The March Eurodollar futures price is $96.55.

Strike	March Call	March Put
96.25	0.34	0.05
96.50	0.16	0.12
96.75	0.05	0.26

Compute the actual prices of the $96.50 call and put. Using the appropriate contract, illustrate how interest rates can be capped at 3.5 percent. Plot an appropriate profit diagram illustrating the cost of the loan under different LIBOR scenarios that evolve when the option expires.

6. A firm plans on issuing $5 million of commercial paper with a maturity of 180 days. If the firm issued the paper today, it would receive $4.8 million for the obligation of paying back $5 million in six months. Unfortunately, the issue date is in three months. The firm is concerned that interest rates may increase and would like to hedge against this event. The current quoted price of a three-month ED futures contract is $96.

   a. Use a duration-based hedging model to establish how many futures contracts should be traded.

   b. What assumptions did you make in the above analysis?

7. A trader sells one T-bond futures contract for 120-01. What view on interest rates does this trader have? What commitment does this trader have? If the final futures price is 118-02, then ignoring interest earned on accrued profits and losses, what is the dollar profit or loss?

8. The cheapest-to-deliver bond is currently a 10 percent coupon bond. It makes payments on March 15 and August 15 each year. The term structure is flat at 12 percent per year, with semiannual compounding. The current date is March 16, and the bond matures in exactly 16 years. The face value of the bond is $100,000. The conversion factor of the bond is 1.50. The repo rate is 12 percent and the delivery date is 60 days away. Compute the futures price.

9. A portfolio manager owns a $10 million T-bond portfolio that has a yield to maturity of 10.5 percent and a duration of 9.4 years. The manager is concerned that interest rates will rise and would like to reduce the duration to 2 years. The current information is summarized below.

Portfolio duration	9.4 years
Target duration	2 years
Bond futures price	120-12
Portfolio value	$10 million
BPV of futures	$60.02
Portfolio yield to maturity	10.5%

  a. Compute the modified duration of the portfolio and the BPV.
  b. Compute the ideal BPV, and use this value to establish the number of futures contracts to sell.
  c. Is this strategy better than rebalancing the portfolio so that its new duration is two years? Can you identify a situation where rebalancing the portfolio may be preferable?

10. A portfolio manager plans to purchase $10 million in face value of T-bonds in three months. The particular T-bond is currently the cheapest-to-deliver bond. The manager is concerned that prices will increase in the interim period and therefore decides to hedge by buying T-bond futures. The following information is available.

Price of T-bond (cheapest to deliver)	126-00
Basis point value per $100,000	$122
Conversion factor	1.3256
T-bond futures price	90-25

  a. Determine the BPV of the T-bond futures contract.
  b. Determine the number of futures contracts to buy.
  c. Assume after three months the bond price has increased by 100 basis points and the futures price has increased by 104 basis points. Compare the costs of the unhedged and hedged positions.

11. A firm plans to issue a $100 million face value 10-year coupon bond in three months. The firm expects interest rates to rise over this interim period and would like to fix the financing costs at current rates. The firm decides to cross hedge using the 10-year T-note futures. As part of the analysis, the firm estimates the BPV of the corporate debt issue to be $65 per $100,000 face value. The current cheapest-to-deliver bond has a BPV of $64.52 and a conversion factor of 1.1062. A regression analysis of yield changes of similar corporate bonds against yield changes of the cheapest-to-deliver bond indicates a slope coefficient of 0.820. Based on this analysis, a 100-basis-point change in Treasuries should have an 82-basis-point effect on corporates. Management's opinions concur with this estimate.

  a. Compute the BPV of the 10-year T-note futures contract.
  b. Determine the number of futures contracts to sell.
  c. Assume over the three-month period the T-note futures price dropped 100 basis points and that the corporate debt was issued at 11 percent rather than 10.5 percent (that is, at 50 basis points higher). Compute the approximate additional cost of issuing this debt, and compute the profit on the futures position. Finally, establish the effective borrowing rate from using the hedge.

CHAPTER 21

Interest Rate Swaps and Other Over-the-Counter Interest Rate Products

The main advantages of exchange-traded products come from the liquidity benefits of standardization and the institutional features put in place to ensure that all parties perform. Liquidity allows positions to be unwound at low cost, and the institutional features of exchange-traded contracts eliminate the need for participants to investigate the creditworthiness of the party taking the other side. As discussed, the disadvantage of exchange-traded products is that there are only a small set of contracts from which to choose. As a result, a significant mismatch can materialize between the firm's exposure and the contract used to manage the exposure. That is, the basis risk can be substantial. To some extent this can be resolved by monitoring hedges very closely and adjusting the hedge ratios over time. However, monitoring such hedges and implementing dynamic hedging schemes can be expensive. The alternative to exchange-traded derivatives is to purchase tailor-made products from a commercial or investment bank. The advantage of doing this is that precise instruments can be designed to manage the very specific situation. Of course, this customization comes at a cost. Moreover, if circumstances change and the firm wants to unravel its position, the cost of accomplishing this will typically be much higher than the cost of unwinding hedges using exchange-traded instruments. It can be difficult to decide whether to use exchange-traded derivatives or customized over-the-counter derivatives.

In the last decade, interest in products offered in over-the-counter derivatives markets has mushroomed. Products that once were considered highly specialized and custom-designed for specific applications have now become more standardized. Initially, these products were offered at significant markups. However, as they became more common, dealers began making markets in them by continuously offering to buy and sell them. The increased liquidity and competition between dealers forced the bid-ask spreads to narrow. As this process occurred, the liquidity benefits of using exchange-traded products diminished, making this market more attractive to firms that had previously been reluctant to use them. Of course, since these contracts are between two specific parties, credit risk still remains. Although the tightening of the bid-ask spread reduced the profit margin to the dealers, to some extent this was compensated by the increased volume. Meanwhile, market makers continue to search for new innovative products that will more precisely meet the risk management needs of certain clients than the array of existing products.

Perhaps the most important products that emerged from the 1980s were the "standard vanilla" interest rate swap and a variety of other "nonstandard" swaps. Swaps are so pervasive that in the United States nearly 75 percent of corporations with revenues of at least $3 billion have used these products. Clearly, such successful products must be meeting needs that otherwise were not being met at all or were being met at a higher cost. This market is massive, but since it is an over-the-counter market, the creditworthiness of the counterparty is an important issue that needs to be carefully addressed. Indeed, while the number of firms entering into swaps continues to increase, a growing number of deals are rejected due to the perception that the credit risk of the counterparty is excessive. Indeed, over 80 percent of corporate chief financial officers who have done swaps claim that they have rejected deals solely because the credit risk of the partner was considered too high. This chapter examines the swap market and other over-the-counter interest rate derivatives. The primary thrust is to describe the nature of the products, the way in which they are traded, the participants, and the pricing of these products.

In the first part of this chapter we discuss forward rate agreements. Such contracts can be viewed as the simplest of swaps. In the second part we describe the swap market, starting with "plain vanilla" swaps and then building up to more complex agreements. We investigate the pricing of interest rate swaps and address default risk exposure. In the third part of this chapter we describe other over-the-counter contracts.

The primary objectives of this chapter are the following:

- To discuss forward contracts on interest rates (forward rate agreements);
- To discuss the interest rate swap market;
- To investigate pricing and default risk exposure in swaps; and
- To discuss other over-the-counter contracts.

Forward Rate Agreements

Forward rate agreements, or FRAs, are forward contracts on interest rates. Such contracts exist in most major currencies, although the market is dominated by U.S. dollar contracts. The market is primarily an interbank market, and the major traders communicate their quotes via electronic quotation systems.

An FRA is a cash-settled contract between two parties where the payout is linked to the future level of a designated interest rate, such as 3-month LIBOR. The two parties agree on an interest rate to be paid on a hypothetical "deposit" that is to be initiated at a specific future date. The buyer of an FRA commits to pay interest on this hypothetical loan at a predetermined fixed rate and in return receives interest at the actual rate prevailing at the settlement date.

Let $f_0(m)$ represent the annualized fixed m-period rate determined at date 0, and let $v_T(m)$ represent the reference m-period rate, also in annualized form, that prevails at the settlement date, T. The net cash payment to the buyer of an FRA is based on a quantity $Q_T(m)$, given by

$$Q_T(m) = [v_T(m) - f_0(m)]NP[m/360] \qquad (21.1)$$

Here NP is the hypothetical deposit quantity, which is a predetermined fixed constant usually referred to as the **notional principal**, and m represents the "deposit" period in days.

Actual settlement of this payment can occur in one of two ways. In one form of FRA, the actual cash payment is made m days after the cash determination date, T. This contract is often preferred by corporations but is not that common. The more usual approach is to settle the contract at date T. In this case the actual cash flow is taken to be the present value of $Q_T(m)$, where the reference rate is used as the discount factor. That is, the cash payment at date T is $Q_T(m)/[1 + v_T(m)(m/360)]$. These advance payment contracts are more common among banks. Exhibit 21.1 identifies the timing for the two alternatives.

EXAMPLE 21.1   Suppose a bank needs to lock in an interest rate for $10 million six-month LIBOR-based funding that commences in three months. That is, in three months the bank will lend $10 million to a client for a period of six months. The client, however, needs a rate commitment from the bank. The bank in turn is reluctant to commit itself to a rate unless it can lock in the cost of its funds. The bank approaches a market maker in FRAs. Assume current six-month LIBOR is quoted at 8 percent. The bank asks the market maker for a quote on "three-month against nine-month" LIBOR. This quote convention identifies the point in time when the contract begins (in three months) and ends (in nine months). In industry shorthand the FRA term would be denoted "3 × 9" and read as "three by nine." Assume the market maker is offering the required contract at 8.5 percent. The bank accepts this offer. Based on its lending policy for its best-rated customers, the bank turns around and offers a locked-in rate of 9 percent to its client.

Suppose that interest rates rise over the next three months and six-month LIBOR is 9.2 percent. While the bank loses money on the actual lending of funds over the six-month period, since it is hedged, it actually comes out ahead. The loss

$f_0(m)$ set	$v_T(m)$ determined	Payment of $Q_T(m)$ made
0	T	$T+m$

$f_0(m)$ set	$v_T(m)$ determined	Payment of $Q_T(m)/[1 + v_T(m)(m/360)]$
0	T	$T+m$

EXHIBIT 21.1   Cash Flows for Forward Rate Agreements

after nine months on the actual lending is $(0.092 - 0.09)(\$10,000,000) \times (180/360) = \$10,000$. However, the payoff from the FRA is $(0.092 - 0.085) \times (\$10,000,000)(180/360) = \$35,000$, which more than compensates.

In this example, the bank bought an FRA and gained from interest rate increases. In contrast, a long position in a futures contract gains if interest rates decline. Note that if three-month LIBOR is the underlying variable, then buying an FRA is almost identical to selling a Eurodollar (ED) futures contract. Of course, since FRAs are forward contracts, they are not marked to market and hence are more likely to default. Banks can use ED futures to hedge exposed FRAs. Unlike exchange-traded futures, however, the FRA can be customized to closely conform to the specific risk being hedged by the firm.

IMM FRAs and the Pricing of FRAs

IMM FRAs are FRAs that use IMM settlement dates. Strips of Eurodollar futures can be used both to hedge and price these contracts. By pricing an FRA, we mean establishing the fair fixed rate of the contract.

To illustrate how this is accomplished, consider the Eurodollar futures prices that existed at the settlement date in December. The actual three-month spot rate from December to March is 3.48 percent. Recall that this number is based on a 360-day year. The actual return on a three-month ED deposit would be $0.0348 \times m/360$, where m is the number of days until the settlement date of the IMM ED futures contract. From Exhibit 21.2 we see the maturity is 90 days, and the return is 0.87 percent. The implied 3×6 forward rate for three-month LIBOR is 3.46 percent. Again, this yield represents the rate that can be locked in over the next three-month period. Exhibit 21.2 shows the prices of Eurodollar futures with maturities extending out several years into the future.

From the set of implied 3-month ED LIBOR rates, a yield curve of LIBOR can be established and longer-term FRAs can be priced. For example, a 0×9 rate could be established using the appropriate 0×3, 3×6, and 6×9 ED contracts. The actual rate from December to March is $3.48(90/360) = 0.87\%$; the implied rate from March to June is $3.46(92/360) = 0.884\%$; and the rate from June to September is $3.65(92/360) = 0.933\%$. As a result, the implied rate over the nine-month period is $(1.0087)(1.00884)(1.00933) - 1 = 2.711\%$, which when annualized yields the 0×9 rate of 3.56% $(2.711 \times 360/274)$.

The same calculation can be done to compute the price of other FRAs. For example, consider a 12×24 FRA. This contract commences next December and lasts 12 months. Using ED futures contracts, a fixed rate can be locked in for the year starting from December. Hence, to avoid riskless arbitrage, the fair fixed rate for a 12×24 FRA should equal this rate. The price of the FRA is completely determined by the appropriate December, March, June, and September ED contracts. The 12-month implied LIBOR rate is given by the value s, where

EXHIBIT 21.2 Eurodollar Futures Prices

Contract	Price ($)	Implied 3-month LIBOR (%)	Days	Notation	Contract	Price ($)	Implied 3-month LIBOR (%)	Days	Notation
Dec.	96.52	3.48	90	0 × 3	Dec.	94.09	5.91	90	48 × 51
March	96.54	3.46	92	3 × 6	March	94.12	5.88	92	51 × 54
June	96.35	3.65	92	6 × 9	June	94.02	5.98	92	54 × 57
Sept.	96.14	3.86	91	9 × 12	Sept.	93.94	6.04	91	57 × 60
Dec.	95.77	4.23	90	12 × 15	Dec.	93.79	6.21	90	60 × 63
March	95.70	4.30	92	15 × 18	March	93.84	6.16	92	63 × 66
June	95.50	4.50	92	18 × 21	June	93.79	6.21	92	66 × 69
Sept.	95.33	4.67	91	21 × 24	Sept.	93.75	6.25	91	69 × 72
Dec.	95.05	4.95	90	24 × 27	Dec.	93.57	6.43	90	72 × 75
March	95.02	4.98	92	27 × 30	March	93.61	6.39	92	75 × 78
June	94.87	5.13	92	30 × 33	June	93.55	6.45	92	78 × 81
Sept.	94.75	5.25	91	33 × 36	Sept.	93.51	6.49	91	81 × 84
Dec.	94.51	5.49	90	36 × 39					
March	94.51	5.49	92	39 × 42					
June	94.39	5.61	92	42 × 45					
Sept.	94.30	5.70	91	45 × 48					

$$\left(1 + s \times \frac{365}{360}\right) = \left[1 + 0.0423 \times \frac{90}{360}\right]$$
$$\left[1 + 0.0430 \times \frac{92}{360}\right]\left[1 + 0.045 \times \frac{92}{360}\right]\left[1 + 0.0467 \times \frac{91}{360}\right]$$

Solving this equation yields $s = 4.50\%$.

This method of pricing FRAs assumes that there is no difference between futures and forward contracts. Actually, this assumption may not be too bad if the FRA date is less than one or even two years. However, the marking-to-market effect that causes futures to deviate from forward prices may be significant for longer-term contracts. As a result, this type of pricing may not be completely precise for distant FRAs.

Exhibit 21.3 shows the implied LIBOR yields to maturity obtained by setting up strips of the ED futures contracts in Exhibit 21.2. Based on this data Exhibit 21.4 shows the current implied yields that can be locked in for selected time periods.

All the rates in Exhibit 21.4 are simple annual rates based on a 360-day year. If this yield curve is to be compared with a Treasury yield curve, then appropriate adjustments need to be made.

Since FRAs are just forward contracts on interest rates, fair prices with any begin and end dates can readily be computed once the LIBOR term structure is established. For example, the market maker could establish the fixed rates for nonstandard FRAs such as 1 × 4 or 2 × 11 contracts. Of course, such contracts

EXHIBIT 21.3   The LIBOR Yields Constructed from ED Futures

Contract	Notation	LIBOR Yield (%)	Contract	Notation	LIBOR Yield (%)
Dec.	0 × 3	3.480	Dec.	0 × 51	5.228
March	0 × 6	3.485	March	0 × 54	5.338
June	0 × 9	3.562	June	0 × 57	5.450
Sept.	0 × 12	3.662	Sept.	0 × 60	5.558
Dec.	0 × 15	3.806	Dec.	0 × 63	5.671
March	0 × 18	3.924	March	0 × 66	5.779
June	0 × 21	4.045	June	0 × 69	5.885
Sept.	0 × 24	4.164	Sept.	0 × 72	5.987
Dec.	0 × 27	4.298	Dec.	0 × 75	6.099
March	0 × 30	4.416	March	0 × 78	6.207
June	0 × 33	4.534	June	0 × 81	6.314
Sept.	0 × 36	4.649	Sept.	0 × 84	6.420
Dec.	0 × 39	4.772			
March	0 × 42	4.885			
June	0 × 45	4.999			
Sept.	0 × 48	5.110			

cannot be precisely hedged using three-month ED futures, and an appropriate cross hedge involving nearby futures may be required. If the contract needs some customization, then the bank may charge an additional fee. Moreover, since the contract is between two parties, default risk may be a concern. In this case, the fixed rate may be set at an appropriate premium above the computed default-free fair fixed rate.

EXHIBIT 21.4   Implied LIBOR Yields for IMM FRAs

Notation	LIBOR Yield (%)
3 × 6	3.460
3 × 9	3.571
3 × 12	3.689
6 × 9	3.650
6 × 12	3.772
9 × 12	3.860
12 × 15	4.230
12 × 18	4.288
12 × 24	4.500
18 × 24	4.611
24 × 30	4.996

Interest Rate Swaps

As discussed in Chapter 11, a **swap** is a customized agreement between two parties to make periodic payments to each other according to well-defined rules. In the simplest of interest rate swaps, one party periodically pays a cash flow determined by a fixed interest rate and receives a cash flow determined by a floating interest rate.

The swap market consists of two types of participants, counterparties and market makers. A **market maker** maintains a portfolio of swaps and hedges the risk of the portfolio using spot and derivative markets. The market maker bears any residual risk that cannot be hedged. **Counterparties** engage in swaps to gain some efficiency either in financing their operations or in managing some risk, while market makers seek to generate profits from their swap portfolios. Swaps are usually executed between counterparties and market makers or between market makers, not between counterparties.

The cash flows received by a market maker from one swap may provide a hedge, or at least a partial hedge, of the cash flows the market maker must pay in a second swap. A pair of perfectly offsetting swaps provides equal but opposite cash flows that match in amount and timing. A market maker who engages solely in matched swaps functions like a clearinghouse or a futures exchange. By acting as an intermediary between the two sides of these swaps, the market maker bears no risk (provided both counterparties do not default). Since there is no principal balance involved, the default risk borne by the market maker is the risk associated with holding an unmatched position. When one side of the swap defaults, the marketmaker must locate another counterparty or bear the risk of holding an unmatched position. We shall have more to say about default risk later on.

In general, market makers provide swaps to counterparties that are tailor-made to suit their needs. Finding another swap that exactly offsets these cash flows may be difficult. As a result, the portfolio of swap positions accumulated by the market maker is unlikely to be perfectly hedged. The net exposure from an imbalance in the portfolio is often hedged using interest rate futures contracts. As with FRAs, the bid-ask spread must be sufficient to cover the credit and hedging risks assumed by the intermediary.

Mechanics of Interest Rate Swaps

Many banks use a "master" swap document so many swaps can be completed with the same customers under the same master agreements. For example, suppose firm ABC contracts to pay 5 percent to Bank 1 for three years in exchange for six-month LIBOR. The details of the deal would be confirmed as in Exhibit 21.5. Most entries in Exhibit 21.5 are self-explanatory. The fixed rate is determined on an "Actual/365" basis. This convention means that the rate is quoted on a 365-day basis and payments are determined according to the actual number of days in the period. The floating rate of "Actual/360" means that interest payments are based on a 360-day

EXHIBIT 21.5 Swap Confirmation

Contract date	July 12, 1994
Contract type	Interest rate swap
Fixed-rate payer	ABC
Floating-rate payer	Bank 1
Start date	July 14, 1994
Maturity date	July 14, 1997
Notional principal	$10 million
Fixed rate	5%
Floating rate	6-month LIBOR
Payment basis	
Fixed rate	Actual/365
Floating rate	Actual/360
Fixed payment dates	July 15 and Jan. 15 of each year
Floating payment dates	July 15 and Jan. 15 of each year
Payment details	Account details to be agreed
Documentation	See Master Agreement dated March 2, 1991

year. An alternative payment basis could be 30/360. This convention treats the year as 360 days, and each month is assumed to be 30 days long.[1]

Exhibit 21.6 shows the cash flows that would occur if LIBOR rates increased by 0.5 percent per period. Of course, if LIBOR rates had declined, then the net advantage would have been to Bank 1.

EXHIBIT 21.6 Cash Flows for Swap Given a LIBOR Scenario

Payment Date	Days	LIBOR (%)	Variable Amount Owed by Bank 1 ($)	Fixed Amount Owed by ABC ($)	Net Payment to ABC ($)
Jan. 15, 1995	184	5	255,555.55	252,054.79	3,500.76
July 15	181	5.5	276,527.77	247,945.20	28,582.57
Jan. 15, 1996	184	6	306,666.66	252,054.79	54,611.87
July 15	182	6.5	328,611.11	249,315.07	79,296.04
Jan. 15, 1997	185	7	359,722.22	253,424.66	106,297.56
July 15	180	7.5	375,000.00	246,575.34	128,424.66

---

[1] In general, actual/365 and 30/360 rates produce the same annual interest total, but if the payment is semiannual there will be slight differences in the half-year coupon. For example, consider a year in which the coupon periods are divided into 181 and 184 days. On a $10 million borrowing priced at 5 percent semiannual actual/365, the two payments are $247,945 and $252,055, totaling $500,000. On a 30/360 basis, the payments would be $250,000 each.

EXAMPLE 21.2   **Management of Interest Rate Risk**

Swaps can be used by firms who borrow at a floating rate and are concerned that rates will rise. The swap can be used to lock in fixed rates. The exact time and terms of the swap can be determined by the firm. More important, unlike a fixed-rate loan, a swap can readily be reversed. Hence, swaps provide firms with a flexible product that allows them to manage interest rate exposure on an ongoing basis.

Investment Enhancement in a Regulated Market

Interest rate swaps can be used to create a variety of synthetic products and to improve the yield on liquid assets. For example, consider an insurance firm which establishes a pool of short-term deposits representing insurance premiums. Regulations prohibit that these funds be placed in deposits with maturities beyond 1 year. By entering a swap where the insurance firm pays three-month LIBOR and receives a fixed five-year rate, the firm can effectively enhance its yield. At the same time, the cash pool continues to satisfy regulatory requirements, and funds are available for withdrawals at short notice.

Hedging a Swap with Eurodollar Futures Strips

Consider the hedging problem faced by a bank that has just entered into a swap as a fixed-rate payer. The swap is for 12 months, has a notional principal of $200 million, and involves quarterly swaps for three-month LIBOR. The reset dates correspond to the settlement dates of the ED futures contracts, and the initiation date corresponds to the IMM settlement date in December. There are 90 days to the first payment date in March. The relevant ED futures contracts are shown below. The current three-month LIBOR rate is 3.48 percent. Assume the fixed rate is 3.57 percent and is quoted in money market form.[2] (That is, this rate is based on a 360-day year.)

Contract	Price ($)	Implied 3-month LIBOR	Days to Next Payment Date	Notation
March	96.54	3.46	92	3 × 6
June	96.35	3.65	92	6 × 9
Sept.	96.14	3.86	91	9 × 12

The bank is exposed to decreasing ED rates, and in spite of an upward-sloping LIBOR yield curve, it desires to hedge this risk by buying a strip of Eurodollar futures.

---

[2] The usual way to quote the fixed rate is in bond-equivalent form. We shall discuss this shortly.

EXHIBIT 21.7   Gains from the Strip of 200 ED Futures

Contract	Purchase Price ($)	Selling Price ($)	Gain/Loss (Basis Points)	Gain of Futures Position ($)	Adjusted Value 3 Months Later ($)
March	96.54	96.62	8	40,000	
June	96.35	96.72	37	185,000	40,348
Sept.	96.14	96.82	68	340,000	186,598
Dec.					342,733

Recall that the swap payments are made in arrears. That is, the LIBOR rate at the beginning of the quarter determines the payment at the end of the quarter. For example, the three-month LIBOR in March determines the swap settlement in June. As this swap cash flow is intended to be hedged by the ED position in the March futures contract, there is a mismatch in terms of the timings of the cash flows on the swap and hedge. For the moment, we shall not incorporate this feature into our analysis; assume that a simple strip of 200 ED futures for each of the above settlement dates is established. Exhibit 21.7 shows the profit on the strip of futures under the assumption that LIBOR decreased by 10 basis points per quarter, starting from 3.48 percent.

The dollar gain of each futures position held to expiration is shown. We assume the gains on the futures positions are invested in three-month ED deposits. We make these deposits so as to line up the cash flows from the strip to the cash flows from the swap. The last column in Exhibit 21.7 shows the dollar value of these accounts. Exhibit 21.8 shows the profit on the unhedged and hedged positions. The fixed payments are computed by multiplying the rate by the number of days/360 and then multiplying by the notional principal. The fourth column reports the LIBOR rate relevant for the variable payment. For example, the first entry of 3.48 percent is the actual spot LIBOR in December. The LIBOR rates decreased by 10 basis points each quarter, consistent with our assumptions. The size of the variable payments can then be determined. The net cash flows provide the results for the unhedged position. The last two columns add in the effects of the strip of ED contracts.

While the naive hedge does protect the swap against declines in the variable rate, it is not completely effective. A better hedging strategy can be established by a suitable "tailing" of the hedge. The necessary adjustment takes into account the

EXHIBIT 21.8   Comparing the Unhedged and Hedged Strategies

Contract	Days	Fixed Payments ($)	LIBOR Rate for Swap (%)	Variable Payments ($)	Net Swap Cash Flow (Unhedged; $)	Gain of Futures Position ($)	Net Swap Cash Flow (Hedged; $)
March	90	1,785,000	3.48	1,740,000	−45,000		−45,000
June	92	1,824,666	3.38	1,727,555	−97,111	40,348	−56,763
Sept.	91	1,804,833	3.28	1,658,222	−146,611	186,598	39,987
Dec.	90	1,785,000	3.18	1,590,000	−195,000	342,733	147,733

EXHIBIT 21.9   The Tailed Hedge

Contract	Implied Yield for Adjustment (%)	Number of Days for Adjustment	Discount Factor	Adjusted Futures Position
March	3.485	182	0.9827	197
June	3.562	274	0.9736	195
Sept.	3.662	365	0.9642	193

fact that swaps pay out in arrears, as well as the fact that the marking-to-market feature of futures tends to create differences in present value between the swap and the hedge cash flows.

Recall that the usual way of tailing the hedge requires modifying the number of contracts used in the naive hedge by multiplying by the appropriate discount factor for the period of the futures contract. In our analysis, however, the cash flow from the swap is deferred an additional quarter, so the appropriate adjustment involves a longer discount factor. For example, the number of contracts for delivery in March is reduced from 200 to 200 times the discount factor from December to June. The appropriate discount factors are obtained from the LIBOR yield curve and are shown in Exhibit 21.9, together with the adjusted hedge. Of course, for a tailed hedge, the number of futures contracts to buy has to be adjusted over time as the discount factors change. In general, if the hedge is not tailed, the initial number of futures contracts traded will be excessive.

Pricing Schedules

The most common interest rate swap is based on semiannual exchanges where the variable rate is linked to six-month LIBOR. Exhibit 21.10 illustrates a typical indication pricing schedule used by a market maker. For each maturity, the exhibit indicates the number of basis points that should be added onto the Treasury rate, depending on whether the market maker is paying or receiving.

For example, consider a bank negotiating a two-year swap where it receives a fixed rate and pays variable six-month LIBOR. From the schedule in Exhibit 21.10, the add-on or swap spread is seen to be 25 basis points (b.p.) above the current coupon rate of a two-year T-note selling at par. If the counterparty wanted to deal

EXHIBIT 21.10   The Indication Pricing Schedule

Treasury Maturity (Years)	Market Maker Pays Fixed Rate	Market Maker Receives Fixed Rate
2	Treasury + 20 b.p.	Treasury + 25 b.p.
3	Treasury + 25 b.p.	Treasury + 30 b.p.
5	Treasury + 25 b.p.	Treasury + 30 b.p.
7	Treasury + 26 b.p.	Treasury + 32 b.p.
10	Treasury + 30 b.p.	Treasury + 35 b.p.

in the opposite direction, then the bank would be prepared to pay a fixed rate of 20 basis points above the Treasury rate. The bid-ask spread from establishing two offsetting fully hedged positions is 5 basis points per year. The spread between the two represents the compensation the market maker demands for providing services, which include bearing default risk of the counterparty. The bid-ask spreads shown in Exhibit 21.10 are appropriate for counterparties with relatively high-quality credit. For high-risk counterparties, the market maker may require additional collateral (i.e., margin) and/or may widen the spread. In the early days of the swap market, bid-ask spreads as high as 100 basis points were common. However, as these markets have become more liquid, competition has eroded away the size of these margins.

The conventional way to quote a swap rate is relative to the floating index "flat." For example, Exhibit 21.10 lists quotes against six-month LIBOR flat. Swaps can of course be arranged to include a spread above or below the floating rate. For example, the fixed rate could be quoted against LIBOR plus 10 basis points.

Note that the rates are quoted on a Treasury bond basis, that is, a semiannual actual/365 rate. If the fixed-rate payer has to pay on a 360-day rate, we must adjust the rate by multiplying by 365/360.

Pricing Swaps

The interest rate swap market can be segmented into a short-term market (up to seven years) and a medium- to long-term market (beyond seven years). Short-term swaps are usually treated as a package of FRAs at a single fixed rate and are often priced and hedged using Eurodollar futures. A swap dealer who receives fixed and pays variable is exposed to LIBOR increases over the term of the swap. A strip of ED futures can be sold to hedge this risk. The very liquid ED futures market has arisen primarily because of the demand by dealers to hedge their residual risks.

Longer-term swaps are usually hedged by other swaps or by establishing cross hedges using Treasury futures contracts. A receiver of fixed on a 10-year swap is exposed to rising interest rates, which could be hedged by selling short 10-year Treasuries and borrowing this security through a reverse repurchase agreement.

The pricing of an IMM swap is best explained by an example. Reconsider the term structure of LIBOR given in Exhibit 21.2. We shall use these data to establish the fair fixed rate of a semiannual two-year fixed-for-variable swap based on IMM settlement dates. Assume the notional principal is $100 million. The current six-month LIBOR is 3.485 percent, and the consecutive implied six-month LIBOR rates are 3.772, 4.288, and 4.611 percent.

The first step of the analysis is to estimate the variable payments at each of the reset points. The first payment, due in 90 days, is based on the current LIBOR rate of 3.485 percent. The exact payment is $0.0348 \times (182/360) \times \$100,000,000 = \$1,759,333$. The second payment, due in June, is based on the LIBOR rate in March. The current implied forward rate is 3.772 percent. Since this variable rate can be hedged using a strip of two ED futures, the implied forward rate is the certainty equivalent for this rate. That is, for valuation procedures, we can assume that the payment due in June is based on a LIBOR rate of 3.772 percent. This implies a second payment of $0.03772 \times (183/360) \times \$100,000,000 = \$1,917,433$. Similar logic is used for the remaining cash flows. The resulting certainty equivalents are shown below.

Date	Certainty Equivalent ($)
June	1,759,333
Dec.	1,917,433
June	2,167,822
Dec.	2,343,925

The second step is to discount these cash flows using the zero-coupon yield curve to obtain the present value. The prices of discount bonds with face values of $100 and matching the dates of the swap settlement days are shown below.

Maturity Date	Discount Bond Price ($)	Bond-Equivalent Yield (%)
June	98.22	3.625
Dec.	96.30	3.805
June	94.30	3.951
Dec.	92.10	4.157

The present value, computed by discounting the certainty equivalents using the discount factors, is $7,777,516.

The final step is to calculate the annuity that has the same present value. Let F represent the fixed payments. Then we require

$$0.9822F + 0.9630F + 0.9430F + 0.9210F = \$7,777,516$$

Solving this equation yields $F = \$204,115$. Finally, let x represent the fixed interest rate for the swap. The fixed cash flow is $F = (x/2) \times \$100,000,000$. Solving for x, we obtain 4.08 percent. Accordingly, the fair fixed rate for the swap is 4.08 percent.

Of course, this analysis assumes there is no credit risk. Clearly, if the counterparty is not completely creditworthy, then an additional premium will be required.

Pricing Off-Market Interest Rate Swaps

Suppose a counterparty wants to be a fixed-rate payer on a two-year swap with semiannual payments. The current market conditions require a fixed rate of 4.3 percent. The party, however, would like to pay a lower rate of 4 percent. To obtain this lower rate, the party would have to pay the dealer an up-front premium. The size of the premium can easily be determined. Specifically, the difference in the rate is 30 basis points a year. This corresponds to 15 basis points for each payment date. Assume the notional principal is $100 million. The 15 basis points correspond to \$150,000 at each payment date. Since four payments are involved, the present value of this annuity is

$$\$150,000[1/(1.0215) + 1/(1.0215)^2 + 1/(1.0215)^3 + 1/(1.0215)^4] = \$569,086$$

As an alternative to paying this up-front fee to lower the interest rate, the dealer may just adjust the floating side of the swap. Here, the floating rate should be reduced by 30 basis points. The floating rate is based on a bank discount basis, with only 360 days, so the adjustment to the floating rate should be $30 \times 360/365 = 29.589$ basis points.

The above method of pricing off-market interest rate swaps can be used to establish the replacement value of the swap. Assume a five-year swap was entered into three years ago. The fixed rate was set at 4 percent, and the notional principal was set at \$100 million. The swap currently has two years to go, and the fair fixed interest rate is 4.3 percent. From our previous analysis, we know the value of the swap to the fixed-rate payer is \$569,086. That is, if the variable-rate counterparty wanted to terminate the swap, the fixed-rate payer would request compensation of \$569,086 so that this side of the transaction could be replaced without increasing the fixed rate.

A Comparison of Swaps and a Strip of Forward Rate Agreements

Swaps can be compared to a series of FRAs (where the payments are deferred to the period after the settlement date). By purchasing a sequence of FRAs, the firm is committed to exchanging variable-rate cash flows for a set of predetermined fixed, but not necessarily equal, cash flows.[3] At initiation, the value of each FRA is equal to zero, so the value of the portfolio of successive FRAs is zero.

In contrast, with a swap, the fixed-rate payer pays a constant level payment. The constant payment is set such that the present value of all inflows equals the present value of all outflows. Unless the yield curve is flat, the actual current value of each exchange is not equal to zero. With a steep yield curve, the difference between the fixed swap payment and the average FRA fixed payment could be substantial.

Default Risk in Swaps

Consider a fixed-for-variable interest rate swap. The cash flows of this swap are shown on page 506. These cash flows are equivalent to the cash flows involving borrowing at a fixed rate and simultaneously selling at a variable rate.

---

[3]Since each FRA is priced and traded separately, there is no reason for all the FRAs to specify the same fixed rate. Indeed, the series of fixed rates would be the same only if the term structure were flat.

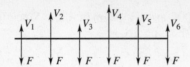

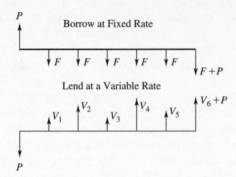

Combining the above loan contracts yields the cash flow from the swap. At first glance, the payer in a fixed-rate swap looks equivalent to a long position in a floating-rate note together with the sale of a fixed-rate security. However, the swap entails lower transaction costs, avoiding the underwriting commissions on a debt issue. Moreover, the swap has a different risk exposure. To see this, suppose a firm bought a floating-rate note and issued a fixed-rate note. If the issuer of the floating-rate note defaults, then the firm is at risk for the coupon and principal payments, while at the same time it has to continue servicing its own debt. In contrast, with a swap, when one party defaults the other party is not obligated to continue its payments.

The standard method for handling default risk of a swap involves establishing the replacement cost of the swap at the time of default. Assume firm A had entered into a swap as the fixed-rate payer with firm B n periods ago at date $-n$. The fixed rate at that time was f_{-n}. It is currently date 0, and the swap still has k periods to go. Suppose that immediately after the cash settlement at date 0, firm B enters bankruptcy and defaults on the remaining k cash flows. Assume that at date 0, the fixed rate on a k-period swap is f_0, a rate that is higher than f_{-n}. As the payer of the fixed rate, firm A experiences a loss equal to the replacement value of the swap, V_0, given by

$$V_0 = \sum_{i=1}^{k} [f_0 - f_{-n}]NP \times P(0, i)$$

If V_0 were negative, implying that f_0 is lower than f_{-n}, then the swap would be valuable to firm B. In this case, firm B would choose not to default on this agreement but would instead attempt to transfer it to a third party at a profit.

Formally, the payment due to the solvent party is the higher of zero or the market value of its position based on prevailing swap rates. This means that exposure is an optionlike function of the value of the contract. Specifically, the exposure is $Max[0,V_0]$, where V_0 is the no-default value of the swap to the solvent firm. This rule is supported by the International Swap Dealers Association. Under the standard swap documentation rules, the replacement cost, V_0, is determined by the solvent counterparty, who is required to obtain at least three market quotes for replacing the swap. V_0 is determined by the average of these quotes, where the highest and lowest quotes are removed. The settlement amount is then the higher of V_0 and 0.

The asymmetric treatment of the solvent and insolvent parties under a default event partially offsets the need for credit-sensitive swap spreads. If firm B defaults and the swap has positive value to B, then A benefits. That is, the stronger counterparty benefits by this asymmetric rule. The impact of this provision, however, is somewhat diluted because solvent parties tend to make at least partial payments for any negative market quotations, and the solvent party may obtain only a fraction of the settlement amount in bankruptcy proceedings.

After default by firm B at date 0, firm A's actual risk exposure, $RE_A(0)$, can be summarized by

$$RE_A(0) = \begin{cases} \sum_{i=1}^{k} [f_0 - f_{-n}]NP \times P(0, i) & \text{if } f_0 > f_{-n} \\ 0 & \text{otherwise} \end{cases}$$

The exposure depends on the joint occurrence of default by the counterparty and an adverse move in interest rates.

Default risk exposure varies over time, depending on the replacement swap rate and the number of cash flows remaining. The greater the divergence between the contracted fixed rate and the replacement rate and the greater the number of remaining cash flows, the greater the potential risk exposure. Early in the life of the swap, when the number of remaining periods is high, the contracted rate and the replacement rate will be fairly close to each other, and the risk exposure will be small. At the other extreme, when the number of remaining periods is fairly small, the chances are greater that the replacement rate deviates significantly from the contracted rate. In this case the risk exposure is small again. Overall, the risk exposure is likely to reach a maximum at some time between the origination date and the final maturity date.

In summary, the asymmetric handling of swaps at bankruptcies favors the higher-rated firm, making the need for establishing credit-sensitive swap spreads less critical. However, if credit risk is a concern to either or both parties, then additional terms may be written into the swap contract. These include credit triggers and marking-to-market requirements.

Credit Triggers   Most long-term swap arrangements contain credit triggers. A typical trigger specifies that if either counterparty falls below investment grade (BBB rating), the other counterparty has the right to have the swap cash-settled. This protection is quite important—very few firms go bankrupt prior to being downgraded. The less creditworthy the counterparty is, the greater the value of this implicit option.

Marking-to-Market Requirements   Rather than quoting higher swap spreads to weaker credits, swap agreements require such counterparties to provide collateral to support the swap.

Swap Portfolio Considerations

There is another reason swap spreads may not be extremely sensitive to credit risk. Dealers carefully monitor the market value of all their swap positions. The typical distribution of the marked-to-market value of all swaps held by a market maker, as a percent of their notional principal, is bell-shaped; a small proportion of swaps show large losses and a small proportion show large profits.

In addition, the distribution of clients in a market maker's portfolio is important. Hopefully, the portfolio is not heavily exposed to any single client. By diversifying their swap positions, market makers are able to sustain the economic consequences of any single default.

In summary, then, we have seen that credit risk imbalances between counterparties motivate adjustments in the fixed rate of the swap or requests for collateral, accomplished through credit triggers and marking-to-market requirements. The keen competition between market makers, together with the fact that they can efficiently diversify credit risk by holding many swaps with different counterparties, leads to credit spread differentials that are smaller than they would be if market makers' activities were restricted.

Most swap market makers are either commercial or investment banks. Commercial banks are in the credit risk-bearing business and hence are more likely to price default risk explicitly into the fixed rate of the swap. In contrast, investment banks are not in the business of bearing the credit risk of clients over the long term. Consequently, they tend to use collateral requirements and credit triggers to raise the effective credit standings of weaker counterparties.

The Wide Variety of Interest Rate Swaps

Interest rate swaps emerged in the early 1980s. The growth of the market has been spectacular. Indeed, no other market has grown as rapidly as the swap market. (Appendix 21A discusses several theories that have been put forward to explain the enormous growth of the swap market.) In 1993 the notional principal of interest rate swaps exceeded $2 trillion. The plain vanilla fixed-for-variable interest rate swap that we have just discussed has given way to hundreds of variants, all designed to serve specific needs.

Contingency Features in Swaps

Some swaps may have specific contingencies built into them. For example, the initiation date could be delayed, or the final settlement date could be adjusted, at the discretion of one of the counterparties. In this section we investigate some of the more common contingency features.

Forward Swaps and Futures Swaps   In the standard swap arrangement, the initiation date is two business days after the swap has been agreed upon by both parties. Some contracts have a delayed start. For example, the counterparties may commit to the exact terms of the contract today, with the initiation date starting at some future date. In other words, a forward contract is entered into, where the underlying commodity is a swap.[4]

Swap Rate Locks and Treasury Rate Locks   The quoted swap rate consists of two components, namely, the prevailing Treasury yield and the swap spread. When there is a large demand from traders wanting to pay the fixed rate, the swap spread tends to increase. Conversely, when there is a large demand from traders wanting to receive the fixed rate, the spread declines. By purchasing a **spread lock**, the firm locks into the spread over Treasuries for a predetermined period.

EXAMPLE 21.3   Suppose firm XYZ plans to issue a floating-rate note in the next six months, which will then be swapped into fixed payments. The firm suspects that interest rates may decline in the interim period, causing an increased demand from fixed-rate payers. This extra demand will force swap spreads higher. To avoid this possibility, the firm enters into a spread lock contract to guarantee the spread over Treasuries for the next six months. When Treasury yields are low enough, the firm issues the floating-rate note and swaps it into fixed payments at this low rate plus the prearranged swap spread.

Rather than lock into the spread component, a firm may want to lock into the current Treasury rate. Such a contract is called a **Treasury lock**. For example, if the firm plans on being a fixed-rate payer in the future but suspects that in the interim interest rates will increase, a Treasury rate lock may be purchased.

The **swap rate lock** is a combination of a Treasury lock and a spread lock that must be exercised at the same time. If the date for exercising the swap rate lock is fixed, then we have a forward swap. If the date for exercising the swap rate lock is not specified but is defined only as being between two fixed dates, then the holder has additional flexibility regarding establishing the initiation date.

Swaptions   Market makers not only offer forward contracts on swaps; they also offer options on swaps. Such contracts are called **swaptions.** The buyer of a **receiver swaption** has the right to receive fixed and pay floating rates. The buyer of a **payer swaption** has the right to pay fixed and receive floating rates. As with any other options, the lifetime of the contract is predetermined, as are the times at which it can be exercised.

---

[4] In 1992 organized trading of futures contracts on three- and five-year swap contracts was introduced. These contracts were not successful and were withdrawn. Plans for trading futures contracts on longer-term swaps have been discussed. However, at this time, hedging swaps is mainly done using ED futures and futures options.

EXAMPLE 21.4 **Receiver Swaptions**

A firm knows that it will need to enter into a five-year variable-rate agreement in one year. The firm plans to swap the variable-rate for a fixed-rate loan. The firm wants to establish a floor for the fixed rate that it can obtain. By purchasing a one-year option to swap variable rate for a given fixed rate of 8 percent per year for a period of five years from the expiration date, the firm establishes a floor for the fixed rate. If rates decline over the year, then the option moves into the money, and at expiration it will be exercised. However, if the fixed rate turns out to be greater than 8 percent, the firm will not exercise the option but rather will swap and obtain the higher rate.

Buyout Options   Options that grant a party the right to terminate the swap under given terms are referred to as **buyout options.** For example, a **callable swap** gives the fixed-rate payer the right to terminate the swap early. A **puttable swap** allows the floating-rate payer to terminate the swap early.

EXAMPLE 21.5 Suppose a counterparty entered into a vanilla fixed-for-variable swap as the fixed payer. Assume the swap had seven years to maturity. The fixed payer, however, was given the option to terminate the swap after three years. In this case the fixed-rate payments are guaranteed only for the first three years. The fixed-rate payer has a European option on a four-year fixed-for-variable swap with a maturity of three years. If the fixed-rate payments at initiation are 10 percent, and after three years the new fixed-rate payments on four-year swaps are 8 percent, then the option will be exercised.

Extendable Options   Contingency features can be built to extend the term of the swap. In an **extendable swap,** one party has the right to extend the maturity of the swap beyond its scheduled termination date.

Indices Used in Swaps

So far we have considered only a fixed-for-variable swap. However, many other variants exist.

Basis Swaps   A **basis swap** is a floating-for-floating swap. That is, the two legs of the swap are tied to two different variable indices. For example, one leg may be LIBOR, while the other is the T-bill rate.

EXAMPLE 21.6 Bank A has invested in a two-year floating-rate note that pays it one-month LIBOR plus 50 basis points. The purchase was funded by issuing one-month certificates of deposit (CDs). Since LIBOR and CD rates are not perfectly correlated, basis risk is present. Indeed, it is possible that the bank will pay more on its CDs than it receives from its floating-rate notes. To avoid this risk, a basis swap is entered into with a market maker. The market maker agrees to pay the one-month CD composite rate less 10 basis points in exchange for LIBOR flat. If the CD composite rate were perfectly related to the bank's CD rate, the hedge would be perfect.

Yield Curve Swaps   The **yield curve swap** is a variant of the basis swap in which the exchanges are based on a short-term interest rate and a long-term interest rate. For example, a counterparty could contract to make semiannual floating-rate payments based on a six-month T-bill yield and receive floating-rate payments based on a 10-year Treasury note yield.

Swaps with Caps and Floors on the Index   In a **rate-capped swap,** the floating rate has a cap. When the variable rate is higher than the cap rate, the variable payer pays the cap rate. A floor rate could also be specified. If the floating rate fell below the floor rate, the payments would be based on the floor rate.

Off-Market Swaps and Zero-Coupon Swaps

Rather than committing to exchanging a fixed periodic payment for a variable payment, the fixed-rate payer may want to defer some or all of the payments until future periods. For example, suppose we have a fixed-for-floating swap where the fixed payer pays at 10 percent. A fixed payer may prefer a lower rate, say 8 percent, followed by a lump-sum payment at the end. The value of the lump sum would of course equal the value of the deferred obligations by the fixed-rate payer. An extreme example would involve deferring all obligations until one specific date. Of course, the size of the terminal payment would have to be large enough to compensate for the deferment in payments. These types of contracts are referred to as **off-market swaps**, with the extreme case called a **zero-coupon swap**. Of course, rather than defer payments, the fixed-rate payer may want to accelerate payments.

Swaps with Varying Notional Principals

So far we have assumed that the notional principal remains constant over the life of the swap. However, this requirement is not necessary. That is, the notional principal can change over time.

   In **amortizing swaps** the notional principal is reduced one or more times prior to the termination of the swap, while in **accreting swaps** the notional principal increases according to a given schedule. The schedule could be fixed, or it could depend on the evolution of an index such as six-month LIBOR rates; the amortization schedule could increase more rapidly as interest rates dropped. This type of swap is often encountered as a hedging instrument in mortgage markets.

EXAMPLE 21.7 Consider a swap in which the notional principal decreases by $10 million at each reset point, from an initial $100 million to $50 million over the three-year time period. The fixed rate for this amortizing swap is easy to establish, since the notional principal in each period is certain.

Now consider a swap in which the notional principal in the next period is determined by the level of LIBOR in the existing period. For example, if LIBOR is below 4 percent, the notional principal drops by 50 percent of its existing level, and if LIBOR is above 4 percent, the notional principal does not change. Such swaps, with notional principals that vary with the path, are more complex to price. These very common contracts are referred to as **index amortization swaps**.

Other Over-the-Counter Interest Rate Contracts

A fairly large over-the-counter market exists for options on interest rates.

Caplets and Floorlets   A **caplet** is a European interest rate call option. At the expiration date, T, the payout quantity, $Q(T)$, is determined as

$$Q(T) = \text{Max}[L(T) - X, 0] \times (m/360) \times NP$$

Here $L(T)$ is the underlying interest rate at date T, expressed in annualized decimal form, and X is the strike price. The interest rate is an m-day interest rate. The multiplier for the contract, or notional principal, is NP. As with FRAs, the actual payment date may be deferred m days to the maturity date of the "underlying."

EXAMPLE 21.8 A three-month caplet on six-month LIBOR has a strike of 7 percent and a notional principal of $10 million. The expiration date is 90 days away ($T = 90$), and the number of days in the six-month period for the underlying is 182 ($m = 182$). The option costs $20,000. Current six-month LIBOR is 7 percent.

Assume that at the expiration date LIBOR is 8 percent. The payoff of the caplet is $(0.08 - 0.07)(182/360)\$10,000,000 = \$50,555$. This quantity is received 182 days later. Alternatively, the present value of this amount is received at the expiration date: $(\$50,555)/(1 + 0.08(182/360)) = \$48,589.80$.

A **floorlet** is just a put option on an interest rate. Like a caplet, a floorlet has deferred payments that occur at the maturity date of the underlying interest rate.

EXAMPLE 21.9 A three-month floorlet on six-month LIBOR has a strike of 7 percent and a notional principal of $10 million. The expiration date is 90 days away ($T = 90$), and the number of days in the six-month period for the underlying is 182 ($m = 182$). The option costs $20,000. Current 6-month LIBOR is 7 percent.

Assume that at the expiration date, LIBOR is 6 percent. The payoff of the caplet is $(0.07 - 0.06)(182/360)\$10,000,000 = \$50,555$. This quantity is received 182 days later. Equivalently, the present value of this amount is received at the expiration date: $(\$50,555)/(1 + 0.06(182/360)) = \$49,066.60$.

Note that a caplet combined with the sale of a floorlet, with strikes of X, has the same payouts as an FRA to borrow at the rate X.

Caps and Floors   A **cap** is a series of caplets, and a **floor** is a series of floorlets.

EXAMPLE 21.10   Consider a two-year cap on six-month LIBOR at 8 percent and notional principal of $10 million. The reset dates at which the payouts are determined are January 15 and July 15. The contract was entered into January 15. There are three reset points covered in the contract. Indeed, the contract can be viewed as a portfolio of three caplets, with expiration date on July 15, on January 15, and in July of the following year. The actual payout of the last caplet occurs in two years. The strike prices of all the caplets are the same.

Caps and Swaptions   A cap gives the holder the option at each reset date to borrow at the lower of the market rate or the strike price. Contrast this to an option on a swap that has a term equal in length to that of the cap. This latter contract offers the holder the one-time option of borowing at a fixed rate over the remaining lifetime of the swap. Clearly, this contract provides less flexibility than the cap, and as a result it should be less valuable. Indeed, an option on a swap can be viewed as an option on a portfolio, while a cap is a portfolio of options. As we have seen, a portfolio of options is more valuable than an option on a portfolio.

EXAMPLE 21.11   Reconsider our two-year cap in Example 21.10 and compare it to a six-month option on a two-year fixed-for-floating rate swap. Assume the LIBOR rates in consecutive six-month periods were 9, 8, and 7 percent. If the swap option was exercised, then the interest rates would be 8, 8, and 8 percent. If the option was not exercised, the interest rates would be 9, 8 and 7 percent. In contrast, with the cap the borrowing rates would be 8, 8, and 7 percent. Regardless, the borrowing costs are lower with the cap. Hence, the cap must be more valuable than the option.

Calls on Interest Rates and Puts on Discount Bonds   The terminal payout of a caplet with a notional principal of $NP = \$1$ is determined by the quantity $Q(T)$, where

$$Q(T) = \text{Max}[L(T) - X, 0] \times (m/360)$$

The terminal value of the contract is $C(T)$, where

$$C(T) = Q(T)/[1 + L(T)(m/360)]$$

Substituting for $Q(T)$, the terminal value can be expressed as

$$C(T) = \text{Max}\left[\frac{l - x}{1 + l}, 0\right]$$

where $l = L(T)m/360$ and $x = X(m/360)$.

Now consider a pure discount bond that matures at date $T + m$. At date T, this bond is priced at $1/(1 + l)$. Consider a put option with strike Y and settlement date T that trades on this discount bond. Its terminal value is $P(T)$, where

$$P(T) = \text{Max}[Y - 1/(1 + l), 0]$$

Assume the strike price is chosen such that $Y = 1/(1 + x)$. Then

$$\begin{aligned}
P(T) &= \text{Max}[1/(1 + x) - 1/(1 + l), 0] \\
&= \text{Max}[(l - x)/\{(1 + l)(1 + x)\}, 0] \\
&= \frac{1}{1 + x}\text{Max}\left[\frac{l - x}{1 + l}, 0\right] \\
&= \frac{1}{1 + x}C(T)
\end{aligned}$$

Hence, a caplet must have the same price as a portfolio of $(1 + x)$ put options on a discount bond with strike $1/(1 + x)$.

EXAMPLE 21.12 Consider a caplet with a strike of 8 percent. The option expires in 161 days. The underlying interest rate is a 182-day LIBOR rate. The notional principal is $1. Then $x = X(m/360) = 0.08(182/360) = 0.0404$ and $Y = 1/(1 + x) = 0.96113$. The caplet is equivalent to 0.96113 European put options on a discount bond. The maturity of the underlying bond is $(161 + 182)$ days, and the expiration date is 161 days. If the notional principal were $10 million, then the caplet would be 10 million times more valuable then the computed put portfolio.

The result illustrated in Example 21.12 suggests that if we had a pricing model for options on bonds, we could obtain prices for caplets. We shall consider pricing models for bond options in Chapter 23.

Collars A **collar** is a contract that can be viewed as a long position in a cap with strike x and a short position in a floor with a lower strike of y. If interest rates rise above x, the holder can borrow at x. However, if interest rates fall below y, the holder is forced into paying the higher rate of y. Collars are usually set up so that the cost of the cap can be subsidized by the revenue from the floor.

Conclusion

This chapter has discussed over-the-counter interest rate derivative products. Of particular importance is the enormous interest rate swap market. This market has expanded dramatically over the last decade. The basic mechanisms of this market were analyzed, together with hedging and pricing of swaps. The variety of swaps is endless, and this chapter has only touched upon some of the more important types. Other over-the-counter products, including forward rate agreements, caps, and floors, were also discussed.

References

Risk magazine has ongoing articles about swaps. These articles are usually very readible and address issues of importance. The textbooks of Marshall and Kapner and Campbell and Kracaw contain additional information on swaps.

Abken, P. "Beyond Plain Vanilla: A Taxonomy of Swaps." *Economic Review* (March 1991).

Arak, M., A. Estrella, L. Goodman, and A. Silver. "Interest Rate Swaps: An Alternative Explanation." *Financial Management* 17 (Summer 1988): 12–18.

Bicksler, J., and A. Chen. "An Economic Analysis of Interest Rate Swaps." *Journal of Finance* 41 (1986): 645–55.

Brown, K., and D. Smith. "Recent Innovations in Interest Rate Risk Management and the Reintermediation of Commercial Banking." *Financial Management* 18 (1988): 45–58.

⸺. "Default Risk and Innovations in the Design of Interest Rate Swaps." *Financial Management* 22 (1993): 94–105.

Campbell, T., and W. Kracaw. "Intermediation and the Market for Interest Rate Swaps." *Journal of Financial Intermediation* 3 (December 1991): 362–84.

⸺. *Financial Risk Management*. New York: Harper Collins, 1992.

Cooper, I. A., and A. S. Mello. "The Default Risk of Swaps." *Journal of Finance* 46 (June 1991): 597–620.

Marshall, J., and K. Kapner. *The Swaps Market*. Miami: Kolb, 1993.

Smith, C., C. Smithson, and L. Wakeman. "The Evolving Market for Swaps." *Midland Corporate Finance Journal* 3 (1986): 20–32.

Sun, T. S., S. Sundaresan, and C. Wang. "Interest Rate Swaps: An Empirical Investigation." *Journal of Financial Economics* 34 (1993): 77–99.

Turnbull, S. "Swaps: A Zero-Sum Game?" *Financial Management* 15 (1987): 15–21.

Wakeman, L. M. "The Portfolio Approach to Swaps Management." Unpublished manuscript, Chemical Bank Capital Markets Group, May 1986.

Wall, L. "Interest Rate Swaps in an Agency Theoretic Model with Uncertainty Interest Rates." *Journal of Banking and Finance* 13 (1989): 261–70.

Wall, L., and J. Pringle. "Alternative Explanations of Interest Rate Swaps: A Theoretical and Empirical Analysis." *Financial Management* 18 (1989): 59–73.

Wolmsley, J. *The New Financial Instruments*. New York: Wiley, 1988.

Exercises

1. Use the data in Exhibit 21.2 to compute the implied nine-month ED LIBOR rate starting in month 21. How could you lock into this rate?

2. a. Use the data in Exhibit 21.2 to compute all the certainty equivalents for a two-year fixed-for-variable swap, based on three-month LIBOR. The swap terms are agreed upon today (December), but the two-year term begins from March, with the first cash settlement date in June. Assume the notional principal is $50 million.

   b. Use the LIBOR yields in Exhibit 21.3 to construct the discount function for the certainty equivalents in Exercise 2a, and then use these discount rates to compute the fair fixed rate for the swap. Comment on using these discount rates versus using rates obtained from Treasuries.

3. A swap is entered into by I AM, Inc. The current LIBOR rate is 5 percent.

Contract date	August 10, 1994
Contract type	Interest rate swap
Fixed-rate payer	YOU ARE bank
Floating-rate payer	I AM, Inc.
Start date	Aug. 12, 1994
Maturity date	Aug. 12, 1997
Notional principal	$50 million
Fixed rate	5%
Floating rate	6-month LIBOR
Payment basis	
Fixed rate	Actual/365
Floating rate	Actual/360
Fixed payment dates	Aug. 12 and Feb. 12 of each year
Floating payment dates	Aug. 12 and Feb. 12 of each year

   a. Compute the cash flows that would occur if LIBOR increased by 0.5 percent per period.

   b. Compute the cash flows that would occur if LIBOR decreased by 0.5 percent per period.

4. Explain why default risk of a swap usually is maximized near the middle of the lifetime of the contract.

5. A firm knows that if a particular project is awarded to the firm, it will need to borrow funds for a five-year period. It can obtain financing at a variable rate linked to LIBOR. The firm is concerned that LIBOR will expand over the five-year period. The award of the project will be made in six months. Explain how this firm could benefit by using swaptions.

6. A firm is exposed to a significant twist risk. In particular, if the yield curve steepens, the firm will encounter severe losses. Explain how a yield curve swap could be helpful to the firm.

7. A three-month caplet on six-month LIBOR has a strike of 8 percent and a notional principal of $50 million. The expiration date is 50 days away, and the number of days in the six-month period is 181. Assume the LIBOR rate at the expiration date is 10 percent. Compute the value of the caplet at that date.

8. Provide an explanation for the high liquidity of the ED futures contracts for maturities as distant as seven years.

9. Compare a cap to an option on a swap that has a term equal to that of the cap.

10. A firm plans on borrowing $10 million from the bank in three months. The loan is for six months, starting in March. Interest payments are in June and September. The interest rates are based on three-month LIBOR rates in March and June. Assume the interest rate determination dates correspond to the settlement dates of the ED futures contracts in Exhibit 21.2. The firm is concerned about rising LIBOR rates and is considering using FRAs to lock in a rate.
    a. Discuss which FRAs to use.
    b. Compare strategies of using FRAs and using ED futures.
    c. If the firm only wants to place a cap on its interest rate expenses, what product should it be interested in?
    d. If the cost of capping interest rate expenses in June and December are too high, what could the firm do to reduce its cost? Explain the ramifications.

11. Firms A and B can obtain the following rates for a 10-year loan of $50 million.

	Firm A	Firm B
Fixed rate	8%	9.5%
Variable rate	LIBOR + 0.5%	LIBOR + 1%

Firm A requires a variable-rate loan while firm B requires a fixed-rate loan. Design a swap that both parties may find equally attractive.

12. Explain the nature of the risk that a market maker is faced with when entering into two offsetting swaps.

APPENDIX 21A

Motivation for Entering Swaps

The success of the swap market must be attributed to the fact that the market serves specific needs that were not well served before the existence of swaps. Swaps help firms reduce their cost of capital and enable them to more efficiently manage interest rate risk exposure. They create a link between distinct markets and between firms with different access to funding sources. Finally, they enable firms to minimize the costs of regulation.

The Simple Credit Arbitrage Hypothesis

One of the early motivations for entering into a swap was to take advantage of a specific arbitrage opportunity so as to reduce the cost of debt. The basis of this arbitrage was thought to stem from different credit spreads that existed in short-term and long-term markets. For example, compare the borrowing costs for AAA- and BBB-rated firms.

	AAA	BBB	Spread
Cost of borrowing fixed	11%	12%	100 b.p.
Cost of borrowing floating	LIBOR + 25 b.p.	LIBOR + 50 b.p.	25 b.p.

Assume AAA would like short-term financing while BBB likes longer-term financing. Directly, these two firms could enter into a swap where the fixed-rate payer is the less creditworthy counterparty. The results of the swap are summarized below.

AAA		BBB	
Receives fixed rate	11.25%	Pays fixed rate	11.25%
Pays floating rate	LIBOR	Receives floating rate	LIBOR
Borrows fixed rate	11%	Borrows floating rate	LIBOR + 50 b.p.
Net cost of funding	LIBOR − 25 b.p.	Net cost of funding	11.75%
(Savings = 50 b.p.)		(Savings = 25 b.p.)	

The total savings equals the difference in the spread differential ($100 - 25 = 75$ basis points). In this example, the savings for AAA was 50 basis points and the savings for BBB was 25 basis points.

If such an apparent arbitrage opportunity existed, competition in debt and swap markets would very rapidly arbitrage it away, and the spread differential based on credit quality would soon disappear. If the credit arbitrage hypothesis were true, swap market activity would decrease over time, not increase.

Of course, there have to be reasons for differential quality spreads existing between short- and long-term markets. The following theories have been postulated.

Comparative Advantage

It is often said that the quality spread results from firms having comparative advantages in different markets. In particular, AAA-rated companies have a comparative advantage in fixed-rate markets, while BBB firms may have a comparative advantage in floating-rate markets. Interest rate swaps are then set up to exploit these comparative advantages, with savings to both firms. This comparative advantage story makes little sense, however, since it ignores arbitrage. In integrated capital markets, BBB-rated firms will have access to fixed-rate funds, either directly or indirectly. In the latter case, AAA-rated firms may relend long-term raised funds to the BBB firm. Such activity would soon cause the comparative advantage to disappear.

Differential Prepayment Options

In our example the low-quality firm could either borrow directly at 11 percent or borrow floating and swaps to fixed at a cost of 10.5 percent. If capital markets are efficient, then it must be the case that the strategy of borrowing at 11 percent provides more flexibility or more value than the less costly alternative. Indeed, this is the case. When a firm borrows directly, it has the option to prepay the loan. If interest rates drop, then the firm will exercise this option to prepay and refinance at a lower rate. In contrast, if the firm borrows floating and swaps to fixed, then the obligations to make the fixed payments are complete. Indeed, early termination of the swap agreement requires that the remaining contract be marked to market and paid in full.

The credit arbitrage hypothesis does not really explain the continued growth of swap markets. Below we provide more plausible explanations motivated by the needs of short-term borrowers who swap into fixed-rate agreements.

Asymmetric Information and Unbundling Interest Rate and Credit Risks

Consider a firm that has a low-quality rating. Assume the managers have inside information indicating that its credit ratings will improve in the future. Finally, assume that the firm believes interest rates are likely to increase. By entering into a long-term financing contract, the firm locks into an interest rate that includes a risk premium based on its low ratings.

By issuing short-term debt and swapping this for fixed payments, the low-rated firm has protection against increasing interest rates. At the same time, the firm avoids locking into a risk premium based on its current quality rating. The swap therefore provides a mechanism for decoupling interest rate risk and credit risk. The expected savings for entering into this swap would of course be divided up between the firm and the counterparty.

Under information asymmetries, it is reasonable to assume the firm has more accurate information about its prospects than investors. If the firm views its prospects more favorably than the market does, it will follow the above strategy. On the other hand, if the firm views its future prospects less favorably than the market does, it may choose to issue a long-term fixed-rate note. The nature of the firm's financing then clearly signals important information. A firm's choice of short-term borrowing combined with a swap signals favorable information while straight long-term financing signals unfavorable information. A firm with poor prospects that attempts to mimic a good firm will pay the price with higher expected short-term financing costs.

The above argument suggests that synthetic fixed-rate financing enhances investors' perceptions of the firm's future credit prospects and lowers the cost to other firms of financing.

Agency Costs and Reducing Bad Investment Strategies

Consider a firm that issues debt before it has fully decided how these funds are to be spent. If the firm is in a fairly precarious state, the shareholders may favor using the funds in very risky investments. In fact, the shareholders may even favor projects with negative net present value if the future uncertainty is sufficiently great. The reason is that if the project fails, the firm defaults on the debt and the bondholders lose; however, if the project succeeds, the shareholders will reap the benefits. Of course, the bondholders will be alarmed if the firm uses the funds for investments more risky than they had anticipated.

Since bondholders suspect that a low-quality firm may adopt risky projects, they will assume the worst case and price the debt accordingly. Alternatively, the bondholders may want constraints imposed on the possible projects that can be funded. **Agency costs** refer to the charges imposed by the potential conflict of interest between shareholders and bondholders. In general, the agency costs of using long-term debt will be higher for low-credit-quality firms. If this is the case, a sensible strategy for a low-credit-quality firm that wants long-term financing is to borrow short term and then swap the floating-rate obligation for a fixed-rate obligation. With this strategy, the agency costs are kept low. In particular, since the low-rated firm must continually come back to the credit market, it will not be in a position to reallocate long-term borrowed funds for extremely risky ventures. At the same time, by swapping, the firm can control interest rate risk. The savings of this agency cost of debt is a real saving to the firm that may be shared with the counterparty.

Completing Markets

The swap market has contributed to making financial markets more integrated. In many cases, swaps can be designed to provide a set of cash flows to the user in a cheaper way than any other alternative. This is accomplished either by reducing transaction costs or by avoiding certain costs of regulation and tax laws.

A U.S. firm can issue yen-denominated debt and structure the issue so that it has favorable tax treatment under the Japanese tax code and can avoid much of the U.S. securities regulation. At the same time, the firm could enter into a contract in which the yen coupon payments are swapped into fixed U.S. dollar payments. In this way, the firm can reduce its costs without bearing any exchange rate risk.

Other Reasons

If swaps are financial contracts, then assuming there are no asymmetries of information, equilibrium prices should be set such that the contracts have zero net present value. That is, the swaps themselves should transfer no value between the firms involved. Of course, the swap could alter the nature of the cash flows of the firm and hence transfer value between bondholders and shareholders. Indeed, in a single-period framework, Cooper and Mello show that wealth can be transferred from shareholders to bondholders. In a multiperiod framework, the transfer of wealth between bondholders and shareholders depends on multiple factors, the most important of which is the relationship between the maturity of the bond and the timing of the cash flows. The important point here, however, is that shareholders may be able to identify situations under which entering into a carefully designed swap could lead to wealth transfers.

PART SIX

Advanced Topics

in Interest Rate

Derivatives

In Chapter 22, the first chapter in Part 6, we consider the term structure of interest rates. We first study the theory of the term structure in a certain world. In this economy, with no shifts in the yield curve, future spot rates equal the initial forward rates. In an uncertain world, however, the relationship between forward rates and future spot rates is unclear. We investigate theories of the term structure that relate forward rates to future expected spot rates and try to establish whether forward rates are useful in predicting future spot rates.

In describing theories of the term structure, we derive some results that are helpful for pricing interest rate claims. For examples, to prevent riskless arbitrage, we can always compute the prices of interest rate claims as if the local expectations hypothesis holds. This result is useful in the same way as the risk-neutral valuation property we used to price stock options.

Chapter 23 explores ways in which the uncertainty of interest rates can be represented by a stochastic process. In order to price any interest-rate-contingent claim, we must first specify this process. In the case of stock options, for example, we assumed the stock prices followed a geometric Wiener process with a volatility that remains constant. For interest rate claims, the underlying process is more complex. As a bond gets closer to maturity, its price converges toward its face value. Bond volatility also depends on the coupon rate. High-coupon bonds pay back more of their value earlier; hence, they are effectively shorter-term instruments than lower coupon bonds of the same maturity. There are may ways of representing the stochastic process for the yield curve. In Chapter 20 we assumed the yield curve was flat and shocks affected all yields in the same way. In Chapter 23 we investigate alternative approaches for modeling the stochastic process of the term structure. With a model for the underlying process, we can price claims on interest rates; we investigate some models for the pricing of bonds, interest rate options, and futures.

Chapter 24 considers some of the more recent developments in the modeling of interest rate claims. The majority of claims in the over-the-counter market are priced and quoted relative to an existing term structure. In particular, it has become increasingly important to adopt a single coherent model that not only relates today's term structure with the expectation of future spot rates, but also represents the comovements of all bond prices in such a way that information from the existing term structure is more fully reflected in prices. The models discussed in Chapter 21 fail to use much of the available information on the term structure; they use information on the initial short-term rate but ignore information on other rates. This chapter investigates some of the models that incorporate more observable information in their analysis. Heath, Jarrow, and Morton, for example, have developed a mechanism for pricing interest rate claims that is analogous to the Black-Scholes stock option model. As in the Black-Scholes model, the only inputs that are necessary are the underlying and a measure of its volatility. Here, the underlying is the entire term structure, and the volatility describes how this term structure fluctuates over time. Thus, the initial term structure is taken as an input in the same way as the stock price is input in the Black-Scholes analysis. This chapter investigates these types of models and illustrates their use. Their pricing approach is investigated.

CHAPTER 22

Pricing Relationships and the Theory of the Term Structure

In this chapter we consider theories that attempt to explain the term structure of interest rates. Understanding the theory is helpful to a manager of a firm who is deciding whether to obtain funds with short-term or longer-term debt. Given a yield curve that is upward-sloping, the firm may decide that short-term financing is favorable. However, if long-term rates are determined largely by the market's expectations of future spot term rates, then, as we shall see, the firm cannot expect to save by borrowing at the short-term rate.

Forward rates provide managers with benchmark numbers they can use to assess alternative strategies. For example, if the firm's forecast of interest rates in the future deviates significantly from forward rates, the manager might surmise that certain strategies could be attractive. Alternatively, firms with no expertise in forecasting interest rates may believe that forward rates provide a consensus opinion on what the future expected interest rate is. We investigate whether there is any validity to such a claim.

Our analysis of the theory of the term structure begins by first considering a certain world where there are no shifts in the yield curve. In this economy, future spot rates equal their initial forward rates. When uncertainty is introduced into the economy, the relationship between forward rates and future spot rates is less obvious. We investigate theories of the term structure that relate forward rates to future *expected* spot rates and consider whether forward rates, by themselves, serve as useful predictors of future spot rates.

In the process of describing theories of the term structure, we will uncover some useful results that will be very helpful for pricing interest rate claims. In particular, if there is no riskless arbitrage, the prices of interest rate claims can always be computed as if the local expectations hypothesis holds. This result is analogous to the risk-neutral valuation property that was used to price stock options.

The primary objectives of this chapter are the following:

- To analyze the relationship between forward rates and future spot rates in an uncertain world; and

- To introduce the local expectations hypothesis and identify its use in pricing interest rate claims.

The Term Structure in a Certain Economy

Consider a time period split up into intervals of width Δt and labeled $0, 1, 2, 3, \ldots$. Let $f_0[t, t + 1]$ be the annualized forward rate at date 0 for the time increment beginning at period t. (That is for the time $t \, \Delta t$ to $(t + 1) \, \Delta t$.) The forward rate at date t for the time increment $[t, t+1]$ is just the one period spot rate, y_t (1) say.

In a world with no interest rate uncertainty, the forward rate for any particular period would not change over time. Indeed, to avoid riskless arbitrage, all future spot rates would equal their original forward rates. That is,

$$f_0[t, t + 1] = f_t[t, t + 1] = y_t(1) \tag{22.1}$$

Equivalently, the forward price for a discount bond to be delivered at time t must be set equal to the price of the bond that is known to occur at that time. That is,

$$F_0[t, T] = P(t, T) \tag{22.2}$$

EXAMPLE 22.1   Suppose time periods are split up into six-month intervals. The annualized spot rates over the first two periods are $y_0(1) = 7\%$ and $y_0(2) = 8\%$. The prices of one- and two-period discount bonds are given by

$$P(0, 1) = e^{-0.07(1)0.5} = \$0.965605$$

$$P(0, 2) = e^{-0.08(2)0.5} = \$0.923116$$

Hence, the current price of a six-month T-bill with face value \$10,000 is \$9,656.05. If the yield curve remained unchanged over a six-month period, the investor would anticipate paying \$9,656.05 for a six-month T-bill.

The forward price is $F_0[1, 2] = P(0,2)/P(0,1) = 0.95600$, and the annualized forward rate is $f_0[1, 2] = 9\%$. The investor can lock into a price of a \$10,000 face value six-month T-bill for delivery in six months at a price of \$10,000 $\times$ $F_0[1,2] = \$9,560$. This amount represents a \$96.05 discount over the current price of a six-month T-bill. Equivalently, the trader could lock into a forward rate for the next six-month period at 9 percent per year, which is 2 percent higher than the current rate.

If it were certain that the future (next-period) price of a six-month T-bill would be \$9,660, then the astute investor would buy the forward contract, wait one period, take delivery at \$9,560, and sell the bond at its market price of \$9,660 for a \$100 profit. In a world of certainty, such opportunities would soon be closed off and the forward price would adjust to \$9,660.

From equation (22.2) and the definition of the forward price, we have

$$P(0, T)/P(0, t) = P(t, T)$$

Rearranging this equation yields

$$P(0, T) = P(0, t)P(t, T) \tag{22.3}$$

The left-hand side of equation (22.3) represents the price paid at time 0 to get $1 at time T. The right-hand side represents an alternative way to guarantee $1 at time T. First invest in $N = P(t, T)$ bonds that mature in period t. The cash obtained at time t, namely $P(t, T)$ dollars, is then used to purchase a bond that matures at time T. The terminal value of this strategy is $1, which equals the value of the first strategy. Unless the left-hand side equals the right-hand side, an arbitrage opportunity exists. Equation (22.3) suggests that in a world of certainty, investment strategy makes no difference to terminal wealth. That is, rolling over short-term bonds will produce the same wealth as purchasing and holding long-term bonds. In particular,

$$P(0, T) = P(0, 1)P(1, 2)P(2, 3) \ldots P(T - 1, T)$$

The price of a bond is always given by

$$P(0, T) = e^{-\sum_{j=0}^{T-1} f_j[j, j+1]\Delta t} \tag{22.4}$$

In a world of certainty, future spot rates are equal to forward rates, so equation (22.4) reduces to

$$P(0, T) = 1 \, e^{-\sum_{j=0}^{T-1} y_j(1)\Delta t} \tag{22.5}$$

That is, the bond's price is fully determined by the future sequence of one-period rates that are known to occur.

Let $M(T)$ be the price of a money market account that rolls funds over at the one-period spot rate. The account is initialized at time 0 with a $1 investment. Then

$$M(0) = 1$$

$$M(1) = e^{y_0(1)\Delta t}$$

and

$$M(T) = e^{y_0(1)\Delta t + y_1(1)\Delta t + \ldots + y_{T-1}(1)\Delta t}$$

or

$$M(T) = e^{\sum_{j=0}^{T-1} y_j(1)\Delta t} \tag{22.6}$$

Comparing this equation to equation (22.5), we see that with no interest rate uncertainty,

$$P(0, T) = 1/M(T) \tag{22.7}$$

Note that the value of a bond at time t relative to the money market account, $M(t)$, is given by

$$\frac{P(t, T)}{M(t)} = e^{-\sum_{j=t}^{T-1} y_j(1)\Delta t} \, e^{-\sum_{j=0}^{t-1} y_j(1)\Delta t} = e^{-\sum_{j=0}^{T-1} y_j(1)\Delta t}$$

The right-hand side equals $P(0, T) = P(0, T)/M(0)$. It also equals $1/M(T) = P(T, T)/M(T)$. Therefore,

$$\frac{P(0, T)}{M(0)} = \frac{P(t, T)}{M(t)} = \frac{P(T, T)}{M(T)} \tag{22.8}$$

Equation (22.8) states that in a world of certainty, the future price of any bond relative to the money market account remains constant.

Before we depart from our world of certainty, consider the value of any contingent claim that is certain to pay out $c(T)$ at time T. For example, $c(T)$ could be the terminal value of an option on a bond that matures at date τ. At the expiration date,

$$c(T) = \text{Max}[P(T, \tau) - X, 0] \tag{22.9}$$

where X is the strike price of the option. In a certain world, $c(T)$ is fully determined at date 0. The payout of this claim could be replicated by a portfolio of $c(T)$ pure discount bonds with maturity T. The value of the option at time t is therefore given by

$$c(t) = c(T)P(t, T)$$

Multiplying both sides by $P(0, t)$, we obtain

$$c(t)P(0, t) = c(T)P(0, t)P(t, T) = c(T)P(0, T)$$

Finally, using equation (22.7), we obtain

$$c(t)/M(t) = c(T)/M(T) \tag{22.10}$$

Equation (22.10) states that in a world of certainty, the price of a contingent claim relative to the money market account remains constant.

Summarizing the results for a certain economy, we have

Investment strategy makes no difference to terminal wealth:

$$P(0, T) = P(0, t)P(t, T) \tag{22.11}$$

Forward prices are perfect predictors of future bond prices:

$$P(t, T) = F_0[t, T] \tag{22.12}$$

Forward rates are perfect predictors of future spot rates:

$$y_t(1) = f_0[t, t + 1] \tag{22.13}$$

Bond prices are constant relative to money market accounts:

$$\frac{P(t, T)}{M(t)} = \frac{P(T, T)}{M(T)} = \frac{1}{M(T)} \tag{22.14}$$

Option prices are constant relative to money market accounts:

$$\frac{c(t, T)}{M(t)} = \frac{c(T, T)}{M(T)} \tag{22.15}$$

We now consider analogies to these equations in a world where interest rates are uncertain.

Term Structures in an Uncertain Economy

When uncertainty is introduced into the economy, the interpretation of forward rates and prices is more complex. By and large, theories of the term structure under uncertainty have taken the certainty model as the starting point and have then examined stochastic generalizations under assumptions of risk preferences of market participants. Most of these theories place predominant emphasis on the expected value of future spot rates. Indeed, there are various hypotheses regarding the behavior of expected interest rates over time and their connection to observed forward rates. In this section we briefly examine a few of these theories.

The Unbiased Expectations Hypothesis

One of the simplest hypotheses postulates that the implied forward rates are equal to the expected spot rates. Thus, forward rates observed from the yield curve should be unbiased estimators of future spot rates. In a world of uncertainty, equation (22.13) is replaced by

$$f_0[t, t + 1] = E_0\{\tilde{y}_t(1)\} \tag{22.16}$$

where viewed from time 0, $\tilde{y}_t(1)$ is a random variable representing the future single-period rate for $[t, t + 1]$. Note that under this theory, equation (22.4) reduces to

$$P(0, T) = e^{-\sum_{j=0}^{T-1} E(\tilde{y}_j(1)) \Delta t} \tag{22.17}$$

EXAMPLE 22.2   Under the unbiased expections hypothesis, the expected one-period yield from period 1 to period 2 in Example 22.1 is given by the forward rate $f_0[1, 2] = 9\%$.

A General Expectations Hypothesis of the Term Structure

Although the unbaised expectations hypothesis of the term structure is a straightforward extension of the certainty case where expectations are used instead of certain values, it is rather mechanical and lacks economic rationale. Moreover, the unbaised expectations hypothesis has been criticized because it assumes investors are capable of forecasting very distant future spot rates. Perhaps a more desirable property would be to characterize an equilibrium by requiring the expected returns on all possible default-free bond strategies to be equal for all holding periods. That is, for any holding period $[0, t]$, the total return obtained on any feasible series of investments should have the same expectation. Unfortunately, such a characterization of an equilibrium cannot be valid; it demands too much, as is illustrated by the following example.

EXAMPLE 22.3   Assume a two-period investment horizon. First, consider the following two strategies.

1. Buy a two-period bond.
2. Roll over two successive one-period bonds.

With strategy 1 the expected total return is $1/P(0, 2)$; with strategy 2 the expected total return is $E_0[(1/P(0, 1))(1/\tilde{P}(1, 2))]$. Hence, for the expected returns to be equal, we require

$$1/P(0, 2) = (1/P(0, 1)E_0[1/\tilde{P}(1, 2)]$$

or $$E[1/\tilde{P}(1, 2)] = P(0, 1)/P(0, 2) \qquad (22.18)$$

Now consider a one-period holding period with strategies 3 and 4.

3. Buy a one-period bond.
4. Buy a two-period bond; sell it after one year.

With strategy 3 the expected total return is $1/P(0, 1)$; with strategy 4 the expected total return is $E_0[\tilde{P}(1, 2)]/P(0, 2)$. Equating these two expected returns yields

$$E_0[\tilde{P}(1, 2)] = P(0, 2)/P(0, 1) \qquad (22.19)$$

Equations (22.18) and (22.19) imply that

$$E_0[1/\tilde{P}(1, 2)] = 1/E_0[\tilde{P}(1, 2)] \qquad (22.20)$$

But equation (22.20) is not true, except in the case of certainty.

EXAMPLE 22.4   Suppose the price of a one-period bond in the next period will either be 0.7 or 0.9. Both events are equally likely. To compute the right-hand side of equation (22.20), first we must compute the expected price of the bond in the future. Specifically, $E_0[\tilde{P}(1, 2)] = 0.5(0.7) + 0.5(0.9) = 0.8$, and the inverse of this price is 1.25. On the other hand, the left-hand side of equation (22.20) is $E_0[1/\tilde{P}(1, 2]] = 0.5(1/0.7) + 1/2(1/0.9) = 1.27$.

The Local Expectations Hypothesis

Example 22.4 clearly illustrates that an equilibrium characterized by equal expected returns over arbitrary holding periods, independent of trading strategy, is not possible. This problem can be avoided if it is postulated that all expected returns are equal only for one specific holding period. Perhaps the most natural choice of holding period is the shortest period.

Under the **local expectations theory,** the expected rate of return of any bond over a single period should equal the prevailing single-period spot rate. Under this theory,

$$E_0[\tilde{P}(1, T)]/P(0, T) = e^{y_0(1)\Delta t}$$

Here a tilde is placed above the bond price, $P(1, T)$, to emphasize the fact that viewed from date 0, the price is a random variable. Rearranging this equation yields

$$P(0, T) = E_0[\tilde{P}(1, T)] e^{-y_0(1)\Delta t}$$

Hence

$$P(0, T) = E_0[\tilde{P}(1, T)]P(0, 1) \qquad (22.21)$$

Equation (22.21) is similar to equation (22.11) with $t = 1$ except that the expectations term replaces the certain term. Moreover, dividing by $P(0,1)$, we obtain

$$E_0[\tilde{P}(1, T)] = F_0[1, T] \qquad (22.22)$$

Equation (22.22) is similar to equation (22.12) with $t = 1$ Here, the set of forward prices for the next period are unbiased estimators for the expected bond prices.

The price of a bond at time $t + 1$ is linked to the price of the bond at time $t + 2$ and the spot rate over the period $[t + 1, t + 2]$. That is, viewed from time t, equation (22.21) becomes

$$P(t, T) = E_t[\tilde{P}(t + 1, T)] e^{-y_t(1)\Delta t} \qquad (22.23)$$

Now, the price of a bond at time $t + 1$ is linked to the price of the bond at time $t + 2$ and the spot rate over the period $[t + 1, t + 2]$. That is, viewed from date t,

$$\tilde{P}(t + 1, T) = \tilde{P}(t + 2, T)e^{-\tilde{y}_{t+1}(1)\Delta t} \qquad (22.24)$$

Substituting equation (22.24) into equation (22.23), we obtain

$$P(t, T) = E_t[e^{-(y_t(1) + \tilde{y}_{t+1}(1))\Delta t}\tilde{P}(t + 2, T)]$$

Continuing this process recursively, we eventually obtain

$$P(t, T) = E_t[e^{-\Sigma_{j=t}^{T-1} \tilde{y}_j(1)\Delta t}P(T, T)] = E_t[e^{-\Sigma_{j=t}^{T-1} \tilde{y}_j(1)\Delta t}]$$

Dividing both sides by $M(t)$, we obtain

$$P(t, T)/M(t) = E_t\{P(T, T)/\tilde{M}(T)\} \qquad (22.25)$$

Equation (22.25) states that the *expected* terminal bond price relative to the terminal money market fund equals the current bond price relative to the current money market. That is, under the local expectations hypothesis, the expected bond price relative to the money market account remains constant. The process $P(t, T)/M(t)$ is referred to as a **martingale process**. Equation (22.14) is the certainty equivalent of this equation.

EXAMPLE 22.5   1.   Assume the discount function at time t is $P(t, \cdot)$. In the next period the discount function moves to $P^+(t + 1, \cdot)$ with probability θ or to $P^-(t + 1, \cdot)$ with probability $1 - \theta$. Then, if the local expectations hypothesis holds, $E_t[P(t + 1, s)] = F_t[t + 1, s]$. That is,

$$\theta P^+(t + 1, s) + (1 - \theta)P^-(t + 1, s) = F_t[t + 1, s] = \frac{P(t, s)}{P(t, t + 1)}$$

2.   The current one-year spot rate is 6 percent. In one year the yield curve will be flat at either 8 percent or 4 percent. The probability of each of these events is one-half. Under the local expectations hypothesis, the expected return on holding any bond for one year is 6 percent. The bond price $P(0, 1) = \exp^{-0.06} = 0.94176$. The future prices of selected bonds are shown under the assumption that interest rates increase.

$$P^+(1, 10) = e^{-0.72} = 0.48675$$

$$P^+(1, 11) = e^{-0.8} = 0.44932$$

Similarly, if rates decline, then

$$P^-(1, 10) = 0.69767$$

$$P^-(1, 11) = 0.67032$$

The expected prices of the bonds in period 1, viewed from date 0, are computed using the formula

$$E_0[P(1, t)] = 0.5P^+(1, t) + 0.5P^-(1, t)$$

In particular, we have

$$E_0[P(1, 10)] = 0.59221$$

$$E_0[P(1, 11)] = 0.55982$$

Note from equation (22.22) that these expected prices are also forward prices. Furthermore, using equation (22.23), we have

$$P(0, t) = E_0[P(1, t)]P(0, 1)$$

In particular,

$$P(0, 10) = 0.557726$$

$$P(0, 11) = 0.52722$$

Using this information, the forward price, $F_0[10, 11]$, is given by $F_0[10, 11] = 0.94530$, and the forward rate is $f_0[10, 11] = 0.0562$ or 5.62 percent.

Note that the expected future spot rate for every period is 6 percent. Hence, under the local expectations hypothesis, with the reference period equal to one year, forward rates are not unbiased estimators of future expected spot rates.

The Return-to-Maturity Expectation Hypothesis*

The local expectations hypothesis claims that the expected rate of return over the next holding period is the same for all default-free bonds. Other theories are based on other trading strategies. For example, under the **return-to-maturity hypothesis,**

---

*This section provides advanced material and is optional reading for students.

the assumption is made that on average, an investor would earn the same return by either rolling over a series of one-period bonds for t periods or buying and holding a t-period bond until maturity.

A \$1 investment will grow to $M(1)$ dollars after the first period. Reinvested in the second period, this investment will grow to $M(2)$ dollars. At time t, the total return on the investment will be $M(t)$. Equating the total expected return of this strategy to the total return from holding a t-period bond to maturity yields

$$\frac{1}{P(0, T)} = E_0\{M(t)\} \qquad (22.26)$$

Under the local expectations hypothesis, from equation (22.25), we have

$$P(0, t) = E_0\{1/M(t)\} \qquad (22.27)$$

Since equations (22.26) and (22.27) are incompatible, this theory is incompatible with the local expectations hypothesis.

Other hypotheses could be developed that link expected returns under different investment strategies. The local expectations hypothesis, however, is extremely important, not because it describes investment behavior but because it has important applications in the pricing of interest rate claims. Before discussing other theories of the term structure and providing empirical evidence, we investigate properties of the local expectations hypothesis that have important ramifications for pricing.

Self-Financing Strategies and the Local Expectations Hypothesis

Assume an economy existed in which the local expectations hypothesis held. In such an economy, would it be possible for riskless arbitrage opportunities to exist? The answer is no. That is, it is not possible to establish any self-financing strategy that requires no net initial investment and guarantees a positive return.

To see this, assume that the local expectations hypothesis holds. Now consider the value of a self-financing trading strategy relative to the money market account. At any point in time, the portfolio is composed of a combination of discount bonds. Hence, the value of this portfolio relative to the money market account must be a martingale. Being a martingale, if a trading strategy has zero initial investment, it must have a zero expected value in the future. Hence, if a zero-initial-investment self-financing strategy has a positive probability of making money, it must have a positive probability of losing money. Under the local expectations hypothesis, then, no self-financing strategy can be established to create riskless arbitrage profits.

EXAMPLE 22.6   The current one-period interest rate is 10 percent. In each period this rate can either increase or decrease by 2 percent. The lattice of rates over the first two periods is shown below.

$$r_0 = 10\% \quad \substack{\nearrow \\ \searrow} \quad \substack{r_{11} = 12\% \\ \\ r_{10} = 8\%} \quad \substack{\nearrow r_{22} = 14\% \\ \searrow r_{21} = 10\% \\ \nearrow \\ \searrow r_{20} = 6\%}$$

Single-period bond prices can readily be computed. Let $P_{ij}(1) = e^{-r_{ij}}$ represent the one-period discount bond price at node (i, j). Then

$$P_0(1) = \$0.9048 \quad \substack{\nearrow \\ \searrow} \quad \substack{P_{11}(1) = \$0.8869 \\ \\ P_{10}(1) = \$0.9231} \quad \substack{\nearrow P_{22}(1) = \$0.8693 \\ \searrow P_{21}(1) = \$0.9048 \\ \nearrow \\ \searrow P_{20}(1) = \$0.9418}$$

Assume the actual probability of an upmove is $p = 0.5$. Then the expected spot rate is 10 percent for all future periods. If the local expectations hypothesis were true, then

$$P_{11}(2) = \left[\frac{1}{2}P_{22}(1) + \frac{1}{2}P_{21}(1)\right]P_{11}(1) = \$0.7868$$

$$P_{10}(2) = \left[\frac{1}{2}P_{21}(1) + \frac{1}{2}P_{20}(1)\right]P_{11}(1) = \$0.8523$$

$$P_0(2) = \left[\frac{1}{2}P_{11}(1) + \frac{1}{2}P_{10}(1)\right]P_0(1) = \$0.8189$$

$$P_0(3) = \left[\frac{1}{2}P_{11}(2) + \frac{1}{2}P_{10}(2)\right]P_0(1) = \$0.7416$$

The forward price is $F_0[2, 3] = P_0(3)/P_0(2) = \$0.9056$. This implies that the forward rate is $f_0[2, 3] = 9.92\%$. As in Example 22.5, note that this is not equal to the expected future spot rate, which is 10 percent. The bond prices computed under the local expectations hypothesis are set such that there are no possibilities of establishing riskless arbitrage.

No Arbitrage and the Local Expectations Hypothesis

Under the local expectations hypothesis, no self-financing strategy can be established to create riskless arbitrage. Actually, it turns out that the reverse condition is also true. That is, for an arbitrage-free process of bond prices to exist, it must be the case that a probability measure exists such that the local expectations hypothesis holds with respect to that measure. *Therefore, in any economy that closes off riskless arbitrage opportunities, regardless of whether the local expectations hypothesis holds, a probability measure must exist such that all bonds can be priced as if the local expectations hypothesis were true. If such a measure cannot be constructed, then riskless arbitrage opportunities must exist.* An intuitive "proof" of this remarkable result is provided in Example 22.7.

EXAMPLE 22.7 Assume interest rates and the one-period bond prices are given as in the lattices in Example 22.6. However, we shall not assume that the probability of an upmove is given or that the local expectations hypothesis holds. For the moment assume that all other bond prices are given and that a trader is attempting to identify whether or not riskless arbitrage opportunities are present. Consider an initial portfolio consisting of X_1 bonds of maturity one period and X_n bonds that mature in n periods. (X_1 or X_n could be negative.) The cost of this portfolio is C_0, where

$$C_0 = X_1 P_0(1) + X_n P_0(n)$$

The value of this portfolio in the next period is

$$1X_1 + P_{11}(n - 1)X_n \quad \text{if interest rates rise}$$
$$1X_1 + P_{10}(n - 1)X_n \quad \text{if interest rates fall}$$

The trader attempts to choose X_1 and X_n such that regardless of the state that occurs, the total portfolio value is positive. Hence, X_1 and X_n satisfy the constraints

$$1X_1 + P_{11}(n - 1)X_n \geq 0$$
$$1X_1 + P_{10}(n - 1)X_n \geq 0$$

Of all such portfolios, the trader chooses the one that minimizes the initial cost. That is, the trader solves the following linear programming problem:

$$\text{Minimize } C_0 = X_1 P_0(1) + X_n P_0(n)$$
$$\text{subject to} \quad 1X_1 + P_{11}(n - 1)X_n \geq 0$$
$$1X_1 + P_{10}(n - 1)X_n \geq 0$$

Clearly, riskless arbitrage is present if the initial cost is negative. Indeed, if the price system is meaningful, then the minimum-cost portfolio should be the portfolio with X_1 and X_n both zero!

The result says that no riskless arbitrage opportunities exist if a probability measure can be identified under which all bonds can be priced as if the local expectations hypothesis holds. Specifically, there must exist a probability value for an upmove, π_1 say, such that for a bond with any maturity, n say,

$$P_0(n) = [P_{10}(n - 1)(1 - \pi_1) + P_{11}(n - 1)\pi_1]P_0(1)$$

Moreover, if no π_1 can be identified, then it must be the case that the current set of prices permits riskless arbitrage.

To see this result, first consider changing the right-hand side of the first constraint to $1 and re-solving the problem. Denote by e_1 the value of the portfolio that provides $1 in the up state and $0 in the down state. Then we have

Similarly, let e_0 represent the minimum-cost portfolio that leads to $1 in the down state and $0 in the up state.

Clearly, $0 < e_0 \leq 1$ and $0 \leq e_1 \leq 1$. If a trader purchased one unit of each of these portfolios at a cost of $e_0 + e_1$, the terminal payouts would be

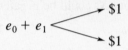

Since this portfolio gives the same payout as a one-period bond, by the law of one price, we have

$$e_0 + e_1 = P_0(1)$$

Now consider a strategy of buying $P_{11}(n - 1)$ units of e_1 and $P_{10}(n - 1)$ units of e_0. The initial and terminal values after one period are

$$P_{10}(n - 1)e_0 + P_{11}(n - 1)e_1 \begin{cases} P_{11}(n - 1) \\ P_{10}(n - 1) \end{cases}$$

This portfolio produces the same payouts as that of an n-period bond. Hence, to avoid riskless arbitrage,

$$P_{11}(n - 1)e_1 + P_{10}(n - 1)e_0 = P_0(n)$$

The fact that there are no riskless arbitrage opportunities implies the existence of e_0 and e_1 with

$$e_0 + e_1 = P_0(1)$$

$$P_{10}(n - 1)e_0 + P_{11}(n - 1)e_1 = P_0(n)$$

Now let $\pi_0 = e_0/P_0(1)$ and $\pi_1 = e_1/P_0(1)$. The preceding two equations can now be written as

$$\pi_0 + \pi_1 = 1$$

$$P_{10}(n - 1)\pi_0 + P_{11}(n - 1)\pi_1 = P_0(n)/P_0(1)$$

Equivalently, the bond price, $P_0(n)$, can be written as

$$P_0(n) = [P_{10}(n - 1)\pi_0 + P_{11}(n - 1)\pi_1]P_0(1)$$

or $$P_0(n) = E\{P_1(n - 1)\}P_0(1)$$

where $E\{P_1(n - 1)\}$ is the expected value of the bond price in one period's time and the probability of an upmove is assumed to be π_1. Note that π_1 does not depend on the maturity of the bond. Hence, to avoid riskless arbitrage opportunities, there must exist a probability π_1 such that all bonds can be priced as if the local expectations hypothesis held. Moreover, if no π_1 can be identified, then it must be the case that the current set of prices permits riskless arbitrage.

The Preferred Habitat and Liquidity Premium Theories of the Term Structure

Unlike the local expectations hypothesis, other theories of the term structure attempt to explain the expected returns of bonds of different maturities using risk arguments. In this section we briefly discuss two competing theories. First we need to understand investment risks as they relate to a particular holding period.

The preferred habitat hypothesis attempts to take risk into account when explaining the difference between expected rates of return of bonds across different maturities. This theory argues that the riskiness of a bond depends on the holding periods required by investors. A riskless strategy is to hold a discount bond with maturity equal to that of the holding period. Longer-term bonds carry price risk while shorter-term bonds carry reinvestment risk. Under the preferred habitat theory, investors will demand higher expected returns on bonds with maturities shorter or longer than their stated holding periods.

The liquidity premium theory is an older theory that can be viewed as a special case of the preferred habitat theory. According to this theory, lenders have shorter investment horizons than borrowers. Lenders thus demand a risk premium as compensation for holding long-term bonds. In terms of the preferred habitat theory, investors have a habitat of a single period, and the shortest-term bond is the safest. In this theory forward rates are related to future expected spot rates by the equation

$$f_0[t, t + 1] = E_0\{y_t(1)\} + \pi_0(t) \tag{22.28}$$

Here $\pi_0(t)$ is the risk or term premium required to compensate lenders for bearing risk. Under the liquidity premium hypothesis, this risk premium increases with maturity. According to equation (22.28), forward rates could be high because investors anticipate future spot interest rates to be high or because they require a larger premium for holding longer-term bonds. Although it may be tempting to infer from a rising yield curve that investors believe interest rates will increase, this may be inaccurate. Rather, the upward slope is caused by the increasing liquidity or risk premiums.

The Use of Yield Curves for Extracting Forecasts of Future Spot Rates

The above theories suggest that forward rates do not provide a perfect estimate of the market's expectations of future short-term interest rates. An important empirical issue is to try to capture the magnitude of the liquidity premiums that are incorporated in the term structure.

Several studies have been performed to establish whether forward rates are useful predictors of future spot rates. Perhaps the simplest test is to compare two estimators of the future spot rate. The first estimator is the forward rate, while the second estimator is the current level of the spot rate. Using historical data, Fama (1976) has shown that the forward rate is *not* necessarily superior to the current spot rate. Of course, the above comparisons ignored the important fact that forward rates contain risk premiums that make them biased estimators of future spot rates. A more satisfactory method of forecasting may be to measure the term premiums and then to extract them from forward rates to obtain the market's true consensus forecast of the future spot rate. In principle this sounds sensible. However, in practice extracting the term premiums has proved to be difficult. The general approach requires measuring the differences between forward rates and actual future spot rates and then averaging these differences. However, the deviations between these two values tend to be large and unpredictable, primarily because of unanticipated economic events in the interim that affect the short rate. Moreover, there is no reason to assume that the risk premium remains constant over time. As a result, averaging these differences may not be appropriate. Naturally, the existence and magnitude of term premiums have been the subjects of an enormous amount of theoretical and empirical analysis.

Term premiums appear to change over time. Several explanations for this time-varying behavior have been put forth. One hypothesis is that the magnitude of term premiums depends on the level of the short-term interest rate relative to its normal level. Under this theory, when interest rates are very high relative to their normal levels, there is a high chance that rates in general will be more likely to shrink than expand. As a result, risk-averse investors with long-term horizons will actively seek investments, thereby reducing the magnitude of the term premiums. Conversely, when interest rates are lower than their normal level and hence are more likely to rise than to fall, the term premiums must expand to entice long-term investors to lend money. If this hypothesis is true, then term premiums should vary inversely with the level of interest rates. Of course, this hypothesis is based on the assumption that interest rate behavior is mean-reverting. That is, as interest rates deviate further from their normal levels, there is increased pressure for them to revert to their normal levels.

Other theories for explaining time-varying term premiums have been put forward. For example, instead of relating term premiums to the relative level of interest rates, recent research has attempted to relate term premiums to interest rate volatility, the idea being that the greater the volatility, the greater the magnitude of the term premium.

In summary, empirical evidence confirms the important role of expectations in explaining the term structure. There is also evidence of an upward bias in forward rates, consistent with the notion of term premiums. Term premiums do appear to change over time. Although there is some evidence that term premiums vary inversely with the level of interest rates and according to the volatility of interest rates, the overall evidence here is still unclear.

Conclusion

In a world of certainty, forward rates will be set equal to the future spot rates. In a world of uncertainty, however, it is not clear whether forward rates will be set equal to expected spot rates. Under the local expectations hypothesis, the expected returns of all bonds over the next time increment should be equal. Under alternative hypotheses, the expected return of a bond could carry a risk premium that depends on the term of the bond. The magnitude of risk premiums may vary over time and according to the level of interest rates.

Of course, the construction of the term structure and the extraction of forward rates are still immensely important. First, the zero-coupon yield curve provides the appropriate discount rates for certain cash flows. Second, forward rates provide interest rate managers with benchmark numbers to use in assessing alternative strategies. For example, if forecast interest rates deviate significantly from forward rates, managers might surmise that the risk premium is more than sufficient compensation for implementing a particular strategy.

We have seen that from a pricing perspective, even if the local expectations hypothesis does not hold, it must be the case that a probability measure exists under which all interest rate claims can be priced as if the hypothesis did hold. Indeed, from a pricing perspective, this result is similar to the risk-neutral valuation relationship that was useful for pricing options on stocks. Chapter 23 deals more closely with pricing interest rate derivatives and returns to this point.

References

Campbell, J. "A Defense of Traditional Hypotheses About the Term Structure of Interest Rates." *Journal of Finance* 41 (March 1986): 617–30.

Cox, J., J. Ingersoll, and S. Ross. "A Reexamination of Traditional Hypotheses about the Term Structure of Interest Rates." *Journal of Finance* 36 (September 1981): 769–99.

Culbertson, J. "The Term Structure of Interest Rates." *Quarterly Journal of Economics* 71 (November 1957): 485–517.

Elliot, J., and M. Echoles. "Market Segmentation, Speculative Behavior, and the Term Structure of Interest Rates." *Review of Economics and Statistics* 57 (May 1975): 190–200.

Fabozzi, F. *The Handbook of Fixed Income Securities*, 3rd ed. Burr Ridge, Ill.: Business One–Irwin, 1991.

Fama, E. "Forward Rate as Predictors of Future Spot Interest Rates." *Journal of Financial Economics* 3 (October 1976): 361–77.

———. "The Information in Term Structure." *Journal of Financial Economics* 13 (December 1984): 509–28.

———. "Term Premiums in Bond Returns." *Journal of Financial Economics* 13 (December 1984): 529–46.

Gilles, C., and S. Leroy. "A Note on the Local Expectations Hypothesis: A Discrete Time Exposition." *Journal of Finance* 51 (September 1986): 975–79.

Heath, D., R. Jarrow, and A. Morton. "Contingent Claim Valuation with a Random Evolution of Interest Rates." *Review of Futures Markets* 9 (1990): 54–76.

Jarrow, R. "Liquidity Premiums and the Expectations Hypothesis." *Journal of Banking and Finance* 5 (December 1981): 539–46.

Lutz, F. "The Structure of Interest Rates." *Quarterly Journal of Economics* 55 (November 1940): 36–63.

McCallum, J. "The Expected Holding Period Return, Uncertainty, and the Term Structure of Interest Rates." *Journal of Finance* 30 (May 1975): 307–23.

McCulloch, J. H. "An Estimate of the Liquidity Premium." *Journal of Political Economy* 83 (February 1975): 95–119.

Modigliani, F., and R. Sutch. "Innovations in Interest Rate Policy." *American Economic Review* 56 (May 1966): 178–97.

Shiller, R. "The Volatility of Long Term Interest Rates and Expectations Models of the Term Structure." *Journal of Political Economy* 87 (December 1979): 1190–1219.

Van Horne, J. *Financial Market Rates and Flows,* 4th ed. Englewood Cliffs, N.J.: Prentice-Hall, 1994.

Exercises

1. The term structure in a certain economy has annualized forward rates given by $f_0[t, t + 1] = \text{Min}[2 + t/2, 10]$, for $t = 0, 1, 2, \ldots$. Each time interval is one year. (For example, $f_0[3, 4] = 3.5\%$.)
   a. Compute the price of a pure discount bond that matures at date $t = 3$.
   b. Compute the price of a pure discount bond at date $t = 2$. The bond matures at date $t = 4$.
   c. What is the forward price at date 0, which requires delivery at date $t = 2$, of the above bond?
   d. What is the short-term interest rate at date $t = 2$, and what is the value of the money market account?
   e. In the context of this exercise, illustrate that the bond price divided by the money market account remains constant.

2. The current spot interest rate is 5 percent. After one period, the entire term structure is flat at either 6 percent or 4 percent. The probabilities of these events are equal. Assume the local expectations hypothesis holds.
   a. Compute the prices of one-, two-, and three-period discount bonds at date 0.
   b. Compute the forward price of a contract that requires delivery of a one-period bond in two-periods' time.
   c. Compute the price of a futures contract that requires delivery of a one-period bond in two-periods' time.
   d. Use the information that you have developed to compute the forward rate $f_0[2, 3]$. Compare this number to the expected spot interest rate for period $[2, 3]$, viewed from date 0.

3. The current one-period rate is 8 percent. In each of the next three periods, rates can increase or decrease by 1.5 percent.
   a. Develop the lattice of possible one-period rates over three periods. Use these rates to compute the one-period bond prices at all nodes.
   b. Assume that the probability of an upmove at each node is 0.5 and that the local expectations hypothesis holds. Compute the two- and three-period bond prices at date 0.
   c. Is it possible to mesh bonds together such that riskless arbitrage profits can be obtained? Explain.

4. Reconsider the lattice in Exercise 2. Assume now that the liquidity premium hypothesis holds. In particular, the required risk premium is 0.1 percent per period, with a cap of 3 percent. That is, on a percentage basis, $\pi(t) =$ Min$[0.1(t - 1), 3]$ for $t = 0, 1, 2, \ldots$. For example, the risk premium for holding a three-period bond over one period is 0.2 percent.

   a. Compute the prices of one-, two-, and three-period bonds, under the assumption that up- and downmoves are equally likely.

   b. Compute the forward price of a contract that requires delivery of a one-period bond in two-periods' time.

5. The term structure is flat at 8 percent. In the next period the term structure is flat at either 11 percent or 7 percent. Use a one-period bond, a five-period bond, and a ten-period bond in the following problems.

   a. Formulate a linear programming problem that establishes whether or not riskless arbitrage is possible over the single period.

   b. Use a linear programming package to identify a riskless arbitrage strategy.

6. "For a set of bond prices to be arbitrage-free on a binomial lattice, it must be the case that at each node, a unique probability exists under which all bonds can be priced as if the local expectations hypothesis holds." Discuss this statement. In particular, explain how the result is useful in establishing a feasible representation of prices on a lattice.

CHAPTER 23

Single-Factor Models for Pricing Interest Rate Claims

In order to price any interest-rate-contingent claim, it is first necessary to specify the process that drives the underlying source of uncertainty. For stock options this was straightforward because the process selected was the underlying stock price, and the statistical description for the behavior of prices over the lifetime of the option was assumed to be known. For example, the Black-Scholes model assumes that stock prices follow a geometric Wiener process with a constant volatility. For interest rate claims, the underlying process is more complex because the behavior of bond prices changes over the life of the option. Specifically, as a bond gets closer to maturity, its price becomes more predictable as it converges toward its face value. The volatility of the bond also depends on the coupon rate. High-coupon bonds may be more predictable than low-coupon bonds of the same maturity since they pay back more of their value earlier and hence effectively are shorter-term instruments. Indeed, as we saw in Chapter 20, the volatility of a bond may well be proportional to its duration.

In order to analyze the behavior of bond prices over time, we must investigate how the entire yield curve shifts over time. This analysis is necessary because a coupon bond can be viewed as a portfolio of discount bonds, where the value of each discount bond depends on yields drawn from the yield curve. There are many ways to represent the stochastic process for the yield curve. In Chapter 20 we implicitly assumed that the yield curve was flat and that shocks to the curve affected all yields in the same way (i.e., parallel shifts). In this chapter we discuss other approaches. One simple approach is to assume that all yields, and hence all pure discount bond prices, are affected by movements in the short-term rate. When the short-term rate rises, it not only affects the price of short-term bonds but also provides a signal that rates are likely to be higher in the future. Therefore, the yields and prices of all maturities are affected. Such models are referred to as single-state models because changes in bond prices are assumed to arise solely from the change in the state of short-term rates. In this chapter we shall investigate some single-factor models for the pricing of bonds, interest rate options, and futures.

The primary objectives of this chapter are the following:

- To present models of the behavior of short-term interest rates;

- To use a binomial lattice for pricing complex contracts; and

- To discuss empirical issues involved in modeling the behavior of interest rates.

Single-Factor Models

The evolution of the short-term rate, r, is given by

$$dr(t) = \mu(r) \, dt + \sigma(r) \, dw(t) \quad \text{with } r_0 \text{ given} \tag{23.1}$$

where $dw(t)$ is a standard Wiener increment. If we assume that interest rate processes follow a geometric Wiener process, then after time T, the level of the interest rate, $r(T)$, would be lognormal. While such a model was reasonable for stock prices, it is not suitable for interest rates. The reason is that when interest rates get very high or very low, there is an increased tendency for their levels to regress toward some long-run "average" rate. This mean-reverting behavior can be captured by defining the drift term $\mu(r)$ such that $\mu(r) = \kappa(\mu - r)$. Here μ and κ are positive scalars: μ is called the long-run average of the short rate, and κ is the mean reversion factor which reflects the speed of adjustment of the interest rate toward μ. When $r = \mu$, the drift is zero. When interest rates are high ($r > \mu$), the drift is negative, and when rates are low ($r < \mu$), the drift is positive. The greater the value of κ, the greater the force that pushes the level of interest rates back to their long-run mean, μ.

If the volatility is independent of the level of the rate, $\sigma(r) = \sigma$, we have

$$dr = \kappa(\mu - r) \, dt + \sigma \, dw \tag{23.2}$$

This process is called the **Ornstein-Uhlenbeck process** or the **mean-reverting Wiener model.** Given that the interest rate at time 0 is $r(0)$, at time T the expected value and variance of this process for date T can be shown to be

$$E\{r(T) \mid r(0)\} = r(0)e^{-\kappa T} + \mu(1 - e^{-\kappa T}) \tag{23.3}$$

$$\text{Var}\{r(T) \mid r(0)\} = \sigma^2\{1 - e^{-2\kappa T}\}/2\kappa \tag{23.4}$$

and the distribution of $r(T)$ is normal.

The disadvantage of this process is that since interest rates are normal, it is possible that they could become negative. However, if we choose a positive speed-of-adjustment parameter, κ, the mean and variance will not grow linearly with time but instead will be bounded. Indeed, from equations (23.3) and (23.4), we can see that as T becomes very large, the expected interest rate level tends to μ and the variance tends to $\sigma^2/2\kappa$. Hence, the probability of interest rates becoming negative is largely mitigated.

It is possible to avoid the negative-interest-rate problem by placing boundaries that restrict movements on the stochastic process. For example, it is possible to set up a boundary at zero that has the property that whenever interest rates fall to zero, the probability is 1 that the interest rate will move up. Such a boundary is termed a **reflecting boundary,** since it reflects the variable away from it. An alternative to placing a reflecting barrier on the process is to redefine the process such that barriers are not necessary. As an example, consider the process

$$dr = \kappa(\mu - r) \, dt + \sigma r \, dw \tag{23.5}$$

Here interest rates are mean-reverting and the volatility depends on the level of interest rates. Specifically, the volatility is directly proportional to the interest rate level, decreasing to zero when interest rates tend to zero. Note, however, that when $r = 0$, the drift term is positive, which implies that in the next instant the rate returns to a positive level. The above model is termed the **proportional mean-reverting model.** A more general model is given by

$$dr = \kappa(\mu - r) \, dt + \sigma r^\gamma \, dw \qquad (23.6)$$

When $\gamma = 1$, we have the proportional model, while $\gamma = 0$ provides the absolute or mean-reverting Wiener process. When $\gamma = 0.5$, the model is termed the **square root model.** This latter model is often encountered in financial economics. It can be shown that conditional on $r(0)$, the expected value and variance of the interest rate at time T are given by[1]

$$E\{r(T) \mid r(0)\} = r(0)e^{-\kappa T} + \mu(1 - e^{-\kappa T}) \qquad (23.7)$$

$$\mathrm{Var}\{r(T) \mid r(0)\} = r(0)\frac{\sigma^2}{\kappa}(e^{-\kappa T} - e^{-2\kappa T}) + \frac{\mu\sigma^2}{2\kappa}(1 - e^{-\kappa T})^2 \qquad (23.8)$$

Binomial Approximation Models for the Square Root Interest Rate

To approximate the square root process by a binomial lattice, we first split up the interval $[0, T]$ into n equal pieces, each of width Δt. Over each time increment, the interest rate can either increase to a particular level or decrease to another level. Recall that in Chapter 8, over each time increment we approximated the geometric Wiener process by an upmove factor, u, equal to $e^{\sigma\sqrt{\Delta t}}$, and a downmove factor, d, equal to $1/u$. For the stock price dynamics, the volatility, σ, was assumed constant. As a result, an upmove followed by a downmove returned the price to the same location as a downmove followed by an upmove. For the square root model, the volatility is not constant but varies with the level of the spot rate. Using the same approximation scheme implies that the upmove factor when the interest rate is r is given by $e^{\sigma\sqrt{r(t)}\sqrt{\Delta t}}$.

As a result, an upmove followed by a downmove does not return the interest rate to the same location as a downmove followed by an upmove. This means that after two jumps there are four possible interest rates, and more generally, after n jumps there are 2^n possible outcomes. If $n = 20$, this implies that the number of states exceeds 1 million. In contrast, for the path-reconnecting scheme, after 20 jumps, there are 21 possible outcomes. Another difficulty concerns the computation of the probability. When the volatility is constant, the probability of an upmove is given by a constant, $(e^{\mu \Delta t} - d)/(u - d)$, which does not vary from node to node on the lattice. However, when the volatility varies with the level of the

---

[1] The actual distribution of the interest rate at time T, $r(T)$, is a noncentral chi-squared distribution with $2q + 2$ degrees of freedom and noncentrality parameter λ where $q = 2\kappa\mu/\sigma^2 - 1$; here $\lambda = 4\kappa r(0)e^{-\kappa s}/[\sigma^2(1 - e^{-\kappa T})$. Actually, to prevent the interest rate from being absorbed at zero, the parameters of the process need to be constrained. In particular, for interest rates to stay positive, $2\kappa\mu \geq \sigma^2$.

spot rate, then the probability of an upmove has to be recomputed at each node. This in itself is not particularly difficult. However, if the resulting value falls outside the interval $[0, 1]$, the lattice is said to be *unstable*, and the approximation fails. As a result, approximating a square root model by the same type of procedure as in Chapter 8 is problematic. In this section we describe a three-step procedure for approximating the process by a path-reconnecting lattice.

The first step involves transforming the process to one where the volatility is constant. The second step involves approximating the transformed process by a simple lattice. Finally, the third step involves modifying the probabilities on the lattice when their computed values are negative or exceed one.

Let the transformed variable be x. That is, $x = g(r)$. For the square root process the transform is

$$x = g(r) = 2\sqrt{r}/\sigma \qquad (23.9)$$

and

$$r = f(x) = \sigma^2 x^2/4 \qquad (23.10)$$

In Appendix 23A it is shown that this transformation results in a new process with a constant volatility equal to 1. This new process can be written as

$$dx = \mu(x)\, dt + dw \qquad (23.11)$$

The exact form of $\mu(x)$ can be established but will not be required.

In the second step a binomial approximation is made to the transformed process. In each increment the approximation for equation (23.11) is given by

$$x \begin{cases} x^+ = x + \sqrt{\Delta t} \\ x^- = x - \sqrt{\Delta t} \end{cases}$$

Given the values on the x lattice, we can recover the dynamics of the spot rate on its lattice.

$$r = f(x) \begin{cases} r^+ = f(x^+) \\ r^- = f(x^-) \end{cases}$$

We now can construct a lattice for the x values.

$$x \begin{cases} x^+ = x + \sqrt{\Delta t} \begin{cases} x^{++} = x^+ + \sqrt{\Delta t} \\ x^{+-} = x \end{cases} \\ x^- = x - \sqrt{\Delta t} \begin{cases} x^{+-} = x \\ x^{--} = x^- - \sqrt{\Delta t} \end{cases} \end{cases}$$

Equivalently, we could construct the lattice for r values.

$$r = f(x) \begin{cases} r^+ = f(x^+) \begin{cases} r^{++} = f(x^{++}) \\ r^{+-} = f(x) \end{cases} \\ r^- = f(x^-) \begin{cases} r^{+-} = f(x) \\ r^{--} = f(x^{--}) \end{cases} \end{cases}$$

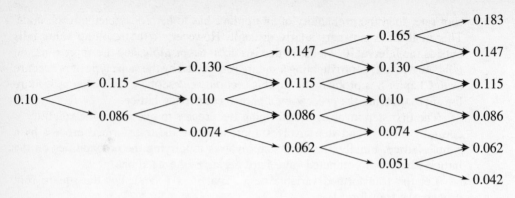

EXHIBIT 23.1   Interest Rate Lattice

The probability of an upmove is computed by

$$p(r) = \frac{\kappa(\mu - r)\,\Delta t + (r - r^-)}{(r^+ - r^-)} \tag{23.12}$$

Note that the probability of an upmove depends on the level of r and the values of r^+ and r^-.

The third step involves modifying the second step when the probability computed in equation (23.12) falls out of the range $[0, 1]$. In particular, as r moves to zero, the probability may exceed 1. When this occurs, we set the probability exactly equal to 1.

The three-step procedure is best illustrated by example.

EXAMPLE 23.1   Consider a one-year period split into five intervals, each of width 0.2 years. The initial spot interest rate is $r(0) = 0.10$. The dynamics of the spot rate are given by the square root model, with $\sigma = 0.10$, $\kappa = 0.1$, and $\mu = 0.10$. Using the transform, the lattice of annualized one-period interest rates is shown in Exhibit 23.1.

Consider the value of the interest rate, given an initial upmove. From equation (23.9), $x = 6.32$ and $\sqrt{\Delta t} = 0.447$. Hence, $x^+ = 6.77$. Using equation (23.10), $r^+ = 11.50$ percent.

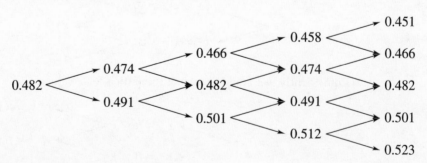

EXHIBIT 23.2   Probabilities of Upmoves

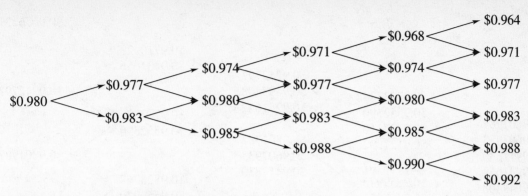

EXHIBIT 23.3   One-Period Discount Bond Prices

The probabilities of upmoves, computed using equation (23.12), at each node are shown in Exhibit 23.2. Note that as interest rates increase, the probability of an upmove decreases, and as interest rates decline, the probability of an upmove increases. This is consistent with the property of mean reversion. Note that in Exhibit 23.2 all the probabilities fall between 0 and 1, so there is no need to modify the values. As the partition of this lattice is refined, the evolution of interest rates becomes indistinguishable from the square root process.

The one-period bond prices at each node can be computed using the information in the interest rate lattice. For example, in the third period, given two upmoves, we have

$$P_{32}(1) = e^{-r_{32}(1)\Delta t} = e^{-(0.115)0.20} = 0.977$$

Exhibit 23.3 illustrates these prices.

Bond Pricing Under the Local Expectations Hypothesis

Given the interest rate process, under the local expectations hypothesis, longer-term bond prices can also be computed.

EXAMPLE 23.2   **Pricing Bonds on Binomial Lattices**

Continuing Example 23.1, starting in the fourth period at any node, we know the bond prices that mature in the fifth period. These are shown at the extreme right of the lattice in Exhibit 23.4. Now, consider the node in the third period, given two upmoves have occurred. The one-period bond price, $P_{32}(1)$ say, is given by $P_{32}(1) = 0.9773322$. To compute the price $P_{32}(2)$, recall that under the local expectations hypothesis

$$P_{32}(2) = [\theta P_{43}(1) + (1 - \theta)P_{42}(1)]P_{32}(1)$$

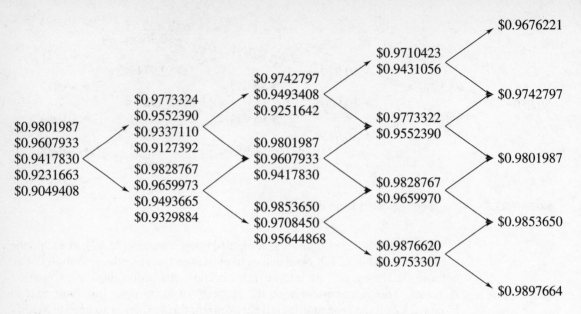

EXHIBIT 23.4   Constructing Bond Prices of Different Maturities at Each Node

where θ is the probability of an upmove, at this node 0.4774. Computing this value leads to $P_{32}(2) = 0.9552390$. In the third period, the one- and two-period bond prices are recorded at each node. These are shown in the last columns in Exhibit 23.4. With these prices we can now compute all two- and three-period bond prices for the nodes in the second period. Then we can compute two-, three-, and four-period bond prices at all nodes in the first period. Finally, we can price two-, three-, four-, and five-period bonds at time 0. The set of bond prices at time 0 is shown in Exhibit 23.4. For example, $P(0, 5) = 0.9049408$.

As the time increment of the lattice gets smaller, the interest rate process given by the binomial lattice converges to the true continuous-time square root process, and the prices of bonds of all maturities stabilize. Actually, analytical solutions exist for the bond prices at each interest rate level. In particular, the theoretical price at date t of a bond that matures at date T is given by

$$P(t, T) = A(t, T) \, e^{-\beta(t, T)r(t)} \tag{23.13}$$

where $\quad A(t, T) = \left[\dfrac{\phi_1 \, e^{\phi_2(T-t)}}{\phi_2(e^{\phi_1(T-t)} - 1) + \phi_1}\right]^{\phi_3} \tag{23.14}$

$$\beta(t, T) = \left[\dfrac{(e^{\phi_1(T-t)} - 1)}{\phi_2(e^{\phi_1(T-t)} - 1) + \phi_1}\right] \tag{23.15}$$

and $\quad \phi_1 = \kappa^2 + 2\sigma^2$

$\phi_2 = (\kappa + \phi_1)/2$

$\phi_3 = \dfrac{2\kappa\mu}{\sigma^2}$

Let $y(t, T)$ be the yield to maturity from time t to date T. That is,

$$P(t, T) = e^{-y(t, T)(T-t)}$$

Under the square root model,

$$y(t, T) = [\alpha(t, T) - \beta(t, T)]/(T - t) \qquad (23.16)$$

with

$$\alpha(t, T) = \ln A(t, T)$$

If the local expectations hypothesis holds, and if interest rates are generated by this single-factor model, then the observed yields to maturity should be given by equation (23.16).

The fact that analytical solutions for bond prices are available is quite attractive because they allow several measures of interest rate risk to be computed. For example, the sensitivity of bond prices to interest rate movements can be established. Differentiating equation (23.13) with respect to r yields

$$dP(t, T)/dr = -\beta(t, T)P(t, T)$$

or

$$dP(t, T)/P(t, T) = -\beta(t, T) \, dr$$

Recall that the modified duration of a bond, $\mathbb{D}_m$, is defined as

$$dP(t, T)/P(t, T) = -\mathbb{D}_m \, dr$$

Hence

$$\mathbb{D}_m = \beta(t, T) \qquad (23.17)$$

EXAMPLE 23.3   1.   Given the parameter values for the square root model in Example 23.2, the analytical prices of one-, two-, three-, four-, and five-period bonds can be computed. Recall that the width of the time periods is 0.2 years. Using equation (23.13), the bond prices turn out to be very close to the values on the lattice. For example, the five-period bond is priced at \$0.904977. The lattice, therefore, provides a good proxy for the bond price dynamics.

2.   Assume the same parameter values in Example 23.2. An investor holds a \$10,000 T-bill that matures in one year (five periods). The theoretical price of the T-bill is therefore \$9,049.77. The modified duration of this bond is given by equation (23.17). In particular $\mathbb{D}_m = 0.95012$. This means that if interest rates change by one basis point the bond is expected to depreciate by

$$(0.95012)(0.01) = 0.095012\%$$

Equation (23.13) shows that under the square root process and local expectations hypothesis, the price of any bond at any date t depends on the spot interest rate at that time and on the maturity of the bond. It can be shown that the dynamics of the bond price are given by

$$\frac{dP(t, T)}{P(t, T)} = \mu_p(t, T) \, dt + \sigma_p(t, T) \, dw(t) \qquad (23.18)$$

where $\mu_p(t, T)$ and $\sigma_p(t, T)$ are the instantaneous drift and volatility of the bond. The drift term is the expected return that is anticipated from holding the bond over the next time increment. Under the local expectations hypothesis, this expected return should be the same for all bonds and of course equal to the instantaneous riskless rate $r(t)$. In Appendix 23B we show that the instantaneous variance is

$$\sigma_p^2(t, T) = \beta^2(t, T)\sigma^2 r(t) \tag{23.19}$$

Note that the volatility of the bond depends on the level of the spot interest rate and on the modified duration of the bond. As the bond nears maturity, the duration, $\beta(t, T)$, converges to zero, and the price process becomes more predictable.

If the underlying interest rate process is the mean-reverting Wiener model, then under the local expectations hypothesis, the limiting bond price can be shown to be

$$P(t, T) = e^{\alpha(t, T) - \beta(t, T)r(t)} \tag{23.20}$$

where $\alpha(t, T) = \sigma^2[4 e^{-\kappa\tau} - e^{2\kappa\tau} + 2\kappa\tau - 3]/4\kappa^3 - \tau\mu$

$$-\mu(1 - e^{-\kappa\tau})/\kappa$$

$\beta(t, T) = [1 - e^{-\kappa\tau}]/\kappa$ and $\tau = T - t$

This is called the Vasicek model.

The Equilibrium Pricing of Bonds

The above analysis relied on the local expectations hypothesis. In a more general setting, bond prices will depend not only on expectations about future levels of the interest rate but also upon investors' attitudes toward risk. In order to establish bond prices without invoking the local expectations hypothesis, we need an alternative specification of how risk premiums are established.

In our one-factor setting, all prices are fully determined by the short-term interest rate. In any meaningful equilibrium there should be no possibility of forming a portfolio of bonds with a return that is free of risk unless its rate of return is equal to the current riskless rate. This necessary condition imposes a particular structure for the expected return, $\mu_p(t, T)$, on any bond. In particular, it can be shown that the ratio of excess expected return on any bond relative to its standard deviation, $\sigma_p(t, T)$ say, must be the same regardless of the maturity of the bond. That is,

$$\frac{\mu_p(t, T) - r(t)}{\sigma_p(t, T)} = \lambda(t) \tag{23.21}$$

The ratio $\lambda(t)$ is referred to as the **market price of interest rate risk.** The equation can be rewritten as

$$\phi(t, T) \equiv \mu_p(t, T) - r(t) = \lambda(t)\sigma_p(t, T) \tag{23.22}$$

This equation states that the risk premium of any bond, $\phi(t, T)$, is directly proportional to its volatility. Equivalently, the expected return of any bond equals the riskless return plus a risk premium. The risk premium depends on the market price of interest rate risk and on the volatility of the bond. This requirement is somewhat similar to the capital asset pricing model, in which the risk premium is proportional to the beta coefficient. The market price of interest rate risk at any point in time is constant and the same for all bonds. In general, however, the market price of interest rate risk could vary over time, and its magnitude could depend on the level of interest rates.

The market price of risk will in general be negative. This follows from the fact that returns on stocks and bonds are negatively related to changes in interest rates. As a result, the addition of any security into a portfolio whose price is positively correlated with interest rates will tend to reduce the risk in the portfolio.

To obtain the required risk premium for bonds at each maturity, an explicit form for the market price of interest rate risk must be supplied. In principle, the structure for this function cannot be chosen arbitrarily; it should come from an equilibrium model that begins by making assumptions regarding investors' beliefs and tastes. Before we consider how bond prices are set when such specific assumptions are made, we first consider the simplest of cases, when the local expectations hypothesis holds. In this case $\lambda(t) = 0$, and the instantaneous expected return for bonds of all maturities is the riskless rate, $r(t)$. As we have seen, the prices of all bonds can then easily be obtained.

Given particular assumptions about the economy and about preferences and beliefs of investors in the economy, Cox, Ingersoll, and Ross showed that the spot interest rate would follow the square root model. They also showed that the market price of interest rate risk was of the form

$$\lambda(t) = \lambda \sqrt{r}/\sigma \tag{23.23}$$

Under their assumptions, then, viewed from time t, the risk premium on a bond that matures at date T is given by

$$\phi(t, T) = \mu_p(t, T) - r(t) = \lambda \sqrt{r}\beta(t, T) \tag{23.24}$$

where $\beta(t, T)$ is given in equation (23.15).

Once the risk premium for each bond is known, we can construct binomial lattices for the **true interest rate process** and can then price bonds by discounting future values at their appropriate discount rates.

The equilibrium bond prices developed on the binomial lattice converge as the partition is more closely refined. Since preference assumptions were made regarding the structure of the market price of risk, an additional parameter, λ, is required in addition to the parameters of the interest rate process.

In Chapter 22 we saw that to prevent riskless arbitrage, a probability measure must exist under which we could value claims by pretending the local expectations hypothesis holds. If we could identify this probability measure, we could proceed to value claims as in the previous examples. This idea is similar to what we did when we valued options on stocks. There, a two-step procedure was followed. In the first step the drift term of the true process was adjusted. In the second step valuation proceeded as if investors were risk-neutral.

Cox, Ingersoll, and Ross have provided the rules for identifying the appropriate probability measure (see Appendix 23B). In particular, they showed that the adjustment to the interest rate process is accomplished by modifying the drift term from its original form, $\mu(r)$ say, to $\mu^*(r)$, where

$$\mu^*(r) = \mu(r) - \lambda(t)\sigma(r) \tag{23.25}$$

and leaving the volatility term untouched. The resulting **risk-neutralized interest rate process** is

$$dr = \mu^*(r)\,dt + \sigma(r)\,dw \tag{23.26}$$

Once this process is identified, we can value bonds by *pretending the local expectations hypothesis holds.*

The Cox-Ingersoll-Ross Bond Pricing Model

Under the Cox-Ingersoll-Ross (CIR) assumptions, the true interest rate process is derived to be

$$dr = \mu(r)\,dt + \sigma\sqrt{r}\,dw$$

where $\mu(r) = \kappa(\mu - r)\,dt$. Further, the market price of interest rate risk, $\lambda(t)$, is shown to be of the form $\lambda(t) = \lambda\sqrt{r}/\sigma$. The drift term of the risk-neutralized process is therefore given by

$$\mu^*(r, t) = [\kappa(\mu - r) - \lambda r]$$

or
$$\mu^*(r, t) = \kappa^*(\mu^* - r) \tag{23.27}$$

where κ^* and μ^* are given by

$$\kappa^* = \kappa + \lambda \tag{23.28}$$

$$\mu^* = \frac{\kappa\mu}{\kappa + \lambda} \tag{23.29}$$

Equilibrium bond prices in the CIR economy can then be computed by pretending that the local expectations hypothesis holds and that the spot rate dynamics are given by

$$dr = \kappa^*(\mu^* - r)\,dt + \sigma\sqrt{r}\,dw$$

Fortunately, we have already computed bond prices under a square root process. In particular, bond prices are given by equation (23.13); here κ^* and μ^* replace κ and μ. In addition, bonds can be priced on a binomial lattice that approximates this risk-neutralized process by pretending the local expectations hypothesis holds.

EXAMPLE 23.4   Assume the market-price-of-risk parameter, λ, is -0.05. The mean reversion parameter, κ, is 0.150, and the long-run average of the short-term interest rate, μ, is 0.0666. The initial spot rate, $r(0)$, is 10 percent, and the volatility parameter is $\sigma = 0.10$.

To establish the prices of any interest rate claim, we must first identify the parameters of the risk-neutralized process. From equations (23.28) and (23.29) we have $\kappa^* = 0.10$ and $\mu^* = 0.10$. We now can construct the lattice of interest rates using the same procedure as before. Note that since the parameters of the risk-neutralized process are exactly equal to the parameters we used in Examples 23.1 and 23.2, the resulting analysis is identical, and the prices of bonds obtained on the lattice are exactly those in Example 23.2. Of course, these are approximate prices, with the true prices being equal to those computed in Example 23.3. Note, however, that in the analysis here we did not assume the local expectations hypothesis holds in the economy. Rather, our analysis was developed under the assumptions of the CIR model.

Pricing of Options on Bonds

Provided the underlying interest rate process is adjusted by modifying the drift according to equation (23.22), we can value any bond by pretending the local expectations hypothesis holds true. A bond is just one type of interest rate claim that can be valued this way. Indeed, once the approximating binomial lattice for the risk-neutralized process has been established, any interest-rate-contingent claim can be priced. For example, European and American call and put options on bonds can easily be priced on a binomial lattice.

EXAMPLE 23.5   1.   Reconsider the information on prices provided in Example 23.2. All forward prices and forward rates can be extracted from the initial discount function. For example, the forward price of a contract that requires delivery of a one-period bond after two periods is $F_0[2, 3] = P(0.3)/P(0, 2) = 0.9802$. Hence, the fair forward price for delivery of a one-period T-bill with a face value of $10,000 in two periods is $9,802.

2.   Consider a call option that gives the owner the right to purchase a one-period discount bond with a face value of $10,000 in the second period for a price set equal to the forward price, $0.9802. The exercise value of the claim in each node in the second period can easily be computed. Then, using the probabilities shown in the lattice in Exhibit 23.2 and the discount factors in Exhibit 23.3, the backward procedure can be invoked to price the claim. The lattice of prices is shown below. Since there is only a small probability of ending up in the money, the option has very little value.

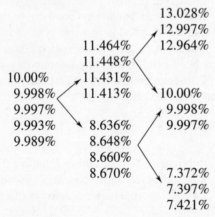

As the partition for the binomial lattice becomes finer, the option prices converge to a unique price. Cox, Ingersoll, and Ross developed analytical solutions for the call option on a discount bond. Since there are many interest rate claims that do not have analytical solutions, the lattice procedure is very useful. For example, the lattice can be used to price American put options on bonds. In addition, options can be computed on interest rate indices.

EXAMPLE 23.6   Exhibit 23.5 shows the yields to maturity corresponding to the discount bond prices in Exhibit 23.4. Consider a two-period contract that provides the holder with the option to profit based on the differential between three-period rates and one-period rates. Specifically, the payout of the option is $1000 \times$ $\text{Max}[0, y_{2j}(1) - y_{2j}(3) - X]$, for $j = 0, 1, 2$. Here X is the strike, which we assume to be equal to the current spread $y_0(1) - y_0(3)$, and the yields are taken to be in

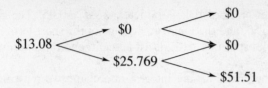

EXHIBIT 23.5   Yields to Maturity

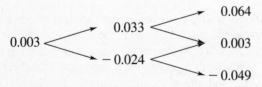

EXHIBIT 23.6   Interest Rate Differentials

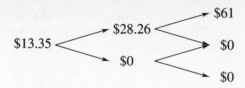

EXHIBIT 23.7   European Options on Differentials

percentage form. Hence, $X = 10.0 - 9.997 = 0.003$. The interest rate differentials are shown in Exhibit 23.6. The prices of the European options are shown in Exhibit 23.7.

Note that if the claim were American, early exercise would be optimal if the term structure moved up in the first period. In particular, the exercise value in the up state is $30, which exceeds the value unexercised. If the contract were American, the initial price would be $30 \times 0.482 \times 0.980 = \$14.17$.

Equilibrium Futures Prices

The binomial lattice for the risk-neutralized process can be used to price futures contracts on bonds or futures contracts on yields.

EXAMPLE 23.7   The futures price that requires delivery of a one-period discount bond with face value $1000 in two-periods' time can be computed as the expected price of a one-period bond at settlement under the risk-neutralized process. Exhibit 23.8 shows the calculations of the expected value. First, the probabilities in Exhibit 23.3 are used to compute the likelihood of each path. The price of the bond at the end of each path is shown in the last column. These values are taken from Exhibit 23.4. The futures price is computed by weighting each outcome by its probability and adding the values. The computed futures price is $979.95. Note that the forward price for this contract is $F_0[2, 3] = P(0, 3)/P(0, 2) = \$980$. The difference between the two prices reflects the cost of marking to market. In this example the cost is just $0.05. Actually, since we used only two periods, the futures contract we priced was marked to market only once before the delivery date. For longer-term

EXHIBIT 23.8   Computing the Futures Price

Path	Probability	Final Bond Price
Up-up	$0.482 \times 0.474 = 0.2286$	974
Up-down	$0.482 \times 0.526 = 0.2535$	980
Down-up	$0.518 \times 0.491 = 0.2543$	980
Down-down	$0.518 \times 0.509 = 0.2636$	985

contracts, and for finer partitions on the lattice, the futures price will fall further below the forward contract. The example nonetheless does serve to illustrate the difference between forwards and futures.

Calibrating Single-Factor Models

The prices of all default-free bonds produced by the single-factor Cox-Ingersoll-Ross model depend solely on the level of the spot interest rate. Given the spot rate dynamics and the structure for the market price of interest rate risk, default-free bonds of all maturities can be priced.

To implement the model, we must estimate the interest rate risk premium and the parameters of the interest rate process. There are three ways to obtain estimates: the pure time-series, pure cross-sectional, and joint time-series and cross-sectional approaches.

Pure Time-Series Approach

In this approach the time series of short-term interest rates is observed and used to estimate the parameters of the process. At best, this approach can be used to validate whether interest rates follow the hypothesized process. However, it provides no way to estimate the risk premium parameter, λ. In addition, it ignores information available from bond prices. Indeed, the estimated parameters may lead to theoretical bond prices that are quite different from observable prices. Finally, a large number of observations are necessary to ensure that the power of the estimation procedure is high. Lengthy estimation periods, however, increase the likelihood that parameters are nonstationary.

Pure Cross-Sectional Approach

Another approach infers the parameters by using a cross section of observable bond prices. First a discount function is established; then values of the parameters are selected so that the theoretical set of bond prices closely approximates the actual set. Once the estimates are obtained, they can be used to price other contemporaneous interest-rate-contingent instruments that are not included in the estimation period.

Choosing the parameters so that the theoretical term structure fits the observed term structure is extremely important if the model is going to be used to price and hedge specific interest rate claims, such as call options on bonds. The theoretical call price has little meaning if it is set relative to a bond price that does not equal the observed price. This procedure of choosing the parameters so that the resulting bond prices are "close" to the observed set of prices is referred to as calibrating the model.

Unlike the pure time-series approach, the cross-sectional approach is unable to separate out the interest rate risk premium from the individual parameters of the interest rate process. The approach does not constrain the interest rate parameters to be stable over time. Instead, it allows the parameters to be completely nonstationary from period to period. If the resulting estimates were stable from period to period, this approach would have merits; unfortunately, empirical evidence indicates that these estimates are quite unstable.

Joint Time-Series and Cross-Sectional Approach

In this approach the parameters are estimated by combining time-series and cross-sectional information. This approach attempts to price bonds as accurately as the cross-sectional approach while producing estimates that are more stable over time.

In Chapter 24 we shall have more to say about the difficulties of estimation and the process of calibration.

Conclusion

In this chapter we have assumed bond prices are fully determined by the short-term interest rate. The evolution of bond prices is therefore fully characterized once the evolution of short-term rates has been specified. We first explored the behavior of the short-term rate. Short-term rates are mean-reverting. We presented a few models of interest rates and discussed binomial approximations to these models. Once the short-term rate process is established, we can easily generate bond prices under a local expectations hypothesis. We developed an equilibrium framework that allowed bonds to be priced if a structure for the market price of risk was specified. Examples include the Vasicek model and the Cox-Ingersoll-Ross model, for which binomial approximations exist.

Once bond prices are established, we can readily develop option prices as well as futures and forward prices. While analytical solutions are available for a few interest rate claims, the easiest way to price most claims is to use a binomial lattice methodology. We priced several claims on the lattice, including American call and put options on bonds and some yield options and futures. We provided examples using a binomial lattice to price a complex contract. Given these interest rate claim models, we can readily compute measures of the sensitivity of prices to interest rate changes such as duration and convexity. In the last section of this chapter we briefly discussed some of the empirical issues associated with this type of approach.

References

This chapter has focused on single-factor models of the term structure. In particular, we have emphasized the single-factor, Cox-Ingersoll-Ross (1985) model and its binomial lattice implementation. The implementation that we have followed is credited to Tian. For two-factor models, the Brennan and Schwartz reference is useful.

Brennan, M., and E. Schwartz. "A Continuous Time Approach to the Pricing of Bonds." *Journal of Banking and Finance* 3 (July 1979): 133–55.

Brown, S., and P. Dybvig. "The Empirical Implications of the Cox, Ingersoll, Ross Theory of the Term Structure of Interest Rates." *Journal of Finance* 41 (July 1986): 617–30.

Courtadon, G. "The Pricing of Options on Default-Free Bonds." *Journal of Financial and Quantitative Analysis* 17 (March 1982): 75–100.

Cox, J., J. Ingersoll, and S. Ross. "A Re-Examination of Traditional Hypotheses about the Term Structure of Interest Rates." *Journal of Finance* 36 (September 1981): 769–99.

———. "An Intertemporal General Equilibrium Model of Asset Prices." *Econometrica* 53 (March 1985): 363–84.

———. "A Theory of the Term Structure of Interest Rates." *Econometrica* 53 (1985): 385–407.

Daves, P., and M. Erhardt. "Joint Cross-Section/Time Series Maximum Likelihood Estimation for the Parameters of the Cox, Ingersoll, Ross Bond Pricing Model." *The Financial Review* 28 (February 1993): 203–37.

Dothan, L. "On the Term Structure of Interest Rates." *Journal of Financial Economics* 6 (January 1978): 59–69.

Longstaff, F. "A Nonlinear General Equilibrium Model of the Term Structure of Interest Rates." *Journal of Financial Economics* 23 (August 1989): 195–224.

Marsh, T., and E. Rosenfeld. "Stochastic Processes for Interest Rates." *Journal of Finance* 38 (May 1983): 635–45.

Richard, S. "An Arbitrage Model of the Term Structure of Interest Rates." *Journal of Financial Economics* 6 (March 1978): 33–57.

Tian, Y. "A Simplified Binomial Approach to the Pricing of Interest Rate Contingent Claims." *Journal of Financial Engineering.* 1 (1993): 14–37.

Vasicek, O. "An Equilibrium Characterization of the Term Structure." *Journal of Financial Economics* 5 (1977): 177–88.

Exercises

1. Explain why modeling interest rates by a geometric Wiener process may not be appropriate.

2. Describe the generalized Wiener process with mean reversion as a model for interest rates. What are its advantages and disadvantages?

3. Describe the square root model used in the Cox-Ingersoll-Ross model. Explain its advantages.

4. The initial interest rate is 8 percent. Interest rates follow a square root process with $\kappa = 0.01$, $\sigma = 0.20$, $\mu = 0.10$. The three-period lattice of one-year rates ($\Delta t = 1$ year) on an approximating lattice are shown below. The one-period probabilities of an upmove are shown under the rates in parentheses.

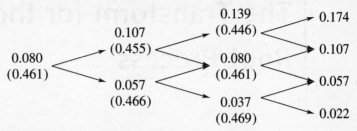

a. Compute the one-period bond prices on the lattice.
b. Compute the two- and three-period bond prices at date 0, based on the assumption that the local expectations hypothesis holds.
c. Compute the price of a two-period call option on a one-period yield that occurs at expiration. The strike price is set at the initial forward rate, and the multiplier is 100. That is, the payout is Max[0, $r - x$]100, where r is in percent and x is the forward rate in percent.

5. Use the lattice in Exercise 4 to price a two-period forward rate agreement on a one-period rate.

6. Interest rates follow a square root process with $r(0) = 10\%$, $\kappa = 0.01$, $\mu = 0.09$, $\sigma = 0.20$, and $x = -0.10$.

a. Establish the risk-neutralized process under which all claims can be priced under the local expectations hypothesis.
b. For $\Delta t = 0.5$ years, compute a one-period lattice for the interest rate. Identify the probability of an upmove.
c. Compute the fair price of a claim that pays $1 in the up state and $0 in the down state.

7. Explain how you could use information on the term structure to calibrate the CIR model. In particular, how could you use this information to estimate the parameters?

APPENDIX 23A

The Transform for the Square Root Process

Assume the interest rate follows the square root process given by

$$dr = \kappa(\mu - r)\, dt + \sigma\sqrt{r}\, dt$$

Consider the process of $x = g(r) = 2\sqrt{r}/\sigma$. Using Ito's rule we have

$$dx = g_r\, dr + \frac{1}{2} g_{rr}\sigma^2 r\, dt$$

Now, $g_r = 1/\sigma\sqrt{r}$, and $g_{rr} = -(1/2\sigma)r^{-3/2}$. Substituting into the above equation and simplifying, using the fact that $r = \sigma^2 x^2/4$, yields equation (23.11):

$$dx = \mu(x)\, dt + dw$$

where $\quad \mu(x) = \dfrac{2}{\sigma^2 x}[\kappa(\mu - \sigma^2 x^2/4) - \sigma^2/2]$

APPENDIX 23B

Pricing Bonds Under the Local Expectations Hypothesis

Consider the following general process for the short rate:

$$dr = \mu(r, t)\, dt + \sigma(r, t)\, dw \qquad (23B.1)$$

Clearly, all the interest rate models we have considered are special cases of this equation. We assume the bond price is fully characterized once the spot rate is known. Let $P(t, T)$ be the price at time t of a pure discount bond that pays \$1 at time T. We assume the dynamics of the bond are determined by the dynamics of the spot rate. From Ito's lemma,

$$dP = P_r\, dr + P_t\, dt + \frac{1}{2}\sigma^2(r, t)P_{rr}\, dt$$

$$= P_r[\mu(r, t)\, dt + \sigma(r, t)\, dw] + P_t\, dt + \frac{1}{2}\sigma^2(r, t)P_{rr}\, dt$$

Hence,
$$dP/P = \mu_p\, dt + \sigma_p\, dw \qquad (23B.2)$$

where $\quad \mu_p = \left[\frac{1}{2}\sigma^2(r, t)P_{rr} + \mu(r, t)P_r + P_t\right]\Big/ P \qquad (23B.3)$

$$\sigma_p = P_r\sigma(r, t)/P \qquad (23B.4)$$

The instantaneous return on the bond follows an Ito process with drift μ_p and volatility σ_p. Now, if the expected return on the bond, μ_p, was known, then from equation (23B.3) the bond price could be obtained by solving the following partial differential equation subject to the appropriate boundary conditions:

$$\frac{1}{2}\sigma^2(r, t)P_{rr} + \mu(r, t)P_r - \mu_p P + P_t = 0 \qquad (23B.5)$$

subject to $\quad P(r, T, T) = 1$

Unfortunately, the expected instantaneous return on the bond, μ_p, is not known. However, if we appeal to the local expectations hypothesis, then the return on all bonds over the smallest time increment equals the riskless return. That is, $\mu_p = r$. Substituting this into equation (23B.5), the partial differential equation, leads to

$$\frac{1}{2}\sigma^2(r, t)P_{rr} + \mu(r, t)P_r - rP + P_t = 0 \qquad (23B.6)$$

subject to $\quad P(T, T) = 1$

Of course, the solution to equation (23B.6) depends on the specific structure selected for the interest rate process. If the process is a square root process, then the solution is given by equation (23.13). If the process is a mean-reverting Gaussian process, then the solution is given by equation (23.18). Given the bond pricing equation, the volatility of the bond, as given by equation (23B.4), can be computed and is given by equation (23.19).

APPENDIX 23C

The Equilibrium Pricing of Bonds

In our one-factor setting, all prices are fully determined by the short-term interest rate. In any meaningful equilibrium there should be no possibility of forming a portfolio of bonds whose return is free of risk unless its rate of return is equal to the current riskless rate. This necessary condition imposes a particular structure for the expected return, μ_p, on a bond. To see this, consider a hedge portfolio containing two default-free bonds of different maturities (T_1 and T_2). Let x_j be the number of dollars invested in bond j ($j = 1, 2$). The dollars invested in the bonds are financed by borrowing at the instantaneous rate, r. Then the instantaneous dollar return, dV, is given by

$$dV = x_1(dP_1/P_1) + x_2(dP_2/P_2) - (x_1 + x_2)r\, dt$$

$$= [x_1(\mu_{p_1} - r) + x_2(\mu_{p_2} - r)]\, dt + [x_1\sigma_{p_1} + x_2\sigma_{p_2}]\, dw$$

Now, we choose x_1 and x_2 such that there is no uncertainty in the instantaneous return. That is,

$$x_1\sigma_{p_1} + x_2\sigma_{p_2} = 0 \tag{23C.1}$$

To avoid riskless arbitrage, it must follow that the return on this portfolio is zero. Hence,

$$x_1(\mu_{p_1} - r) + x_2(\mu_{p_2} - r) = 0 \tag{23C.2}$$

For a nontrivial solution to exist for equations (23C.1) and (23C.2), it follows that

$$\frac{\mu_{p_1} - r}{\sigma_{p_1}} = \frac{\mu_{p_2} - r}{\sigma_{p_2}} = \lambda(r, t) \tag{23C.3}$$

That is, the ratio of excess expected return relative to standard deviation of bonds is always equal to some constant, $\lambda(r, t)$ say, regardless of the maturity of the bond. Substituting for the volatility, from equation (23B.4) we obtain

$$\mu_p - r = \lambda(r, t)\sigma(r, t)\frac{P_r}{P} \tag{23C.4}$$

This condition is somewhat similar to the capital asset pricing model, in which the risk premium is proportional to the beta coefficient. Here the risk premium is proportional to a factor that captures the sensitivity of the bond price change with respect to the instantaneous short rate. Substituting equation (23B.3) for μ_p into equation (23C.4) and simplifying leads to

$$\frac{1}{2}\sigma^2(r, t)P_{rr} + [\mu(r, t) - \lambda(r, t)\sigma(r, t)]P_r - rP + P_t = 0 \quad (23C.5)$$

with $P(r, T, T) = 1$

Clearly, to solve this partial differential equation, we must place structure on the interest rate process and on the market price of risk, $\lambda(r, t)$. We shall return to equation (23C.5).

The Martingale Method for Pricing Bonds

Given that interest rates are generated by

$$dr = \mu(r, t)\, dt + \sigma(r, t)\, dw \quad (23C.6)$$

recall that under the local expectations hypothesis, discount bond prices are given by

$$\frac{P(0, T)}{M(0)} = E_0\left[\frac{P(T, T)}{M(T)}\right]$$

Here $M(T)$ is the value of a money fund initialized with \$1 at date 0; it earns interest at the instantaneous short-term interest rate. Hence, $M(0) = 1$, and

$$M(T) = e^{\int_0^T r(s)\, ds}$$

Since $P(T, T) = 1$, the above equation can be expressed as

$$P(0, T) = E_0[1/M(T)] = E_0[e^{-\int_t^T r(s)\, ds}]$$

More generally, under the local expectations hypothesis, the bond price at date t is linked to the future interest rates through the relationship

$$P(t, T) = E_t[e^{-\int_t^T r(s)\, ds}] \quad (23C.7)$$

We have seen that under the local expectations hypothesis the bond price is the solution of partial differential equation (23B.6). The fact that the expectation given in equation (23C.7) can be obtained by solving the partial differential equation (23B.6) is called the Feynman-Kac result. Conversely, the solution to equation (23B.6) can be expressed as an expectation of the form in equation (23C.6), taken under the process given in equation (23C.6).

Now we can return to the problem of solving the partial differential equation (23C.5). By comparing equations (23C.5) and (23B.6), we observe that the only difference is the coefficient of P_r, which has been changed from $\mu(r, t)$ to $\mu(r, t) - \lambda(r, t)\sigma(r, t)$. If we write

$$dr = [\mu(r, t) - \lambda(r, t)\sigma(r, t)]\, dt + \sigma(r, t)\, dw \quad (23C.8)$$

then the solution to equation (23C.5) can be written as

$$P(t, T) = \overline{E}_t[e^{-\int_t^T r(s)\,ds}] \tag{23C.9}$$

where the expectation is taken with respect to the modified stochastic process given by equation (23C.8).

Hence, if we knew the structure for the market price of risk, then we can make an appropriate adjustment to the drift term and obtain the value of the bond by *pretending* that the local expectations hypothesis holds true. The process given in equation (23C.8) is referred to as the risk-neutralized process.

Pricing of Options on Bonds

A bond is just one type of interest rate claim. The argument leading to equation (23C.5) holds true for other interest-rate-derivative securities, the only difference being the specification of the boundary conditions. For example, consider a European call option with strike X and expiration date T. The bond underlying the call matures at time T_1. Then, as with equation (23C.5), we obtain the fundamental partial differential equation

$$\frac{1}{2}\sigma^2(r, t)C_{rr} + [\mu(r, t) - \lambda(r, t)\sigma(r, t)]C_r - rC + C_t = 0$$

which together with the boundary condition

$$C(r, T) = \text{Max}[P(T, T_1) - X, 0]$$

provides a unique solution for the option. The solution can be expressed as

$$C(r, t) = \overline{E}_t[C(r, T)e^{-\int_t^T r(s)\,ds}]$$

where the expectation is taken with respect to the risk-neutralized process. The above equation states that a call option on a bond can be valued as if the local expectations hypothesis holds true, provided the underlying interest rate process is the risk-neutralized process.

Equilibrium Futures Prices

Again assume the short-term interest rate follows an arbitrary diffusion process of the form in equation (23C.6). Let $F(r, t)$ be the futures price on a pure discount bond with settlement date T. The maturity of the underlying bond is T_1. Applying Ito's rule to $F(r, t)$, we obtain

$$dF = \mu_F\,dt + \sigma_F\,dw$$

where $\quad \mu_F = \dfrac{1}{2}\sigma^2(r, t)F_{rr} + \mu(r, t)F_r + F_t \tag{23C.10}$

$$\sigma_F = \sigma(r, t)F_r$$

Now consider a position consisting of n_1 futures contracts with settlement date T_1 and n_2 futures contracts with settlement date T_2. Let dV be the instantaneous change in value of this position due to continuous marking to market. Then

$$dV = n_1\, dF_1 + n_2\, dF_2$$

$$= n_1(\mu_{F1} + \sigma_{F1}\, dw) + n_2(\mu_{F2} + \sigma_{F2}\, dw)$$

$$= (n_1\mu_{F1} + n_2\mu_{F2})\, dt + (n_1\sigma_{F1} + n_2\sigma_{F2})\, dw$$

Following the same procedure as before, we choose n_1 and n_2 such that the coefficient of the stochastic term vanishes. That is,

$$n_1\sigma_{F1} + n_2\sigma_{F2} = 0 \qquad (23C.11)$$

Since the position requires no investment and incurs no risk, to prevent riskless arbitrage, its return should be zero:

$$dV = n_1\mu_{F1} + n_2\mu_{F2} = 0 \qquad (23C.12)$$

A nontrivial solution exists to equations (23C.11) and (23C.12) if

$$\mu_F = \lambda(r, t)\sigma_F \qquad (23C.13)$$

Equation (23C.13) states that the ratio μ_F/σ_F is the same for all futures contracts, regardless of their settlement dates. This ratio, $\lambda(r, t)$, could depend on the level of interest rates and on time. Substituting $\mu_F = \lambda(r, t)\sigma_F$ into equation (23C.10) yields the fundamental valuation equation for futures:

$$\frac{1}{2}\sigma^2(r, t)F_{rr} + (\mu(r, t) - \lambda(r, t)\sigma(r, t))F_r - F_t = 0 \qquad (23C.14)$$

subject to $F(r, T) = P(r, T, T_1)$

This partial differential equation differs from that for bonds and options in that the coefficient of F in equation (23C.14) is zero. It can be shown that the solution to equation (23C.14) can be written as

$$F(r, t) = \bar{E}_{r,t}[F(r, T)] \qquad (23C.15)$$

where the expectation is taken under the risk-neutralized process given in equation (23C.8).

CHAPTER 24

Term Structure–Constrained Interest Rate Claim Models

In the last decade, over-the-counter trading in interest rate derivatives has dramatically expanded to involve more than a \$14 trillion market of notional principal. In this market, the majority of claims are priced and quoted relative to an existing term structure. The complexity of such contracts has placed new demands on models of the terms structure. In particular, it has become increasingly more important to adopt a single coherent model that not only relates today's term structure with the expectation of future spot rates, but also represents the comovements of all bond prices in such a way that information from the existing term structure is more fully reflected in prices. The single-factor models we presented in Chapter 23 disregard much available information. Indeed, the models we described used only information on the initial short-term rate and ignored other information, such as other rates drawn from the yield curve.

In this chapter we investigate some models that incorporate more information. First we highlight the importance of this problem. Then we establish some simple lattice-based models that attempt to address this issue. We explain why the approach is quite controversial. Then we present a simple version of the Heath-Jarrow-Morton (HJM) paradigm. These authors have developed a mechanism for pricing interest rate claims that is analogous to the Black-Scholes stock option model. As in the Black-Scholes model, the only inputs necessary are the underlying and a measure of its volatility. Here, the underlying is the entire term structure, and the volatility describes how this term structure fluctuates over time. Thus, the initial term structure is taken as an input in the same way as the stock price is input in the Black-Scholes analysis. Under certain assumptions, the HJM analysis simplifies, and analytical solutions can be developed for interest rate claims. In general, however, the analysis is computationally intensive. The reason for this is described, and recent models that attempt to resolve the computational intensity are discussed.

The primary objectives of this chapter are the following:

· To develop pricing models that incorporate information from the term structure;

· To describe the Heath-Jarrow-Morton paradigm for pricing interest rate claims;

- To identify some of the implementation problems of term structure–constrained models; and

- To introduce a lattice-based method for pricing a wide variety of interest-sensitive claims.

Single-State Models and the Pricing of Interest Rate Claims

If the goal of the analysis is to price interest rate claims relative to a term structure, then it is extremely important for the model to price discount bonds so that they match the observed term structure. If theoretical and actual bond prices do not match, the prices of interest rate claims produced by the model are said to be inconsistent. Such models could indicate that arbitrage opportunities exist when in fact they do not. Example 24.1 illustrates how single-factor models can produce inconsistent results.

EXAMPLE 24.1   1.   Consider the prices of European put and call options on discount bonds that mature at date T. The options have strike X and expiration date s, where $s < T$. From put-call parity we know that the price of a call less the price of a put equals the underlying bond price less the present value of the strike. Hence

$$P_0^E = C_0^E + XP(0, s) - P(0, T)$$

Any model for the put option must know about s- and T-period yields if it is to price the put correctly. Single-state models, such as the Cox-Ingersoll-Ross (CIR) model, have the property that whenever the short rate returns to a previous value, the entire term structure returns to its previous shape. Such models do not explicitly take into account the observed prices of discount bounds. If the model uses theoretical values for $P(0, s)$ and $P(0, T)$ that are different from the observed values, then the resulting theoretical put price will be flawed.

2.   For American options on coupon bonds, early exercise is a possibility. We must compare the benefits from early exercise against deferring exercise. In turn, we need to know the alternative yields available; this information is currently available from the yield curve. Any consistent model of option prices must therefore fully reflect information on the current set of yields available.

Interest Rate Models with Time-Varying Parameters

Models like the CIR model contain only a few parameters and hence are capable only of producing term structures that have limited shapes. As a result, a precise matching of the yield curve may not be possible. Cox, Ingersoll, and Ross recognized this weakness and recommended modifying the interest rate process so that an exact matching was possible. In particular, they proposed representing the interest rate process by

$$dr(t) = \kappa(\mu(t) - r(t)) \, dt + \sigma \sqrt{r(t)} \, dw(t)$$

In this formulation the drift term, $\mu(\,\cdot\,)$, is time-varying. The idea is to use the set of observable bond prices to back out the values for the $\mu(\,\cdot\,)$ function. This observation has led to the development of models of interest rate claims that incorporate many initial conditions into the analysis. These models are called **term structure–constrained** models and are discussed next.

Term Structure–Constrained Models

We noted that it may be desirable for an interest rate claim model to produce discount bond prices that match the observable prices. In addition, it may be desirable to incorporate additional information, such as information on the volatilities of yields. For example, the volatility of short-term interest rates is usually much greater than the volatility of longer-term rates, and the user of the model may want to incorporate specific volatility assumptions into the model. In what follows, we develop procedures in which the prices of successively larger-maturity Treasuries are used sequentially, and in conjunction with volatility information, to establish a process for interest rates and a pricing model for interest rate claims.

The Black-Derman-Toy Paradigm

The prices of zero-coupon Treasuries of differing maturities are taken as inputs. Exhibit 24.1 shows the prices of discount bonds maturing in years 1, 2, and 3. For simplicity, we have chosen the time increments between periods to be one year. In practice, shorter intervals would be used. Given the bond prices in Exhibit 24.1, the continuously compounded yields to maturity can be obtained. Exhibit 24.1 shows these yields as well as their volatilities. The volatility numbers are inputs and will be described soon. The goal is to use this information to establish a binomial lattice for interest rates that produces a term structure at the origin equal to the observed term structure. Once this lattice is developed, then the prices of any interest rate claim can be computed, using the appropriate backward recursion method.

We shall construct a binomial lattice using the short-term rate as the state variable. From Chapter 23 we know that to avoid riskless arbitrage it must be the

EXHIBIT 24.1   Initial Term Structure Information

Maturity (Years)	Bond Price ($)	Yield to Maturity (%)	Volatility
1	0.92312	8.0	—
2	0.83527	9.0	0.010
3	0.74082	9.5	0.009

case that a probability measure exists under which prices can be computed as if the local expectations hypothesis holds. We shall assume that in the lattice the probability measure is given as 0.50. That is, the up- and downmove probability value is exactly 0.50. Unlike the case with the binomial lattice in Chapter 23, however, we do not know the size of the jump. Actually, we shall compute the size of the price moves in such a way that when the lattice is used to price a discount bond, it will lead to the observed prices in Exhibit 24.1.

We are given the initial spot interest rate, $r_0(1) = 8\%$. Assume that after one year this rate moves with equal probability to $r_{11}(1)$ or $r_{10}(11)$:

$$r_0(1) = 8\% \diagdown \begin{matrix} \nearrow r_{11}(1) \\ \\ \searrow r_{10}(1) \end{matrix}$$

The idea is to choose $r_{11}(1)$ and $r_{10}(11)$ so that the price of a two-year bond at date 0, $P_0(2)$ say, is given by $P_0(2) = \$0.83527$, and the volatility of the yield is 0.010.

At nodes $(1, 0)$ and $(1, 1)$ the prices of one-period bonds are

$$P_{10}(1) = e^{-r_{10}(1)}$$

$$P_{11}(1) = e^{-r_{11}(1)}$$

Further, the price of a two-period bond at date 0 is related to the future one-period prices by

$$P_0(2) = [\tfrac{1}{2}P_{11}(1) + \tfrac{1}{2}P_{10}(1)]P_0(1)$$

Hence, $r_{11}(1)$ and $r_{10}(1)$ must be chosen so that

$$P_0(2)/P_0(1) = \tfrac{1}{2} e^{-r_{11}(1)} + \tfrac{1}{2} e^{-r_{10}(1)} \tag{24.1}$$

Substituting values for $P_0(2)$ and $P_0(1)$, we obtain

$$\$1.8097 = e^{-r_{11}(1)} + e^{-r_{10}(1)} \tag{24.2}$$

Viewed from time 0, the future one-period yields are uncertain. Let $\sigma_0^2(1)$ represent the variance viewed from date 0 of the one-period yield to maturity after one year. The variance calculation depends on assumptions made regarding the interest rate process. If we assume that the true short-term interest rates are normally distributed, then on the binomial lattice, the variance of future one-period rates should be computed by the formula

$$\text{Var}_0\{r_1(1)\} = \sigma_0^2(1) = p(1 - p)[r_{11}(1) - r_{10}(1)]^2 \tag{24.3}$$

where $p = 1/2$ is the probability of an upmove. Substituting for p and taking the square root yields the volatility of one-period rates, $\sigma_0(1)$, as

$$\sigma_0(1) = [r_{11}(1) - r_{10}(1)]/2 \tag{24.4}$$

If instead we assume short-term rates are lognormally distributed, then the logarithms of the rates follow a normal distribution, and the appropriate variance calculation is given by

$$\text{Var}_0\{r_1(1)\} = \sigma_0^2(1) = p(1 - p)[\ln(r_{11}(1) - \ln(r_{10}))]^2$$
$$= p(1 - p)[\ln(r_{11}(1)/(r_{10}))]^2$$

Hence, for $p = 1/2$,

$$\sigma_0(1) = \ln[r_{11}(1)/(r_{10}(1)]/2 \qquad (24.5)$$

A lognormal representation for interest rates may be more attractive than a normal representation, since the latter representation permits negative interest rates. In what follows we shall assume that the volatility numbers given in Exhibit 24.1 correspond to calculations based on the first formula. Specifically, the volatility of one-year rates is assumed to be 0.010 (i.e., 1% per year). The binomial lattice model that results from this assumption was first developed by Ho and Lee.[1] In our case, we have

$$0.01 = [r_{11}(1) - r_{10}(1)]/2 \qquad (24.6)$$

Solving equations (24.2) and (24.6) leads to

$$r_{10}(1) = 0.09$$

$$r_{11}(1) = 0.11$$

The prices of one-year discount bonds in the first period are therefore given by

$$P_{11}(1) = 0.8958$$

$$P_{10}(1) = 0.9139$$

We now proceed to the two-period problem. We have

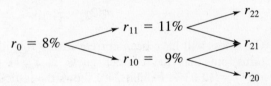

The idea is to identify r_{22}, r_{21}, and r_{20} such that the theoretical value produced by the lattice for the three-year bond matches the observed value and the volatility of yields to maturity of three-period bonds, one period later. Note that we have also required that the lattice reconnect. That is, a downmove followed by an upmove leads to the same value as an upmove followed by a downmove. As a result, after two price moves there are only three possible values. This requirement is equivalent to restricting one-period spot rate volatilities in each time period to be independent of their level of spot rates. As a result, the volatility of one-period rates viewed from node $(1, 1)$ must equal the volatility of spot rates viewed from node $(1, 0)$. That is,

$$\sigma_{11}(1) = \sigma_{10}(1) \qquad (24.7)$$

For the Ho-Lee model, this implies[2]

---

[1] If the volatility numbers were based on equation (24.5), then the model originally developed by Black, Derman, and Toy would be obtained.

[2] For the Black-Derman-Toy model, the path-independent condition that results from equation (24.7) is $\ln(r_{22}/r_{21}) = \ln(r_{21}/r_{20})$, from which $r_{21} = [r_{22}r_{20}]^{1/2}$.

$$[r_{22}(1) - r_{21}(1)]/2 = [r_{21}(1) - r_{20}(1)]/2$$

or
$$r_{21}(1) = [r_{22}(1) + r_{20}(1)]/2$$

(24.8)

For the moment, let us guess values for $r_{22}(1)$ and $r_{20}(1)$. Then $r_{21}(1)$ is computed by equation (24.8). The one-period bond prices could then be computed for each of the nodes in the second period $(P_{2j}(1) = e^{-r_{2j}}$ for $j = 0, 1, 2)$. Given these prices, together with the one-period bond prices in the first period, the two-period bond prices in the first period could be obtained. Specifically,

$$P_{11}(2) = [\tfrac{1}{2}P_{22}(1) + \tfrac{1}{2}P_{21}(1)]P_{11}(1)$$

$$P_{10}(2) = [\tfrac{1}{2}P_{21}(1) + \tfrac{1}{2}P_{20}(1)]P_{10}(1)$$

Once these prices are obtained, the corresponding two-period yields to maturity can be computed $(r_{1j}(2) = -\ln[P_{1j}(2)]/2)$, $\alpha = 1,2$.

Clearly, the values of $P_{11}(2)$ and $P_{10}(2)$ and the equivalent yields to maturity will depend on our original guesses for $r_{22}(1)$ and $r_{20}(1)$. For our guesses to be "right," the theoretical three-period bond price computed using the following equation must match the observed bond price:

$$P_0(3) = [\tfrac{1}{2}P_{11}(2) + \tfrac{1}{2}P_{10}(2)]P_0(1)$$

(24.9)

Further, the volatility of two-period yields to maturity must match the required input. Specifically, the volatility on the lattice is given by

$$\sigma_0(2) = \frac{1}{2}[r_{11}(2) - r_{10}(2)]$$

(24.10)

Our guess will have been correct if this volatility matches the input of 0.009. It turns out that the correct guess is $r_{20}(1) = 8.90\%$, $r_{21}(1) = 10.50\%$, and $r_{22}(1) = 12.03\%$. Exhibit 24.2 shows the lattice of yields to maturity.

Exhibit 24.3 shows the lattice of discount bonds for three periods.

This procedure can be used repeatedly with successively larger maturities. In the above models, the *initial* term structure and *initial* volatilities were sufficient to construct the lattice for all future spot rates and bond prices. Once the lattice is established, then all types of interest rate claims can be readily priced.

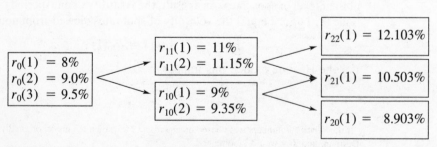

EXHIBIT 24.2   Lattice of Yields of Maturity

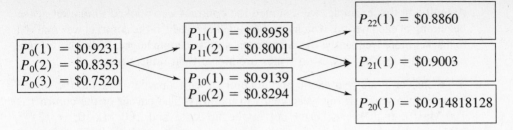

EXHIBIT 24.3   Lattice of Prices of Discount Bonds

EXAMPLE 24.2   1.   Consider a two-period call option that requires delivery of a one-year discount bond. The strike price of the option is set equal to the current forward price. That is, $X = P(0, 3)/P(0, 2) = \$0.9003$. The terminal payouts in the second period are computed by $Max[0, P_{2j}(1) - X]$ for $j = 0$, 1, and 2. Using backward recursion, the call prices can be computed; they are shown in Exhibit 24.4 with the two-period European put option prices.

An alternative way to compute the put price is to use the put-call parity relationship, which for this problem is

$$c_0 = p_0 - P_0(3) - P_0(2)X$$

Substituting the *observed* three-period and two-period bond prices into the above equation, as well as the computed call value, we obtain $p_0 = \$0.003$. Note that when the strike price is taken to be equal to the forward price, the put-call parity condition simplifies to

$$c_0 = p_0 - P_0(3) - P_0(2)P_0(3)/P_0(2) = p_0$$

2.   Consider a futures contract that requires delivery of a one-year discount bond in the second period. The fair futures price is F^*, where

$$F^* = E\{\tilde{P}_2(1)\} = \tfrac{1}{4}P_{20}(1) + \tfrac{1}{2}P_{21}(1) + \tfrac{1}{4}P_{22}(1) = \$0.897$$

Note that the fair futures price differs from the forward price, which is \$0.900.

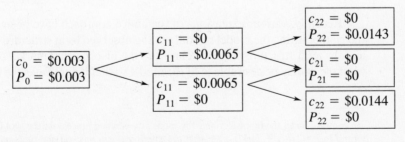

EXHIBIT 24.4   Lattice of Option Prices

Actually, in this example, we assumed the contract was marked to market at the beginning of each period, which corresponded to a year. If the contract was marked to market more frequently, the differences would become larger. With interest rate uncertainty, forward prices on bonds are higher than futures prices.

3.   Consider a one-year exotic option contract with a payout linked to the spread between two-year and one-year yields to maturity. The payout of the contract is $100 \, \text{Max}[0, \, (r_{11}(2) - r_{11}(1)) - X]$ in the up state and $100 \, \text{Max}[0, \, (r_{10}(2) - r_{10}(1)) - X]$ in the down state, where the strike price X equals \$0.025 and interest rates are expressed in decimal form rather than in percentage form. The terminal payouts of this spread option are \$0 in the up state and \$10 in the down state. The value of the claim at date 0 is therefore $\$10 \times 0.5 \times 0.9231 = \$4.62$.

Of course, the construction of the lattice depends critically on the initial term structure and on the initial volatility specification of yields to maturity. Finally, to get the paths reconnecting, the assumption that spot rate volatility depends only on time and not on the level of the spot rate is important.

It can be shown that as the partition gets smaller, the interest rate process under the Ho-Lee assumptions converges to

$$dr(t) = \mu(t) \, dt + \sigma(t) \, dw(t) \qquad (24.11)$$

That is, changes in interest rates are normally distributed.[3]

In the above models, the *initial volatilities of yields* for different maturities were provided. Given the initial term structure and these initial volatilities, an interest rate lattice was constructed. Actually, in the above procedure, the initial conditions were sufficient to uniquely characterize the statistical process for the short-term interest rate over time. In particular, the future short-term rate volatility at each node is completely determined, as are future volatilities of yields to maturity.

EXAMPLE 24.3   Reconsider the lattice shown in Exhibit 24.3. Viewed from node $(1, 1)$, the one-period volatility of the spot interest rate is given by equation (24.4) as 0.008. By construction, this is also the volatility at node $(1, 0)$. Hence, the lattice construction implies that the future one-period volatility will decrease.

Recently, various extensions of the above approach have been developed with the goal of fitting the model not only to the observed term structure of interest rates and the term structure of yield volatilities but also to other market observables. For example, it may be desirable to fit the model so that it duplicates the observed prices

---

[3] In contrast, under the Black-Derman-Toy model, the limiting process for the spot interest rate has the form $d \ln r = [\mu(t) + \alpha(t) \ln r] + \sigma(t) \, dz$, where $\alpha(t)$ is a time-varying function determined by the initial volatilities.

of certain interest rate options. Alternatively, users of the model may want to curtail the future values of short-term rate volatilities. All these efforts allow traders to incorporate a host of market observables and opinions into a model in such a way that the resulting prices of claims are consistent with that information.

EXAMPLE 24.4   **Term Structure Models of Hull and White**

If the initial volatility of yields is specified as a declining function, then the above models have the property that the future short-term spot rate volatility declines over time. Conversely, if the future short-term rate volatility is specified as a constant, then the initial volatility of all yields will be fully determined. This feature may not be desirable. Ideally, we would like to decouple these specifications, so that the volatility of yields can be initialized as well as the future level of short-term spot rate volatility. Hull and White provide a model of accomplishing this by introducing another time-varying function into the analysis. In particular, they assume the risk-neutralized process for the spot interest rate is of the form

$$dr(t) = [\theta(t) - \phi(t)r(t)] \, dt + \sigma(t) \, dw(t)$$

The function $\theta(\cdot)$ is used to match the term structure. The other two time-varying functions can be used to describe the volatility structure. One of these serves the same purposes as in the above analysis. That is, it permits the model to fit current spot rate volatilities. The additional time-varying function enables the future variance of the short-term spot rate to be specified independent of other data. The capability of fitting a third term structure of observables is achieved by using a third branch at each node of the tree.

Criticisms of Term Structure Models

A significant amount of research has been conducted in developing models that are consistent with a wide variety of market observables. While these efforts certainly provide a high cross-sectional accuracy in that they do fit a host of market observables, this fitting exercise is accomplished at the high cost of introducing time-varying functions into the analysis.

   If the parameters of the model change from period to period, then the dynamic behavior of these models could be poor. Dynamic accuracy is important, especially if hedges are to be constructed and replicating strategies implemented. Indeed, the term structure–constrained models have been criticized because of their ad hoc nature. Most implementations of these models work as follows. At each point in time, perhaps at the beginning of each trading day, the initial conditions are determined. This involves establishing the term structure and other relevant prices and volatilities that will be used to calibrate the model. With these inputs, all the time-varying functions are then estimated. An implicit assumption in this part of the analysis is that the time-varying parameters never change. That is, the parameters for date t, viewed from date s, $0 < s < t$, should be identical to parameters used for date t, viewed from date 0. Once the parameters are estimated, the model is used to price new claims and to establish appropriate hedge portfolios. At the beginning of the next day the entire procedure is started again.

The unreasonable feature of this approach is that at every date the entire model is changed. That is, the time-varying functions obtained at the second date may have no bearing on the set obtained earlier. In particular, at the second date, the parameters used for a future date, date t say, may have no bearing to the parameter values used for date t in the prior period.

Put another way, at each date, based on observable information, an entire statistical process for the future risk-neutralized spot rate process is identified. Then, at the next date, that process is thrown away and an entire new process is created, consistent with a new set of observables. With so much parameterization involved to obtain the spot rate dynamics, the intertemporal behavior of these models is suspect. Indeed, many academicians view these models as nothing more than sophisticated **interpolators,** which, at best, may be useful to traders who want to price a derivative that is not actively traded, relative to a large information set that includes the prices of other bonds and options. However, there is a serious concern when it comes to using these models for intertemporal hedging and risk management.

Heath-Jarrow-Morton Models

Heath, Jarrow, and Morton have developed a mechanism for pricing interest rate claims that is analogous to the Black-Scholes stock option model. As in the Black-Scholes model, the only inputs that are necessary are the underlying and a measure of its volatility. Here, the underlying is the entire term structure, and the volatility describes how this term structure fluctuates over time. Thus, the initial term structure is taken as an input in the same way as the stock price is input in the Black-Scholes analysis.

The basic building blocks in the Heath-Jarrow-Morton (HJM) paradigm consist of the set of all forward rates. Divide the time interval into trading intervals of length Δt. In previous chapters we let $f_t[T, T + 1]$ be the forward rate, observed at the beginning of time period t, for the period $[T, T + 1]$, where the width of the period is Δt. Since in this chapter our forward rates will always refer to one-period forward rates, we could simplify the notation. Let $f(t, T)$ be the forward rate at date t for the time period $[T, T + \Delta t]$. We shall also assume that the time indices t and T are expressed in real time as opposed to the time period. That is, the indices t and T are multiples of Δt.

Exhibit 24.5 shows the set of forward rates at time 0 for several periods. Over the time increment Δt, new information arrives that causes the term structure to change. Let $f(t + \Delta t, T)$ be the new forward rate at date $t + \Delta t$ for the period $[T, T + \Delta t]$. Exhibit 24.6 shows the set of old forward rates (solid lines) and the new forward rates (dashed lines) for the different time increments.

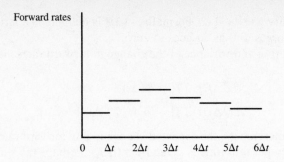

EXHIBIT 24.5   Single-Period Forward Rates at Date 0

The actual magnitude of the change in each forward rate may depend on the forward rate itself, on its maturity date, and on other factors. The change in forward rates need not be constant for all maturities. Let $\Delta f(t, T)$ represent the change in the forward rate for the time period $[T, T + \Delta t]$ from date t to date $t + \Delta t$. That is

$$\Delta f(t, T) = f(t + \Delta t, T) - f(t, T) \qquad (24.12)$$

Recall that the Black-Scholes analysis began by specifying a statistical process for the underyling stock. In the same way, the HJM analysis begins by specifying how these changes in forward rates evolve over time. We start with an initial forward rate curve, $\{f(0, T), T = 0, \Delta t, 2\,\Delta t, \ldots, n\,\Delta t\}$, chosen to match the observed term structure at date 0. Note that $f(0, 0)$ is just the spot rate for the immediate period. Over each time increment, the forward rates change as follows:

$$f(t + \Delta t, T) = \begin{cases} f(t, T) + \sigma_f(t, T)\sqrt{\Delta t} & \text{with probability } p(\Delta t) \\ f(t, T) - \sigma_f(t, T)\sqrt{\Delta t} & \text{with probability } 1 - p(\Delta t) \end{cases} \qquad (24.13)$$

where $p(\Delta t) = 1/2 + o(\Delta t)$

Each forward rate can change to one of two values. The magnitude of the change is given by $\sigma_f(t, T)\sqrt{\Delta t}$. The value of $\sigma_f(t, T)$ could depend on information available at date t. We shall have more to say about this later. The probability of an upmove is $p(\Delta t)$. This value depends on the width of the time increment and has the property that when the time increment gets very small (i.e., as Δt approaches

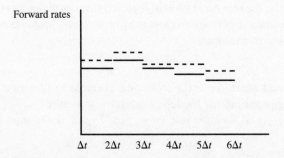

EXHIBIT 24.6   Single-Period Forward Rates at Date Δt

0), the probability goes to $1/2$. Formally, $o(\Delta t)$ is defined as a term that depends on Δt and converges to 0 as Δt goes to zero.

The expectation and variance of the change in forward rates viewed from date t are given by

$$E_t[\Delta f(t, T)] = o(\Delta t) \tag{24.14}$$

$$\text{Var}_t[\Delta f(t, T)] = \sigma_f^2(t, T) \, \Delta t + o(\Delta t) \tag{24.15}$$

For small time increments, the expected change in any forward rate is almost zero and the volatility per unit time is given by $\sigma_f(t, T)$. Perhaps the simplest volatility structure is obtained by letting $\sigma_f(t, T)$ be a constant, σ say, for all maturities, T. In this case, all forward rates have the same volatility, so the entire forward rate curve is continuously subjected to upward or downward parallel shocks. In this case, since the magnitude of the shock is independent of the level of the forward rate, it is permissible for rates to become negative.

A more realistic volatility structure for forward rates is obtained by permitting volatility to depend on the forward rate's maturity, namely, $T - t$. For example,

$$\sigma_f(t, T) = \sigma \, e^{-\kappa(T-t)} \tag{24.16}$$

This exponentially dampened volatility structure exploits the fact that near-term forward rates are more volatile than distant forward rates. However, as in the constant volatility structure, the exact magnitude of volatility is independent of the level of the forward rate. Other forward rate volatility functions that have intuitive appeal include

$$\sigma_f(t, T) = \sigma f(t, T)^\gamma \tag{24.17}$$

$$\sigma_f(t, T) = \sigma r(t)^\gamma e^{-\kappa(T-t)} \tag{24.18}$$

The structure described by equation (24.17) permits the volatility to depend on the level of the forward rate. The structure described by equation (24.18) permits the volatility to vary according to the spot interest rate and the forward rate maturity. Note that when $T = t$, the volatility reduces to that of the short-term spot rate. For $\gamma = 0$, equations (24.17) and (24.18) state that the volatility of the spot rate is constant, as in the Vasicek model. For $\gamma = 0.5$, the volatility of the spot rate is given by the square root model, as in the single-factor Cox-Ingersoll-Ross model. Finally, for $\gamma = 1$, the volatility is proportional to the level of the spot rate, as in most implementations of the Black-Derman-Toy model.

Unfortunately, the representation of forward rates as given by equation (24.13) is inappropriate since it permits riskless arbitrage strategies to be initiated. This is best illustrated by an example.

EXAMPLE 24.5   Heath, Jarrow, and Morton use the following example to illustrate why the above process is not appropriate for modeling the term structure.

Suppose the initial forward rate curve $f(0, T)$ is flat and equal to 0.10 for all T. Let

$$f(\Delta t, T) = \begin{cases} 0.12 & \text{with probability } p \\ 0.08 & \text{with probability } 1 - p \end{cases}$$

where Δt is one year. Bond prices can easily be computed under the term structures at date 0 and at date Δt. For example, at date 0, the price of a one-year bond is $P(0, 1) = e^{-0.10} = 0.9048374$. Under this structure an arbitrage profit can be generated. Specifically, buy n_1 bonds maturing at time Δt, sell n_2 bonds maturing at time $2\Delta t$, and buy n_3 bonds maturing at time $3\Delta t$, where $n_1 = 0.452509559$, $n_2 = 1$, and $n_3 = 0.552474949$. The initial value of this portfolio is 0, and a final positive value of 0.000180938 is obtained regardless of which state occurs. Hence, a parallel shift in the term structure as given above is not admissible.

Since equation (24.13) is not appropriate, it needs to be modified in such a way that riskless arbitrage will not be present. The idea is to add an adjustment term, $\mu_f(t, T) \Delta t$ say, that removes all possible arbitrage opportunities. In particular, consider the process

$$f(t + \Delta t, T) = \begin{cases} f(t, T) + \mu_f(t, T) \Delta t + \sigma_f(t, T)\sqrt{\Delta t} & \text{with prob. } p(\Delta t) \\ f(t, T) + \mu_f(t, T) \Delta t - \sigma_f(t, T)\sqrt{\Delta t} & \text{with prob. } 1 - p(\Delta t) \end{cases}$$

where $p(\Delta t) = 1/2 + o(\Delta t)$ (24.19)

The expectation and variance of the change in forward rates are given by

$$E_t[\Delta f(t, T)] = \mu_f(t, T) \Delta t + o(\Delta t) \tag{24.20}$$

$$\text{Var}_t[\Delta f(t, T)] = \sigma_f^2(t, T) \Delta t + o(\Delta t) \tag{24.21}$$

Note that the adjustment leaves the variance unchanged but changes the expected forward rates over the period.

Recall from our discussion in Chapter 23 that to avoid arbitrage opportunities, it must be the case that a probability measure exists under which all claims can be priced as if the local expectations hypothesis holds. We shall replace the true probability, $p(\Delta t)$, by $\theta(\Delta t)$ and construct the adjustment term, $\mu_f(t, T) \Delta t$, so that the local expectations hypothesis holds under the new probabilities. If this can be done, then our original process is arbitrage-free. Assume $\theta(\Delta t) = 1/2$. Then Heath, Jarrow, and Morton have shown that the adjustment term is given by[4]

$$\mu_f(t, T) \Delta t = \tanh(\omega) \times \sigma_f(t, T)\sqrt{\Delta t} \tag{24.22}$$

where

$$\omega = \left[\int_{t+\Delta t}^{T} \sigma_f(t, u) \, du \right] \sqrt{\Delta t}$$

and

$$\tanh(\omega) = \frac{e^{\omega} - e^{-\omega}}{e^{\omega} + e^{-\omega}}$$

If we pretend the probability of an upmove is $1/2$, and define $\mu_f(t, T)$ as above, then

---

[4] A proof of this result is given in Appendix 24A.

the price we obtain for any interest rate claim on the lattice using the local expectations hypothesis is a fair price that does not permit riskless arbitrage. If the price is set at any other value, then arbitrage is possible.

EXAMPLE 24.6 Assume $f(0, T) = 10\%$, a volatility structure $\sigma_f(t, T) = \sigma = 0.02$, and a time partition $\Delta t = 1$ year. Then

$$\omega = \int_{t+1}^{T} \sigma \, du = (T - t - 1)\sigma$$

Here $\mu_f(0, T) = \tanh(\omega) \times \sigma$. In particular, the adjustment terms at date 0 can be computed. The specific terms for the first three forward rates are

$$\mu_f(0, 1) = \tanh(0) \times (0.02) = 0$$

$$\mu_f(0, 2) = \tanh(0.02) \times (0.02) = 0.0004$$

$$\mu_f(0, 3) = \tanh(0.04) \times (0.02) = 0.0008$$

EXAMPLE 24.7 Consider a three-period HJM model. The volatility structure is given by equation (24.18) with $\gamma = 1$ and $\kappa = 0.02$. The time increment is one year, and the initial term structure is taken to be flat at 4 percent. Selected forward rates for this proportional volatility structure are shown in Exhibit 24.7. The computations are based on equation (24.22).

Only a few spot and forward rates are provided. Of course, the entire term structure at each date could have been computed. This feature has the advantage over the Black-Derman-Toy paradigm because the term structure at each node need not be built up sequentially. That is, at date 1, the entire term structure for all future dates can be immediately computed.

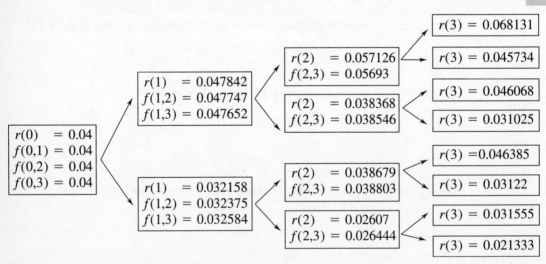

EXHIBIT 24.7   HJM Lattice for the Term Structure in Example 24.7

Note that in the HJM paradigm the calculation of contingent claims requires knowledge of the initial term structure, $\{f(0, T)$ for $T = 0, \Delta t, 2\Delta t, \ldots n\,\Delta t\}$; the volatility structure, $\sigma_f(t, T)$ of forward rates; and the adjustment term, $\mu_f(t, T)$. However, from equation (24.22) we see that the adjustment term is completely determined by the volatility structure. Hence, as in the Black-Scholes analysis, the important inputs are just the underlying term structure and its volatility.

Continuous Time Limit of the Discrete Model

As the partition Δt in the above lattice becomes smaller, the drift term, $\mu_f(t, T)$, converges to the following expression:[5]

$$\mu_f(t, T) = \sigma_f(t, T)\sigma_p(t, T) \tag{24.23}$$

where

$$\sigma_p(t, T) = \int_t^T \sigma_f(t, u)\,du \tag{24.24}$$

Actually, $\sigma_p(t, T)$ has an economic interpretation. It is the date t volatility of a discount bond that matures at date T.

EXAMPLE 24.8   **Constant Volatility Structure**

For the constant volatility structure of forward rates, $\sigma_f(t, T) = \sigma$. Hence,

$$\sigma_p(t, T) = \int_t^T \sigma_f(t, u)\,du = \int_t^T \sigma\,du = \sigma(T - t)$$

The drift term as given in equation (24.23) is

$$\mu_f(t, T) = \sigma_f(t, T)\sigma_p(t, T) = \sigma^2(T - t)$$

Interest rate claims can then be priced under the local expectations hypothesis, using the arbitrage-free process for forward rates given by

$$\Delta f(t, T) = \sigma^2(T - t)\,\Delta t + \sigma\,\Delta w(t) \tag{24.25}$$

Exponentially Dampened Volatility Structure

For the exponentially dampened volatility structure, $\sigma_f(t, T) = \sigma e^{-\kappa(T-t)}$. Hence,

$$\sigma_p(t, T) = \int_t^T \sigma_t(t, u)\,du = \int_t^T \sigma\,e^{-\kappa(T-u)}\,du = \frac{\sigma}{\kappa}[1 - e^{-\kappa(T-t)}]$$

and

$$\mu_f(t, T) = \sigma_f(t, T)\sigma_p(t, T) = \frac{\sigma^2}{\kappa}[e^{-\kappa(T-t)} - e^{-2\kappa(T-t)}]$$

---

[5] A proof of this result is provided in Appendix 24A.

The evolution of forward prices is given by

$$\Delta f(t, T) = \frac{\sigma^2}{\kappa} [e^{-\kappa(T-t)} - e^{-2\kappa(T-t)}] \Delta t + \sigma e^{-\kappa(T-t)} \Delta w(t) \qquad (24.26)$$

We should emphasize that the processes given in equations (24.25) and (24.26) are not the true processes of forward rates. Rather, they represent the risk-neutralized processes under which all interest rates can be priced as if the local expectations hypothesis holds.

EXAMPLE 24.9   Continuing Example 24.7, we see that the lattice representation of forward rates in Exhibit 24.7 has the property that it does not admit arbitrage opportunities. Consider the problem of pricing a one-year cash-settled yield option based on the two-year yields to maturity after one year. The terminal payout is given by $C = \$1000 \times \text{Max}[y_1(2) - X, 0]$, where $y_1(2)$ is the yield to maturity on a two-year discount bond at date 1. At the up node the yield is $y_1(2) = (4.7937 + 4.7842)/2 = 4.78895\%$, while at the down node the value is 3.20475%. Assume the strike price is taken to be the current yield to maturity of 4 percent. Then the value of this claim is $\$1000[0.78895 \times 0.5 + 0 \times 0.5]e^{-0.04} = \$379.01$.

Path Dependence and State Variables

In the HJM paradigm, the future term structure may depend on the entire path of prices since the term structure was initialized. For example, the interest rate at date $(t + \Delta t)$ may not only depend on its level at date t but on previous levels along its path going all the way back to date 0. Moreover, the interest rate may not act as the single state variable. That is, knowledge of the interest rate, $r(t)$, at date t may not be sufficient for the determination of all the forward rates at date t. Indeed, knowledge of many points on the term structure at date t may not be sufficient for the identification of other forward rates at that time. This path-dependent property, together with the fact that there may not be a finite number of state variables, creates pricing difficulties. In particular, lattice procedures may not recombine, and it may be necessary to keep track of all paths. A lattice with 20 partitions, for example, will have $2^{20} = 1,048,576$ unique paths to terminal nodes. If the partition is increased to 21, then the number of unique paths doubles to 2,097,152. This exploding lattice could cause computational problems, especially if long-term interest rate claims, such as mortgage-related products, need to be priced and a fine partition over long periods is required.

Fortunately, there are some cases where simplifications do occur. In particular, if the volatility structure of forward rates is restricted to certain classes, the path dependence is eliminated. We consider some of these cases.

The Generalized Vasicek Models

If the volatility structures of forward rates are constant, or exponentially damp-ened, then the path dependence is eliminated and simplifications occur. Indeed, for these structures it can be shown that given the spot interest rate at any date t, the entire set of forward rates can be recovered. In particular,

$$f(t, T) = f(0, T) + e^{\kappa(T-t)}[r(t) - f(0, t) + \beta(t, T)\phi(t)] \qquad (24.27)$$

where $\beta(t, T) = \dfrac{1}{\kappa}[1 - e^{-\kappa(T-t)}]$

$$\phi(t) = \frac{\sigma^2}{2\kappa}[1 - e^{-2\kappa t}]$$

In addition, the bond prices at date t are related to the state variables through the pricing equation:

$$P(t, T) = \frac{P(0, T)}{P(0, t)}\, e^{-\beta(t, T)[r(t) - f(0, t)] - \beta^2(t, T)\phi(t)/2} \qquad (24.28)$$

Equation (24.28) states that bond prices at date t, equal their original forward prices, multiplied by an adjusting factor which depends on the interest rate that occurs at date t. Using equation (24.28) modified duration and convexity measures can be obtained for straight bonds. For example, it can be easily shown that at date t, the modified duration of a discount bond that matures at date T is $\mathbb{D}_m$ where

$$\mathbb{D}_m = \beta(t, T)$$

As a practical matter, equations 24.27 and 24.28 are very useful. They suggest that we need only track the spot interest rate over time. Actually, for the exponen-tially dampened volatility structure, the exact dynamics of the spot rate can be established. In particular, it can be shown that

$$dr(t) = \mu(r, t)dt + \sigma\, dw(t) \qquad (24.29)$$

where

$$\mu(r, t) = -\kappa[r(t) - f(0, t)] + \frac{\partial}{\partial t}f(0, t) + \phi(t) \qquad (24.30)$$

Equation (24.29) characterizes the evolution of the interest rate under the risk neutralized process. As a result, if a lattice can be developed for equation (24.29) then at each interest rate node, the entire term structure can be recovered using equations (24.27) and (24.28). Also, since the underlying process is the risk neutralized process, claims can be priced as if the local expectations hypothesis holds true.

The resulting models are called generalized Vasicek models. Like the Vasicek model, discussed in the previous chapter, the spot rate volatility is a constant. However, unlike the Vasicek model, the drift term is specified so that it fully incorporates information on the existing yield curve.

It can be shown that, viewed from date 0, the interest rate at date t under the risk neutralized process is a normal random variable with expected value and variance given by

$$E_0\{\tilde{r}(t)\} = f(0, t) + \frac{\sigma^2}{2\kappa^2}[1 - e^{-\kappa t}]^2 \tag{24.31}$$

$$\text{Var}_0\{\tilde{r}(t)\} = \phi(t) \tag{24.32}$$

Note that under the risk neutralized process the forward rate is not an unbiased estimate of the expected spot rate in the future. However, if there is no uncertainty, that is $\sigma = 0$, then the future spot rate $r(t)$ does equal the forward rate. Since the distribution is easily characterized, it is not surprising that analytical solutions can be obtained for almost all common interest rate claims such as futures prices, options on bonds, forward rate agreements, options on interest rates and options on futures. Below we provide a few examples.

The Futures Price on a Discount Bond

Here the futures contract settles at date s while the underlying bond settles at date $T^*(T^* \geq s)$. The theoretical price is $FU(0)$, where

$$FU(0) = \frac{P(0, T^*)}{P(0, s)}e^{-\beta(s, T^*)\eta(s)} \tag{24.33}$$

We already defined $\beta(s, T^*)$ and

$$\eta(s) = \frac{\sigma^2}{2\kappa^2}[1 - e^{-2\kappa s}]^2$$

Note that the first term in equation (24.30) is the forward price of the underlying bond. Hence, the futures price equals the forward price multiplied by an adjustment term that is strictly smaller than one, unless the volatility structure is zero (in which case there is no interest rate uncertainty).

Options on Futures Contracts

Consider an option contract on the above futures contract. Assume the option contract matures at date τ, where $\tau \leq s \leq T^*$. The strike price of the option is X. Then

$$C(0) = P(0, \tau)\frac{P(0, T^*)}{P(0, s)}e^{q+\delta}N(d_1 + \delta/v) - P(0, \tau)XN(d_2 + \delta/v) \tag{24.34}$$

where $d_1 = \dfrac{\ln[\{P(0, T^*)/P(0, s)\}/X] + \mu + v^2]}{v}$

$d_2 = d_1 - v$

$q = \mu + v^2/2$

$\mu = \dfrac{\phi(t)}{2}[\beta^2(\tau, T^*) - \beta^2(\tau, s)]$

$v^2 = [\beta(\tau, T^*) - \beta(\tau, s)]^2\phi(\tau)$

$\phi(\tau) = \dfrac{\sigma^2}{2\kappa}[1 - e^{-2\kappa\tau}]$

Equation (24.34) can be used to price options on T-bill futures contracts.

Options on Discount Bonds

If the settlement date of the forward contract, s, coincides with the expiration date of the option, τ, then the European option on the futures contract reduces to an option on a discount bond and equation (24.34) reduces to the following model, first developed by Jamshidian.

$$C(0) = P(0, T^*)N(d_1) - XP(0, \tau)N(d_2) \tag{24.35}$$

where $\quad d_1 = \dfrac{\ln[\{P(0, T^*)/P(0, \tau)\}/X] + v^{2/2}]}{v}$

$$d_2 = d_1 - v$$

$$v^2 = \beta(\tau, T^*)^2 \phi(\tau)$$

Equation (24.35) can be used to price options embedded in callable discount bonds.[6]

Forward Rate Agreements

The fair price of a forward rate (FRA) agreement to purchase a yield that is determined by the τ rate that exists at date s is given by $fr(0)$, where

$$fr(0) = f_0[s, s + \tau] + \frac{\beta^2(s, s + \tau)\phi(s)}{2\tau} \tag{24.36}$$

Note that the first term is the forward rate for the period. That is, it is the rate that can be locked into today for a loan that begins at date s and ends at date $(s + \tau)$. The above contract, of course, is a cash-settled contract with a terminal payout at date s that is linked to the actual τ yield at date s.

The fair price of a futures contract to purchase the τ yield at date s, $fu(0)$ say, is given by

$$fu(0) = fr(0) + \frac{\beta(s, s + \tau)\eta(s)}{\tau} \tag{24.37}$$

One could use equation (24.37) to price Eurodollar futures contracts provided the initial term structure corresponded to the LIBOR curve rather than the Treasury curve.

Options on Yields

Consider the price of an option on a yield. The expiration date is s, and the terminal payout is based on the yield of a τ-year discount bond at that date. As before, the

---

[6] Actually, Jamshidian has shown that the equation can be modified so as to be useful for pricing options embedded in callable coupon bonds.

strike price is X. The fair price of the call is

$$C(0) = P(0, s)v[M(q) - q] \tag{24.38}$$

where $v^2 = \dfrac{\beta^2(s, s + \tau)\phi(s)}{\tau^2}$

$q = [X - f_0[s, s + \tau] - v^2\tau/2]/v$

and $M(q) = \displaystyle\int_{-\infty}^{q} N(x)\, dx$

Pricing American Claims Under the Generalized Vasicek Model

While analytical solutions do exist for many interest rate claims, others can be approximated using simple lattice procedures. These lattices also permit American claims to be priced. The lattice procedure is quite similar to the one we used for the Cox, Ingersoll, and Ross models in Chapter 23.

Actually, instead of taking the spot interest rate as the state variable, it is easier to work with the transformed variable, $Y(t)$, defined as

$$Y(t) = R(t) - \Phi(t) \tag{24.39}$$

where $R(t) = r(t) - f(0, t)$ \hfill (24.40)

and $\Phi(t) = \dfrac{\sigma^2}{2\kappa}\left[t + \dfrac{e^{-2\kappa t}}{2\kappa} - \dfrac{1}{2\kappa} \right]$

We now partition the interval $[0, T]$ into n subintervals each of length $\Delta t = T/n$ and set up a reconnecting lattice for the Y-variable. Let $Y_0 = 0$ be the initial values of the approximating process with $\Phi_0 = 0$. In each time increment the Y-variable can move from its location to one of two points. Specifically, given the value at time $i\Delta t$ is Y, then the two possible values at time $(i + 1)\Delta t$ are Y^+ or Y^- where

$$Y \left\langle \begin{array}{l} Y^+ = Y + \sigma\sqrt{\Delta t} \\[2mm] Y^- = Y - \sigma\sqrt{\Delta t} \end{array} \right.$$

Given the lattice of the Y values, the spot rates can be recovered. In particular, the spot rate at date $t = i\Delta t$, $r(t)$ say, when $Y(t) = Y$ is given by

$$r(t) = Y + f(0, t) + \Phi(t)$$

The second step is to compute the probabilities at each node. The probability of an up-jump, p say, is given by

$$p = 1/2 - \frac{\mu(R, t)\sqrt{\Delta t}}{2\sigma}$$

where $\mu(R, t) = \kappa R(t) + \phi(t)$.

As long as this probability is between 0 and 1 there is no problem. This is the usual case, especially if the time increment, Δt, is small. However, if the probability falls outside this range, then an adjusted jump may be necessary. To illustrate this, assume $p > 1$. In this case, replace the normal jump

$$Y \begin{cases} Y^+ = Y + \sigma\sqrt{\Delta t} \\ Y^- = Y - \sigma\sqrt{\Delta t} \end{cases}$$

with

$$Y \begin{cases} Y^{++} = Y + 2\sigma\sqrt{\Delta t} \\ Y^+ = Y + \sigma\sqrt{\Delta t} \end{cases}$$

and compute p, the probability of an up-jump to Y^{++}, as

$$p = \frac{\mu(R, t)\sqrt{\Delta t}}{\sigma} - 1$$

Alternatively, if $p < 0$ then replace the usual jump with the jump

$$Y \begin{cases} Y^- = Y - \sigma\sqrt{\Delta t} \\ Y^{--} = Y - 2\sigma\sqrt{\Delta t} \end{cases}$$

where $p = 2 + \dfrac{\mu(R, t)\sqrt{\Delta t}}{\sigma}$ is the probability of a jump to Y^-.

We illustrate this procedure with a 5 period example.

EXAMPLE 24.10   Assume the yield curve is flat at 10%, and that $\kappa = 0.20$, $\sigma = 0.01$ and $\Delta t = 1$ year. A five year option on a six year discount bond is to be priced. The strike price is the current forward price. The face value of the discount bond is $100,000. The strike price is $X = [P(0, 6)/P(0, 5)]100,000 = \$904,837$.

The Y-lattice is shown in Exhibit 24.8, together with the Φ-values for each time period.

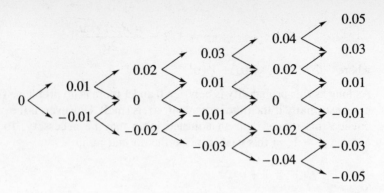

EXHIBIT 24.8   The Y-lattice

$$\Phi(t) = \frac{\sigma^2}{2\kappa}\left[t + \frac{e^{-2\kappa t}}{2\kappa} - \frac{1}{2\kappa}\right]$$

Hence $\Phi(0) = 0,\quad \Phi(1) = 0.00004395,\quad \Phi(2) = 0.00015583,$
$\Phi(3) = 0.00081325,\quad \Phi(4) = 0.00050119,\quad \Phi(5) = 0.00070959.$

Now $R(t) = Y(t) + \Phi(t)$

and $r(t) = Y(t) + f(0, t) + \Phi(t).$

The interest rate lattice, computed from the Y-lattice, is shown in Exhibit 24.9. Under each interest rate is the probability for an up-jump. These values are in parentheses.

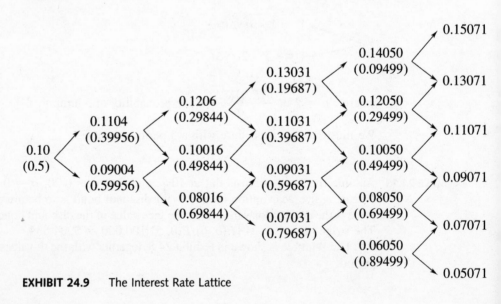

EXHIBIT 24.9   The Interest Rate Lattice

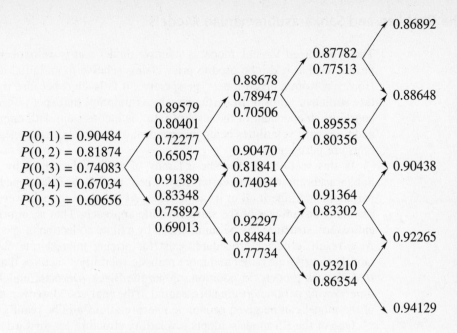

EXHIBIT 24.10   The Discount Function Lattice

The lattice of selected discount bond prices are shown in Exhibit 24.10. At each node, the top value is the price of a single period bond, and the values below this number represent the prices of bonds with longer maturities.

Exhibit 24.11 shows the lattice of prices of a five period at the money European call option on a bond that matures in period 6. As the partition is refined, prices of European options, for example, do converge to their analytical values. The lattice permits American style contracts to be computed.

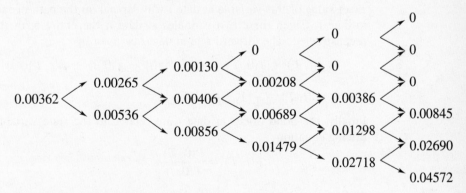

EXHIBIT 24.11   Option Price Lattice

The Ritchken and Sankarasubramanian Models

The generalized Vasicek model is a simple model that is well-specified and quite flexible in that it can be used to price claims relative to an initial term structure. However, from a practitioners' perspective, it falls short because it does not capture sufficient realism. In particular, the assumption that spot rate volatilities are constant, independent of the level of rates, is inconsistent with empirical data. In addition, with volatilities being independent of the level of rates, negative forward rates are permissible.

In this section we describe a family of models developed by Ritchken and Sankarasubramanian (hereafter RS). Their models are developed in the HJM paradigm and inherit all of its advantages. At the same time, however, they retain the many advantages of the **state variable** approach. That is, information on the entire term structure can be summarized by a finite collection of specific variables. As a result, efficient procedures exist for pricing interest rate claims. The RS models incorporate richer and more realistic volatility structures than the generalized Vasicek models. In addition, unlike the Black, Derman, and Toy approach, time-varying parameters are not essential in the analysis. Moreover, the parameters of the model can be given economic interpretations and be readily estimated.

One of the RS models adopts a volatility structure for forward rates given by equation (24.18). For this structure, it can be shown that the dynamics of all forward rates can be linked to exactly two state variables. All future forward rates and bond prices are completely determined at date t, once the levels of the spot rate, $r(t)$, and a path-dependent statistic, $\phi(t)$, are known. The exact specification of the second state variable, $\phi(t)$ is

$$\phi(t) = \int_0^t r(u)^{2\gamma} e^{-2\kappa(t-u)} \, du \qquad (24.41)$$

Note that as interest rates change, the statistic $\phi(t)$ will change. That is, the exact value of this variable at date t will depend on the path of rates from date 0 to date t. Given these two variables at date t, the entire term structure can be reconstructed. The forward rate at date t is given by

$$f(t, T) = f(0, T) + e^{-\kappa(T-t)}[r(t) - f(0, t) + \beta(t, T)\phi(t)] \qquad (24.42)$$

where $\beta(t, T) = \dfrac{1}{\kappa}[1 - e^{-\kappa(T-t)}]$

Finally, the bond prices at date t are related to the state variables through the pricing equation

$$P(t, T) = \frac{P(0, T)}{P(0, t)} e^{-\beta(t, T)[r(t) - f(0, t)] - \beta^2(t, T)\phi(t)/2} \qquad (24.43)$$

At first glance, this equation looks exactly the same as equation (24.28). Indeed, if $\gamma = 0$, then the two equations are identical. However, unlike the exponentially dampened case, where the ϕ variable at date t was a specific constant, in the case when $\gamma \neq 0$ the ϕ variable is a term that is determined by the path of spot interest values over the period $[0, t]$. As a result, knowledge of the spot rate $r(t)$ by itself is not sufficient to characterize the term structure at date t. However, the spot rate $r(t)$ and $\phi(t)$ are sufficient to completely characterize the term structure. RS show that the dynamics of the two state variables are given by

$$dr(t) = \mu(r, \phi, t) \, dt + \sigma[r(t)]^\gamma \, dw(t) \tag{24.44}$$

$$d\phi(t) = [\sigma^2[r(t)]^{2\gamma} - 2\kappa\phi(t)] \, dt \tag{24.45}$$

where $\quad \mu(r, \phi, t) = \kappa[f(0, t) - r(t)] + \dfrac{\partial}{\partial t} f(0, t) + \phi(t) \tag{24.46}$

Unfortunately, analytical solutions for interest rate claims are not readily available. However, the RS model can be easily implemented using lattice procedures. Equation (24.43), however, does allow modified duration and convexity measures to be obtained for straight bonds. For example, it can be easily shown that at date t, the modified duration of a discount bond that matures at date T is $\mathbb{D}_m$ where

$$\mathbb{D}_m = \beta(t, T)$$

The Proportional RS Model

We describe a lattice procedure developed by Li, Ritchken, and Sankarasubramanian, which can be used to implement the RS models. To make matters specific, we consider the proportional model where $\gamma = 1$ in equation (24.18). Like the binomial lattice approximation of the single-factor CIR model, the procedure begins by transforming the interest rate process into a form that has constant volatility. For the proportional model where $\gamma = 1$, the appropriate transform is

$$Y(t) = g(r(t)) = \ln r(t)/\sigma \tag{24.47}$$

Given any value of $Y(t)$, the corresponding value of $r(t)$ is given by

$$r(t) = e^{\sigma Y(t)} \tag{24.48}$$

We now partition the interval $[0, T]$ into n subintervals, each of length $\Delta t = T/n$, and set up a reconnecting lattice for the Y variable. Let (Y_0, ϕ_0) be the initial values of the approximating process, with $Y_0 = g(r_0)$ and $\phi_0 = 0$. In each time increment Y can move to one of two points. Specifically, Y_i can move to Y_{i+1}^+ or Y_{i+1}^-, where

$$Y_i \begin{cases} Y_{i+1}^+ = Y_i + \sqrt{\Delta t} \\ Y_{i+1}^- = Y_i - \sqrt{\Delta t} \end{cases}$$

Let $r_i = \exp^{\sigma Y_i}$. Then, on the interest rate lattice, we have

$$r_i = e^{\sigma Y_i} \begin{cases} r_{i+1}^+ = e^{\sigma Y_{i+1}^+} = e^{\sigma(r_i + \sqrt{\Delta t})} \\ r_{i+1}^- = e^{\sigma Y_{i+1}^-} = e^{\sigma(r_i - \sqrt{\Delta t})} \end{cases}$$

The probability of an upmove is given by

$$p(r_i, \phi_i, i\,\Delta t) = \frac{\mu(r_i, \phi_i, i\Delta t)\Delta t - r_i + r_{i+1}^-}{r_{i+1}^+ - r_{i+1}^-} \tag{24.49}$$

where $\mu(r_i, \phi_i, i\,\Delta t)$ is the drift term in equation (24.46).

The number of unique ϕ values on the lattice at time $i\,\Delta t$, if j upmoves have occurred, is given by the number of distinct paths that lead to node (i, j). This number is $\binom{i}{j}$ which can be very large, especially when i is large and the number of upmoves, j, is near $i/2$. Rather than keep track of all these values, we identify the two paths from the origin to each vertex (i, j), which yield the maximum and minimum values for the state variable. Let $\overline{\phi}_{i+1,j}$ and $\phi_{i+1,j}$ represent these two values. Clearly, these two values will vary for each node, and only on the edges of the lattice will these two values equal each other. In general, the maximum ϕ value at node (i, j) occurs when the interest rate path jumps up j consecutive times and then jumps down $(i - j)$ consecutive times. The minimum ϕ value occurs when the interest rate moves down the first j periods and then moves up the remaining $(i - j)$ periods. At each node of the lattice, the interval between the largest and smallest ϕ values is partitioned into m equidistant points. Let $\phi_{ij}(k), k = 1, 2, \ldots, m$ represent the m points at a particular node (i, j). Exhibit 24.12 illustrates the lattice structure where $m = 5$. From node (i, j) the interest rate can either move up to node $(i + 1, j + 1)$ or move down to node $(i + 1, j)$. The probability of an upmove depends on $r_{i,j}$ as well as on the second state variable and can be computed from equation (24.49).

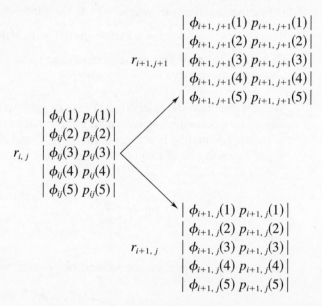

EXHIBIT 24.8   The Jump Structure for the Lattice Implementation of the Proportional RS Models

Given the levels of the two state variables at any node, we can compute the term structure using equation (24.43). Moreover, the value of the probability of an upmove can be computed at each $(r_{ij}, \phi_{ij}^{(k)})$ combination.

To illustrate this process, assume the initial term structure is flat at 10 percent. The volatility structure for forward rates is given by equation (24.18), with $\gamma = 1$, $\sigma = 10\%$, and $\kappa = 0\%$. The time partition Δt is one-third of a year. Exhibit 24.13 shows the evolution of the state variables on the lattice over the first three time periods. At each node, the interest rate is indicated as well as the ϕ values. In this example, the maximum number of ϕ values at any node is restricted to 3. In particular, given the maximum and minimum ϕ value to a node, we can take the third value to be the midpoint. Along the edges of the lattice, there is, of course, only one ϕ value at each node. The lattice shows the interest rate at each node together with the ϕ variables. The interest rate values are in percentage units, while the ϕ values are in percentage squared units. The lattice is constructed in a forward direction using the transform in equation (24.47). As an example, in the first period $r = 0.10$, and hence $y = \ln(r)/\sigma = -23.0258$; with $\Delta t = 1/3$, $y^+ = y_0 + \sqrt{1/3} = -22.4485$. Hence, $r^+ = \exp(\sigma y^+) = 10.59434\%$. The initial value of ϕ is 0. We compute the ϕ value at the next time increment using a discrete approximation to equation (24.40). In general, given (r, ϕ), the next ϕ is given by

$$\phi_{\text{next}} = \phi + [\sigma^2 r^2 - 2\kappa\phi]\,\Delta t \tag{24.50}$$

Using this equation, with $\phi = 0$, leads to an updates value of ϕ, of 0.333. Since ϕ is locally deterministic, this value is used in the up and down node. In this example, after three periods, there are 8 distinct (r, ϕ) states.

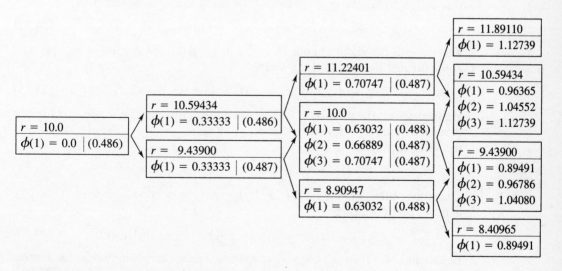

EXHIBIT 24.13   Construction of the Lattice

The probability values are shown for state in parenthesis. For example, the probability of an upmove at the first node is 0.486. In this example, the probability values do not vary that much. This is due to the fact that the initial term structure was taken to be flat, and the parameter, κ, was taken to be zero. The value κ is referred to as the **mean reversion parameter**. As its value increases, the probabilities of upmoves increase for low-interest rate nodes and decrease for high-interest rate nodes. As the Δt partition gets finer, the lattice converges to the continuous time dynamics given in equations (24.44) and (24.45).

Once the lattice for the state variables is constructed, we can price interest rate claims. In particular, at each (r, ϕ) location we can compute the entire term structure using equation (24.43). If the time period at which the valuation is done coincides with the expiration date of the claim, then we can establish the terminal value of the claim. Once this is done, we can use the usual backward recursion procedure to obtain the fair value of the claim.

Let $C_{i+1, j}(k), k = 1, \ldots, m$ be the value of the claim at node $(i + 1, j)$ when the interest rate is $r_{i+1, j}$ and the ϕ variable is $\phi_{i+1, j}(k)$. Similarly, let $C_{i+1, j+1}(k)$ be the value of the claim at node $(i + 1, j + 1)$ when the interest rate is $r_{i+1, j+1}$ and the ϕ value is $\phi_{ij}(k)$. If the values of the claims at these nodes are known, then we can obtain the values of the interest rate claim at node (i, j), conditional on the ϕ values. In particular, assume $C_{ij}(k)$ is to be computed. The ϕ value at time $(i + 1) \Delta t$ is updated using equation (24.50) as follows:

$$\phi_{\text{next}} = \phi_{ij}(k) + [\sigma^2 r_{ij}^2 - 2\kappa\phi_{ij}(k)] \qquad (24.51)$$

We now go to the up node, $(i + 1, j + 1)$, and search the table for the ϕ value equal to ϕ_{next}. Unfortunately, the exact value may not exist in the table; hence the closest value that is lower than ϕ_{next} is identified. Let $\phi_{i+1, j+1}(\ell)$ be the value. Then $\phi_{i+1, j+1}(\ell) \le \phi_{\text{next}} \le \phi_{i+1, j+1}(\ell + 1)$. Define q as the value such that

$$\phi_{\text{next}} = (1 - q)\phi_{i+1, j+1}(\ell) + q\phi_{i+1, j+1}(\ell + 1) \qquad (24.52)$$

The value of the claim at node $(i + 1, j + 1)$, given the ϕ value is ϕ_{next}, is now approximated by $C_{i+1, j+1}(\phi_{\text{next}})$, where

$$C_{i+1, j+1}(\phi_{\text{next}}) = qC_{i+1, j+1}(\ell + 1) + (1 - q)C_{i+1, j+1}(\ell) \qquad (24.53)$$

We next repeat the procedure for the down node. Specifically, let $\phi_{i+1, j}(\ell)$ be the ϕ value at node $(i + 1, j)$ such that $\phi_{i+1, j}(\ell) \le \phi_{\text{next}} \le \phi_{i+1, j}(\ell + 1)$. Define q as the value such that

$$\phi_{\text{next}} = (1 - q)\phi_{i+1, j}(\ell) + q\phi_{i+1, j}(\ell + 1) \qquad (24.54)$$

The value of the claim at node $(i + 1, j)$, given the ϕ value at node (i, j) is $\phi_{ij}(k)$, is now approximated by

$$C_{i+1, j}(\phi_{\text{next}}) = qC_{i+1, j}(\ell + 1) + (1 - q)C_{i+1, j}(\ell) \qquad (24.55)$$

Equations (24.53) and (24.55) are just simple linear interpolation rules for approximating the option values at ϕ values, for which option prices are not available at time $(i + 1) \Delta t$.

We now can perform backward recursion and price the interest rate claim. Specifically,

$$C_{i,j}(k) = [pC_{i+1,j+1}(\phi_{\text{next}}) + (1 - p)C_{i+1,j}(\phi_{\text{next}})]P(r_{ij}, \phi_{ij}(k)) \qquad (24.56)$$

where p is the appropriate probability of an upmove at node (i, j), computed using equation (24.49) with $r = r_{ij}$ and $\phi = \phi_{ij}(k)$, and $P(r_{ij}, \phi_{ij}(k))$ is the discount factor at the node (i, j) for one period, given $\phi = \phi_{ij}(k)$.

As the Δt partition gets finer, the prices of the interest rate claim converge to a continuous time limit. The convergence behavior of this algorithm has been investigated by Li, Ritchken, and Sankarasubramanian and has been found to be very rapid. They show that for almost any type of interest-sensitive claim, a lattice limited to 25 ϕ values at each node produces fairly precise answers. The number of time partitions depends on the type of claim. In general, the computational effort is about 25 times greater than pricing a stock option using a binomial lattice with the same number of time partitions.

Pricing Interest Rate Exotics

Below, we use our three-period example to illustrate how the lattice can be used to price an exotic interest rate claim. In particular, we examine the pricing of a Constant Maturity Treasury (CMT), which is a bond that has coupons fully determined by a specific Treasury coupon at the time the coupon is due. For example, each coupon could be based on the yield to maturity of a newly issued 10-year T-bond. To illustrate the pricing of such a security, consider the CMT that has coupons every period (i.e., every four months) for the next three periods. The coupon payment is based on the current 10-year Treasury coupon rate. After one year, the principal of $100 is paid out with the last coupon.

The value of the CMT is indicated at the top row of each node in the lattice of Exhibit 24.14. In addition, the cash payment at each node is indicated. The third entry, shown in parentheses, represents the probability of an upmove. These probabilities are reproduced from Exhibit 24.13.

At the expiration date in the third period, the value of the underlying bond in each state is shown. We compute the value by adding the face value of $100 to the final coupon payment. The coupon payment at any node is computed by using the discount function at the node, to establish the coupon yield on a 10-year semiannual coupon bond, that prices the bond at par. (The discount function is computed using equation (24.43).) This coupon rate is then adjusted to a four-month rate to establish the actual coupon for the security at the node.

Having identified the terminal value of the CMT, we now proceed with the backward induction to find the current value of the claim. In particular, consider the central node, one period prior to maturity where $r = 10\%$ and $\phi(k) = 0.66889$ as shown in Exhibit 24.13. Using equation (24.50) we find that $\phi_{\text{next}} = 1.0022247$ percent squared. From Exhibit 24.13, this then implies that in the up node, $\phi(\ell) = 0.96365$ and $\phi(\ell + 1) = 1.04552$. The interpolation probability, q, in equation

(24.52) is then computed as 0.47116452. Using equation (24.51) we can compute the effective value of the CMT in the up node as

$$(103.62606)(0.47116452) + (103.62361)(1 - 0.47116452) = 103.62476$$

In a similar fashion, we obtain that for the down node $\phi(\ell) = 0.96786$ and $\phi(\ell + 1) = 1.0408$, which implies that the interpolation probability is 0.47116452 and the effective value of the CMT in the down node is 103.22913.

The one-period discount factor is 0.9672125, based on the value of $r = 10\%$ and $\phi = 0.66889$, using equation (24.43). The coupon payment on the claim is therefore $(10.232)/3 = 3.411$. Hence, the value of the claim at this node is given by

$$3.411 + \{(0.48749717)(103.62476)$$
$$+ (1 - 0.48749717)(103.22913)\}0.9672125 = 103.442$$

This number is reported in Exhibit 24.14. Proceeding in the above fashion, we find that the current value of the CMT is 100.060.

Note that as the state variables change, the coupon changes. Not surprisingly, when the spot rate increases, the value of the coupon increases. Of course, the spot interest rate does not by itself fully determine the coupon. For example, the coupon is at three different possible levels after eight months, when the spot rate is 10 percent. Of course, the coupon is fully determined once both the the spot rate, $r(t)$, and the second state variable, $\phi(t)$, are given.

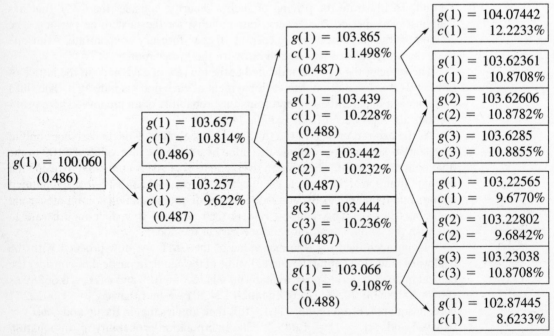

EXHIBIT 24.14   Construction of CMT Prices

The RS models improve upon the generalized Vasicek models in that they permit a richer and more realistic class of volatility structures to be incorporated into the analysis. The resulting models are flexible enough to cover most situations that arise in practice. In particular, the models can be readily initialized to any observable forward rate curve. The models are simple enough in that they can compute answers in reasonable time. This property stems from the fact that there are only two state variables, and hence all path information does not need to be tracked. In addition, analytical measures, such as modified duration, are available, and hedge ratios, including deltas, gammas, thetas, etc., can be estimated from the lattice. The models are well specified, in that required inputs can be observed or readily estimated. Indeed, all the parameters have economic interpretations. Time-varying parameters are not required in the analysis. The models are also realistic, in that negative interest rates can be avoided, and volatilities in general can depend on the level of rates.

Conclusion

The importance of pricing interest rate claims relative to an observable term structure has become more apparent over the last decade. Although many single-factor models, such as the CIR model, can be adapted to yield prices consistent with the term structure, they involve the ad hoc introduction of time-varying parameters into the analysis. The HJM paradigm provides a way to generate consistent prices without requiring time-varying parameters. This approach requires that the volatility structure for forward rates be specified. If the volatility structure is constant or exponentially dampened, then analytical solutions are available for almost all types of European claims. For more realistic volatilty structures, implementing the HJM models becomes complex because of path dependence and exploding lattices. If the volatility structure belongs to the class identified by RS, then the evolution of the term structure can be captured by two state variables, and efficient lattice-based models can be used to price all types of interest rate contracts. The general HJM models are particularly useful for pricing short-term claims. In this case, the path dependence may not be an issue. However, for the pricing of longer-term claims, including interest-sensitive corporate securities such as callable bonds, structured notes, as well as a host of exotics, the RS models are useful. Multifactor extensions of all these models do exist. However, such topics remain beyond the scope of this text.

References

Amin, K., and J. Bodurtha. "Discrete Time Valuation of American Options with Stochastic Interest Rates." *Review of Financial Studies* (1998): 193–234.

Amin, K. and R. Jarrow. "Pricing Foreign Currency Options Under Stochastic Interest Rates." *Journal of International Money and Finance* 10 (1991): 310–330.

Amin, K. and A. Morton. "Implied Volatility Functions in Arbitrage Free Term Structure Models." *Journal of Financial Economics* 35 (1994): 141–80.

Black, F., E. Derman, and W. Toy. "A One Factor Model of Interest Rates and Its Application to Treasury Bond Options." *Financial Analysts Journal* 46 (1990): 33–39.

Black, F. and P. Karasinski. "Bond and Option Pricing When Short Rates Are Lognormal." *Financial Analysts Journal* (1991): 52–59.

Caverhill A. "When Is the Short Rate Markovian?" *Mathematical Finance* 4 (1994): 305–312.

Chan, K., G. Karolyi, F. Longstaff, and A. Sanders. "An Empirical Comparison of Alternative Models of the Term Structure of Interest Rates." *Journal of Finance* 47 (1992): 1209–28.

Cheyette O. "Term Structure Dynamics and Mortgage Valuation." *Journal of Fixed Income* (1992): 28–41.

Heath, D., R. Jarrow, and A. Morton. "Bond Pricing and the Term Structure of Interest Rates: A Discrete Time Approximation." *Journal of Financial and Quantitative Analysis* 25 (1990): 419–40.

_____. "Contingent Claim Valuation with a Random Evolution of Interest Rates." *Review of Futures Markets* 9 (1990): 54–76.

_____. "Bond Pricing and the Term Structure of Interest Rates: A New Methodology for Contingent Claims Valuation." *Econometrica* 60 (1992): 77–105.

Heath, D., R. Jarrow, A. Morton, and M. Spindel. "Easier Done Than Said." *Risk Magazine* 5 (1992): 77–80.

Ho, T., and S. Lee. "Term Structure Movements and Pricing Interest Rate Contingent Claims." *Journal of Finance* 41 (1986): 1011–30.

Hull, J., and A. White. "Pricing Interest Derivative Securities." *Review of Financial Studies* 3 (1990): 573–92.

_____. "Bond Option Pricing on a Model for the Evolution of Bond Prices." *Advances in Options and Futures Research* 6 (1993): 1–13.

_____. "One Factor Interest Rate Models and the Valuation of Interest Rate Derivative Securities." *Journal of Financial and Quantitative Analysis* 28 (1993): 235–54.

Jamshidian, F. "An Exact Bond Option Formula." *Journal of Finance* 44 (1989): 205–09.

Li, A., P. Ritchken, and L. Sankarasubramanian. "Lattice Models for Pricing Interest Rate Claims." *Journal of Finance* (1995):

Ritchken, P., and L. Sankarasubramanian. "Pricing the Quality Option in Treasury Bond Futures." *Mathematical Finance* 2 (1992): 197–214.

_____. "Averaging and Deferred Payment Yield Agreements." *The Journal of Futures Markets* 13 (1993): 23–41.

_____. "Volatility Structures of Forward Rates and the Dynamics of the Term Structure." *Mathematical Finance* (1995): 55–72.

Vasicek, O. "An Equilibrium Characterization of the Term Structure." *Journal of Financial Economics* 5 (1977): 177–88.

Exercises

1. Explain the problems in using a simple Cox-Ingersoll-Ross model to price an interest rate claim when the term structure is provided.

2. Explain the basic idea behind the Black-Derman-Toy model. In particular, what assumptions are made? Explain the advantages of this approach from the perspective of a trader of interest rate claims.

3. What are the biggest disadvantages of models like the Black-Derman-Toy model? Under what conditions is this problem minor?

4. "The Heath-Jarrow-Morton models are similar to the Black-Scholes models in that the underlying is taken as given and the volatility structure is specified." Explain what the "underlying" and the "volatility" refers to in the Black-Scholes model and in the HJM approach. Carefully explain the volatility structure for HJM and comment on how it could be measured using historical data.

5. What do we mean by a state-variable model of the term structure? Explain why the HJM models, in general, are not state-variable models. What complexity do models of the term structure possess if they do not have a finite number of state variables?

6. Explain the advantages of the generalized Vasicek model. What is its single biggest weakness?

7. Explain the general idea behind the Ritchken-Sankarasubramanian models of the term structure. Under what circumstances are these models likely to prove useful to practioners interested in pricing interest rate claims?

8. Use the information in Exhibits 24.1 to 24.3 to price a claim that pays \$1 only if two consecutive upmoves occur.

9. Use the HJM model and the information in Exhibit 24.7 to price a call option that allows the holder to buy a one-period discount bond after one period for the current forward price for the time period $[1, 2]$.

10. Use the RS model and the information in Exhibits 24.9 and 24.10 to price a two-period call option on the spot rate. The strike price for the claim is the initial forward rate for the third period. Assume the contract is a cash-settled contract and has a multiplier of 100.

APPENDIX 24A

Derivation of the Correction Term in Equation (24.22)

Under the local expectations hypothesis, we have

$$P(t, T) = E_t\{\tilde{P}(t + \Delta t, T)\}P(t, t + \Delta t)$$

Hence,
$$\frac{P(t, T)}{P(t, t + \Delta t)} = E_t\{\tilde{P}(t + \Delta t, T)\}$$

Now,
$$P(t, T) = e^{-\int_t^T f(t, u)\, du}$$

Substituting this expression into the left-hand side of the above equation yields

$$e^{-\int_t^T f(t, u)\, du}\, e^{-\int_t^{t+\Delta t} f(t, u)\, du} = e^{-\int_{t+\Delta t}^T f(t, u)\, du}$$

Computing the expectation on the right-hand side yields

$$\tfrac{1}{2}\, e^{-\int_t^T f(t, u) + \mu_f(t, u)\,\Delta t + \sigma_f(t, u)\sqrt{\Delta t}\, du} + \tfrac{1}{2}\, e^{-\int_t^T f(t, u) + \mu_f(t, u)\Delta t - \sigma_f(t, u)\sqrt{\Delta t}\, du}$$

which simplifies to

$$\tfrac{1}{2}\, e^{-\int_{t+\Delta t}^T f(t, u) + \mu_f(t, u)\, du}\Big[e^{-\int_{t+\Delta t}^T \sigma_f(t, u)\sqrt{\Delta t}\, du} + e^{\int_{t+\Delta t}^T \sigma_f(t, u)\sqrt{\Delta t}\, du}\Big]$$

Equating the left-hand side to the right-hand side, we obtain[7]

$$e^{\int_{t+\Delta t}^T \mu_f(t, u)\,\Delta t\, du} = \cosh\left[\int_{t+\Delta t}^T \sigma_f(t, u)\sqrt{\Delta t}\, du\right]$$

Taking natural logarithms and differentiating with respect to T yields

$$\mu_f(t, T)\,\Delta t = \frac{\partial}{\partial T} \ln \cosh\left[\int_{t+\Delta t}^T \sigma_f(t, u)\sqrt{\Delta t}\, du\right]$$

$$= \tanh\left[\int_{t+\Delta t}^T \sigma_f(t, u)\sqrt{\Delta t}\, du\right]\sigma_f(t, T)\sqrt{\Delta t}$$

---

[7] By definition, $\cosh(x) = (e^{-x} + e^x)/2$.

Now, the $\tanh(x)$ function can be represented by the following expansion:

$$\tanh(x) = x - \frac{x^3}{3} + \frac{2x^5}{15} - \frac{17x^7}{315} + \cdots$$

Applying the series expansion to the above equation with $x = \int_{t+\Delta t}^{T} \sigma_f(t, u) \, du \sqrt{\Delta t}$ yields

$$\mu_f(t, T) \, \Delta t = \sigma_f(t, T)\sqrt{\Delta t}\left[\int_{t+\Delta t}^{T} \sigma_f(t, u) \, du \sqrt{\Delta t} \cdots \right]$$

$$= \sigma_f(t, T) \, \Delta t \int_{t+\Delta t}^{T} \sigma_f(t, u) \, du + o(\Delta t)$$

Dividing both sides by Δt and taking the limit yields

$$\mu_f(t, T) = \sigma_f(t, T) \int_{t}^{T} \sigma_f(t, u) \, du = \sigma_f(t, T)\sigma_p(t, T)$$

Index